# THE LAW OF AMERICAN STATE CONSTITUTIONS

# THE LAW OF AMERICAN STATE CONSTITUTIONS

Second Edition

ROBERT F. WILLIAMS
LAWRENCE FRIEDMAN

Oxford University Press is a department of the University of Oxford. It furthers the University's objective of excellence in research, scholarship, and education by publishing worldwide. Oxford is a registered trade mark of Oxford University Press in the UK and certain other countries.

Published in the United States of America by Oxford University Press
198 Madison Avenue, New York, NY 10016, United States of America.



CIP data is on file at the Library of Congress

ISBN 978-0-19-006880-6

DOI: 10.1093/oso/9780190068806.001.0001

Printed by Integrated Books International, United States of America

*For Alaine, Sarah, Tyler, Lakshmi, Ķali, and Mila*
*RFW*

*For Elizabeth, Piper, and Keir*
*LF*

# CONTENTS

## PART IV. UNIQUE INTERPRETATION ISSUES IN STATE CONSTITUTIONAL LAW

## PART V. STATE CONSTITUTIONAL AMENDMENT AND REVISION

# PREFACE TO THE SECOND EDITION

The 2009 edition of this book sought to provide readers a single-volume treatment of the many issues that regularly arise in state constitutional law. Now, more than ten years have passed and a number of significant new developments have taken place. Further, Professor Robert Williams was able to convince Professor Lawrence Friedman, who assisted on the first edition, to join him as a coauthor on this second edition and remains grateful for his assistance and commitment to this important field of law.

The first edition was reviewed favorably,[1] and was the subject of a symposium in the *New England Law Review*.[2] We are gratified that the volume has been put to use by students, scholars, and judges.

Now, with the composition of the federal judiciary, including the U.S. Supreme Court, being so dramatically affected by President Donald Trump, we expect another wave of interest in state constitutions, particularly in the area of individual rights, similar to that which occurred with the advent of the Burger Court. At the same time, the developments of the last decade show more clearly than ever that the importance of state constitutionalism goes far beyond judicial protection of individual rights and civil liberties. Significant attention has been paid to the area of separation of powers and checks and balances under state constitutions in this era of increasingly polarized state and local government. The area of local government home rule has evolved as a significant battlefield for these contending forces, some of which operate from the national level.

Further, the recognition of the special role of positive rights guarantees in state constitutions has continued to evolve. The readily available avenues of state constitutional amendment continue to be utilized by government reformers as well as contending political forces. The topic of state constitutional amendment processes has also captured the attention of academics. And, not least, a new generation of jurists and political science scholars has turned its attention to state

[1] Sanford Levinson, *America's "Other Constitutions": The Importance of State Constitutions for Our Law and Politics*, 45 Tulsa L. Rev. 813 (2010); Peter Buchsbaum, *The Law of American State Constitutions*, 42 The Urban Lawyer 761 (Summer 2010); Jim Rossi, *Assessing the State of State Constitutionalism*, 109 Mich. L. Rev. 1145 (2011).

[2] *Symposium: The Law of American State Constitutions*, 45 New Eng. L. Rev. 797 (2011).

constitutionalism after G. Alan Tarr[3] and John Dinan[4] "reopened the study of state constitutionalism."[5]

Much of the "stuff" of state constitutional law is, of course, the decisions of the state high courts interpreting state constitutions. We have, where appropriate, included new cases in the text of footnotes and, in some areas, removed references to older cases. In an effort to orient readers, this edition begins with an introductory chapter focusing on the issue of same-sex marriage and the ways in which that issue illustrates many of the aspects of state constitutional law discussed at greater length throughout the book. Finally, we have added a brief epilogue that looks at state constitutional issues likely to arise in the wake of a retreat from rights enforcement at the federal level, as well as efforts to use state constitutions as a means to effectuate policies disfavored or ignored at the federal level.

Robert F. Williams
Camden, New Jersey
Lawrence Friedman
Boston, Massachusetts
August 2022

[3] G. Alan Tarr, Understanding State Constitutions (1998).
[4] John J. Dinan, The American State Constitutional Tradition (2006).
[5] Robinson Woodward-Burns, *The State Constitutions' Influence on American Political Development*, 81 J. Pol. e85 (2019). Recent works on state constitutional law include Jeffrey S. Sutton, 51 Imperfect Solutions: States and the Making of Constitutional Law (2018), and Jeffrey S. Sutton, Who Decides: States as Laboratories of Constitutional Experimentation (2021).

# PREFACE TO THE FIRST EDITION AND ACKNOWLEDGMENTS

This book is the result of over forty years that I have been interested in and studying state constitutions. I became interested in the field in the spring of 1967—before going to law school and while I was serving as a legislative aide to Representative Bob Graham in the Florida House of Representatives. The Florida Legislature stayed in session all summer and revised the 1885 Florida Constitution. The revisions were submitted to the voters, approved, and took effect in 1968. Several years later, I wrote my law review Note about the new state constitution's property tax provisions.

Since beginning my academic career in 1980 at Rutgers, I have taught and written about state constitutions. I have learned immeasurably from the Rutgers law students' class discussions and research papers in my State Constitutional Law course over almost thirty years. Many of these lessons and insights are reflected in my *State Constitutional Law: Cases and Materials* (4th ed. 2006) and, now, in this book.

I thank first John Kincaid, director of the former Advisory Commission on Intergovernmental Relations, which published the first edition of my casebook on state constitutional law; and next, Lexis Law Publishing, which has provided excellent support for the second, third, fourth, and hopefully, future editions. The work I have done keeping that book updated is reflected directly in this one.

I have had the opportunity to lecture before, and interact with, hundreds of state judges over the years in programs presented by the Conference of Chief Justices, the American Bar Association's Appellate Judges Seminar Series, New York University's Institute for Judicial Administration, the Roscoe Pound Civil Justice Institute, and many state and regional continuing judicial education programs. All of these interactions were extremely informative for me, and I am deeply indebted to the many state judges who have shared, and continue to share, their considerable insights and work product with me. These experiences have reinforced my view of the importance of this work.

I have been blessed to be one-half of an extraordinary, interdisciplinary academic collaboration with my Rutgers political science colleague, G. Alan Tarr, the author of *Understanding State Constitutions* (1998). Alan and I have worked closely for over twenty-five years on state constitutional law matters in New Jersey, in much of the United States, and in federal countries abroad. We created the Rutgers Center for State Constitutional Studies (https://statecon.cam

den.rutgers.edu/), which operates under his directorship. His academic brilliance, energy, generous collegiality, and friendship are reflected in many ways throughout this book. I have learned a great deal from, and with, Alan.

The *Rutgers Law Journal*'s Annual Issue on State Constitutional Law, beginning in 1989 (at the suggestion of my colleague, Earl Maltz), has provided me with another extremely interesting, satisfying, and stimulating faculty-student relationship. Serving for twenty years as faculty editor for this annual student publication has enabled me to interact with some of our best students, year after year, for our mutual benefit. Together we look at virtually every state constitutional law case in the country every year. We believe that we have contributed in a major way to the development of a substantial body of high-quality, interdisciplinary student, and professional scholarship on state constitutionalism. The opportunity to spend time with the invited authors of the Forewords for each of these annual issues has been extremely enlightening for me.

Since I began my academic career at Rutgers in 1980, through the indulgence of numerous law review editors and the thoughtfulness of law review symposium planners, I have published many articles on state constitutional law. Some of these articles now form a substantial portion of this book, after being reorganized, integrated, and updated.

I was fortunate to receive the Chamberlain Fellowship from the Legislative Drafting Research Fund at Columbia University School of Law for a year of graduate legal study for 1979–1980. It was there that I began to organize my academic approach to state constitutional law. A generous fellowship from the American Council of Learned Societies, for the academic year 1987, supported the original research now reflected in Chapter 2. And Rutgers University research leaves over the years have enabled me to delve into a wide range of topics in state constitutional law.

The Ford Foundation provided generous support for the Center for State Constitutional Studies' multiyear project, "State Constitutions for the Twenty-first Century." Many of the insights from that work are reflected in this book.

Finally, I want to give special thanks to several academic supporters who helped and guided me over the years: Professor L. Herald Levinson, from whom I took a course in state constitutional law at the University of Florida College of Law in 1969; the late Professor William Swindler of William and Mary and Professor A.E. Dick Howard of the University of Virginia, both of whom provided invaluable encouragement and support early in my academic career; Justice Hans A. Linde of Oregon, who has been supportive, encouraging, and always the teacher throughout my academic career; and Frank P. Grad of Columbia Law School, my generous mentor, friend, and coauthor.

Lawrence Friedman provided very useful advice and suggestions on several of the early chapters. My dean, Rayman Solomon, has been unwaveringly supportive, including scheduling a sabbatical so I could finish the book. Chris Collins at Oxford University Press has been encouraging, helpful, and enthusiastic since the first moment he heard about this project. David Batista, research librarian at Rutgers Law School's library in Camden, provided invaluable assistance with sources for this low-tech legal researcher. Finally, Denise Johnson-Steinert never seemed to tire of the new and reorganized versions of chapters, renumbered footnotes, and dealt with hundreds of other minor technical details that go into a project like this one. I can see clearly the mark of all of these people in this book.

A number of chapters include material I previously published, much of it copyrighted, and portions of the following materials are used here with permission: *A "Row of Shadows": Pennsylvania's Misguided Lockstep Approach to Its State Constitutional Equality Doctrine*, 3 WIDENER J. PUB. L. 343 (1993); *Equality Guarantees in State Constitutional Law*, 63 TEXAS L. REV. 1195 (1985); *State Constitutional Limits on Legislative Procedure: Problems of Judicial Enforcement and Legislative Compliance*, 17 PUBLIUS: THE JOURNAL OF FEDERALISM 91 (1987), reprinted in 48 U. PITT. L. REV. 797 (1987); *Rhode Island's Distribution of Powers Question of the Century: Reverse Delegation and Implied Limits on Legislative Powers*, 4 ROGER WILLIAMS U.L. REV. 159 (1998); *Juristocracy in the American States*, 65 MD. L. REV. 883 (2006); *Comment: On the Importance of a Theory of Legislative Power Under State Constitutions*, 15 QUINNIPIAC L. REV. 57 (1995); *The State Constitutions of the Founding Decade: Pennsylvania's Radical 1776 Constitution and Its Influences on American Constitutionalism*, 62 TEMPLE L. REV. 541 (1989); *State Courts Adopting Federal Constitutional Doctrine: Case by Case Adoptionism or Prospective Lockstepping?* 46 WM. & MARY L. REV. 1499 (2005); *In the Glare of The Supreme Court: Continuing Methodology and Legitimacy Problems in Independent State Constitutional Rights Adjudication*, 72 NOTRE DAME L. REV. 1015 (1997); *The Brennan Lecture: Interpreting State Constitutions as Unique Legal Documents*, 27 OKLA. CITY U.L. REV. 189 (2002); *"Traces of Its Labors": The Constitutional Commission, the Legislature, and Their Influence on the New Jersey State Constitution*, 1873–1875, 33 RUTGERS L.J. 929 (2002); *Introduction: The Third Stage of the New Judicial Federalism*, 59 N.Y.U. ANN. SURV. AM. L. 211 (2003); *The State of State Constitutional Law: The New Judicial Federalism and Beyond*, 72 RUTGERS U.L. REV. 949 (2020).

There is still much to learn about American state constitutions. It is my hope that this book is a step in the right direction.

Robert F. Williams
Camden, New Jersey
March 2009

# INTRODUCTION

> *State constitutions . . . have been studied almost exclusively from a reformist perspective—to recommend the elimination of presumed deficiencies. Relatively little attention has been given to the underlying political theories and philosophic assumptions of the fifty state constitutions and their colonial predecessors.*[1]
>
> *If we are ever to produce a complete and accurate American constitutional history, we must recognize that without the state constitutions in force in 1789 the national Constitution is an incomplete text. They must all be read together. These state constitutions together contain and embody a coherent political theory which is, in important respects, at variance with Federalist theory which underlies the United States Constitution. Nevertheless, the idea for a written national constitution, as well as the basic elements and institutions within it, come from the state documents.*[2]

Working effectively with state constitutions requires an understanding of their origins and evolution over time—how they intertwine with, and are limited by, the federal Constitution; how their rights and distribution of powers provisions differ from those in the federal Constitution; how the branches of state government are constituted; the unique approaches to their judicial interpretation; the mechanisms for their revision and amendment; and the state judicial involvement in those processes of change. These are the purposes of this book.

This book does not suggest a single, grand theory of interpretation for state constitutions, but rather describes a bundle of approaches or ways to think about questions of state constitutions and state constitutional interpretation. In addition, it provides some prescriptive views on a number of matters.

[1] Daniel J. Elazar, *The Principles & Traditions Underlying State Constitutions*, 12 Publius: The J. Federalism 11, 11 (Winter 1982).

[2] Donald S. Lutz, *From Covenant to Constitution in American Political Thought*, 10 Publius: The J. Federalism 101, 101–02 (Fall 1980) (footnotes omitted); *see also* John Kincaid, *State Constitutions in the Federal System*, 496 Annals Am. Acad. Pol. & Soc. Sci. 12, 13, 15–16 (1988).

*The Law of American State Constitutions.* Robert F. Williams and Lawrence Friedman, Oxford University Press.
 DOI: 10.1093/oso/9780190068806.003.0001

State constitutions are low-visibility constitutions in the United States. Political scientist John Kincaid referred to state constitutions as the "dark side of the moon."[3] The study of American constitutional law has been dominated by a virtually exclusive focus on the federal Constitution and its judicial interpretation. In a 1988 national poll conducted by the Advisory Commission on Intergovernmental Relations (ACIR), 52 percent of the respondents did not know that their state had its own constitution.[4] An ACIR report the following year concluded that lawyers tended to be unaware of their state constitutions and that classes in public schools, universities, and even law schools seldom mentioned state constitutions.[5] A 1991 poll by ACIR found the same results.[6] "Out of a hundred persons who can identify James Madison as the putative 'Father of the Constitution,'" observed one commentator, "could more than half a dozen name the principal author of the oldest written constitution still in operation?"[7] This situation has improved only somewhat in the ensuing generations.

The main cause of the increasing interest in state constitutions has been the "New Judicial Federalism" (NJF), whereby state courts have interpreted their state constitutions to provide more protective rights than those recognized by the U.S. Supreme Court under the federal Constitution, together with the increased use of state constitutional amendments to advance national political goals.[8]

This leads to an interesting paradox in American constitutionalism. The federal Constitution is much more familiar in our country, but it is in fact remote and out of reach for any significant public involvement. State constitutions, on the other hand, are much closer to the people and are realistically accessible to popular involvement through a number of avenues. Yet, as noted, state constitutions are still not well understood by the public or even many legal or political professionals.

Legal scholars, political scientists, and the media have contributed to ignorance about state constitutions by their preoccupation with federal constitutional matters as defined by the U.S. Supreme Court. The federal Constitution,

[3] John Kincaid *Early State History and Constitutions*, *in* The Oxford Handbook of State and Local Government 239, 240 (Donald P. Haider ed., 2014).

[4] John Kincaid, *The New Judicial Federalism*, 61 J. State Gov't 169 (Sept./Oct. 1988).

[5] Advisory Commission on Intergovernmental Relations, State Constitutions in the Federal System: Selected Issues and Opportunities for State Initiatives 2 (1989). *See also* Jill Rosen, JHU Survey: Americans Don't Know Much About State Government, Johns Hopkins University (Dec. 11, 2016), *available at* https://releases.jhu.edu/2018/12/11/jhu-survey-americans-dont-know-much-about-state-government/ (one-half of American don't know if their state has a constitution).

[6] G. Alan Tarr, Understanding State Constitutions 1–2 (1998).

[7] Don E. Fehrenbacher, Constitutions and Constitutionalism in the Slaveholding South 2 (1989) (referring to John Adams of Massachusetts).

[8] *See generally* Robert F. Williams, *The State of State Constitutional Law; The New Judicial Federalism and Beyond*, 72 Rutgers U.L. Rev. 949 (2020).

however, is "incomplete"[9] in the sense that it relies extensively on mechanisms established in, and pursuant to, state constitutions, and leaves nearly all matters within the sphere of state power to be regulated by state constitutions and laws. In the words of a leading expert on American federalism:

> Although the term "American Constitution" is often used synonymously with "Constitution of the United States," the operational American constitution consists of the federal Constitution and the 50 state constitutions. Together, these 51 documents comprise a complex system of constitutional rule for a republic of republics.[10]

We actually live in a system of dual constitutionalism, as well as dual constitutional traditions in terms of constitutional design and practice.[11] We share this constitutional characteristic with other *federal* countries because a "federal nation is, as it were, an unfinished nation."[12] The study of state, or *subnational*, constitutions in other federal countries has begun to emerge, but it is far behind even the tentative American developments and is beyond the scope of this book.[13] Most Americans' daily lives are governed much more directly by *state* rather than federal laws, as enacted (and limited) pursuant to the provisions of the fifty state constitutions. Each of these state constitutions structures ("constitutes") and limits the state government and contains rights that the individual state's residents possess regardless of their federal constitutional rights, as they may be interpreted by the U.S. Supreme Court.

Each of the states (plus Puerto Rico) has a constitution. All of these documents, although varying widely as to detail and length, perform the same general function in our federal system of law and government. This function is very different from that of the Constitution of the United States—the constitution usually thought of when we refer to "constitutional law."

[9] Donald S. Lutz, *The Purposes of American State Constitutions*, 12 Publius: The J. Federalism 27, 38–42 (Winter 1982); *The United States Constitution as an Incomplete Document*, 496 Annals Am. Acad. Pol. & Soc. Sci. 23 (1988).

[10] Kincaid, *supra* note 2, at 13. *See also* Donald S. Lutz, The Origins of American Constitutionalism 96 (1988) ("Obviously, the United States Constitution assumes, in fact requires, the existence of state constitutions if it is to make any sense.").

[11] Tarr, *supra* note 6, at 6.

[12] Ivo D. Duchacek, Comparative Federalism: The Territorial Dimension of Politics 192 (1987).

[13] Robert F. Williams & G. Alan Tarr, *Subnational Constitutional Space: A View from the States, Provinces, Regions, Länder, and Cantons*, *in* Federalism, Subnational Constitutions and Minority Rights 3 (G. Alan Tarr, Robert F. Williams, & Josef Marko eds., 2004); *see also* Ronald L. Watts, *Foreword: States, Provinces, Länder, and Cantons: International Variety Among Subnational Constitutions*, 31 Rutgers L.J. 945 (2000); James A. Gardner, *In Search of Sub-National Constitutionalism*, 4 Eur. Const. L. Rev. 325 (2008); Robert F. Williams, *Teaching and Researching Comparative Subnational Constitutional Law*, 115 Penn St. L. Rev. 1109 (2011).

A state constitution serves as a charter of law and government for the state—the supreme law of the state—and prescribes in more or less detail the structure and functions of state and, sometimes, local government. Further, it provides *limitations* on the otherwise plenary, residual, sovereign power of states to make law and govern themselves. At the outset, this fundamental point regarding the legal and political function and effect of state constitutions must be understood. By contrast, the federal Constitution is a *grant of* enumerated powers upon which all exercises of federal power must be based. The states delegated to the federal government certain powers and agreed to restrain themselves with respect to other powers and functions. Such restraints are found in the federal and state constitutions.

The study of state constitutional law, of powers and restraints it embraces, has been and will continue to be, evolving. In 1988, two commentators on the status of state constitutional law scholarship observed: "[M]ost of the literature, like many of the state cases themselves, offers more in terms of approval and encouragement than of analytical insight and innovation. . . . More attention must be devoted to *new* conceptualizations in constitutional doctrine."[14]

Dr. G. Alan Tarr noted in 1991:

> The new judicial federalism, now middle-aged, can no longer be sustained by the sense of discovery that sparked it initially. If advances are to be made in state constitutional law, they will come through more sustained reflection about the nature of state constitutions and through a dialogue with scholars outside the field of state constitutional law.[15]

In 1992, Professor James A. Gardner asserted that "state constitutional law today is a vast wasteland of confusing, conflicting, and essentially unintelligible pronouncements"[16] and that "state constitutional discourse is impoverished and inadequate to the tasks that any constitutional discourse is designed to accomplish."[17] Gardner's central focus was on rights cases.[18] Although the reemergence of state constitutional law in rights cases is not new, it is not very old either. It remains a fairly "rough sea," where there may be more than one "anchor" available to a state court.[19]

[14] Ronald K.L. Collins & David M. Skover, *The Future of Liberal Legal Scholarship*, 87 MICH. L. REV. 189, 217–18 (1988).

[15] G. Alan Tarr, *Constitutional Theory and State Constitutional Interpretation*, 22 RUTGERS L.J. 841, 861 (1991).

[16] James A. Gardner, *The Failed Discourse of State Constitutionalism*, 90 MICH. L. REV. 761, 763 (1992).

[17] *Id.* at 766.

[18] *But see id.* at 808–10.

[19] *See* Vito J. Titone, *State Constitutional Interpretation: The Search for an Anchor in a Rough Sea*, 61 ST. JOHN'S L. REV. 431 (1987).

After having concluded that state constitutional discourse was impoverished, Professor Gardner asserted that this was caused by the failure of state constitutionalism generally.[20] He pointed to the inclusion of mere statutory detail in state constitutions (reflecting political compromise) and the frequency with which they are amended or revised to conclude that state constitutionalism is a failed enterprise.[21] The "poverty of state constitutional discourse merely reflects the limited narrative possibilities that state constitutions offer to erstwhile interpreters."[22] A truly diverse set of independent constitutional values, at least in rights cases, was even said to be dangerous to our national community.[23] Ultimately, Professor Gardner contended that "the communities in theory defined by state constitutions simply do not exist, and debating the meaning of a state constitution does not involve defining an identity that any group would recognize as its own."[24]

These were strong and provocative conclusions. They stimulated a useful new and continuing discussion of what state constitutional law is all about.[25] Much of that discussion continues to analyze state constitutional law as it relates to federal constitutional law, in comparative or relational terms. This volume is intended to contribute further to the dialogue about state constitutions, and although it had its origins long before Professor Gardner's article, it is intended to provide a partial refutation to Professor Gardner.[26]

By 1994, Dean Neil H. Cogan could state:

> The legal literature of state fundamental law was, but is no longer, sparse. This is due in part to a new realization by lawyers and judges that the form of most state fundamental law is progressive rather than static, and also to an awakening within many communities that state fundamental law may be revised by amendment as well as construction.[27]

[20] Gardner, *supra* note 13, at 812 ("the failure of state constitutionalism itself to provide a workable model for the contemporary practice of constitutional law and discourse on the state level").

[21] *Id.* at 818–22.

[22] *Id.* at 822.

[23] *Id.* at 827.

[24] *Id.* at 837. *See also* James A. Gardner, *What Is a State Constitution?* 24 RUTGERS L.J. 1025 (1993).

[25] *Roundtable: Responses to James A. Gardner, The Failed Discourse of State Constitutionalism*, 24 RUTGERS L.J. 927 (1993).

[26] Professor Gardner's article also generated a wide, earlier response. *See, e.g.*, Robert F. Utter, *The Practice of Principled Decision-Making in State Constitutionalism: Washington's Experience*, 65 TEMPLE L. REV. 1153 (1992); David Schuman, *The Failed Critique of State Constitutionalism*, 91 MICH. L. REV. 274 (1992); Jeffrey A. Parness, *Failed or Uneven Discourse of State Constitutionalism? Governmental Structure and State Constitutions*, 5 ST. THOMAS L. REV. 155 (1992); Neil H. Cogan, *In Praise of Diverse Discourse*, 5 ST. THOMAS L. REV. 173 (1992). *See also* James A. Gardner, *Discourse and Difference—A Reply to Parness and Cogan*, 5 ST. THOMAS L. REV. 193 (1992).

[27] Neil H. Cogan, *Moses and Modernism*, 92 MICH. L. REV. 1347, 1353 (1994) (reviewing three books on state constitutional law).

By 1998, Dr. Tarr had concluded that "doubts about the viability of state constitutional jurisprudence have not prevented its development."[28] In 2005, Professors Jim Gardner and Jim Rossi noted that, after undergoing an "understandable overcompensation" in reaction to the dominance of federal constitutional law, scholars "have turned toward developing more nuanced theories of the interaction of state and federal constitutional law."[29] In the ensuing decades, the field has continued to grow in sophistication, making this an appropriate time for the publication of a new edition of this book.

Indeed, in the last several generations, there have been striking developments in state constitutional law. We have experienced a now maturing "constitutional revolution" in the judicial interpretation of individual rights provisions of state constitutions since the early 1970s. The era of major state constitutional innovation prior to the turn of the last century was, by contrast, concerned primarily with changes in constitutional texts. Similarly, the wave of state constitutional change that took place during the Progressive Era and between 1945 and 1970 dealt with revisions to, and modernization of, the constitutions themselves. The rediscovery of state constitutional law beginning around 1970, however, involves *judicial* interpretation of the rights guarantees in state constitutions (the NJF) and, more recently, provisions establishing governmental structure and policies.

As discussed at length in the following, the 2003 same-sex marriage decision by the Massachusetts Supreme Judicial Court, *Goodridge v. Department of Public Health*, thrust the field of state constitutional law onto the national stage in a way that had never happened before.[30] California's and Connecticut's similar 2008 decisions, followed by Iowa's 2009 decision,[31] and the adoption in many states of opposing constitutional amendments banning same-sex marriages, kept the issue on the national agenda.[32] California's Proposition 8, overturning that state's same-sex marriage decision and the ensuing litigation challenging its validity, further heightened the national interest in state constitutions. The U.S. Supreme

[28] Tarr, *supra* note 6, at 208.

[29] James A. Gardner & Jim Rossi, *Foreword: The New Frontier of State Constitutional Law*, 46 Wm. & Mary L. Rev. 1231, 1234 (2005). *See also* Robert K. Fitzpatrick, Note, *Neither Icarus Nor Ostrich: State Constitutions as an Independent Source of Individual Rights*, 79 N.Y.U. L. Rev. 1833 (2004).

[30] 798 N.E.2d 941 (Mass. 2003). *Symposium on Goodridge v. Department of Public Health*, 14 B.U. Pub. Int. L.J. 1 (2004); Jeffrey M. Shaman, Equality and Liberty in the Golden Age of State Constitutional Law 185–210 (2008).

[31] *In re* Marriage Cases, 183 P.3d 384 (Cal. 2008); Kerrigan v. Commissioner of Public Health, 957 A.2d 407 (Conn. 2008); Varnum v. Brien, 763 N.E.2d 862 (Iowa 2009). *See* Mary Bonauto, *Equality and the Impossible—State Constitutions and Marriage*, 68 Rutgers U. L. Rev. 1481 (2016).

[32] William C. Duncan, *Revisiting State Marriage Recognition Provisions*, 38 Creighton L. Rev. 233 (2005); *Symposium: State Marriage Amendments*, 7 Fla. Coastal L.J. 221 (2005); Mark Strasser, *State Marriage Amendments and Overreaching: On Plain Meaning, Good Public Policy, and Constitutional Limitations*, 25 Law & Inequality 59 (2007). *See also* 1 Jennifer Friesen, State Constitutional Law: Litigating Individual Rights, Claims and Defences, app. 2A (2006).

Court ended the marriage equality debate in 2015,[33] but at this writing there are concerns that this precedent might be narrowed or overturned, as we discuss in the epilogue. Indeed, President Donald Trump's appointment of several originalists to the Supreme Court has resulted in *Roe v. Wade*[34] being overruled,[35] a development that has cast increasing attention on state constitutions and their interpretation by state courts.[36]

State constitutional law remains a source of lesser-known battles. Debates about "tort reform" have been and continue to be waged in the state legislatures and state courts, applying state constitutional limits.[37] The U.S. Supreme Court's 2005 decision in *Kelo v. City of New London*,[38] permitting the taking of property for economic development, spurred a wave of consideration of the issue by state legislatures, and by courts under their analogous state constitutional provisions.[39] And, after Hurricane Katrina, should any of us be surprised that levees have been the subject of state constitutional treatment in Louisiana for many years?[40]

The U.S. Supreme Court also influenced the development of the NJF as a result of its hands-off approach to federal constitutional litigation concerning equal and adequate funding for public schools.[41] This left, literally, *no federal*

[33] Obergefell v. Hodges, 576 U.S. 644 (2015).

[34] 410 U.S. 113 (1973).

[35] *See* Dobbs v. Jackson Women's Health Organization, 597 U.S. ___ (2022).

[36] *See, e.g.*, Ronald K.L. Collins, *Is There "Life" (or "Choice") After Roe?* 3 Const. Commentary 91 (1986); Note, *State Constitutions: The New Battlefield of Abortion Rights*, 10 Harv. Women's L.J. 284–94 (1987); Harry Tepker, *Abortion, Privacy and State Constitutional Law: A Speculation If (or When) Roe v. Wade Is Overturned*, 2 Emerging Issues in State Const. L. 173 (1989); Amy Johnson, *Abortion, Personhood, and Privacy in Texas*, 68 Tex. L. Rev. 1521 (1990); Scott A. Moss & Douglas M. Raines, *The Intriguing Federalist Future of Reproductive Rights*, 88 B.U. L. Rev. 175 (2008); Linda J. Wharton, Roe *at Thirty-six and Beyond: Enhancing Protections for Authority Through State Constitutions*, 15 Wm. & Mary J. Women & L. 469 (2009); Paul Benjamin Linton, Abortion Under State Constitutions: A State-by-State Analysis (3d ed. 2020).

[37] *See Symposium, Tort Reform and State Constitutional Law*, 32 Rutgers L.J. 897 (2001); Vega v. Jordan Valley Medical Center, L.P., 449 P.3d 31 (Utah 2019); Yankos v. UMPC, 218 A.3d 1214 (Pa. 2019); Hilburn v. Enerpipe, Ltd., 442 P.3d 509 (Kan. 2019); McClay v. Airport Management Services, Inc., 596 S.W., 3d 686 (Tenn. 2020).

[38] 545 U.S. 469 (2005).

[39] David Schultz, *Economic Development and Eminent Domain After* Kelo: *Property Rights and "Public Use" Under State Constitutions*, 11 Alb. L. Envtl. Outlook J. 41 (2006); Maureen E. Brady, *The Domino Effect in State Takings Law: A Response to 51 Imperfect Solutions*, 2020 U. Ill. L. Rev. 1455 (2020); *see* Gabriel I. Chacón, *Comment*, 36 Rutgers L.J. 1313 (2005) (County of Wayne v. Hathcock, 684 N.W.2d 765 (Mich. 2004)); Marshall T. Kizner, *Comment*, 38 Rutgers L.J. 1379 (2007) (City of Norwood v. Horney, 853 N.E.2d 1115 (Ohio 2006)); Bd. of Co. Commissioners of Muskogee Co. v. Lowrey, 136 P.3d 639, 651 (Okla. 2006); St. Bernard Port, Harbor & Terminal Dist. v. Violet Dock Port, 239 So.3d 243, 250 (La. 2018).

[40] La. Const. art. VI, §§ 38 & 39.

[41] San Antonio Indep. Sch. Dist. v. Rodriguez, 411 U.S. 1, 44 (1973) (indicating hesitance to make a uniform requirement for all fifty states); Jeffrey S. Sutton, San Antonio Independent School District v. Rodriguez *and Its Aftermath*, 94 Va. L. Rev. 1963, 1971–77 (2008). Professor Scott Bauries has suggested that constitutional separation of powers concerns and textual analysis are less helpful in understanding education finance litigation in state courts than the varying conceptions of the nature of education rights. *See generally* Scott R. Bauries, *Is There an Elephant in the Room? Judicial*

constitutional avenue for this type of litigation and resulted in a near-immediate round of landmark *state* constitutional law decisions on education funding.[42] Professor A.E. Dick Howard noted that this view of the federal Constitution's limits also served as a stimulus for continuation of the extensive doctrines of substantive due process and equal protection in challenges to economic regulation, which had been alive and well in the states even before the NJF.[43]

Although state constitutional law predated federal constitutional law and has always been important in areas of civil litigation such as state taxation and eminent domain, and in areas of criminal procedure such as bail rights, a broader spectrum of the private bar and a growing number of law professors, political scientists, students, and the media and the public have begun to discover state constitutional law for the first time. This is attributable directly to the NJF and the many "evasion cases"[44] of the past five decades—in other words, state supreme courts relying on their own constitutions (1) to provide greater civil liberties protections for their citizens than are required by U.S. Supreme Court interpretations of the federal Constitution, or (2) to insulate their decisions, based on state law grounds, from Supreme Court review.

Recently, controversial government structure and separation of powers matters under state constitutions have gained wide national attention. For example, California's 2003 gubernatorial recall and simultaneous election of Arnold Schwarzenegger;[45] the increased controversy over, and expense of, state judicial elections;[46] and the rise of plebiscite lawmaking and state constitutional

*Review of Educational Adequacy and the Separation of Powers in State Constitutions*, 61 ALA. L. REV. 701, 701–02 (2010); *see also* Scott R. Bauries, *The Education Duty*, 47 WAKE FOREST L. REV. 705, 718–25, (2012). For a different view, compare William E. Thro & R. Craig Wood, *The Constitutional Text Matters: Reflections on Recent School Finance Cases*, 251 EDUC. L. REP. 510, 529–32 (2010). For an examination of the ways which the state and federal conceptions of education rights under constitutions have converged in school finance cases, see Scott R. Bauries, *State Constitutions and Individual Rights: Conceptual Convergence in School Finance Litigation*, 18 GEO. MASON L. REV. 301, 351–65 (2011).

[42] *See* Robinson v. Cahill, 303 A.2d 273, 281–82 (N.J. 1973); Serrano v. Priest, 557 P.2d 929, 951–52 (Cal. 1976).

[43] A.E. Dick Howard, *State Courts and Constitutional Rights in the Day of the Burger Court*, 62 VA. L. REV. 873, 881–82 (1976).

[44] Donald E. Wilkes, *More on the New Federalism in Criminal Procedure*, 63 KY. L.J. 873 n. 2 (1975).

[45] LARRY N. GERSTON & TERRY CHRISTENSEN, RECALL! CALIFORNIA'S POLITICAL EARTHQUAKE (2004); Vickram D. Amar, *Adventures in Direct Democracy: The Top Ten Constitutional Lessons from the California Recall Experience*, 92 CAL. L. REV. 927 (2004); Kira L. Klatchko, *The Progressivist Origins of the 2003 California Gubernatorial Recall*, 35 MCGEORGE L. REV. 701 (2004); Floyd Feeney, *The 2003 California Gubernatorial Recall*, 41 CREIGHTON L. REV. 37 (2007).

[46] G. Alan Tarr, *Politicizing the Process: The New Politics of State Judicial Elections*, *in* BENCH PRESS: THE COLLISION OF COURTS, POLITICS, AND THE MEDIA 52 (2007). *See* Douglas Keith, Patrick Berry, & Eric Velasco, *The Politics of Judicial Elections, 2017–2018: How Dark Money, Interest Groups, and Big Donors Shape State High Courts* (Brennan Center 2019), https://www.brennancenter.org/our-work/research-reports/politics-judicial-elections-2017-18.

amendment through the initiative in a number of states have cast light on the unique government structures and processes established by state constitutions.

The 2020 coronavirus pandemic, in the absence of strong *federal* leadership, pushed to the fore *state* governments and their legal authority to respond to the emergency. Of particular concern was governors' use, or nonuse, of emergency powers. Especially in states with divided executive and legislative political control, a welter of litigation arose concerning such public health measures such as mask mandates, stay-at-home orders, business (including religious institutions) closing and capacity restriction requirements, and school closings.[47] At the same time, as the 2020 presidential election approached and passed, a new wave of litigation arose over election-related concerns like mail-in votes, extended due dates for ballots, and the processes for counting votes. Many of these cases were litigated in state courts, under state constitutions.[48]

In respect to the pandemic and the election, consider, for example, the Colorado Supreme Court ruling that the legislature, rather than being constitutionally limited to the number of "calendar days" in the constitution, could meet on "working calendar days" because of the pandemic.[49] The Pennsylvania Supreme Court held that mail-in votes could be counted for three days after the election based on the state constitution's "free and equal elections" clause.[50] That same court upheld the governor's executive order compelling the closure of all non-life-sustaining businesses against a separation-of-powers challenge.[51] The Wisconsin Supreme Court struck down on, among other things, separation of powers grounds, the governor's executive order postponing the primary election.[52] The Michigan Supreme Court struck down the governor's executive order prohibiting healthcare providers from performing nonessential procedures, on the ground that the statute authorizing such orders was an unconstitutional delegation of legislative authority.[53] The Pennsylvania Supreme Court held that a statute purporting to authorize the legislature to terminate a state of emergency by a concurrent resolution without presentation to the governor violated the

[47] For a preliminary assessment, see 50 Am. Rev. Pub. Admn. 450–808 (Aug.–Oct. 2020).

[48] For an argument for continued judicial review of government action during emergencies, see Lindsay Wiley & Stephen Vladeck, *Coronavirus, Civil Liberties, and the Courts: The Case Against "Suspending" Judicial Review*, 133 Harv. L. Rev. F. 179 (July 2020).

[49] *In re* Interrogatory on House Joint Resolution, 20-1006, 500 P.3d 1053 (Colo. 2020).

[50] Pennsylvania Democratic Party v. Boockvar, 238 A.3d 345 (Pa. 2020).

[51] Friends of Danny DeVito v. Wolf, 227 A.2d 872 (Pa. 2020).

[52] Wisconsin Legislature v. Palm, 942 N.W.2d 900 (Wis. 2020).

[53] *In re* Certified Questions from United States District Court, Western District of Michigan, 958 N.W.2d 1 (Mi. 2020). *Contra* Beshear v. Acree, 615 S.W.3d 780 (Ky. 2020). *See generally* Kelly J. Deere, *Governing By Executive Order During the COVID-19 Pandemic: Preliminary Observations Concerning the Proper Balance Between Executive Orders and More Formal Rulemaking*, 86 Mo. L. Rev. 721 (2021).

state constitution's presentation clause.[54] There was more: partisan "power plays" gained national political and scholarly attention as, for example, outgoing political parties in North Caroline and Wisconsin sought to decrease dramatically the power of the incoming governor of the other party.[55]

All of these developments continue to capture the attention of the legal and political community, as well as the media and the public, in ways that a state constitutional convention's increase in gubernatorial powers or modernization of fiscal and budgetary provisions never could. Such structural or political reforms has captured the attention of political scientists and state government experts, whose interests have included the structure and power allocations of state and local government, as well as the ways in which such powers actually are exercised. Lawyers, judges, and law teachers, by contrast, have tended to be concerned with the extent and limit of governmental powers and with the interpretation of constitutional provisions in litigation. It is no surprise, therefore, that the state bill of rights "explosion" of the NJF attracted the interest of a wide array of lawyers, judges, and legal scholars, and that this attention had both broadened and accelerated in recent years.

At the same time, the field of state constitutional law, like federal constitutional law, is by no means limited to cases involving the application of state bills of rights. State constitutions and their interpretation affected the structure and power of state and local governments, state-local relations, state legislative, executive and judicial systems, taxation and public finance, the environment and natural resources, public education, and the processes of amendment and revision. Furthermore, many of the issues governed by state constitutions, except for some regional variations, do not differ substantially from one state to another. Despite this fact, state constitutional law has not generally been treated as a matter of political or legal theory or as a subject for comparative treatment; rather, it usually has been thought of as a parochial, state-specific matter. The recurring themes and issues found throughout state constitutional law, however, do make it susceptible in this book to treatment on a comparative or "all-states" basis. This could be referred to, in Professor Daniel Rodriguez's terminology, as a "trans-state" constitutionalism.[56]

A study of state constitutional law, while pointing out similarities, also highlights the differences among the legal and governmental systems of our fifty states. In the famous words of Justice Louis Brandeis:

[54] Wolf v. Scarnati, 233 A.3d 679 (Pa. 2020). *Accord* Kelly v. Legislative Coordinating Council 460 P.3d 832 (Kan. 2020).

[55] *See* Miriam Siefter, *Judging Power Plays in The American States*, 97 Tex. L. Rev. 1217 (2019).

[56] State constitutions "raise similar stakes and have more or less similar shapes." Daniel B. Rodriguez, *State Constitutional Theory and Its Prospects*, 28 N.M. L. Rev. 271, 301 (1998).

> It is one of the happy incidents of the federal system that a single courageous State may, if its citizens choose, serve as a laboratory; and try novel social and economic experiments without risk to the rest of the country.[57]

Many common themes appear in the constitutional law of all states. They touch upon the same or similar issues, despite differences in how such issues may be resolved under any specific state constitution. It is the purpose of this book to focus on these common themes and issues, which are likely to arise in any jurisdiction. This approach, in turn, highlights the importance of the unique language and judicial interpretation of the constitutions of each of the states in the resolution of specific issues.

This book is not intended to provide an exhaustive catalog of the provisions in the fifty American state constitutions. Nor does it analyze all of the judicial decisions and the interpretation techniques they reflect, expounding on the meaning of all the states' constitutional provisions. It is not arranged by the substantive topics in state constitutions. Rather, it provides a selective, general survey of the origins, evolution, and functions of the state constitutions; a comparative and illustrative analysis of the contents of the state constitutions; a detailed consideration of their rights provisions that operate simultaneously with federal constitutional rights provisions; a review of state constitutional structure and distribution of powers together with consideration of the nature, powers, and interrelationships of each of the three branches; examples of policy matters that have been inserted into state constitutions; and the processes of state constitutional amendment and revision. Techniques of judicial interpretation in each of these areas will be considered because state constitutional law, like its federal counterpart, is comprised of both constitutional text and judicial interpretation. In some instances, case studies from specific states are used to illustrate common themes. The book functions, in many instances, as a reference tool and therefore need not be read through from start to finish; indeed, some of the central themes are cross-referenced or recur in several places.

The discussion of, and citation to, many of the judicial decisions on state constitutional law must be somewhat decontextualized. This is because space simply does not allow for a full discussion of each case and because, often, the reference

[57] New State Ice Co. v. Liebmann, 285 U.S. 262, 311 (1932) (Brandeis, J., dissenting). Justice Oliver Wendell Holmes referred to "social experiments that an important part of the community desires, in the insulated chambers afforded by the several States . . ." Truax v. Corrigan, 257 U.S. 312, 344 (1921) (Holmes, J., dissenting).

Scholars have debated the relevance of Brandeis's use of the "experimental laboratory" metaphor. *See, e.g.*, Earl M. Maltz, *Lockstep Analysis and the Concept of Federalism*, 496 Annals Am. Acad. Pol. & Soc. Sci. 98, 100–01 (1988); James A. Gardner, *The "States-as-Laboratories" Metaphor in State Constitutional Law*, 30 Val. U. L. Rev. 475 (1996); G. Alan Tarr, *Laboratories of Democracy? Brandeis, Federalism and Scientific Management*, 31 Publius: The J. Federalism 37 (Winter 2001).

to the decision is not based on its *substantive conclusion* but rather on its *technique of analysis* and potential for issue recognition. This is particularly true with Chapter 12 on techniques of interpretation and Part II on state constitutional rights adjudication. The reader can then utilize these techniques of analysis in the specific contexts where they appear to be useful. Further, a study of the cases cited here will illustrate and review the differing techniques of state constitutional interpretation discussed specifically in the book.

Again, this book is not arranged around substantive topics like criminal procedure, free speech or privacy, public finance and taxation, education, or local government, as are some other books on state constitutional law.[58] The structure of the book is based on the theory that state constitutional law is multifaceted: proper understanding and interpretation of state constitutions must take account of the history of state constitutional provisions, the possibility that they were modeled on other states' provisions or are similar to, or different from other states' provisions, their evolution over time, their similarity to federal provisions, the possibility that they can be changed, and their function as a matter of state constitutional law. These are the interlocking parts of this book.

Judge Thomas Cooley's 1868 *A Treatise on the Constitutional Limitations Which Rest Upon the Legislative Power of the States of the American Union*, the eighth and final edition of which was published in 1927,[59] became "the most popular and influential constitutional law treatise of the late nineteenth century. For over forty years, it was regarded as 'an indispensable companion for every one interested in constitutional problems.'"[60] Although Cooley's work was the "first important treatise on state constitutional law,"[61] it has been, for over a century, "unreliable."[62] There is a need for a volume that considers state constitutions, and

[58] *See, e.g.*, SHAMAN, *supra* note 30; BARRY LATZER, STATE CONSTITUTIONAL CRIMINAL LAW (1995); JENNIFER FRIESEN, STATE CONSTITUTIONAL LAW: LITIGATING INDIVIDUAL RIGHTS, CLAIMS AND DEFENSES (2 vols., 4th ed. 2015).

[59] "The last major constitutional law treatise that discussed the law contained in the state bills of rights was published in 1927." Charles Douglas, *Federalism and State Constitutions*, 13 VT. L. REV. 127, 133 n.40 (1988).

[60] Stephen A. Siegel, *Historism in Late Nineteenth-Century Constitutional Thought*, 1990 WIS. L. REV. 1431, 1487 (*quoting* 4 DICTIONARY OF AM. BIOGRAPHY 393 (A. Johnson & D. Malone eds., 1930)).

[61] *Developments in the Law—The Interpretation of State Constitutional Rights*, 95 HARV. L. REV. 1324, 1465 (1982).

[62] Thomas Reed Powell, *Book Review*, 41 HARV. L. REV. 272 (1927); William Swindler, *State Constitutional Law: Some Representative Decisions*, 9 WM. & MARY L. REV. 166, 166 (1967) ("now obsolete").

Max Lerner and many others had linked the publication of Cooley's treatise and the emergence of post–Civil War laissez-faire capitalism. Max Lerner, *The Supreme Court and American Capitalism*, 42 YALE L.J. 668, 692 (1933). *See also* PHILLIP S. PALUDAN, A COVENANT WITH DEATH: THE CONSTITUTION, LAW AND EQUALITY IN THE CIVIL WAR ERA 249–73 (1975) (analyzing Cooley's influence). For an in-depth analysis, and defense, of Cooley's treatise, see ALAN R. JONES, THE CONSTITUTIONAL CONSERVATISM OF THOMAS MCINTYRE COOLEY: A STUDY IN THE HISTORY OF IDEAS 122–65 (1987).

the interpretation problems they present, as a discrete subject. As with statutory or federal constitutional interpretation, no single interpretational theory or approach will suffice. Each interpretational problem should be looked at from a variety of perspectives.

The approach of this book is similar to, but in important respects different from, that of Judge Thomas Cooley more than a century ago—that state constitutional law could be analyzed as a general topic. Professor Paul Kahn elaborated this point as follows:

> Cooley looked to the cases coming from the different state courts to find the common principles of state constitutionalism—and, ultimately, of American constitutionalism. Just as his contemporaries looked to the case law from different jurisdictions to find the common principles of tort or contract, Cooley aimed to describe an American constitutionalism that was the common object of each state court's interpretive effort. The diversity of state courts, each claiming a unique authority, did not prevent their engagement in a common interpretive enterprise.[63]

James Gardner further described Cooley's project:

> With this treatise, Cooley essentially invented—or certainly formalized—the field of "state constitutional law." In his hands, it was a distinctly anti-positivist invention. It treated its subject not in the positivist sense of a body of particular commands issued by the sovereign people of particular states, but in the universalist sense of an undifferentiated body of general principles existing independent of any particular constitution and available to courts construing individual constitutions whenever useful to decision in individual cases.[64]

Cooley's treatise is still cited by some state courts as a doctrinal authority.[65] We tend to disagree with his approach to state constitutional law, as Gardner described it—"an undifferentiated body of general principles existing independent of any particular constitution"—because of the importance we attribute to each state's constitutional text. As Justice Hans A. Linde has pointed out, state constitutions are not "common law."[66] Nonetheless, the same textual

[63] Paul Kahn, *Interpretation and Authority in State Constitutionalism*, 106 HARV. L. REV. 1147, 1162–63 (1993).

[64] James A. Gardner, *The Positivist Revolution That Wasn't: Constitutional Universalism in the States*, 4 ROGER WILLIAMS U. L. REV. 109, 126–27 (1998).

[65] *Id.* at 127–28. *See* Curious Theater Co. v. Colo. Dept. of Health and Environment, 220 P.3d 544, 551 (Colo. 2009).

[66] Hans A. Linde, *State Constitutions Are Not Common Law: Comments on Gardner's Failed Discourse*, 24 RUTGERS L.J. 927 (1993).

application and interpretation matters are likely to arise in any state, and therefore state constitutions and their interpretation can be studied as a general or "all-states" matter and not only on a provincial, state-specific basis. Certainly, in specific states, based on differences in state constitutional text, constitutional history, judicial precedent, or judicial philosophy, the resolution of interpretation questions will differ.

As noted, President Trump's campaign pledge to nominate only federal judges who were recommended by the Federalist Society may well result in another 1970s-like rush to the state courts and state constitutions.[67] The U.S. Supreme Court's recent "hands-off" ruling on partisan gerrymandering may provide another similar stimulus.[68] Not for the first time, the Court referred those dissatisfied with its decision to state law remedies: "Provisions in state statutes and state constitutions can provide standards and guidance for state courts to apply."[69]

The attention that the NJF increasingly brought to state constitutions, initially with respect to arguments for *rights protections* beyond the federal constitutional minimum standards, has now led to an emerging recognition of the additional elements of state constitutional law that are fundamentally important to our governance and to the protection of our citizens. Now that the role of state constitutional rights in American constitutionalism is more clearly understood (we still have a ways to go), separation of powers, the role of state constitutional revision and amendment, and local government under state constitutions are also emerging from the "gravitational pull"[70] or "shadow"[71] of federal constitutional law.

[67] We discuss this possibility at greater length in the epilogue.

[68] Rucho v. Common Cause, 139 S.Ct. 2484, 2506–07 (2019); *see, e.g.*, League of Women Voters v. Commonwealth, 178 A.3d 737, 741 (Pa. 2018) (striking down partisan gerrymandering under state constitution); *see also supra* notes 51–53 and accompanying text; Samuel S.-H. Wang et al., *Laboratories of Democracy Reform: State Constitutions and Partisan Gerrymandering*, 22 U. Pa. J. Const. L. 203, 211–13 (2019). *See generally* James A. Gardner, *A Post-*Vieth *Strategy for Litigating Partisan Gerrymandering Claims*, 3 Election L.J. 643 (2004); Schultz, *supra* note 39.

[69] *Rucho*, 139 S.Ct. at 2507.

[70] Scott Dodson, *The Gravitational Force of Federal Law*, 164 U. Pa. L. Rev. 703, 705 (2016) (explaining that federal constitutional interpretations in rights protection and beyond often exert a kind of "gravitational pull" on interpretations of identical or similar state constitutional provisions). However, according to Professor Scott Dodson:

> Constitutional law often involves sensitive and important policy matters, on which local preferences tend to be stronger, more unified, and more extreme than national preferences. Further, state constitutions have a different history and erect a different governmental structure than the federal Constitution. Finally, constitutional governance is the most prominent feature of popular sovereignty, a cherished American ideal. These factors suggest that states should exercise independence in state constitutionalism, relying on the preferences of their particular populaces, with sensitivity to the nuances of their state governmental structures.

*Id.* at 724–25.

[71] Robert F. Williams, *In the Supreme Court's Shadow: Legitimacy of State Rejection of Supreme Court Reasoning and Result*, 35 S.C. L. Rev. 353 (1984).

To illustrate both the point that state constitutions and their interpretation can be studied as a general matter, as well as the point that state-specific differences may be relevant in addressing the resolution of certain constitutional issues, we turn in the remainder of this introduction to a case study of the issue of same-sex marriage. Advocates for same-sex marriage first pressed this issue under the federal Constitution, which initially was held not to protect an individual's right to marry a person of the same sex. Years later, advocates would try again, this time making arguments under *state* constitutional commitments to equality and due process.[72] The timespan between the initial cases raising federal constitutional arguments, through the cases in which plaintiffs made arguments under state constitutions, and, finally, to the overriding 2015 decision from the U.S. Supreme Court in *Obergefell v. Hodges*,[73] holding that bans on same-sex marriage violate the federal Constitution, was relatively short. As the journalist Sasha Issenberg has observed, "[i]n a quarter century, gay marriage went from being a test of the moral and political imagination to settled policy in fifty states and a simple, even banal, fact of everyday life."[74]

A closer look at the issue of same-sex marriage in state courts, and the consequences of state constitutional decision-making in the same-sex marriage cases, reveals many of the facets of state constitutional law that we have noted in this introduction and which we explore in greater detail later in this book. First, the issue of same-sex marriage demonstrates the way in which state courts have embraced the NJF—that is, how some courts, interpreting their own constitutions, have approached the interpretation of their state constitution's individual rights protections in ways that stand in contrast to how the U.S. Supreme Court has approached the same protections under the Fifth and Fourteenth Amendments to the federal Constitution. The issue also shows how different interpretive methodologies may be deployed in various ways by state courts construing their own constitutions, including efforts to "lockstep" state constitutional rights with federal law, as well as the unique interpretation issues that may be raised by idiosyncratic state constitutional provisions.

The issue of same-sex marriage also demonstrates the ways in which state constitutions distribute governing power among the legislative, judicial, and executive branches and, in particular, how the configuration of state governments may differ from the federal plan. An exploration of same-sex marriage further illustrates the use of state constitutional amendment processes to entrench policy positions in state constitutions, how these processes have come to involve

[72] *See generally* Mary Bonauto, *Equality and the Impossible—State Constitutions and Marriage*, 68 Rutgers U. L. Rev. 1481 (2016).

[73] 576 U.S. 644 (2015).

[74] Sasha Issenberg, The Engagement: America's Quarter-Century Struggle over Same-Sex Marriage 14 (2021).

national political issues, the ways in which state courts play an important role in adjudicating procedural challenges to state constitutional change, how state constitutional amendments can "overrule" judicial interpretations, how state constitutional provisions can be invalid under the federal Constitution, and how elected state judges can be held accountable by voters for controversial state constitutional decisions.

Finally, the issue of same-sex marriage implicates the array of direct democracy mechanisms that state constitutions contain—features of political life in the states that have no parallel under the U.S. Constitution.

## I. Same-Sex Marriage and the New Judicial Federalism

The first time a court considered the exclusion of same-sex couples from state marriage laws, the issue arose as a matter of *federal* constitutional law in a *state* court. The plaintiffs in *Baker v. Nelson*, Richard John Baker and James Michael McConnell, applied for a marriage license and were denied by the clerk of court.[75] A Minnesota trial court upheld that action, and the plaintiffs appealed. They argued that they were being denied a fundamental right under the Ninth Amendment to the U.S. Constitution, as well as due process and equal protection under the Fourteenth Amendment.[76] The Minnesota Supreme Court was not impressed. The court concluded that it was not irrational for the state legislature to restrict marriage to couples of the opposite sex, and that there was no irrational or invidious discrimination involved.[77] The plaintiffs did not make, and the court did not consider, any arguments about the legality of the legislative prohibition under the state constitution. The plaintiffs appealed the decision to the U.S. Supreme Court. The court dismissed the appeal "for want of a substantial federal question."[78] This one-sentence decision became the law of the land for decades as far as the legality of same-sex marriage bans under the federal Constitution was concerned.

Two decades later, three same-sex couples in Hawaii sought to challenge the denial of marriage licenses under that state's laws by making explicit arguments about the meaning of equality under the state constitution.[79] By this time, the NJF was not quite so new. Many state courts, particularly in the area of constitutional

[75] 191 N.W.2d 185, 185 (Minn. 1971). *See also* Issenberg, *supra* note 74, at 48–49 (describing the litigation efforts of Baker and McConnell).

[76] *Baker*, 191 N.W.2d at 186.

[77] *See id.* at 186–87.

[78] Baker v. Nelson, 409 U.S. 810 (1972). It is important to remember that this, in contrast to a denial of *certiorari*, constitutes a ruling on the merits.

[79] There were several other challenges to restrictions on access to civil marriage in the interim, none of which squarely addressed the constitutionality of such restrictions under state constitutional law. *See* Jones v. Hallahan, 501 S.W.2d 588 (Ky. Ct. App. 1973) (failing to address equal protection arguments); Singer v. Hara, 522 P.2d 1187 (Wash. 1974) (holding plaintiffs were not denied equal

criminal procedure, had begun to entertain arguments that their state's constitutional commands protected rights to a greater extent than the U.S. Supreme Court had concluded those rights' federal counterparts did. In fact, the plaintiffs' counsel in *Baehr v. Lewin*[80] specifically declined to raise federal constitutional arguments.[81] He believed that he could leverage the first article of the Hawaii Constitution, which states that "the right of the people to privacy is recognized and shall not be infringed without the showing of a compelling state interest,"[82] in his clients' behalf. The complaint also alleged, among other things, that denying the plaintiffs access to civil marriage violated the state constitution's guarantee of equal protection—indeed, the state supreme court ultimately concluded that the trial court's dismissal of the case "r[an] aground on the shoals of the Hawaii Constitution's equal protection clause."[83]

Interestingly, the Hawaii Supreme Court, pointing to textual distinctions between the provisions, made an initial effort to suggest that the scope of the equality guarantee under the state constitution was different from that of the Fourteenth Amendment's promise of equal protection.[84] In the end, the court did not make very much of these distinctions in its analysis of the central issue, and relied upon U.S. Supreme Court cases in determining that, under the Hawaii Constitution, classifications based upon sex should receive heightened judicial scrutiny.[85] The court acknowledged, moreover, that, in ruling in this case on the meaning of the state constitution, it had the authority "to accord greater protections to Hawaii's citizens . . . than are recognized under the United States Constitution."[86]

At the time of its decision in *Baehr*, the Hawaii Supreme Court was interpreting its equal protection guarantee on a relatively clean slate in regard to the issue of same-sex marriage. The court was untroubled by the U.S. Supreme Court's one-sentence opinion in *Baker v. Nelson*, and instead embraced the opportunity to define the meaning of equal protection under the state constitution, without any discernible anxiety over how and whether that definition could be squared with the meaning of equal protection under the Fourteenth Amendment in regard

protection); De Santo v. Barnsley, 476 A.2d 952 (Pa. Super. 1984) (declining to reach equal protection argument because it has not been raised below).

[80] Baehr v. Lewin, 852 P.2d 44 (Haw. 1993).

[81] *See* Issenberg, *supra* note 74, at 66 (noting that plaintiffs' counsel "no longer counted the Supreme Court as a welcoming venue for civil-rights litigation").

[82] Haw. Const., art. I, § 6.

[83] *Baehr*, 852 P.2d at 54.

[84] *See id.* at 59 ("The equal protection clauses of the United States and Hawaii Constitutions are not mirror images of one another."). *See generally* Chapter 7, section II.

[85] *See, e.g.*, *Baehr*, 852 P.2d at 66–67 (relying on sex discrimination cases under Fourteenth Amendment).

[86] *Id.* at 65–66 (footnote omitted). *See generally* Chapter 5.

to the constitutionality of prohibitions on same-sex marriage. In 1996, on remand, the state trial court held that Hawaii's prohibition on same-sex marriage ran afoul of the state constitutional commitment to equality.[87]

Ten years later, the Massachusetts Supreme Judicial Court famously heard a challenge similar to *Baehr* under the Massachusetts Declaration of Rights in *Goodridge v. Department of Public Health*.[88] As noted earlier, *Goodridge* put the project of state constitutionalism before the American public like no other case before it, including *Baehr*. In 2003, the NJF was entering its fourth decade, yet it is fair to say that no other decision of a state court interpreting its state's individual rights protections more generously than the parallel provisions under the federal Constitution attracted the same level of attention as *Goodridge*. In part this was because, at the time *Goodridge* reached the commonwealth's highest court, prohibitions on same-sex marriage had become a matter of national debate: among other developments, since the Hawaii court's decision in *Baehr*, Congress had enacted the Defense of Marriage Act, which allowed states to refuse to recognize foreign same-sex marriages and defined "marriage" under federal law to include only opposite-sex couples; and numerous states had enacted laws defining marriage as confined to opposite-sex couples.[89] A number of states were amending their constitutions to ban same-sex marriage, eliminating the promise of the NJF.

The court in *Goodridge* ultimately concluded that the ban on issuing marriage licenses to same-sex couples violated the guarantee of equality under the Massachusetts Declaration of Rights.[90] Other than its subject matter, however, the decision represented a relatively ordinary application of two principles, one related to state constitutional law and the other to the prevailing judicial philosophy regarding the implementation of equality guarantees. First, the decision vindicated the premise underlying the NJF—that nothing in our federalist governmental system precludes state courts from interpreting their state's constitution to provide citizens greater protection than might be found under the U.S. Constitution. Second, the decision illustrated the long-standing view of the U.S. Supreme Court and the lower federal courts that, in general, heightened judicial scrutiny under equal protection should be employed sparingly.[91] *Goodridge*

[87] Baehr v. Miike, No. CIV. 91-1394, 1996 WL 694235, at *22 (Haw. Cir. Ct. Dec. 3, 1996), *aff'd*, 950 P.2d 1234 (1997), and *rev'd*, 994 P.2d 566 (1999).

[88] 798 N.E.2d 941 (Mass. 2003).

[89] *See* Leonore F. Carpenter & Ellie Margolis, *One Sequin at a Time: Lessons on State Constitutions and Incremental Change From the Campaign for Marriage Equality*, 75 N.Y.U. Ann. Survey Am. L. 255, 282–83 (2020) (discussing federal Defense of Marriage Act and state legislative developments in the wake of *Baehr*).

[90] *See Goodridge*, 798 N.E.2d at 968.

[91] *See* Lawrence Friedman, *The (Relative) Passivity of* Goodridge v. Department of Public Health, 14 B.U. Pub. Int. L.J. 1 (2004); *Ordinary and Enhanced Rational Basis Review in the Massachusetts Supreme Judicial Court: A Preliminary Investigation*, 69 Albany L. Rev. 415 (2006).

was in this way both pathbreaking and conservative: it stands as an example of the NJF at work—for the same result likely would not have been reached under the Fourteenth Amendment's Equal Protection Clause (at least at the time)—and an example of how state courts, even when interpreting their own constitutions, nonetheless tend to revert to federal doctrinal approaches to implementing constitutional commands. As well, the *Goodridge* court notably made reference to international law human rights norms in support of its decision.[92]

*Baehr* and *Goodridge* illustrate and exemplify the virtues of dual constitutionalism. While, as we suggested earlier, state constitutionalism is by no means limited to the NJF or to cases involving the interpretation of state constitutional rights provisions, rights cases are the avenue by which many state constitutional decisions will become known to a wider public. Chapter 5 of this book is devoted to exploring the NJF and the issues that state courts may face when litigants seek either greater protection under their state constitutions than would be available under the U.S. Constitution or, in some instances, protections that do not even exist under the federal charter.

## II. Same-Sex Marriage, Interpretive Methodologies, and Lockstepping

The courts in Hawaii and Massachusetts led the way in regard to the issue of same-sex marriage, but many other state courts soon followed as advocates of same-sex marriage sought to build on their victory in *Goodridge*. The same-sex marriage cases that resulted prior to the settlement of the issue nationally by the U.S. Supreme Court with its decision in *Obergefell*, in addition to illustrating the basic premise of the NJF, also serve as examples of the varying methodological approaches to state constitutional decision making in individual rights cases, including the judicial phenomenon of lockstepping state and federal constitutional interpretation; as well as the interpretive challenges presented by provisions that are unique to a state constitution.

It should be no surprise that methodological approaches to interpreting state constitutional provisions might vary between courts and even from case to case. Whereas the Massachusetts Supreme Judicial Court in *Goodridge* viewed the prohibition on same-sex marriage as unconstitutionally irrational, the Iowa Supreme Court, just six years later in *Varnum v. O'Brien*,[93] adopted the broader view that, under the state constitution, sexual orientation should be considered a

[92] *Goodridge*, 798 N.E.2d at 969. *See generally* Chapter 12, section XII.
[93] 763 N.W.2d 862 (Iowa 2009). *See* Allan Vestal, *Vindication:* Varnum v. O'Brien *at Ten Years*, 67 Drake L. Rev. 563 (2019).

quasi-suspect classification. In retrospect, the *Goodridge* decision can be seen as logically related to the U.S. Supreme Court's determinations in two earlier cases, *Romer v. Evans*[94] and *Lawrence v. Texas*.[95] In *Romer*, the court struck down as irrational a state constitutional amendment prohibiting the enforcement of discrimination protections on the basis of sexual orientation,[96] and in *Lawrence*, the court struck down as irrational state laws prohibiting certain intimate conduct between consenting adults. In all three decisions, the respective courts saw no need to explore whether legislative classifications based upon sexual orientation should be subject to some form of heightened judicial scrutiny.

In contrast to *Romer*, *Lawrence*, and *Goodridge*, the Iowa Supreme Court in *Varnum* adopted a construction of the Iowa Constitution that was more protective of rights than the interpretation of the Massachusetts and U.S. constitutions by the Supreme Judicial Court and the U.S. Supreme Court, respectively. The *Varnum* court notably sought to distinguish its doctrinal analysis under the state constitution, which closely resembled federal doctrine, from the evolution of equal protection doctrine under the U.S. Constitution, as the court observed that Iowa jurisprudence reflected a history of recognizing significant equality concerns before the U.S. Supreme Court had done so.[97] The Iowa court ruled more broadly than the *Goodridge* court, undertaking an analysis as to whether sexual orientation should be considered a suspect classification and concluding that it should.[98] The court went on to conclude that Iowa's ban on same-sex marriage failed to satisfy the test of heightened scrutiny that court applied to suspect and quasi-suspect classifications under the state constitution, because the discrimination in the law did not substantially further any legitimate state objectives.[99]

Although the court in *Varnum* ultimately reached the same result as the court in *Goodridge*, it got there by following a different path, one defined primarily by its more robust enforcement of the state constitutional commitment to equality—and one which could support other challenges to government action aimed at discriminating on the basis of sexual orientation. In this way, *Varnum* is an example of how state courts may endeavor to more fully enforce

[94] 517 U.S. 620 (1996).
[95] 539 U.S. 558 (2003).
[96] *See* Chapter 3.
[97] *See Varnum*, 763 N.W.2d at 877.
[98] *See id.* at 895–96.
[99] *See id.* at 904. The Iowa court was not the first to determine that heightened scrutiny of classifications based upon sexual orientation was appropriate, or that state bans on same-sex marriage failed to satisfy heightened scrutiny. *See In re* Marriage Cases, 183 P.3d 384, 453 (Cal. 2008) (concluding prohibition on same-sex marriage violated equality and due process protections under California Constitution); Kerrigan v. Comm'r of Pub. Health, 957 A.2d 407 (Conn. 2008) (concluding prohibition on same-sex marriage violated equality protections under Connecticut Constitution).

rights guarantees that under federal law go underenforced because of the U.S. Supreme Court's deference to the states—or that under a state constitution may go underenforced because a state court has, in a particular case or as a practice, followed the minimalist approach to rights enforcement favored by the Supreme Court. We discuss the ways in which the underenforcement of federal constitutional rights may play a role in the implementation of state constitutional rights in Chapter 6.

Recall that nothing in the U.S. Constitution requires state courts to interpret their constitutions in line with the U.S. Supreme Court's interpretation of the federal Constitution. Nonetheless, some state courts, in particular cases or as a matter of course, seek to walk in lockstep with the U.S. Supreme Court in regard to the interpretation and application of parallel individual rights provisions. An illustration of this phenomenon in the context of same-sex marriage is the decision of the New York Court of Appeals in *Hernandez v. Robles.*[100] In *Hernandez,* New York's high court concluded that the state constitution did not "compel recognition of marriages between members of the same sex."[101] The court found that the only question was whether excluding same-sex couples from marriage was rational—precisely the test of constitutionality, in other words, that a federal court would have applied at the time if it had faced the same question under the Fourteenth Amendment, and indeed that a federal court would have applied to any statutory rule that did not classify individuals on the bases of such protected categories as race, sex, or the deprivation of a fundamental interest. In fact, the *Hernandez* court expressly linked its understanding of equality under the New York Constitution to the Supreme Court's approach to equal protection under the federal Constitution.[102]

The *Hernandez* decision is an example of a state court determining that the interpretation and application of a provision of its state constitution should be linked to federal jurisprudence on the same issue. This kind of lockstepping is a familiar approach to state constitutional law in many states, with courts explicitly seeking to follow rather than diverge from federal law where individual rights protections are concerned. There are different varieties of lockstepping; *Hernandez* represents the common occurrence of a state court essentially "borrowing" a doctrinal analysis and mode of reasoning from the U.S. Supreme Court and applying it the correlative rights protection contained in the state

[100] 855 N.E.2d 1 (N.Y. 2006).

[101] *Id.* at 5.

[102] *See id.* at 9 (noting that New York equality guarantee "is no broader in coverage than the identical Federal provision" (*quoting* Under 21, Catholic Home Bur. For Dependent Children v. City of New York, 482 N.E.2d 1 (1985))); *id.* at 11 (relying upon federal equal protection jurisprudence). *See generally* Chapter 7, section II.

constitution. This and the other forms of lockstepping are discussed at length, and critiqued, in Chapter 7.

Finally, an early challenge to a state law limiting marriage to opposite-sex couples illustrates the phenomenon of state constitutional protections that lack a counterpart under the federal Constitution. In *Baker v. State*,[103] the plaintiffs alleged that Vermont's marriage law violated the state constitution's Common Benefits Clause, the text of which scarcely resembles the Fourteenth Amendment's Equal Protection Clause.[104] The state supreme court concluded that the concept of equality at the core of this clause "was not the eradication of racial or class distinctions," as under federal law, "but rather the elimination of artificial government preferments and advantages."[105] The court embraced a straightforward analysis to evaluate allegations that the clause had been violated: as outlined in the *Baker* decision, a reviewing court must determine "whether the omission of a part of the community from the benefit, protection, and security of the challenged law bears a reasonable and just relation to the governmental purpose."[106] Applying this test, the court held that same-sex couples had been unreasonably excluded from the benefits and protections of marriage, though in the end the court deferred to the legislature as to how best to remedy this exclusion.[107]

As Professor Williams has explained, the Vermont court's decision in *Baker* may be seen in many ways as a kind of primer on how state courts should approach the interpretation of state constitutional rights provisions for which there is no federal parallel.[108] Some of the themes related to independent state constitutionalism addressed in *Baker* include the relevance of textual differences, the historical context in which a provision was framed, existing judicial precedent, and the importance of referring to the interpretation of similar provisions in other state constitutions.[109] The potential sources and techniques that are

[103] 744 A.2d 864 (Vt. 1999).

That government is, or ought to be, instituted for the common benefit, protection, and security of the people, nation, or community, and not for the particular emolument or advantage of any single person, family, or set of persons, who are a part only of that community; and that the community hath an indubitable, unalienable, and indefeasible right, to reform or alter government, in such manner as shall be, by that community, judged most conducive to the public weal.

[104] VT. CONST., ch. 1, art. VII.

[105] *Baker*, 744 A.2d at 876.

[106] *Id.* at 878–79. For a discussion of this standard and how it compares to equal protection doctrine under the Fourteenth Amendment, see Lawrence Friedman & Charles H. Baron, Baker v. State *and the Promise of the New Judicial Federalism*, 43 B.C. L. REV. 125, 141–49 (2001).

[107] *Baker*, 744 A.2d at 886.

[108] *See* Robert F. Williams, *Old Constitutions and New Issues: National Lessons from Vermont's State Constitutional Case on Marriage of Same-Sex Couples*, 43 B.C. L. REV. 73 (2001).

[109] *See id.* at 78–99.

relevant to the interpretation of state constitutions, some of which the Vermont court relied upon in *Baker*, are explored in Chapter 12.

## III. Same-Sex Marriage and the Distribution of Powers in State Constitutions

In addition to the insight they offer into the interpretation of state constitutional individual rights protections, the same-sex marriage cases serve as a lens through which to view the ways in which state constitutions configure governmental arrangements and the distribution of authority, as well as how those arrangements may stand in contrast to the structure of government created by the U.S. Constitution.[110] The various decisions on same-sex marriage that we discuss in this introduction each led to questions that fell to the political departments of state government, which responded in a variety of ways, from proposing legislation or constitutional amendments, to, in one instance, requesting an advisory opinion on a proposed remedy (Massachusetts).

Some state court same-sex marriage decisions either explicitly or implicitly invited a legislative response. Consider *Baker v. State*, in which the Vermont Supreme Court expressly referred the matter to the legislature to devise a remedy for the constitutional problem created by the exclusion of same-sex couples from civil marriage.[111] The Vermont Legislature responded with a law allowing same-sex couples to enter into civil unions, which provided them the benefits and protections of marriage,[112] if not the status itself.[113] In New York, by contrast, the state legislature responded to the decision of the Court of Appeals in *Hernandez v. Robles*, which upheld the exclusion of same-sex couples from marriage, by enacting the Marriage Equality Act in 2011.[114] That law provided a statutory basis for marriage equality; in addition to legalizing same-sex marriage, the law forbids state and local courts and governments from punishing religious and religious-supervised institutions, their employees, and their clergy for failing to recognize such marriages should they be contrary to particular

[110] *See generally* Norman R. Williams, *Executive Review in the Fragmented Executive: State Constitutions and Same-Sex Marriage*, 154 U. Pa. L. Rev. 565 (2006); Vikram David Amar, *Lessons from California: Of Mayors, Governors, Controllers, and Attorneys General*, 59 Emory L.J. 469 (2009).

[111] *Baker*, 744 A.2d at 886. *See also* Lewis v. Harris, 908 A.2d 196 (N.J. 2006) (declaring ban on same-sex marriage unconstitutional but leaving choice of marriage or civil unions to legislature).

[112] *See* Vt. Stat. Ann. Tit. 15, §§ 1201–07 (2001).

[113] *See* Jes Krause, Note, *Monkey See, Monkey Do: On* Baker, Goodridge, *and the Need for Consistency in Same-Sex Alternatives to Marriage*, 26 Vt. L. Rev. 959, 974–75 (2002) (discussing critiques of civil unions as remedy for state constitutional violation in *Baker*).

[114] *See In the* Matter of Kelly S. v. Farah M., 139 A.D. 90, 97–98 (N.Y. 2016) (discussing Marriage Equality Act and legislative intent to treat opposite- and same-sex couples equally in regard to marriage).

religious beliefs or practices. The New York example is a reminder, too, that states may raise individual rights protections above the federal floor not just through judicial decisions interpreting state constitutional provisions.

Decisions overturning same-sex marriage bans have led to other legislative responses. The reaction to the Hawaii Supreme Court's initial decision in *Baehr* illustrates a legislative reaction to state constitutional decision-making centered around constitutional amendment. Following the trial court's ruling on remand in *Baehr* that the prohibition on same-sex marriage violated the state constitution, the legislature proposed a state constitutional amendment to preclude the state's judiciary from addressing the issue of marriage equality; voters passed the amendment in 1998.[115] The next year, as Professors Leonore Carpenter and Ellie Margolis have written, "the Hawaii Supreme Court, which had stalled in its enforcement of marriage equality pending the outcome of the amendment process, officially ended the *Baehr* litigation by admitting that the passage of the constitutional amendment had rendered Hawaii's same-sex marriage ban constitutional."[116] Chapters 8 and 9 discuss, respectively, the distribution of powers across state government and the legislature's broad authority under state constitutions to address remedial concerns and legislate in public interest.

Massachusetts saw a different kind of response to the Supreme Judicial Court's decision in *Goodridge v. Department of Public Health* holding the Commonwealth's same-sex marriage ban unconstitutional. In *Goodridge*, the court seemed to assume that, following its decision, the legislature would respond with implementing legislation.[117] Instead, the legislature drafted a law like Vermont's, which would have allowed same-sex couples to enter into civil unions providing the same benefits and privileges as marriage does or opposite-sex couples. The legislature then requested an advisory opinion from the court as to the constitutionality of such a scheme.[118] While the court rejected this proposal, the legislative request illustrates the availability of a mechanism for dialogue between the branches of state governments—the advisory opinion—that has no federal equivalent.[119] Following *Goodridge*, moreover, the Massachusetts attorney general, elected separately from the governor under the state constitution, declined the governor's request to seek a stay of the decision, illustrating another signal difference between state and federal governmental plans—the plural

[115] *See* Carpenter & Margolis, *supra* note 89, at 286.

[116] *Id.*

[117] *See* Goodridge v. Dep't of Public Health, 798 N.E.2d 941, 970 (Mass. 2003) (allowing legislature 180 days "to take such action as it may deem appropriate in light of" the court's decision).

[118] *See In re* Opinions of the Justices to the Senate, 802 N.E.2d 565, 566 (Mass. 2004).

[119] For an examination of advisory opinions under state constitutions, see Jonathan D. Persky, *"Ghosts That Slay": A Contemporary Look at State Advisory Opinions*, 37 CONN. L. REV. 1155 (2005). *See also* Chapter 10, section VII.

executive.[120] In Chapter 10, we examine advisory opinions, and in Chapter 11 we address the nature of executive power under state constitutions, including the plural executive.

Chapter 10 also covers judicial selection and retention, another area in which constitutional rules in many states diverge markedly from the federal system—and another area in which the issue of same-sex marriage under state constitutions provides a pointed illustration of divergence between state and federal law. As we noted earlier, the Iowa Supreme Court in *Varnum v. O'Brien* concluded that the state constitutional equality guarantee required courts to subject classifications based upon sexual orientation to rigorous judicial review and, applying such scrutiny, the state's ban on same-sex marriage did not pass muster. Under the Iowa Constitution, judges, following their initial appointment, must stand for retention elections; the political and popular reaction to *Varnum* centered on a concerted effort to remove three of the justices who joined the majority—an effort that ultimately was successful.[121] Professor Todd Pettys has speculated that that the judges' ouster might have resulted from thc roadblocks to constitutional amendment confronting critics of *Varnum*; regardless, as he put it, the justices "did not lose their jobs by violating widely embraced conventions of constitutional reasoning," but "by reaching a conclusion that many citizens found morally and politically objectionable."[122]

## IV. Same-Sex Marriage and State Constitutional Amendment via Direct Democracy

One of the most significant distinguishing features of state constitutions, as compared to the federal Constitution, is the relative ease with which they can be amended, particularly through popular democratic mechanisms, like citizen initiatives. Indeed, in nearly every state, direct democracy plays some part in the constitutional amendment process. While the Hawaii legislature led the way in proposing a constitutional amendment to divest the state courts of authority in regard to marriage following the *Baehr* decision, other efforts to amend have originated with citizens who objected to their judiciary's involvement (or potential involvement) in defining marriage for constitutional purposes; these efforts were launched at times either in advance of or in response to state supreme court marriage equality decisions.

120 *See* Mark C. Miller, *Conflicts Between the Massachusetts Supreme Judicial Court and the Legislature: Campaign Finance Reform and Same-Sex Marriage*, 4 Pierce L. Rev. 279, 304 (2006).

121 *See* Todd E. Pettys, *Letter from Iowa: Same-Sex Marriage and the Ouster of Three Justices*, 59 Kansas L. Rev. 715, 716–17 (2011).

122 *Id.* at 717.

In California, for example, the effort to amend the constitution to prevent same-sex marriage proceeded in parallel with litigation over the issue in the state courts.[123] By the time the California Supreme Court issued its decision in *In re Marriage Cases*, in May 2008, the movement to amend the state constitution to prohibit same-sex marriage was well underway. The court in *In re Marriage Cases* concluded both that laws discriminating on the basis of sexual orientation should be subject to the most rigorous judicial review and that state bans on same-sex marriage were unconstitutional.[124] Following that decision, in November 2008, voters approved Proposition 8, which amended the state constitution to confine marriage to opposite-sex couples.[125] Ruling on a challenge to the amendment under the state constitution, the court in *Strauss v. Horton* upheld the amendment, rejecting arguments that the proposal violated the state constitutional requirements for modifying the constitution through the initiative process.[126]

California's amendment was soon challenged in federal district court, in a case called *Perry v. Schwarzenegger*.[127] Concluding that Proposition 8 violated the Fourteenth Amendment to the U.S. Constitution, the district court observed that the amendment failed "to advance any rational basis in singling out gay men and lesbians for denial of a marriage license."[128] The Ninth Circuit Court of Appeals subsequently wrestled with the question of who might challenge the district court's ruling on appeal, since the principal named defendants, Governor Arnold Schwarzenegger and Attorney General Jerry Brown, had declined to do so. Ultimately, without addressing the merits of the case, the U.S. Supreme Court determined that the backers of Proposition 8 lacked standing to appeal the district court's decision.[129]

The sequence of judicial and political events associated with the issue of same-sex marriage in California illustrates a number of points about the nature of state constitutional law, state constitutional change, and the ways in which state constitutional law operates in tandem with federal law. As an initial matter, there is the California Supreme Court's conclusion, in *In re Marriage Cases*, that, under

[123] Following the Massachusetts Supreme Judicial Court's decision in *Goodridge*, voters in Arkansas, Michigan, Montana, North Dakota, Ohio, and Oregon all approved proposals to amend their state constitutions to prohibit same-sex marriage. *See* Carlos A. Ball, *The Backlash Thesis and Same-Sex Marriage: Learning from* Brown v. Board of Education *and Its Aftermath*, 14 Wm. & Mary Bill Rts. J. 1493, 1513 (2006).

[124] *See In re* Marriage Cases, 183 P.3d 384, 453 (Cal. 2008).

[125] *See* Strauss v. Horton, 207 P.3d 48 (Cal. 2009).

[126] *See id.* at 101 (concluding that "it is evident" that because Proposition 8 works no qualitative change in the California Constitution, "it does not constitute [an invalid] constitutional revision"). *See generally* Chapter 14.

[127] Perry v. Schwarzenegger, 704 F. Supp.2d 921 (N.D. Cal. 2010).

[128] *Id.* at 1003.

[129] Hollingsworth v. Perry, 570 U.S. 693, 708 (2013) ("Article III standing is not to be placed in the hands of 'concerned bystanders,' who will use it simply as a vehicle for the vindication of value interests" (internal quotations omitted)).

the state constitution, classifications on the basis of sexual orientation are subject to strict judicial scrutiny—a conclusion later echoed by the Iowa Supreme Court and other state courts. As well, the sequence of events in California shows both how direct democracy can be an engine of constitutional change at the state level through the initiative process and the ways in which the state courts may review such efforts. Finally, in the context of same-sex marriage in California, the federal litigation shed light on another dimension of popular democratic state constitutional change—namely, the question of who, among a state's officials, has the authority to represent the interests of the state in regard to citizen-initiated statutes and amendments in a situation where the people's elected representatives and officials are not primarily responsible for the law or amendment in question. This is another question that simply does not arise in federal practice, where there is no option for popular lawmaking, much less constitutional amendment.[130]

The processes of state constitutional amendment, including questions about the requirements for valid modification of a state's constitution through the mechanisms of direct democracy, as well as the role of the judiciary in evaluating the same, are discussed in Chapters 13 and 14.

## V. Conclusion

Following the U.S. Supreme Court's decision in *Obergefell v. Hodges*, in 2015, the issue of whether states can prohibit same-sex marriage, via either statute or constitutional amendment, is no longer a subject of litigation in state courts, at least at this writing. In some ways, the *Obergefell* decision can be viewed as a culmination of the efforts of advocates in many states to press the issue of marriage equality under state constitutions. However, as we hope this brief survey shows, the issue as litigated in numerous state courts also implicates numerous other aspects of state constitutional practice well beyond the issue of discrimination, none of which were the object of the Supreme Court's attention in *Obergefell*.

The multifaceted nature of state constitutional law as a distinct body of law is the focus of this book. As we observed in the first part of this introduction, we seek to explore the issues of constitutional application and interpretation that extend to all state constitutions and to explain the ways in which individual state constitutions, owing to differences in text, history, judicial precedent, or judicial philosophy, may have relevance to the citizens who live under them. As the issue of same-sex marriage demonstrates, state courts and state constitutions can be at

130 For a discussion of the tensions between citizen-led initiatives and the federal approach to constitutional standing in cases where initiatives are challenged in federal court, see Scott L. Kafker & David A. Russcol, *Standing at a Constitutional Divide: Redefining State and Federal Requirements for Initiatives After* Hollingsworth v. Perry, 71 WASH. & LEE L. REV. 229 (2014).

the cutting edge of constitutional litigation, paving the way for the consideration of common issues by the U.S. Supreme Court under the federal Constitution. At the same time, the issue of same-sex marriage shows the critical role of state constitutional law as the source of governing principles for a particular state—principles that may well distinguish one state's constitutional law from that of other American constitutions, both state and federal.

In short, the issue of same-sex marriage as litigated in state courts reveals not just *how* state constitutional law operates but *why* it is such an important feature of the American constitutional system. The rest of this book is devoted to expanding on these propositions. Because the importance of state constitutional law, to our daily lives and as a field of study, is now generally accepted, we are confident that it will continue to be developed—by state courts, and also through all the other means by which constitutional change occurs.

## PART I

# STATE CONSTITUTIONS IN AMERICAN CONSTITUTIONAL FEDERALISM

In this first part of the book, the characteristics of state constitutions, in contrast to the more familiar federal Constitution, will be introduced. Chapter 1 provides a broad-brush description of state constitutions as *real* constitutions, interconnected and operating in tandem with the "incomplete" federal Constitution, but different in many respects from the federal model. Chapter 2 covers the development of the early state constitutions, before the adoption of the federal Constitution, and their varying influences on the development of the federal document. The wide range of alternative, and now somewhat unfamiliar, visions of the structure of state governments are covered. Chapter 3 gives a picture of the evolution of state constitutions, which are much easier to amend, including the federal influences over them exerted during the process of admitting new states to the Union. This evolution reflects a very different set of constitutional traditions from those that are more familiar in connection with the federal Constitution. Finally, Chapter 4 reviews the limits placed on state constitutions by the federal Constitution and laws which are, of course, the supreme law of the land. The two kinds of constitutions are interconnected, but it is not an equal relationship.

# 1
# THE OTHER AMERICAN CONSTITUTIONS

*The State Constitutions are the oldest things in the political history of America, for they are continuations and representatives of the royal colonial charters, whereby the earliest English settlements in America were created.... Their interest is all the greater, because the succession of Constitutions and amendments to Constitutions from 1776 till today enables the annals of legislation and political sentiment to be read in these documents more easily and succinctly than in any similar series of laws in any other country. They are a mine of instruction for the natural history of democratic communities.*[1]

*One might almost say that the romance, the poetry, and even the drama of American politics are deeply embedded in the many state constitutions promulgated since the publication of Paine's Common Sense, the Declaration of Independence, and the Virginia Bill of Rights.*[2]

When thinking about American constitutional law, we almost always have a unitary focus on federal constitutional law. The more accurate view is that we have two kinds of constitutional law in the United States: federal and state.[3] Federal constitutional law, however, has received the lion's share of academic and judicial analysis. Most of the attention brought to bear on state constitutional law in the last several generations has centered on rights cases and whether state courts should interpret their constitutions to be more protective than the federal Constitution.[4] These matters are covered in Part II. While state constitutional

[1] 1 JAMES BRYCE, THE AMERICAN COMMONWEALTH 413, 434 (2d ed. 1891).

[2] JAMES QUAYLE DEALEY, GROWTH OF AMERICAN STATE CONSTITUTIONS II (1915; reprint, 1972). Dealey also referred to state constitutions as "a cinematoscope of the times." *Id.* at 2.

[3] This is true also in other systems of constitutional federalism. *See* Robert F. Williams, *Comparative Subnational Constitutional Law: South Africa's Provincial Constitutional Experiments*, 40 S. TEX. L. REV. 625 (1999). *See also infra* note 26.

[4] *See, e.g.*, G. Alan Tarr, *Constitutional Theory and State Constitutional Interpretation*, 22 RUTGERS L.J. 841 (1991); James A. Gardner, *The Failed Discourse of State Constitutionalism*, 90 MICH. L. REV. 761 (1992); James Gray Pope, *An Approach to State Constitutional Interpretation*, 24 RUTGERS L.J.

*The Law of American State Constitutions*. Robert F. Williams and Lawrence Friedman, Oxford University Press.
 DOI: 10.1093/oso/9780190068806.003.0002

rights adjudication is extremely important and the sophistication of this area of the law has developed substantially,[5] state constitutional law extends beyond rights cases. State constitutions are unique legal instruments—real constitutions but different in significant ways from the federal Constitution.[6] In the United States, a system of constitutional federalism, it is therefore important to study, analyze, and describe "comparative American constitutional law."[7]

As Chief Judge Judith Kaye of New York pointed out, the New York Constitution "is a curious document—particularly when compared with the U.S. Constitution."[8] She continued:

> Given its laborious detail, our Constitution may not in every phrase ring with the majesty of Chief Justice Marshall's declaration: "it is *a constitution* we are expounding." But it *is* a constitution we are expounding, and its commands are therefore entitled to the particular deference that courts are obliged to accord matters of constitutional magnitude. To borrow former Chief Judge Breitel's eloquent words . . . "it is a Constitution that is being interpreted and as a Constitution it would serve little of its purpose if all that it promised, like the elegantly phrased Constitutions of some totalitarian or dictatorial Nations, was an ideal to be worshipped when not needed and debased when crucial."[9]

State constitutions, in fact, can be difficult to appreciate. Justice Hans A. Linde of Oregon explained:

> Most state constitutions are dusty stuff—too much detail, too much diversity, too much debris of old tempests in local teapots, too much preoccupation with

985 (1993); Paul W. Kahn, *Interpretation and Authority in State Constitutionalism*, 106 HARV. L. REV. 1147 (1993); Thomas Morawetz, *Deviation and Autonomy: The Jurisprudence of Interpretation in State Constitutional Law*, 26 CONN. L. REV. 635 (1994); Robert F. Williams, *In the Glare of the Supreme Court: Continuing Methodology in Legitimacy Problems in Independent State Constitutional Rights Adjudication*, 72 NOTRE DAME L. REV. 1015 (1997); Robert A. Schapiro, *Identity and Interpretation in State Constitutional Law*, 84 VA. L. REV. 389 (1998); Daniel B. Rodriguez, *State Constitutional Theory and Its Prospects*, 28 N.M. L. REV. 271 (1998); Jack L. Landau, *Hurrah for Revolution: A Critical Assessment of State Constitutional Interpretation*, 79 OR. L. REV. 793 (2000); Lawrence Friedman, *The Constitutional Value of Dialogue and the New Judicial Federalism*, 28 HAST. CONST. L.Q. 93 (2000).

[5] *See* Part II.

[6] *See* Graham Maddox, *A Note on the Meaning of "Constitution,"* 76 AM. POL. SCI. REV. 806 (1982).

[7] I am indebted to Gisbert H. Flanz for pointing out the applicability of the term "comparative constitutional law" to the study of American state constitutional law. *See* J. Michael Medina, *The Origination Clause in the American Constitution: A Comparative Survey*, 23 TULSA L.J. 165 (1987) (comparing state constitutional origination clauses with each other and with the federal clause).

[8] Judith S. Kaye, *Dual Constitutionalism in Practice and Principle*, 61 ST. JOHN'S L. REV. 399, 408 (1987). *See also* People v. Trueluck, 670 N.E.2d 977, 979 (N.Y. 1996) ("To be sure, the State Constitution in the overall is a lengthy and highly detailed document.").

[9] *Id.* at 411 (footnotes omitted).

> offices, their composition and administration, and forever with money, money, money. In short, no grand vision, no overarching theory, nothing to tempt a scholar aspiring to national recognition. Serious theorists understandably care about methods, principles, and outcomes that have nationwide importance. They are willing to let the states pursue their local peculiarities by statutes, by common law, or by interpreting or amending state constitutions; and who can blame them?
>
> *Yet I think this is a loss to theory.*[10]

These observations are relevant to state constitutions in general. State constitutions are curious, indeed, when compared with the more familiar U.S. Constitution. But they were not meant to be compared so much with the federal Constitution. Since 1787, when the federal Constitution was framed while taking into account the state constitutional experiments of 1776–1787,[11] state constitutions have evolved on paths distinct from federal constitutional law.[12]

## I. INTERRELATED CONSTITUTIONS

American state constitutions are *subnational* constitutions that operate internally within a *national constitution*, creating a relationship based on *imperium in imperio* (sovereignty within sovereignty or empire within empire).[13] They structure a measure of self-rule within a system of shared rule.[14] State constitutions

[10] Hans A. Linde, *E Pluribus—Constitutional Theory and State Courts*, 18 GA. L. REV. 165, 196–97 (1984) (emphasis added). With respect to American state constitutions, one commentator lamented:

> The explanation for the comparatively small amount of intensive professional and scholarly interest in at least the basic study of comparative state constitutional provisions lies to a great extent in the nature of the state constitutional documents themselves. . . . With some exceptions, the state constitutions are not notable as masterpieces of legal draftsmanship or literary style.

Morris M. Goldings, *Massachusetts Amends: A Decade of State Constitutional Revision*, 5 HARV. J. LEGIS. 373, 373 (1968).

[11] *See* Chapter 2.

[12] *See* Chapter 3.

[13] *See, e.g.*, FORREST MCDONALD, STATES' RIGHTS AND THE UNION: IMPERIUM IN IMPERIO, 1776–1833 (2000). Constitutions of the United States territories, where authorized by Congress under Article IV, Section 3, Clause [2] of the federal Constitution, are also *subnational* constitutions. *See* José Julián Alverez-Gonzalez, *The Protection of Civil Rights in Puerto Rico*, 6 ARIZ. J. INT'L & COMP. L. 89 (1989). Congress has provided for territorial constitution making in the U.S. Virgin Islands and Guam. Public Law 94-584, Statutes at Large, 90 2899–2900 (1976). For a critique of American territorial administration, see Christina Duffy Burnett, *United States: American Expansion and Territorial Deannexation*, 72 U. CHI. L. REV. 797 (2005). For a close look at the Puerto Rico Constitution and the island's constitutional relationship with the United States, see RAFAEL COX ALOMAR, THE PUERTO RICO CONSTITUTION (2022).

[14] DANIEL J. ELAZAR, EXPLORING FEDERALISM 4–5 (1987). *See also* Daniel J. Elazar, *A Response to Professor Gardner's The Failed Disclosure of State Constitutionalism*, 24 RUTGERS L.J. 975 (1993).

are essential in "designing democracy" in federal countries but for component, subnational polities rather than for the national polity.[15] The state constitutions are constrained by, and constitute integral parts of, the federal Constitution. Each of the constitutions forms an interlocking, interdependent element of the other. They are, as Professor James Gardner describes them, each part of our larger, continuously evolving federal constitutional structure:

> A realistic account of states and their powers must begin from the recognition that the American states are not free-standing, independent polities, but rather are embedded in a nationally created system of federalism. The apparatus of federalism exists for a purpose: to protect the liberty of all Americans. Federalism does so by constructing two levels of government, state and national; granting each level considerable overlapping authority; and charging each level of government with a duty not only to monitor the behavior of the other, but actively to resist it when it takes actions that threaten public welfare.[16]

Thus, in analyzing American constitutional federalism, Professor Louis Bilionis concluded that the federal and state constitutions should be evaluated together as an interconnected whole:

> Each is a distinct force which helps shape our national constitutional environment. Each force, however, is also dependent upon, limited by, and to some extent the product of, that very same environment. Federal and state constitutions thus are interdependent features of a greater *American* constitutional structure, the web of social institutions and practices the American people employ, sometimes unwittingly, to articulate and effectuate their highest ideals.[17]

For example, the Guarantee Clause[18] of the federal Constitution mandates a "republican form of government" for the states' structures of government,

[15] *See* CASS R. SUNSTEIN, DESIGNING DEMOCRACY: WHAT CONSTITUTIONS DO (2001). For an analysis of state constitutions as "political technology," see Donald S. Lutz, *The Purposes of American State Constitutions*, 12 PUBLIUS: THE J. FEDERALISM 27, 31 (Winter 1982).

[16] JAMES A. GARDNER, INTERPRETING STATE CONSTITUTIONS: A JURISPRUDENCE OF FUNCTION IN A FEDERAL SYSTEM 18 (2005).

[17] Louis D. Bilionis, *On the Significance of Constitutional Spirit*, 70 N.C. L. REV. 1803, 1805 (1992). *See also* ELAZAR, *supra* note 14, at 174 ("In fact, the constitutions of constituent states are part and parcel of the total constitutional structure of federal systems and play a vital role in giving the system direction."). According to Donald Lutz "[t]he states are mentioned explicitly or by direct implication 50 times in 32 separate sections of the U.S. Constitution . . ." Donald S. Lutz, *The United States Constitution as an Incomplete Document*, 496 ANNALS AM. ACAD. POL. & SOC. SCI. 23, 32 (1988).

[18] U.S. CONST. art. IV, § 4:

> The United States shall guarantee to every State in this Union a Republican Form of Government, and shall protect each of them against Invasion; and on Application of the

or constitutions. The Supremacy Clause[19] makes specific mention of state constitutions in its unequivocal declaration that federal law is the "supreme law of the land." Article VI, Clause [3] requires state legislative, executive, and judicial officers to support the federal Constitution by oath or affirmation. Article I, Section 2 adopts voting and citizenship qualifications of the states for the U.S. House of Representatives. The original version of Article I, Section 3 provided for the election of U.S. senators by state legislators.[20] Article I, Section 4 leaves the "Times, Places and Manor of holding Elections for Senators and Representatives" to the state legislatures, which are, in turn, governed by the state constitutions. Article I, Section 10 places significant, direct limitations on state actions, such as coining money, impairing the obligation of contracts, passing ex post facto laws, keeping troops in time of peace, or laying import or export duties—all of which were sovereign powers the states gave up. An additional set of limitations on state actions was included in the Civil War Amendments, numbers 13 through 15.

The Full Faith and Credit Clause requires each state to enforce the "Public Acts, Records, and judicial Proceedings of every other State."[21] The Privileges and Immunities Clause requires each state to accord its privileges and immunities to citizens of other states.[22] Article II, Section I, Clause [2] requires the state legislatures to determine how the electors for President will be chosen—a clause made famous by the U.S. Supreme Court's decision in *Bush v. Gore*,[23] and in the wake of the 2020 presidential election.

These are the provisions of a national, *federal* Constitution.[24] All of the activities of the states that are necessary to complete the structure and functioning

> Legislature, or of the Executive (when the Legislature cannot be convened) against domestic Violence.

*See* William M. Wiecek, The Guarantee Clause of the United States Constitution (1972). *See* Chapter 4.

[19] U.S. Const. art. VI, cl. [2]:

> This Constitution, and the Laws of the United States which shall be made in Pursuance Thereof; and all treaties made, or which shall be made, under the Authority of the United States, shall be the Supreme Law of the Land; and the Judges in every state shall be bound thereby, anything in the *Constitution* or Laws of any State to the Contrary notwithstanding.

[20] The Seventeenth Amendment, in 1913, changed this to popular election within each state. Clause [2] of the Seventeenth Amendment, as we saw so vividly in 2008–2009, relies on the state executive or state elections in filling Senate vacancies. Prior to 1913 some states had already amended their constitutions to move toward direct elections of U.S. senators. *See* Vikram D. Amar, *Indirect Effects of Direct Election: A Structural Examination of the Seventeenth Amendment*, 49 Vand. L. Rev. 1347, 1354–55 (1996).

[21] U.S. Const. art. IV, § 1.

[22] U.S. Const. art. IV, § 2.

[23] 531 U.S. 98 (2000). *See* James A. Gardner, *The Regulatory Role of State Constitutional Structural Constraints in Presidential Elections*, 29 Fla. St. U. L. Rev. 625 (2001); Robert A. Schapiro, *Conceptions and Misconceptions of State Constitutional Law in Bush v. Gore*, 29 Fla. St. U. L. Rev. 661 (2001).

[24] *See generally* 1 A Global Dialogue on Federalism: Constitutional Origins, Structure, and Change in Federal Countries (John Kincaid & G. Alan Tarr eds., 2005).

of the federal government under the federal Constitution are, within federal limits, subject to the specific design and process set forth in each *state* constitution. As long as a state's constitution, or the legislative, executive, or judicial implementation of its provisions, does not contravene the federal Constitution or federal law under the Supremacy Clause,[25] the states are free to devise their own arrangements for performing these federal functions as well as other ones reserved to them under our system of constitutional federalism.

Further, from the top down, or center vantage point of the American federal Constitution, it would appear that the states would perform these federal functions, as well as their other reserved powers, in a uniform, or "symmetrical" manner. This is, however, not the case. Despite the general similarity of American state constitutions, when viewed from the bottom up, or peripheral vantage point of the states themselves, there is a good deal of variation ("asymmetry"). Some of these variations are quite important in the details of their rights provisions, governmental arrangements, and policy-oriented provisions.[26]

Assessment of American constitutionalism is usually based on the U.S. Constitution and its interpretation by the Supreme Court, leading to the conclusion that America is "exceptional" when compared to those other national constitutions that are not static and do contain positive rights. However, Mila Versteeg and Emily Zackin have recently pointed out the error of this point of view:

> Our analysis reveals three important features of state constitutions that should prompt reconsideration of U.S. constitutional exceptionalism. First, like most of the world's constitutions, state constitutions are rather long and elaborate, and they include detailed policy choices. The exceptional American taste for constitutional brevity, it turns out, is confined to the federal document alone. Second, like most of the world's constitutions, state constitutions are frequently amended, overhauled, and replaced. Thus, the textual stability of the over-two-century-old federal Constitution is exceptional compared not only with other national constitutions but also with the constitutions of the American states, which are characterized, in part, by a commitment to progress and change. Third, like most of the world's constitutions, state constitutions contain positive rights, such as a right to free education, labor rights, social welfare rights, and environmental rights. While the federal Constitution arguably omits

[25] *See* Chapter 4.

[26] This is true, to a greater or lesser extent, in all systems of constitutional federalism that utilize subnational constitutions. *See* Robert F. Williams & G. Alan Tarr, *Subnational Constitutional Space: A View from the States, Provinces, Regions, Länder, and Cantons*, *in* FEDERALISM, SUBNATIONAL CONSTITUTIONS, AND MINORITY RIGHTS 3 (G. Alan Tarr et al. eds., 2004). *See generally* PATRICIA POPELIER, GIACOMO DELLEDONNE, & NICHOLAS ARONEY, ROUTLEDGE HANDBOOK OF SUBNATIONAL CONSTITUTIONS AND CONSTITUTIONALISM (2022).

> explicit declarations of these rights, they are not foreign to the American *constitutional tradition*. On all these dimensions, it is at the federal level only that Americans' constitutional practices appear exceptional. When we include the writing and revision of state constitutions in our assessment, it becomes clear that American constitutionalism is not nearly as distinctive as most comparative studies and political commentators have suggested.[27]

Versteeg and Zackin continued their important reinterpretation of American constitutionalism by evaluating the question of "entrenchment" in constitutions.[28]

> A dominant theme of the constitutional theory literature is that successful constitutions must not only constrain those in power, but must do so over long time horizons, establishing constraints durable enough to bind across generations. . . . By entrenching commitments, constitutions serve as a mechanism for overcoming the inconsistency of preferences over time.[29]

They recount the reasons scholars insist that entrenchment is necessary, including removing matters from the political agenda and allowing political parties to form new democracies with established rules. Entrenched constitutions are "spare frameworks," rigid, and characterized by "generality and abstraction."[30] Again, they suggest that this is too narrow a view of other nations' constitutions and, more importantly here, the American state constitutions:

> The model of an entrenched and spare document, which changes meaning primarily through judicial interpretation, successfully describes the U.S. Constitution. However, it does a poor job of depicting most other national democratic constitutions, or even U.S. state constitutions. As we will demonstrate, specific and unentrenched constitutions developed over the course of the nineteenth and twentieth centuries, and are now the dominant form of constitutionalism across the globe, and within the U.S. states. We argue that these polities' flexible and detailed constitutional texts embody an alternative model of constitutionalism. Rather than entrenching constraints through spare and stable texts, these constitutions provide officeholders—judges, legislatures

[27] Mila Versteeg & Emily Zackin, *American Constitutional Exceptionalism Revisited*, 81 U. Chicago L. Rev. 1641, 1644–45 (2014). *See also* Emily Zackin, Looking for Rights in All the Wrong Places: Why State Constitutions Contain America's Positive Rights (2013); Jonathan L. Marshfield, *America's Misunderstood Constitutional Rights*, 170 U. Pa. L. Rev. 853 (2022).

[28] Mila Versteeg & Emily Zackin, *Constitutions Unentrenched: Toward an Alternative Theory of Constitutional Design*, 110 Am. Pol. Sci. Rev. 657 (2016).

[29] *Id.*

[30] *Id.* at 658.

> and executives—with specific and frequently modified instructions. Although these flexible constitutions do not entrench commitments over long time horizons, we argue that they are nonetheless attempts to constrain the exercise of political power by leaving empowered actors with fewer choices about which policies to pursue.[31]

Versteeg and Zackin are beginning an important theoretical assessment of the differences between our federal and state constitutions, something Alan Tarr called for years ago.[32] These scholarly conclusions demonstrate clearly that our state constitutions are not simply little versions of our federal Constitution. Indeed, another way of characterizing state constitutions is as "hybrid" constitutions, containing "selective entrenchment."[33]

Interestingly, political science research seems to indicate that members of the public recognize, and support, the view of state constitutions as presented by Versteeg and Zackin.

> This finding implies a Jeffersonian view of state constitutions as practical governing documents rather than pedestalized relics, where respect for the constitution hinges on its democratic legitimacy. Second, we find that informing participants of their state constitution's high amendment rate does more than increase respect—it also prompts desire for reform. Although the exact nature of that reform cannot be ascertained from these data, it seems likely that one element of it is the need for a document to be changed and altered for a given generation (for "the living" as Jefferson would put it).
>
> * * *
>
> Perhaps Madison was right to say that the (national) constitution requires veneration that is "breathed" by "the voice of the people." This kind of allegiance should not be treated lightly, and, as Madison suggested, it may even be crucial to our political system. But we must also understand that the system of

[31] *Id. See also* ROBINSON WOODWARD-BURNS, HIDDEN LAWS: HOW STATE CONSTITUTIONS STABILIZE AMERICAN POLITICS (2021) (in the United States, national issues and conflicts can be decentralized to the states and their easier-to-amend constitutions thereby preserving our federal constitutional stability). Dr. Adam Brown contends, based on significant statistical evidence, that more specific (and therefore longer) state constitutions have negative effects on states. These include the necessity of more amendments, more statutes invalidated through judicial review, and limitations on "policy performance, resulting in lower incomes per capita, higher unemployment rates, greater economic inequality, and reduced policy innovativeness generally." ADAM R. BROWN, DEAD HAND'S GRIP: HOW LONG CONSTITUTIONS BIND STATES 2 (2022).

[32] G. Alan Tarr, *Constitutional Theory and State Constitutional Interpretation*, 22 RUTGERS L.J. 841, 842 (1991).

[33] *Cf.* David Landau, *Selective Entrenchment in State Constitutional Law: Lessons from Comparative Experience*, 69 ARK. L. REV. 425, 427 (2016).

government generated by the founders has multiple levels and Jefferson's vision of constitutions amended and changed to fit the times and retain their legitimacy clearly appeals to people thinking about their state constitutions. At the state level, Americans crave reform and change. They do not want a state constitution of antiquity but a state constitution of the present. Perhaps it is a fitting tribute to the founding generation's efforts that the thinking of American citizens—two and a quarter centuries later—is not uniform but changes depending upon the level of government and the purpose of the document.[34]

## II. DIFFERING STATE CONSTITUTIONS

State constitutions are *sui generis*, differing from the federal Constitution in their origin, function, form, and quality.[35] They are not miniature versions of the federal Constitution, nor are they clones of it. They originate from a very different process from that which led to the ratification of the federal Constitution. State constitutions perform functions that are different from the federal Constitution. They do not look or work like the federal Constitution. They are longer, more detailed, and cover many more topics: taxation and finance, local government, education, and corporations. The constitutional conversation at the state level is considerably different from the federal constitutional conversation.[36]

There are many policy decisions that have been directly embedded in state constitutions. As Professor G. Alan Tarr has noted:

> During the nineteenth century, state constitutions became more polished and professional, as their framers built upon the constitutional experience of their own states and developments in sister states. The shape of the documents and their contents also changed. Over the course of the century, state constitutions increasingly became instruments of government rather than merely frameworks for government.[37]

[34] Adam R. Brown & Jeremy C. Pope, *Measuring and Manipulating Constitutional Evaluations in the States: Legitimacy Versus Veneration*, 47 Am. Pol. Res. 1135 (2018).

[35] This section owes an obvious debt to Frank P. Grad, *The State Constitution: Its Function and Form for Our Time*, 54 Va. L. Rev. 928 (1968). *See also* Frank P. Grad & Robert F. Williams, 2 State Constitutions for the Twenty-First Century: Drafting State Constitutions, Revisions and Amendments 7–30 (2006).

[36] *See* G. Alan Tarr, *State Constitutional Design and State Constitutional Interpretation*, 72 Mont. L. Rev. 7 (2011).

[37] G. Alan Tarr, Understanding State Constitutions 132 (1998). *See also id.* at 20–21.

Political scientist Christopher Hammons elaborates on the distinction between "framework-oriented" and "policy-oriented" provisions in state constitutions.[38] He analyzed all of the state constitutions according to this distinction and concluded that policy-oriented provisions constituted about 40 percent of the provisions in state constitutions.[39] Dr. Hammons concluded that the longer and more policy-oriented a state constitution is, the longer it endures before replacement.[40] Of course, what constitutes a policy-oriented provision, rather than a framework-oriented provision, can be in the eyes of the beholder, and neutral, academic observers may not appreciate the important historic and political reasons why state constitutions contain certain detailed provisions.[41]

In fact, there has also been a major shift in the idea of what the basic function of a state constitution should be and what matters are important enough to be contained therein. Professor Christian Fritz noted this shift in the attitudes of state constitution makers during the nineteenth century as the American society and economy became more complex, particularly with the rise of powerful corporations. These constitution makers believed that they needed to include more material in state constitutions, even in areas that could, theoretically, be governed by legislation.[42] Professor Fritz concluded:

[38] Christopher W. Hammons, *State Constitutional Reform: Is It Necessary?* 64 ALB. L. REV. 1327, 1338 (2001) [hereinafter *State Constitutional Reform*]:

> *Framework provisions* are those provisions that deal exclusively with the principles, institutions, powers, and processes of government. They provide the basic building blocks of government. *Policy provisions* are defined as those provisions that deal with "statute law" or "public-policy" type issues, do not relate to the establishment of the government, are rather specific, typically do not apply to all citizens, and often provide differential benefits. It is these provisions that most political scientists and legal scholars consider "extra-constitutional."

*See also id.* at 1351 (examples of each type of provision); Christopher W. Hammons, *Was James Madison Wrong? Rethinking the American Preference for Short Framework-Oriented Constitutions*, 93 AM. POL. SCI. REV. 837, 846–47 (1999) [hereinafter *Was James Madison Wrong?*] (more detailed list of examples), 848 (referring to policy-oriented provisions as "particularistic").

[39] Hammons, *State Constitutional Reform*, *supra* note 38, at 1333; *see also* Hammons, *Was James Madison Wrong?*, *supra* note 38, at 840 (39 percent).

[40] Hammons, *State Constitutional Reform*, *supra* note 38 at 1338–41; Hammons, *Was James Madison Wrong?*, *supra* note 38, at 845. For another view on the issue of state constitutional length, see BROWN, *supra* note 31.

[41] For each provision in a state constitution, no matter how seemingly trivial, there is a story to be told. It may be a political story rather than an epic, "constitutional" story. As the legal historian, Lawrence M. Friedman, stated, "[t]here was a point to every clause in these inflated constitutions. Each one reflected the wishes of some faction or interest group, which tried to make its policies permanent by freezing them into the charter. Constitutions, like treaties, preserved the terms of compromise between warring groups." LAWRENCE M. FRIEDMAN, A HISTORY OF AMERICAN LAW 119 (2d ed. 1985).

[42] *See* Christian G. Fritz, The *American Constitutional Tradition Revisited: Preliminary Observations on State Constitution-Making in the Nineteenth-Century West*, 25 RUTGERS L.J. 945, 964–71 (1994) [hereinafter *The American Constitutional Tradition*]; Christian G. Fritz, *Rethinking the American Constitutional Tradition: National Dimensions in the Formation of State Constitutions*, 26 RUTGERS L.J. 969 (1995) (book review).

> The key to explaining the growing length of nineteenth-century constitutions lies in the delegates' understanding of the purpose of constitutions. There was common agreement that the nature and object of constitutions extended beyond fundamental principles to what delegates called constitutional legislation. Delegates willingly assumed an institutional role that occasionally supplanted the ordinary legislature.
>
> . . .
>
> Restraining corporations and limiting governmental debt provided the most dramatic expression of the role of the conventions acting in lieu of legislatures. In the case of controlling corporate power, including the railroad companies, conventions claimed that legislatures were institutionally unable to respond. Moreover, many delegates regarded the control of corporations and debt as matters on which the people had given conventions a mandate to act.[43]

A similar shift occurred several generations later, when the state constitutions of the Progressive Era were formed.[44]

Professor Stephen M. Griffin provides another thoughtful analysis of state constitutional change.[45] He noted that these documents evolved into "long legislative codes" because, during the nineteenth century, almost all of the new functions of government took place at the state level, while at the same time there developed a "popular distrust of state legislatures." The federal and state systems accordingly developed differing models of constitutional change. At the state level, there was no hesitation to make frequent, statute-like changes in response to social, economic, and technological changes; and their influence on state politics was important.

Griffin concluded:

> Earlier we asked why the states adapted their constitutions by making them into legislative codes. The New Deal experience points the way to answering this question. Passing a broad amendment to preserve the framework character of the document runs the risk of overreacting to a specific policy problem by changing some fundamental power of government. With a broad amendment there is a greater risk of unforeseen effects. The safe way to proceed is to pass a narrow amendment that deals with the specific problem at hand. In addition, as set out earlier, revision of state constitutions was partly motivated by distrust

[43] Fritz, *The American Constitutional Tradition*, *supra* note 42, at 964–65, 968.

[44] *See generally* John Dinan, *Framing a "People's Government": State Constitution-Making in the Progressive Era*, 30 RUTGERS L.J. 933 (1999). *See generally* HISTORICAL DICTIONARY OF THE PROGRESSIVE ERA, 1890–1920 (John D. Buenker & Edward R. Kantowicz eds., 1988).

[45] STEPHEN M. GRIFFIN, AMERICAN CONSTITUTIONALISM: FROM THEORY TO POLITICS 33–42 (1996).

> of state legislatures. The people of the states wanted to make the restrictions on the legislature as specific as possible in order to prevent particular abuses of power.[46]

These changing conceptions of state constitutional function account for the transition to "instruments of government rather than merely frameworks for government."[47] State constitutions can be used as "instruments of lawmaking. . . ."[48] This transition from framework to framework plus instruments reflects the rough and evolving dichotomy between core, or framework-oriented provisions, and policy-oriented provisions.

It remains, though, that a continuing criticism of state constitutions has been that they contain a wealth of nonfundamental policy matters that would be better relegated to statutory law. Professor James Pope has made this point in the following way:

> At bottom, the problem with state constitutionalism is—as James Gardner has thoroughly, ruthlessly, and humorously shown—that state constitutions just aren't all that constitutional. How can anyone expect judges to develop independent constitutional jurisprudence on a textual foundation that changes with every legislative or popular whim, obsesses in excruciating detail over pecuniary matters, and declares the law on such fundamentals as golf course tax exemptions and bingo regulation?[49]

Professor Pope, nonetheless, went on to respond that there have been, in fact, a number of very important "vital provisions" that are "weight(y) (enough) to alter the field of state constitutional interpretation."[50] He noted this by way of examples of truly constitutional provisions: Jacksonian democracy, the populist-progressive movement for direct democracy, and the guarantees of free public schools. Professor Pope differentiated the *constitutional* provisions of state constitutions from those that are merely constitutional because they have been included in the state constitution.[51]

There is the view that a state constitution should legitimately limit itself to provisions structuring and allocating governmental powers and limiting those

[46] *Id.* at 40.

[47] TARR, *supra* note 37, at 132. *See also id.* at 20–21: "Relatively few provisions of the federal Constitution directly address public-policy issues . . . State constitutions, in contrast, deal directly with matters of public policy, sometimes in considerable detail. State governments share common policy responsibilities, and these are reflected in state constitutions."

[48] Robert F. Williams, *State Constitutional Law Processes*, 24 WM. & MARY L. REV. 169, 175 (1983).

[49] Pope, *supra* note 4, at 985 (footnote omitted).

[50] *Id.* at 1007. *See also id.* at 991 ("episodes of determined popular deliberation and struggle over issues of high principle.").

[51] *Id.* at 988.

powers to protect the people. This is, of course, the dichotomy between fundamental constitutional material, on the one hand, and mere legislative detail on the other.[52] While this distinction is always important, it must be considered in light of the political situation and the specific constitutional context within a state. As two commentators noted:

> First, one must include certain "core" subjects that common experience and tradition support as basic for the proper functioning of state government, and second, one must—depending on the particular circumstances in a state at a given time—necessarily include other matters deemed so important to that particular state as to call for constitutional treatment.[53]

In any event, the limitation of a state constitution to "fundamental" matters is inevitably subject to political reality, past constitutional practice within the state, and the acknowledged additional function of a state constitution as an "instrument of lawmaking,"[54] utilized to entrench certain matters in a way to remove them from legislative discretion.

State constitutions, in addition to a variety of policy-based provisions, often contain positive or affirmative rights, or even mandates, while federal constitutional rights are primarily negative in nature.[55] State courts interpreting state constitutions are therefore thrust more deeply and more often into the affairs of the coordinate branches of government than when they or federal courts are interpreting the federal Constitution. Put simply, at the state level, there is just more constitutional text *there* to interpret! All of these differences lead to unique research requirements and approaches to advocacy and interpretation in state constitutional cases.

In sum, the primary characteristics upon which we may differentiate state constitutions from the federal model are their length, which results partially from the broader range of state plenary authority, and the inclusion of many policy

[52] *See* Grad & Williams, *supra* note 35, at 15, stating:

> [A] consideration of the problems and criteria of constitutional inclusion and exclusion must concern itself with a balancing of the purposes of the constitution and the needs of government, rather than with an attempt to supply a fixed meaning for the valuative terms "fundamental" and "legislative." Although there is a more or less agreed on "core" area of constitutional content, criteria of inclusion and exclusion must take account of the needs of government as conditioned by time and place.

[53] *Id.*

[54] *See* Williams, *supra* note 48, at 175–77; *see also* Robert F. Williams, *The Anatomy of Law Reform: Dissecting a Decade of Change in Florida in Forma Pauperis Law*, 12 Stetson L. Rev. 363, 386 n.127 (1983).

[55] *See generally* Burt Neuborne, *Foreword: State Constitutions and the Evolution of Positive Rights*, 20 Rutgers L.J. 881 (1989); Helen Hershkoff, *Positive Rights and State Constitutions: The Limits of Federal Rationality Review*, 112 Harv. L. Rev. 1131 (1999); Zackin, *supra* note 27; Chapter 5.

matters that could be treated by legislation, as well as state constitutions' relative ease of amendment and revision. Although these characteristics effectively distinguish state constitutions from the federal charter, they do not make state constitutions, as is often argued, *less* constitutional. Rather, state constitutions are simply *different kinds* of constitutions—and they are constitutions that are unique in the American federal system. They reflect two distinct constitutional functions and traditions. Because of their relative ease of amendment, state constitutions could be modified through trial and error over the years concerning matters that, for all practical purposes, remain frozen in the federal Constitution.[56]

## III. STATE CONSTITUTIONAL ORIGINS

State constitutions have unique origins, differentiating them in important ways from the federal Constitution. State constitutions owe their legal validity and political legitimacy to the state electorate, not to "Framers" or state ratifying conventions, as with the federal Constitution.[57] This was not always the case. Many of the early state constitutions of the Revolutionary period and up into the mid-nineteenth century were put into effect without such a vote of the people. Slowly, however, the amendment and revision mechanisms in state constitutions have matured to the point of requiring popular ratification for changes in, or revisions of, the state's basic charter. Therefore, for most constitutional provisions adopted since the mid-nineteenth century, it can legitimately be said that they gain their legal force—their pedigree or *constitutional* status—through an affirmative vote of the electors in the state who are to be bound by the state constitution. This point has very important implications for judicial interpretation of state constitutions—a matter that is treated in Chapter 12.

[56] John Dinan thoroughly analyzes the differing state and federal constitutional traditions in a number of key areas in John J. Dinan, The American State Constitutional Tradition 5 (2006):

> To summarize my principal conclusions, therefore, I show that a number of federal governing principles and institutions have been revised or rejected in the course of state conventions; I demonstrate that state constitution makers' departures from the federal model are primarily attributable to the flexibility of state amendment processes and the resulting opportunities to benefit from institutional knowledge and experience throughout American history; and I argue that the state convention debates are in many ways a better expression of the considered judgment of the American constitutional tradition than can be found in the eighteenth-century federal sources.

[57] Linde, *supra* note 10, at 197 ("State constitutions have . . . drafters, yes, but no 'Founders'; no Federalist Papers. . . ."). *See generally* Christian G. Fritz, *Alternative Visions of American Constitutionalism: Popular Sovereignty and The Early American Constitutional Debate*, 24 Hastings Const. L.Q. 287 (1997).

State constitutions, ratified by the electorate, are therefore characterized by state courts as the "voice of the people."[58] The New Jersey Supreme Court put it this way:

> It is a familiar rule of construction that where phraseology is precise and unambiguous there is no room for judicial interpretation or for resort to extrinsic materials. The language speaks for itself, and where found in our State Constitution the language is the *voice of the people*. As this Court said some twenty years ago,
>
> [T]he Constitution derives its force, not from the Convention which framed it, but from the people who ratified it: and the intent to be arrived at is that of the people.[59]

These perspectives apply in forty-nine of the states. In Delaware, the state constitution can be amended without a vote of the people. There, an amendment may be proposed by either house and if approved by two-thirds of the elected members of each house, published before the next general election, and then readopted by the same supermajority in each house, it becomes of part of the Delaware Constitution.[60] The calling of a constitutional convention, by contrast, is submitted to the voters.[61] Delaware has never required popular ratification of amendments, in part to avoid hasty changes, and in part to protect the more sparsely populated regions from being outvoted by the more populous areas.[62] There was substantial debate of these mechanisms in the 1897 Delaware Constitutional Convention.[63]

## IV. STATE CONSTITUTIONAL FUNCTIONS

One of the other major factors distinguishing state constitutions from the federal Constitution is that they are often referred to as documents of limitation

[58] Vreeland v. Byrne, 370 A.2d 825, 830 (N.J. 1977) (emphasis added). Delaware is the only state that does not require a popular referendum on proposed state constitutional amendments. *See* Opinion of the Justices, 264 A.2d 342 (Del. 1970).

[59] *Vreeland*, 370 A.2d at 830, *quoting* Gangemi v. Berry, 134 A.2d 1, 9 (N.J. 1957) (emphasis added). Interestingly, the *Gangemi* court quoted from *U.S. v. Sprague*, 282 U.S. 716, 731 (1931), a case interpreting the *federal* Constitution, stating: "The Constitution was written to be understood by the voters. . . ." *See also* McKenna v. Williams, 874 A.2d 217, 242 (R.I. 2005) (Suttel, J., concurring in part and dissenting in part).

[60] Del. Const. art. XVI, § 1.

[61] Del. Const. art. XVI, § 2.

[62] Randy J. Holland, The Delaware State Constitution: A Reference Guide 229–31 (2002); Dinan, *supra* note 56, at 38–39.

[63] William T. Quillen, *Amendments and Conventions: Article XVI*, *in* The Delaware Constitution of 1897: The First One Hundred Years 201 (Randy J. Holland ed., 1997).

rather than documents granting powers.[64] Limitations in state constitutions may be either express or implied.[65] Thus, the basic legal and political function of state constitutions differs from that of the federal Constitution. Although this distinction is oversimplified,[66] it does describe a major structural, and therefore interpretational, difference between state and federal Constitutions. As political scientist Walter Dodd pointed out many years ago, based on this distinction:

> The preceding discussion has suggested a real antithesis between constitutional construction as it relates to the national government on the one side and constitutional construction as it relates to the state government on the other. With respect to the United States, emphasis has been upon powers, and perhaps the most important single manifestation of judicial action has been the doctrine of implied powers. With respect to the states, emphasis has been upon limitations, and the most important single manifestation of judicial action has been the doctrine of implied limitations.[67]

## V. STATE CONSTITUTIONAL FORM

The function of state constitutions, not surprisingly, dictates their form. Generally speaking, because of the necessity to enunciate specific limitations on otherwise virtually unlimited ("plenary") governmental power, state constitutions contain a high level of detail and specificity, in contrast to the federal Constitution, with respect to the structure and operations of government. For example, most state constitutions contain long articles on taxation and finance, two of the most important functions of any government. These provisions restrict state government taxing and spending power in a range of ways that is unfamiliar in the federal government.

Professor G. Alan Tarr observed:

[64] "The constitution is not a grant but a limitation upon the lawmaking power of the state legislature and it may enact any law not expressly or inferentially prohibited by state and federal constitutions." State v. Hy Vee Food Stores, Inc., 533 N.W.2d 147 (S.D. 1995) (*quoting* Kramar v. Bon Homme County, 155 N.W.2d 777, 778 (S.D. 1968)). *See also* Utah Sch. Bds. Ass'n v. Utah State Bd. of Educ., 17 P.3d 1125, 1128 (Utah 2001).

[65] Caddo-Shreveport Sales & Use Tax Comm'n v. Office of Motor Vehicles, 710 So.2d 776, 779–80 (La. 1998) ("constitutional limitation on legislative power may be either express or implied").

[66] *See* Robert F. Williams, *Comment: On the Importance of a Theory of Legislative Power Under State Constitutions*, 15 QUINNIPIAC L. REV. 57, 60 (1995); Williams, *supra* note 48, at 178–79.

[67] Walter F. Dodd, *Implied Powers and Implied Limitations in Constitutional Law*, 29 YALE L.J. 137, 160 (1919). Dodd recognized that a number of state constitutional provisions are not actually limits. *Id.*

> Currently, the unamended text of the typical state constitution remains over three times as long as that of the federal constitution, and state constitutions on average contain over 120 constitutional amendments.[68]

Professor Tarr reports that the state constitutions vary greatly in length: the longest (at this writing) remains Alabama's, which is over twenty-six times the length of Vermont's, the shortest.[69] While there has only been one federal Constitutional Convention, as of 2018, there had been 233 state constitutional conventions,[70] and the state constitutions have been amended close to six thousand times, with almost as many amendments being rejected by the voters.[71] Most states have had three or more constitutions, including Louisiana with eleven and Georgia with ten. Only nineteen operate under their original constitution.[72] In a very real sense, an important element of state governance is through constitutional amendment.[73]

As we will see in Chapter 13, the texts of state constitutions are much easier to change than their federal counterpart, and they are subject to amendment and revision from a number of different sources, including legislative proposals, initiative amendments (in some states), and proposals submitted to the voters by constitutional conventions. Because of this malleability of state constitutional text, formal amendment and revision is a much greater force for constitutional change at the state level than with respect to the federal Constitution.[74]

There have been a wide variety of motivations for using the state constitution as a lawmaking mechanism, rather than resorting to ordinary legislation or common-law development. First, of course, entrenching a provision or policy in the state constitution makes it more permanent than statutory law and removes the matter from legislative discretion and, as a consequence, moves issues of interpretation to the courts. In a circumstance in which the state legislature will not propose a certain change, a constitutional convention or, in those states that permit it, a constitutional amendment proposed through the initiative provides

68 Tarr, *supra* note 37, at 10.

69 *Id.* at 10–11.

70 *See* John Dinan, State Constitutional Politics: Governing by Amendment in the American States 95 (2018).

71 Tarr, *supra* note 37, at 24.

72 *Id.* at 23.

73 *See generally* John Dinan, *supra* note 70; Chapter 13.

74

> One of the most striking features of state constitutional politics is the tendency to pursue constitutional change through formal mechanisms of constitutional change, through amendment or replacement of the constitution, rather than through litigation. The contrast with federal constitutional politics, in which amendment is rare and revision unheard of, could hardly be sharper.

G. Alan Tarr, *State Constitutional Politics: An Historical Perspective, in* Constitutional Politics in the States: Contemporary Controversies and Historical Patterns 3 (G. Alan Tarr ed., 1996).

an "alternative channel for law-making."[75] Also, in addition to bypassing the legislature, state constitutional change can also be used to "overrule" judicial interpretations of the state constitutions.[76] State constitutional amendments can "overrule," or invalidate, *statutes*.[77] Changes to the state constitution can eliminate doubt about a particular matter, even before any state constitutional litigation.[78] Any such view of the federal Constitution as a tool of lawmaking would be completely foreign.

Because of such motivations, coupled with the fact that state constitutions are easier to amend than the federal Constitution, they have accumulated many layers of limiting and policy-based details reflecting the concerns of citizens during the various eras of American history. For example, evidence of the periods of distrust of the legislature, Jacksonian democracy, the Civil War and Reconstruction, the Industrial Revolution, the Progressive Movement, the settling of the West, bankruptcy in public finance, concern for efficient management, and many other matters, can be seen clearly in any modern state constitution.

Under the "historical-movement model," state constitutions reflect "not distinctive state political cultures but rather the political forces prevailing nationally at the time they were adopted."[79] A good example of this phenomenon was the adoption by thirty-five states of "continuity of government" provisions during the seven-year period (1959–1966) at the height of the Cold War and the shared fears about the threat of nuclear attack.[80]

Given the wide range of possibilities for state constitutions, however, and beyond differences in length and specific details, they are remarkably similar.[81] Political scientist Daniel Elazar identified and described patterns of regional variation among the state constitutions.[82] At least one court has relied on this typology in interpreting its state constitution.[83]

[75] JAMES WILLARD HURST, THE GROWTH OF AMERICAN LAW: THE LAW MAKERS 243 (1950).

[76] *Id.* at 245. *See also* Walter Dodd, *The Function of a State Constitution*, 30 POL. SCI. Q. 201, 213 (1915); John Dinan, *Foreword: Court-Constraining Amendments and the State Constitutional Tradition*, 38 RUTGERS L.J. 983 (2007); State v. Hartmann, 700 N.W.2d 449, 455 (Minn. 2005); People v. McClanahan, 729 N.E.2d 470, 473 n. 1 (Ill. 2000); State v. Goins, 423 P.3d 1236, 1241 (Utah 2017).

[77] Consulting Engineers & Land Surveyors of California, Inc. v. Professional Engineers in California Government, 169 P.3d 903, 909 (Cal. 2007); Hendrick v. Walters, 865 P.2d 1232, 1235, 1240–43 (Okla. 1993).

[78] Tucker v. Toia, 371 N.E.2d 449, 451 (N.Y. 1977); PETER J. GALIE, ORDERED LIBERTY: A CONSTITUTIONAL HISTORY OF NEW YORK 238 (1996).

[79] Tarr, *supra* note 74, at 4.

[80] Eric R. Daleo, *State Constitutions and Legislative Continuity in a 9/11 World: Surviving an "Enemy Attack,"* 58 DEPAUL L. REV. 919 (2009).

[81] GRAD & WILLIAMS, *supra* note 35, at 13.

[82] Daniel J. Elazar, *The Principles and Traditions Underlying State Constitutions*, 12 PUBLIUS: THE J. FEDERALISM 11, 13–22 (Winter 1982). *See also* TARR, *supra* note 37, at 127–32. *But see* James A. Gardner, *Southern Character, Confederate Nationalism, and the Interpretation of State Constitutions: A Case Study in Constitutional Argument*, 76 TEX. L. REV. 1219 (1998) (concluding that the Southern state constitutions do not reflect a distinctive southern character).

[83] Benning v. State, 641 A.2d 757, 758 (Vt. 1994).

## VI. STATE CONSTITUTIONAL QUALITY

Based on the limited function of the federal Constitution and the plenary or residual powers of the states under their constitutions, the *quality* of matters contained in these constitutions differs. Daniel Elazar explained:

> Were the federal constitution to stand alone, one could conclude that morality and government were entirely separated in the new American constitutional order. This is not, in fact, the case. Since the federal constitution and the government it creates are both incomplete and need the states to be complete, we must also look at the state constitutions to see what kind of liberty they are committed to protecting and fostering. Certainly in the revolutionary period most of the state constitutions were designed to foster commonwealths rather than marketplaces, that is to say, polities that were both republican and committed to a shared moral vision. It is not unfair to say that the federal constitution could emphasize individualism and the marketplace precisely because the founders could count upon the state constitutions to emphasize community and commonwealth.[84]

In fact, therefore, the state constitutions, since the Revolution, have dealt with state citizens' character, virtue, and even morality.[85] Political scientist John Dinan, after analyzing the state constitutional debates on these issues, concluded that, despite the absence of such provisions in the federal Constitution, "state constitutionmakers have frequently concluded that government should take an active role in shaping citizen character and that this role should be constitutionalized."[86] Provisions on "support for religious institutions, compulsory education, prohibition of lotteries, and regulation of liquor" appear in state constitutions either to fulfill the expectations of the federal framers or in opposition to the view "that character formation should not be the concern of a republican polity."[87]

In a number of important ways, the state constitutions can be considered more "democratic" than the federal Constitution.[88] Professor Sanford Levinson

[84] Daniel J. Elazar, The American Constitutional Tradition 169 (1988).

[85] Dinan, *supra* note 56, at 222–70, 274.

[86] *Id.* at 274.

[87] *Id. See also* Daniel J. Elazar, *The Moral Compass of State Constitutionalism*, 30 Rutgers L.J. 849 (1999); Lawrence G. Sager, *Cool Federalism and the Life-Cycle of Moral Progress*, 46 Wm. & Mary L. Rev. 1385 (2005).

[88] *See generally* Jessica Bulman-Pozen & Miriam Seifter, *The Democracy Principle in State Constitutions*, 119 Mich. L. Rev. 859 (2021); Jessica Bulman-Pozen & Miriam Seifter, *Countering the New Election Subversion: The Democracy Principle and the Role of State Courts* Wis. L. Rev. 1337 (2022). *See also* Woodward-Burns, *supra* note 31 at 193 ("These state constitutions, unlike their federal counterpart, are democratically responsive. Through the states, Americans secure popular sovereignty.").

pointed out a number of features of the federal Constitution that are "undemocratic."[89] While this criticism can also be leveled at state constitutions, they do involve the public in decision-making in many ways that are unrecognizable in federal constitutional law. One major criticism of the federal Constitution leveled by Levinson and others centers on the structure of the Senate, with two senators from each state, regardless of its population.[90] The upper chambers in the forty-nine states that have them (Nebraska has a unicameral legislature), albeit by U.S. Supreme Court mandate, must follow the one-person, one-vote principle for their elections. Further, in many states, executive officials other than the governor are elected directly by the people.

Most modern state constitutions are, as noted earlier, themselves products of "popular sovereignty" in that they were proposed by constitutional conventions authorized by the voters, drafted by delegates elected by the voters, and then ratified at a referendum of the voters (the "voice of the people"). Further change through amendment or revision involves another round of voter participation.[91] Within state constitutions, important governmental decisions such as assuming debt[92] and authorizing new forms of gambling[93] are subject to referendum or plebiscite.

The texts of virtually all state constitutions proclaim their foundation in popular sovereignty, with provisions such as those in North Carolina's Article I:

> Section 2
> Sovereignty of the people. All political power is vested in and derived from the people; all government of right originates from the people, is founded upon their will only, and is instituted solely for the good of the whole.
>
> Section 3
> Internal government of the State. The people of this State have the inherent, sole, and exclusive right of regulating the internal government and police thereof, and of altering or abolishing their Constitution and form of government whenever it may be necessary to their safety and happiness; but every such right shall be

[89] Sanford Levinson, Our Undemocratic Constitution: Where the Constitution Goes Wrong (And How We the People Can Correct It) (2006).

[90] *Id.* at 49–62. *See also* Frances E. Lee & Bruce I. Oppenheimer, Sizing Up the Senate: The Unequal Consequences of Equal Representation (1999); Lynn A. Baker & Samuel H. Dinkin, *The Senate: An Institution Whose Time Has Gone?* 13 J.L. & Pol. 21 (1997).

[91] Chapter 13.

[92] Richard Briffault, *Foreword: The Disfavored Constitution: State Fiscal Limits and State Constitutional Law*, 34 Rutgers L.J. 907, 916 (2003).

[93] *See, e.g.*, N.J. Const. art. IV, § VII, ¶ 2; Atlantic City Racing Assoc. v. Attorney General, 489 A.2d 165 (N.J. 1985); R.I. Const. art. VI, § 22.

exercised in pursuance of law and consistently with the Constitution of the United States.

Provisions such as North Carolina's are present in virtually all of the state constitutions, expressing the "basic, philosophical point that the people are . . . political sovereigns with the power to create government to achieve peace, safety, and well being."[94] They are, generally, expressions of political philosophy, but they can have a role in resolving questions of judicial interpretation of the state constitution.[95]

A number of state constitutions, of course, involve the public in both constitution making and lawmaking through the initiative, referendum, and recall. All of these mechanisms of popular voter participation in governing and constitution making are the direct descendants of America's revolutionary approach to the people governing themselves,[96] or government by consent.[97] This is very different from the federal constitutional tradition.

Dr. Douglas Reed has described a new theory of state constitutional meaning that emanates not exclusively from courts, but rather from an "exchange between popular mobilization and judicial interpretation."[98] One form of this he refers to as "legal mobilization through public interest litigation."[99] Dr. Reed also reviewed the so-called "down and out" scholarship by those who seek to "decenter" the courts as the exclusive source of constitutional meanings[100] and applied those theories to state constitutional law:

[94] William P. McLauchan, The Indiana State Constitution: A Reference Guide 33 (1996). *See generally* Christian G. Fritz, American Sovereigns: The People and America's Constitutional Tradition Before the Civil War (2008).

[95] Chapter 12.

[96] *See* Fritz, *supra* note 94. James Henretta called this "activist popular sovereignty." James A. Henretta, *Foreword: Rethinking the State Constitutional Tradition*, 22 Rutgers L.J. 819, 826 (1991).

[97] Donald S. Lutz, Popular Consent and Popular Control: Whig Political Theory in the Early State Constitutions (1980).

[98] Douglas S. Reed, *Popular Constitutionalism: Toward a Theory of State Constitutional Meanings*, 30 Rutgers L.J. 871, 875 (1999). *See also* Daniel B. Rodriguez, *State Constitutionalism and the Domain of Normative Theory*, 37 San Diego L. Rev. 523, 530 (2000) ("[I]f the centrality—or, at least the exclusivity—of constitutional adjudication as a method for framing constitutional discourse is replaced by legislative, administrative, and citizen/grass-roots action, then the pressure groups who regularly participate in state constitutional politics will organize their strategies accordingly."); John J. Dinan, Keeping the People's Liberties: Legislators, Citizens, and Judges as Guardians of Rights (1998).

[99] Reed, *supra* note 98, at 875. Reed concluded: "The interpreter of state constitutions, under popular constitutionalism, is less likely to be a judge and more likely to be a mobilized and politically active citizenry." *Id.*

[100] *Id.* at 881; *see also* Michael Paris, *Legal Mobilization and the Politics of Reform: Lessons from School Finance Litigation in Kentucky, 1984–1995*, 26 Law & Soc. Inquiry 631 (2001) (using a similar approach).

> The meanings of state constitutions are frequently forged outside judicial confines because state constitutions give great credence and power to democratic majorities, which invites political contestation and dispute. This political responsiveness of state constitutions, in conjunction with the expansion of the state judicial agenda under the "new judicial federalism," has made state constitutional politics an increasingly dynamic and energetic form of political contestation in recent times.[101]

Once again, this view of constitutionalism could not be applied to the difficult-to-amend federal Constitution.

State constitutional rights provisions, by contrast to the federal guarantees we think of as protecting *minority* and unpopular people, sometimes actually provide *majoritarian* protections. The bans on special privileges and special laws, discussed in the context of equality guarantees in Chapter 7, serve to protect the majority from legislative favoritism for powerful economic interests. Even the discredited "*Lochner*-era" federal substantive due process doctrines, applied in behalf of powerful economic interests to overturn economic regulation, are still in vogue in some states, but more often used to protect the majority from "special-interest" legislation.[102] This was noted by the *Harvard Law Review* editors as early as 1982:

> Both courts and commentators have largely ignored the possibility that judicial review might play a radically different role—that of safeguarding the interests of majorities. State constitutional law could be dramatically divorced from its federal counterpart if state courts were to reconceive their purpose in terms of elaborating and employing a theory of majoritarian, rather than anti-majoritarian, review. In fact, there is reason to believe that state courts already have undertaken something very much like this change of direction in one area: the review of economic regulation.[103]

## VII. STATE CONSTITUTIONS' ALTERNATIVE VOICES

Seen from a related perspective, by contrast to the federal Constitution's character as an admirable but also slavery-affirming product of an all-white (and

[101] *Id.* at 885.

[102] The literature and cases are collected and analyzed in Anthony B. Sanders, *The "New Judicial Federalism" Before Its Time: A Comprehensive Review of Economic Substantive Due Process Under State Constitutional Law Since 1940 and the Reasons for Its Recent Decline*, 55 AM. U. L. REV. 457 (2005). Chapter 6.

[103] *Developments in the Law—The Interpretation of State Constitutional Rights*, 95 HARV. L. REV. 1324, 1498–99 (1982).

male) constitutional convention,[104] state constitutions (many of which also affirmed slavery and racism) also reflect the impact of a much wider variety of alternative voices to the original, elite white-male, federal constitutionalism. For example, in New York's 1846 constitutional convention, poor farmers continued their "Rent Wars," successfully challenging the continued extraction of quitrents rather than the availability of fee simple ownership.[105] The California Constitution bears marks to this day of the 1879 women's rights proposals of Clara Foltz, the first woman lawyer on the West Coast.[106] The Reconstruction Era state constitutional conventions included many African American delegates, leading to the term "Black and Tan" constitutional conventions.[107] The Granger Movement, reflecting the interests of farmers, made itself felt in the 1870 Illinois Constitutional Convention, as well as others.[108]

The 1947 New Jersey Constitutional Convention was influenced in important ways by the single African American delegate[109] and the women who made up 10 percent of the delegates.[110] Native Americans had a significant impact on Oklahoma's constitution making in 1908.[111] There was a very substantial and influential presence of Hispanic delegates at the 1910 New Mexico Constitutional Convention:

[104] Thurgood Marshall, *Reflections on the Bicentennial of the United States Constitution*, 101 HARV. L. REV. 1, 2 (1987):

> For a sense of the evolving nature of the Constitution we need look no further than the first three words of the document's preamble: "We the People." When the Founding Fathers used this phrase in 1787, they did not have in mind the majority of America's citizens. "We the People" included, in the words of the framers, "the whole Number of free Persons." On a matter so basic as the right to vote, for example, Negro slaves were excluded, although they were counted for representational purposes—at three-fifths each. Women did not gain the right to vote for over a hundred and thirty years.

[105] William M. Wiecek, *State Protection of Personal Liberty: Remembering the Future*, *in* TOWARD A USABLE PAST: LIBERTY UNDER STATE CONSTITUTIONS 371, 379–80 (Paul Finkelman & Stephen E. Gottlieb eds., 1991); CHARLES W. MCCURDY, THE ANTI-RENT ERA IN NEW YORK LAW AND POLITICS, 1839–1865, 260–63 (2001).

[106] Barbara Allen Babcock, *Clara Shortridge Foltz: Constitution-Maker*, 66 IND. L.J. 849 (1991).

[107] Richard L. Hume, *Carpetbaggers in the Reconstruction South: A Group Portrait of Outside Whites in the "Black and Tan" Constitutional Conventions*, 64 J. AM. HIST. 313 (1977). *See also* Peggy Cooper Davis, *Introducing Robert Smalls*, 69 FORD. L. REV. 1695, 1701–04 (2001). Chapter 3.

[108] *See, e.g.*, James C. Harrington, *Free Speech, Press, and Assembly Liberties Under the Texas Bill of Rights*, 68 TEX. L. REV. 1435, 1439–40 (1990).

[109] Bernard K. Freamon, *The Origins of the Anti-Segregation Clause of the New Jersey Constitution*, 35 RUTGERS L.J. 1267 (2004).

[110] Maxine Lurie, *The Twisted Path to Gender Equality: Women and the 1947 Constitution*, 117 N.J. HIST. 39 (Spring/Summer 1990); Barbara Burns Petrick, *Mary Philbrook, Lawyer and Feminist: Opening the Practice of Law to Women and Establishing a Constitutional Basis for Sex Equality in New Jersey*, 4 WOMEN'S RTS. L. REP. 253 (1978).

[111] ROBERT L. TSAI, AMERICA'S FORGOTTEN CONSTITUTIONS: DEVIATIONS OF POWER AND COMMUNITY 152–84 (2014); DANNEY GOBLE, PROGRESSIVE OKLAHOMA: THE MAKING OF A NEW KIND OF STATE 187–227 (1980).

> The New Mexico Constitutional Convention was many-sided and colorful, being as it was on the borderline where two civilizations had met, fused and developed a society of its own composed of the Anglo American from the States and the Spanish American who had come up through Mexico. The membership stood at 35 members of Spanish decent and 65 members of the so called Anglo American decent.[112]

The California Constitutional Convention of 1849 also had an important Hispanic presence.[113] Nonetheless, it should not be overlooked that many state constitutions also bear the marks of some extremely reprehensible anti-immigrant[114] and racial bias[115] over the years.

Obviously, many of the unique perspectives on evaluating state constitutions are expressed in comparison or by contrast to what we know about the federal Constitution. State constitutions, therefore, are most often considered in relational terms, juxtaposed against the federal Constitution. It is no longer likely, however, that scholars will characterize state constitutions as reflecting a "pallid me-tooism"[116] or conclude that "[i]t is doubtful, that any major new ideas in constitutional law . . . have originated in the state courts or have been first devised as a reading of some state constitution."[117]

## VIII. CONCLUSION

For all these reasons, state constitutions need to be understood, evaluated, and utilized on their own terms and not through the commonly unfavorable comparisons to the more familiar federal Constitution. They have different origins, functions, forms, and qualities from the federal document, all for rational reasons. As a consequence, questions about drafting[118] and interpreting[119] these documents by the courts and others, attitudes about their proper content,

[112] Reuben W. Heflin, *New Mexico Constitutional Convention*, 21 N. Mex. Hist. Rev. 60, 61 (Jan. 1946).

[113] *See, e.g.*, Myra K. Saunders, *California Legal History: The California Constitution of 1849*, 90 Law Libr. J. 447 (1998).

[114] Babcock, *supra* note 106, at 858; Harry N. Scheiber, *Race, Radicalism, and Reform: Historical Perspective on the 1879 California Constitution*, 17 Hast. Const. L.Q. 35, 42–44, 49, 68–69 (1989).

[115] Chapter 3.

[116] Jerome Frank, *Book Reviews*, 63 Tex. L. Rev. 1339, 1340 (1985).

[117] Lawrence M. Friedman, *State Constitutions in Historical Perspective*, 496 Annals Am. Acad. Pol. & Soc. Sci. 33, 40 (1988).

[118] *See generally* Grad & Williams, *supra* note 35.

[119] Chapter 12.

and approaches to their amendment and revision must be considered in a specific *state* constitutional context. Lawyers, judges, legislators, constitutional convention delegates, students, and other citizens need to understand these characteristics leading to the unique character of American state constitutions if they are to work effectively within this other, less visible but nevertheless important constitutional tradition in the United States.

# 2

# THE PRE-FEDERAL "STATE" CONSTITUTIONS

## THE FOUNDING DECADE

> *America in the 1780s had Constitutions—a baker's dozen of them—but not a culture of constitutionalism. As yet there had developed no special aura around the notion of a constitution. . . . In several states the constitutions themselves had become the focal point of controversy. Veneration of constitutions did not figure prominently in public discourse, and campaigns to rewrite the state constitutions had begun with their ratification.*[1]

Constitutional scholars have long recognized that the framers of the U.S. Constitution modeled many of its features on the earlier state constitutions.[2] John Adams indicated contemporary recognition of this with his boast: "I made a Constitution for Massachusetts, which finally made the Constitution of the

[1] Joyce Appleby, *The American Heritage: The Heirs and the Disinherited*, 74 J. AM. HIST. 798, 800 (1987).

[2] *See, e.g.*, Richard Beeman, *Introduction* to BEYOND CONFEDERATION: ORIGINS OF THE CONSTITUTION AND AMERICAN NATIONAL IDENTITY 3, 18 (Richard Beeman, Stephen Botein, & Edward Carter eds., 1987) ("[I]t is now becoming apparent that it may only be through studies of legal and constitutional development in the individual *states* that we will be able to discover where we have been.") (emphasis in original); MAX FARRAND, THE FRAMING OF THE CONSTITUTION OF THE UNITED STATES 128–29, 203–04 (1913) (state constitutions continually drawn upon); CHARLES WARREN, CONGRESS, THE CONSTITUTION AND THE SUPREME COURT 22–39 (1925).

For example, Peter Hoffer and Natalie Hull have observed:

> The transformation of impeachment from a check against monarchical misdeeds to an instrument of republican government was first explored in state governments before 1787, and fully realized in the federal Constitution. Between 1776 and 1787, state politicians drafted and tested various provisions for impeachment. Delegates to the federal convention—Madison, Randolph, Paterson, Mason, and Hamilton—supported by the voices and votes of other knowledgeable state leaders, fashioned national impeachment provisions along lines laid down in the states' constitutions.

PETER HOFFER & NATALIE HULL, IMPEACHMENT IN AMERICA, 1635–1805, 68 (1984) (footnote omitted).

*The Law of American State Constitutions*. Robert F. Williams and Lawrence Friedman, Oxford University Press.
 DOI: 10.1093/oso/9780190068806.003.0003

United States."[3] Although an oversimplification, Adams's claim contains an important element of truth. Still, he was probably more accurate when he said in 1788, "What is the Constitution of the United States . . . but that of Massachusetts, New York and Maryland! There is not a feature of it which can not be found in one or the other."[4]

Alexander Hamilton, not surprisingly, relied on positive modeling in the very first number of *The Federalist*, where he assured New Yorkers that the new federal Constitution was an "analogy to your own State constitution. . . ."[5] There are references, both favorable and unfavorable, to the state constitutions throughout *The Federalist*. For example, James Madison criticized the state constitutions for their failure to separate governmental powers adequately.[6]

This influence of the early "state" constitutions on the federal constitutional discussions is clear, despite controversies over the reliability of federal Constitutional Convention records,[7] or their relevance in determining the "intent" of the Framers with respect to specific issues.[8] Justice Felix Frankfurter, for example, in interpreting the federal Constitution's congressional immunity provision, noted, "The provision in the U.S. Constitution was a reflection of the political principles already firmly established in the States. Three State Constitutions adopted before the Federal Constitution specifically protected the privilege."[9]

The fifty-five delegates who attended the 1787 Constitutional Convention in Philadelphia already had wide experience, either directly or indirectly, with constitutional theory and constitution making.[10] One scholar estimated that "one-third to one-half of the members of the federal Convention had been members of the conventions which framed the several state constitutions, and a very large number of the members of the various ratifying conventions had also had a part in the formation of the respective state constitutions."[11] By the

[3] Letter from John Adams to Mercy Warren (July 28, 1807), *quoted in* RONALD PETERS, THE MASSACHUSETTS CONSTITUTION OF 1780, 14 (1978).

[4] CATHERINE BOWEN, MIRACLE AT PHILADELPHIA 199 (1966).

[5] THE FEDERALIST No. 1, at 6 (Alexander Hamilton) (Modern Library ed. 1937).

[6] *Id.* No. 47, at 316–20 (J. Madison); *id.* No. 48, at 323–26 (J. Madison). *See infra* note 172.

[7] *See, e.g.*, Christopher Collier, *The Historians versus the Lawyers: James Madison, James Hutson, and the Doctrine of Original Intent*, 112 PA. MAG. HIST. & BIOG. 137 (1988) (discussing views of accuracy of federal Constitutional Convention records and their relationship to the doctrine of original intent); James H. Hutson, *The Creation of the Constitution: The Integrity of the Documentary Record*, 65 TEX. L. REV. 1 (1986) (same).

[8] *See, e.g.*, H. Jefferson Powell, *The Modern Misunderstanding of Original Intent*, 54 U CHI. L. REV 1513 (1987) (discussing debate over role of original intent in constitutional interpretation).

[9] Tenny v. Brandhove, 341 U.S. 367, 373 (1951).

[10] *See generally* Robert F. Williams, *Experience Must Be Our Only Guide: The State Constitutional Experience of the Framers of the Federal Constitution*, 15 HASTINGS CONST. L.Q. 403 (1988). *See also* RICHARD B. MORRIS, THE FORGING OF THE UNION, 1781–1789, 267, 269 (1987).

[11] W.C. Webster, *Comparative Study of the State Constitutions of the American Revolution*, 9 ANNALS AM. ACAD. POL. & SOC. SCI. 380, 417 (1897). *See also* 1 JAMES BRYCE, THE AMERICAN COMMONWEALTH 32 (rev. 2d ed. 1889) (similar estimate); JOHN JAMESON, AN INTRODUCTION TO THE STUDY OF THE CONSTITUTIONAL AND POLITICAL HISTORY OF THE STATES 18 (1886) (same).

time the federal Convention met, the thirteen newly independent colonies had debated, framed, adopted, rejected, modified, and continued to debate at least twenty "state" constitutions in the period since 1775. Of course, these entities were not yet "states" as we know them now—members of the American federal constitutional structure—but they functioned from the beginning in an evolving confederation.[12]

My count of twenty includes Vermont's constitution (although Vermont was not formally admitted to the Union until 1791); Massachusetts' failed 1778 constitution; South Carolina's two constitutions; and the Connecticut and Rhode Island charters, which were modified and retained instead of the formal adoption of state constitutions. Scholars have given different numbers of state constitutions during the founding decade. Political scientist Donald Lutz observed, "The institutions written into the American Constitution were heavily dependent on colonial experience and practice, as well as upon the framers' experience of having written and lived under eighteen state constitutions between 1776 and 1786."[13] It is not, of course, the exact number that matters but rather the fact that many state constitutions predated the federal Constitution.

[12] Richard Morris contended that the states were creations of the Continental Congress. Morris, *supra* note 10, at 76. Mark Graber treats the ambiguity of the early "state" constitutions as both national and subnational in *State Constitutions As National Constitutions*, 69 Ark. L. Rev. 371, 372 (2016) ("The first late eighteenth century American state constitutions were also unambiguously national constitutions.") *But see* Craig Green, *United/States: A Revolutionary History of American Statehood*, 119 Mich. L. Rev. 1, 8 (2020):

> On the contrary, legal characteristics of American states and statehood were created and negotiated in the same historical moments as the United States' central government, often through the same legal documents. States and the United States repeatedly leaned on one another for support and recognition, operating and functioning together, of necessity and also by design. Both layers of government jointly manufactured structures to organize populations and territory even as they struggled with one another over particular substantive points.

[13] Donald Lutz, Popular Consent and Popular Control: Whig Political Theory in the Early State Constitutions 1 (1980). *See also* Sydney G. Fisher, The Evolution of the Constitution of the United States 8 (1897). Fisher lists seventeen state constitutions, including those that were rejected. Lutz adds the Massachusetts Charter, under which that state operated from 1776 until 1780, to reach his total of eighteen.

For excellent summaries of this decade of state constitution making, see generally Willi Paul Adams, The First American Constitutions: Republican Ideology and the Making of State Constitutions in the Revolutionary Era 63–93 (1980); Elisha Douglass, Rebels and Democrats: The Struggle for Equal Political Rights and the Majority Rule During the American Revolution (1955); Jackson Turner Main, The Sovereign States, 1775–1783, 143–95 (1973); Gordon S. Wood, The Creation of the American Republic, 1776–1787, 125–255 (1969).

# I. STATE CONSTITUTIONAL EXPERIMENTS

In the decade following Independence, the states, in the words of American historian Jackson Turner Main, "became the laboratories for testing theories, trying the institutions in the various forms that presently appeared in the constitutions of the United States and other countries."[14] Contemporaries of this period also understood the experimental nature of those efforts at constitution making. In 1778, for example, Thomas Paine applauded "the happy opportunity of trying a variety, in order to discover the best. . . . By diversifying the several constitutions, we shall see which State flourish the best, and out of the many posterity may choose a model. . . ."[15] The author of the 1776 pamphlet, *Four Letters on Interesting Subjects*, now believed to be Paine, argued:

> Perhaps most of the Colonies will have two houses, and it will probably be of benefit to have some little difference in the forms of government, as those which do not like one, may reside in another, and by trying different experiments, the best form will the sooner be found out, as the preference at present rests on conjecture.[16]

The "founding decade" of 1776–1787,[17] half of it while the Revolution was still in progress,[18] included what was possibly the most intense and concentrated focus in the history of written constitutional theory and practice. Political scientist William Morey observed in 1893 that "the most eventful constitution-making epoch in our history was not the year 1787 but an antecedent period extending

[14] Jackson Turner Main, *The American States in the Revolutionary Era*, *in* Ronald Hoffman & Peter Albert, Sovereign States in an Age of Uncertainty 1, 23 (1981).

Justice Brandeis' better-known description of the states as "laboratories" was made in reference to state legislative innovations at the beginning of the twentieth century. New State Ice Co. v. Liebmann, 285 U.S. 262, 311 (1932) (Brandeis, J., dissenting).

[15] *A Serious Address to the People of Pennsylvania on the Present Situation of Their Affairs*, *in* *Pennsylvania Packet* (Dec. 1, 1778), *reprinted in* 2 Philip S. Foner, The Complete Writings of Thomas Paine 277, 281 (1969).

[16] *Four Letters on Interesting Subjects* (Philadelphia 1776), *reprinted in* 1 American Political Writing During the Founding Era, 1760–1805, 368, 387 (Charles Hyneman & Donald Lutz eds., 1983).

[17] The term "founding decade" was apparently first used by Martin Diamond. *See* Diamond, *Decent, Even Though Democratic*, *in* Robert Goldwin & William A. Schambra, How Democratic Is the Constitution? 18, 24 (1980).

[18] When one is reading the first state constitutions, it is easy to forget that most of them were drafted and adopted during wartime. Cecelia Kenyon noted:

> It is difficult for us to imagine Washington or Jefferson captured by the British and shot or hanged as traitors, it is even more difficult to remember that every member of the state assemblies or conventions that drafted constitutions was publicly committing himself to the Revolution and therefore placing his life in jeopardy should the Revolution fail.

Cecelia M. Kenyon, *Constitutionalism in Revolutionary America*, *in* Nomos XX: Constitutionalism 84, 91–92 (J. Roland Pennock & John W. Chapman eds., 1979).

from 1776 to 1780."[19] The founding decade witnessed an internal political struggle over, in historian Carl Becker's terms, "who should rule at home," as well as the Revolutionary War struggle for "home rule."[20] The issues of independence and military confrontation had a major impact on many of the state constitution drafters, particularly in Pennsylvania and New York.[21] Certainly, no similar statement could be made about the delegates to the Constitutional Convention in 1787.

The central controversies over the first state constitutions had little to do with rights. Rather, the focus was on how the new state governments would be structured and which groups in society would have the dominant policymaking role under the new governments. The question of rights as we think of them today was not at the forefront of these debates.[22]

Several important points have become much clearer since earlier studies of the first state constitutions. First, we now know that there was far more fundamental controversy, as well as diversity of opinion and interest, in the state constitution-making processes during the founding decade than was earlier thought.[23] Although we should generally avoid the tendency to analyze historical events on the basis of oversimplified dichotomies,[24] two competing views of

[19] William Morey, *The First State Constitutions*, 4 ANNALS AM. ACAD. POL. & SOC. SCI. 201, 201 (1893). Harry Cushing asserted: "In the history of the use of the written constitution as a basis of government, no period, so brief has been marked by such activity in constituent proceedings and by such political pathbreaking as the decade of the American Revolution." Harry Cushing, *The People, The Best Governors*, 1 AM. HIST. REV. 284, 284 (1896). *See also* BENJAMIN F. WRIGHT, CONSENSUS AND CONTINUITY, 1776–1787, 8–9 (1958) (1787 Convention would have been a failure without "the example, experience, and the constructive achievements of 1776 and the years immediately thereafter").

[20] CARL L. BECKER, THE HISTORY OF POLITICAL PARTIES IN THE PROVINCE OF NEW YORK, 1760–1776 (1909).

From 1765 to 1776, therefore, two questions, about equally prominent, determined party history. The first was whether essential colonial rights should be maintained; the second was by whom and by what methods they should be maintained. The first was the question of home rule; the second was the question, if we may so put it, of who should rule at home.

*Id.* at 22.

[21] *See* EDWARD COUNTRYMAN, A PEOPLE IN REVOLUTION: THE AMERICAN REVOLUTION AND POLITICAL SOCIETY IN NEW YORK, 1760–1790, 163–65 (1981).

[22] *See* DOUGLASS, *supra* note 13, at 133:

> The bills of rights in the first state constitutions were valuable as the basis for restricting the sphere of governmental authority and as expressions of liberal political philosophy, but they did nothing to make government more responsive to the people. The attainment of democracy required political equality and majority rule. . . .

*See also* WOOD, *supra* note 13, at 62 (discussing early understanding of rights).

[23] *See, e.g.*, Harry C. Black, *The Formation of the First State Constitutions*, 7 CONST. REV. 22, 31 (1923) (noting "[r]eady. acceptance of closely parallel institutions"). For an analysis of the debates, see CHRISTIAN G. FRITZ, AMERICAN SOVEREIGNS: THE PEOPLE AND AMERICA'S CONSTITUTIONAL TRADITION BEFORE THE CIVIL WAR 9–46 (2008).

[24] Cecelia M. Kenyon, *Republicanism and Radicalism in the American Revolution: An Old Fashioned Interpretation*, 19 WM. & MARY Q. 153, 154–55 (3d Ser. 1962); ADAMS, *supra* note 13, at 147.

governmental structure emerged in the framing of the state constitutions during the founding decade. Controversy surrounded both *substantive* questions of state constitutional content and *procedural* questions concerning the process of drafting and adopting the state constitutions. Social and economic interests, and the political and constitutional theories underlying their alternative visions of state constitutions, were very divergent.

The ultimate outcomes of the state constitutional battles were much closer and less predetermined than has been commonly recognized. Most studies of the early state constitutions focus exclusively on the documents as finally adopted.[25] Those whose ideas did not prevail have largely been forgotten[26] in much the same way that the Anti-Federalists were, until fairly recently, forgotten.[27] Investigating the various constitutional theories and political positions of the time calls for including views of early state constitution making "from the bottom up,"[28] or for "listening to the inarticulate."[29] Despite their relative obscurity today, the unsuccessful arguments that surfaced during the framing of the state constitutions, and the experience with government structures that seemed in retrospect not to work well, were not lost on the Philadelphia delegates in 1787. By studying such ideas and institutions, we, as well, may find an important alternative perspective on what is too often portrayed as a consensus view of the proper constitution of government during the founding decade.[30]

## II. TWO WAVES OF STATE CONSTITUTION MAKING

Historians[31] and political scientists[32] have identified two major "waves" of state constitution making during the founding decade. The first wave's crest was the

[25] *See, e.g.*, Morey, *supra* note 19 (analyzing early state constitutions); Webster, *supra* note 11 (analyzing early state constitutions).

[26] Donald Lutz pointed out the importance of ideas that were rejected at the state constitutional conventions, in addition to those that were adopted. LUTZ, *supra* note 13, at 1. These rejected ideas undoubtedly were fresh in the minds of the delegates to the federal Constitutional Convention in 1787.

[27] *See* CECELIA M. KENYON, THE ANTIFEDERALISTS (1966); HERBERT STORING, THE COMPLETE ANTIFEDERALIST (1981); SAUL CORNELL, THE OTHER FOUNDERS: ANTI-FEDERALISM AND THE DISSENTING TRADITION IN AMERICA, 1788–1828 (1999). Difficult as it was to collect the materials for the Anti-Federalists, the task is multiplied many times when one is examining the state constitutions.

[28] Jesse Lemisch, *The American Revolution Seen from the Bottom Up*, *in* TOWARDS A NEW PAST: DISSENTING ESSAYS IN AMERICAN HISTORY 16 (Barton J. Bernstein ed., 1968).

[29] Jesse Lemisch, *Listening to the "Inarticulate": William Widger's Dream and the Loyalties of America Revolutionary Seamen in British Prisons*, 3 J. SOC. HIS. 1 (1969–1970).

[30] Donald Lutz has observed the tendency to emphasize the continuities in constitutional development between 1776 and 1787. He concluded: "A careful examination of state constitutions written in the period . . . will reveal that the discontinuities are more important." LUTZ, *supra* note 13, at xv.

[31] *See, e.g.*, WOOD, *supra* note 13, at 435.

[32] *See, e.g.*, LUTZ, *supra* note 13, at 44–45; DONALD LUTZ, THE ORIGINS OF AMERICAN CONSTITUTIONALISM 103–08 (1988).

Pennsylvania Constitution of 1776[33]—it was a direct stimulus for the second wave. The Massachusetts Constitution of 1780 was the central feature of the second wave. "The 1780 Massachusetts Constitution," asserted Donald Lutz,

> was the most important one written between 1776 and 1789 because it embodied the Whig theory of republican government, which came to dominate state level politics; the 1776 Pennsylvania Constitution was the second most important because it embodied the strongest alternative. The Massachusetts document represented radical Whiggism, moderated somewhat by the form of mixed government if not the actual substance. Pennsylvania Whigs wrote the most radical constitution of the era, one lacking even a bow in the direction of mixed government.[34]

## A. The First Wave

The first wave of state constitutions is generally seen to include those adopted during the first year after Independence.[35] For the most part, legislative bodies hastily drafted these new constitutions, which did not differ substantially from the colonial charters they replaced, except in providing for weakened executive power and, sometimes, the inclusion of declarations of rights. The drafters gave little consideration to permanency or to structural mechanisms to check dominant legislatures. South Carolina's constitution of 1776 contained an absolute gubernatorial veto, but it remained in effect for only two years.[36] Most of these constitutions also created upper houses within their legislative branches. Although the 1776 Pennsylvania Constitution did not fit this basic pattern, because it was promulgated in a more leisurely fashion by a convention elected for that purpose and did not include an upper house, it represented the culmination of the first wave and provided a counterpoint to the second.

[33] The text of Pennsylvania's 1776 Constitution is reprinted in 8 SOURCES AND DOCUMENTS OF UNITED STATES CONSTITUTIONS 227 (William F. Swindler ed., 1979) [hereinafter SOURCES AND DOCUMENTS].

[34] LUTZ, *supra* note 13, at 129. *See also* KENYON, *supra* note 27, at xxx (noting that some commentators focus on differences among state constitutions "emerging from sharp conflict between democratic and antidemocratic forces, with the constitutions at Pennsylvania and Massachusetts representing respectively the victories of the two sides"); Kenyon, *supra* note 18, at 92 (same).

For a discussion of Whig political thought, see Donald Elfenbein, *The Myth of Conservatism as a Constitutional Philosophy*, 71 IOWA L. REV. 401, 468–79 (1986).

[35] *See, e.g.*, 2 SOURCES AND DOCUMENTS, *supra* note 33, at 197 (1776 Delaware Constitution); 6 SOURCES AND DOCUMENTS, *supra* note 33, at 449 (1776 New Jersey Constitution); 10 SOURCES AND DOCUMENTS, *supra* note 33, at 48 (1776 Virginia Constitution).

[36] 8 SOURCES AND DOCUMENTS, *supra* note 33, at 464 (1776 South Carolina Constitution, art. VII).

The second wave lasted longer than the first, from 1777, when the New York Constitution was adopted, to 1780, when Massachusetts adopted the constitution that remains in place today.[37] The second wave could even be seen as lasting until 1784, when New Hampshire, after much trial and error, adopted its revised state constitution.[38] These state constitutions were adopted in a more deliberate fashion, often by specially elected conventions. The second-wave documents reflected a direct concern with mechanisms to check the dominant legislative branches.

The Pennsylvania Constitution, adopted in September 1776, played two important roles in the development of American constitutionalism. On the one hand, this constitution and the political arguments supporting it provided the basis for persons in most of the states to argue for a simple people's government that would contain no elements of "aristocracy." In other words, the document's lack of effective checks on the powerful unicameral assembly was lauded as imposing no "undemocratic" restraints on the expressed will of the people. Checks and balances of the usual sort, such as an upper house and executive veto, were not part of Pennsylvania's first constitution.

This radically democratic Pennsylvania Constitution, according to historian Richard Ryerson, "marked the outer limits of the Revolution."[39] It was very influential during the founding decade, but not necessarily in positive ways. Because the Continental Congress met in Philadelphia, delegates were aware of the Pennsylvania Constitution and the controversy surrounding it, and therefore these events received immediate national attention.[40] The constitutions of other states, even draft versions, were published in Philadelphia newspapers,[41] and all of the well-known pamphlets on state constitutions were available to the Continental Congress delegates.[42] Philadelphia thus became the epicenter of state constitutional debate. As early as July 1776, for example, Dr. Josiah Bartlett, a statesman from New Hampshire (which had already adopted a state constitution in January 1776), wrote home from Philadelphia to John Langdon, a future delegate to the federal Constitutional Convention, that the constitutions "of

[37] *See, e.g.*, 5 SOURCES AND DOCUMENTS, *supra* note 33, at 92 (1780 Massachusetts Constitution); 7 SOURCES AND DOCUMENTS, *supra* note 33, at 168 (1777 New York Constitution).

[38] 6 SOURCES AND DOCUMENTS, *supra* note 33, at 344.

[39] Richard A. Ryerson, *Republican Theory and Partisan Reality in Revolutionary Pennsylvania: Toward a New View of the Constitutionalist Party*, *in* HOFFMAN & ALBERT, *supra* note 14, at 96.

[40] ADAMS, *supra* note 13, at 94 n.111.

[41] HELEN H. MILLER, GEORGE MASON: GENTLEMAN REVOLUTIONARY 154 (1975).

[42] JOHN P. SELSAM, THE PENNSYLVANIA CONSTITUTION OF 1776: A STUDY IN REVOLUTIONARY DEMOCRACY 171 n.11, 173–75 (1936). Those delegates from other states took a special interest in the drafting of the Pennsylvania Constitution. *Id.* at 171 (*quoting* PA. EVE. POST, July 30, 1776). *See also* DOUGLAS M. ARNOLD, A REPUBLICAN REVOLUTION: IDEOLOGY AND POLITICS IN PENNSYLVANIA, 1776–1790 (1989).

*Virginia* and *New-York* are in this city. . . . I shall send them forward, and the Constitutions of the other Colonies as they are formed, as possibly something may be taken from them to amend our own."[43]

Pennsylvania's constitution was not the only manifestation of a very different vision of the proper structure of government from that which ultimately prevailed. It mirrored a broader debate on the nature of republicanism and the distribution of authority within government. There is evidence of a fairly widespread, radically democratic vision of the proper state constitution, which arose to some extent during the framing of virtually all of the state constitutions. Jesse Lemisch, a historian of the "inarticulate," has noted that "there existed in 1776 a body of political thought which did not endorse deference" to traditional elites.[44] Although this assertion is controversial among historians, there is some documentation of this body of thought, particularly in Pennsylvania. Even in the absence of documentation, Lemisch asserts that less articulate people must have shared these ideas "directly out of the experience of their lives."[45] The Pennsylvania Constitution of 1776 and the political theory supporting it reflect the less well-known constitutional theory of those whose ideas did not prevail and who, like the Anti-Federalists, have tended to be forgotten in constitutional history.

In its resolution of May 10 and 15, 1776,[46] the Second Continental Congress

> recommended to the respective assemblies *and conventions* of the United Colonies, where no government sufficient to the exigencies of their affairs, has been hitherto established, to adopt such Government as shall, in the Opinion of the Representatives of the People, best conduce to the Happiness and Safety of their Constituents in particular and America in general.[47]

Now that it was time to frame the new state governments, the stakes surrounding who was to rule at home were very high. Independence, resulting in drastic changes in the political system of the past, was worrisome to those who previously had held power. To those who sought new power, independence without real change in the makeup of internal political power was not worth the effort. This

[43] Robert A. Rutland, The Birth of the Bill of Rights, 1776–1791, 52 (1962) (emphasis in original). Bartlett's reference to the New York Constitution must have been to a draft version because New York's Constitution was not finally adopted until April 1777.

[44] Lemisch, *supra* note 28, at 16.

[45] *Id.* at 16. *See also* Jesse Lemisch, *Radical Plot in Boston (1770): A Study in the Use of Evidence*, 84 Harv. L. Rev. 485 (1970) (reviewing Hiller B. Zobel, The Boston Massacre (1970)).

[46] The resolution was adopted May 10, 1776, and a preamble was added on May 15, 1776. Adams, *supra* note 13, at 61. John Adams served with Edward Rutledge of South Carolina and Richard Henry Lee of Virginia on the committee that drafted the resolution. *Id.*

[47] Adams, *supra* note 13, at 61 (*quoting* 4 Journals of the Continental Congress 342, 357–58 (1904–37)) (emphasis supplied).

tension would form the basis for the struggles over framing and implementing state constitutions from 1776–1786, and on into the next century. Quite literally, control over the new governments, which would exercise plenary power without any higher authority, was up for grabs. As historian Elisha Douglass has noted:

> Large numbers of those unable to vote or hold political office felt that the primary purpose of the struggle was to abolish the political institutions by which privilege had been maintained in the colonial governments. Thus when the question of home rule was succeeded by the question of who would rule at home, these groups of humbler rebels attempted to obtain equal consideration for themselves by demanding that democratic reforms be written into the new state constitutions.[48]

In no state would a greater transition of internal power take place than in Pennsylvania.[49] The Pennsylvania Constitution of 1776 reflected the extreme shift in the internal political structure of the state (a shift evidenced especially by the political importance of the city of Philadelphia), and the constitution proved influential beyond the state. The controversies over governmental structure illustrate the wide range of opinions concerning the details of the new state governments within what can be viewed as a consensus on the advisability of "republicanism." The colonists had many different reasons for supporting republicanism and, in fact, actually supported many different variations of republicanism. As Professor Robert Shalhope pointed out:

> Only one thing was certain, Americans believed that republicanism meant an absence of an aristocracy and a monarchy. Beyond this, agreement vanished—what form a republican government should assume and, more important, what constituted a republican society—created disagreement and eventually bitter dissension. This was a consensus that promoted discord rather than harmony. . . .[50]

[48] DOUGLASS, *supra* note 13, at vi. *See also* GARY B. NASH, THE URBAN CRUCIBLE: SOCIAL CHANGE, POLITICAL CONSCIOUSNESS, AND THE ORIGINS OF THE AMERICAN REVOLUTION 340 (1979) (internal struggle for new social order).

[49] For the pre-independence evidence of this internal power struggle, see Robert Gough, *Charles H. Lincoln, Carl Becker, and the Origins of the Dual-Revolution Thesis*, 38 WM. & MARY Q. 97 (3d Ser. 1981); CHARLES H. LINCOLN, THE REVOLUTIONARY MOVEMENT IN PENNSYLVANIA, 1760–1776 (1901); Charles J. Stille, *Pennsylvania and the Declaration of Independence*, 13 PA. MAG. HIST. & BIOG. 385 (1889); THEODORE THAYER, PENNSYLVANIA POLITICS AND THE GROWTH OF DEMOCRACY, 1740–1776 (1953).

[50] Robert E. Shalhope, *Toward a Republican Synthesis: The Emergence of an Understanding of Republicanism in American Historiography*, 29 WM. & MARY Q. 49, 72 (3d Ser. 1972). *See also* ROBERT E. SHALOPE, THE ROOTS OF DEMOCRACY: AMERICAN THOUGHT AND CULTURE, 1760–1800, 44–52 (1990); Morton J. Horwitz, *Republicanism and Liberalism in American Constitutional Thought*, 29 WM. & MARY L. REV. 57 (1987); Frank I. Michelman, *Foreword: Traces of Self-Government*, 100 HARV. L. REV. 4, 17–55 (1986).

The Pennsylvania Constitution of 1776 lasted only until 1790. As the focal point of controversy over the proper structure of the new state government, it mirrored the broader debate taking place in the other states during the decade prior to the federal Constitutional Convention of 1787. Dr. Benjamin Rush was an opponent of Pennsylvania's radical constitution. The depth of his feelings, which were not unique to him, was revealed when he wrote to Timothy Pickering toward the close of the federal Convention: "The new federal government like a new Continental waggon will overset our State dung cart, with all its dirty contents . . . and thereby restore order and happiness to Pennsylvania."[51] These are strong words of condemnation for Pennsylvania's first constitution, the central features of which many others strongly supported. Yet the hostility toward the constitution within the state spilled over to influence constitution making elsewhere. The framers of the U.S. Constitution ultimately embraced a structure of government reflecting a political philosophy very different from that prevailing in Pennsylvania from 1776 to 1790—an implicit, and at times explicit, rejection of Pennsylvania's first constitution. At the same time, elements of Pennsylvania's early constitutional experience were incorporated into the federal Constitution and became basic elements of American constitutionalism.[52]

Thomas Paine's *Common Sense*, probably the most influential political pamphlet in American history, was published in Philadelphia on January 9, 1776.[53] It made a strong case for establishing simple, republican governments, operated by unicameral legislatures with a wide elective franchise in each of the colonies.[54] Paine, an English tradesman, had come to Philadelphia in 1774 and worked with many of the political newcomers (former outsiders) who had recently become active in the revolutionary committees.[55] Together, they developed in Philadelphia an "urban variant of republicanism that fostered egalitarianism as well as economic enterprise."[56]

[51] 4 MAX FARRAND, THE RECORDS OF THE FEDERAL CONSTITUTIONAL CONVENTION OF 1787, 75 (Rev. ed. 1937).

[52] *See infra* notes 181–82 and accompanying text, for a discussion of the positive influences of the 1776 Pennsylvania Constitution on the federal Constitution.

[53] 1 FONER, *supra* note 15, at 4.

[54] ERIC FONER, TOM PAINE AND REVOLUTIONARY AMERICA 75 (1976). *See also* A. OWEN ALDRIDGE, THOMAS PAINE'S AMERICAN IDEOLOGY 24 (1984) (discussing *Common Sense*); Jack P. Greene, *Paine, America, and the "Modernization" of Political Consciousness*, 93 POL. SCI. Q. 73, 84–86 (1978) (same).

[55] For a description of Paine and these politicians, see generally FONER, *supra* note 54, at 107–44; CHARLES S. OLTON, ARTISANS FOR INDEPENDENCE: PHILADELPHIA MECHANICS AND THE AMERICAN REVOLUTION (1975); Sharon V. Salinger, *Artisans, Journeymen, and the Transformation of Labor in Late Eighteenth-Century Philadelphia*, 40 WM. & MARY Q. 62 (3d Ser. 1983).

[56] Robert E. Shalhope, *Republicanism and Early American Historiography*, 39 WM. & MARY Q. 334, 341 (3d Ser. 1982).

In *Common Sense*, Paine initiated a "new political language" to portray a "utopian image of an egalitarian republican society."[57] He wrote for a mass audience, appealing to conservatives as well as radicals.[58] This message was, of course, favorably received by, and articulated the feelings of, many of the newly active political participants and simply confirmed their recent experiences with the committees and, to a lesser extent, with the prior limited self-government in the colonies. *Common Sense* reached the mass audience for which Paine aimed; it was read by hundreds of thousands of people and read aloud to many more.[59]

Those who seized power in Pennsylvania and wrote the new constitution emphasized values that were new. Although these values had pre-Revolutionary origins,[60] they gained vitality when their adherents assumed political power in Pennsylvania. They called for a people's government, unencumbered by interference from what they saw as the "aristocratic" elements of society that would be represented by either a second house of the legislature or a powerful executive and that would seek to limit the political participation of ordinary people. Any excesses of such a simple government were to be checked by its mandated openness and required legislative and public deliberation on measures, together with annual elections, rotation in office, and periodic review of legislative activity by specially elected overseers.[61] These "democratic" values and approaches were shared by groups in other states as well, intent on achieving newfound political power. Of course, the traditional elites in other states were well aware of, and disturbed by, the influence of Pennsylvania's democratic constitutional movement.

Pennsylvania's 1776 constitution followed Paine's recommendation and established a "simple" government. Paine later referred to it as "a generous Constitution . . . which considers mankind as they came from their maker's hands—a *mere* man, before it can be known what shall be his fortune or his state. . . ."[62] It contained a separate Declaration of Rights and Frame of Government. The Declaration of Rights was patterned after Virginia's, but Article XII contained among the broadest statements of speech and press freedom: "The people have a right to freedom of speech, and of writing, and publishing their

[57] FONER, *supra* note 54, at xvi. For a wide-ranging critique of Paine's political theories over the years, see Cecelia M. Kenyon, *Where Paine Went Wrong*, 45 AM. POL. SCI. REV. 1086 (1951). Kenyon concluded that Paine was "incurably naive." *Id.* at 1094.

[58] FONER, *supra* note 54, at 82–84, 99.

[59] *Id.* at 79–80.

[60] See *supra* note 49 for materials tracing the pre-Revolutionary origins of Pennsylvania's radical political ideas.

[61] Kenyon, *supra* note 18, at 101, 103; ADAMS, *supra* note 13, at 249–51; SELSAM, *supra* note 42, at 184–85. *See generally* JOSEPH S. FOSTER, IN PURSUIT OF EQUAL LIBERTY: GEORGE BRYAN AND THE REVOLUTION IN PENNSYLVANIA 59–76 (1994).

[62] 2 FONER, *supra* note 15, at 285 (emphasis in original). *See* STEVEN ROSSWURM, ARMS, COUNTRY AND CLASS: THE PHILADELPHIA MILITIA AND THE "LOWER SORT" DURING THE AMERICAN REVOLUTION, 1775–1783, 86–87 (1987).

sentiments; therefore the freedom of the press ought not to be restrained." Article XVI provided: "That the people have a right to assemble together, to consult for their common good, to instruct their representatives, and to apply to the legislature for redress of grievances, by address, petition or remonstrance."

Interestingly, the Frame of Government protected various other rights as well. For example, Section 35 specified, "The printing presses shall be free to every person who undertakes to examine the proceedings of the legislature, or any part of government."[63] Professor Robert Palmer has argued that rights specified in both the Declaration of Rights and the Frame of Government were aimed more at reinforcing republican government than at guaranteeing individual rights:

> The Pennsylvania Constitution, even in its declaration of rights, was not oriented directly to individual fulfillment; it considered the communal right to qualify liberties as important as the individual's right to be free from governmental interference. The constitution thus established a republican form of government, majoritarian in emphasis and liberty-enhancing in intention.
>
> * * *
>
> Liberties in this constitution were social contract liberties, all qualified by entry into society. Those provisions that seem unqualifiable, such as the printing presses to be free to examine government, take on a less unique, less expansive flavor when perceived not as personal liberties but rather as provisions necessary to preserve republican government.[64]

The provisions of the Pennsylvania Constitution reflected the values of those who pushed for its adoption. An analysis of the actions and influence of the "lower sorts," acting "out of doors," concluded:

> Thus, Pennsylvania had enshrined many of the mechanisms of mobilization that had brought the province to this point. The constitution gave the people freedom of expression through the press and petitions, allowed input from the politicized masses, and opened up avenues for out-of-door politicking.[65]

[63] Despite these guarantees, however, a major libel action was pursued by Chief Justice Thomas McKean against newspaper publisher Eleazar Oswald for published criticisms of the Chief Justice. *See* Leonard W. Levy, *On the Origins of the Free Press Clause*, 32 UCLA L. REV. 177, 188–91 (1984); JEFFREY A. SMITH, PRINTERS AND PRESS FREEDOM: THE IDEOLOGY OF EARLY AMERICAN JOURNALISM 37–38, 155–56, 165 (1988); Dwight L. Teeter, *The Printer and the Chief Justice: Seditious Libel in 1782–1783*, 45 JOURNALISM Q. 235 (1968).

[64] Robert C. Palmer, *Liberties as Constitutional Provisions, 1776–1791*, *in* WILLIAM E. NELSON & ROBERT C. PALMER, LIBERTY AND COMMUNITY: CONSTITUTION AND RIGHTS IN THE EARLY AMERICAN REPUBLIC 55, 64, 68 (1987) (footnotes omitted).

[65] BENJAMIN L. CARP, REBELS RISING: CITIES AND THE AMERICAN REVOLUTION 210 (2007).

From the moment it was implemented, controversy raged over whether the Pennsylvania Constitution should be changed. Many qualified persons boycotted the new government by refusing to hold office or to practice law in the courts.[66] This ongoing controversy, which was highly visible and followed by observers in other states, dominated most elections in Pennsylvania until the 1790 constitution was substituted as part of the overall movement that led to the federal Constitution.[67] This period of controversy generated rich newspaper and pamphlet literature, with Paine contributing several newspaper articles in support of the 1776 constitution.[68]

Interested persons in other states spoke out on both sides of the debate over Pennsylvania's unique constitutional theory and practice. Almost immediately after *Common Sense* appeared, John Adams published his influential *Thoughts on Government*[69] as, among other things, a response to Paine. Adams wrote in his autobiography, sometime later, the following about *Common Sense*:

> The other third part relative to a form of Government I considered as flowing from simple Ignorance, and a mere desire to please the democratic Party in Philadelphia, at whose head were Mr. Matlock, Mr. Cannon and Dr. Young. I regretted, however, to see so foolish a plan recommended to the People of the United States, who were all waiting only for the countenance of Congress, to institute their State Governments. I dreaded the Effect so popular a pamphlet might have, among the People, and determined to do all in my Power, to counter Act the effect of it.[70]

[66] Thomas R. Meehan, *Courts, Cases and Counselors in Revolutionary and Post-Revolutionary Pennsylvania*, 91 PA. MAG. HIST. & BIOG. 3, 4–10 (1967).

[67] *See generally* OWEN S. IRELAND, RELIGION, ETHNICITY, AND POLITICS: RATIFYING THE CONSTITUTION IN PENNSYLVANIA (1995); FOSTER, *supra* note 61, at 141–51; ROBERT L. BRUNHOUSE, THE COUNTER-REVOLUTION IN PENNSYLVANIA, 1776–1790, 17 (1942) ("The Constitution became the center of the political warfare. . . ."); Ryerson, *supra* note 39 (tracing controversy surrounding Pennsylvania Constitution); WOOD, *supra* note 13, at 226–37, 438–46 (same).

For an argument that the conflicts over the Pennsylvania Constitution of 1776 were essentially religious, see Owen S. Ireland, *The Crux of Politics: Religion and Party in Pennsylvania*, 1778–1789, 42 WM. & MARY Q. 453 (3d Ser. 1985). *See also* Wayne Bockelman & Owen S. Ireland, *The Internal Revolution in Pennsylvania: An Ethnic-Religious Interpretation*, 41 PA. HIST. 125 (1974).

On the movement for a federal Constitution in Pennsylvania, see Steven R. Boyd, *Antifederalists and the Acceptance of the Constitution: Pennsylvania*, 1787–1792, 9 PUBLIUS: THE J. FEDERALISM 123 (Spring 1979); PENNSYLVANIA AND THE FEDERAL CONSTITUTION 1787–1788 (John B. McMaster & Frederick D. Stone eds., 1970).

[68] See *supra* notes 15–16 and accompanying text for references to some of these pamphlets and newspaper articles. *See also* FONER, *supra* note 54, at 142–43 (same).

[69] *Reprinted in* 1 AMERICAN POLITICAL WRITING DURING THE FOUNDING ERA, 1760–1805, 401 (Charles Hyneman & Donald Lutz eds., 1983).

[70] AUTOBIOGRAPHY AND DIARY (OF JOHN ADAMS) 332–33 (L.H. Butterfield ed., 3d ed. 1961), *quoted in* ALDRIDGE, *supra* note 54, at 198.

While in Philadelphia at the Continental Congress, Adams had been asked by two North Carolina delegates for his views concerning the structure of the new state governments; his response was later published as *Thoughts on Government*.[71] There, Adams set forth an alternative vision of how the new state governments should be constituted, a vision less radical than the Pennsylvania system. He proposed a model based on "balanced government," or checks and balances, in which bicameralism and executive power counterbalanced the lower house, which "should be in miniature an exact portrait of the people at large. It should think, feel, reason, and act like them."[72] He also advocated property requirements for holding office and voting.[73]

Adams remained highly critical of the Pennsylvania Frame of Government. As Dr. Benjamin Rush recalled:

> So great was [Adams's] disapprobation of a government composed of a single legislature, that he said to me upon reading the first constitution of Pennsylvania "The people of your state will sooner or later fall upon their knees to the King of Great Britain to take them again under his protection, in order to deliver them from the tyranny of their own government."[74]

Rush wrote to Adams: "From you I learned to discover the danger of the Constitution of Pennsylvania."[75]

Thus, as early as 1776, arising out of the constitutional theories being developed in Pennsylvania, the crucial issues of the founding decade were joined: How would the new governments be structured? Who would participate in the new governments, directly as office holders, and indirectly as voters? Paine's ideas carried the day in a few states, primarily Pennsylvania, and influenced constitutional debate in most other states, but Adams's ideas ultimately prevailed. Historian Elisha Douglass, concluding that Adams's *Thoughts on Government* was probably the "paramount guide" for constitution making in at least five

[71] Aldridge, *supra* note 54, at 200. It has been asserted that the defense of unicameralism in *Four Letters on Interesting Subjects* was Paine's response to Adams. *Id.* at 233. *See* 1 American Political Writing During the Founding Era, *supra* note 69, at 384–87 (reprinting *Four Letters on Interesting Subjects*) (defense of unicameration found in fourth letter).

[72] 1 American Political Writing During the Founding Era, *supra* note 69, at 403.

[73] Adams argued in favor of property qualifications:

> New claims will arise; women will demand a vote; lads from twelve to twenty-one will think their rights not enough attended to; and every man who has not a farthing, will demand an equal voice with any other, in all acts of state. It tends to confound and destroy all distinctions, and prostrate all ranks to one common level.

Adams, *supra* note 13, at 207.

[74] Foner, *supra* note 54, at 142.

[75] Letters of Benjamin Rush, 1761–1792, at 114–15 (L.H. Butterfield ed., 1951), *quoted in* John M. Coleman, Thomas McKean: Forgotten Leader of the Revolution 203 n.56 (1975).

states, observed, "When it is considered that the state constitutions, particularly that of Massachusetts—were the greatest single influence on the Federal Constitution, the full importance of the pamphlet should be evident."[76]

Interestingly, both Paine in *Common Sense* and Adams in *Thoughts on Government* revealed the sense of exhilaration felt by constitution makers at the beginning of the founding decade. Paine proclaimed:

> [W]e have every opportunity and every encouragement before us, to form the noblest purest constitution on the face of the earth. We have it in our power to begin the world over again. A situation similar to the present, hath not happened since the days of Noah until now. The birthday of a new world is at hand. . . .[77]

Adams's more familiar comment in *Thoughts* is remarkably similar:

> You and I, my dear friend, have been sent into life at a time when the greatest lawgivers of antiquity would have wished to live. How few of the human race have ever enjoyed an opportunity of making an election of government . . . for themselves or their children! When, before the present epocha, had three millions of people full power and a fair opportunity to form and establish the wisest and happiest government that human wisdom can contrive?[78]

These statements reflect an enthusiasm and optimism that would be difficult to find a decade later, at the opening of the federal Constitutional Convention.[79] Beyond this shared enthusiasm, however, there was no real consensus between Paine's and Adams's views regarding how the new governments should be structured and who should participate in them.

Because Philadelphia was at the center of state constitutional debate, Pennsylvania's experience was watched with great interest and concern in

[76] DOUGLASS, *supra* note 13, at 32. For a full analysis of John Adams's views as they changed during the founding decade, see WOOD, *supra* note 13, at 567–92. *See also* Joseph Dorfman, *The Regal Republic of John Adams*, 59 POL. SCI. Q. 227 (1944) (tracing development of Adams's political philosophy).

[77] PHILIP FONER, THE LIFE AND MAJOR WRITINGS OF THOMAS PAINE 45 (1974), *quoted in* ALDRIDGE, *supra* note 54, at 2.

[78] 1 AMERICAN POLITICAL WRITING DURING THE FOUNDING ERA, *supra* note 69, at 408–09. *See also* DANIEL J. HULSEBOSCH, CONSTITUTING EMPIRE: NEW YORK AND THE TRANSFORMATION OF CONSTITUTIONALISM IN THE ATLANTIC WORLD, 1664–1830, 170 (2005) ("Not since the English Civil War had Anglophone people tried to frame a republic: a representative government with no king.").

[79] ADAMS, *supra* note 13, at 22–26 (describing the "Founding Spirit"); BERNARD BAILYN, THE IDEOLOGICAL ORIGINS OF THE AMERICAN REVOLUTION 19–21 (1967) (noting the "vast release of American energies"); Kenyon, *supra* note 18, at 114–15 (describing the "attitude of founding").

other states,[80] as well as in Europe.[81] In an effort to avoid adopting a constitution like Pennsylvania's, traditional leaders in various states adopted a strategy of delay. In their focus on the apparent "rush" to adopt state constitutions after Independence, historians sometimes miss this fact. In North Carolina, for example, an early 1776 meeting of the Provincial Congress constitutional drafting committee resolved "to establish a purely democratic form of government" and had prepared an anti-aristocratic draft.[82] As a defensive response by conservatives, which has been called a defeat for the "democratic faction,"[83] the constitution-making process was intentionally slowed down. Samuel Johnson wrote on May 2, 1776, that "affairs have taken a turn within a few days past. All ideas of forming a permanent Constitution are, at this time, laid aside."[84]

The radical faction in North Carolina had its roots in the back-country Regulator movement of the prior decade.[85] The November 1776 instructions given by Orange and Mecklenburg County representatives to their Provincial Congress delegates reflected the same notions of a simple, popular government as those advocated by Paine and the Pennsylvania Constitutionalists.[86] These instructions were, "taken together . . . among the most complete and articulate statements of democratic aspirations to come out of North Carolina during the Revolutionary period."[87]

[80] *See* SELSAM, *supra* note 42, at 215–16 (Maryland man equated Pennsylvania government with "system of slavery"). William Hooper, a North Carolina delegate to the Continental Congress wrote that the Pennsylvania Constitution "made more tories than the whole treasury of Britain would have done in the same space of time." Letter from William Hooper to Joseph Hewes (Oct. 27, 1776), *reprinted in* 5 LETTERS OF DELEGATES TO CONGRESS, 1774–1789, at 407, 410 (Paul H. Smith ed., 1980).

[81] The Pennsylvania Constitution stimulated great interest in Europe, especially France. *See generally* Albert Blaustein, *Our Most Important Export: The Influence of the United States Constitution Abroad*, 3 CONN. J. INT'L L. 15, 18 (1987); Henrey E. Bourne, *American Constitutional Precedents in the French National Assembly*, 8 AM. HIST. REV. 466 (1903); J. Paul Selsam & Joseph G. Rayback, *French Comment on the Pennsylvania Constitution of 1776*, 76 PA. MAG. HIST. & BIOG. 311 (1952); J. Paul Selsam, *Brissot de Warville on the Pennsylvania Constitution of 1776*, 72 PA. MAG. HIST. & BIOG. 25 (1948).

[82] Elisha P. Douglass, *Thomas Burke, Disillusioned Democrat*, 26 N.C. HIST. REV. 150, 157 (1950); DOUGLASS, *supra* note 13, at 119–20.

[83] DOUGLASS, *supra* note 13, at 121, 123, 129.

[84] Letter from Samuel Johnston to James Iredell (May 2, 1776), *quoted in* ADAMS, *supra* note 13, at 81–82. A month earlier he had written, "We are going to the devil without knowing how to help ourselves." Letter from Samuel Johnston to James Iredell (Apr. 4, 1776), *quoted in* Douglass, *supra* note 82, at 157.

[85] DOUGLASS, *supra* note 13, at 71–99.

[86] 1 THE FOUNDERS' CONSTITUTION 56–58 (Philip Kurland & Ralph Lerner eds., 1987). *See also* M. VILE, CONSTITUTIONALISM AND THE SEPARATION OF POWERS 141 (1967) (instructions reflected pure doctrine of separation of powers).

[87] For discussion of the Orange and Mecklenburg County instructions, see Douglass, *supra* note 13, at 15; Douglass, *supra* note 82, at 159–60; ADAMS, *supra* note 13, at 107, 246–47. The Orange County instructions had been drafted by Thomas Burke, leader of the radical faction in the Provincial Congress. Douglass, *supra* note 82, at 159. Burke, like Paine, formed the basis for his radical political outlook prior to leaving England. DOUGLASS, *supra* note 13, at 150, 159–60.

After the delay in drafting a constitution, *Thoughts on Government* arrived in North Carolina, was considered by the drafting committee, and made its mark. The outcome was a compromise constitution, which included a bicameral legislature but also an expanded franchise.[88] Historian Merrill Jensen concluded that, in the final product of North Carolina's 1776 constitution, "more than a fourth of the sections . . . dealt with and embodied reforms that had been demanded by the Regulators."[89]

One of North Carolina's delegates to the Continental Congress, also a member of the Provincial Congress working on the North Carolina Constitution, wrote to Samuel Johnson:

> You have seen the constitution of Pennsylvania—the motley mixture of limited monarchy and an execrable democracy—a beast without a head. The mob made a second branch of the legislature. Laws subjected to their revisal in order to refine them. A washing in ordure by way of purification. Taverns and dram shops are the councils to which the laws of this state are referred for approbation before they possess a binding influence.[90]

Elisha Douglass explained that the noted "'washing in ordure' to which [the writer] referred was the provision in the Pennsylvania Constitution that all legislation after passage must be published to the people at large before it could become law."[91] This was what Staughton Lynd referred to as "bicameralism from below."[92]

## B. The Second Wave

In early 1777, New York's delegates to the Continental Congress in Philadelphia wrote home about the controversy over the Pennsylvania Constitution of 1776:

> The unhappy Dispute about their Constitution is the fatal Rock on which they have split, and which threatens them with Destruction. We ardently wish that in our own State the utmost Caution may be used to avoid a like calamity. Every

[88] DOUGLASS, *supra* note 13, at 31, 120, 124–25.

[89] MERRILL JENSEN, THE ARTICLES OF CONFEDERATION: AN INTERPRETATION OF THE SOCIAL-CONSTITUTIONAL HISTORY OF THE AMERICAN REVOLUTION, 1774–1781, 26 (1940).

[90] Letter from William Hooper to Samuel Johnson (Sept. 1776), *quoted in* Douglass, *supra* note 82, at 158. *See also* Letter from William Hooper to Joseph Hewes (Oct. 27, 1776), *reprinted in* 5 LETTERS OF DELEGATES TO CONGRESS, *supra* note 80, at 407, 410 (referring to 1776 Pennsylvania Constitution as the "Monster which they called a Government").

[91] DOUGLASS, *supra* note 13, at 158 n.33. Hooper recommended the Delaware, South Carolina, and New Jersey constitutions as models. *Id.* at 159.

[92] STAUGHTON LYND, INTELLECTUAL ORIGINS OF AMERICAN RADICALISM 171 (1968).

> wise Man here wishes that the establishment of new Forms of Government had been deferred. . . .[93]

The committee drafting the New York Constitution, headed by Abraham Yates Jr., who later became a leading Anti-Federalist,[94] stretched out the process for eight months.[95] Robert R. Livingston, one of New York's conservative leaders, contrasted what he viewed as the failure in Pennsylvania with New York's moderate outcome, which he said was made possible by "swimming with a Stream which it is impossible to stem." Concerning Pennsylvania, he continued, "I long ago advised that they should yield to the torrent if they hoped to direct its course—you know nothing but well timed delays, indefatigable industry, and a minute attention to every favorable circumstance, could have prevented our being exactly in their situation."[96]

The "stream" to which Livingston referred included pressure from the Committee of Mechanics in New York City and a writer called "Spartanus," who was influenced by Paine.[97] The June 1776 *Respectful Address of the Mechanics in Union*[98] responded to a statement by the Provincial Congress indicating that it might adopt a constitution without direct involvement of the people either through a convention or ratification of the finished product.[99] The Address represents one of the earliest examples, like that in Pennsylvania, of an argument for separating the process of constitution making from that of ordinary legislation. Further, it reflects some of the early political positions taken on state constitutional issues by "lesser merchants, tradesmen, mechanics, and laborers,"

[93] Letter from Philip Livingston, James Duane, and William Duer to Abraham TenBroeck (Apr. 29, 1777), *reprinted in* 6 LETTERS OF DELEGATES TO CONGRESS, *supra* note 80, at 686–87, *quoted in* GEORGE DARGO, LAW IN THE NEW REPUBLIC: PRIVATE LAW AND THE PUBLIC ESTATE 10 (1983) (citations omitted).

[94] STAUGHTON LYND, CLASS CONFLICT, SLAVERY AND THE UNITED STATES CONSTITUTION 217 (1967).

[95] *See* LUTZ, *supra* note 13, at 45 (discussing delay in New York Constitution drafting); BERNARD MASON, THE ROAD TO INDEPENDENCE: THE REVOLUTIONARY MOVEMENT IN NEW YORK, 1773–1777, 219–20 (1966) (constitutional committee successfully evaded deadlines); ALFRED F. YOUNG, THE DEMOCRATIC REPUBLICANS OF NEW YORK: THE ORIGINS, 1763–1797 (1967) (discussing delay in New York Constitution drafting). Regarding New York's first constitution, see generally WILLIAM A. POLF, 1777: THE POLITICAL REVOLUTION AND NEW YORK'S FIRST CONSTITUTION (1977); DON R. GERLACH, PHILIP SCHUYLER AND THE AMERICAN REVOLUTION IN NEW YORK, 1733–1777, at 292–300 (1964); PETER J. GALIE, ORDERED LIBERTY: A CONSTITUTIONAL HISTORY OF NEW YORK 36–63 (1996); HULSEBOSCH, *supra* note 78, at 170–202.

[96] Letter from Robert R. Livingston to William Duer (June 12, 1777), *quoted in* MASON, *supra* note 95, at 231; YOUNG, *supra* note 95, at 15.

[97] COUNTRYMAN, *supra* note 21, at 162–64.

[98] New York Gazette, June 14, 1776, *reprinted in* HEZEKIAH NILES, PRINCIPLES AND ACTS OF THE REVOLUTION IN AMERICA 441–44 (1822). This document was apparently influenced by Paine's work. LYND, *supra* note 92, at 92–98. *See also* ADAMS, *supra* note 13, at 84–85 (discussing Address); COUNTRYMAN, *supra* note 21, at 162–63 (same).

[99] MASON, *supra* note 95, at 154–56.

and, in addition, it "by implication . . . raised the question of class power and condemned rule by an elite."[100]

New York's 1777 constitution, with its elected governor (for a three-year term with no limit on re-election), senate, and Council of Revision that could veto bills, represented the beginning of the second wave of state constitution making. It provided a model based on a blending of governmental powers that appealed to many of those who opposed the Pennsylvania Constitution. The Council of Revision, with Chief Justice John Jay as a member, went on to veto fifty-eight legislative enactments prior to the federal Constitutional Convention.[101] Its veto provision served as a model for the presidential veto in the federal Constitution.[102]

Jay, who had been one of the principal drafters of New York's 1777 constitution, wrote home in 1779 from Philadelphia to New York's Governor George Clinton:

> The exceeding high opinion entertained of your Constitution and the wisdom of your Counsels, has made a deep impression on many People of wealth and Consequence in this State, who are dissatisfied with their own; and unless their opinions should previously be changed, will remove to New York the moment the Enemy leave it.[103]

But New York's moderate 1777 constitution had been a hard-fought victory over those pushing for radical change. John Jay reported that the final product was so delicately balanced that "another turn of the winch would have cracked the cord."[104] Historian Alfred Young described the polar positions that led to what he described as the "middle of the road" New York Constitution of 1777. It is representative of the diversity of opinion generally concerning state constitutions during the founding decade:

> The [New York] constitution of 1777 retained many "aristocratic" features. . . . At the same time the constitution made several democratic departures from provincial precedent. . . . Had extreme conservatives had their way, they would

[100] *Id.* at 156, 158. *See also* Staughton Lynd & Alfred Young, *After Carl Becker, the Mechanics and New York City Politics, 1774–1801*, 5 LAB. HIST. 215 (1964) (discussing political activities of New York City mechanics).

[101] CHARLES THACH JR., THE CREATION OF THE PRESIDENCY, 1775–1789, 39 (1923, reprint 1969). For a detailed study of these vetoes, see 1 FRANK W. PRESCOTT & JOSEPH F. ZIMMERMAN, THE POLITICS OF THE VETO OF LEGISLATION IN NEW YORK STATE 19–34 (1980).

[102] THACH, *supra* note 101, at 110–16; DOUGLASS, *supra* note 13, at 65.

[103] Letter from John Jay to George Clinton (Oct. 7, 1779), *quoted in* THACH JR., *supra* note 101, at 54. Jay went on to describe the Pennsylvania Constitution of 1776 as "whimsical." *Id.* Jay had earlier called the Pennsylvania Constitution "premature." Letter from John Jay to Gourverneur Morris and R.R. Livingston (Apr. 29, 1777), *quoted in* MASON, *supra* note 95, at 230.

[104] *Quoted in* MAIN, *supra* note 13, at 176.

> have gotten elections at four-year intervals by voice voting, an upper house indirectly chosen, a governor elected by an upper house, and a governor with more of the powers of his royal predecessors. Had the most democratic elements had their way, there would have been taxpayer suffrage, a secret ballot for all elections . . . annual election of all state officials, and popular election of county and local officials; furthermore the appointive power would have been vested exclusively in the assembly and the governor's veto power would have been eliminated.[105]

Maryland constitutional framers in 1776 sought the advice of Pennsylvanian John Dickinson on how to avoid a constitution like Pennsylvania's. Thomas Stone, a Maryland delegate to the Continental Congress, wrote Dickinson that he thought "it not improbable that a well-formed government in a state so near as Maryland might tend to restore the affairs of . . . [Pennsylvania] from that anarchy and confusion which must attend any attempt to execute their present no plan of polity."[106] Dickinson did not visit Maryland but apparently did send his comments on the Maryland draft.[107] Despite significant "anti-aristocratic" pressures, Maryland's 1776 constitution ended up being the most conservative of the founding decade.[108] Many of the features of radical democracy seen in Pennsylvania were contained in the published constitutional proposal and instructions of the Ann Arundel County militia company to its county's delegates to the Convention framing the 1776 constitution. Nevertheless, the delegates, in publishing their response, rejected the radical proposals.[109] Furthermore, despite strict property requirements for voting for Convention delegates, many radical Ann Arundel County taxpayers and militia members voted by threat of arms.[110]

"A Watchman" wrote in the August 15, 1776, *Maryland Gazette*:

> A constitution formed without this important right of free voting being preserved to the people, would be despotic, and the people mere beasts of burden. It would be unjust and oppressive in the extreme to shut out the poor in having

[105] Young, *supra* note 95, at 20–21. For similar general descriptions of the opposing viewpoints on state constitutions, see Lemisch, *supra* note 28, at 11, 16; Main, *supra* note 13, at 184–85; Mason, *supra* note 95, at 231–34; Stephen E. Patterson, *The Roots of Massachusetts Federalism: Conservative Politics and Political Culture Before 1787*, *in* Hoffman & Alpert, *supra* note 14, at 42–43.

[106] Letter from Thomas Stone to John Dickinson, *quoted in* Edward C. Papenfuse & Gregory A. Stiverson, The Decisive Blow Is Struck: A Facsimile Edition of the Proceedings of the Constitutional Convention of 1776 and the First Maryland Constitution 4–5 (1977).

[107] Papenfuse & Stiverson, *supra* note 106, at 5 (unnumbered pages). *See also* Douglass, *supra* note 13, at 124 (Dickinson's involvement with drafters of Maryland's constitution).

[108] Ronald Hoffman, A Spirit of Dissention: Economics, Politics and the Revolution in Maryland 170–83, 269 (1973).

[109] *Id.* at 173.

[110] *Id.* at 170.

> a share in declaring who shall be the lawgivers of their country, and yet bear a very heavy share in the support of government. Would not the rich complain grievously if they had no power of electing representatives?[111]

The experience of Massachusetts from 1776 to 1780 represents the best example of the second wave of state constitution making. In contrast to most of the other states,[112] including Pennsylvania, the processes leading to the well-known Massachusetts Constitution of 1780 are well documented.[113] The availability of documentation is primarily because of the influence of local governments in the New England political structure at that time.[114] The responses of Massachusetts towns from 1776 to 1780 "on constitutional issues comprise the most important single source for any study of democratic ideas among the common people during the revolutionary period."[115] Professor Willi Paul Adams has asserted that the intensity and sophistication of the public debate on republican constitutionalism in Massachusetts in 1778 rivaled the federal constitutional debate of 1787–1789.[116] It seems, however, that Pennsylvania's less well-documented experience must be a close second.

As one historian has observed, in Massachusetts:

> [The] overriding issue of the 1770's was the question of a state constitution. From the very moment the reins of government were taken up by a provincial congress in the fall of 1774, conservatives feared the unchecked democracy it seemed to represent, eagerly sought the reinstatement of the constitution of 1691 which gave coequal powers to a council and a house of representatives,

[111] *Quoted in* MERRILL JENSEN, THE AMERICAN REVOLUTION WITHIN AMERICA 86 (1974).

[112] Kenyon, *supra* note 18, at 92 (early state constitution-making process not well documented).

[113] *See, e.g.*, OSCAR & MARY HANDLIN, POPULAR SOURCES OF POLITICAL AUTHORITY: DOCUMENTS ON THE MASSACHUSETTS CONSTITUTION OF 1780 (1966); PROVINCE IN REBELLION: A DOCUMENTARY HISTORY OF THE FOUNDING OF THE COMMONWEALTH OF MASSACHUSETTS 1774–1775 (L. Kevin Wroth ed., 1975); ROBERT J. TAYLOR, MASSACHUSETTS FROM COLONY TO COMMONWEALTH: DOCUMENTS ON THE FORMATION OF ITS CONSTITUTION, 1775–1780 (1961).

[114] LUTZ, *supra* note 13, at 75–77.

[115] DOUGLASS, *supra* note 13, at 163. The historian of the town of Pittsfield, Massachusetts, noted:

> As the anticipations of independence strengthened, what ideas should lie at the foundations of the new States—when the Colonies should assume that rank—became the subject of earnest and often of profound consideration, not only in legislative halls, but in country villages; and not less so were the constitutional provisions by which vitality could best be given to those ideas. We may be sure that rarely anywhere were these subjects earlier or more intelligently discussed than in the little meeting-house under the Pittsfield elm.

1 JOSEPH A. SMITH, HISTORY OF PITTSFIELD, MASSACHUSETTS 335 (1869).

[116] ADAMS, *supra* note 13, at 5. For a discussion of the process leading to the Massachusetts Constitution, see generally Alexander J. Cella, *The People of Massachusetts, A New Republic, and the Constitution of 1780: The Evolution of Principles of Popular Control of Political Authority, 1774–1780*, 14 SUFFOLK U. L. REV. 975 (1980).

> and denounced the various reformist demands for a unicameral legislature and no governor.[117]

Delay became the tactic of proponents of this view.[118]

The Reverend Thomas Allen, one of the leaders of the radical Berkshire Constitutionalists, was deeply influenced by Paine's *Common Sense*.[119] In February 1776, he read the pamphlet aloud to the Berkshire Committee of Inspection.[120] The Constitutionalists argued for popular participation in the constitution-making process and against aristocratic limitations on the legislature. The traditional elites, however, labeled the Berkshire Constitutionalists—who had closed the courts—as lawless mobs who sought to avoid paying their debts.[121]

The Berkshire Constitutionalists fought hard not only for the *content* of the state constitution but the proper *process* for adopting one. In this sense, their arguments for popular involvement in constitution making are comparable to the earlier Pennsylvania, North Carolina, Maryland, and New York arguments. The pressure for a legitimate state constitution led to the unsuccessful legislatively proposed 1778 Massachusetts Constitution,[122] and ultimately, to the famous Massachusetts Constitution of 1780, the oldest American constitution and a document bearing the personal mark of John Adams.[123]

Many of the themes contained in *Common Sense* and implemented in the 1776 Pennsylvania Constitution appeared the same year in New England in the anonymous pamphlet *The People the Best Governors*.[124] The pamphlet warned, "Let it not be said in future generations that money was made by the founders of the American states an essential qualification in the rulers of a free people."[125] Many of the New England clergy, especially the Calvinists, cited this pamphlet in state constitutional debates and sermons.[126] The May 19, 1777, instructions of

[117] Patterson, *supra* note 105, at 39.

[118] *Id.* "For four more years they succeeded in putting off a constitutional settlement, fearing it would generate, and perhaps even consolidate, social and political revolution." *Id.* at 39–40.

[119] DOUGLASS, *supra* note 13, at 151 (Allen influenced by Paine); Theodore M. Hammet, *Revolutionary Ideology in Massachusetts: Thomas Allen's "Vindication" of the Berkshire Constitutionalists, 1778*, 33 WM. & MARY Q. 514 (3d Ser. 1976); SMITH, *supra* note 115, at 347; TAYLOR, *supra* note 113, at 84.

[120] SMITH, *supra* note 115, at 347. *See also* ALICE M. BALDWIN, THE NEW ENGLAND CLERGY AND THE AMERICAN REVOLUTION 140–45 (1928).

[121] Hammett, *supra* note 119, at 514–16; TAYLOR, *supra* note 113, at 80.

[122] HANDLIN, *supra* note 113, at 190. This proposed constitution and its rejection are ably discussed in STEPHEN E. PATTERSON, POLITICAL PARTIES IN REVOLUTIONARY MASSACHUSETTS 171–96 (1973).

[123] *See generally* PETERS, *supra* note 3, for a thorough discussion of the Massachusetts Constitution.

[124] The author of this pamphlet called himself "a friend to the popular government." Cushing, *supra* note 19, at 285. *See also* DOUGLASS, *supra* note 13, at 15 (comparing the pamphlet with Paine's ideas).

[125] *The People, The Best Governors*, *quoted in* DOUGLASS, *supra* note 13, at 16.

[126] ALAN HEIMERT, RELIGION AND THE AMERICAN MIND FROM THE GREAT AWAKENING TO THE REVOLUTION 510–23 (1966). Heimert entitled his tenth chapter "The People, The Best Governors."

Wilbraham, Massachusetts to the town's representatives included the following direction: "That in all their proceedings they have Special recourse (as an assistance) to a Little book or Pamphlet Intitled, The People the best Governors or a Plan of Government, etc. . . ."[127] Similar radically democratic ideas appeared in instructions, newspaper essays, pamphlets, and arguments in state constitutional conventions in all the other states. Even in states where the Pennsylvania model was not adopted, its underlying theory and Paine's ideas formed a platform for outsiders pushing for change.

Constitutional debates in New Hampshire raised arguments similar to those in Pennsylvania and Massachusetts. In the July 1776 "College Hall Address," the towns in Grafton County asserted that they had reverted to a state of nature, and, "As for ourselves, we are determined not to spend our blood and treasure, in defending against the chains and fetters, that are forged and prepared for us abroad, in order to purchase some of the like kind of our own manufacturing."[128] The address opposed both property requirements for representatives and the executive veto and reflected the radically democratic constitutional platform that had prevailed in Pennsylvania and that was reflected in *The People the Best Governors.*[129]

The drafters of the 1776 Pennsylvania Constitution sent copies to representatives of Vermont, who came to Philadelphia to lobby the Continental Congress to recognize their statehood.[130] Dr. Thomas Young, a key Pennsylvania radical constitutionalist and longtime friend of Vermont's Ethan Allen, published a letter, addressed to Vermonters, on April 11 and 12, 1777, offering the Pennsylvania Constitution "as a model, which, with very little alteration, will, in my opinion, come as near perfection as anything yet concocted by mankind."[131] Upon their return to Vermont, the representatives took up the question of a state constitution. After concluding that the recent New York Constitution of 1777 was a "horrible example," they proposed a constitution modeled closely after Pennsylvania's.[132]

For materials on the involvement of the clergy in state constitutional debates of the founding decade, see Baldwin, *supra* note 120, at 79.

[127] *Quoted in* Cushing, *supra* note 19, at 285 n.1.

[128] 10 Provential and State Papers of New Hampshire 229–35, *quoted in* Baldwin, *supra* note 120, at 151.

[129] Baldwin, *supra* note 120, at 151–52.

[130] Adams, *supra* note 13, at 94.

[131] Matthew B. Jones, Vermont in the Making, 1750–1777, at 379 (1939, reprint ed. 1968). Appended to Young's letter was a copy of the Continental Congress Resolutions of May 10 and 15, 1776. *Id.* at 380. For discussion of Young's letter, see also Selsam, *supra* note 42, at 184 n.56. On Vermont during this period, see William Brewster, The Fourteenth Commonwealths: Vermont and the States That Failed (1960).

[132] Main, *supra* note 13, at 177; Jones, *supra* note 131, at 382 ("The straw that broke the opposition to an independent state and overcame the loyalty to New York . . . was the adoption by New York in April of a conservative state constitution"). *See also* Vile, *supra* note 86, at 140 (discussing Vermont constitution).

Georgia was the only state other than Pennsylvania and Vermont to adopt a unicameral legislature. As Elisha Douglass noted, "Relatively little is known about the Revolutionary movement in Georgia, but from the available evidence it would appear that it was accompanied by an internal revolution comparable to that of Pennsylvania."[133] More recently, however, information has been uncovered about Georgia's radical 1777 constitution. This constitution was strongly influenced by Button Gwinnett, one of Georgia's delegates to the Continental Congress in Philadelphia, where in 1776 he was exposed to the wide range of state constitutional drafts, pamphlets, and arguments.[134] Dr. Benjamin Rush noted that Gwinnet had taken the Pennsylvania Constitution back to Georgia.[135] Historian Edward Cashin has asserted:

> Gwinnett's legacy to Georgia was the radically democratic constitution of 1777. Gwinnett was president of the convention and chairman of the committee that drafted the constitution; it provided for a unicameral assembly, a plural executive, virtually universal suffrage, and provisions for compulsory voting. One Savannah conservative scoffed at the new constitution as the work of a small clique "at a nightly meeting in a Tavern."[136]

## III. LEGISLATIVE DOMINANCE

Most of the early state constitutions, though expressly recognizing the doctrine of separation of powers,[137] "tended to exalt legislative power at the expense of the executive and the judiciary."[138] This increased legislative dominance came primarily at the expense of the executive, which had come to be identified with the British Crown, against which the colonial assemblies had struggled but never succeeded in achieving anything more than shared power.[139] With the advent of

[133] DOUGLASS, *supra* note 13, at 340.

[134] Edward Cashin, *"But Brothers, It Is Our Land We Are Talking About": Winners and Losers in the Georgia Backcountry*, *in* RONALD HOFFMAN, THAD W. TATE, & PETER J. ALBERT, AN UNCIVIL WAR: THE SOUTHERN BACKCOUNTRY DURING THE AMERICAN REVOLUTION 240, 254–55 (1985). *See also* Jackson, *The Rise of the Western Members: Revolutionary Politics and the Georgia Backcountry*, *in* HOFFMAN, TATE, & ALBERT, *supra*, at 276, 295–301 (discussing Georgia constitution).

[135] BENJAMIN RUSH, THE AUTOBIOGRAPHY OF BENJAMIN RUSH 153 (George Corner ed., 1948).

[136] Cashin, *supra* note 134, at 254–55.

[137] Edward S. Corwin, *The Progress of Constitutional Theory Between the Declaration of Independence and the Meeting of the Philadelphia Convention*, 30 AM. HIST. REV. 511, 514 (1924–1925).

[138] WILLIAM M. WIECEK, THE GUARANTEE CLAUSE OF THE U.S. CONSTITUTION 21 (1972). *See also* Gerhard Casper, *An Essay in Separation of Powers: Some Early Versions and Practices*, 30 WM. & MARY L. REV. 211, 216 (1989): "As one reviews the state constitutions adopted between 1776 and 1787 for the ways in which they implement separation of powers notions, one is struck by the fact that the particulars display an exceedingly weak version of separation of powers." *Id.*

[139] For a summary of the powers of the colonial executive, see MAIN, *supra* note 13, at 99–103.

Independence, this conflict with the colonial executive could be finally ended;[140] the states were free to structure their governments as they saw fit. James Wilson, a key federal Convention delegate, ruefully noted the "excessive partiality" to the state legislature, "into whose lap, every good and precious gift was profusely thrown."[141]

Even though bicameral legislatures were created in the majority of states, the lower houses were clearly the most important.[142] Not only was membership in the lower houses expanded to include "new men" through reapportionment and lower suffrage and office-holding requirements, these bodies also assumed powers formerly exercised by colonial officials.[143]

The upper houses in the Revolutionary state constitutions descended directly from the colonial governor's councils, which performed both executive and legislative functions.[144] After the Revolution, the senators no longer owed their seats to the Crown but were responsible to the electorate.[145] Donald Lutz has described the general picture: "The overall result was that senates were somewhat more conservative than lower houses and protected property more carefully; but they failed to provide a consistent check on lower houses, as had been intended."[146]

The senators began to respond to the electorate in basically the same manner as members of the lower houses. Most states found themselves in the position Alfred Young described in New York:

> From a conservative point of view it was apparent that the state constitution was not functioning as it was supposed to. . . . The senators, presumably the protectors of property, "are more eager in the pursuit of popularity than the Assembly," Livingston complained. "The democratical part of the government is always encroaching."[147]

The first state constitutions profoundly transformed the governorship, from an instrument of British policy during the colonial period with prerogative powers that included an absolute veto of legislative acts, to a legislatively appointed office almost totally beholden to the newly dominant state legislatures.[148] After the

[140] *Id.* at 143–44.

[141] 1 The Works of James Wilson 357 (Robert G. McCloskey ed., 1967).

[142] Main, *supra* note 13, at 200.

[143] *Id.* at 205. *See also* Wood, *supra* note 13, at 162–63.

[144] Fisher, *supra* note 13, at 72–73.

[145] In addition to indirect elections, other conservative features of state senates included high property qualifications for office, longer terms than the lower house, and staggered terms. Lutz, *supra* note 13, at 89.

[146] *Id.* at 92. *See also* Wood, *supra* note 13, at 503–04.

[147] Young, *supra* note 95, at 62 (citations omitted).

[148] Fisher, *supra* note 13, at 17; Jensen, *supra* note 89, at 107; Main, *supra* note 13, at 102. The exception to this rule was Rhode Island, where neither the governor nor the Crown had veto power over

newly independent states had struggled so long against powerful governors, it would have been politically impossible for them to then turn around and adopt strong governorships.[149]

The second wave of state constitution making during the founding decade established a pattern of gradual transition from early legislative dominance, or "omnipotence," toward an increased role for both the executive and judicial branches. In the early years of the Revolution, the judiciary had almost been forgotten. If anything, it was considered part of the executive power, which was the target of intense hostility in the early state constitutions.[150] As experience with the dominant legislative branches developed, however, the judiciary and the executive came to be viewed as a necessary checks on potential legislative encroachments upon the rights guaranteed by the constitutions and upon the prerogatives of the other branches.[151]

Although the split in Pennsylvania over the constitution, between what came to be known as the Constitutionalist and Republican "parties,"[152] was the most extreme of any of the states, it reflected in a general sense the controversies that would surround the new state constitutions. The two basic factions that developed in each of the states during the battles over the state constitutions,[153] and which argued over the franchise, legislative structure, and executive powers, carried over into the legislative politics of the founding decade. In virtually all of the states, two "parties," described by Jackson Turner Main as the "Localists" and the "Cosmopolitans,"[154] clashed again and again over key legislative issues. These

assembly acts. This led one scholar to assert that the "Rhode Island General Assembly was among the most nearly autonomous legislative bodies in the British Empire." PATRICK CONLEY, DEMOCRACY IN DECLINE: RHODE ISLAND'S CONSTITUTIONAL DEVELOPMENT, 1776–1841, 45 (1977).

149 MAIN, *supra* note 13, at 143–44.

150 DONALD L. ROBINSON, "TO THE BEST OF MY ABILITY": THE PRESIDENCY AND THE CONSTITUTION 36–58 (1987).

151 WOOD, *supra* note 13, at 452. On the rise of judicial power during the founding decade, see generally *id.* at 453–63; VILE, *supra* note 86, at 157–58.

152 Ryerson, *supra* note 39, at 96.

153 Pennsylvania provided the clearest example of parties contending over the state constitution. RICHARD RYERSON, THE REVOLUTION IS NOW BEGUN: THE RADICAL COMMITTEES OF PHILADELPHIA, 1765–1776, 251 n.9 (1978); SELSAM, *supra* note 42, at 247. However, early party formation took place over constitutional development in many other states.

154 JACKSON TURNER MAIN, POLITICAL PARTIES BEFORE THE CONSTITUTION 24 (1973). Main concluded:

> Our investigation has disclosed the existence, in every state, of two legislative blocs or parties similarly composed and expressing . . . the same attitudes toward major issues of the period. The "Cosmopolitans" and "Localists" of Massachusetts, Maryland, and the Carolinas appear almost identical with the anti-Clintonians and Clintonians of New York, the Republicans and Constitutionalists in Pennsylvania and the Northern Neck and Southside blocs of Virginia. Even the West-East division in New Jersey about 1785 took a similar form, and we can trace the same political alignments in New Hampshire, Connecticut, Rhode Island, and Delaware.

*Id.* at 365.

issues included the treatment (and punishment) of Loyalists, price regulation, issuance of paper money, payment of the public debt, taxation policy, debtor/creditor relations, public spending, and a range of social and cultural issues.[155] Not all states faced all of these issues or resolved them the same way, but, as Main has observed, the various "states faced many of the same problems, and these problems stimulated a similar response, notably the emergence in each state of two major, opposing political blocs."[156] According to Professor Gordon Wood, those who found themselves on the losing side of these controversial issues began to realize that these legislative policies "were not the decrees of a tyrannical and irresponsible magistracy, but laws enacted by legislatures which were probably as equally and fairly representative of the people as any legislatures in history."[157] Main concluded that the clashes over these issues "reached a climax in the most momentous question of the decade: the ratification of the Federal Constitution."[158] The adoption of the U.S. Constitution, he continued, "involved not merely relations between the states and the central government but the many internal disputes that divided the legislatures—paper money, the court system, debts, slavery, taxes, land policy, and ultimately many more."[159]

## IV. STATE CONSTITUTIONAL INFLUENCE ON THE FEDERAL CONSTITUTION

There are many and varying accounts of the reasons for the move toward the federal Constitution and the abandonment of the Articles of Confederation. Westward expansion and territorial controversies; the payment of creditors; Shay's Rebellion in Massachusetts; and the failure of the "states" to respond to the mandatory requisitions of revenue (primarily for the war and war debts) imposed by the Continental Congress, together with other causes, have been suggested.[160] To this list may be added dissatisfaction with the way the states were functioning under their constitutions.

[155] *Id.* at 44–79. *See also* FORREST MCDONALD, NOVUS ORDO SECLORUM? THE INTELLECTUAL ORIGINS OF THE CONSTITUTION 143–79 (1985) (describing range of legislative controversies during founding decade); Janet Riesman, *Money, Credit, and Federalist Political Economy*, *in* BEYOND CONFEDERATION: ORIGINS OF THE CONSTITUTION AND NATIONAL IDENTITY, *supra* note 2, at 128 (same). *See generally* A. BECANSON, PRICES AND INFLATION DURING THE AMERICAN REVOLUTION: PENNSYLVANIA, 1770–1790 (1951); LOUIS HARTZ, ECONOMIC POLICY AND DEMOCRATIC THOUGHT: PENNSYLVANIA, 1776–1860, 7–8, 229 (1948).

[156] MAIN, *supra* note 154, at 321.

[157] WOOD, *supra* note 13, at 404.

[158] MAIN, *supra* note 154, at 79.

[159] *Id.*

[160] CALVIN H. JOHNSON, RIGHTEOUS ANGER AT THE WICKED STATES: THE MEANING OF THE FOUNDERS' CONSTITUTION 15–39, 202–22 (2005). *See also* ROGER H. BROWN, REDEEMING THE REPUBLIC: FEDERALISTS, TAXATION AND THE ORIGINS OF THE CONSTITUTION (1993); FRITZ, *supra* note 23, at 131–38.

Those who had opposed Pennsylvania's 1776 constitution, but repeatedly failed to change it, began to turn their sights to the national level to accomplish reform of state governments. For example, James Wilson of Pennsylvania expressed this view when he spoke before the 1787 Constitutional Convention on June 16: "Where do the people look at present for relief from the evils of which they complain? Is it from an internal reform of their Govt.? No. Sir, it is from the Natl. Councils that relief is expected."[161] Wilson had been an opponent of the 1776 Pennsylvania Constitution and many of the legislative policies of the period.[162] Partly as a result of this opposition, his Philadelphia home was the scene of fatal shootings in a clash between a militia company supporting price regulation and opponents of such legislative policies in 1779.[163] Following the Convention, Wilson told the Pennsylvania ratifying convention that "the greatest potential threats to popular rule were state governments themselves."[164]

Many participants in other states began to follow the same approach. James Madison, a longtime critic of even the relatively moderate Virginia constitution,[165] noted that it was the problems with how state governments were operating, rather than merely defects in the Articles of Confederation, that led to the federal Convention.[166] Likewise, Edmund Randolph, in introducing the Virginia Plan to the Convention, argued, "Our chief danger arises from the democratic parts of our state constitutions.... None of the constitutions have provided sufficient checks against the democracy."[167] Madison, like Randolph, singled out state legislatures for criticism. He argued that the state legislative branch had become "omnipotent" because "experience has proved a tendency in our governments

[161] FARRAND, *supra* note 51, at 253 (statement of James Wilson, Constitutional Convention, June 16, 1787). *See also* John C. Roche, *The Founding Fathers: A Reform Caucus in Action*, 55 AM. POL. SCI. REV. 799, 800 (1961) (*quoting* Wilson).

[162] CHARLES P. SMITH, JAMES WILSON, FOUNDING FATHER, 1742–1798, 107–15, 129–31, 296–306 (1956). A letter by Wilson published in the *Pennsylvania Gazette* attacked the 1776 constitution and responded to the charge that those seeking changes in it were attempting to establish themselves as a House of Lords. Wilson noted the long list of Republicans signing the letter and asked, "*Are we all desirous of becoming Lords?*" Letter from James Wilson to the *Pennsylvania Gazette*, Mar. 24, 1779, *quoted in* Smith, *The Attack on Fort Wilson*, 78 PA. MAG. HIST. & BIOG. 177, 177–78 (1954) (emphasis in original).

[163] *See generally* John K. Alexander, *The Fort Wilson Incident of 1779: A Case Study of the Revolutionary Crowd*, 31 WM. & MARY Q. 589 (3d Ser. 1974); SMITH, *supra* note 162; ROSSWURM, *supra* note 62, at 205–47. Robert Brunhouse referred to this event as "the highwater mark of Radical democracy in Pennsylvania during the revolutionary period." BRUNHOUSE, *supra* note 67, at 75. On the price regulation issues, see Ronald Schultz, *Small Producer Thought in Early America: Philadelphia Artisans and Price Control* (pt. 1), 54 PA. HIST. 115 (1987).

[164] *Quoted in* WIECEK, *supra* note 138, at 69.

[165] Madison told the federal Convention: "I would always exclude inconsistent principles in framing a system of government. The difficulty of getting its defects amended are great and sometimes insurmountable. The Virginia state government was the first which was made, and though its defects are evident to every person, we can not get it amended." 1 FARRAND, *supra* note 51, at 475–76. Interestingly, this passage appears in Yates' notes but not in Madison's.

[166] 1 FARRAND, *supra* note 51, at 134–36. *See also* Appleby, *supra* note 1, at 800–01, 811.

[167] 1 FARRAND, *supra* note 51, at 26–27.

to throw all power in to the legislative vortex."[168] One of the Founding Fathers, Gouverneur Morris of Pennsylvania, targeted his own state's legislature when he argued, "Every man of observation had seen in the democratic branches of the State Legislatures . . . excesses against personal liberty, private property and personal safety. What qualities are necessary to constitute a check in this case?" He continued, "Ask any man if he confides in the State of Penna. If he will lend his money or enter into contract? He will tell you no. He sees no stability. He can repose no confidence."[169]

Among the most influential delegates at the Constitutional Convention, Madison, Randolph, Wilson, and Morris saw the existing state constitutions, with Pennsylvania's as the most extreme example, as unable to provide checks against wide-ranging assaults on liberty and property by the relatively unfettered state legislatures. Concluding that meaningful change was unlikely at the state level, they began to see a new federal Constitution as the source of workable restrictions on state legislative action. It was significant for the fate of the Pennsylvania model at the federal Convention that the Pennsylvania delegation, which exercised considerable influence, consisted of persons who opposed the Pennsylvania Constitution of 1776. As yet unable to redraw the constitutional and political framework in Pennsylvania, they looked for relief at the federal Convention in Philadelphia.

As issues arose in the Convention regarding the structure of the new federal government, the framers rejected most of the fundamental features of the Pennsylvania Constitution, either explicitly or implicitly. For example, when rotation in office, a key feature of Pennsylvania's constitution, was debated, Gouverneur Morris opposed it, arguing, "A change of men is ever followed by a change of measures. We see this fully exemplified in the vicissitudes among ourselves, particularly in the State of Pena."[170] In discussing a proposed prohibition on members of the House holding other offices, Wilson was reported to have "observed that the State of Penna. which has gone as far as any State into the policy of fettering power, had not rendered the members of the Legislature ineligible to offices of the Govt."[171]

[168] 2 Farrand, *supra* note 51, at 35 (statement of James Madison, July 17, 1787). *See also id.* at 74 (additional similar comments of Madison). Ryerson referred to the Pennsylvania Constitution of 1776 as "America's most un-Madisonian Constitution." Ryerson, *supra* note 39, at 98.

Madison's concerns about state legislatures led him to propose, unsuccessfully, that the federal Congress be empowered to veto any state statute. *See* Larry D. Kramer, *Madison's Audience*, 112 Harv. L. Rev. 611, 627–628 (1999); Charles F. Hobson, *The Negative on State laws: James Madison, the Constitution and the Crisis in Republican Government*, 36 Wm. & Mary Q. 215 (3d Ser. 1979); James S. Liebman & Brandon L. Garrett, *Madisonian Equal Protection*, 104 Colum. L. Rev. 837, 843–49 (2004).

[169] 1 Farrand, *supra* note 51, at 511–13 (statement of Gouverneur Morris, July 1, 1787).

[170] 2 Farrand, *supra* note 51, at 112–13 (statement of Gouverneur Morris, July 25, 1787).

[171] *Id.* at 288 (statement of James Wilson, Aug. 14, 1787).

In debating the need for some form of executive veto in the federal Constitution, Morris reminded the delegates:

> The Report of the Council of Censors in Pennsylvania points out that many invasions of the legislative department on the Executive numerous as the latter is, within the short term of seven years, and in a State where a strong party is opposed to the Constitution, and watching every occasion of turning the public sentiments agst. It.[172]

Wilson had argued earlier that the federal executive needed an absolute veto because "[w]ithout such a self-defense the Legislature can at any moment sink it into non-existence."[173] In contrast to Pennsylvania's plural executive, Wilson also "moved that the Executive consist of a single person."[174]

One of the earliest—and most resolute—decisions of the federal Constitutional Convention was in favor of bicameralism, another direct response to Pennsylvania's frame of government. There was no real controversy over this point. In adopting bicameralism, a key element of the Virginia plan, Madison recalled later that it was only the Pennsylvania delegation that dissented, "probably from complaisance to Docr. Franklin who was understood to be partial to a single House of Legislation."[175] George Mason was sure that the "mind of the people of America" was

> Settled . . . in an attachment to more than one branch in the legislature. . . . Their constitutions accord so generally . . . that they seem almost to have been a miracle, or have resulted from the genius of the people. The only exceptions to the establishment of two branches in the Legislature are the State of Pa. and Congs.[176]

Although the nature of representation in the federal two-branch legislature led to the almost fatal large-small state split and eventually to the Great Compromise, it was clear from the debates that the delegates thought that the federal Senate needed to be a stronger check than state upper houses had been[177] on what many

[172] *Id.* at 299–300 (statement of Gouverneur Morris, Aug. 15, 1787). On several occasions in *The Federalist*, Madison pointed to the Pennsylvania Council of Censors, noting its failure to prevent violations of the constitution. The Federalist Nos. 48 & 50 (J. Madison) (Modern Library ed. 1937).

[173] 1 Farrand, *supra* note 51, at 98 (statement of James Wilson, June 4, 1787).

[174] *Id.* at 65–66 (statement of James Wilson, June 1, 1787).

[175] *Id.* at 48 (statement of James Madison, May 31, 1787).

[176] *Id.* at 339 (statement of George Mason, June 20, 1787).

[177] Jackson Turner Main concluded that "[e]ven those senates that were intended to be aristocratic were indelibly marked by the vigorous democratic movement." Jackson Tuner Main, The Upper House in Revolutionary America, 1763–1788, 99 (1967). *See also supra* notes 144–47 and accompanying text for a discussion of the functioning of senates under state constitutions.

delegates viewed as an "excess of democracy"[178] or "the turbulence and follies of democracy."[179] John Dickinson clearly expressed this view.[180]

Several features of Pennsylvania's constitutional experience found favor among the delegates at the Constitutional Convention. For example, Section 9 of the Frame of Government set forth the powers of the legislature but concluded that it "shall have no power to add to, alter, abolish, or infringe any part of this constitution." This important statement of the principle of constitutional supremacy was unusual in 1776, when most state constitutions were drafted and promulgated by legislatures and could be changed by mere legislative action. Nonetheless, it was embodied in the federal Constitution of 1787.

Pennsylvania's 1776 constitution also had introduced such concepts as the taxpayer franchise, reapportionment based on taxpayer population, and expanded eligibility for office-holding—notions that were controversial in 1776 but that Richard Ryerson reminded us, were "casually accepted in twentieth-century America." He continues, "Pennsylvania was America's cutting edge of democracy, advancing that political condition to a Jacksonian level fifty years before Jackson.... Pennsylvania's Constitutionalists contributed dearly and heavily to the equality-of-opportunity democracy that Americans like to think they have created."[181] Even the idea of a specialized constitutional convention itself, followed by a separate mechanism for popular ratification, which was a more commonly accepted, albeit by no means universal, procedure by 1787, was the product of a painstaking period of trial and error with state constitution-making processes,[182] beginning with Pennsylvania's specially elected constitutional convention in 1776.

Much of Wilson's well-known support for a powerful, popularly elected president mirrored arguments that were being developed within Pennsylvania by the opponents of the 1776 constitution during the decade before the federal Constitution. Wilson was a prominent member of this opposition group which warned that, contrary to the rhetoric of 1776, an unchecked legislative branch could actually constitute a danger to liberty.[183] As this argument evolved,

[178] 1 FARRAND, *supra* note 51, at 48 (statement of Elbridge Gerry, May 31, 1787). *See also id.* at 123 (Gerry's comments on Shays' demand for abolition of Massachusetts Senate and establishment of powerful unicameral legislature as reflecting "the wildest ideas of government in the world.").

[179] *Id.* at 51 (statement of Edmund Randolph, May 31, 1787). William Pierce recorded Randolph's comments as referring to the "fury of democracy." *Id.* at 58.

[180] *Id.* at 150, 158 (statements of John Dickinson, June 7, 1787).

[181] Ryerson, *supra* note 39, at 132–33.

[182] *See generally* ADAMS, *supra* note 13, at 63–98; Thad W. Tate, *The Social Contract in America 1774–1787: Revolutionary Theory as a Conservative Instrument*, 22 WM. & MARY Q. 375 (1965) (describing evolution of constitution-making process).

[183] *See supra* notes 161–64 and accompanying text for a description of Wilson's opposition to the 1776 Pennsylvania Constitution. *See also* Morton M. Rosenberg, *In Search of James Wilson*, 55 PA. HIST. 107 (1988) (tracing Wilson's political philosophy).

it began to separate government officials from the people themselves and to contend that checks on legislative power were necessary to protect the people's interests from the misuse of power.[184] Checks such as an upper house and a more powerful, single executive elected by the people were portrayed as logical republican mechanisms to represent more effectively the popular will by avoiding various kinds of legislative abuses. According to republican logic, an elected governor exercising effective power was a representative of the people, while an upper house was necessary to divide legislative power that had been abused.[185] If nothing else, Wilson's argument at the convention recast arguments that Republicans previously had leveled against the 1776 Pennsylvania Constitution.

Perhaps the most important contribution of Pennsylvania's first constitution was to provide a highly visible, national focal point for the competing arguments on the key constitutional issue of the founding decade—namely, the relationship between separation of powers and checks and balances. The Pennsylvania Constitutionalists were acutely aware of the separation of, and the differences among, governmental powers. It was the not yet fully understood concept of checks and balances, which they associated with monarchical government, that they rejected. Professor John Vile makes this point as follows:

> It is often stated that the Constitution of Pennsylvania did not embody the separation of powers, whereas in fact it was the basis for the whole Constitution. It is the failure to distinguish clearly between the separation of powers on the one hand, and checks and balances on the other, which leads to the confusion. The founders of the 1776 Constitution were bitterly opposed to any semblance of the checks and balances of the monarchic or aristocratic constitution.[186]

## V. CONCLUSION

The 1776 Pennsylvania Constitution, as we have seen, has had a broad and lasting importance. It represented a model of government that seems quite unrelated to what we now think of as American constitutionalism, one that has almost been forgotten. Its place in the evolution of constitutional ideas in this country, however, should not continue to be overlooked. Although ultimately unsuccessful, it represented an important, and legitimate, early model of government for the newly independent states. It was a major focal point of debates in all of the state constitutional conventions following it during the founding decade.

[184] Peter Onuf, *State Politics and Ideological Transformation: Gordon S. Wood's Republican Revolution*, 44 Wm. & Mary Q. 612, 614 (3d Ser. 1987).
[185] Wood, *supra* note 13, at 438–53.
[186] Vile, *supra* note 86, at 136.

This constitution and the experiences with government under it also provided a major stimulus for the federal Constitution and for the development of more effective mechanisms of checks and balances, which are now considered one of America's unique contributions to constitutional theory and practice. Gordon Wood put it clearly:

> Not only did the formation of the new state constitutions in 1776 establish the basic structures of our political institution, their creation also brought forth the primary conceptions of America's political and constitutional culture that have persisted to the present.[187]

In 2021, Dr. Wood amplified his conclusion:

> But the Revolutionary state constitutions created in 1776 were far more important in shaping America's understanding of constitutionalism than was the federal Constitution framed a decade later. Our single executives, our bicameral legislatures, our independent judiciaries, our idea of separation of powers, our bills of rights, and our unique use of constitutional conventions were all born in the state constitution-making period between 1775 and the early 1780s, well before the framing of the federal Constitution of 1787. In fact, the new federal government of 1787—its structure and form—was derived from what had taken place in the making of the state governments in the previous decade. In the first crucial years of independence, the states—not the federal government—were the focus of interest for most Americans.[188]

[187] Gordon S. Wood, *Foreword: State Constitution-Making in the American Revolution*, 24 RUTGERS L.J. 911, 911 (1993).
[188] GORDON S. WOOD, POWER AND LIBERTY: CONSTITUTIONALISM IN THE AMERICAN REVOLUTION 32 (2021). *See also id.*, ch. 2; ROBINSON WOODWARD-BURNS, HIDDEN LAWS: HOW STATE CONSTITUTIONS STABILIZE AMERICAN POLITICS 24 (2021):

> The drafting and survival of the national Constitution was not a matter of "accident and force." State constitutional drafting, failure, and adaptation answered national questions on legislative sovereignty and design, slavery and franchise law, and the enumeration of rights. This state constitutional experience guided the framing of the federal Constitution.

# 3

# THE EVOLVING AMERICAN STATE CONSTITUTIONS

*New States may be admitted by the Congress into this Union; but no new State shall be formed or erected within the jurisdiction of any other State; nor any State be formed by the Junction of two or more States, or Parts of States, without the Consent of the Legislatures of the States concerned as well as of the Congress.*

*The Congress shall have Power to dispose of and make all needful Rules and Regulations respecting the Territory or other Property belonging to the United States; and nothing in this Constitution shall be so construed as to Prejudice any Claims of the United States, or of any particular State.*

—U.S. Constitution, Article IV, Section 3

The American Revolution changed the society, economy, and political philosophy of the nation in countless ways. These changes continued after the end of the Revolution and the adoption of the federal Constitution.[1] Indeed, the modern American state constitutions reflect a pattern of constitutional evolution in theory and practice over two centuries that is quite distinct from those of the federal Constitution. These state constitutional developments are worthy of study in their own right, both as a counterpoint to federal constitutional development and in comparison to the evolution of state constitutions in other countries.[2] They can also inform the interpretation processes of current state constitutions.

The evolution of state constitutions over time and space reflects a mixture of national and regional issues and influence, together with matters of immediate,

[1] *See generally* Gordon S. Wood, The Radicalism of the American Revolution (1991). *See also* Alfred F. Young, *Afterword: How Radical Was the American Revolution*, *in* Beyond the American Revolution: Explorations in the History of American Radicalism (Alfred F. Young ed., 1993).

[2] Lawrence M. Friedman, *State Constitutions in Historical Perspective*, 496 Annals of Am. Acad. Pol & Soc. Sci. 33, 34 (Mar. 1988). *See generally* John Kincaid, *Early State History and Constitutions*, *in* The Oxford Handbook of State and Local Government 239 (Donald Haider ed., 2014).

*The Law of American State Constitutions*. Robert F. Williams and Lawrence Friedman, Oxford University Press.
 DOI: 10.1093/oso/9780190068806.003.0004

local concern. The states generally took the advice of Thomas Jefferson concerning the periodic amendment and revision of the state constitutions. Jefferson wrote:

> And, lastly, let us provide in our constitution for its revision at stated periods . . . Each generation is as independent as the one preceding, as that was of all which had gone before. It has then, like them, a right to choose for itself the form of government it believes most promotive of its own happiness; consequently, to accommodate to the circumstances in which it itself, had received from its predecessors; and it is for the peace and good of mankind, that a solemn opportunity of doing this every nineteen or twenty years, should be provided by the constitution; so that it may be handed on, with periodic repairs, from generation to generation, to the end of time, if anything human can so long endure.[3]

Jefferson spoke from long experience with the Virginia Constitution of 1776, which he considered deficient in many ways. In later years, a number of state constitutions were amended to include provisions facilitating automatic review.[4]

## I. POST-FEDERAL CONSTITUTIONAL EVOLUTION

After the ratification of the federal Constitution, the majority of governmental activity continued to take place in the states. "Between the ratification of the federal Constitution and the Civil War," according to Professor Daniel J. Hulsebosch, "constitutionally, the emphasis in the United States was on the *states*. The primary instrument of popular constitutionalism was the state convention. . . ."[5] He continued:

[3] Letter from Thomas Jefferson to Samuel Kercheval (July 12, 1816), *in* THOMAS JEFFERSON, WRITINGS 1395, 1402 (Library of America ed., 1984). For a complete analysis of Jefferson's attitudes toward constitutional change, see JOHN R. VILE, THE CONSTITUTIONAL AMENDING PROCESS IN AMERICAN THOUGHT 59–78 (1992). *See also* Merrill D. Peterson, *Mr. Jefferson's "Sovereignty of the Living Generation,"* 52 VA. Q. REV. 437 (1976).

[4] Robert J. Martineau, *The Mandatory Referendum on Calling a State Constitutional Convention: Enforcing the People's Right to Reform their Government*, 31 OHIO ST. U. L. REV. 421 (1970); Gerald Benjamin, *The Mandatory Constitutional Convention Question Referendum: The New York Experience in National Context*, *in* 1 STATE CONSTITUTIONS FOR THE TWENTY-FIRST CENTURY: THE POLITICS OF STATE CONSTITUTIONAL REFORM 145 (G. Alan Tarr & Robert F. Williams eds., 2006); John Dinan, *The Political Dynamics of Mandatory State Constitutional Convention Referendums: Lessons from 2005 Regarding Obstacles and Pathways to Their Passage*, 71 MONT. L. REV. 395 (2010).

[5] DANIEL J. HULSEBOSCH, CONSTITUTING EMPIRE: NEW YORK AND THE TRANSFORMATION OF CONSTITUTIONALISM IN THE ATLANTIC WORLD, 1664–1830, 259 (2005).

> After the Revolution, each state was nearly omnipotent within its borders. This authority manifested itself in many ways. In New York, the state was the primary lawmaker, the source of most patronage, and the largest property owner. Through legislation, public offices, and land grants, the government interacted with ordinary people every day. This power, however, also made it the target of popular grievances. Petitions and resistance were most often directed at the state government, and this ensured that it, rather than the federal government, was the site of most constitutional change in the first half of the nineteenth century.

Most of these constitutional changes actually *weakened* state government.[6] The vast majority of the expansion of state constitution making through the admission of new states, as well as the revision of the original states' constitutions, took place after the adoption of the federal Constitution. The ratification of the U.S. Constitution in 1787–1789 imposed some constraints on the sovereignty of states, as the status of the former colonies changed from independent entity to *imperium in imperio*.[7] As early as 1777, however, agitation began for the creation of new states, with their own constitutions, most often within the territory of the existing, newly independent "states."

The Pennsylvania Constitution of 1776 proved influential beyond that state, particularly in Vermont.[8] As noted in Chapter 2, the Pennsylvania Constitution was provided to representatives of Vermont,[9] who were in Philadelphia asking the Continental Congress to recognize their statehood.[10] Dr. Thomas Young, one of the key Pennsylvania radical constitutionalists, published a letter, addressed to Vermonters,[11] suggesting the Pennsylvania Constitution "as a model, which, with very little alteration, will, in my opinion, come as near perfection as anything yet concocted by mankind."[12] He even claimed that Congress was disposed to grant Vermont statehood.[13] After rejecting the recent,

[6] *Id.* at 260.

[7] *See* Chapter 1.

[8] *See* Chapter 2.

[9] *See* WILLIAM C. HILL, THE VERMONT STATE CONSTITUTION: A REFERENCE GUIDE 4 (1992); Paul Gillies, *Not Quite a State of Nature: Derivations of Early Vermont Law*, 23 VT. L. REV. 99, 107 (1998).

[10] *See* WILLIAM BREWSTER, THE FOURTEENTH COMMONWEALTH: VERMONT AND THE STATES THAT FAILED 27–28 (1960).

[11] BREWSTER, *supra* note 10, at 9; MATT BUSHNELL JONES, VERMONT IN THE MAKING, 1750–1777, 379 (1939); Gary J. Aichele, *Making the Vermont Constitution 1777–1824*, 56 VT. HIST. 166, 178–79 (1988).

[12] *See* JONES, *supra* note 11, at 380; Gillies, *supra* note 9, at 107. *But see* Aichele, *supra* note 11, at 175–76 (contending that the 1777 Vermont Constitution did not adhere as closely to Pennsylvania's as is commonly thought).

[13] *See* HILL, *supra* note 9, at 4; Aichele, *supra* note 11, at 179; Gillies, *supra* note 9, at 107.

more conservative New York Constitution of 1777,[14] Vermonters embraced a constitution very similar to Pennsylvania's.[15] Thus began the long and continuing, process of existing state constitutions providing models and ideas for other states' constitutions.

Vermont's origins as a future state arose from the "authority of squatter sovereignty."[16] In rebelling against the authority of New York and New Hampshire, the state engaged in a "double revolution—a rebellion within a rebellion."[17] Vermonters' attempts at convincing the Continental Congress to grant statehood, based on many of the same self-determination arguments supporting the Revolution against England, failed: Congress was more interested in preserving peace with and between New York and New Hampshire than it was in admitting a new state over their objections and potentially shifting the balance of power in New England.[18] As one historian put it, "When Vermont became independent, it became independent of all the world, and remained so until 1791 when it finally admitted to the union."[19] Therefore, he concluded, "Vermont was the only true American republic, for it alone had truly created itself."[20]

The Pennsylvania Constitution apparently was influential in the drafting of the constitution of the "state" of "Frankland,"[21] in what is now part of Eastern Tennessee and which was, of course, never admitted into the Union. Such "jurisdictional controversies" within the existing colonies, as illustrated by the Vermont experience, all included constitution drafting as a central element. Professor Peter Onuf observed:

> The early constitutional history of the United States was shaped by jurisdictional struggles within and among the states....
>
> ....

[14] BREWSTER, *supra* note 10, at 29; *see also* JONES, *supra* note 11, at 382 ("The straw that broke the opposition to an independent state and overcame the loyalty to New York . . . was the adoption by New York in April of a conservative state constitution.").

[15] *See* WILLI PAUL ADAMS, THE FIRST AMERICAN CONSTITUTIONS: REPUBLICAN IDEOLOGY AND THE MAKING OF STATE CONSTITUTIONS IN THE REVOLUTIONARY ERA 94 (1980); JACKSON TURNER MAIN, THE SOVEREIGN STATES, 1775–1783, 176 (1973); M.J.C. VILE, CONSTITUTIONALISM AND THE SEPARATION OF POWERS 140 (1967).

[16] BREWSTER, *supra* note 10, at xi.

[17] Baker v. State, 744 A.2d 864, 876 (Vt. 1999). *See generally* ROBERT E. SHALHOPE, BENNINGTON AND THE GREEN MOUNTAIN BOYS: THE EMERGENCE OF LIBERAL DEMOCRACY IN VERMONT, 1760–1850 (1996). Vermont's 1777 Constitution contained grievances against both England and New York, HILL, *supra* note 9, at 6.

[18] *See* ADAMS, *supra* note 15, at 103–25; *see generally* PETER S. ONUF, THE ORIGINS OF THE FEDERAL REPUBLIC: JURISDICTIONAL CONTROVERSIES IN THE UNITED STATES, 1775–1787, 103–25 (1983).

[19] *See* ONUF, *supra* note 18, at 127.

[20] *Id.* at 145.

[21] WALTER F. DODD, THE REVISION AND AMENDMENT OF STATE CONSTITUTIONS 34 n.10 (1910, reprint 1970). On Frankland, see BREWSTER, *supra* note 10, at 181–96.

> Pressure for the creation of new states—reflecting the new political aspirations of frontier populations—challenged state authority both directly and indirectly. Separatists helped reduce the large states to less threatening proportions: sponsored separatism in Kentucky and the western land Cessions were designed to preempt the kind of involuntary dismemberment that New York suffered in Vermont.[22]

At this point, of course, there were no federal limitations on the content of a "state" constitution; the Articles of Confederation were not even adopted until 1781. Although no new states were actually created prior to the adoption of the federal Constitution, there was a good deal of state constitutional discussion and drafting in areas agitating to become new states, as well as congressional consideration of the creation and admission of new states.[23]

The questions surrounding the status of western lands, some claimed by the original colonies, some claimed by land speculators, and some claimed by their residents as potential new states, was one of the major factors that delayed the adoption of the Articles of Confederation until 1781.[24] Article II, as finally adopted, provided that "no other colony shall be admitted into the same [the Union], unless such admission be agreed to by nine states." No new state, however, was admitted under this provision, but Congress made several steps toward establishing a process for admission of new states prior to the adoption of the federal Constitution in 1789.

In the mid-1780s, Congress began to focus on guidelines and procedures for the creation of new states. In 1784, it enacted the Territorial Governance Act, which "created a binding, entrenched system of reciprocal obligations, committing the existing states to future admission of new states whose rights and duties would mirror those of the established members of the Confederacy, even as it obligated the formative new states to adopt five core principles of republican governance and society."[25] Still, no new states were admitted under the 1784 statute.

The Northwest Ordinance of 1787 put another plan in place for the creation of new states.[26] Then, the federal Constitution provided not only a mechanism

[22] ONUF, *supra* note 18, at 3, 39–40.

[23] CHRISTIAN G. FRITZ, AMERICAN SOVEREIGNS: THE PEOPLE AND AMERICA'S CONSTITUTIONAL TRADITION BEFORE THE CIVIL WAR 47–79 (2008).

[24] MERRILL JENSEN, THE ARTICLES OF CONFEDERATION: AN INTERPRETATION OF THE SOCIAL-CONSTITUTIONAL HISTORY OF THE AMERICAN REVOLUTION, 1774–1781, 150–60, 198–224 (1970).

[25] William G. Merkel, *Jefferson's Failed Anti-Slavery Proviso of 1784 and the Nascence of Free Soil Constitutionalism*, 38 SETON HALL L. REV. 555, 561 (2008).

[26] PETER S. ONUF, STATEHOOD AND UNION: A HISTORY OF THE NORTHWEST ORDINANCE (1787); Denis Duffey, Note, *The Northwest Ordinance as a Constitutional Document*, 95 COLUM. L. REV. 929 (1995); Douglas Laycock, *Equal Citizens of Equal and Territorial States: The Constitutional Foundations of Choice of Law*, 92 COLUM. L. REV. 249, 288–89 (1992).

for the creation of new states in Article IV, Section 3, Clause 1, but in Clause 2 it empowered Congress "to dispose of and make all needful Rules and Regulations respecting the Territory or other Property belonging to the United States." Thus, the new Constitution gave Congress exclusive control over both the administration of federal territories and the admission of new states.[27]

Pursuant to this grant of congressional authority over the admission of new states, acceptance of a new state's constitution by Congress became a central feature of the statehood process. Governing the nonstate territories, and controlling their progression toward statehood, was part of the new country's "colonial" power:

> This last point—that independence freed the United States to govern its own colonial territories and subjugated populations—speaks to the country's distinct identity as a settler nation. Sometimes called "second world" countries, settler nations such as the United States, Canada, Australia, New Zealand, Ulster, South Africa, and Israel negotiate double identities of belonging to both European first world traditions and non-western "third world" regions. These settler societies possess an ambivalent double history as both colonized and colonizers. And, on gaining freedom from their imperial rulers, settler states acquire a new kind of political "doubleness" as postcolonial nations that have now assumed sovereign colonial rule over appropriated domestic territories. Political independence, then, liberated settler nations to claim their domestic colonies for themselves alone.[28]

One recent analyst of Wisconsin's statehood constitution-making process stated:

> Western state formation, even in its concrete form of constitutional conventions and founding texts, required a touch of fiction.... For the writing of a constitution necessitated that Wisconsin citizens imagine their state in its future life. In other words, they had to engage in a kind of (political) science fiction.[29]

[27] *See generally* GARY LAWSON & GUY SEIDMAN, THE CONSTITUTION OF EMPIRE: TERRITORIAL EXPANSION AND AMERICAN LEGAL HISTORY (2004); ONUF, *supra* note 18; JACK E. EBLEN, THE FIRST AND SECOND UNITED STATES EMPIRES: GOVERNORS AND TERRITORIAL GOVERNMENT, 1784–1912 (1968).

[28] BETHEL SALER, THE SETTLERS' EMPIRE: COLONIALISM AND STATE FORMATION IN AMERICA'S OLD NORTHWEST 2 (2015).

[29] *Id.* at 249 (footnotes omitted); *see also id.* at 2 (describing the United States as a "settler nation." "These settler societies possess an ambivalent double history as both colonized and colonizers.").

## II. FEDERAL INFLUENCE ON STATE CONSTITUTION MAKING

Under these federal constitutional arrangements, the constitutions of new states were subject, quite literally, to the whims of Congress as part of its decision-making concerning the admission of new states. After the formation of the Union, there was often congressional, and even presidential,[30] influence over state constitutions during the admission process. Such federal influence, of course, could not have been exerted over the constitutions of the original states.[31] Further, from the state perspective, the constitutions of newly created (from the territory of existing states) or newly admitted (from federally controlled territory) states might now reflect either reactions against the governmental control of the state from which it was created, or the governmental control of the federal territorial administration exercised by the U.S. government.[32] The constitutions of the original states, in contrast, reflected reactions against the control exercised by Britain.

State constitution making was the "central event of political incorporation" into the Union for the admission of new states and the Westward Movement.[33] The doctrine of Manifest Destiny envisioned state constitution making. In fact, Professor Edward S. Corwin argued that America's federal system, including state sovereignty reflected in, among other things, the states' constitutions, actually contributed to the Westward Movement through its promise of self-government.[34] Tracing the Westward Movement of constitutional concepts in the original state constitutions as they were copied and modified by newly admitted states can be an important component of interpreting present-day

[30] John D. Leshy, *The Making of the Arizona Constitution*, 20 ARIZ. ST. L.J. 1, 7–27 (1988). Some new states were admitted through enabling acts passed ahead of time by Congress, and some were admitted without such enabling acts. DENNIS C. COLSON, IDAHO'S CONSTITUTION: THE TIE THAT BINDS 5 (1991). "Congressional practice early conditioned the entrance of a new state on the adoption of a constitution satisfactory to Congress." JAMES WILLARD HURST, THE GROWTH OF AMERICAN LAW: THE LAW MAKERS 201 (1950).

[31] The U.S. Supreme Court has acknowledged, in passing, this distinction between the original and the other states. *See* Reynolds v. Sims, 377 U.S. 533, 574 (1964); Alden v. Maine, 527 U.S. 706, 712–13 (1999). We are indebted to Professor Williams's colleague, Perry Dane, for pointing this out.

[32] Ohio, for example, in reaction to a territorial governor who was perceived to be too autocratic, drafted its first state constitution in 1802 specifically to minimize the authority of the governor by dispersing executive power over a range of independent executive branch officers.

William P. Marshall, *Break Up the Presidency? Governors, State Attorneys General, and Lessons from the Divided Executive*, 115 YALE L.J. 2446, 2451 (2006).

[33] DAVID ALAN JOHNSON, FOUNDING THE FAR WEST: CALIFORNIA, OREGON, AND NEVADA, 1840–1890, 3 (1992).

[34] Edwin S. Corwin, *The Passing of Dual Federalism*, 36 VA. L. REV. 1, 22 (1950) ("For one of the greatest lures to the westward movement of population was the possibility which federalism held out to the advancing settlers of establishing their own undictated political institutions, and endowing them with the generous powers of government for local use.").

constitutions.[35] There is evidence, in fact, that constitutional ideas were being developed and implemented by the settlers as they made their way West.[36] Yet if western constitutions were influenced by earlier Eastern models, the relationship was reciprocal. The Eastern states, in the words of historian Frederick Jackson Turner, felt the "stir in the air raised by the Western winds of Jacksonian democracy."[37] Thus, the winds of state constitutional change blew not only to the West but back to the East.

As detailed in Chapter 4, congressional authority (albeit implicit) over the content of the constitutions of newly created or admitted states influenced the content of such state constitutions in ways that are still felt today. Either through prospective conditions imposed by Congress in "enabling acts" or conditions applied prior to admission, Congress (as well as the president), has exercised its influence over the content of state constitutions in ways that were impossible in the context of the original thirteen states.

The influence of Senator Albert J. Beveridge of Indiana over Arizona's admission is illustrative:

> Mindful of Arizona's maverick tendencies and its Democratic domination, he took pains to ensure that its constitution (as well as New Mexico's) would not escape careful review in Washington. His Committee on Territories inserted in the bill providing for New Mexico and Arizona's admission as separate states, a provision requiring them to submit their constitutions to the federal government for approval prior to each state's first general election. Such a condition was unusual.
>
> Moreover, Senator Beveridge was not eager to leave approval solely up to the divided Congress, where the House was dominated by the Democrats and substantial statehood sympathy existed in his own chamber. His committee therefore required the new constitution to be submitted for the approval of both the President and Congress, in effect giving the President a veto over admission.[38]

In fact, President Howard Taft did veto the admission of Arizona, based on his objection to the judicial recall provision in its constitution.[39] Arizona removed

[35] William Swindler, *State Constitutional Law: Some Representative Decisions*, 9 WM. & MARY L. REV. 166, 173 (1967) ("Historically, new states in the westward movement of the nation borrowed in whole or in part from the constitutions of older states in preparing their first constitutions."). *See, e.g.*, Sterling v. Cupp, 625 P.2d 123 (Or. 1981), State v. Kessler, 614 P.2d 94, 95–99 (Or. 1980); Los Angeles Alliance for Survival v. City of Los Angeles, 993 P.2d 334, 341–42 (Cal. 2000); State v. Hirsch, 114 P.3d 1104, 1118 (Or. 2005).

[36] *See* John Phillip Reid, *Governance of the Elephant: Constitutional Theory on the Overland Trails*, 5 HASTINGS CONST. L.Q. 421 (1978).

[37] FREDERICK JACKSON TURNER, THE FRONTIER IN AMERICAN HISTORY 192 (1920). *See also id.* at 252.

[38] Leshy, *supra* note 30, at 18.

[39] Veto Message of August 11, 1911, 47 CONG. REC. 3964.

the provision, gained admission as a state on "equal footing," and promptly reinserted the clause into its constitution.[40] This feature of American state constitutionalism has, until recently, received very little study.[41] The equal footing doctrine, a seemingly all-or-nothing approach to the admission of new states, is not as simple as it seems, as we will discover in the next chapter.

An exhaustive analysis by Professor Eric Biber of the conditions imposed on states, the "Price of Admission," concluded:

> A review of the types of conditions that have been imposed on admitted states, and the historical context for those conditions, reveals a significant pattern: Congress has imposed conditions on the admission of states where it has concerns about whether the citizenry of the new state can be assimilated as a loyal, democratic unit of government within the United States, sometimes because that citizenry has been perceived as fundamentally different from mainstream American politics and society. These concerns have been expressed in a variety of ways, and thus in a variety of conditions, depending on the historical context. Basic civil liberties, language, religion, race relations, and the structure of the family and marriage have all been elements that Congress has used as touchstones in attempting to reassure itself that the new state will be a loyal member of a homogeneous American federal democratic state. For example, admitted states that had conditions imposed upon them for their admission (or in some cases, readmission) to the Union include Louisiana (predominantly French at the time of its admission in the early 1800s), the Southern states during Reconstruction, Utah (populated by Mormons that were perceived as disloyal and different from the rest of the Union), and New Mexico (with a substantial Mexican population). These conditions have also often been part of a broader process of assimilation and "Americanization" which the admitted state went through—voluntarily or not—in order to become a member of the Union.[42]

## III. STATEHOOD AND STATE CONSTITUTIONS

About half of the newly admitted states followed the requirements of a congressional enabling act. The legal effect of such acts is discussed in Chapter 4. Other states, by contrast, organized their campaigns for statehood without enabling acts and presented their cases to Congress. For example, Hawaii proceeded

[40] John D. Leshy, The Arizona State Constitution: A Reference Guide 17–18 (1993).
[41] *See* Chapter 4.
[42] Eric Biber, *The Price of Admission: Causes, Effects, and Patterns of Conditions Imposed on States Entering the Union*, 46 Am. J. Legal Hist. 119, 120 (2004).

without an enabling act, holding a constitutional convention in 1950 at which it adopted its "Hope Chest" constitution (in the hope it would convince Congress of its adoption of American governmental practices), and was not admitted until 1959.[43] This strategy, often called the "Tennessee Plan," based on Tennessee's successful approach in the 1790s, was also followed a century and a half later in Alaska.[44]

Many states held multiple constitutional conventions before finally attaining statehood. This was true in states like Colorado,[45] South Dakota,[46] and Washington,[47] as well as others. In such states, the "original" statehood constitution was often deeply influenced by the earlier draft state constitutions. This influence may well continue to the present day.

Given that the original state constitutions provided very substantial models for the new federal Constitution, one might ask whether the new federal Constitution then provided a model for later state constitutions. In contrast to the founding decade, when it was the federal Constitution that was influenced by the earlier state constitutions, in this later period a partial reversal took place.[48] In 1790, Pennsylvania replaced its radical 1776 constitution with one modeled directly on the new federal Constitution.[49] Several other original states, such as Georgia (1789) and South Carolina (1790), also revised their revolutionary state constitutions to reflect many of the principles of the federal Constitution.

Political scientist James Dealey made an interesting observation about the reciprocal modeling of provisions from the first state constitutions to the federal Constitution, and then back again:

> On the other hand, it might be said in behalf of the theory of the imitation of the national constitution by the states, that in so far as certain features found in the constitutions of the states under the confederation were selected for insertion in the national constitution, these, so to speak, became *standardized*, thus forming natural patterns for later imitation.[50]

[43] ANNE FEDER LEE, THE HAWAII STATE CONSTITUTION: A REFERENCE GUIDE 7–10 (1993).

[44] GERALD A. MCBEATH, THE ALASKA STATE CONSTITUTION: A REFERENCE GUIDE 6–7 (1997).

[45] DALE A. OESTERLE & RICHARD B. COLLINS, THE COLORADO STATE CONSTITUTION: A REFERENCE GUIDE 1–6 (2002).

[46] John Lauck, *"The Organic Law of the Great Commonwealth": The Framing of the South Dakota Constitution*, 53 S.D. L. REV. 203 (2008).

[47] State v. Norman, 40 P.3d 1161, 1169 (Wash. 2002).

[48] Friedman, *supra* note 2, at 37.

[49] OWEN S. IRELAND, RELIGION, ETHNICITY, AND POLITICS: RATIFYING THE CONSTITUTION IN PENNSYLVANIA 217–77 (1995); Joseph Foster, *The Politics of Ideology: The Pennsylvania Constitutional Convention of 1789–1790*, 59 PA. HIST. 122 (Apr. 1992); DOUGLAS M. ARNOLD, THE REPUBLICAN REVOLUTION: IDEOLOGY AND POLITICS IN PENNSYLVANIA, 1776–1790, 288–327 (1989).

[50] JAMES Q. DEALEY, GROWTH OF AMERICAN STATE CONSTITUTIONS 10 (1915) (emphasis in original).

The admission of Kentucky in 1792 indicated that national issues could be fought out in state constitutional conventions. "[I]t is perhaps significant that Kentucky," observed historian Don Fehrenbacher, "which led the way in erecting a constitutional barrier against legislative emancipation, did so after a fierce struggle between proslavery and antislavery forces in the constitutional convention of 1792."[51]

## IV. EVOLVING STATE CONSTITUTIONAL TRADITIONS

Professor G. Alan Tarr identified three general, recurring concerns or issues as the state constitutions evolved over the centuries: (1) distributing and redistributing political power among groups and regions of the state, through the franchise and reapportionment; (2) defining (and limiting) the scope of state governmental authority through adjusting the balance of the branches and the advent of substantive and procedural limits on the legislature; and (3) adjusting the relationship of the state to private economic activity through both direct government involvement and indirect promotion and regulation.[52] These issues were considered in virtually all of the state constitutional conventions in both the original and the new states.

Political scientist John Dinan traced, in a number of areas, the evolution of state constitutional traditions that are widely divergent from the federal constitutional tradition.[53] He located and analyzed the debates of 114 state constitutional conventions between 1776 and 2005.[54] Dinan evaluated the states' consideration of (and compared with federal doctrine) the contending arguments, over time and across states, concerning mechanisms of amendment and revision, the basis of representation, separation of powers, bicameralism, rights, and state involvement in citizens' character and virtue. In each of these areas, partially because of the difficulty in amending the federal Constitution, the state constitutional tradition evolved in quite different directions from the federal constitutional tradition:

> To summarize my principal conclusions, therefore, I show that a number of federal governing principles and institutions have been revised or rejected in

[51] Don E. Fehrenbacher, Constitutions and Constitutionalism in the Slaveholding South 28 (1989); Joan Wells Coward, Kentucky in the New Republic: The Process of Constitution Making 36–45 (1979).

[52] G. Alan Tarr, Understanding State Constitutions 4, 65, 101 (1998). *See also* James A. Henretta, *The Rise and Decline of "Democratic Republicanism": Political Rights in New York and the Several States*, 53 Alb. L. Rev. 357 (1989).

[53] John J. Dinan, The American State Constitutional Tradition (2006).

[54] *Id.* at 28.

> the course of state conventions; I demonstrate that state constitution makers' departures from the federal model are primarily attributable to the flexibility of state amendment processes and the resulting opportunities to benefit from institutional knowledge and experience throughout American history; and I argue that the state convention debates are in many ways a better expression of the considered judgment of the American constitutional tradition than can be found in the eighteenth-century federal sources.[55]

This evolution reveals evidence of a number of important themes that continue to have a major influence today in the area of state constitutionalism. The constitutional laboratories of the states continued to work out the separation of powers and checks and balances problems, as well as others that were inadequately treated in the first state constitutions.[56] Issues such as legislative reapportionment, expansion of political participation through wider eligibility for voting and office holding, broadening the range of elected offices, and many other similar issues were considered in almost every state constitutional convention in the late 1700s and early 1800s.[57] Some of the old revolutionary state constitution drafters continued their involvement, but also a new generation of state constitutional practitioners and theorists participated. For example, in the Massachusetts Constitutional Convention of 1820–1821, Joseph Story and Daniel Webster were major figures.[58] The aging Chancellor James Kent figured prominently in New York's 1821 Constitutional Convention, as did the young Martin Van Buren.[59] Thaddeus Stevens served as a delegate to the 1837 Pennsylvania Constitutional Convention.[60] This has continued up through the present.[61]

The Virginia Constitutional Convention of 1829, deemed by one commentator as "the most famous of all state constitutional conventions," included the "fiercest battle over suffrage and representation, conducted by a group of delegates including two former Presidents, one future President, and the incumbent Chief

55 *Id.* at 5. For an assessment of influences on the state constitutions of former colonies of *civil law* countries, see Daniel Berkowitz & Karen Clay, *American Civil Law Origins: Implications for State Constitutions*, 7 AM. L. & ECON. REV. 61 (2005).

56 JAMES M. BURNS, THE VINEYARD OF LIBERTY 28, 134, 261 (1982).

57 James A. Henretta, *Foreword: Rethinking the State Constitutional Tradition*, 22 RUTGERS L.J. 819 (1991).

58 MERRILL PETERSON, DEMOCRACY, LIBERTY, AND PROPERTY: THE STATE CONSTITUTIONAL CONVENTIONS OF THE 1820'S, 6, 77–108 (1966).

59 MARVIN MEYERS, THE JACKSONIAN PERSUASION: POLITICS AND BELIEF 181–89 (1957). *See generally* PETER J. GALIE, ORDERED LIBERTY: A CONSTITUTIONAL HISTORY OF NEW YORK 71–94 (1996); HULSEBOSCH, *supra* note 5, at 259–73.

60 ROSALIND L. BRANNING, PENNSYLVANIA CONSTITUTIONAL DEVELOPMENT 23 (1960).

61 DINAN, *supra* note 53, at 13–14.

Justice of the United States."[62] Professor Merrill Peterson also had high praise for the 1829 Virginia Convention:

> The Virginia Convention of 1829–1830 was the last of the great constituent assemblies in American history. As an arena of ideological encounter it was unexcelled. It was a seemingly inexhaustible exercise in political erudition—the last gasp of Jeffersonian America's passion for political disputation. It was a dazzling forensic display of more than three months' duration.[63]

Many of the compromises struck in the revolutionary state constitutions were revisited. Attention was also directed to new issues at the state level that were developing in the growing new country. According to Professor Tarr:

> Different issues dominated the constitutional agendas of state and nation. Issues salient in many states included the extension of the franchise, the curtailment of legislative power, state governmental participation in promoting economic development and allocating natural resources, and the relations between state and local governments. None of these issues figured prominently in federal constitutional politics.[64]

Key local issues such as New York's "Rent Wars" beginning in the 1830s led poor farmers to focus on the 1846 constitutional convention for a solution to their inability to obtain fee simple title to their lands. Professor William Wiecek stated:

> The farmers of the region resented the quitrents that they were obligated to pay to the descendants of the Dutch patrons who had engrossed so much land in the Hudson and Mohawk valleys. The farmers demanded fee simple ownership of their holdings. Their inability to secure changes in the patterns of ownership of agricultural land led them to take matters into their own hands and revive the eighteenth century tradition of "the people out of doors," as it was then called, whereby controlled mobs took purposive action to secure political goals with a minimum of violence.
>
> The farmers' grievances expressed in the Rent Wars were redressed in the nineteenth century's most innovative and influential constitutive document, the New York Constitution of 1846. Itemizing some changes wrought by this instrument will demonstrate how significant constitutional change at the state level was for the protection of individual liberty before the Civil War. Among

[62] FEHRENBACHER, *supra* note 51, at 13.
[63] PETERSON, *supra* note 58, at 271.
[64] TARR, *supra* note 52, at 94–95.

> other things, the 1846 Constitution abolished legislative divorce; prohibited lotteries; did away with feudal tenures (the focus of the Rent Wars grievances), replacing them with fee simple tenure of allodial land and prohibiting long-term agricultural leases. . . .[65]

State constitutional development was also influenced by the major national movements such as Jeffersonian democracy, Jacksonian democracy, the Depression of 1837–1842, the Civil War and Reconstruction, the Depression of the 1870s, and the Progressive Movement.[66] The state constitutions of these periods evidence the beginnings of the "waves" of influence and change in state constitutions across the country. These national influences operated together with the internal, or unique state influences, on the state constitutions of this period. In the decade of 1844–1853, alone, constitutional conventions met in more than half of the states.[67]

The crucial issues of slavery and African-Americans, of course, were important intrastate, state constitutional policy matters in the antebellum period.[68] For example, the Illinois Constitutional Convention of 1847 proposed a "Negro exclusion" provision and the voters adopted it:

> When the subject of the state's black population was first raised during the 1847 convention, the delegates unanimously supported a provision, drawn from the 1818 statehood constitution, which prohibited slavery and involuntary servitude. But ultimately the delegates included a constitutional provision that banned the immigration of free blacks into Illinois and prohibited masters from bringing their slaves into the state for purposes of manumission. This joint provision was presented to voters as a separate proposition in March 1848, when they cast ballots on the ratification of the constitution as a whole. The Negro exclusion provision was adopted by a 70–30 percent margin.[69]

65 William M. Wiecek, *State Protection of Personal Liberty: Remembering the Future*, *in* TOWARD A USABLE PAST: LIBERTY UNDER STATE CONSTITUTIONS 371, 379–80 (Paul Finkelman & Stephen E. Gottlieb eds., 1991). *See generally* CHARLES W. MCCURDY, THE ANTI-RENT ERA IN NEW YORK LAW AND POLITICS, 1839–1865 (2001); GALIE, *supra* note 59, at 98–107.

66 DINAN, *supra* note 53, at 9–10; John J. Wallis, *Constitutions, Corporations, and Corruption: American States and Constitutional Change*, 65 J. ECON. HIST. 211 (2005).

67 TARR, *supra* note 52, at 94 ("an era of permanent constitutional revision").

68 *See* EARL M. MALTZ, SLAVERY AND THE SUPREME COURT, 1825–1861, 71–75 (2009).

69 Jerome B. Meites, *The 1847 Illinois Constitutional Convention and People of Color*, 108 J. ILL. ST. HIST. SOC. 266, 267 (Fall/Winter 2015). Historian Dr. Silvana R. Siddali has analyzed the Black exclusion debates as well as those concerning banking, judicial selection, land rights, and married women's rights in the antebellum state constitutional conventions of the "old Northwest." FRONTIER DEMOCRACY: CONSTITUTIONAL CONVENTIONS IN THE OLD NORTHWEST (2016). She concludes:

> Many of the bitterly fought-over provisions were overturned, some within twenty years. The constitutional prohibitions that prevented black families from migrating into Illinois and Indiana, and that deprived black men of the franchise everywhere in the region, were all gone (at least from the state conventions) by the early 1870s.

Dr. Paul E. Herron had the following to say about the antebellum southern state constitutions:

> While the South might have appeared to follow the nation in state constitutional development, slavery actually had a profound impact on the fundamental law. Southern elites only agreed to democratize suffrage, office holding, the amendment process, and elective offices in exchange for the explicit textual protection of slavery in state constitutions.[70]

The question of free coinage of silver was both an important national issue from the 1890s through the first decade of the twentieth century and a key local issue in statehood and state constitution making in Arizona.[71] Water rights were, not surprisingly, considered to be of constitutional magnitude in some of the arid Rocky Mountain states.[72] A number of states admitted to the Union or revising their constitutions during the Jacksonian and Progressive eras included substantial limitations on corporate and banking power.[73] The influence of Jacksonian democracy and the rise of the professional bar led to the spread of the elected judiciary, a central feature of many revised state constitutions.[74]

*Id.* at 382. Dr. Paul E. Herron has analyzed the "American Paradox," where antebellum state constitutions expanded democratic rights such as voting for white men while protecting slavery and limiting democratic participation by Black people in *Slavery and Freedom in American State Constitutional Development*, 27 J. POL'Y HIST. 301, 301–02 (2015) (footnote omitted):

> [D]uring the first half of the nineteenth century, greater access to the vote for white men came with limitations and outright restrictions on access to the vote for black men. This unfortunate phenomenon took place in new and old states, North and South. There was, however, another similarly disturbing development in state constitutions. In slave states, the expansion of rights for white men, including universal male suffrage, was dependent on the continued dominance of black men, so democratization came at a cost: the constitutional protection of slavery. The cost was borne exclusively by African Americans. Few southern whites were abolitionists, so the exchange of additional slaveholding security for new political power seemed to be a bargain without a downside.

[70] PAUL E. HERRON, FRAMING THE SOLID SOUTH: THE STATE CONSTITUTIONAL CONVENTIONS OF SECESSION, RECONSTRUCTION, AND REDEMPTION, 1860–1902, 32 (2017); *see also id.* at 37–71 (antebellum Southern state constitutions); *see also* ROBIN L. EINHORN, AMERICAN TAXATION, AMERICAN SLAVERY 200–50 (2006) (evidence that Southern states constitutionalized wider suffrage and representation in return for tax protection of slavery).

[71] Leshy, *supra* note 30, at 8–9.

[72] GORDON MORRIS BAKKEN, ROCKY MOUNTAIN CONSTITUTION MAKING, 1850–1912, 65–73 (1987).

[73] *Id.* at 75–84; JOHNSON, *supra* note 33, at 102–03; MELVIN MYERS, THE JACKSONIAN PERSUASION: POLITICS AND BELIEF 199–204 (1957); Deborah Scott Engelby, Note, *The Corporation Commission: Preserving Its Independence*, 20 ARIZ. ST. L.J. 241, 242–44 (1988); Leshy, *supra* note 30, at 88–91; Robert L. Stone, *Article Nine of the Constitution of the State of Oklahoma of 1907 and Comparative Constitutional Law*, 17 OKLA. CITY U. L. Rev. 89 (1992); Gerawan Farming, Inc. v. Kawamura, 90 P.3d 1179, 1187–88 (Cal. 2004).

[74] Kermit L. Hall, *Progressive Reform and the Decline of Democratic Accountability: The Popular Election of State Supreme Court Judges, 1850–1920*, 1984 AM. BAR F. RES. J. 345 (1984).

## V. STATE CONSTITUTIONAL MODELS

As the nation expanded, the pattern of using other state constitutions as models continued,[75] even through the most recent American state constitutions.[76] This practice has obvious implications for interpreting state constitutional provisions imported from the constitutions of other states.[77] The item veto, now so prevalent in state (but not the federal) constitutions and the envy of every sitting president, traces its origins to the Constitution of the Confederate States of America![78] Further, evidence indicated that the initiative and referendum provisions of the Oregon Constitution were based on an idea of direct democracy reflected in the constitutions of the Cantons of Switzerland.[79] A commentator on the 1849 California Constitution noted the initial, albeit unrealistic view of the delegates: "The weight of opinion had it that other, recently composed state constitutions were suited perfectly to California, requiring only minor emendation."[80] It turned out, however, that the task was much greater for the delegates than simply copying existing state constitutional texts.

As Professor Christian Fritz has noted, the reference to, and adoption of, other state constitutional provisions was a calculated, educated process:[81]

> The fact that the delegates carefully canvassed, studied, and ultimately chose provisions from many preexisting state constitutions supports the idea that they recognized they were engaged in the important process of constitution building. The comparative analysis of state constitutions within the convention, which occurred on a broader scale than many have realized, is a measure of their seriousness of purpose.[82]

[75] Friedman, *supra* note 2, at 37; JOHNSON, *supra* note 33, at 102, 108, 121, 140–43, 178.

[76] *See* P. Allan Dionisopoulos, *Indiana, 1851, Alaska, 1956: A Century of Difference in State Constitutions*, 34 INDIANA L.J. 34, 34 (1958) ("Embodied in the Alaska Constitution are 180 years of accumulated experience in constitution-making. . . .").

[77] *See* G. Alan Tarr, *Understanding State Constitutions*, 65 TEMP. L. REV. 1169, 1190–91 (1992). *See* Chapter 12.

[78] Richard Briffault, *The Item Veto in State Courts*, 66 TEMP. L. REV. 1171, 1176 n.19 (1993). On the Constitution of the Confederate States, see James A. Gardner, *Southern Character, Confederate Nationalism, and the Interpretation of State Constitutions: A Case Study in Constitutional Argument*, 76 TEX. L. REV. 1219, 1260–67 (1998).

[79] David Schuman, *The Origin of State Constitutional Direct Democracy: William Simon U'Ren and the "Oregon System,"* 67 TEMP. L. REV. 947, 950 (1994).

[80] JOHNSON, *supra* note 33, at 102.

[81] Christian G. FRITZ, *More Than "Shreds and Patches": California's First Bill of Rights*, 17 HAST. CONST. L.Q. 13 (1990).

[82] *Id.* at 18. *But see* David O. Porter, *The Ripper Clause in State Constitutional Law: An Early Urban Experiment—Part I*, 1969 UTAH L. REV. 287, 311 (1969) (several states adopted a clause aimed at protecting municipal powers when they had no cities that had experienced such problems).

Thus, state conventions built on the state constitutional experience of other states. Several years before Charles A. Beard gained his place in history with his controversial economic analysis of the federal Constitution,[83] he wrote an article analyzing the 1908 Oklahoma Constitution. He concluded that, despite widespread criticism, the Oklahoma Constitution was not a "radical departure from American principles and practice." He stated:

> The American people are not given to sailing the ship of state by the stars or to deducing rules of law from abstract notions; and every important clause of the Oklahoma Constitution has been tried out in the experience of one or more of the older commonwealths.[84]

This process of modeling, or copying, state constitutional provisions from others is one of the most significant and, upon reflection, understandable features of the evolution of state constitutions. Professor Willard Hurst explained, "There was a sort of *stare decisis* about this making of constitutions; it was altogether natural in a country in which men moved about readily, taking with them the learning and institutions of their former homes."[85]

## VI. STATE CONSTITUTION-MAKING PROCESSES

During the period after the adoption of the federal Constitution, the *processes* of state constitution making continued to be refined. Mechanisms for proposal of amendments, state constitutional conventions, and the ratification by voters of the proposed amendments and revisions continued to be worked out in the constitutional laboratories of the states.[86] These processes were not born of idealism and philosophy but rather of pragmatism and experience. As Willard Hurst has observed, "we built our constitution-making procedures out of a generation of practice, rather than out of the logical development of any clear-cut idea of

[83] CHARLES A. BEARD, AN ECONOMIC INTERPRETATION OF THE CONSTITUTION OF THE UNITED STATES (1913).

[84] Charles A. Beard, *The Constitution of Oklahoma*, 24 POL. SCI. Q. 95, 114 (1909).

[85] HURST, *supra* note 30, at 224–25. *See also* JOHNSON, *supra* note 33, at 104–05 (describing "migratory habits" of delegates to California Constitutional Convention of 1849); DEALEY, *supra* note 50, at 9–10.

[86] *See generally* Albert L. Sturm, *The Development of American State Constitutions*, 12 PUBLIUS: THE J. FEDERALISM 57 (Winter 1982); Janice C. May, *State Constitutions and Constitutional Revision: 1988–89 and the 1980s*, 28 THE BOOK OF THE STATES 20 (1991); DODD, *supra* note 21; Michael G. Colantuono, *The Revision of American State Constitutions: Legislative Power, Popular Sovereignty, and Constitutional Change*, 75 CAL. L. REV. 1473 (1987).

constitutionalism."[87] The question of whether state constitutions should be easy or difficult to amend was hotly debated, often against the background of existing provisions that interest groups sought to preserve in state constitutions.[88] This reflects the infancy of the American philosophy of constitutionalism, which was still grappling with clarifying the fundamental nature of constitutions as a higher source of law than ordinary legislation.

Another key element in the growth of state constitutions, both within existing states and in territories moving toward admission to the Union, was the question of whether formal, established processes had to be followed or whether "the people" could follow their own processes in adopting state constitutions. Extralegal constitutional conventions were an important part of state constitutional development, particularly in the first half of the nineteenth century, as Professor James Henretta noted:

> Established politicians, fearing the potential power of propertyless voters and rapidly-growing western regions, resisted demands for constitutional revision or insisted that it be done only by the legislature. The result was political conflict and a new constitutional doctrine of activist popular sovereignty. Between 1818 and 1821, dissident citizens in Connecticut, Massachusetts, and New York successfully insisted on the use of popularly-elected conventions to revise their existing constitutions. However, the struggle for constitutional revision had only begun. In 1816 and again in 1825, dissident Virginians met in extra-legal conventions and demanded a plebescite. They were not successful until 1828, and even then, the sitting legislature apportioned delegates to give eastern areas a majority in the convention that met in 1829–30.
>
> This pattern of events was repeated in many states during the subsequent three decades. In 1833, Pennsylvania Democrats called an extra-legal reform convention in Harrisburg and sat as a shadow constitutional body, recommending a list of amendments as part of its call for a plebescite. The shadow convention met again in 1834, finally forcing a plebescite in 1835 which authorized a Constitutional Convention in 1837. Similar extra-legal reform conventions took place in North Carolina, Georgia, Maryland, and once again in Virginia. In each case, a plebescite and a popular majority for the constitutional convention was finally won.[89]

[87] Hurst, *supra* note 30, at 202. *See also* Lawrence M. Friedman, A History of American Law 100–09 (1973).

[88] Dinan, *supra* note 53, at 29–47.

[89] Henretta, *supra* note 57, at 827–28. *See also* Tarr, *supra* note 52, at 103.

Supporters of these extralegal conventions relied on popular-sovereignty and self-governance arguments that were virtually identical to those supporting independence from England.[90] How could prior generations bind the current generation to follow specified, limiting processes if the authority for government originated in the people themselves? Early state constitutions expressly embraced these doctrines. These controversies, noted by Henretta, led to the famous Dorr Rebellion from 1841 to 1842 in Rhode Island.[91] The arguments of "the people" were met by counterarguments of the "Law and Order" forces, who contended that the established constitutional processes for change were binding and had to be followed.[92]

The question of statehood itself, with its complementary issues of state constitution making, was often caught up in national political concerns. For example, the question of Kansas statehood in 1857, as part of the pre–Civil War free-state, slave-state battle, featured a national debate on the question of whether the proslavery "Lecompton Constitution" should be submitted to the Kansas voters for ratification.[93] President James Buchanan was at the center of the controversy, and there were extensive debates in the Senate (featuring Stephen A. Douglas) and the House.[94]

Several years later, renewed efforts to admit Nevada during the Civil War apparently had their origins in the Nation's Capital.

> The 1864 constitutional convention in Nevada was as different as could be from the meeting that took place seven years earlier in Oregon. In the latter territory, statehood originated in the desire of political men to settle local disputes and insulate themselves from national solutions to the sectional crisis.... In Nevada, to the contrary, statehood came in the midst of the Civil War and an economic crisis in the mines.... This territory's constitutional convention was, for all intents and purposes, a product of plots hatched in Washington, D.C.—plots fully apparent to the assembled delegates.[95]

[90] FRITZ, *supra* note 23, at 240 ("From the start, constitutional conventions meeting without the authorization of legislatures routinely sought legitimacy from the inherent rights of the people.").

[91] *Id.* at 246–76. With respect to the "Dorr Rebellion," *see* GEORGE M. DENNISON, THE DORR WAR: REPUBLICANISM ON TRIAL 1831–1861 (1975); MARVIN GETTLEMAN, THE DORR REBELLION: A STUDY IN AMERICAN RADICALISM, 1833–1849 (1973); John M. Schuchman, *The Political Background of the Political-Question Doctrine: The Judges and the Dorr War*, 16 AM. J. LEGAL HIST. 111 (1972).

[92] FRITZ, *supra* note 23, at 275.

[93] KENNETH M. STAMPP, AMERICA IN 1857: A NATION ON THE BRINK 266–94 (1990).

[94] *Id.* at 295–322.

[95] JOHNSON, *supra* note 33, at 189. For very useful, fifty-state coverage of the processes by which each of the states was formed, its constitution developed, and it was admitted to the Union, see THE UNITING STATES: THE STORY OF STATEHOOD FOR THE FIFTY UNITED STATES (3 vols., Benjamin Shearer ed., 2004).

## VII. RECONSTRUCTION STATE CONSTITUTIONS

The state of West Virginia was created out of part of Virginia, and its constitution was approved in 1863 *during* the Civil War.[96] The Civil War, Reconstruction, and the aftermath left indelible marks on the state constitutions of the southern states. First, the seceding states rewrote their constitutions in an interesting replication of the wartime Revolutionary period state constitutions almost a century earlier, during the Founding Decade. An initial round of state constitution making under Presidential Reconstruction, which had minimal requirements, resulted in new constitutions resolving a number of local issues about political representation and other issues that had nothing to do with Civil War issues.[97]

A central feature of Radical Reconstruction was to require, subject to congressional approval, the southern states to revise their constitutions, according to federally imposed requirements, as a condition of *readmission* to the Union. Pursuant to the Reconstruction Act, the "first task," historian Eric Foner noted, "of the southern states was to hold conventions to draft new state constitutions."[98] This important element of Reconstruction, therefore, can be seen as re*constituting* the southern state polities. For southern states among the original thirteen, this was the first direct federal influence on their constitutions; for the southern states that had been admitted to the Union after the ratification of the federal Constitution, this was their second experience with such influence. The Reconstruction requirements were more rigidly imposed, and the readmission process was an element of military conquest rather than territorial administration, but this was another example of federal influence over both the process and content of state constitutions. For the first time Congress imposed requirements concerning "integral matters of state government. . . ."[99] As Professor Eric Biber concluded, "The conditions were in part the result of partisan political efforts by the Republicans to ensure they would become a majority party nationwide; yet, they also reflected a deep sense of principled ideology."[100]

These southern constitutional conventions included about one-third African-American delegates among the dominant Republicans and "were the first biracial governmental bodies in American history."[101] The opposition press

[96] James M. McPherson, Battle Cry of Freedom: The Civil War Era 297–304 (1988). *See generally* Vasan Kesavan & Michael Stokes Paulsen, *Is West Virginia Unconstitutional?* 90 Cal. L. Rev. 291 (2002).

[97] Eric Foner, Reconstruction: America's Unfinished Revolution 192–95 (1988). *See also* Herron, *supra* note 70.

[98] Eric Foner, Forever Free: The Story of Emancipation and Reconstruction 143 (2005). Tennessee was an exception, being readmitted after amending its constitution to abolish slavery, before the Reconstruction Act was passed. Michael W. McConnell, *Originalism and the Desegregation Decisions*, 81 Va. L. Rev. 947, 962 n.132 (1995).

[99] Biber, *supra* note 42, at 140.

[100] *Id.*

[101] Foner, *supra* note 98, at 143.

ridiculed these conventions as "Bones and Banjo Conventions,"[102] and opposition delegates supported the values of the Confederacy.[103] Most of the African-American delegates were "recently freed slaves, had little education or political experience and took little part in convention debates."[104] One conservative Arkansas newspaper complained that the purpose of the 1868 constitutional convention was

> giving silly negroes and dishonest white men an opportunity of seeing a big town, free of expense directly to themselves, and to sit in arm chairs in the state house, and look as knowingly as owls, board at the Anthony House, go to see old Governor Murphy, at will, and listen to long "loyal talks."[105]

These conventions produced "progressive documents" "in a region where government had previously done little more than secure an owner's control over his slaves."[106] The constitutions proclaimed equal civil rights for all; established free public schools (attendance was compulsory in some states); new prisons; and even in some states, relief for the poor, while abolishing whipping, imprisonment for debt, and reducing the number of capital crimes.[107] There was disagreement, however, about integrated schools.[108] Professor Michael McConnell concluded that "constitutional language and actual practice were far apart" and that when the states were readmitted with "colorblind" constitutions, many of them enacted statutes requiring segregated schools, with little or no reaction in Congress.[109] Conservatives and Democrats continued their bitter opposition to both the constitution-making processes and the resulting content of the state constitutions. One Democratic newspaper promised:

> These constitutions and governments will last just as long as the bayonets which ushered them into being, shall keep them in existence, and not one day longer.[110]

Reconstruction, of course, did come to an end. As the Revolutionary state constitutions had reacted to British rule and the constitutions of newly admitted states reacted to federal territorial administration, the post-Reconstruction,

[102] FONER, *supra* note 97, at 317.
[103] *Id.*
[104] FONER, *supra* note 98, at 143. Foner noted that Louisiana and South Carolina were exceptions.
[105] THOMAS S. STAPLES, RECONSTRUCTION IN ARKANSAS, 1862–1874, 218 (1964).
[106] FONER, *supra* note 98, at 143–44. For a review of the conventions, debates, and constitutions, see FONER, *supra* note 97, at 316–33.
[107] FONER, *supra* note 98, at 143–44.
[108] *Id.* at 144.
[109] McConnell, *supra* note 98, at 962–67.
[110] FONER, *supra* note 97, at 333.

"Redeemer" state constitutions reacted to federal control and federal mandates for state constitutions. Evaluating Virginia's 1902 constitution, Professor Wythe Holt concluded:

> Virginia's new Constitution of 1902 terminated a revolutionary experiment in participatory democracy. Recently-freed blacks and whites from the lower socioeconomic strata of society had been forcibly franchised by federal troops in 1869 pursuant to the carpetbagger Underwood Constitution, in order that the planter class be directly threatened. The planters and other members of the elites opposed enfranchisement of the masses, particularly of the blacks, and they worked throughout the period between 1869 and 1902 to reduce the size and the power of this dangerous group of voters.[111]
>
> * * *
>
> The undemocratic new Constitution, and the sluggish, unexciting Convention that produced it, symbolized and epitomized the counter-revolution that had taken place in the Old Dominion. These events marked the culmination of the reestablishment by Virginia's elites, old and new, of control over a troublesome and assertive group of lower class elements who for three short decades had exercised the power of the franchise to attempt to alter their miserable conditions.[112]

## VIII. STATE CONSTITUTIONAL ISSUES AND EPICS

Throughout this long period, and continuing now, the issues of the day, be they national or local, arose in state constitutional conventions. As commentators on state constitutional conventions have observed:

> Doubtless one could take a cluster of constitutional conventions in any era—the Jacksonian period, the years of reconstruction or postreconstruction, the turn-of-the-century progressive era—and find patterns of issue uniformity in each. In other words, there are broad areas of agreement in any one period as to what "modern," "effective," "democratic" state government consists of, but little such agreement over time. Conventions in one era meet to undo the careful reforms of an earlier generation.[113]

[111] WYTHE HOLT, VIRGINIA'S CONSTITUTIONAL CONVENTION OF 1902, 254 (1990).

[112] *Id.* at 257. *See also* MALCOLM COOK MCMILLAN, CONSTITUTIONAL DEVELOPMENT IN ALABAMA: A STUDY IN POLITICS, THE NEGRO, AND SECTIONALISM (1955).

[113] ELMER E. CORNWELL JR., JAY S. GOODMAN, & WAYNE R. SWANSON, STATE CONSTITUTIONAL CONVENTIONS: THE POLITICS OF THE REVISION PROCESS IN SEVEN STATES 203 (1975).

These constitutional debates, including the popular referenda on ratification of successfully proposed state constitutional changes, took place within the broader context of a state's political scene.[114] This was little different from the political nature of the framing of the first state constitutions during the Revolutionary era.[115] State constitutions became established tools of lawmaking or policymaking, albeit of a special nature, within the legal technology of the states.[116] The special character of this technique of lawmaking is its reflection of "activist popular sovereignty," described by Professor Henretta:

> In his much-quoted treatise, *The American Commonwealth*, first published in 1888, Lord Bryce perceived a "conscious relish for power" among ordinary Americans, "an unmistakable wish in the minds of the people to act directly [by amending their constitutions] rather than through their representatives in legislation." In drawing attention to this culturally pervasive populist sentiment, Bryce identified a vital part of the state constitutional tradition, activist popular sovereignty.[117]

Through the exercise of this form of activist popular sovereignty, generations of Americans have had an actual voice in state constitution making, in approving or disapproving constitutional convention calls, electing delegates, and ratifying or rejecting proposed constitutional changes. The issues range from those of major national importance to what may seem to many of us to be the most trivial, provincial question of state constitutional change. Each of these voices was raised with respect to *contemporary* issues of the day.[118] And, throughout the states, there were diverse voices heard, even if they were not always heeded.

For each provision in a state constitution, no matter how seemingly trivial, there is a story to be told. It may be a political story rather than an apparently lofty, "constitutional" story. As the legal historian, Professor Lawrence M. Friedman, put it:

[114] *Id.* at 33, 192, 204.

[115] As Willard Hurst noted:

> Men framed, fought over, and adopted the first state constitutions . . . in an atmosphere of the utmost political realism. They saw they were dealing with the balance of power between interests, and they were frankly skeptical of the permanency of what they had done. . . . Like their successors, the first makers of constitutions saw their work in terms of contests for power and advantage, or the security of power and advantage already won.

HURST, *supra* note 30, at 203, 204.

[116] Robert F. Williams, *State Constitutional Law Processes*, 24 WM. & MARY L. REV. 169, 175–77 (1983); HURST, *supra* note 30, at 243.

[117] Henretta, *supra* note 57, at 826.

[118] *See, e.g.*, JOHNSON, *supra* note 33, at 138 (California Constitutional Convention of 1849 "in the process they explored, through without resolving, the *central dilemmas of their time as only contemporaries could*.") (emphasis added).

> There is a point to every clause in these inflated constitutions. Each one reflected the wishes of some faction or interest group, which tried to make its policies permanent by freezing them into the charter. Constitutions, like treaties, preserved the terms of compromise between warring groups.[119]

"For every constitution there is an epic. . . ."[120] The *text* of the federal Constitution formally reflects just three epics: 1787, 1791, and 1868. Other federal constitutional epics have been judge-made. The more numerous state constitutional stories, or "narratives,"[121] may not have the national recognition or "constitutional" majesty we are used to with the federal Constitution. But they are important and *constitutional*, just the same.

There are countless interesting "epics" in the broad flow of state constitution making and change. Consider the alleged role of the Harvard Law School Professor, James B. Thayer in drafting the pro-railroad "Williams Constitution" debated in the 1889 North Dakota Constitutional Convention.[122] Or, how Montana, during the interim between its 1884 and 1889 constitutional conventions, resolved the issues of a mining tax and taxation of irrigation corporations and "wrote a long constitution full of details designed to protect the new state from the corruption of the east by attempting to ensure frugality and honesty in government."[123] The 1857 Minnesota Constitutional Convention actually proposed, and the people ratified, *two* not entirely identical Republican and Democratic state constitutions, both of which remained in effect for many years.[124] Utah evolved from the Mormon State of Deseret with its constitution of 1849 (patterned on the Illinois Constitution of 1818), amidst opposition from the federal government, into statehood some fifty years later in 1896.[125]

[119] FRIEDMAN, *supra* note 87, at 104

In 1960, the Supreme Court of Michigan noted: "The words of a Constitution normally carry the gloss of history. They come to us not as the apt alliterations of the moment of draftsmanship but as the verbal symbols of political turmoil."

Stoliker v. Waite, 101 N.W.2d 299, 301 (Mich. 1960).

[120] Robert M. Cover, *Foreword: Nomos and Narrative*, 97 HARV. L. REV. 4, 4 (1983).

[121] *Id. See also* Robert F. Williams, *Introduction: The Stories of State Constitutional Law*, 18 NOVA L. REV. 715 (1994).

[122] Robert Vogel, *Sources of the 1889 North Dakota Constitution*, 65 N.D. L. REV. 331, 332–36 (1989); Herbert L. Meschke & Lawrence D. Spears, *Digging for Roots: The North Dakota Constitution and the Thayer Correspondence*, 65 N.D. L. REV. 343 (1989).

[123] Richard Roeder, *The 1972 Montana Constitution in Historical Context*, 51 MONT. L. REV. 260, 262–63 (1990). For interesting discussions of the 1889 Montana Constitution, see also Harry W. Fritz, *The 1972 Montana Constitution in a Contemporary Context*, 51 MONT. L. REV. 270 (1990). On Wyoming's Constitution, see Michael J. Horan, *The Wyoming Constitution: A Centennial Assessment*, 26 LAND & WATER L. REV. 13 (1991).

[124] Fred L. Morrison, *An Introduction to the Minnesota Constitution*, 20 WM. MITCHELL L. REV. 287, 295–97 (1994); State v. Lessley, 779 N.W.2d 825, 838–40 (Minn. 2010).

[125] John J. Flynn, *Federalism and Viable State Government—The History of Utah's Constitution*, 1966 UTAH L. REV. 311 (1966); KEN VERDOIA & RICHARD FIRMAGE, UTAH: THE STRUGGLE FOR STATEHOOD (1966); Society of Separationists, Inc. v. Whitehead, 870 P.2d. 916 (Utah 1993).

Another interesting story concerns the proposed 1905 constitution of the State of Sequoyah, strongly influenced by Native Americans in eastern Oklahoma and which formed a model for parts of Oklahoma's progressive 1908 constitution.[126] These are just a few examples.

As of 2017, there have been 233 separate state constitutional conventions and thousands of amendments to existing state constitutions in the United States.[127] In 1862, the visiting Englishman Edward Dicey observed:

> At the period of my visit, Illinois was undergoing one of those periodical revolutions which seem so strange to English politicians. The whole state was about to throw off its Constitution as a snake casts its slough. . . .[128]

Strange as this prospect might have seemed to a visiting Englishman, it was not strange to Americans and remains a central feature of state constitutionalism. Many important amendments and revisions were rejected by the voters but still stimulated substantial, ongoing constitutional debate and even later acceptance.[129] For example, voters defeated progressive post–Civil War state constitutional revisions in Michigan (1867), New York (1867), Nebraska (1871), and Ohio (1873); among the rejected ideas were compulsory education, longer terms of office, and taxation of church property.[130] Postwar reform then took a negative direction, limiting what had become active state governments.[131] The Texas Constitution of 1876, for example, reflected a broader theme than just a reaction to Reconstruction:

> Contrary to recent popular historical views, the 1875 convention reflected a nationwide philosophical movement, more than a reaction to Reconstruction.

[126] Robert L. Tsai, America's Forgotten Constitutions: Deviant Visions of Power and Community 152–184 (2014); Danny M. Adkison & Lisa McNair Palmer, The Oklahoma State Constitution: A Reference Guide 4, 8, 241 (2001); Danny Goble, Progressive Oklahoma: The Making of a New Kind of State 187–227 (1980).

[127] John Dinan, State Constitutional Politics: Governing by Amendment in the American States 95 (2018).

[128] Edward Dicey, Spectator of America 230 (Rev. ed. 1971). Dicey's prediction was incorrect, however, because the Illinois voters rejected the proposed 1862 revision, and it was not until 1870 that Illinois got a revised constitution. Dealey, *supra* note 50, at 81.

[129] *See, e.g.*, John P. Wheeler Jr. & Melissa Kinsey, Magnificent Failure: The Maryland Constitutional Convention of 1967–68 (1970); Calvin R. Ledbetter et al., Politics in Arkansas: The Constitutional Experience (1972); Henrik N. Dullea, Charter Revision in the Empire State: The Politics of New York's 1967 Constitutional Convention (1997); Robert B. McKay, *Constitutional Revision in New York State: Disaster in 1967*, 19 Syracuse L. Rev. 207 (1967); Thomas G. Pullen Jr., *Why the Proposed Maryland Constitution Was Not Approved*, 10 Wm. & Mary L. Rev. 378 (1968); Dan Friedman, *Magnificent Failure Revisited: Modern Maryland Constitutional Law from 1967 to 1998*, 58 Md. L. Rev. 528 (1999).

[130] Morton Keller, Affairs of State: Public Life in Late Nineteenth Century America 111–12 (1977).

[131] Kermit L. Hall, The Magic Mirror: Law in American History 102–05 (1989).

The convention was a revolt, of sorts, away from the empowered government exemplified in the federal constitution toward a more restrictive "hands off," even antigovernment, approach.[132]

Professor Morton Keller noted:

> The ultimate thrust of constitutional revision after the Civil War was not to enhance the power of the state, but rather "a grand design to reduce the field of state law and withhold from it every subject which it is not necessary to concede." New and revised constitutions in the 1870s substantially reduced legislative authority. Illinois forbade its legislature to act in twenty items of local or private concern, Pennsylvania in forty, California in thirty-three. The areas enjoined covered a wide range of government functions: social (name changes, divorce, adoption, minors' rights, inheritance); economic (interest rates, tax exemption, special incorporation acts, local indebtedness); and political (county seats, town incorporation, the conduct of elections, the powers of local officials, grand juries, municipal improvements). The judiciary became the determining authority in most of these instances.[133]

Some of these rejected ideas were later adopted, after more experience and discussion.[134] It can fairly be said that textual change has been a prominent a component of state constitutional development—at least as important as evolving judicial interpretation.[135]

In contrast to this postwar negativism reflected in state constitutions in the East and Midwest, state constitution making in the West can be characterized as much more positive. Dr. Amy Bridges examined the western constitutional conventions in the last quarter of the nineteenth century, concluding:

> My reading of western state constitutions and the deliberations at the conventions where they were written, leads me to the conclusion that this [negative] consensus view is incomplete. Although delegates were wary of state

[132] James C. Harrington, *Free Speech, Press, and Assembly Liberties Under the Texas Bill of Rights*, 68 TEX. L. REV. 1435, 1439 (1990). *See also* John Walker Mauer, *State Constitutions in a Time of Crisis: The Case of the Texas Constitution of 1876*, 68 TEX. L. REV. 1615 (1990).

[133] KELLER, *supra* note 130, at 112 (*quoting* Simeon E. Baldwin). *See also* Henretta, *supra* note 55, at 824.

[134] *See, e.g.*, Steven J. Uhlfelder & Robert A. McNeely, *The 1978 Constitution Revision Commission: Florida's Blueprint for Change*, 18 NOVA L. REV. 1489 (1994); G. Theodore Mitau, *Constitutional Change by Amendment: Recommendations of the Minnesota Constitutional Commission in Ten Year's Perspective*, 44 MINN. L. REV. 461 (1959).

[135] ELMER E. CORNWELL ET AL., *supra* note 113, at 8 ("As a method of constitutional change, it is probably true that interpretation has been less important than the more formal processes of amendment and revision.").

> legislatures, and denied them many powers, at the Gilded Age conventions I present here, delegates affirmed and expanded the prerogatives and authority of state government. They created new institutions for managing their economies and wrote property law for settlement and growth. They also greatly expanded bills of rights, creating positive rights, which mandated activity by state government. John Hicks read the constitutions of the Northwest states similarly. He saw that in the Gilded Age ". . . people were confronted . . . by the need of an immediate expansion of state activities to meet new and unprecedented conditions." The result was that "undoubtedly, the sentiment of the country favored more government, not less," and more elected officials, not fewer.[136]

Bridges's conclusion followed analysis of the debates leading to state constitutional provisions mandating active state involvement in water rights, railroad and corporate regulation, and protection of labor.[137]

The one-person, one-vote revolution of the 1960s stimulated a major round of state constitutional revision.

> State legislatures have once again become relatively democratic and representative bodies as a result of the reapportionment revolution begun in *Baker v. Carr*. Not accidentally, that decision spurred a wave of constitutional revision. No fewer than thirteen states revised their basic charters between 1963 and 1976, reviving at least in part, the tradition of activist popular sovereignty.[138]

## IX. CONCLUSION

A more detailed account, chronological and analytical, of the more than two centuries of American state constitutional evolution is beyond the scope of this chapter.[139] This sketch reflects a picture of general, regional, and state-specific

[136] Amy Bridges, *Managing the Periphery in the Gilded Age: Writing Constitutions for the Western States*, 22 STUD. AM. POL. DEVEL. 32, 36 (2008). *See also* AMY BRIDGES, DEMOCRATIC BEGINNINGS: FOUNDING THE WESTERN STATES (2015); PAUL E. HERRON, *Upon the Shore's of an Unknown Sea*, 69 RUTGERS U. L. REV. 1433 (2017).

[137] *Id.* at 43–57.

[138] Henretta, *supra* note 57, at 839.

[139] For an introduction to the rich, but relatively unknown, literature, see Friedman, *supra* note 2; Henretta, *supra* note 57; Sturm, *supra* note 86; FLETCHER M. GREEN, CONSTITUTIONAL DEVELOPMENT IN THE SOUTH ATLANTIC STATES, 1776–1860 (1930); Dealey, *supra* note 50; Morton Keller, *The Politics of State Constitutional Revision, 1820–1930*, *in* KERMIT L. HALL, HAROLD M. HYMAN, & LEON V. SIGAL, THE CONSTITUTIONAL CONVENTION AS AN AMENDING DEVICE 67 (1981); PETERSON, *supra* note 58; Kermit L. Hall, "*Mostly Anchor and Little Sail: The Evolution of American State Constitutions*," *in* Paul FINKELMAN & STEPHEN E. GOTTLIEB, TOWARD A USABLE PAST: LIBERTY UNDER STATE CONSTITUTIONS 388 (1991).

processes and substance of constitution making that is starkly different from the stable, venerated, and rarely amended text of the U.S. Constitution, evolving primarily through practice and judicial interpretation. These processes, in turn, have yielded American state constitutions that may be distinguished in form, content, function, and quality from their federal counterpart. "State constitution-makers," Professor Alan Tarr concluded, "came to view constitutionmaking as a progressive enterprise, requiring the constant readjustment of past practices and institutional arrangements in light of changes in circumstance and political thought."[140] The evolution of these state constitutions is a continuing process, ever unfolding.[141]

[140] TARR, *supra* note 52, at 97.
[141] DONALD S. LUTZ, THE ORIGINS OF AMERICAN CONSTITUTIONALISM 167 (1988) (referring to our "unfinished constitutional traditions").

# 4
# FEDERAL LIMITS ON STATE CONSTITUTIONS

*This Constitution, and the Laws of the United States which shall be made in Pursuance thereof; and all Treaties made, or which shall be made, under the Authority of the United States, shall be the supreme law of the Land; and the Judges in every State shall be bound thereby, any Thing in the Constitution or laws of any State to the Contrary notwithstanding.*

—U.S. Constitution Article VI, Clause 2

American state constitutions are, as we have seen, interlocked with the federal Constitution. State constitutions are not only *integral to* the federal constitutional scheme, they are also *limited by* the federal Constitution and laws. Further, the content of state constitutions has been subject to federal influence in a variety of ways through the processes of admitting new states (from existing states and territories) and readmitting existing states after the Civil War, all with required congressional and presidential approval of their state constitutions. Limits also arise as consequences of U.S. Supreme Court decisions invalidating state constitutional provisions or requiring their modification.

Based on the language of the Supremacy Clause quoted at the beginning of this chapter, the state constitutions are also *subject to* contrary restrictions by, or conflicts with, any form of federal law, not just the federal Constitution. Therefore, even lesser forms of federal law, such as statutes, administrative regulations, and even federal common law, can trump the highest source of state law—the state constitution.

Justice Oliver Wendell Holmes Jr. famously observed:

> I do not think the United States would come to an end if we lost our power to declare an Act of Congress void. I do think the Union would be imperiled if we could not make that declaration as to the laws of the several States.[1]

[1] Oliver Wendell Holmes, Collected Legal Papers 295–96 (1920).

*The Law of American State Constitutions.* Robert F. Williams and Lawrence Friedman, Oxford University Press.
 DOI: 10.1093/oso/9780190068806.003.0005

The first case in which the U.S. Supreme Court declared a state constitutional provision to be in violation of the federal Constitution was *Dodge v. Woolsey*, in 1856, in which the court held Ohio state constitutional and statutory provisions impaired the state's prior contractual obligation.[2]

When the U.S. Supreme Court evaluates the constitutionality of a state constitutional provision, it does not seem to differentiate between state constitutions and statutes.[3] For example, in *Reynolds v. Sims*, the Court stated: "With respect to the operation of the Equal Protection Clause, it makes no difference whether a State's apportionment scheme is embodied in its constitution or in statutory provisions."[4]

## I. FEDERAL CONSTITUTIONAL LIMITS

In June 2017, the U.S. Supreme Court held, in *Trinity Lutheran Church of Columbia, Inc. v. Comer*,[5] that the state of Missouri's refusal to award a grant to a church to resurface its preschool and daycare playground, because of limitations in its state constitution,[6] violated the Free Exercise Clause of the First Amendment.[7] Application of a common state constitutional limit was invalidated under the Supremacy Clause. Speaking for the Court, Chief Justice John Roberts reasoned that "the Department's policy expressly discriminates against otherwise eligible recipients by disqualifying them from a public benefit

[2] 59 U.S. 331 (1856). *See* Harold M. Hyman & William M. Wiecek, Equal Justice Under Law: Constitutional Development, 1835–1875, 68 (1982) ("But *Dodge v. Woolsey* was no ordinary bank-tax case. Here, for the first time in its history, the United States Supreme Court held a provision of a state Constitution—not just an ordinary statute—void because of a conflict with the federal Constitution.").

[3] For Supreme Court jurisdictional purposes a state constitution is treated as a "statute" under 42 U.S.C. § 1252(b). Pruneyard Shopping Ctr. v. Robins, 447 U.S. 74, 79 (1980).

[4] 377 U.S. 533, 584 (1964). *See also* Fisk v. Police Jury of Jefferson, 116 U.S. 131, 135 (1885); Railway Employees Department v. Hanson, 351 U.S. 225, 232 (1956). But, in 1991 the Court stated, in rejecting an Equal Protection challenge to Missouri's state constitutional mandatory retirement provision for judges:

> In this case, we are dealing not merely with government action, but with *a state constitutional provision approved by the people of Missouri as a whole*. This constitutional provision reflects both the considered judgment of the state legislature that proposed it and that of the citizens of Missouri who voted for it. "[W]e will not overturn such a [law] unless the varying treatment of different groups or persons is so unrelated to the achievement of any combination of legitimate purposes that we can only conclude that the [people's] actions were irrational."

Gregory v. Ashcroft, 501 U.S. 452, 471 (1991) (emphasis added). The Court cited two Equal Protection cases that did not concern state constitutional provisions.

[5] 582 U.S. ___ (2017).

[6] Missouri Const. art. I, § 7.

[7] *Trinity Lutheran*, 137 S.Ct. at 2024. Two subsequent cases expanded on this holding: Espinoza v. Montana Dep't of Revenue, 591 U.S. ___ (2020), and Carson v. Makin, 596 U.S. ___ (2022).

solely because of their religious character."[8] The Court also concluded that this would not violate the Establishment Clause.[9]

Justice Sotomayor noted in her dissenting opinion that "thirty-eight States have a counterpart to Missouri's Article I, §7. The provisions, as a general matter, date back to or before the States' original Constitutions."[10] Accordingly, as a consequence of *Trinity Lutheran*, the provisions of thirty-eight states' constitutions barring governmental aid to religious institutions were invalidated (at least in part). In 2018, the Supreme Court of New Jersey notably decided that *Trinity Lutheran* did not invalidate application of the *state constitution*'s Religious Aid Clause[11] in a case involving taxpayer funds to restore and preserve the actual facilities of churches themselves. The court further distinguished *Trinity Lutheran* on the ground that, in that case, the grants were for playground renovation rather than the actual church buildings,[12] concluding that the grants in question violated the New Jersey Constitution. The county and the churches sought review in the U.S. Supreme Court, which denied their petition for certiorari in March 2019.[13] Justice Brett Kavanaugh, however, attached a "Statement" to the denial indicating that he believed the record inadequate to evaluate New Jersey's decision and suggesting that "the decision of the New Jersey Supreme Court is in serious tension with this Court's religious equality precedents." He continued:

> In my view, prohibiting historic preservation grants to religious organizations simply because the organizations are religious would raise serious questions under this Court's precedents and the Constitution's fundamental guarantee of equality."[14]

This progression of cases dealing with inconsistencies between state and federal constitutional commitments illustrates the potential complexity and unpredictability of Supremacy Clause adjudication concerning the validity of state constitutional provisions and their application. *Trinity Lutheran* seems to be an example of a Supreme Court decision establishing, in the words of Professors Marc

[8] *Trinity Lutheran*, *supra* note 7.

[9] *Id.* at 2018, 2019. *See generally* Douglas Laycock, *Churches, Playgrounds, Government Dollars—And Schools*, 131 HARV. L. REV. 133 (2017).

[10] *Id.* at 2037.

[11] N.J. CONST. art. I, ¶ 3 ("[n]o person shall . . . be obligated to pay taxes . . . for building or repairing any church or churches, place or places of worship, or for the maintenance of any minister or ministry."). *See* ROBERT F. WILLIAMS, THE NEW JERSEY STATE CONSTITUTION 62 (2d ed. 2012).

[12] Freedom From Religion Foundation v. Morris County Board of Chosen Freeholders, 181 A.3d 992, 993 (N.J. 2018).

[13] 586 U.S. ___ (2019)

[14] *Id.* (Justices Alito and Gorsuch joined)

Miller and Ronald Wright, "leaky floors"—that is, a lack of clear and predictable guidelines limiting state law, including state constitutions.[15] They explain:

> Lawyers, teachers, and scholars who speak of the "meaning" of particular U.S. Supreme Court decisions have long recognized the pliability of both language and logic that leaves some "play" in almost any case. American law schools routinely teach students to ask about the "narrowest" or "broadest" plausible readings of a decision. To this extent, regardless of politics, we are all legal realists. Deconstructionists today wield the tools that make us doubt the meaning of any text.[16]

The Supreme Court's use of multifactor tests, general language, and standards such as "totality of the circumstances," leave many circumstances in which the federal "floor" is not as clear as a "national minimum standard" might be expected to appear.

In 2020, the Supreme Court decided *Espinosa v. Montana Department of Revenue*, a case similar to *Trinity Lutheran*.[17] That decision cast further doubt on the validity of many state constitutional religion provisions. Alan Tarr critiqued the Supreme Court's "unseemly eagerness in *Espinoza* to intervene and impose a federal solution" that short-circuited debate about state school choice policies; the decision, he concluded, was "not a victory for self-government or a vibrant federalism or, indeed, for proper judicial modesty."[18]

To be sure, the Supreme Court has on occasion noted the significance of a state embedding a policy in its constitution. In 1967, for example, the Court struck down an amendment to the California Constitution that purported to authorize a person to sell or rent property to anybody he chose "in his absolute discretion."[19] The Court concluded that by *constitutionalizing* the right to discriminate, the California constitutional provision amounted to intentional race discrimination in violation of the Equal Protection Clause of the Fourteenth Amendment.[20] Similarly, in 1985, the Court invalidated a provision of the Alabama Constitution barring persons convicted of a "crime involving moral turpitude" from voting.[21] Although this provision was neutral on its face, a review of the records of the 1901 Alabama Constitutional Convention revealed evidence of intent to discriminate

[15] Marc L. Miller & Ronald F. Wright, *Leaky Floors: State Law Below Federal Constitutional Limits*, 50 Ariz. L. Rev. 227 (2008).

[16] *Id.* at 238.

[17] 591 U. S.___ (2020).

[18] G. Alan Tarr, Espinoza *and the Misuses of State Constitutions*, 73 Rutgers U. L. Rev. 1109, 1144 (2021).

[19] Reitman v. Mulkey, 387 U.S. 369, 370–73 (1967).

[20] *Id.* at 380–81.

[21] Hunter v. Underwood, 471 U.S. 222, 224, 233 (1985).

against African-American citizens, thereby supporting a finding of intentional racial discrimination in violation of the federal Equal Protection Clause.[22] Finally, in 1996, the Court declared an amendment to the Colorado constitution, adopted by initiative, that would have barred local or state legislation protecting lesbians and gay men from discrimination, unconstitutional because it violated the Fourteenth Amendment's Equal Protection Clause.[23]

In a Florida decision, a federal district court reviewed the process of ratification of the Federal Equal Rights Amendment (ERA). After the U.S. Congress proposed the ERA, the state legislature in Florida took up the question of ratification. The Florida Constitution, however, provided that the legislature "shall not take action on any proposed amendment to the constitution of the United States unless a majority of the members thereof have been elected after the proposed amendment has been submitted for ratification."[24] The federal court declared this provision unconstitutional because it conflicted with Article V of the federal Constitution.[25] By the time this decision was rendered, however, after an earlier delay in the litigation,[26] the political situation had changed, and the ERA was never ratified in Florida.

The U.S. Court of Appeals for the Eighth Circuit relied on the dormant commerce clause to strike down a Nebraska state constitutional ban on corporate-owned farming operations.[27] Nonresident farming interests successfully argued that the state constitutional ban, in prohibiting their corporate ownership, discriminated against them.

Another important federal constitutional limit on state constitutions appears in the Guarantee Clause, Article IV, Section 4:

> The United States shall guarantee to every State in this Union a Republican Form of Government, and shall protect each of them against Invasion; and on

[22] *Id.* at 229.

[23] Romer v. Evans, 517 U.S. 620 (1996). *See also* Rice v. Cayetano, 528 U.S. 495, 523–24 (2000) (concluding that a Hawaii constitutional provision limiting voting for trustees of the office of Hawaiian Affairs to "native Hawaiians" was race discrimination in voting, in violation of the Fifteenth Amendment); Cook v. Gralike, 531 U.S. 510 (2001) (striking down a Missouri state constitutional amendment directing congressional candidates to support a federal term limits amendment as being beyond states' power to regulate federal elections); Honda Motor Co. v. Oberg, 512 U.S. 415 (1994) (striking down an Oregon constitutional provision that had been interpreted to prohibit appellate review of punitive damages awards by juries as violating the federal Due Process Clause). *See* Chapter 9, section XI.

[24] FLA. CONST. art. X, § 1.

[25] Trombetta v. Florida, 353 F. Supp. 575 (M.D. Fla. 1973). The leading U.S. Supreme Court decisions on this point were *Hawke v. Smith*, 253 U.S. 221 (1920), and *Leser v. Garnett*, 258 U.S. 130 (1922). *See also* State *ex rel.* Harper v. Waltermire, 691 P.2d 826 (Mont. 1984).

[26] Trombetta v. Florida, 339 F. Supp. 1359 (M.D. Fla. 1972).

[27] Jones v. Gale, 470 F.3d 1261 (8th Cir. 2006), *cert. denied*, 127 S.Ct. 1912 (2007).

> Application of the Legislature, or of the Executive (when the Legislature cannot be convened) against domestic violence.[28]

The U.S. Supreme Court has held that challenges to state government arrangements on Guarantee Clause grounds are nonjusticiable political questions, and it is up to Congress to enforce the provision.[29] At the same time, it has been argued that this view need not constrain *state* courts from enforcing the federal provision as a limit on state constitutions,[30] although this approach has not been much pursued.

The possibility of a federal constitutional challenge to a state constitutional provision, if rejected by the U.S. Supreme Court, may actually *validate* the type of provision, stimulating its inclusion in other states' constitutions. For example, when Illinois included an entire article on "Warehouses" (reflecting the Granger movement) in its 1870 constitution, authorizing governmental regulation of grain elevators, it was upheld in *Munn v. Illinois*.[31] The case, and the possibilities it held for business regulation, was then a major topic at the 1879 California Constitutional Convention. Professor Gordon Bakken noted:

> This put on the legislative agenda a vast array of opportunities to interpose the will of the people through legislation to regulate the rates charged to consumers. The regulatory agenda made possible by this decision challenged the vested rights of private property so dear to conservative Americans.[32]

## II. FEDERAL STATUTORY LIMITS

As indicated earlier, not only may the federal *Constitution* trump a state constitutional provision; federal *statutes* may also supersede state constitutional provisions. One example of this is where a federal statute preempts a state

[28] U.S. Const. art. IV, § 4. *See generally* William M. Wiecek, The Guarantee Clause of the United States Constitution (1972).

[29] Pacific States Tel. & Tel. Co. v. Oregon, 223 U.S. 118 (1912). *See* Elizabeth R. Leong, Note, *Ballot Initiatives & Identifiable Minorities: A Textual Call to Congress*, 28 Rutgers L.J. 677 (1997); Catherine Engberg, Note, *Taking the Initiative: May Congress Reform State Initiative Lawmaking to Guarantee a Republican Form of Government?* 54 Stan. L. Rev. 569 (2001).

[30] Van Sickle v. Shanahan, 511 P.2d 223 (Kan. 1973); State v. Wagner, 752 P.2d 1136, 1197 n.8 (Or. 1988) (Linde, J., dissenting). In 1997, the Oregon Supreme Court reiterated its view that guarantee clause claims were nonjusticiable even in state courts. State *ex rel.* Huddleson v. Sawyer, 932 P.2d 1145 (Or. 1997), *cert. denied*, Sawyer v. Oregon, 522 U.S. 994 (1997).

[31] 94 U.S. 113 (1876). *See generally* Harry N. Scheiber, *The Road to Munn: Eminent Domain and the Concept of Public Purpose in the State Courts*, 5 Pers. in Am. Hist. 329 (1971).

[32] Gordon Morris Bakken, *Becoming Progressive: The California Supreme Court, 1880–1910*, 64 Historian 551, 556 (2002). *See also* Amy Bridges, *Managing the Periphery in the Gilded Age: Writing Constitutions for the Western States*, 22 Stud. in Am. Pol. Dev. 32, 50 (2008).

constitutional provision. For instance, unionized workers in California sought to resist a random drug testing policy adopted by their employer by relying on the privacy clause of the California Constitution. The employer, however, argued that that provision was preempted because it conflicted with the federal Labor Management and Relations Act. The U.S. Court of Appeals for the Ninth Circuit agreed with the employer and declared that the California constitutional provision was preempted under circumstances that were governed by national labor policy.[33] In other labor relations contexts, federal statutory labor law may preempt state constitutional provisions guaranteeing the right to collective bargaining.[34] The West Virginia Supreme Court of Appeals ruled that a federal civil rights statute preempted the state constitutional sovereign immunity provision, even when that statute was being applied by a *state* administrative agency.[35] Pennsylvania courts have held that the federal Fair Labor Standards Act can preempt state constitutional provisions prohibiting the expenditure of state funds in the absence of a legislative appropriation if state employees work into a new fiscal year without a new state budget, or where the federal law (the Social Security Act) has been interpreted to require welfare payments even if a budget has not been adopted.[36]

Federal statutes based on the Spending Clause of the federal Constitution[37] often impose extensive conditions that, although not mandatory (or preemptive) on the states, because they do not have to accept federal dollars, can come into conflict with state constitutional provisions. The U.S. Supreme Court has held that Spending Clause conditions may not amount to excessive congressional coercion of the states,[38] but it has only found that Congress employed such coercion once, in 2012.[39] The U.S. Congress, for example, enacted a program that

[33] Utility Workers of America v. S. Cal. Edison Co., 852 F.2d 1083 (9th Cir. 1988), *cert. denied*, 489 U.S. 1078 (1989). *See* John C. Barker, *Constitutional Privacy Rights in the Private Workplace, Under the Federal and California Constitutions*, 19 Hastings Const. L.Q. 1107 (1992). *See also* Garnett v. Renton Sch. Dist. No. 403, 987 F.2d 641 (9th Cir. 1993) (Federal Equal Access Act preempts state constitutional requirement that public schools be free from sectarian control or influence); Bartlett v. Strickland, 556 U.S. 1 (2009) (Voting Rights Act does not preempt state constitutional limits on splitting local governments in redistricting).

[34] Richard A. Goldberg & Robert F. Williams, *Farmworkers' Organizational and Collective Bargaining Rights in New Jersey: Implementing Self-Executing State Constitutional Rights*, 18 Rutgers L.J. 729, 742 (1987).

[35] Kerns v. Bucklew, 357 S.E.2d 750, 758 (W. Va. 1987).

[36] *See* Council 13, AFSCME v. Commonwealth of Pa., 986 A.2d 63 (Pa. 2009).

[37] *See generally* David E. Engdahl, *The Spending Power*, 44 Duke L.J. 1 (1994); Lynn A. Baker, *Conditional Federal Spending After Lopez*, 95 Colum. L. Rev. 1911 (1995); Lynn A. Baker, *The Spending Power and the Federalist Revival*, 4 Chap. L. Rev. 195 (2001).

[38] South Dakota v. Dole, 483 U.S. 203, 207–09 (1987) (conditions must be "related" to a "federal interest").

[39] Nat'l Fed. Of Independ. Business v. Sebelius, 567 U.S. 519, 577–78 (2012) (striking down the condition of loss of Medicaid funds if states did not expand significantly their Medicaid programs); James F. Blumstein, *Enforcing Limits on the Affordable Health Care Act's Mandated Medicaid Expansion: The Coercion Principle and the Clear Notice Rule*, Cato Sup. Ct. Rev. 67 (2011–2012). *See generally* Roderick M. Hills Jr., *Dissecting the State: The Use of Federal Law to Free State and Local*

offered health-care funds to the states on the condition that they enact a "certificate of need" statute. The Supreme Court of North Carolina, however, had already declared that such a certificate of need statute violated the North Carolina Constitution's ban on monopolies.[40] In these circumstances, the state of North Carolina instituted a lawsuit seeking a declaration that it did not have to comply with the condition of receiving federal funds because its state constitution prohibited that from happening.[41] A three-judge federal district court denied relief, finding that the federal condition was not "coercive."[42] The court made the following observation:

> It is unfortunate that its Constitution, as presently phrased and interpreted, might prevent compliance by North Carolina with the federally established condition. Simply because one State, *by some oddity* of its Constitution may be prohibited from compliance is not sufficient ground, though, to invalidate a condition which is legitimately related to a national interest sought to be achieved by a federal appropriation and which does not operate adversely to the rights of the other States to comply. Were this not so, any State, dissatisfied by some valid federal condition on a federal grant could thwart the congressional purpose by the expedient of amending its Constitution or by securing a decision of its own Supreme Court. The validity of the power of the federal government under the Constitution to impose a condition on federal grants made under a proper Constitutional power does not exist at the mercy of the State Constitutions or decisions of State Courts.[43]

In 1985, the Oregon Supreme Court observed that the "legislature cannot violate the State's Constitution in order to qualify for a benefit that Congress leaves optional. . . . [T]he [s]tate cannot violate its own Constitution in order to satisfy a federal program that Congress has not made obligatory under the Supremacy Clause."[44] Thus a conflict may arise. This is a generally accepted principle, although it has been the subject of some academic criticism.[45]

*Officials from State Legislatures' Control*, 97 MICH. L. REV. 1201 (1999); Dennis Murashko, Comment, *Accountability and Constitutional Federalism: Reconsidering Federal Conditional Spending Programs in Light of Democratic Political Theory*, 101 NW. U. L. REV. 931 (2007); Rebecca E. Zeitlow, *Federalism's Paradox: The Spending Power and Waiver of Sovereign Immunity*, 37 WAKE FOREST L. REV. 141 (2002).

[40] *In re* Certificate of Need for Aston Park Hospital, 193 S.E.2d 729, 736 (N.C. 1973); Edward C. Winslow III, *Hospital Regulation After Aston Park: Substantive Due Process in North Carolina*, 52 N.C. L. REV. 763 (1974).

[41] N.C. *ex rel.* Morrow v. Califano, 445 F. Supp. 532 (E.D. N.C. 1977).

[42] *Id.* at 535.

[43] *Id.* (emphasis added).

[44] Salem College & Academy, Inc. v. Employment Div. 695 P.2d 25, 30, 34 (Or. 1985).

[45] William Van Alstyne, *"Thirty Pieces of Silver" for the Rights of Your People: Irresistible Offers Reconsidered as a Matter of State Constitutional Law*, 16 HARV. J.L. & PUB. POLICY 303, 317–18

In certain circumstances, Congress may foresee a potential conflict between state constitutions and a condition attached to the receipt of federal funds under a Spending Clause statute. For example, in 1974, the U.S. Supreme Court recognized that Congress did not intend for federal funds under Title I of the Elementary and Secondary Education Act of 1965 to be utilized in violation of state constitutional restrictions on the use of public money in religious schools.[46]

In most circumstances of preemption, or conflict between conditions attached to federal spending and state constitutions, it is unlikely that Congress foresaw or considered the potential collision between dominant federal statutory law and subservient state constitutional provisions. On at least one occasion, however, Congress has intentionally utilized its authority to displace a state constitutional provision. In the late 1970s, an era of high inflation and very high interest rates, the Arkansas state constitution's limit on the legal rate of interest (a policy-oriented provision) served to block the lending of funds for many purposes within the state and to encourage people to move their funds out of state. Under these circumstances, the Arkansas congressional delegation sought the introduction of legislation specifically aimed at preempting their own state constitutional provision![47] The legislation was enacted, pursuant to congressional authority to regulate interstate commerce, and it directly displaced the Arkansas constitutional provision.[48] A similar congressional method was utilized by Congress in its regulation of gambling on Indian reservations.[49]

## III. OTHER FEDERAL LIMITS

A lesser form of federal law—federal administrative regulations—can also trump state constitutional provisions if it is validly promulgated. The U.S. Supreme

(1993); Ilya Somin, *Closing the Pandora's Box of Federalism: The Case for Judicial Restriction of Federal Subsidies to State Governments*, 90 GEO. L.J. 461 (2002).

[46] Wheeler v. Barrera, 417 U.S. 402, 417 (1974).

[47] 125 CONGRESSIONAL RECORD—HOUSE, at 993 (daily ed. Feb. 29, 1979).

[48] With respect to this interest rate legislation, see Maxine Master Long, *Trends in Usury Legislation—Current Interest Overdue*, 34 U. MIAMI L. REV. 325 (1980); Mark Barry Riley, *Usury Legislation—Its Effects on the Economy and a Proposal for Reform*, 33 VAND. L. REV. 199, 204–05 (1980). In *McInnis v. Cooper Communities, Inc.*, 611 S.W.2d 767 (Ark. 1981), the Arkansas Supreme Court ruled, in a divided opinion, that Congress had validly exercised its commerce power.

[49] In 1988, Congress passed the Indian Gaming Regulatory Act, 18 U.S.C. §§ 1166–68; 25 U.S.C. §§ 2701–21. This act operates to displace certain state constitutional restrictions on gambling. *See* Dalton v. Pataki, 835 N.E.2d 1180 (N.Y. 2005); Florida House of Representatives v. Crist, 990 So.2d 1035 (Fla. 2008); Wesley D. Huber, *Gambling—Vice or Virtue?: The Federal Indian Gaming Regulatory Act Preempts the New York Constitution's Ban on Commercial Gambling*, Comment, 37 RUTGERS L.J. 1317 (2006); Kathryn R.L. Rand, *Caught in the Middle: How State Politics, State Law, and State Courts Constrain Tribal Influence over Indian Gaming*, 90 MARQ. L. REV. 971 (2007).

Court has stated that "[f]ederal regulations have no less preemptive effect than federal statutes."[50]

Indeed, judge-made "federal common law" can take precedence over state constitutional provisions. In 1938, the U.S. Supreme Court held that state constitutional provisions on water rights must give way to federal common law.[51] In 1931, in *Herron v. Southern Pac. Co.*,[52] the U.S. Supreme Court concluded that a federal court sitting in Arizona could direct a verdict for the defendant on the grounds of contributory negligence or assumption of the risk, despite the following Arizona constitutional provision: "The defense of contributory negligence or of assumption of risk shall, in all cases whatsoever, be a question of fact and shall, at all times, be left to the jury."[53]

The federal government's entry into treaty relationships can have the effect of overriding the constitutions of the states.[54] At least one commentator speculated that this was possible under North American Free Trade Agreement, which has since been replaced by the substantially similar United States–Mexico–Canada Agreement.[55]

Finally, an interstate compact entered into by a state, particularly one that has received the consent of Congress, potentially may operate to supersede state constitutional provisions.[56] In an interesting 1951 decision, West Virginia officials argued that their state constitution prohibited them from complying with an interstate compact that the state had entered. The justices of the U.S. Supreme Court disagreed on whether to step in and simply interpret the state constitution themselves as providing no impediment, or to declare the interstate compact a *federal* statute that trumped the state constitutional provisions.[57] Two well-known commentators on interstate compacts made the following observations on the theory of Justice Reed's concurring opinion in the case:

> If this construction were to be accepted, the government of a state, by making a compact with another state, could in effect amend the state constitution without regard to the requirements for amendment, such as ratification by

50 Fidelity Fed. Sav. & Loan Ass'n. v. de la Cuesta, 458 U.S. 141, 153–54 (1982).

51 Hinderlider v. LaPlata River & Cherry Creek Ditch Co., 304 U.S. 92 (1938).

52 283 U.S. 91 (1931).

53 *Id.* at 92.

54 Missouri v. Holland, 252 U.S. 416, 433 (1920); 1 LAWRENCE H. TRIBE, AMERICAN CONSTITUTIONAL LAW 645 (3d ed. 2000). *See* Charles A. Lofgren, *Missouri v. Holland in Historical Perspective*, 1975 SUP. CT. REV. 77 (1975); Johanna Kalb, *Human Rights Treaties in State Courts: The International Prospects of State Constitutionalism After Medellin*, 115 PENN. ST. L. REV. 1051 (2011). *See* Chapter 12, section XII.

55 G. Alan Tarr, *NAFTA and Federalism: Are They Compatible?* 2 NORTEAMÉRICA 133, 143–44 (July–Dec. 2007).

56 *See* West Virginia *ex. rel.* Dyer v. Sims, 341 U.S. 22 (1951).

57 *Id.* at 32.

> popular referendum; similarly a state government could accomplish by compact what it could not by statute under the constitution of the state.[58]

James Blumstein and Thomas Cheeseman have more recently argued for the use of interstate compacts:

> First, in the face of regional polarization that has often hampered Congress's ability to craft nationwide legislation addressing important issues, interstate compacts provide a means for states to partner with Congress to address those issues on a regional, rather than a national, basis..... [s]uch an approach allows for a "sensitivity to geographically-based sub-national majorities" so that different interests can be accommodated without the need for a national resolution or consensus on important issues.[59]

They point out that an interstate compact which receives consent from Congress is transformed into *federal law*, and they argue that it need not be presented to the president for veto. Importantly, this kind of federal law would take precedence over state law under the Supremacy Clause.

## IV. ENABLING ACT LIMITS

Returning to the federal influence on state constitutions during the process of admission to the Union,[60] such influences can be of a lasting but limiting nature. For example, Congress, in its Enabling Act for Oklahoma's admission, required that the state capital be located temporarily in the city of Guthrie. The Oklahoma Constitutional Convention adopted a separate, irrevocable "ordinance" accepting this and other conditions, which was ratified along with the constitution by the voters. After its admission as a state, on "equal footing" with existing states, Oklahoma took steps to move its capital. In *Coyle v. Smith*, the

[58] Frederick L. Zimmermann & Mitchell Wendell, *The Interstate Compact and* Dyer v. Sims, 51 Colum. L. Rev. 931, 937 (1951). *See also id.* at 943 n.61. *See generally* Duncan B. Hollis, *Unpacking the Compact Clause*, 88 Tex L. Rev. 741 (2010). Jim Rossi explores state constitutional separation of powers issues in state governments entering into interstate compacts in *Constitutional Isolationism and the Limits of State Separation of Powers as a Barrier to Interstate Compacts*, 90 Marq. L. Rev. 721 (2007). Dan Rodriguez explores the possibility of interstate cooperation in the context of public health emergencies like the pandemic in *Public Health Emergencies and State Constitutional Quality*, 72 Rutgers U. L. Rev. 1223, 1242–45 (2020).

[59] James F. Blumstein & Thomas J. Cheeseman, *State Empowerment and the Compact Clause*, 27 Wm. & Mary Bill Rts. J. 775, 778 (2019), *citing* James F. Blumstein, *Federalism and Civil Rights: Complimentary and Competing Paradigms*, 47 Vand. L. Rev. 1251, 1252–53 (1994).

[60] *See* Chapter 3.

U.S. Supreme Court upheld its power to do so, against the claim that the enabling act condition was binding.[61]

The Court, however, clearly accepted the power of Congress initially to require certain conditions in a state constitution upon pain of denial of membership in the Union.[62] It went on to note that binding, enduring requirements could be extracted if they were based on a congressional power, other than over the admission of new states, such as regulating interstate commerce, commerce with Indians, or federal public lands.[63] Since the question of where a state is to locate its capital is purely a state law matter, and the power to admit new states did not add to the other legislative powers of Congress, the enabling act requirement was not binding after Oklahoma's admission to the Union on "equal footing" with the other states.[64]

In areas where Congress *does* have valid legislative authority, as recognized by the Court in *Coyle*, conditions of admission can have a lasting, limiting influence. A 1990 Arizona case illustrates these points clearly.[65] At the time of Arizona's admission to the Union in 1910, Congress in the enabling act granted large tracts of federal land, over which it had legislative authority, to Arizona in trust, on the conditions that such lands be used to support public schools and could only be sold or leased to the highest bidder at public auction.[66] Arizona was required to accept these conditions and not deviate from them without consent of Congress. Arizona then included these provisions in its constitution.[67]

Over the ensuing years, based on requests from the states, Congress amended the enabling act (illustrating its continuing relevance) to permit more flexible approaches to school trust lands, including permission for Arizona to engage in *exchanges* of such lands, in addition to sale and lease. This is an unusual circumstance where states must seek congressional *permission* to amend their constitutions. But Arizona never amended its constitution to authorize such alternatives.[68] Litigation arose over a proposed exchange, and the Arizona

[61] 221 U.S. 559 (1911). For discussions of the nonoriginal states and the conditions of their admission to the Union, see Julien C. Monnet, *Violation by a State of the Conditions of Its Enabling Act*, 10 Colum. L. Rev. 591 (1910); George W. Wickersham, *New States and Constitutions*, 21 Yale L.J. 1 (1911); John Hanna, *Equal Footing in the Admission of States*, 3 Baylor L. Rev. 519 (1951); Peter S. Onuf, *New State Equality: The Ambiguous History of a Constitutional Principle*, 18 Publius: The J. Federalism 53 (Fall 1988).

[62] *Coyle*, 221 U.S. at 568. For an example of a "compact" with the United States, inserted in a state constitution, see N.M. Const. art. XXI.

[63] 221 U.S. at 574.

[64] *Id.*

[65] Fain Land & Cattle Co. v. Hassell, 790 P.2d 242 (Ariz. 1990). *See also* State *ex rel.* King v. Lyons, 248 P.3d 878, 882 (N.M. 2011) ("The Act was adopted during New Mexico's constitutional convention, making it "fundamental law to the same extent as if it had been directly incorporated into the Constitution.").

[66] *Id.* at 243–44. *See also* Office of Hawaiian Affairs v. Housing and Community Devel. Corp., 177 P.3d 884, 891–92 (Haw. 2008), *rev'd* 556 U.S.163, (2009).

[67] *Fain Land & Cattle Co.*, 790 P.2d at 244.

[68] *Id.* at 245.

Supreme Court held that the Arizona Constitution was binding until changed pursuant to congressional permission and that the amendment to the enabling act did not, of its own force, amend or preempt the Arizona constitutional provisions.[69]

A related dispute arose in Colorado; there, changes made to the state's land trust for public schools conformed to the restrictions Congress had originally imposed in the Colorado Enabling Act, which led the U.S. Court of Appeals for the Tenth Circuit to conclude that the there was no Supremacy Clause issue.[70] This opinion also provides a detailed analysis of the relationship of enabling act provisions based on Congress's legislative powers and state constitutional provisions in response. An interesting Washington case confronted the question of the actual location of the state's northern border under the enabling act and the state constitution, concluding that there was a need to determine *congressional* intent when a state constitutional provision was mandated by an enabling act.[71] Similar relationships between state constitutions and congressional enabling acts will exist in the area of "Indian lands."[72]

Thus, the federal government can, under certain circumstances, exert continuing control of segments of state constitutionalism in the thirty-seven nonoriginal states, despite the apparent all-or-nothing equal footing doctrine, in ways that were never available in the original thirteen. As one analyst observed:

> By ruling in *Coyle* that Congress could only impose conditions that it otherwise had the power to enact against all of the states through its other constitutional powers, the Supreme Court did make a powerful statement about the enforceability and validity of many of these conditions. But on the other hand, the line that the Court drew was not entirely protective of state sovereignty in the admission process—while Congress might be limited in the tools that it could use (such as the use of conditions that prohibited changes in state constitutions or laws after admission), Congress nonetheless had enormous power through its land grant authority and its regulation of federal lands within the states to control the admitted states. By granting lands to the new states with certain conditions, and restricting the power that the states had over lands that

[69] *Id.* at 247–50. *See also* Tacy Bowlin, *Rethinking the ABCs of Utah's School Trust Lands*, 1994 Utah L. Rev. 923; C. Maison Heidelberg, *Closing the Book on School Trust Lands*, 45 Vand. L. Rev. 1581 (1992).

[70] Branson Sch. Dist. Re-82 v. Romer, 161 F.3d 619 (10th Cir. 1998); PPL Montana, LLC. v. State, 229 P.3d 421 (Mont. 2010); Jones Co. School Dist. v. Dept. of Revenue, 111 So.3d 588 (Miss. 2013); State v. Mathis, 233 P.3d 1119 (Utah 2009).

[71] State v. Norman, 40 P.3d 1161, 1168 (Wash. 2002).

[72] William P. Schwartz, Comment, *State Disclaimers of Jurisdiction over Indians: A Bar to the McCarran Amendment?* 18 Land & Water L. Rev. 175 (1983). *See also* Peter Nicolas, *American-Style Justice in No Man's Land*, 36 Ga. L. Rev. 895, 912–14 (2002).

continued to be under federal control, the federal government retained significant powers over the new states—the secularization of New Mexico schools in the 1950s in part because of the conditions on state school land grants is a reminder of the importance of conditions that continue to be enforced by the courts today, and the degree with which they can intrude into state government.

***

The reliance of the Supreme Court on *Coyle* as it has constructed a vision of state sovereignty as protected in certain inviolable ways is therefore extremely problematic. How can *Coyle* stand for the proposition that the Court has cited it for, when the Court's holding in *Coyle* seems almost irrelevant compared to the enormous political and social changes that some member states of the Union have gone through in order to be admitted, changes that were caused in part by the admission conditions themselves? Indeed, the facts of *Coyle*—where the Court refused to enforce an admission condition that restricted the movement of a state capital—are significantly less egregious than other conditions—official language, the banning of polygamy are the most obvious examples—that Congress has successfully imposed on newly-admitted states, and which have been part of a process that led to significant social and political changes in those states.[73]

Even in areas where Congress arguably does not have any continuing legislative power over a state's constitution after it is admitted to the Union, often provisions inserted in the state constitution to gain admission simply remain there after admission. The "Blaine Amendments" are a good example of this phenomenon. These were amendments required to be included in state constitutions, at the insistence of Representative James G. Blaine of Maine, after he failed in his bid to amend the federal Constitution, requiring public schools to be "free from sectarian control."[74] Serious questions have been raised about state Blaine Amendments based on arguments that they reflected anti-Catholic bias when they were adopted and therefore might violate the First Amendment.[75] When Washington education officials interpreted Article I, Section 11, of their constitution to prohibit the use of state-financed scholarships for university religious

[73] Eric Biber, *The Price of Admission: Causes, Effects, and Patterns of Conditions Imposed on States Entering the Union*, 46 Am. J. Legal Hist. 119, 194, 198 (2004).

[74] *See* Frank J. Conklin & James M. Vache, *The Establishment Clause and the Free Exercise Clause of the Washington Constitution—A Proposal to the Supreme Court*, 8 U. Puget Sound L. Rev. 411, 431–33, 436–42, 459–60 (1985); Joseph P. Viteritti, *Blaine's Wake: School Choice, The First Amendment, and State Constitutional Law*, 21 Harv. J. L. & Pub. Pol'y 657, 659, 670–74 (1998); Steven K. Green, *The Blaine Amendment Reconsidered*, 36 Am. J. Legal. Hist. 38 (1992); Kyle Duncan, *Secularism's Laws: State Blaine Amendments and Religious Persecution*, 72 Fordham L. Rev. 493 (2003); Toby J. Heytens, Note, *School Choice and State Constitutions*, 86 Va. L. Rev. 117 (2000).

[75] *See* Mitchell v. Helms, 530 U.S. 793, 828–29 (2000) (Thomas, J., plurality opinion).

studies, this was upheld against a First Amendment free-exercise challenge in *Locke v. Davey*.[76] The Court noted that the challenged provision of the Washington Constitution was not a "Blaine Amendment, and therefore not potentially in violation of the federal Constitution."[77] As discussed at the start of this chapter, more recently the U.S. Supreme Court has been skeptical about the constitutionality of state laws that allegedly discriminate on the basis of religion in the provision of public educational benefits.

## V. STATE CONSTITUTIONAL PROVISIONS THAT HAVE BEEN INVALIDATED

Of course, provisions in state constitutions that have been invalidated based on the conflicts identified in this chapter are not automatically removed from the constitutional text. Often they linger on for many years, apparently continuing as part of the constitution despite being unenforceable. Professor Maureen Brady classifies these provisions as "zombie constitutional provisions," which she describes as "clearly or arguably unenforceable clauses and amendments that stick with us, toward sometimes unclear effect and with potentially harmful consequences."[78]

Professor Allan Vestal has identified a particular set of such unenforceable state constitutional provisions that he refers to as "badges of inferiority."[79] Examples of such provisions are religious tests for office, mandates of segregated schools, bars to marriage equality and religious tests for witness competency.[80] He contends that these badges of inferiority are "diminished, but not eliminated, when the state constitution provisions were rendered unenforceable, but not removed from the state constitutions."[81] The problem he identifies, however, is that provisions such as bars to marriage equality are difficult to remove because some supporters of these provisions harbor a hope that the U.S. Supreme Court will change its mind about their invalidity under the U.S. Constitution.[82]

In the context of same-sex marriage, for example, state legislatures may hesitate to suggest such removal through amendment out of desire not to offend remaining opponents of same-sex marriage.[83] Indeed, the Supreme Court gave

[76] 540 U.S. 712 (2004).

[77] *Id.* at 723 n.7.

[78] Maureen E. Brady, *Zombie State Constitutional Provisions*, 2021 Wis. L. Rev. 1063, 1065.

[79] Allan W. Vestal, *Removing State Constitution Badges of Inferiority*, 22 Lewis & Clark L. Rev. 1151 (2018).

[80] *Id.* at 1156–64.

[81] *Id.* at 1163.

[82] *Id.* at 1190.

[83] *Id.* at 1187–94.

support to this position in *Dobbs v. Jackson Women's Health Organization*,[84] holding that the Fourteenth Amendment does not protect a woman's right to choose. Concurring in the decision, Justice Clarence Thomas expressly invited challenges to other decisions that turned on substantive due process, including *Obergefell v. Hodges*,[85] in which the Court ruled that the U.S. Constitution affords same-sex couples the right to marry.

## VI. CONCLUSION

State constitutions interact with, and specific provisions may be limited by, or in violation of, the federal Constitution and laws. This can occur in a fairly wide variety of circumstances, often not obvious at first glance. This subservient position for state constitutions is part of the original structure of our federal Constitution and will continue to impose important limitations on the content of state constitutions.

84 597 U.S. ___ (2022).
85 576 U.S. 644 (2015).

# PART II

# RIGHTS GUARANTEES UNDER STATE CONSTITUTIONS

## *THE NEW JUDICIAL FEDERALISM*

Part II covers the New Judicial Federalism, the development of state court interpretations of some state constitutional rights provisions to be more protective than the same or similar federal constitutional provisions as interpreted by the U.S. Supreme Court. This has been the driving force in the increased interest in, and relevance of, state constitutions in the past several generations.

Because state constitutional interpretation in *rights* cases has been so dominated by concerns over whether state courts should follow or diverge from federal constitutional doctrine, this part treats these issues separately from the more general interpretation issues dealt with in Part IV. There is some overlap with techniques of interpretation arising here in the rights cases and with some rights cases considered in Part IV as part of the treatment of interpreting state constitutions as unique legal documents.

Once again, this part is not arranged by the *substantive* content of state constitutional rights guarantees. Rather, the focus is on techniques of analysis in the very important area of America's dual enforcement of constitutional norms.

# 5
# THE NEW JUDICIAL FEDERALISM

*Rediscovery by state supreme courts of the broader protections afforded their own citizens by their state constitutions . . . is probably the most important development in constitutional jurisprudence in our times.*

—Justice William J. Brennan Jr.[1]

It has been generally understood that, prior to the U.S. Supreme Court's "selective incorporation" of the federal Bill of Rights into the Fourteenth Amendment, through which most of the Bill's provisions became binding against the states, the only constitutional rights guarantees applicable against the states were in the state constitutions.[2] This is why the New Judicial Federalism (NJF) is referred to as a "rediscovery" of rights provisions. At the same time, recent research has convincingly cast doubt on this assumption.[3] Professor Jason Mazzone reports:

> In a series of cases that are largely forgotten or brushed aside today, early state courts regularly did apply the Federal Bill of Rights to invalidate state laws and otherwise constrain state government. Although as a matter of federal constitutional law enforced by the federal courts, the Bill applied only to the national government, the state courts understood the Bill to set out general constitutional principles applicable to state legislatures and executives alike—even when no provision of the applicable state constitution imposed any such constraint on state government. The jurisdictional limits of the 1789 Judiciary Act protected these state court decisions applying the Bill of Rights from review by the United States Supreme Court.[4]

[1] NATL. L.J., Sept. 29, 1986, at S1, *quoted in* G. ALAN TARR, UNDERSTANDING STATE CONSTITUTIONS 165 (1998). *Accord* William J. Brennan Jr., *Foreword: Remarks of William J. Brennan, Jr.*, 13 VT. L. REV. 11, 11 (1988) (NJF "the most significant development in American constitutional jurisprudence today.").

[2] Barron v. City of Baltimore, 32 U.S. 243 (1833); Timbs v. Indiana, 586 U.S. ___ (2019) (incorporating Eighth Amendment Excessive Fines Clause).

[3] Jason Mazzone, *The Bill of Rights in the Early State Courts*, 92 MINN. L. REV. 1 (2007).

[4] *Id.* at 3.

*The Law of American State Constitutions.* Robert F. Williams and Lawrence Friedman, Oxford University Press.
 DOI: 10.1093/oso/9780190068806.003.0006

In any event, the development described by Justice William Brennan, now known as the NJF,[5] dates from the early 1970s and, of course, has long ceased to be "new."[6] The term describes the fact that state judges in numerous cases have interpreted their state constitutional rights provisions to provide *more* protection than the national minimum standard guaranteed by the federal Constitution. In the American system of constitutional federalism, we have "dual enforcement of constitutional norms."[7] Of course, state constitutions may also be interpreted to provide *less* protection than the federal Constitution, but the national minimum standards must still be enforced.[8]

[5] *See* TARR, *supra* note 1, at 161–70.

[6] *See* Ronald K.L. Collins, *Foreword: Reliance on State Constitutions—Beyond the "New Federalism,"* 8 U. PUGET SOUND L. REV. vi (1985).

[7] *Symposium: Dual Enforcement of Constitutional Norms*, 46 WM. & MARY L. REV. 1231 (2005). Federal courts, of course, may be faced with state constitutional questions under their diversity and supplemental jurisdiction. *See* City of Mesquite v. Aladdin's Castle, Inc., 455 U.S. 283, 291, 293–94 (1982); Robert A Schapiro, *Polyphonic Federalism: State Constitutions in the Federal Courts*, 87 CAL. L. REV. 1409, 1411–12 (1999); ROBERT A. SCHAPIRO, POLYPHONIC FEDERALISM: TOWARD THE PROTECTION OF FUNDAMENTAL RIGHTS 121–50 (2009). For an example of a federal court exercising its discretion not to hear a state constitutional claim asserted under its supplemental jurisdiction (formerly pendent jurisdiction), and dismissing without prejudice under 28 U.S.C. § 1367, see Green v. Zendrian, 916 F. Supp. 493 (D. Md. 1996). *See also* Trump Hotels & Casino Resorts, Inc. v. Mirage Resorts, Inc., 963 F. Supp. 395, 408 (D.N.J. 1997); Snyder v. Murray City Corp., 124 F.3d 1349, 1354–55 (10th Cir. 1997). Such dismissed claims, of course, would not be subject to claim or issue preclusion arguments. Snyder v. Murray City Corp., 73 P.3d 325, 332–33 (Utah 2003).

On state constitutional claims in federal court, see Michael T. Morley, *Litigating Imperfect Solutions: State Constitutional Claims in Federal Court*, 35 CONST. COMM. 401 (2020) (reviewing JEFFREY S. SUTTON, 51 IMPERFECT SOLUTIONS: STATES AND THE MAKING OF AMERICAN CONSTITUTIONAL LAW (2018)). *Compare* Guiney v. Roache, 833 F.2d 1079 (1st Cir. 1987), *with* Guiney v. Police Comm'n., 582 N.E.2d 523 (Mass. 1991).

[8] As the Supreme Court of North Carolina noted:

> Strictly speaking, however, a state may still construe a provision of its constitution as providing less rights than are guaranteed by a parallel federal provision. Nevertheless, because the United States Constitution is binding on the states, the rights *it* guarantees must be applied to every citizen by the courts of North Carolina, so no citizen will be "accorded lesser rights" no matter how we construe the state Constitution. For all practical purposes, therefore, the only significant issue for this Court when interpreting a provision of our state Constitution paralleling a provision of the United States Constitution will always be whether the state Constitution guarantees additional rights to the citizen above and beyond those guaranteed by the parallel federal provision.

State v. Jackson, 503 S.E.2d 101, 103 (N.C. 1998). For other recognitions that the state constitutions are sometimes *less* protective than the federal Constitution, see State v. Ice, 170 P.3d 1049, 1056 (Or. 2007) *reversed sub. nom.* Oregon v. Ice, 555 U.S. 160 (2009) (jury trial rights, reversed on federal ground); Serna v. Superior Court, 707 P.2d 793, 799 (Cal. 1985) (analyzing the right to a speedy trial); State v. Hopper, 822 P.2d 775, 778 (Wash. 1992) (evaluating the requirements for a valid indictment); State v. Smith, 725 P.2d 894 (Or. 1986). *See generally* Earl Maltz, *False Prophet—Justice Brennan and the Theory of State Constitutional Law*, 15 HASTINGS CONST. L.Q. 429, 443–44 (1988); Barry Latzer, *Whose Federalism? Or, Why "Conservative" States Should Develop Their State Constitutional Law*, 61 ALB. L. REV. 1399 (1998); Marc L. Miller & Ronald F. Wright, *Leaky Floors: State Law Below Federal Constitutional Limits*, 50 ARIZ. L. REV. 227 (2008).

Professor Alan Tarr contended that, prior to the beginning of the 1970s, the conditions were not right for the development of an expansive state constitutional rights jurisprudence. He noted:

> What was missing was a model of how state judges could develop a civil liberties jurisprudence. Because Americans had not come to rely on courts to vindicate civil liberties, state courts throughout the 19th and early 20th centuries gained little experience in interpreting civil liberties guarantees. Nor could they look to federal courts for guidance in interpreting their constitutional protections.... Only when circumstances brought a combination of state constitutional arguments, plus an example of how a court might develop constitutional guarantees, could a state civil liberties jurisprudence emerge. Put differently, when the Burger Court's anticipated—and to some extent actual—retreat from Warren Court activism encouraged civil liberties litigants to look elsewhere for redress, the experience of the preceding decades had laid the foundation for the development of state civil liberties law.
>
> This, in turn, suggests that, paradoxically, the activism of the Warren Court, which was often portrayed as detrimental to federalism, was a necessary condition for the emergence of a vigorous state involvement in protecting civil liberties.[9]

Dr. John Kincaid pointed out that President Richard Nixon's 1969 appointment of Chief Justice Warren E. Burger reflected the president's campaign promise to turn the U.S. Supreme Court in a more conservative direction. Most analysts agree that the appointment was one of the other moving forces behind the NJF.[10] If it was concern about a conservative trend on the highest court in the land, interestingly that Court has actually encouraged recourse to state constitutions.[11]

These developments have made it clear that, with respect to federal constitutional rights, decisions of the U.S. Supreme Court may be divided into two categories: decisions ruling in *favor* of asserted federal constitutional rights become the supreme law of the land and must be followed everywhere in the

[9] G. Alan Tarr, *The Past and Future of the New Judicial Federalism*, 24 PUBLIUS: THE J. FEDERALISM 63, 72–73 (Spring 1994). *See also* TARR, *supra* note 1, at 161–65.

[10] John Kincaid, *Foreword: The New Federalism Context of the New Judicial Federalism*, 26 RUTGERS L.J. 913, 914–15 (1995).

[11] For an early pre-NJF statement by the Court of the truism that state courts may interpret their state constitutions to be more protective than the federal Constitution, see Chase Securities Corp. v. Donaldson, 325 U.S. 304, 312–13 (1945) ("Many have, as they are privileged to do, so interpreted their own easily amendable constitutions to give restrictive clauses a more rigid interpretation than we properly could impose upon them from without by construction of the federal instrument which is amendable only with great difficulty and with the cooperation of many States."). *See infra* notes 46–50, and accompanying text. For more examples, see Robert F. Williams, *State Constitutional Protection of Civil Litigation*, 70 RUTGERS U. L. REV. 905, 910–11 (2018).

United States. Decisions ruling *against* asserted federal constitutional rights, on the other hand, do not end the matter but rather leave the question, quite literally, to the fifty states (and Puerto Rico) for their own decisions based on judicial interpretation of their respective state constitutions, statutory enactments, or some other form of state lawmaking.

There are really at least six different kinds of state constitutional rights that must be distinguished from each other and evaluated by state courts engaging in the NJF:

1. State constitutional provisions that are textually identical to their federal counterparts. Many criminal procedure protections such as those on search and seizure and right to counsel are identical.
2. State constitutional rights provisions that are only slightly different textually from their federal counterparts. Good examples are taking clauses that provide that property may not be taken *or damaged*;[12] provisions banning cruel *or* unusual punishment;[13] and confrontation clauses requiring *face-to-face* testimony.[14] Professor Harry Scheiber attributes the first example to a reaction to a line of cases that found "consequential" or "indirect" damage caused by railroads not to be compensable in eminent domain.[15]
3. State constitutional rights provisions that are substantially different from their federal counterparts. Some of the best examples of these kinds of provisions are the free speech guarantees that are often stated *affirmatively*[16] and the variety of religion clauses that are much more detailed than the First Amendment.[17]

   Professor Burt Neuborne has argued that state courts are better equipped than federal courts to enforce state constitutional affirmative rights.[18]

[12] Henderson v. City of Columbus, 827 N.W.2d 482, 490 (Neb. 2013).

[13] People v. Anderson, 493 P.2d 880 (Cal. 1972); State v. Bullock, 485 N.W.2d 866 (Mich. 1992); Bear Cloud v. State, 275 P.3d 377, 412 (Wyo. 2012); State v. Juarez, 837 N.W.2d 473, 482 (Minn. 2013); Matter of Williams, 496 P.3d 289 (Wash. 2021); State v. Kelliher, 873 S.E.2d 366 (N.C. 2022).

[14] Commonwealth v. Ludwig, 594 A.2d 281 (Pa. 1991); People v. Fitzpatrick, 633 N.E.2d 685 (Ill. 1994). Both of these decisions, requiring face-to-face confrontation for child abuse victims, were overturned by constitutional amendment. *See* Thomas Conklin, Note, People v. Fitzpatrick: *The Path to Amending the Illinois Constitution to Protect Child Witnesses in Criminal Sexual Abuse Cases*, 26 Loy. U. Chi. L.J. 321 (1995).

[15] Harry N. Scheiber, *Race, Radicalism, and Reform: Historical Perspective on the 1879 California Constitution*, 17 Hast. Const. L.Q. 35, 63 (1989).

[16] 1 Jennifer Friesen, State Constitutional Law: Litigating Individual Rights, Claims and Defenses Appendix 5 (4th ed. 2006); Bierman v. Weier, 826 N.W.2d 436, 451 (Iowa 2013); Beeman v. Anthem Prescription Management, LLC 315 P.3d 71, 78–79 (Cal. 2013).

[17] *Id.* at ch. 4; Robert F. Williams, *State Constitutional Religion Clauses: Lessons from the New Judicial Federalism*, VII U. St. Thomas J.L. & Pub. Pol'y 192 (2013); G. Alan Tarr, *Church and State in the States*, 64 Wash. L. Rev. 73 (1989); Christine M. Durham, *What Goes Around Comes Around: The New Relevancy of State Constitutional Religion Clauses*, 38 Val. U. L. Rev. 353 (2004); Kent Greenawalt, *The Concept of Religion Under State Constitutions*, 8 Campbell L. Rev. 437 (1986).

[18] Burt Neuborne, *Foreword: State Constitutions and the Evolution of Positive Rights*, 20 Rutgers L.J. 881, 891 (1989).

Noting the distinctions between federal and state constitutions and judicial review under each, he relied on the presence of more positive rights texts in state constitutions, the broader lawmaking function of state courts ("generative ethos"), local flexibility, and the "democratic imprimatur" of state judges chosen by the electorate, to argue that state courts were more suited to enforcing positive rights.[19] Professor Lawrence Sager makes a similar point.[20] Professor Helen Hershkoff has urged an approach to judicial interpretation and enforcement of state constitutional positive rights that differs from federal constitutional interpretation.[21] Hershkoff has also set forth a compelling case for the adoption of new positive rights by state constitutional reformers—a recommendation clearly not aimed at courts.[22]

4. State constitutional rights provisions with no federal counterpart or federal "analog." There are, of course, a wide range of such provisions, but a few examples are civil litigation protections that are very important in the battle over "tort reform,"[23] the most important of which are the "right to remedy," or "access to court" guarantees;[24] explicit privacy

[19] *Id.*

[20] Lawrence Gene Sager, *Foreword: State Courts and the Strategic Space Between the Norms and Rules of Constitutional Law*, 63 TEX. L. REV. 959, 973–76 (1985).

[21] Helen Hershkoff, *Positive Rights and State Constitutions: The Limits of Federal Rationality Review*, 112 HARV. L. REV. 1131, 1136–38 (1999). *See also* Helen Hershkoff, *"Just Words": Common Law and the Enforcement of State Constitutional Social and Economic Rights*, 62 STAN. L. REV. 1521 (2010); EMILY ZACKIN, LOOKING FOR RIGHTS IN ALL THE WRONG PLACES: WHY STATE CONSTITUTIONS CONTAIN AMERICA'S POSITIVE RIGHTS (2013); Jeffery S. Sutton, *Courts as Change Agents: Do We Want More—Or Less?* 127 HARV. L. REV. 1419 (2014) (reviewing Zackin book); Lawrence Friedman, *Testing the Limits: Judicial Enforcement of Positive State Constitutional Rights*, 53 DUQUESNE L. REV. 437 (2015). For judicial treatment, see Butte Cmty. Union v. Lewis, 712 P.2d 1309, 1311 (Mont. 1986) (applying heightened scrutiny to classifications restricting welfare benefits because of the positive rights found in the Montana Constitution); Tucker v. Toia, 371 N.E.2d 449, 451–53 (N.Y. 1977) (relying on the positive rights found in the New York Constitution to strike down a limitation on public assistance even though the legislature had a rational reason to enact the limitation); McCleary v. State, 269 P.3d 227, 247–48 (Wash. 2012) (distinguishing positive and negative rights).

[22] Helen Hershkoff, *Foreword: Positive Rights and the Evolution of State Constitutions*, 33 RUTGERS L.J. 799, 805–09 (2002).

[23] Robert F. Williams, *Foreword: Tort Reform and State Constitutional Law*, 32 RUTGERS L.J. 897 (2001); Victor Schwartz & Leah Lorber, *Judicial Nullification of Civil Justice Reform Violates the Fundamental Federal Constitutional Principle of Separation of Powers: How to Restore the Right Balance*, 32 RUTGERS L.J. 907, 939–76 (2001); Robert S. Peck, *Tort Reform's Threat to an Independent Judiciary*, 33 RUTGERS L.J. 835 (2002); John Fabian Witt, *The Long History of State Constitutions and American Tort Law*, 36 RUTGERS L.J. 1159 (2005).

[24] FRIESEN, *supra* note 16, at ch. 6; David Schuman, *The Right to a Remedy*, 65 TEMP. L. REV. 1197 (1992); Jonathan M. Hoffman, *Questions Before Answers: The Ongoing Search to Understand the Origins of the Open Courts Clause*, 32 RUTGERS L.J. 1005 (2001). *See* Robert F. Williams, *State Constitutional Protection of Civil Litigation*, 70 RUTGERS U. L. REV. 905 (2018); *Can State Constitutions Block the Workers' Compensation Race to the Bottom?* 69 RUTGERS U. L. REV. 1081 (2017); Petersen v. Utah Labor Comm., 416 P.3d 583 (Utah 2017); Gibby v. Hobby Lobby Stores, Inc., 404 P.3d 44 (Okla. 2017); Hilburn v. Enerpipe Ltd., 42 P.3d 509 (Kan. 2019); Yanakos v. UMPC, 218 A.3d 1214 (Pa. 2019); Dan Friedman, Jackson v. Dackman Co.: *The Legislative Modification of Common Law Tort Remedies Under Article 19 of the Maryland Declaration of Rights*, 77 MD. L. REV. 949 (2018).

rights;[25] collective bargaining rights;[26] rights of arrestees and prisoners, the most well-known of which is the right not to be treated with "unnecessary rigor";[27] victims' rights;[28] the right to vote;[29] and environmental rights.[30]

[25] Friesen, *supra* note 16, at ch. 2; Jeffrey M. Shaman, Equality and Liberty in the Golden Age of State Constitutional Law 121–62 (2008); Ken Gormley & Rhonda G. Hartman, *Privacy and the States*, 65 Temp. L. Rev. 1279 (1992).

[26] Richard A. Goldberg & Robert F. Williams, *Farmworkers' Organizational and Collective Bargaining Rights in New Jersey: Implementing Self-Executing State Constitutional Rights*, 18 Rutgers L.J. 729 (1987); Alaine S. Williams, *Alternatives to the Right to Strike for Public Employees: Do They Adequately Implement Florida's Constitutional Right to Collectively Bargain?* 7 Fla. St. U. L. Rev. 475 (1979); United Public Workers, AFSCME v. Yogi, 58 P.3d 649 (Haw. 2002); Independence-National Education Assoc. v. Independence School Dist., 223 S.W.3d 131 (Mo. 2007).

[27] Sterling v. Cupp, 625 P.2d 123 (Or. 1981); State v. Lane, 826 S.E.2d 657 (W. Va. 2019); Worden v. Montana Bd. Pardons and Parole, 962 P.2d 1157 (Mont. 1998); *In re Lasure*, 666 S.E.2d 228 (S.C. 2008); People v. Sharpe, 839 N.E.2d 492 (Ill. 2005) (proportionate penalties); State v. Stanislaw, 65 A.3d 1242 (Me. 2013); State *ex rel.* Hatcher v. McBride, 656 S.E.2d 789 (W. Va. 2007); Washington Water Jet Workers Assoc. v. Yarbrough, 61 P.3d 309 (Wash. 2003) (prison labor); State v. Houston, 353 P.3d 55, 71–72 (Utah 2015); Scott Sandberg, Note, *Developing Jurisprudence on the Unnecessary Rigor Provision of the Utah Constitution*, 1996 Utah L. Rev. 751; Edgardo Rotman, *Criminal Law: Do Criminal Offenders Have a Constitutional Right to Rehabilitation?* 77 Crim. L. & Criminology 1023, 1062 (1986); Thomas A. Balmer, *Some Thoughts on Proportionality*, 87 Or. L. Rev. 783 (2008). *See also* Marcus Alexander Gadson, *Constitutionalizing Rehabilitation Did Not Work: Lessons from Indiana and Oregon and a Way Forward*, 54 Willamette L. Rev. 269 (2018); Richard Frase, *Limiting Excessive Prison Sentences Under Federal and State Constitutions*, 11 U. Pa. J. Const. L. 39 (2008); 2 Friesen, *supra* note 16, at ch. 13. Professor Caroline Davidson provides a comprehensive analysis of these and other related provisions in *State Constitutions and the Humane Treatment of Arrestees and Pretrial Detainees*, 19 Berkeley J. Crim. L. 1 (2014). *See also* Gregory S. Schneider, Note, *Sentencing Proportionality in the States*, 54 Ariz. L. Rev. 241 (2012); State v. Stanislaw, 65 A.3d 1242 (Me. 2013) (sentencing proportionality). More recent amendments have added purposes like public safety and retribution to these provisions. Michele Cotton, *Back with a Vengeance: The Resilience of Retribution as an Articulated Purpose of Criminal Punishment*, 37 Am. Crim. L. Rev. 1313 (2000).

[28] *See* Paul G. Cassell, *Balancing the Scales of Justice: The Case for and the Effects of Utah's Victims' Rights Amendment*, 1994 Utah L. Rev. 1373 (1994); *Symposium: The Unnecessary Victims' Rights Amendment*, 1999 Utah L. Rev. 443 (1999); Alice Koskela, *Victims' Rights Amendments: An Irresistible Political Force Transforms the Criminal Justice System*, 34 Idaho L. Rev. 157 (1997); Jeffrey A. Parness, Laura Lee, & Edmund Lanbe, *Monetary Recoveries for State Crime Victims*, 58 Clev. St. L. Rev. 819 (2010); *In re* Issuance of Summons, 908 N.W.2d 160, 165–67 (S.D. 2018); State v. Carlin, 249 P.3d 752, 758–59 (Alaska 2011).

[29] Joshua A. Douglas, *The Right to Vote Under State Constitutions*, 67 Vand. L. Rev. 89 (2014); Michael T. Morley, *Rethinking the Right to Vote Under State Constitutions*, 67 Vand. L. Rev. En Banc 189 (2014); *State Judges and the Right to Vote*, 77 Ohio St. L.J. 1 (2016); Derek T. Miller, *Complexity Confronting State Judges and the Right to Vote*, 71 Ohio St. L.J. Furthermore 65 (2016); David Schultz, *Voting Rights and the 2020 Election: New Judicial Federalism for the Right to Vote*, 104 Minn. L. Rev. Headnotes 41 (2020). *See* Chelsea Collaborative, Inc. v. Secretary of the Commonwealth, 100 N.E.3d 326, 330 nn.17–19 (Mass. 2018) (discussing right to vote under state constitution); League of Women Voters v. Commonwealth, 178 A.3d 737 (Pa. 2018) (striking down partisan gerrymandering). *Compare* Gentges v. State Election Bd., 419 P.3d 224 (Okla. 2018) (upholding voter ID requirement), *with* Applewhite v. Comm., 54 A.3d 1 (Pa. 2012) (remanding for trial on photo ID requirement).

[30] State constitutions contain a number of environmental rights provisions. *See* Barton H. Thompson Jr., *Environmental Policy and State Constitutions: The Potential Role of Substantive Guidance*, 27 Rutgers L.J. 863 (1996). After a period of nonenforcement, the Pennsylvania Supreme Court applied its environmental rights provision in the context of fracking. Robinson Twp. v. Commonwealth, 83 A.3d 901 (Pa. 2013). *See* John C. Dernbach, Kenneth T. Kristl, & James R. May, *Recognition of Environmental Rights for Pennsylvania Citizens:* Pennsylvania Environmental Defense Foundation v. Commonwealth of Pennsylvania, 70 Rutgers U. L. Rev. 803 (2018).

5. Limitations or mandates on government, such as the bans on special laws enacted by the legislature[31] or requirements that the legislature provide for a "uniform" or "thorough and efficient" education,[32] that are not contained within the Declaration of Rights but which are enforced by the courts as if they are rights provisions.[33]
6. "Unenumerated rights" provisions that are similar to the Ninth Amendment to the federal Constitution. Many state constitutions contain such provisions, some but not all of which were linked to natural law concepts.[34]

Finally, some state constitutions do not contain all of the rights that appear in the federal Constitution.[35] These are the kinds of distinctions between federal and state constitutional rights provisions that must be taken into account by state courts attentive to the lessons of the NJF.

Thus, it is now clear that state constitutional rights claims may be made either under provisions that are the same as, or similar to, federal constitutional rights guarantees or, rather, under state constitutional rights provisions that are quite different from federal constitutional rights guarantees. Often, in this latter situation, claims that may have been asserted under more familiar federal provisions may be repackaged under the less familiar state constitutional provisions.[36]

[31] *See* Chapter 9.

[32] INSTITUTE FOR EDUCATIONAL EQUITY AND OPPORTUNITY, EDUCATION IN THE 50 STATES: A DESKBOOK OF THE HISTORY OF STATE CONSTITUTIONS AND LAWS ABOUT EDUCATION (2008); Scott R. Bauries, *The Education Duty*, 47 WAKE FOREST L. REV. 705 (2012); *A Common Law Constitutionalism for the Right to Education*, 48 GA. L. REV. 949 (2014). *See* Jonathan Feldman, *Separation of Powers and Judicial Review of Positive Rights Claims: The Role of State Courts in an Era of Positive Government*, 24 RUTGERS L.J. 1057 (1993); Paul L. Tractenberg, *The Evolution and Implementation of Educational Rights Under the New Jersey Constitution of 1947*, 29 RUTGERS L.J. 827, 896–902, 933 (1998); Justin R. Long, Comment, *Enforcing Affirmative State Constitutional Obligations and* Sheff v. O'Neill, 151 U. PA. L. REV. 277 (2002).

[33] TARR, *supra* note 1, at 22. For an exhaustive catalog of rights present in each state constitution at the time the Fourteenth Amendment was ratified, see Steven G. Calabresi & Sarah E. Agudo, *Individual Rights Under State Constitutions When the Fourteenth Amendment Was Ratified in 1868: What Rights Are Deeply Rooted in American History and Tradition?* 87 TEX. L. REV. 7 (2008). *See also* Steven G. Calabresi et al., *Individual Rights Under State Constitutions in 2018: What Rights Are Deeply Rooted in a Modern-Day Consensus of the States?* 94 NOTRE DAME L. REV. 49 (2018).

[34] *See* Louis Karl Bonham, Note, *Unenumerated Rights Clauses in State Constitutions*, 63 TEX. L. REV. 1321 (1985); McCraken v. State, 518 P.2d 85 (Alaska 1974); Pro-Choice Mississippi v. Fordice, 716 So.2d 645 (Miss. 1998); Atwood v. Vilsack, 725 N.W.2d 641, 651–52 (Iowa 2006). *See also* Suzanna Sherry, *Natural Law in the States*, 61 U. CINN. L. REV. 171 (1992); Suzanna Sherry, *Foreword: State Constitutional Law: Doing the Right Thing*, 25 RUTGERS L.J. 935 (1994); Anthony B. Sanders, *Baby Ninth Amendments and Unenumerated Individual Rights in State Constitutions Before the Civil War*, 68 MERCER L. REV. 389 (2017); *Baby Ninth Amendments Since 1860 the Unenumerated Rights Americans Repeatedly Want (and Judges Often Don't*, 70 RUTGERS U. L. REV. 857 (2018).

[35] *See, e.g.*, State v. Michael J., 875 A.2d 510, 529 (Conn. 2005). *See also* Brennan Mancil, *Reviving Elusive Rights: State Constitutional Unenumerated Rights Clauses as Bounded Guarantors of Fundamental Liberties*, GEO. J.L. & PUB. POL'Y 281 (2021).

[36] *See* Robert F. Williams, *State Constitutional Law Processes*, 24 WM. & MARY L. REV. 169, 190–91 (1983).

Particularly in the first circumstance, where the state right is the same as, or similar to, the federal guarantee, legitimacy questions have been raised about state courts reaching results that are more liberal or protective of rights than those rendered under the federal Constitution.[37] Professor Tarr noted:

> For federal constitutional law, the primary legitimacy concern has involved the relation between the Unites States Supreme Court and other purportedly more democratic branches, such as Congress or state legislatures. For state constitutional law, in contrast, the major legitimacy concern has involved the relation between state courts and the U.S. Supreme Court: when can a state court interpret its state guarantees to reach a result different from that obtained by the Supreme Court interpreting the Federal Constitution?[38]

## I. THE FIRST STAGE: THE THRILL OF DISCOVERY

There were a number of factors contributing to the rise of the NJF. Probably the most important early case was *People v. Anderson*,[39] decided in 1972, where the California Supreme Court declared the death penalty unconstitutional under its state constitutional prohibition against cruel *or* unusual punishment.[40] This decision stimulated a substantial academic response and an initiated state constitutional amendment reinstating the death penalty,[41] as well as a dawning recognition by many lawyers, judges, and academics that state courts could "evade" decisions of the U.S. Supreme Court by relying on their own state constitutions.[42] In 1973, the wave of litigation on equality and adequacy in school finance was launched in California and New Jersey,[43] and it is still going on today.[44]

[37] G. Alan Tarr, *Constitutional Theory, and State Constitutional Interpretation*, 22 RUTGERS L.J. 841, 853 (1991). *See also* TARR, *supra* note 1, at 175.

[38] Tarr, *Constitutional Theory*, *supra* note 37, at 853.

[39] 493 P.2d 880 (Cal. 1972).

[40] *Id.* at 899. In 2012, the Connecticut Legislature abolished capital punishment prospectively. Then, in 2015, the Connecticut Supreme Court declared that pre-2012 death penalties violated the state constitutional cruel and unusual punishments clause. State v. Santiago, 122 A.3d 1 (Conn. 2015).

[41] *See, e.g.*, Scott H. Bice, *Anderson and the Adequate State Ground*, 45 S. CAL. L. REV. 750 (1972); Jerome B. Falk Jr., *Foreword: The State Constitution: A More Than "Adequate" Nonfederal Ground*, 61 CAL. L. REV. 273 (1973); Donald R. Wright, *The Role of the Judiciary: From Marbury to Anderson*, 60 CAL. L. REV. 1262 (1972); Edward L. Barrett Jr., *Comment, Anderson and the Judicial Function*, 45 S. CAL. L. REV. 739 (1972). *Anderson* was overruled by Article I, Section 27 of the California Constitution, ratified only a few months later. *See infra* note 99 and accompanying text.

[42] Donald E. Wilkes Jr., *The New Federalism in Criminal Procedure: State Court Evasion of the Burger Court*, 62 KY. L. REV. 421, 425 (1974).

[43] Jeffrey S. Sutton, San Antonio Independent School District v. Rodriguez *and Its Aftermath*, 94 VA. L. REV. 1963 (2008); Tractenberg, *supra* note 32, at 892–930.

[44] *See* Abbott v. Burke, 960 A.2d 360 (N.J. 2008) (concerning the most recent education finance statute); Abbott v. Burke, 798 A.2d 602 (N.J. 2002) (issuing an additional order in New Jersey's ongoing school finance litigation governing the 2002–2003 school year); Tractenberg, *supra* note 32, at

These and a number of other, primarily criminal procedure cases, both resulted from, and further stimulated, a flash of insight, or click of a light bulb, that state courts could, in fact, disagree with the decisions of the U.S. Supreme Court that declined to recognize *federal* constitutional rights. It was as though there was a parallel universe of constitutional law that had always been there but that had gone unrecognized. It was, of course, not identical to the universe of federal constitutional law. Notwithstanding the many ways in which it was different, it could be brought to bear on almost all of the constitutional questions that had been submitted as matters of federal constitutional law. The arguments had to be limited *spacially* to state-by-state presentation, but *substantively*, this alternative state constitutional law universe was there waiting to be explored. This was a very exciting, and sometimes daunting, prospect for lawyers and state judges.

In 1980, the U.S. Supreme Court decided *PruneYard Shopping Ctr. v. Robins*, upholding, against federal constitutional challenge, the California Supreme Court's recognition of free speech rights under the California Constitution in privately owned shopping malls.[45] In this way, the U.S. Supreme Court placed its early imprimatur on the NJF.

The following 1982 statement by Justice Stevens for a Supreme Court *majority* is important:

> As a number of recent State Supreme Court decisions demonstrate, a state court is entirely free to read its own State's constitution more broadly than this Court reads the Federal Constitution, or to reject the mode of analysis used by this Court in favor of a different analysis of its corresponding constitutional guarantee.[46]

As indicated by this quotation, the high court was comfortable, or even in a sense encouraging, in its acknowledgment that state courts are free, under their own state constitutions or even statutes, court rules, and common law, to render decisions that are more protective than the Supreme Court's interpretations

930–36 (discussing history of New Jersey's school finance litigation); EDUCATION LAW CENTER, THE HISTORY OF ABBOT V. BURKE, (https://edlawcenter.org/litigation/abbott-v-burke/abbott-history.html) (last visited Nov. 18, 2019).

[45] 447 U.S. 74 (1980).

[46] City of Mesquite v. Aladdin's Castle, Inc., 455 U.S. 283, 293 (1982) (*citing* William J. Brennan Jr., *State Constitutions and the Protection of Individual Rights*, 90 HARV. L. REV. 489 (1977)). Justice John Paul Stevens went on to write a number of opinions like Justice Brennan, encouraging state courts to develop independent state constitutional interpretation in rights cases. *See, e.g.*, Pennsylvania v. Finley, 481 U.S. 551, 570–72 (1987) (Stevens, J., dissenting); Delaware v. Van Arsdall, 475 U.S. 673, 689–708 (1986) (Stevens, J., dissenting); Michigan v. Long, 463 U.S. 1032, 1065–72 (1983) (Stevens, J., dissenting). *See generally* Ronald K.L. Collins, *Justice Stevens Becomes Advocate of States' Role in the High Court*, 6 NAT'L. L.J. 1 (1984).

of federal constitutional rights, which establish a national minimum standard under the U.S. Constitution's Supremacy Clause.[47] Opinions of members of the majority of the U.S. Supreme Court therefore were in line with the *dissenting opinions* of justices in other cases encouraging state courts to "diverge" from the national minimum standard of rights.[48] Again, state judges should take heed of statements such as those quoted earlier, and similar statements, such as: "Our reasoning in *Lloyd*, however, does not *ex proprio vigore* limit the authority of the State to exercise its police power or its sovereign right to adopt in its own Constitution individual liberties more expansive than those conferred by the Federal Constitution."[49] Justice Scalia, in a death penalty sentencing case, noted: "The state courts may experiment all they want with their own constitutions, and often do in the wake of this Court's decisions."[50] Based on all of these statements, state judges should not feel any discomfort in "going beyond" the Supreme Court or even in disagreeing with it in the process of interpreting their own state constitutions.

As noted at the start of this chapter, Justice William J. Brennan Jr. can be credited with first stimulating the re-emergence of state constitutional law.[51] His 1977 *Harvard Law Review* article, *State Constitutions and the Protection of Individual Rights*,[52] has already taken its place among "the most frequently cited law review articles of modern times."[53] In that article, Justice Brennan noted the

[47] *See* U.S. CONST. art. VI, cl. 2.

[48] *See, e.g.*, Michigan v. Mosley, 423 U.S. 96, 120 (1975) (Brennan, J., dissenting); *see also* William J. Brennan Jr., *In Defense of Dissents*, 37 HASTINGS L.J. 427, 430 (1986). As Professor Williams has observed:

> Supreme Court dissents can and do have a significant impact upon state courts confronting the same constitutional problem the dissenter believes the Court decided incorrectly. In this sense, state courts have become a new audience for Supreme Court dissents on federal constitutional questions that may also arise under state constitutions. Thus, dissenters may be vindicated more quickly, but only on a state-by-state basis.

Robert F. Williams, *In the Supreme Court's Shadow: Legitimacy of State Rejection of Supreme Court Reasoning and Result*, 35 S.C. L. REV. 353, 375–76 (1984). *See* State v. Mattson, 226 P.3d 482, 496 (Haw. 2010); State v. Mandon, 219 P.3d 1126, 1153–54 (Haw. 2009).

[49] Pruneyard Shopping Ctr. V. Robbins, 447 U.S. 74, 81 (1980); *accord* Florida v. Powell, 559 U.S. 50, 59 (2010); Arizona v. Evans, 514 U.S. 1, 8 (1995); Harmelin v. Michigan, 501 U.S. 957, 982 (1991); Nichols v. United States, 511 U.S. 738, 748–49 n.12 (1994); Oregon v. Hass, 420 U.S. 714, 719 (1975); Cooper v. California, 386 U.S. 58, 62 (1967); Minnesota v. National Tea Co., 309 U.S. 551, 557 (1940).

[50] Kansas v. Carr, 136 S.Ct. 633, 641 (2016). *See also* Montejo v. Louisiana, 556 U.S. 778 (2009), and *supra* notes 11 and 46.

[51] *See, e.g.*, James A. Gardner, *The Failed Discourse of State Constitutionalism*, 90 MICH. L. REV. 761, 762 (1992). For accounts and assessments of the origins of the NJF, see G. Alan Tarr, *The New Judicial Federalism in Perspective*, 72 NOTRE DAME L. REV. 1097 (1997); Robert F. Williams, *Foreword: Looking Back at the New Judicial Federalism's First Generation*, 30 VAL. U. L. REV. at xiii (1996).

[52] William J. Brennan Jr., *State Constitutions and the Protection of Individual Rights*, 90 HARV. L. REV. 489 (1977).

[53] Ann Lousin, *Justice Brennan: A Tribute to a Federal Judge Who Believes in State's Rights*, 20 J. MARSHALL L. REV. 1, 2 n.3 (1986) (*citing* Fred R. Shapiro, *The Most-Cited Law Review Articles*, 73 CAL. L. REV. 1540, 1550 (1985), "which found [in 1985] Brennan's article to be the nineteenth

rise of federal constitutional rights protections and the influence of that development on the work of state courts. He also criticized the trend toward lesser protections reflected in the U.S. Supreme Court's pronouncements and pointed out that state courts had been "step[ping] into the breach" by interpreting their state constitutions to provide more rights protections than required under the federal Constitution.[54] In now oft-quoted words, he stated:

> State constitutions, too, are a font of individual liberties, their protections often extending beyond those required by the Supreme Court's interpretation of federal law. The legal revolution which has brought federal law to the fore must not be allowed to inhibit the independent protective force of state law—for without it, the full realization of our liberties cannot be guaranteed.[55]

Fittingly, since he had begun his judicial career as a New Jersey judge, it is important to note that Justice Brennan had a deep, earlier interest in state constitutional law, and the 1977 article was the text of a speech he had delivered to the New Jersey State Bar Association on May 22, 1976.[56] Justice Stewart G. Pollock of New Jersey referred to Brennan's article as "the Magna Carta of state constitutional law."[57]

Reviewing the NJF and Justice Brennan's impact, California Supreme Court Justice Godwin Liu concluded that the "redundancy" in the federal and state rights guarantees is an extremely positive attribute of American constitutionalism.[58] Justice Liu said: "The redundancies built into our structure of government largely serve to channel and manage conflict rather than to facilitate permanent resolution."[59] He continued:

most-frequently-cited law review article of those published in the last forty years"). There were, however, several earlier, important contributions. *See, e.g.*, Robert Force, *State "Bills of Rights": A Case of Neglect and the Need for a Renaissance*, 3 VAL. U. L. REV. 125 (1969); John M. Steel, *The Role for a Bill of Rights in a Modern State Constitution*, 45 WASH. L. REV. 453 (1970); *Project Report: Toward an Activist Role for State Bills of Rights*, 8 HARV. C.R.-C.L.L. REV. 271 (1973); Donald E. Wilkes Jr., *The New Federalism in Criminal Procedure: State Court Evasion of the Burger Court*, 62 KY. L.J. 421, 425 (1974); Donald E. Wilkes Jr., *More on the New Federalism in Criminal Procedure*, 63 KY. L.J. 873 (1975); Donald E. Wilkes Jr., *The New Federalism in Criminal Procedure Revisited*, 64 KY. L.J. 729 (1976); A.E. Dick Howard, *State Courts and Constitutional Rights in the Day of the Burger Court*, 62 VA. L. REV. 873 (1976).

[54] *See* Brennan, *supra* note 52, at 502–03.

[55] *Id.* at 491.

[56] Robert F. Williams, *Justice Brennan, The New Jersey Supreme Court, and State Constitutions: The Evolution of a State Constitutional Consciousness*, 29 RUTGERS L.J. 763, 765 (1998).

[57] Stewart G. Pollock, *State Constitutions as Separate Sources of Fundamental Rights*, 35 RUTGERS L. REV. 707, 716 (1983).

[58] Honorable Goodwin Liu, *Brennan Lecture, State Constitutions and the Protection of Individual Rights: A Reappraisal*, 92 N.Y.U. L. REV. 1307 (2017); *see also* Jeffrey S. Sutton, *A Response to Justice Goodwin Liu*, 128 YALE L.J. 936, 937, 941 (2019).

[59] *Id.* at 1335.

> State constitutionalism is properly understood as a mechanism by which ongoing disagreement over fundamental principles is acknowledged and channeled in our democracy. Far from endangering the legitimacy of constitutional law, interpretive pluralism is a source of its resilience and deep resonance with our diverse citizenry. When a state court departs from Supreme Court precedent to secure greater protection for individual rights under a parallel provision of its state constitution, the state court "registers a forceful and often very public dissent." Whether or not it influences other states or eventually induces the Supreme Court to reconsider its precedent, the state decision carries forward a dialogue over the meaning of our basic liberties. In short, state constitutionalism is one way in which our structure of government provides an outlet for constitutional conflict.[60]

Between the 1920s and the late 1940s, the *American Political Science Review* published an annual article on state constitutional law.[61] A development, probably attributable to the NJF is the increased interest of political scientists in the area of state constitutionalism. After Alan Tarr[62] and John Dinan[63] "reopened the study of state constitutionalism,"[64] they have been followed by Emily Zackin,[65] Amy Bridges,[66] Paul Herron,[67] John Dinan again,[68]

[60] *Id.* at 1336.

[61] *See, e.g.*, Jacobus tenBroek & Howard Jay Graham, *State Constitutional Law in 1945–1946*, 40 Am. Pol. Sci. Rev. 703 (1946); J. Alton Burdine, *Basic Materials for the Study of State Constitutions and State Constitutional Development*, 48 Am. Pol. Sci. Rev. 1140 (1954). *See also* William F. Swindler, *State Constitutions for the 20th Century*, 50 Neb. L. Rev. 577, 587 n.54 (1971) ("[T]his excellent twenty-year series of annual surveys was discontinued in 1949. The present writer has hopes of seeing the series revived in the near future."). The series has not been revived and your authors, many years later, still maintain a similar hope.

[62] G. Alan Tarr, Understanding State Constitutions (1998).

[63] John J. Dinan, The American State Constitutional Tradition (2006).

[64] Robinson Woodward-Burns, *The State Constitutions' Influence on American Political Development*, 81 J. Pol. e85, e85 (2019).

[65] Emily Zackin, Looking for Rights in All the Wrong Places: Why State Constitutions Contain America's Positive Rights (2012);Mila Versteeg & Emily Zackin, *American Constitutional Exceptionalism Revisited*, 81 U. Chi. L. Rev. 101 (2014); Mila Versteeg & Emily Zackin, *Constitutions Unentrenched: Toward an Alternative Theory of Constitutional Design*, 110 Am. Pol. Sci. Rev. 657 (Nov. 2016).

[66] Amy Bridges, Democratic Beginnings: Founding the Western States (2015); Amy Bridges *Managing the Periphery in the Gilded Age: Writing Constitutions for the Western States*, 22 Stud. Am. Pol. Dev. 32 (2008).

[67] Paul E. Herron, Framing the Solid South: The State Constitutional Conventions of Succession, Reconstruction, and Redemption, 1860–1902 (2017); Paul E. Herron, *Upon the Shores of an Unknown Sea*, 69 Rutgers U. L. Rev. 1433 (2017) (reviewing Amy Bridges, Democratic Beginnings: Founding the Western States (2015)).

[68] John Dinan, State Constitutional Politics: Governing by Amendment in the American States (2018).

Robinson Woodward-Burns,[69] Adam Brown,[70] Keith Whittington,[71] and Sean Beienburg,[72] among others.

But the most important early work on state constitutional rights (and on state constitutional law generally) was that of professor and former justice of the Oregon Supreme Court, Hans A. Linde. His work, both academic and judicial, is a central feature in the growth of the NJF.[73] Linde's achievements in state constitutional law[74] span and also reflect the events of the first generation of the NJF. His work has been described as "one of this century's most important judicial contributions . . ."[75] Professor Sanford Levinson has stated that Justice Linde is "easily one of the three most important state court judges in this century," comparing his work to that of Benjamin Cardozo and Roger Traynor.[76]

Finally, during this first stage of the NJF, the U.S. Supreme Court ironed out questions regarding its jurisdiction in mixed federal and state constitutional cases, with its adoption of the "plain statement" requirement for invoking the adequate and independent state ground doctrine. Pursuant to this doctrine, state court decisions are final, and the U.S. Supreme Court has no jurisdiction to review them when they are based on adequate and independent state law ground such as the state constitution.[77] Because of the dominance of federal constitutional doctrine, it is not surprising that state courts often wrote opinions mixing state and federal doctrine in ways that made it difficult, when U.S. Supreme Court review was sought, to tell if the state decision was based on an adequate and independent state ground. In 1983, the Court sought to resolve the problem; in *Michigan v. Long*,[78] Justice Sandra Day O'Connor announced:

[69] *Supra* note 64; *see* ROBINSON WOODWARD-BURNS, HIDDEN LAWS: HOW STATE CONSTITUTIONS STABILIZE AMERICAN POLITICS (2021).

[70] Adam R. Brown & Jeremy C. Pope, *Measuring and Manipulating Constitutional Evaluations in the States: Legitimacy Versus Veneration*, 47 AM. POL. RES. 1135 (2019).

[71] Keith E. Whittington, *State Constitutional Law in the New Deal Period*, 67 RUTGERS U. L. REV. 1141 (2015); *Some Dilemmas in Drawing the Public/Private Distinction in New Deal Era State Constitutional Law*, 75 MD. L. REV. 1 (2015).

[72] Sean Beienburg, *Contesting the U.S. Constitution Through State Amendments: The 2011 and 2012 Elections*, 129 POL. SCI. Q. 55 (2014).

[73] Joseph R. Grodin, *State Constitutionalism in Practice*, 30 VAL. U. L. REV. 601 (1996).

[74] INTELLECT AND CRAFT: THE CONTRIBUTIONS OF JUSTICE HANS LINDE TO AMERICAN CONSTITUTIONALISM (Robert F. Nagel ed., 1995) [hereinafter INTELLECT AND CRAFT]. There were a number of tributes to Justice Linde in 1984 ANN. SURV. AM. L., at vvi (1984).

[75] Louis H. Pollak, *Judge-Professor Linde*, 70 OR. L. REV. 679, 682 (1991), *quoted in* INTELLECT AND CRAFT, *supra* note 74, at 3 n.2.

[76] Sanford Levinson, *Tiers of Scrutiny—From Strict Through Rational Bases—And the Future of Interests: Commentary on Fiss and Linde*, 55 ALB. L. REV. 745, 746 (1992), *quoted in* INTELLECT AND CRAFT, *supra* note 74, at 3 n.3.

[77] Stewart G. Pollock, *Adequate and Independent State Grounds as a Means of Balancing the Relationship Between State and Federal Courts*, 63 TEX. L. REV. 977 (1985).

[78] 463 U.S. 1032 (1983). *See* Martin H. Redish, *Supreme Court Review of State Court "Federal" Decisions: A Study in Interactive Federalism*, 19 GA. L. REV. 861 (1985); Michael E. Solimine, *Supreme Court Monitoring of State Courts in the Twenty-First Century*, 35 IND. L. REV. 335, 339–44 (2002).

> Accordingly, when, as in this case, a state court decision fairly appears to rest primarily on federal law, or to be interwoven with the federal law, and when the adequacy and independence of any possible state law ground is not clear from the face of the opinion, we will accept as the most reasonable explanation that the state court decided the case the way it did because it believed that federal law required it to do so. If a state court chooses merely to rely on federal precedents as it would on the precedents of all other jurisdictions, then it need only make clear by a *plain statement* in its judgment or opinion that the federal cases are being used only for the purpose of guidance, and do not themselves compel the result that the court has reached. In this way, both justice and judicial administration will be greatly improved. If the state court decision indicates clearly and expressly that it is alternatively based on bona fide separate, adequate, and independent grounds, we, of course, will not undertake to review the decision.[79]

This approach, although criticized by Justice John Paul Stevens[80] and, later, by Justice Ruth Bader Ginsburg,[81] once again called national attention to and validated the field of state constitutional law, while providing guidance for state courts to ensure their state constitutional law rulings were final.

Interestingly, many state constitutional decisions since *Michigan v. Long* have not utilized the simple "plain statement."[82] Dr. Barry Latzer provided a possible explanation for this phenomenon:

> [L]aw-ambiguity may be viewed as a mark of caution: perhaps the failure to "commit" state law to a position is a way of preserving future interpretive options, so that the court could someday say that the previous case was not construing the state constitution after all.[83]

[79] *Long*, 463 U.S. at 1040–41 (emphasis added). *See* Sandra Day O'Conner, *Our Judicial Federalism*, 35 Case W. Res. L. Rev. 1, 5–9 (1984–1985); Friesen, *supra* note 16, at § 1.07.

[80] *Long*, 463 U.S. at 1065–72 (Stevens, J., dissenting). In *Harris v. Reed*, 489 U.S. 255 (1989), the Court expanded the plain statement requirement to habeas corpus. *See also* Coleman v. Thompson, 501 U.S. 722, 735–40 (1991). Justice Stevens continued his criticism in *Brigham City v. Stuart*, 547 U.S. 398, 407 (2006) (Stevens, J., concurring). For Justice Stevens' criticism of cases being brought to the Court even though based on adequate and independent state grounds, see California v. Carney, 471 U.S. 386, 396 (1985) (Stevens, J., dissenting).

[81] Arizona v. Evans, 514 U.S. 1, 24, 30–32 (1995) (Ginsburg, J., dissenting); Ohio v. Robinette, 519 U.S. 33, 40–45 (1996) (Ginsberg, J., concurring).

[82] A survey of over five hundred decisions, from all fifty states, between the 1983 *Michigan v. Long* decision and the beginning of 1988, concluded that "few states have adopted a consistent, concise way of communicating the bases for their constitutional decisions." Felicia A. Rosenfeld, Note, *Fulfilling the Goals of* Michigan v. Long: *The State Court Reaction*, 56 Fordham L. Rev. 1041, 1068 (1988). *See* Mathew G. Simon, Note, *Revisiting* Michigan v. Long *After Twenty Years*, 66 Alb. L. Rev. 969, 970 (2003), for a similar conclusion many years later. *See also* Donna M. Nakagiri, Comment, *Developing State Constitutional Jurisprudence After* Michigan v. Long: *Suggestions for Opinion Writing and Systemic Change*, 1998 Mich. St. L. Rev. 807 (1998); Michael Esler, Michigan v. Long: *A Twenty Year Retrospective*, 66 Alb. L. Rev. 835 (2003); Ken Gormley, *The Silver Anniversary of New Judicial Federalism*, 66 Alb. L. Rev. 797 (2003).

[83] Barry Latzer, *Into the'90s: More Evidence that the Revolution Has a Conservative Underbelly*, 4 Emerging Issues St. Const. L. 17, 31–32 (1991).

By contrast, Professor Ann Althouse has argued that the *Michigan v. Long* "plain statement" requirement eliminates "law ambiguity" as a choice for state judges:

> State judges who want to expand the rights of an unpopular group, such as the criminally accused, may not want to call attention to their independence and thereby make themselves targets for political retaliation. By obscuring the source of the expanded rights they announce, state judges may create the impression that they act under the coercion of federal law and thus deflect voter wrath . . . Justice O'Connor's presumption forces state judges to endure one form of scrutiny or [possible U.S. Supreme Court review] and deprives them of the ability to immunize themselves with ambiguity.[84]

As the NJF has matured, the adequate and independent state ground doctrine has often become a *criminal defendant's* argument, used to shield protective state constitutional judgments from a prosecutor's petition for U.S. Supreme Court review.[85] Prior to the NJF, the doctrine was most often used as a *prosecutor's* argument, used to shield state criminal procedure judgments (arguably below federal constitutional standards) from defendants' petitions for U.S. Supreme Court review.[86]

The field of criminal procedure generally has, in many ways, provided the driving force behind the NJF. It is in this area that state courts first realized they could reach results different from those reached by the U.S. Supreme Court, or at least consider doing so. It is understandable that criminal procedure cases, after the post-incorporation Warren Court years, formed the bulk of the early cases on the NJF. As Professor Jennifer Friesen observed, criminal procedure "cases applying state constitutions are plentiful, in large part because attorneys are paid to file and brief them."[87] She also noted that criminal procedure cases

[84] Ann Althouse, *Variations on a Theory of Normative Federalism: A Supreme Court Dialogue*, 42 Duke L.J. 979, 988–89 (1993) (footnote omitted). Professor Edward Hartnett has provided an elaborate criticism of the U.S. Supreme Court's interpretation of its jurisdictional statutes to permit appeals by *state officials* to the Supreme Court from their own courts' federal constitutional rulings. He argues that this possibility (which he sees as improper under the statutes) militates against use of adequate and independent state grounds by state judges. Edward Hartnett, *Why Is The Supreme Court of the United States Protecting State Judges from Popular Democracy?* 75 Tex. L. Rev. 907 (1997).

[85] Robert C. Welsh, *Whose Federalism?—The Burger Court's Treatment of State Civil Liberties Judgments*, 10 Hastings Const. L.Q. 819 (1983).

[86] *See, e.g.*, Williams v. State, 82 S.E.2d 217 (Ga. 1954), *remanded*, Williams v. Georgia, 349 U.S. 375 (1955), *on remand*, Williams v. State, 88 S.E.2d 376 (Ga. 1955), *cert. denied*, 350 U.S. 950 (1956); Walter Murphy, *Lower Court Checks on Supreme Court Power*, 53 Am. Pol. Sci. Rev. 1017, 1021 (1959).

[87] Jennifer Friesen, *Recovering Damages for State Bills of Rights Claims*, 63 Tex. L. Rev. 1269, 1270 (1985). *See also* Shirley S. Abrahamson, *Criminal Law and State Constitutions: The Emergence of State Constitutional Law*, 63 Tex. L. Rev. 1141, 1148–49 (1985) ("The sheer number of state criminal cases and the relation between the protection offered by state and federal constitutions means that the state courts have many opportunities to rule on both federal and state constitutional issues. Thus, state criminal cases provide a rich source of material to study vertical and horizontal federalism.") (internal footnotes omitted)); Ken Gormley, *Special Project, State Constitutions and Criminal Procedure: A*

were of a "higher visibility and drama" than civil cases.[88] Lawyers are already in court defending criminal charges, so state constitutional criminal procedure arguments are easier to make. Also, often the outcome of some arguments, such as search and seizure, will dictate the disposition of the entire case, and, as Justice Shirley Abrahamson of Wisconsin pointed out, criminal law is of special *state* concern:

> Criminal law is an area of traditional concern for state judges. It is an area of law in which state judges have special experience and expertise. The very bulk of the criminal cases in the state trial court may justify a state's attempt to formulate rules to achieve stability of state law, relatively free of the changes wrought by the United States Supreme Court, and to achieve uniformity within the state judicial system. Because of the state supreme courts' supervisory power over trial courts and procedural rules, it may be easier to develop independence in criminal procedural law than in other areas of constitutional law.[89]

In 1982, the *Harvard Law Review* devoted its prestigious "Developments in the Law" survey to state constitutional rights cases: "The Interpretation of State Constitutional Rights."[90] This recognition provided another important seal of approval on the NJF.

In 1984, an important conference bringing together scholars and state supreme court justices took place at the Marshall-Wythe School of Law of the College of William and Mary, under the co-sponsorship of the Conference of Chief Justices and the National Center for State Courts. The important contributions to the conference were published in book form by West Publishing Company.[91] The next year, another important symposium took place at the University of Texas Law School.[92] In 1987, the National Association of Attorneys General (NAAG) began publishing its *State Constitutional Law Bulletin*, which provided information on recent cases and other developments in state constitutional law and has since been discontinued.[93] NAAG also started an annual law review in 1988, *Emerging Issues in State Constitutional Law*, which has also been discontinued.

*Primer for the 21st Century*, 67 Or. L. Rev. 689, 695 (1988) ("Perhaps the greatest and most immediate impact of state constitutional law has been in the area of criminal law and procedure.").

[88] Friesen, *supra* note 87, at 1270.
[89] Abrahamson, *supra* note 87, at 1150.
[90] *Developments in the Law: The Interpretation of State Constitutional Rights*, 95 Harv. L. Rev. 1324 (1982).
[91] Developments in State Constitutional Law: The Williamsburg Conference (Bradley D. McGraw ed., 1985).
[92] *Symposium: The Emergence of State Constitutional Law*, 63 Tex. L. Rev. 959 (1985).
[93] *See* Friedman v. Commissioner of Pub. Safety, 473 N.W.2d 828, 831 n.1 (Minn. 1991).

In October, 1988, the now-defunct Advisory Commission on Intergovernmental Relations, then under the leadership of Dr. John Kincaid, published the first casebook on state constitutional law, by Williams,[94] the precursor to the current Carolina Academic Press casebook, now in its fifth edition.[95] The *Rutgers Law Journal*, now *Rutgers University Law Review*, in 1989 began publishing its Annual Issue on State Constitutional Law, still an annual publication featuring an invited Foreword, scholarly articles, and student comments on leading state constitutional law cases.[96] Also in 1989, the first issue of the quarterly *State Constitutional Commentaries and Notes* (also now discontinued) appeared, under the editorship of Stanley H. Friedelbaum. Finally, in 1990 Greenwood Press initiated a fifty-state series of single-volume reference works on each state constitution. Oxford University Press acquired the series and has continued it as *The Oxford Commentaries on the State Constitutions of the United States*.

Currently, a small but growing number of law schools offer courses or seminars on state constitutional law that treat the topic on an "all states" rather than a state-specific basis. Virtually all of these courses were developed after the late 1970s, and many more have been developed recently. Many other law schools offer state-specific courses. Although these courses focus primarily on the text, history, and interpretation of a single state's constitution, they are increasingly including comparative materials from other states. In addition, programs on state constitutional law have been held at annual meetings of the Association of American Law Schools.[97]

In what was both a cause and effect of the NJF, there was an explosion of law review literature on a variety of topics in state constitutional law by students, judges, and academic authors. This academic literature built upon itself and led to many symposia in law reviews across the country. These publications analyzed the emerging judicial embrace of state constitutional law and, in turn, were cited by lawyers and the state courts in future decisions. In addition, the literature began to cross state lines ("trans-state"), analyzing certain common provisions in state constitutional law more broadly.[98]

[94] State Constitutional Law: Cases and Materials (Robert F. Williams compiler, 1988, ACIR Publication # M-159).

[95] Robert F. Williams & Lawrence Friedman, State Constitutional Law: Cases and Materials (5th ed. 2015).

[96] *See, e.g.*, Robert F. Williams & G. Alan Tarr, *Rutgers Law Journal: Twenty-Five Years of State Constitutionalism*, 44 Rutgers L.J. 547 (2014).

[97] *See* Shirley S. Abrahamson, *Reincarnation of State Courts*, 36 Sw. L.J. 951, 964 n.46 (1982) (describing "standing room only" AALS program on state constitutional law). Programs on state constitutional law were held at the AALS convention from 1982 to 1988. There are also periodic programs on state constitutional law at the annual meeting of the American Political Science Association.

[98] Daniel B. Rodriguez, *State Constitutional Theory and Its Prospects*, 28 N.M. L. Rev. 271, 301-02 (1998).

## II. THE SECOND STAGE: BACKLASH

Beginning in the 1980s, but tracing its roots in the reaction to the 1972 California decision in *People v. Anderson*,[99] a backlash against the NJF arose. Academics, government officials, and judges spoke out in various forums opposing state decisions "going beyond" the national minimum standards. Prosecutors, particularly those who had been elected, remained especially critical of state constitutional criminal procedure decisions providing more protections than those required by the U.S. Supreme Court.[100] They argued that state court judges' disagreement with the outcome of similar rights claims in the U.S. Supreme Court did not justify substitution of their judgment for those federal outcomes at the state level.[101]

In some states, amendments to state constitutions were proposed to the electorate that would overturn state court interpretations that were more protective than federal constitutional rights. The development of the NJF, therefore, has shown that the exercise of popular sovereignty, or voting by the electorate, cannot only be used to add new rights but to literally overturn or "overrule" judicial interpretations of state constitutional rights guarantees (or, for that matter, other state constitutional provisions). Such overruling can be accomplished either through legislatively proposed amendments; constitutional convention proposals; or, in those states that permit it, popularly initiated constitutional amendments.

There are two different approaches. First, state constitutional decisions can be overruled simply by amending the constitution to say that the judicial interpretation no longer applies. For example, several states, such as California, have overturned state judicial decisions declaring the death penalty unconstitutional by inserting language in the relevant constitutional clauses to indicate that capital punishment will not be deemed to violate the clause.[102] Illustrating a different approach, after some expansive state judicial interpretations, the people in 1982 ratified an amendment to Florida's search and seizure clause

[99] 493 P.2d 880 (Cal. 1972). *See supra* notes 39–40 and accompanying text. Justice Stewart cited the California amendment in his plurality opinion in *Gregg v. Georgia*, 428 U.S. 153, 181 (1976), upholding the death penalty.

[100] *See generally* John B. Wefing, *The New Jersey Supreme Court 1948–1998: Fifty Years of Independence and Activism*, 29 Rutgers L.J. 701, 721 (1998) (noting that as a result of a New Jersey Supreme Court decision finding broader protection for defendants who confessed in police custody than had the U.S. Supreme Court, "a brutal murderer ended up only serving eight years and then was released. If the prosecutor had been running for office that year, he or she would undoubtedly have attacked the court's decision.").

[101] Professor Williams took the position that reasoned disagreement was justified in Robert F. Williams, *In the Supreme Court's Shadow: Legitimacy of State Rejection of Supreme Court Reasoning and Result*, 35 S.C. L. Rev. 353, 389–404 (1984). The Arkansas Supreme Court recognized this point in *Griffin v. State*, 67 S.W.3d 582 (Ark. 2002). *But see* People v. Haley, 41 P.3d 666, 679–80 (Colo. 2001) (Kourlis, J., dissenting).

[102] On November 2, 1982, the Massachusetts voters approved a constitutional amendment that added a second and third sentence to Article 26:

requiring the state courts to interpret the provision the same way as the U.S. Supreme Court interprets the federal clause.[103] This also happened in California to eliminate a line of state constitutional interpretations that went beyond the federal requirements in the area of school busing.[104] This Florida and California "lockstep" or "forced linkage" amendment approach can be seen as undesirable because it constitutes a blanket adoption, *in futuro*, of all interpretations of the U.S. Supreme Court, thereby abdicating a part of a state's sovereignty and

> No provision of the Constitution, however, shall be construed as prohibiting the imposition of the punishment of death. The general court may, for the purpose of protecting the general welfare of the citizens, authorize the imposition of the punishment of death by the courts of law having jurisdiction of crimes subject to the punishment of death.
>
> MASS. CONST. amend. art. CXVI. *See also* CAL. CONST. art. I, § 27; OR. CONST. art. I, § 40. Donald E. Wilkes Jr. described this phenomenon as a "part of the overall trend toward law and order and increased emphasis on crime control, even at the cost of individual rights." Donald E. Wilkes Jr., *First Things Last: Amendomania and State Bills of Rights*, 54 MISS. L.J. 223, 250 (1984). *See also* Lynn A. Baker, *Constitutional Change and Direct Democracy*, 66 U. COLO. L. REV. 143 (1995).

John Dinan calls these kinds of amendments "court-responsive amendments." JOHN DINAN, STATE CONSTITUTIONAL POLITICS: GOVERNING BY AMENDMENT IN THE AMERICAN STATES 109 (2018).

[103] The Florida clause reads as follows:

> The right of the people to be secure in their persons, houses, papers and effects against unreasonable searches and seizures, and against the unreasonable interception of private communications by any means, shall not be violated. . . . This right shall be construed *in conformity with* the 4th Amendment to the United States Constitution, as interpreted by the United States Supreme Court. Articles or information obtained in violation of this right shall not be admissible in evidence if such articles or information would be inadmissible under decisions of the United States Supreme Court construing the 4th Amendment to the United States Constitution.
>
> FLA. CONST. art. I, § 12 (emphasis added). *See also* FLA. CONST. art. I, § 17 (forced linkage for cruel and unusual punishment). *See* Howell v. State, 133 So.3d 511, 516–17 (Fla. 2014); Moreno-Gonzalez, v. State, 67 So.3d 1020 (Fla. 2011). *See generally* Christopher Slobogin, *State Adoption of Federal Law: Exploring the Limits of Florida's "Forced Linkage" Amendment*, 39 U. FLA. L. REV. 653 (1987); Thomas C. Marks Jr., *Federalism and the Florida Constitution: The Self-Inflicted Wounds of Thrown-Away Independence from the Control of the U.S. Supreme Court*, 66 ALB. L. REV. 701 (2003).

[104] The amendment reads:

> A person may not be deprived of life, liberty, or property without due process of law or denied equal protection of the laws; provided, that nothing contained herein or elsewhere in this Constitution imposes upon the State of California or any public entity, board, or official any obligations or responsibilities which exceed those imposed by the Equal Protection Clause of the 14th Amendment to the United States Constitution with respect to the use of pupil school assignment or pupil transportation. In enforcing this subdivision or any other provision of this Constitution, no court of this state may impose upon the State of California or any public entity, board, or official any obligation or responsibility with respect to the use of pupil school assignment or pupil transportation, (1) except to remedy a specific violation by such party that would also constitute a violation of the Equal Protection Clause of the 14th Amendment to the United States Constitution, and (2) unless a federal court would be permitted under federal decisional law to impose that obligation or responsibility upon such party to remedy the specific violation of the Equal Protection Clause of the 14th Amendment of the United States Constitution.
>
> CAL. CONST. art. I, § 7(a).

judicial autonomy. In a few states, notably California,[105] Oregon,[106] and Iowa,[107] campaigns were mounted against judges associated with independent interpretation of the state constitution.

Another feature of this stage of the NJF was the attempt, in a number of states, to develop criteria to guide and limit state courts in their decision about whether to interpret their state constitutions to provide more rights than were guaranteed at the federal level. Professor Williams has described the "criteria approach" as follows:

> Under this methodology, the state supreme court . . . sets forth a list of circumstances (criteria or factors) under which it says it will feel justified in interpreting its state constitution more broadly than the Federal Constitution. These criteria, then, are used by advocates to present, and judges to decide, claims made under the state constitution in cases where there is also a federal claim that is unlikely to prevail. On the one hand, the criteria approach is laudable because it teaches and calls attention to the nature of state constitutional arguments. On the other hand, however, I have been critical of this approach for a number of reasons that I believe have demonstrated themselves in the past fifteen years.[108]

This approach is still attracting adherents today, and it is discussed in depth in Chapter 6.

## III. THE THIRD STAGE: THE LONG HARD TASK

> *[T]o make an independent argument under the state clause takes homework—in texts, in history, in alternative approaches to analysis.*
>
> —Justice Hans A. Linde[109]

[105] Among the most well-known judicial elections was the 1986 California Supreme Court election in which three sitting judges, including Chief Justice Rose Bird, were voted out of office. This election is analyzed by Joseph R. Grodin, himself one of the defeated justices, in JOSEPH R. GRODIN, IN PURSUIT OF JUSTICE: REFLECTIONS OF A STATE SUPREME COURT JUSTICE 162–86 (1989). *See also* John H. Culver & John T. Wold, *Rose Bird and the Politics of Judicial Accountability in California*, 70 JUDICATURE 81 (1987); John T. Wold & John H. Culver, *The Defeat of the California Justices: The Campaign, the Electorate, and the Issue of Judicial Accountability*, 70 JUDICATURE 348 (1987); Robert S. Thompson, *Judicial Retention Elections and Judicial Method: A Retrospective on the California Retention Election of 1986*, 61 S. CAL. L. REV. 2007 (1988).

[106] *See, e.g.*, Fred Leeson, *Oregon Court Seat Fight Gets Bitter*, NAT'L L.J., May 14, 1984, at 3; Wallace Turner, *Law-and-Order Groups Oppose an Oregon Justice*, N.Y. TIMES, Apr. 2, 1984, at A17.

[107] David E. Pozen, *What Happened in Iowa?* 111 COLUM. L. REV. SIDEBAR 90 (2011). *See infra* note 126 and accompanying text.

[108] *See* Robert F. Williams, *In the Glare of the Supreme Court: Continuing Methodology and Legitimacy Problems in Independent State Constitutional Rights Adjudication*, 72 NOTRE DAME L. REV. 1015, 1021–22 (1997). *See* Chapter 6.

[109] Hans A. Linde, *First Things First: Rediscovering the States' Bills of Rights*, 9 U. BALT. L. REV. 379, 392 (1980).

The most vitriolic reactions to the NJF died down by the late 1990s. Currently, the legitimacy concerns have partially subsided. More and more members of the public, lawyers, judges, academics, and members of the media have learned that state constitutions may, in fact, be interpreted to provide more rights than the national minimum. This fact is no longer such a surprise to people as the maturation process of the NJF has continued.[110] Still, independent state constitutional interpretation can, as Justice Linde noted, be difficult work.

Despite the development of the NJF over two generations ago, however, lawyers still fail to argue properly the state constitutional grounds where available. In many states, the courts refuse to reach the state constitutional argument in such circumstances.[111] In this context, the colorful imagery of the Supreme Court of Appeals of West Virginia is relevant: "We have said many times that a skeletal argument, really nothing more than an assertion, does not preserve a claim . . . Judges are not like pigs, hunting for truffles buried in briefs."[112]

Even in the last several years, in case after case around the country, state courts are faced with arguments by lawyers that either do not raise state constitutional claims at all or make them improperly under the guidelines annunciated by such courts. For example, in 2016 the New Mexico Supreme Court made the following statement:

> Because Defendant makes no claim that his rights under the New Mexico Constitution should be interpreted more broadly than those guaranteed by the Fourteenth Amendment of the United States Constitution, "we base our discussion of this issue on the constitutional requirements established under federal law."[113]

[110] *See generally* Randall T. Shepard, *The Maturing Nature of State Constitution Jurisprudence*, 30 Val. U. L. Rev. 421 (1996). Professor Williams noted in 1997 that "the initial thrill of discovery of the existence of state constitutional rights may have given way to the responsibility of determining how to enforce them." Williams, *supra* note 108, at 1018.

[111] *See, e.g.*, State v. Thornton, 929 P.2d 676, 682 n.3 (Ariz. 1996); Jones v. State, 64 S.W.3d 728, 733 (Ark. 2002); State v. Robertson, 760 A.2d 82, 98 n.15 (Conn. 2000); State v. Ross, 924 P.2d 1224, 1225 (Idaho 1996); People v. Emerson, 727 N.E.2d 302, 321 (Ill. 2000); Henderson v. State, 769 N.E.2d 172, 175 n.6 (Ind. 2002); Lockett v. State, 747 N.E.2d 539, 541 (Ind. 2001); Osterberg v. Peca, 12 S.W.3d 31, 40–41 (Tex. 2000); State v. Hayes, 752 A.2d 16, 18 (Vt. 2000); State v. Fire, 34 P.3d 1218, 1224 (Wash. 2001); Martindale v. State, 24 P.3d 1138, 1141 n.2 (Wyo. 2001).

[112] State v. Ladd, 557 S.E.2d 820, 831 n.1 (W. Va. 2001) (internal quotations omitted). As long ago as 1985 the Supreme Court of Idaho proclaimed: "Long gone are the days when state courts will blindly apply United States Supreme Court interpretation and methodology when in the process of interpreting their own constitutions." State v. Newman, 696 P.2d 856, 861 n.6 (Idaho 1985). *See also* State v. Kolvu, 272 P.3d 483, 490 (Idaho 2012).

[113] State v. Thomas, 376 P.3d 184, 189 (N.M. 2016). *See also* State v. Coleman, 890 N.W.2d 284, 286–87 (Iowa 2017); State v. Arlene's Flowers, Inc., 389 P.3d 543, 560 (Wash. 2017); State v. Razzaq, 439 P.3d 903, 907 (Kan. 2019); Commonwealth v. Bell, 211 A.3d 761, 769 (Pa. 2019); Sandoval v. State,

## IV. A FOURTH STAGE? STATE AND FEDERAL CONSTITUTIONAL DIALOGUE

> *Just as it seems strange to lawyers in 1990 that in the early part of the twentieth century the federal Bill of Rights did not extend to protection of individuals against state government, future generations may look back and wonder why state courts have ignored their state constitutions for so long.*
>
> —Justice Shirley S. Abrahamson[114]

A number of scholars and judges have called for a true dialogue among state and federal judges and constitutional scholars. Professor Paul Kahn has argued that state constitutional rights cases should not necessarily "rely on unique state sources of law. Those sources include the text of the state constitution, the history of its adoption and application, and the unique, historically identifiable qualities of the state community."[115] Kahn described constitutionalism, including state constitutional law, as "not a single set of truths" but rather as an ongoing national discourse about "ideas of liberty, equality, and due process."[116] Professor Kahn argued that state and federal courts should work together, using both state constitutions and the federal Constitution to pursue the "common enterprise" of providing interpretive answers to great constitutional questions.[117]

Professor Lawrence Friedman elaborated the elements and benefits of a true constitutional dialogue between state courts and the U.S. Supreme Court on shared constitutional issues,[118] concluding:

441 P.3d 748, 752 (Utah 2019): State v. Lindsey, 881 N.W.2d 411, 427 (Iowa 2016); AFT Michigan v. State of Michigan, 866 N.W.2d 782, 791–92 (Mich. 2015).

[114] Shirley S. Abrahamson, *Divided We Stand: State Constitutions in a More Perfect Union*, 18 Hastings Const. L.Q. 723, 744 (1991).

[115] Paul W. Kahn, *Interpretation and Authority in State Constitutionalism*, 106 Harv. L. Rev. 1147, 1147 (1993).

[116] *Id.* at 1147–48.

[117] *Id.* at 1168. Professor Jim Gardner describes "Human Rights Federalism":

> The protection of human rights is not something that the architecture of federalism assigns exclusively to the national level; it is, on the contrary, a shared function, to be pursued simultaneously at both levels through the identification and active policing of such rights.

James A. Gardner, *Justice Brennan and the Foundations of Human Rights Federalism*, 77 Ohio St. L.J. 355, 380 (2016).

[118] Lawrence Friedman, *The Constitutional Value of Dialogue and the New Judicial Federalism*, 28 Hastings Const. L.Q. 93, 112–23 (2000).

> [I]nsofar as the new judicial federalism reflects attempts by state courts independently to interpret the meaning of cognate textual provisions, its legitimacy is buoyed by the federal constitutional value of dialogue—that is, the value that attaches to discourse about law and governance that occurs between and among the different organs of the federal and state governments.[119]

Still, it must be remembered that each state constitution has its own text. The textual focus is an important way to distinguish the interpretation of a state constitution from the U.S. Supreme Court's interpretations of the federal Constitution. This point was emphasized by Hans Linde, when he cautioned that state constitutions are not common law. He noted:

> [S]tate courts find themselves pulled between fidelity to the state's own charter and the sense that constitutional law is a shared enterprise. Fidelity to a constitution need not mean narrow literalism. Most state bills of rights leave adequate room for modern applications, as well as for comparing similar guarantees elsewhere. But fidelity to a constitution means at least to identify what clause is said to invalidate the challenged law, to read what one interprets, and to explain it in terms that will apply beyond the case at issue, not to substitute phrases that have no analogue in the state's charter. . . . A demand that each state's court reach whatever desired result courts in other states have reached, in the common law manner of generic judge-made formulas, denies significance to the lawmaking act of choosing and adopting the constitutional provisions on which claims of unconstitutionality rest.[120]

The move to overrule state constitutional rights decisions, at this writing, has slowed; this is a positive development. As noted in the introduction to this book, California's Proposition 8 controversy over marriage equality was but an exception to this observation. A constitutional ruling about people's rights is really something quite special, even if it applies in "only" one state. Rights decisions should be seen as different from constitutional rulings about separation of powers, state-local relations, or other matters of state constitutional interpretation. Such matters are extremely important but are qualitatively different from rights rulings. Rulings about rights often protect unpopular people or groups who cannot gain a

[119] *Id.* at 97.

[120] Hans A. Linde, *State Constitutions Are Not Common Law: Comments on Gardner's* Failed Discourse, 24 Rutgers L.J. 927, 955–56 (1993). *See also* Hans A. Linde, *E Pluribus—Constitutional Theory and State Courts*, 18 Ga. L. Rev. 165, 195–97, 199 (1984); Robert A. Schapiro, *Identity and Interpretation in State Constitutional Law*, 84 Va. L. Rev. 389, 393–94 (1998) (arguing that state identity for the purpose of constitutional interpretation is "constituted not by the beliefs of the population of the state, but rather by the ideals defined by the constitution itself").

legislative or electoral majority. If a decision about constitutional rights becomes nothing more than the springboard for a proposed constitutional amendment to overrule it, we can damage our fundamental system of state constitutional rights. That system depends on independent courts for its operation.

Constitutional interpretation, especially in controversial rights cases based on older, generally worded clauses, is not an exact science. This is true despite the assertions of strict constructionists or those jurists and commentators advocating for various kinds or originalist approaches to constitutional interpretation. Decisions based on similar clauses, which rule against the asserted rights, are not necessarily correct, either. Regardless, we should leave those decisions in the hands of independent judges.

Those who disagree with a controversial rights decision often argue that there is no constitutional underpinning for the decision and that the court was just implementing its policy preferences. These people often feel a particular decision cries out for a constitutional amendment to overrule it, even though they may not feel that way about other controversial rights decisions in such areas as free speech, criminal procedure rights, and religious freedom. Those who feel strongly about those other decisions, however, may propose amendments to overrule them. This reaction can have a snowball effect. When those who object to a particular decision are legislators, or ordinary citizens in states where the state constitution can be amended by initiative, the slippery slope problem becomes obvious.

The legislator who believes passionately about a particular amendment and believes just as passionately that the decision to be overruled was rendered without legal basis will need to enlist the support of other legislators, forming a majority or even a supermajority. The situation with initiatives is different but related. If some of these other legislators have amendments about which they are passionate, the stage is set for a logrolling process on constitutional rights. Support for one amendment may depend on, or even stimulate, support for others. This is not a climate that is conducive to independent interpretation of state constitutional rights provisions.

## V. ONLY "TWO CHEERS" FOR THE NEW JUDICIAL FEDERALISM?

In 2010, Dean Erwin Chemerinsky published an article entitled "Two Cheers for State Constitutional Law," in which he concluded "that state constitutional law is a necessary, but inadequate second best to advancing individual liberties when that cannot be accomplished under the United States Constitution."[121] He

[121] Erwin Chemerinsky, *Two Cheers for State Constitutional Law*, 62 Stan. L. Rev. 1695, 1696 (2010). Dean Chemerinsky restated these descriptions of the inherent limits of state constitutional

is correct, of course, in pointing out that, by contrast to a national victory for civil liberties under the U.S. Constitution, such victories within the states under state constitutions are less far-reaching and permanent.

First, of necessity, any state constitutional ruling on civil liberties, or any other issue for that matter, must be limited to that particular state. Second, decisions of state supreme courts interpreting the state constitution are vulnerable to being overturned by an amendment to the state constitution. As Dr. John Dinan has pointed out, although such amendments are extremely rare at the federal level, they have taken place with some regularity in the states.[122] Dinan describes "amendments to *reverse* state court decisions," as well as "amendments to *preempt* rights-expansive state court decisions."[123] Dinan goes on to provide numerous examples of both of these kinds of state constitutional amendments that can affect state courts' individual-liberties rulings. This is far from an everyday occurrence, but its possibility is ever present, and may even affect state supreme court justices' willingness to render individual rights decisions beyond the federal minimum standards.[124] Federal judges, including Justices of the U.S. Supreme Court, have very little to worry about in this regard.

Third, the vast majority of state supreme court justices face the electorate in a variety of ways. In the words of the late California Supreme Court Justice Otto Kraus, deciding controversial cases as an elected justice is "like finding a crocodile in your bathtub when you go in to shave in the morning. You know it's there, and you try not to think about it, but it's hard to think about much else while you're shaving."[125] In one of the most extreme examples of this feature of most state judiciaries, unlike in the federal judiciary, after the Iowa Supreme Court ruled in favor of same-sex marriage, three justices of the Iowa Supreme Court were voted out of office following a negative campaign financed largely with out-of-state funding.[126]

Dean Chemerinsky further noted that U.S. Supreme Court decisions themselves can "impose constitutional limits on government actions," including the interpretation or amendment of state constitutions.[127]

law in 2018, in *Keynote Address: The Alaska Constitution and the Future of Individual Rights*, 35 Alaska L. Rev. 117 (2018).

[122] Chapter 5, section II.

[123] John Dinan, State Constitutional Politics: Governing by Amendment in the American States 111 (2018) (emphasis in original).

[124] Jonathan L. Marshfield, *The Amendment Effect*, 98 B.U. L. Rev. 55 (2018). Neal Devins analyzes a variety of factors state supreme court justices may take into account when deciding to expand state constitutional rights beyond the national minimum (floor). *How State Supreme Courts Take Consequences into Account*, 62 Stan. L. Rev. 1629 (2010).

[125] *Quoted in* Gerald F. Uelmen, *Crocodiles in the Bathtub: Maintaining the Independence of State Supreme Courts in an Era of Judicial Politicization*, 72 Notre Dame L. Rev. 1133, 1133 (1997).

[126] David E. Pozen, *What Happened in Iowa?* 111 Columbia L. Rev. Sidebar 90 (2011); Varnum v. Brien, 763 N.W.2d 862 (Iowa 2009). *See supra* notes 105–07 and accompanying text.

[127] Chemerinsky, *supra* note 121, at 1698. His example was *Citizens United v. FEC*, 557 U.S. 932 (2009).

Having acknowledged the limitations pointed out by Dean Chemerinsky, as one must, there remain numerous positive aspects of state constitutional protection of individual rights and liberties above the federal minimum standards, even outside the state. For example, expansive state individual liberties decisions may serve as persuasive precedent in other states considering the same matter.[128] Further, as we discuss at greater length in the epilogue to this book, in some situations a progression of state constitutional rulings can lead, ultimately, to a change of position by the U.S. Supreme Court itself, as in its same-sex marriage decision.[129]

Professor Neal Devins has also pointed out some realistic limitations on the likelihood of many state supreme courts interpreting state constitutional rights provisions beyond the national minimum standard set by the U.S. Supreme Court, based on a number of factors such as elected versus appointed state supreme courts, party alignment within the state, and so forth.[130] Even taking all of these factors into consideration, there is still great potential for the NJF. Particularly from the standpoint of individual lawyers and their clients, the possibility of a victory in their case, unreviewable by the Supreme Court, remains extremely attractive. In the end, "second best" opportunities to expand civil liberties are better than no chances at all. So maybe state constitutional law is entitled to two and one-quarter or even two and one-half cheers!

## VI. CONCLUSION

The NJF has been, and continues to be, an evolving phenomenon. It is here to stay as a central feature of American federalism and promises to continue through a number of additional stages in the future. Scholars of law, political science, and history, as well as judges and lawyers, will define these stages.

As John Kincaid has observed, federal constitutional arrangements, as in the United States, which permit state constitutional rights (including positive rights) beyond the national minimum standards, result in a "rights terrain" that may be characterized by "peaks and valleys of rights protection" among the different component units.[131] Such an approach is a central feature of a federal system,

[128] Chapter 12, section X.

[129] Obergefell v. Hodges, 576 U.S. 644 (2015); Mary L. Bonauto, *Equality and the Impossible—State Constitutions and Marriage*, 68 Rutgers U. L. Rev. 1481 (2016). *See also* Lawrence v. Texas, 539 U.S. 558 (2003). Dean Chemerinsky acknowledges this possibility. Chemerinsky, *supra* note 121, at 1703.

[130] Neal Devins, *State Constitutionalism in the Age of Party Polarization*, 71 Rutgers U. L. Rev. 1129 (2019). *See also* Jacob M. Grumbach, Laboratories Against Democracy: How National Parties Transformed State Politics (2022) (addressing consequences of increasingly nationalized state politics and party affiliations).

[131] Kincaid, *supra* note 10, at 946.

with a variety of different legal rules in the component units. As the Connecticut Supreme Court put it: " '[T]he law of the land' may not, in a proper state constitutional context, also be 'the law of the state of Connecticut.' "[132]

On the other hand, it is worth considering Professor Jim Gardner's view that, although Justice Brennan's 1977 stimulus "did much to excite the appetite of rights liberals, it had little long-term impact on the practices of state courts."[133] He continues:

> [O]f subnational constitutional independence, grounding it in a Madisonian understanding of federalism as implementing a two-government system of dual agency, a system that is designed to produce permanent contestation between national and subnational governments. In that context, the deployment of independently interpreted constitutional rights can be better understood as merely one tool available to subnational governments in an ongoing practice of intergovernmental struggle over policy. That, in turn, explains why state courts are a priori no more likely to be inclined to prefer rights-expanding interpretations of state constitutional provisions than to prefer rights-contracting ones. When and if state courts choose to issue rights-expanding decisions thus depends largely on how well they believe the federal government is doing its job, a judgment that in today's world is as much about power and partisanship as it is about constitutional jurisprudence.[134]

Gardner points out that still the majority of state-court rights decisions do not diverge from federal standards and that "Justice Brennan's call to arms was thus built around a significantly incomplete view of state constitutional law: he saw the independence, but overlooked the interdependence; he saw human rights protections, but missed the phenomenon of human rights federalism."[135] Whether one agrees with these conclusions, they bear careful consideration going forward. Having acknowledged the limitations pointed out by Dean Chemerinsky and Professors Devins and Gardner, as one must, there can be several aspects of state constitutional law protection of civil liberties above the federal minimum standards outside the state. For example, expansive state individual liberties decisions may serve as persuasive precedent in other states considering the same matter.[136] At least several major decisions by the U.S. Supreme Court were preceded by persuasive lines of state constitutional law decisions on

[132] State v. Dukes, 547 A.2d 10, 19 (Conn. 1988). *See also* Linde, *Common Law?*, *supra* note 120, at 955–56; Donald E. Batterson, *A Trend Ephemeral? Eternal? Neither?: A Durational Look at the New Judicial Federalism*, 42 Emory L.J. 209, 251–52 (1993).

[133] Gardner, *supra* note 117, at 358.

[134] *Id.* at 359.

[135] *Id.* at 374, 380.

[136] Devins, *supra* note 130, at 1175–76.

the same topic. As noted earlier, marriage equality and the decision that sodomy laws are unconstitutional come to mind.[137] The marriage equality decision in the Supreme Court was the culmination of state-constitutional-law-first strategy.[138]

As well, word continues to spread about the NJF and the potential it may hold for rights expansion. A notable 2018 book by U.S. Court of Appeals for the Sixth Circuit Judge Jeffrey Sutton, *51 Imperfect Solutions: States and the Making of American Constitutional Law*,[139] increased awareness of the NJF and state constitutional law in a variety of ways. The book was well received, and Judge Sutton spoke widely about it and the importance of state constitutional law.[140]

Further, state constitutionalism has emerged in the second decade of the twenty-first century to be understood as important far beyond individual rights adjudication.[141] The significantly different distribution of powers and checks and balances arrangements in the states, in contrast to the more familiar federal structures, have gained prominence.[142] Much more attention is being paid to the policy provisions in state constitutions, their differences from ordinary statutes, and their judicial interpretation. The interest of political scientists in state constitutionalism has greatly increased. Finally, study of the use and effects of state constitutional amendment processes advanced dramatically.[143]

[137] *See supra* notes 128–129 and accompanying text; *see also* Derek W. Black, *Unlocking the Power of State Constitutions with Equal Protection: The First Step Toward Education as a Federally Protected Right*, 51 Wm. & Mary L. Rev. 1343, 1380 (2010); Joseph Blocher, *Reverse Incorporation of State Constitutional Law*, 84 S. Cal. L. Rev. 323, 377 (2011); Joseph Blocher, *What State Constitutional Law Can Tell Us About the Federal Constitution*, 115 Penn St. L. Rev. 1035, 1041–42 (2011).

[138] Mary L. Bonauto, *Equality and the Impossible—State Constitutions and Marriage*, 68 Rutgers U.L. Rev. 1481, 1530–32 (2016). Dean Chemerinsky clearly acknowledged this possibility. Chemerinsky, *supra* note 121, at 1703.

[139] Jeffrey S. Sutton, 51 Imperfect Solutions: States and the Making of American Constitutional Law (2018).

[140] Jeffrey S. Sutton, *Foreword: The Enduring Salience of State Constitutional Law*, 70 Rutgers U. L. Rev. 791, 791 (2018).

[141] *See generally* Robert F. Williams, *The State of State Constitutional Law, the New Judicial Federalism and Beyond*, 72 Rutgers U. L. Rev. 949 (2020).

[142] State constitutional separation of powers is discussed in Part III.

[143] State constitutional amendment processes are discussed in Part V.

# 6

# METHODOLOGY IN STATE CONSTITUTIONAL RIGHTS INTERPRETATION

## I. THE POWER OF U.S. SUPREME COURT DECISIONS: THE MISTAKEN PREMISE

Many of the methodological problems that state courts encounter when interpreting state constitutional rights provisions that are analogous to those contained in the federal Bill of Rights arise, in Justice Hans Linde's words, from "the non sequitur that the United States Supreme Court's decisions under such a text not only deserve respect but presumptively fix its correct meaning also in state constitutions."[1] Justice William Brennan noted in 1977 that U.S. Supreme Court decisions rejecting claimed rights under the federal Constitution "are not, and should not be, dispositive of questions regarding rights guaranteed by counterpart provisions of state law. Accordingly, such decisions are not mechanically applicable to state law issues, and state court judges and the members of the bar seriously err if they so treat them."[2] The often unstated premise that U.S. Supreme Court interpretations of the federal Bill of Rights are presumptively correct for interpreting analogous state provisions is simply wrong. But it still exerts a significant amount of intuitive force upon lawyers and judges grappling with problems of state constitutional interpretation. It is important, therefore, to understand the sources of this mistaken premise.

This premise is based on our conception of the power and authority of the U.S. Supreme Court in our legal system. It is still true that many judges and legal practitioners, as well as members of the media, formed their attitudes about the Supreme Court when it was more actively involved in *recognizing* rights. Federal constitutional decisions recognizing new constitutional rights are extremely powerful. Under the Supremacy Clause,[3] these decisions reach into every single

[1] State v. Kennedy, 666 P.2d 1316, 1322 (Or. 1983).

[2] William J. Brennan Jr., *State Constitutions and the Protection of Individual Rights*, 90 Harv. L. Rev. 489, 502 (1977). *See also* Dorothy P. Beasley, *The Georgia Bill of Rights: Dead or Alive?* 34 Emory L.J. 341, 414 (1985) ("The virtual piggybacking of the state clause onto the federal clause renders the former a parasite instead of an independent source of authority.").

[3] U.S. Const. art. VI, cl. 2.

*The Law of American State Constitutions*. Robert F. Williams and Lawrence Friedman, Oxford University Press.
 DOI: 10.1093/oso/9780190068806.003.0007

trial court in the country because state judges must follow them.[4] Based on this experience, it is an odd feeling for lawyers and state judges to think about having a "choice" as to whether they must follow decisions of the U.S. Supreme Court.[5] But, in fact, state courts *do* have a choice as to whether to follow decisions rejecting asserted federal constitutional rights.

First, it is critical to remember that it is very different for the Supreme Court to hold that people *have* certain rights that must be respected under the federal Constitution than for it to hold that people *do not have* such rights. Because both are decisions of the Supreme Court, however, judges and lawyers "feel" both kinds of decisions should have the same force. Upon closer examination, it is clear that, just because some action is not prohibited by the federal Constitution, it is not therefore automatically "'authorized' in the absence of contrary state law, for the Constitution only *limits* the actions of state officials; *authority* to take these actions must be found in state law."[6]

Second, many of the leading decisions in the so-called reemergence of state constitutional law, or the New Judicial Federalism (NJF), have inadvertently contributed to bolstering the mistaken premise. As a matter of methodology, many of these decisions initially focus on the U.S. Supreme Court decision holding against the asserted federal constitutional right and then seek to try and explain why the outcome should be different under the state constitution. These cases are often described as "relying" on state constitutional law as though that were somehow an unusual judicial approach. The state constitution, however, is the binding supreme law of the state. Would a commentator describe, for instance, a criminal case as "relying" on the burglary statute? No one would consider such an approach in an area in which the state constitutional right at issue had no federal analog.[7]

It is understandable, in light of the position and prestige of the Supreme Court in our legal system, that this is the way legal arguments unfold in these cases. It is

[4] This is not entirely true, as demonstrated in political science literature tracing state supreme court compliance with U.S. Supreme Court mandates. *See generally* STEPHEN WASBY, THE IMPACT OF THE UNITED STATES SUPREME COURT (1970); Walter Murphy, *Lower Court Checks on Supreme Court Power*, 53 AM. POL. SCI. REV. 1017 (1959) (examining state court resistance to Supreme Court decisions).

[5] "The power of state supreme courts to reject decisions of the United States Supreme Court seems to contradict our fundamental understanding of constitutional law." Robert F. Williams, *State Constitutional Law Processes*, 24 WM. & MARY L. REV. 169, 185 (1983).

[6] State v. Scharf, 605 P.2d 690, 691 (Or. 1980) (emphasis added). Justice Linde's point in this opinion is very important and should move attention away from limits on actions in either the state or federal constitutions, to the underlying authority for such action. This can be a very different kind of argument, often shifting the focus from constitutional law to statutory law.

[7] Thus, in areas of state constitutional law such as the judiciary's inherent power to compel funding for judicial functions, e.g., Grimsley v. Twiggs County, 292 S.E.2d 675 (Ga. 1982), there is no analogous federal doctrine to complicate matters. *See also* Chapter 8 on state constitutional distribution of powers.

understandable that lawyers arguing cases, or judges writing opinions to justify their decisions, point to differences in text or history justifying different results under the state constitution. The problem with this approach, however, is that it seems to lend validity to the mistaken premise. In other words, it seems to ascribe a presumptive validity to the Supreme Court decision and to make it appear that *only* on the basis of some objective factor or criterion is a state court justified in "disagreeing" with the Court. This approach also can lead to the charge that the state decisions are "reactionary," in the sense that they are seeking only to avoid U.S. Supreme Court decisions and not to develop any principled state constitutional jurisprudence.[8] Thus, often the focus of the state court opinion becomes the grounds or reasons for not following the Supreme Court rather than a reasoned elaboration of state constitutional doctrine. This can incline state courts toward the "criteria" or "factor" approach, as discussed later in this chapter.

Decisions of the U.S. Supreme Court declining to recognize rights should not be accorded special weight in state constitutional interpretation. State courts should consult these decisions, but not accord them any presumptive validity. In fact, it could be argued that sometimes such Supreme Court decisions should be entitled to *less* weight than other state decisions interpreting similar state constitutional law provisions. This is because federalism and other institutional concerns, either explicitly[9] or implicitly, pervade Supreme Court decisions declining to recognize rights *against states*. Thus, such decisions must always be viewed as partially attributable to "underenforcement"[10] of the federal Bill of Rights against the states and, therefore, not of precedential value for state constitutional interpretation beyond the persuasiveness of their reasoning.[11]

## II. LEGITIMACY

*The right question is not whether a state's guarantee is the same as or broader than its federal counterpart as interpreted by the Supreme*

[8] *See* Ronald K.L. Collins, *Commentary: Reliance on State Constitutions—Away from a Reactionary Approach*, 9 HASTINGS CONST. L.Q. 1, 17–18 (1981); Ronald K.L. Collins, *Reliance on State Constitutions: Some Random Thoughts*, 54 MISS. L. REV. 371, 375–76 n.15 (1984). *See also* Paul M. Bator, *The State Courts and Federal Constitutional Litigation*, 22 WM. & MARY L. REV. 605, 606 n.1 (1981) ("I must confess to some misgivings about the extent to which some of this commentary seems to assume that state constitutional law is simply 'available' to be manipulated to negate Supreme Court decisions which are deemed unsatisfactory."); George Deukmejian & Clifford K. Thompson Jr., *All Sail and No Anchor—Judicial Review Under the California Constitution*, 6 HASTINGS CONST. L.Q. 975 (1979) (criticizing California state constitutional decisions as "result oriented").

[9] *See infra* notes 198–99 and accompanying text.

[10] *See infra* notes 200–01 and accompanying text.

[11] *See infra* notes 185–86 and accompanying text.

> *Court. The right question is what the state's guarantee means and how it applies to the case at hand.*
>
> —Justice Hans A. Linde, Oregon Supreme Court[12]

> *In interpreting the New Jersey Constitution, we look for direction to the United States Supreme Court, whose opinions can provide "valuable sources of wisdom for us." . . . But although that Court may be a polestar that guides us as we navigate the New Jersey Constitution, we bear ultimate responsibility for the safe passage of our ship. Our eyes must not be so fixed on that star that we risk the welfare of our passengers on the shoals of constitutional doctrine. In interpreting the New Jersey Constitution, we must look in front of us as well as above us.*
>
> —Justice Robert L. Clifford, New Jersey Supreme Court[13]

Critics have charged as unprincipled and result-oriented decisions of state courts that had interpreted their state constitutions to provide broader rights than those recognized under similar or identical provisions of the federal Constitution. These charges, often coming from dissenters on the state courts themselves, questioned the legitimacy of independent state constitutional decisions. Partially as a result of these criticisms, many state courts began to adopt a criteria, or factor approach, to justify divergence from, or disagreement with, the U.S. Supreme Court's interpretations of the federal Constitution. These concerns have continued and may have actually increased.

The idea that state courts may interpret their "potentially applicable state constitutional provisions"[14] to provide more, or broader, rights protections than are recognized by the Supreme Court under the federal Constitution should no longer be seen as a cute trick,[15] or "simply a flexing of state constitutional

[12] Hans A. Linde, *E Pluribus—Constitutional Theory and State Courts*, 18 GA. L. REV. 165, 179 (1984); *see also id.* at 177.

[13] State v. Hempele, 576 A.2d 793, 800 (N.J. 1990).

[14] Bruce Ledewitz, *The Role of Lower State Courts in Adapting State Law to Changed Federal Interpretations*, 67 TEMP. L. REV. 1003, 1004 n.5 (1994) ("The term 'potentially applicable state constitutional provisions' is superior to terms such as 'analogous,' 'related,' or 'parallel,' which imply a subordinate status for the state constitution.").

[15] H.C. Macgill, *Introduction—Upon a Peak in Darien: Discovering the Connecticut Constitution*, 15 CONN. L. REV. 7, 9 (1982) ("There probably remains some feeling on the bench as well as in the bar that a state constitutional holding is something of a cute trick, if not a bit of nose-thumbing at the federal Supreme Court, and not 'real' constitutional law at all."); *see also* Shirley S. Abrahamson, *Divided We Stand: State Constitutions in a More Perfect Union*, 18 HASTINGS CONST. L.Q. 723, 732 (1991) ("Furthermore, state judges experience a sense of chutzpah in expressing disagreement with the United States Supreme Court."); Robert F. Williams, *The Claus von Bulow Case: Chutzpah and State Constitutional Law?* 26 CONN. L. REV. 711, 712, 718–19 (1994).

muscle."[16] It has now become an accepted, albeit still sometimes controversial, feature of our jurisprudence. Indeed, as has been correctly noted for some time, the NJF is not new anymore.[17] Observers have periodically tallied the increasing numbers of cases in which state courts have, under their own constitutions, recognized rights beyond those in the federal Constitution.[18] There is continuing evidence of state courts actively turning to their state constitutions to reach results beyond those required under the federal Constitution.[19]

On the other hand, as Professor Barry Latzer has reminded us, many state courts, even after *independent analysis* of state constitutional claims, decide to follow the Supreme Court's federal constitutional rights analysis.[20] This reflects a maturing of judicial federalism. Nonetheless, many state courts still continue to collapse state and federal constitutional analysis and to decide cases as though the two constitutions were the same.[21] This will be discussed further in Chapter 7. There is still much work left to be done. Chapter 5 demonstrated that the initial thrill of discovery of the existence of state constitutional rights has given way to the responsibility of determining how to enforce them. The question of whether, and in what circumstances, it is legitimate for state courts to reach conclusions under their state constitutions that are more protective of rights than U.S. Supreme Court decisions is one of the most important questions of American constitutional federalism.

Despite the warning in 1983 by Justice Robert Jones of Oregon that any "lawyer who fails to raise an Oregon Constitution violation and relies solely on parallel provisions under the federal constitution . . . should be guilty of legal malpractice,"[22] many lawyers continue to litigate state constitutional cases

16 State v. Miller, 630 A.2d 1315, 1328 (Conn. 1993) (Callahan, J., concurring in part and dissenting in part).

17 Ronald K.L. Collins, *Foreword: Reliance on State Constitutions—Beyond the "New Federalism,"* 8 U. Puget Sound L. Rev. vi (1985; Ronald K.L. Collins, *Foreword: The Once "New Judicial Federalism" & Its Critics*, 64 Wash. L. Rev. 5 (1989).

18 Ronald K.L. Collins et al., *State High Courts, State Constitutions, and Individual Rights Litigation Since 1980: A Judicial Survey*, 13 Hastings Const. L.Q. 599, 600–01 (1986).

19 *See* Craig F. Emmert & Carol Ann Traut, *State Supreme Courts, State Constitutions and Judicial Policymaking*, 16 Just. Sys. J. 37 (1992) (when state courts base their decisions solely on state constitutional grounds, laws are more often declared unconstitutional than when decisions are based on both federal and state, or only federal, constitutional grounds).

20 Barry Latzer, *Into the '90s: More Evidence that the Revolution Has a Conservative Underbelly*, 4 Emerging Issues St. Const. L. 17 (1991) [hereinafter Latzer, *Into the '90s*]; Barry Latzer, *The Hidden Conservatism of the State Court "Revolution,"* 74 Judicature 190, 190–91 (1991); Barry Latzer, *The New Judicial Federalism and Criminal Justice: Two Problems and a Response*, 22 Rutgers L.J. 863, 864–65 (1991); *see also* Michael Esler, *State Supreme Court Commitment to State Law*, 78 Judicature 25 (1994).

21 The Maryland Court of Appeals, for example, often refers to similar state and federal constitutional provisions as *in pari materia*. *See* Hof v. State, 655 A.2d 370, 373 n.3 (Md. 1995); WBAL-TV Div., Hearst Corp. v. State, 477 A.2d 776, 781 n.4 (Md. 1984). This approach is criticized in Michael R. Braudes, *When Constitutions Collide: A Study in Federalism in the Criminal Law Context*, 18 U. Balt. L. Rev. 55 (1988). *See* Chapter 7.

22 State v. Lowry, 667 P.2d 996, 1013 (Or. 1983) (Jones, J., specially concurring). *See also* Commonwealth v. Kilgore, 719 A.2d 754, 756–57 (Pa. Super. Ct. 1998). Justice Brennan stated: "I

without adequately raising or briefing state constitutional arguments.[23] Neither the threat of a malpractice judgment nor a possible finding of ineffective assistance of counsel, of course, is the primary reason to pay attention to state constitutional law in criminal procedure. These threats do, however, serve as a kind of "bottom line" warning to lawyers.

## III. STATE CONSTITUTIONAL METHODOLOGIES: TEACHING AND SEQUENCE

In the past decades, as the NJF came of age, state courts adopted a variety of methodologies in approaching litigants' arguments that they should be accorded more rights under the state constitution than were currently (or were likely to be) recognized under the federal Constitution. One of the first methodologies was espoused by then Professor Hans A. Linde of the University of Oregon School of Law.[24] Linde applied his approach when he joined the Oregon Supreme Court.[25] This "primacy" approach, or "first things first" method, has appealed to a number of scholars,[26] judges,[27] and even to Justice John Paul Stevens of the U.S. Supreme Court.[28]

Interestingly, this approach contemplates consideration of *subconstitutional* state law claims even prior to the state constitutional law analysis.[29] This point has been made clear by the Oregon court:

suggest to the bar that, although in the past it might have been safe for counsel to raise only federal constitutional issues in state courts, plainly it would be most unwise these days not also to raise the state constitutional questions." Brennan, *supra* note 2, at 502.

[23] *See, e.g.*, State v. Dean, 76 P.3d 429, 432 n.1 (Ariz. 2003); Myers v. State, 839 N.E.2d 1154, 1158 (Ind. 2005); State v. Holzer, 656 N.W.2d 686, 690–91 (N.D. 2003); Custer v. State, 135 P.3d 620, 623–24 (Wyo. 2006); State v. Price, 146 P.3d 1183 (Wash. 2006); Brigham City v. Stuart, 122 P.3d 506 (Utah 2005), *rev'd*, 547 U.S. 398 (2006); State v. Burgess, 639 N.W.2d 564, 567–68 (Iowa 2001).

[24] Hans A. Linde, *Without "Due Process": Unconstitutional Law in Oregon*, 49 OR. L. REV. 125, 133 (1970).

[25] *See, e.g.*, State v. Kennedy, 666 P.2d 1316 (Or. 1983).

[26] *See, e.g.*, 1 JENNIFER FRIESEN, STATE CONSTITUTIONAL LAW: LITIGATING INDIVIDUAL RIGHTS, CLAIMS, AND DEFENSES, ch. 1 (4th ed. 2006).

[27] *See, e.g.*, Traylor v. State, 596 So.2d 957, 961–64 (Fla. 1992); R. Communications, Inc. v. Sharp, 875 S.W.2d 314, 315 (Tex. 1994); State v. Tiedemann, 162 P.3d 1106, 1113 (Utah 2007); *see also* Daniel Gordon, *Good Intentions—Questionable Results: Florida Tries the Primacy Model*, 18 NOVA L. REV. 759 (1994).

[28] *See* Delaware v. Van Arsdall, 475 U.S. 673, 698–708 (1986) (Stevens, J., dissenting); *see also* Massachusetts v. Upton, 466 U.S. 727, 736 (1984) (Stevens, J., concurring); Brigham City v. Stuart, 547 U.S. 398, 407–08 (2006) (Stevens, J., concurring).

[29] Judith S. Kaye, *Foreword: The Common Law and State Constitutional Law as Full Partners in the Protection of Individual Rights*, 23 RUTGERS L.J. 727 (1992); Curtis J. Berger, *PruneYard Revisited: Political Activity on Private Lands*, 66 N.Y.U. L. REV. 633 (1991); Gary v. State, 422 S.E.2d 426 (Ga. 1992); *see also* Mason v. State, 534 A.2d 242, 248 (Del. 1987).

> By now, the appropriate method of resolving properly raised issues of criminal procedure in Oregon should be axiomatic. All issues should first be addressed on a subconstitutional level. Courts then should consider any remaining issues under the Oregon Constitution. Finally, if no state law, including the state constitution, resolves the issues, courts then should turn for assistance to the Constitution of the United States.[30]

Judge-made "prophylactic rules" represent another area of possible state subconstitutional protections.[31]

Following this primacy approach would, most likely, lead state courts to be clearer about whether they intend their decisions to rest on adequate and independent state grounds. Consider the New Hampshire Supreme Court, which has been quite consistent in applying the primacy approach. Since its influential 1983 decision in a search and seizure case, *State v. Ball*,[32] this court has applied the primacy approach. Justice Stevens noted the New Hampshire methodology:

> Since 1983, in over a dozen cases, the New Hampshire Supreme Court has thereby averted unnecessary disquisitions on the meaning of the Federal Constitution.
>
> The emerging preference for state constitutional bases of decision in lieu of federal ones, in my view, is the analytical approach best suited to facilitating the independent role of state constitutions and state courts in our federal system.[33]

New Hampshire has followed this method to the present; a 2003 decision requiring a warrant under the state constitution for the search and seizure of curbside garbage is illustrative.[34] Despite this support for the primacy approach, joined by scholars,[35] it has not been embraced consistently by very many state courts.[36]

[30] State v. Moylett, 836 P.2d 1329, 1332 (Or. 1992); State v. Thompkin, 143 P.3d 530, 534 (Or. 2006); State v. Cable, 51 So.3d 434 (Fla. 2010); State v. Case, 305 P.3d 812 (Mont. 2013). In the speedy-trial context, the Oregon court addresses the state constitution before statutory arguments because under the former, there is a dismissal with prejudice, whereas under the statute there is a dismissal without prejudice. State v. Johnson, 157 P.3d 198, 206–07 (Or. 2007).

[31] *See generally* Honorable Thomas G. Saylor, *Prophylaxis in Modern State Constitutionalism: New Judicial Federalism and the Acknowledged, Prophylactic Rule*, 59 N.Y.U. Ann. Surv. Am. L. 283 (2003). The New Jersey Supreme Court in 2002 engaged in an interesting, and unusually candid, discussion of the merits of a prophylactic rule rather than a state constitutional ruling in a search and seizure case. State v. Carty, 790 A.2d 903 (N.J. 2002), *modified by* 806 A.2d 798 (N.J. 2002).

[32] 471 A.2d 347, 350 (N.H. 1983).

[33] *Van Arsdall*, 475 U.S. at 704 (1986) (Stevens, J., dissenting) (footnote omitted).

[34] State v. Goss, 834 A.2d 316 (N.H. 2003). *See also* State v. McKenna, 103 A.3d 756, 761 (N.H. 2014). *But see* State v. Zidel, 940 A.2d 255, 257 (N.H. 2008) (where federal constitutional result is clear in protecting the right, it will be applied first).

[35] Friesen, *supra* note 26, at ch. 1.

[36] Rachel E. Fugate, *The Florida Constitution: Still Champion of Citizens' Rights?* 25 Fla. St. U. L. Rev. 87, 102–09 (1997); Gordon, *supra* note 27; John W. Shaw, Comment, *Principled Interpretations*

By contrast, a number of scholars and judges have supported analysis of federal constitutional law first, with state constitutional law being used as a supplementary or interstitial source of rights.[37] A number of states follow this methodology, which is the opposite of the primacy approach. Under the supplemental or interstitial approach, the federal constitutional claim is examined first, and if the rights claimant prevails, the decision is based on the federal Constitution and is subject to U.S. Supreme Court review. In the event that the federal claim fails, the state court proceeds to evaluate the state constitutional claim to determine whether it will recognize rights beyond the federal doctrine. When they do recognize rights beyond the national minimum, it can seem results-oriented. It is, therefore, the use of this approach which is most likely to stimulate the state court to search for criteria or factors to *justify* a divergence from federal constitutional doctrine. Virtually all states that subscribe to the criteria or factor approach tend to apply the supplemental or interstitial methodology.

Actually, this method should not be surprising given the prior domination of federal constitutional law. In some sense, the conditioned response of lawyers and judges is to look at the federal Constitution first. Justice Stewart Pollock of the New Jersey Supreme Court explained the rationale of this approach: "One reason for following the supplemental model is that federal constitutional rights . . . establish our national identity. In an increasingly mobile nation, each of us can take comfort in knowing that, throughout the United States, the federal constitution protects a core of basic liberties."[38] In 1997, the Supreme Court of New Mexico specifically adopted the interstitial approach:

> [W]hen federal protections are extensive and well-articulated, state court decisionmaking that eschews consideration of, or reliance on, federal doctrine not only will often be an inefficient route to an inevitable result, but also will lack the cogency that a reasoned reaction to the federal view could provide, particularly when parallel federal issues have been exhaustively discussed by the United States Supreme Court and commentators.[39]

*of State Constitutional Law: Why Don't the "Primacy" States Practice What They Preach?* 54 U. PITT. L. REV. 1019 (1993).

[37] *See, e.g.*, Stewart G. Pollock, *State Constitutions as Separate Sources of Fundamental Rights*, 35 RUTGERS L. REV. 707, 708 (1983) ("The challenge is to develop a jurisprudence of state constitutional law, a jurisprudence that will make more predictable the recourse to and the results of state constitutional law analysis."); *Developments in the Law: The Interpretation of State Constitutional Rights*, 95 HARV. L. REV. 1326, 1361 (1982).

[38] Stewart G. Pollock, *Adequate and Independent State Grounds as a Means of Balancing the Relationship Between State and Federal Courts*, 63 TEX. L. REV. 977, 986 (1985). *See also* FRIESEN, *supra* note 26, at § 1.06 [3].

[39] State v. Gomez, 932 P.2d 1, 7 (N.M. 1997) (*quoting Developments in the Law—The Interpretation of State Constitutional Rights*, 95 HARV. L. REV. 1324, 1357 (1982)). *See also* Montoya v. Ulibarri, 163 P.3d 476, 481 (N. M. 2007); State v. Rowell, 188 P.3d 95, 98–99 (N.M. 2008).

Unlike many courts which utilize the interstitial approach, however, the *Gomez* court specifically rejected use of the "criteria":

> We decline to follow those states that require litigants to address in the trial court specified criteria for departing from federal interpretation of the federal counterpart. However, we note that several state courts have outlined a number of criteria that trial counsel in New Mexico might profitably consult in framing state constitutional arguments.[40]

Finally, others have espoused a dual sovereignty approach, in which both constitutions are examined, and even if the state constitution is interpreted to provide the rights sought by the litigants, the federal Constitution is also analyzed.[41] Justice Robert Utter of the Supreme Court of Washington has advocated this technique.[42] Justice Utter correctly noted that, in fact, many state courts made it a regular practice to rule on both state and federal constitutional grounds.[43] This technique of analyzing constitutional claims based on both constitutions, of course, is what led to the problems in identifying decisions that were based on adequate and independent state grounds. Justice Utter recognized this problem and advocated a clear distinction in state court opinions between federal and state constitutional law.[44] Acknowledging that, if the rights claimant prevailed on the state constitutional claim, any discussion of federal constitutional law would be dictum, Justice Utter contended:

[40] *Gomez*, 932 P.2d at 8 n.3.

[41] *See* Patchogue-Medford Congress of Teachers v. Board of Educ., 510 N.E.2d 325 (N.Y. 1987).

[42] Robert F. Utter, *Swimming in the Jaws of the Crocodile: State Court Comment on Federal Constitutional Issues When Disposing of Cases on State Constitutional Grounds*, 63 Tex. L. Rev. 1025 (1985).

[43] *Id.* at 1049; *see also* Friesen, *supra* note 26, at § 1.04 [4].

[44] Utter, *supra* note 42, at 1050. Scott H. Bice, *Anderson and the Adequate State Ground*, 45 S. Cal. L. Rev. 750, 757 (1972):

> But although the state court's decision of independent state and federal questions may seem to serve political and judicial economy, under the current Supreme Court practice such a course, in addition to preventing Supreme Court review, unfortunately will also have the effect of precluding effective political review of the state court ruling. Decisions based on independent state and federal grounds may substantially discourage any effort to use the state political process to change the relevant state law, because amendment to the state constitution or laws cannot correct the federal defect and therefore cannot change the result of the state court's decision. . . . Thus the present operation of the adequate state ground doctrine allows a state court, which may not be motivated by any considerations of efficiency, to insulate its decision from effective review by either the judicial or political processes for what may be a significant period. If a state court bases a decision on independent state and federal grounds to gain this "insulation effect," its action is illegitimate.

*See* Immuno AG v. J. Moor-Jankowski, 567 N.E.2d 1270, 1285–86 (N.Y. 1991) (Simons, J., concurring), for a similar criticism, relying on Bice's argument. *See also* Mark R. Drozdowski, *Building Castles Out of Sands: An Analysis of the Competing Adjudicative Models Used by the California Supreme Court in Sands v. Morongo Unified School District*, 40 UCLA L. Rev. 253, 270–71 (1992).

> Failure to continue to engage in the federal debate can only weaken the values that underlie our federal system. To engage in the debate can only broaden our understanding of the federal constitution. The result will be a healthy, living document, nourished by the court systems of all fifty states.[45]

The point here is that state courts (and the lawyers who present cases to them) should be cognizant of the sequence in which they raise federal and state constitutional arguments. These methodology questions may serve to highlight other issues in the interpretation of state constitutional rights guarantees. Scholars continue to catalog the different sequential approaches to state and federal constitutional analysis, identifying more complex typologies beyond the three outlined here.[46] In fact, however, it is not the *sequence* that is the most important methodological issue, but rather the focus on truly independent state constitutional interpretation, in whatever sequence it occurs.[47] It is substance, not form, that counts most.

A different approach is reflected in those states in which the highest state court has written a "teaching opinion" alerting the bar and bench to the possibilities of independent state constitutional analysis and educating them in the techniques of making state constitutional arguments. New Jersey Justice Alan B. Handler's 1982 concurring opinion in *State v. Hunt*[48] was probably the first example of such an opinion, followed in 1986 by Washington's *State v. Gunwall* decision.[49] To a certain extent, also, the U.S. Supreme Court's opinions in the *Pruneyard*[50] and *Michigan v. Long*[51] cases are other examples of teaching "from above."

[45] *Id. See* Robert F. Utter & Sanford E. Pitler, *Presenting a State Constitutional Argument: Comment on Theory and Technique*, 20 IND. L. REV. 635 (1987), for a later version of Justice Utter's views. *See* State v. Hayes, 188 S.W.3d 505, 513 (Tenn. 2006), for a Tennessee search and seizure case performing dual analysis.

[46] *See generally* Catherine Greene Burnett & Neil Colman McCabe, *A Compass in the Swamp: A Guide to Tactics in State Constitutional Law Challenges*, 25 TEX. TECH. L. REV. 75 (1993); Wallace P. Carson Jr., *Last Things Last: A Methodological Approach to Legal Argument in State Courts*, 19 WILLAMETTE L. REV. 641 (1983); Ronald K.L. Collins & Peter J. Galie, *Models of Post-Incorporation Judicial Review: 1985 Survey of State Constitutional Individual Rights Decisions*, 16 PUBLIUS: THE J. FEDERALISM 111 (Summer 1986), *reprinted in* 55 U. CINN. L. REV. 317 (1986); Peter J. Galie, *Modes of Constitutional Interpretation: The New York Court of Appeals' Search for a Role*, 4 EMERGING ISSUES ST. CONST. L. 225 (1991); James C. Harrington, *Framing a Texas Bill of Rights Argument*, 24 ST. MARY'S L.J. 399 (1993).

[47] *See* Robert F. Williams, *Methodology Problems in Enforcing State Constitutional Rights*, 3 GA. ST. U. L. REV. 143, 172–73 (1986–1987); *see also* Thomas Morawetz, *Deviation and Autonomy: The Jurisprudence of Interpretation in State Constitutional Law*, 26 CONN. L. REV. 635, 639 n.11 (1994).

[48] 450 A.2d 952, 962 (N.J. 1982). *See infra* note 56.

[49] 720 P.2d 808 (Wash. 1986). *See also* State v. Schwartz, 689 N.W.2d 430, 439–40 (S.D. 2004); Friedman v. Commissioner of Public Safety, 473 N.W.2d 828 (Minn. 1991).

[50] Pruneyard Shopping Ctr. v. Robins, 447 U.S. 74 (1980); *see also* Delaware v. Van Arsdall, 475 U.S. 673 (1986).

[51] 463 U.S. 1032 (1983). *See* Chapter 5.

The most explicit teaching opinion, however, remains that written in 1985 by the late Justice Thomas L. Hayes of Vermont, in *State v. Jewett*.[52] The opinion outlined the approaches to state constitutional interpretation (historical, textual, comparison to sibling jurisdictions, and analysis of economic and social materials), cautioning that "[i]t would be a serious mistake for this Court to use its state constitution chiefly to evade the impact of the decisions of the United States Supreme Court. Our decisions must be principled, not result-oriented."[53] Justice Hayes explained the reasoning behind an opinion aimed at the bar in connection with the court's order that counsel file supplemental briefs on the state constitutional issues in *Jewett*:

> There was some discussion on the court about publishing a law review article advising lawyers to look to the state constitution, but I had the feeling that if we took that course the article would be read by nine students, nine law professors, and the janitor who was cleaning up at night at the law school. I believed an article would not get our message across. Ultimately the court agreed that if we were to tell our lawyers: "Look to your Vermont constitution and, when you do, brief it adequately," we could do so only in a judicial opinion.[54]

The Pennsylvania Supreme Court, in a 1991 opinion by Justice Ralph Cappy, has followed the approach of the Vermont Supreme Court in *Jewett* but included the teaching section within an opinion deciding the merits of a search and seizure case much like New Jersey's *Hunt* decision.[55] Teaching opinions often appear in concurrences,[56]

[52] 500 A.2d 233 (Vt. 1985). The Vermont court reiterated this approach in *State v. DeLaBruère*, 577 A.2d 254, 268 (Vt. 1990); *see also* State v. Zumbo, 601 A.2d 986, 988 (Vt. 1991) ("Defendant fails to provide a substantive analysis as to why the Vermont Constitution should provide a different answer for his argument than the federal constitution."); State v. Jenne, 591 A.2d 85, 89 (Vt. 1991) ("Vermont's constitutional guarantee to a fair cross-section . . . does not, in this case, provide any greater protection than that afforded by the federal constitution.").

[53] *Jewett*, 500 A.2d at 235.

[54] Thomas L. Hayes, *Clio in the Courtroom*, 56 VT. HIST. 147, 149 (1988); *see also* State v. Earl, 716 P.2d 803, 805–06 (Utah 1986).

[55] Commonwealth v. Edmunds, 586 A.2d 887 (Pa. 1991). *See generally* Ken Gormley, *Foreword: A New Constitutional Vigor for the Nation's Oldest Court*, 64 TEMP. L. REV. 215, 217–19 (1991) (discussing *Edmunds*). Other examples of teaching opinions are Traylor v. State, 596 So.2d 957, 961–64 (Fla. 1992); Friedman v. Commissioner of Pub. Safety, 473 N.W.2d 828 (Minn. 1991); Immuno, AG. v. Moor-Jankowski, 567 N.E.2d 1270 (N.Y. 1991).

[56] North Dakota Justice Beryl J. Levine, in a concurring opinion, called attention to the majority's footnote indicating that only the federal constitutional issue was before the court. She noted that "although the footnote serves as a red flag, it may not alert the color blind," and noted the possibility of independent state constitutional interpretation. State v. Thompson, 369 N.W.2d 363, 372–74 (N.D. 1985) (Levine, J., concurring specially); *see also* State v. Wheaton, 825 P.2d 501, 504 (Idaho 1992) (Bistline, J., concurring specially); Gronski v. State, 910 P.2d 561, 565 (Wyo. 1996); Saldana v. State, 846 P.2d 604, 621 (Wyo. 1993) (Golden, J., concurring). State v. Ochoa, 792 N.W.2d 260 (Iowa 2010) (Appel, J.); State v. Baldon III, 829 N.W.2d 785, 803 (Iowa 2013) (Appel, concurring specially); City of West Fargo v. Ekstrom, 938 N.W.2d 915, 921-923 (N.D. 2020) (Tufte, concurring specially).

dissents,[57] and in lower court opinions.[58] The Wyoming Supreme Court included, as an appendix to an opinion, a bibliography of state constitutional law articles.[59]

## IV. THE CRITERIA APPROACH: LOOKING FOR FACTORS TO JUSTIFY DIVERGENCE

A related approach to methodology concerns, typified by New Jersey's *State v. Hunt*,[60] Washington's *State v. Gunwall*,[61] and Pennsylvania's *Edmunds*,[62] is the "criteria" or "factor"[63] approach. Under this methodology, the state supreme court, in what seems like a teaching opinion, sets forth a list of circumstances (criteria or factors) under which it says it will be justified in interpreting its state constitution more broadly than the federal Constitution. These criteria are used by advocates to present, and for judges to decide, claims made under the state constitution in cases where there is also a federal claim that is unlikely to prevail. On the one hand, the criteria approach is laudable because it teaches and calls attention to the nature of state constitutional arguments. On the other hand, however, we have been critical of this approach for a number of reasons that we believe have demonstrated themselves in the past several decades.

In *Hunt*, the New Jersey Supreme Court found a defendant's telephone billing records to be protected from a warrantless search and seizure under the New Jersey Constitution, diverging from a contrary holding by the U.S. Supreme Court as to a pen register listing of numbers dialed in *Smith v. Maryland*.[64] Justice Handler's concurring opinion cautioned:

> There is a danger, however, in state courts turning uncritically to their state constitutions for convenient solutions to problems not readily or obviously

[57] *See, e.g.*, People v. Rister, 803 P.2d 483, 494–98 (Colo. 1990) (Quinn, J., dissenting); *Saldana*, 846 P.2d at 624 (Urbrigkit, J., dissenting); Duffy v. State, 789 P.2d 821, 847–48 (Wyo. 1990) (Urbrigkit, J., dissenting).

[58] *See, e.g.*, State v. Geisler, 594 A.2d 985, 988 (Conn. App. Ct. 1991); Wells v. State, 348 S.E.2d 681, 684–86 (Ga. Ct. App. 1986) (Beasley, J., concurring specially); Nugin v. State, 334 S.E.2d 921, 922 (Ga. Ct. App. 1985) (Beasley, J., concurring specially); State v. Graham, 584 A.2d 878 (N.J. Super. Ct. App. Div. 1991); State v. Mollica, 524 A.2d 1303 (N.J. Super. Ct. App. Div. 1987).

[59] Dworkin v. L.F.P., Inc., 839 P.2d 903, 920–22 (Wyo. 1992).

[60] 450 A.2d 952 (N.J. 1982).

[61] 720 P.2d 808 (Wash. 1986).

[62] Commonwealth v. Edmunds, 586 A.2d 887 (Pa. 1991).

[63] Steve McAllister, Comment, *Interpreting the State Constitution: A Survey and Assessment of Current Methodology*, 35 U. Kan. L. Rev. 593, 605 (1987) ("factor analysis").

[64] 442 U.S. 735 (1979).

> found elsewhere. The erosion or dilution of constitutional doctrine may be the eventual result of such an expedient approach. . . .[65]
>
> It is therefore appropriate, in my estimation, to identify and explain standards or criteria for determining when to invoke our State Constitution as an independent source for protecting individual rights.[66]

Justice Handler's concurring opinion in *Hunt* became the Court's majority position the next year with his opinion in *State v. Williams*.[67] In 1987, Justice Handler, writing for the Court, stated that the state constitution should be interpreted to provide greater rights than those required under federal constitutional law "only when justified by '[s]ound policy reasons.' "[68]

The New Jersey approach, while teaching about state constitutional arguments, also seems to require[69] some objectively verifiable difference between state and federal constitutional analysis—whether textual, decisional, or historical—to justify a state court's interpretational divergence from the federal Constitution. This view, in turn, seems to imply that the U.S. Supreme Court decision is presumptively correct and that, in the absence of one or more of the criteria identified, it is illegitimate for a state court to reject the reasoning or result of a Supreme Court decision in the same or similar context. In fact, Justice Morris Pashman had written separately in *Hunt* to caution against this result.[70]

Under this approach, a state court is compelled to focus on the Supreme Court's decision and to explain, in terms of the identified criteria, why it is not following

[65] *Hunt*, 450 A.2d at 963–64 (Handler, J., concurring). Justice Handler noted the possibility that state court constitutional interpretations could be overruled by state constitutional amendments. *Id.* at 964 n.1 (Handler, J., concurring); *see also* New Jersey Coalition Against War in the Middle E. v. J.M.B. Realty Corp., 650 A.2d 757, 770 (N.J. 1994) (describing origins of New Jersey criteria approach).

[66] *Hunt*, 450 A.2d at 965 (Handler, J., concurring); *see also* Right to Choose v. Byrne, 450 A.2d 925, 932 (N.J. 1982) ("[W]e proceed cautiously before declaring rights under our state Constitution that differ significantly from those enumerated by the United States Supreme Court in its interpretation of the federal Constitution. . . . Our caution emanates, in part, from our recognition of the general advisability in a federal system of uniform interpretation of identical constitutional provisions."); Pollock, *supra* note 37, at 718 (supporting criteria).

[67] 459 A.2d 641, 650–51 (N.J. 1983). The Court noted that it had, in "important cases," relied on the state constitution. "We have not hesitated to recognize and vindicate individual rights under the State Constitution where our own constitutional history, legal traditions, strong public policy and special state concerns warrant such action." *Id.* at 650.

[68] State v. Stever, 527 A.2d 408, 415 (N.J. 1987), *cert. denied*, 484 U.S. 954 (1987), *citing Hunt*, 450 A.2d at 955; *see also* State v. Koedatich, 572 A.2d 622, 627–28 (N.J. 1990).

[69] In a law review article, Justice Handler stated: "I wrote separately in *Hunt* to express my view that resort to the state constitution as an independent source for protecting individual rights is most appropriate when supported by sound reasons of state law, policy or tradition." Alan B. Handler, *Expounding the State Constitution*, 35 Rutgers L. Rev. 202, 204 (1983); *see also id.* at 206 n.29; *Hunt*, 450 A.2d at 967 n.3 (Handler, concurring).

[70] *Hunt*, 450 A.2d at 960 (Pashman, J., concurring) ("Although the factors listed are potentially broad, they impose clear limits."); *see also Right to Choose*, 450 A.2d at 949 (Pashman, J., concurring in part and dissenting in part).

the Supreme Court precedent.[71] It is a relational, or comparative approach, which analyzes the relationship between or comparison of federal and state constitutional law. The stated criteria form a checklist of hurdles or prerequisites for the applicability of a state's highest law. A truly independent state constitutional interpretation "that will stand the test of detached criticism"[72] is, under this approach, not enough.

The requirement of justification in this manner raises several critical issues: (1) Is disagreement over substantive constitutional interpretation illegitimate? (2) Does the persuasive power of Supreme Court decisions depend upon the Court's institutional position, or the soundness of its reasoning? We believe this approach attributes too much to Supreme Court decisions.

The Washington Supreme Court's 1986 adoption of the criteria approach in *State v. Gunwall*[73] further illustrates the problems with this appealing and apparently lawyer- and judge-like technique. *Gunwall* came three years after *State v. Ringer*,[74] and two years after *State v. Coe*,[75] two decisions that generated intense criticism of the Washington Supreme Court's state constitutional jurisprudence and probably contributed, in part, to a change in court personnel in the 1984 election.[76]

*Gunwall*, like New Jersey's *Hunt* decision, dealt with the warrantless seizure of long-distance telephone billing records under circumstances where a warrant would not be required under the federal Constitution. Justice James A. Anderson

[71] *See* Robin B. Johansen, *Note, The New Federalism: Toward a Principled Interpretation of the State Constitution*, 29 STAN. L. REV. 297, 318 (1977) ("The court must convince the legal community and the citizenry at large that it was justified in its disagreements with the Supreme Court and that the state constitution supports different outcomes." (footnote omitted)).

[72] A.E. Dick Howard, *State Courts and Constitutional Rights in the Day of the Burger Court*, 62 VA. L. REV. 873, 934 (1976); *see also* RICHARD A. WASSERSTROM, THE JUDICIAL DECISION: TOWARD A THEORY OF LEGAL JUSTIFICATION 159 (1961). *But see* Hans A. Linde, *Judges, Critics, and the Realist Tradition*, 82 YALE L.J. 227, 248 (1972) (citing the importance of constitutional decisions even when they are vulnerable to academic criticism).

[73] 720 P.2d 808 (Wash. 1986); *see also* State v. Stroud, 720 P.2d 436, 444 (Wash. 1986) (Durham, J., concurring) ("We should adopt an independent analysis of Const. art. I, § 7 on the basis of principles, not results.").

[74] 674 P.2d 1240 (Wash. 1983).

[75] 679 P.2d 353 (Wash. 1984).

[76] For a general description of the 1984 Washington judicial elections, see CHARLES H. SHELDON, A CENTURY OF JUDGING: A POLITICAL HISTORY OF THE WASHINGTON SUPREME COURT 183–85 (1988); *see also* Robert F. Utter, *The Practice of Principled Decision-Making in State Constitutionalism: Washington's Experience*, 65 TEMP. L. REV. 1153, 1159 (1992) ("Four new justices had joined the court.").

Charles Sheldon reports:

> In the 1984 election for seats on the supreme court, a number of the successful candidates spoke of a return to a more balanced approach to the rights of the accused and the rights of society, indicating a reluctance to pursue state constitutional grounds that might add to the protection afforded the accused.
>
> Charles H. Sheldon, *"All Sail and No Anchor" in New Federalism Cases—Attempted Remedial Efforts by the Supreme Court of Washington*, ST. CONST. COMMENTARIES & NOTES, Winter 1990, 8, 10.

stated as an issue the question of when it is "appropriate for this court to resort to independent state constitutional grounds to decide a case, rather than deferring to comparable provisions of the U.S. Constitution as interpreted by the U.S. Supreme Court."[77] He answered:

> The following non-exclusive neutral criteria are relevant in determining whether, in a given situation, the Washington State Constitution should be considered as extending broader rights to its citizens than the United States Constitution: (1) the textual language; (2) differences in the texts; (3) constitutional history; (4) pre-existing state law; (5) structural differences; and (6) matters of particular state or local concern.[78]

These criteria are, of course, strikingly similar to those adopted in New Jersey in *Hunt*, and Justice Anderson, in fact, credited *Hunt* by citing to it. The opinion treats each criterion in some depth. In this sense, this opinion, like that in *Hunt*, serves an important teaching function. The Washington court went on to apply the criteria and conclude that, in fact, this case was one in which it would "resort" to the state constitution to reach a conclusion different from that reached by the U.S. Supreme Court. Like New Jersey, the Washington Supreme Court rejected the U.S. Supreme Court's *Smith v. Maryland*[79] decision.

On the one hand, the court expressed the position that, when it decides whether to disagree with the U.S. Supreme Court's interpretations of the federal Constitution, "it will consider these criteria to the end that our decision will be made for well founded legal reasons and not by *merely substituting our notion of justice* for that of . . . the United States Supreme Court."[80] On the other hand, however, the court characterized the factors on which it would base divergence as "*nonexclusive* neutral criteria."[81]

Calls for, or application of, a criteria or factor approach have also surfaced in other states, including Illinois,[82] Kentucky,[83] Michigan,[84]

[77] *Gunwall*, 720 P.2d at 810.
[78] *Id.* at 811.
[79] 442 U.S. 735 (1979).
[80] *Gunwall*, 720 P.2d at 813 (emphasis added).
[81] *Id.* at 811 (emphasis added).
[82] *See, e.g.*, People v. Levin, 623 N.E.2d 317, 328 (Ill. 1993); People v. DiGuida, 604 N.E.2d 336, 342–47 (Ill. 1992); People v. Tisler, 469 N.E.2d 147, 155–57, 165 (Ill. 1984); People v. Fitzpatrick, 633 N.E.2d 685, 690 (Ill. 1994) (Freeman, J., dissenting); *see generally* Thomas B. McAffee, *The Illinois Bill of Rights and Our Independent Legal Tradition: A Critique of the Illinois Lockstep Doctrine*, 12 S. Ill. U. L.J. 1 (1987); Lawrence Schlam, *State Constitutional Amending, Independent Interpretation, and Political Culture: A Case Study in Constitutional Stagnation*, 43 DePaul L. Rev. 269 (1994).
[83] *See, e.g.*, Commonwealth v. Wasson, 842 S.W.2d 487, 504, 514 (Ky. 1992) (Lambert, J., & Wintersheimer, J., dissenting).
[84] *See, e.g.*, Doe v. Department of Soc. Servs., 487 N.W.2d 166, 176 n.31 (Mich. 1992); People v. Bullock, 485 N.W.2d 866, 871–74 (Mich. 1992); Sitz v. Department of State Police, 506 N.W.2d 209, 216 (Mich. 1993).

Massachusetts,[85] and Connecticut.[86] These calls can be seen as representing, in an important sense, a challenge to the legitimacy of independent state constitutionalism itself.[87]

## V. STATE EXPERIENCE WITH THE CRITERIA APPROACH

After the *Hunt* opinion in New Jersey, the *Gunwall* opinion in Washington, the *Edmunds* opinion in Pennsylvania, and criteria cases in other states, one might have thought that the state constitutional interpretation would have followed a predictable course. This was, after all, one of the primary rationales for the criteria approach. Later cases indicate, however, that this has not happened and that the criteria themselves have taken on a focus of their own.

### A. Washington

In Washington, for example, in *Sofie v. Fibreboard Corp.*,[88] in interpreting the state constitutional civil jury guarantee, Justice Robert Utter noted:

> Chief Justice Callow relies on *Gunwall* and *Hunt* to support his implication that this court should defer to Supreme Court interpretation of a comparable federal provision unless an analysis of the six *Gunwall* criteria indicate that we should take an independent course....
>
> After criticism that the *Gunwall* criteria could be misinterpreted to support the view now espoused by the dissent this court clarified the test in *State v. Wethered*. In *Wethered*, we reemphasized the statement that the *Gunwall* factors were nonexclusive and added that they were to be used as interpretive principles of our state constitution.[89]

[85] *See, e.g.*, Commonwealth v. Amendola, 550 N.E.2d 121, 127 (Mass. 1990) (Nolan, J., dissenting); Guiney v. Police Comm'r of Boston, 582 N.E.2d 523, 527–28 (Mass. 1991) (Nolan, J., dissenting).

[86] *See, e.g.*, State v. Geisler, 610 A.2d 1225, 1232–34 (Conn. 1992); State v. Miller, 630 A.2d 1315, 1323–27 (Conn. 1993); State v. Diaz, 628 A.2d 567, 576–85 (Conn. 1993); State v. Joyce, 639 A.2d 1007, 1011 n.7 (Conn. 1994); *see also* Robert I. Berdon, *An Analytical Framework for Raising State Constitutional Claims in Connecticut*, 14 QUINNIPIAC L. REV. 191 (1994); Michael J. Besso, *Commenting on the Connecticut Constitution*, 27 CONN. L. REV. 185, 217 (1994); Martin B. Margulies, *The Uses and Misuses of History: A Reply to Michael Besso* 27 CONN. L. REV. 231, 234–35 (1994); Wesley D. Dupont, Note, *Automobile Searches and Judicial Decisionmaking Under State Constitutions:* State v. Miller, 27 CONN. L. REV. 699, 715–17, 720 (1995).

[87] *See infra* notes 184–86 and accompanying text.

[88] 771 P.2d 711 (Wash. 1989), *citing* State v. Wethered, 755 P.2d 797 (Wash. 1988).

[89] *Id.* at 725 (citations omitted) (footnote omitted). Chief Justice Callow had criticized the majority for not utilizing the *Gunwall* criteria. *Id.* at 730. Justice Durham dissented, in part because he did not believe *Wethered* in any way clarified the use of the *Gunwall* criteria, nor did it respond to

The criticism to which Justice Utter referred was a law review student Note, arguing that the criteria approach could limit independent state constitutional interpretation.[90] This rigidity and limiting effect of the criteria were predictable. They make it appear, as Chief Justice Keith Callow argued in his *Sofie* dissent, that Supreme Court interpretations should be followed unless one or more of the criteria are met. This is a presumption of correctness. It makes the criteria themselves, and their relationship to the Supreme Court decision casting the "shadow"[91] (or shining the "glare")[92] over the state case, the focus of attention rather than the question of independently interpreting the state constitution. The criteria can distract attention from the real issue before the court: How is that state constitutional provision to be interpreted and applied to the facts of this case?

In another example of this counterproductive fixation on the criteria, the Washington Supreme Court held in several cases that litigants must not only raise[93] state constitutional claims but must also brief and present arguments based on the *Gunwall* criteria. To illustrate, in *Forbes v. Seattle* in 1990, the court stated:

> In *State v. Gunwall* we enumerated several nonexclusive neutral criteria which must be met before this court considers state constitutional analysis. As a matter of policy, examination of the *Gunwall* criteria is essential in order for the process of state constitutional analysis to be "articulable, reasonable and reasoned." Because Forbes has failed to discuss the minimum criteria mentioned in *Gunwall*, we decline to undertake a separate analysis of Const. art. 1, § 5 at this time. Accordingly, Forbes free speech claims will be decided under federal constitutional law.[94]

criticisms of the *Gunwall* criteria. Rather, he contended, *Wethered* simply stated that state constitutional analysis required counsel to brief the *Gunwall* criteria. *Id.* at 737–38.

[90] Linda White Atkins, Note, *Federalism, Uniformity, and the State Constitution*—State v. Gunwall, 62 WASH. L. REV. 569 (1987) (criticizing *Gunwall* approach as limiting and requiring too much focus on federal constitutional doctrine).

[91] Robert F. Williams, *In the Supreme Court's Shadow: Legitimacy of State Rejection of Supreme Court Reasoning and Result*, 35 S.C. L. REV. 353 (1984).

[92] Robert F. Williams, *In the Glare of the Supreme Court: Continuing Methodology and Legitimacy Problems in Independent State Constitutional Rights Adjudication*, 72 NOTRE DAME L. REV. 1015 (1997).

[93] *See, e.g.*, Clark v. Pacificorp, 809 P.2d 176, 188 (Wash. 1991); State v. Long, 778 P.2d 1027, 1030 (Wash. 1989); State v. Herzog, 771 P.2d 739, 742 (Wash. 1989).

[94] 785 P.2d 431, 433–34 (Wash. 1990) (citations omitted); *see also* Halquist v. Department of Corrections, 783 P.2d 1065, 1067–68 (Wash. 1989); State v. Carver, 781 P.2d 1308, 1312 (Wash. 1989); Seattle v. Webster, 802 P.2d 1333, 1340 n.19 (Wash. 1990); City of Spokane v. Douglass, 795 P.2d 693, 695 (Wash. 1990); State v. Motherwell, 788 P.2d 1066, 1074 (Wash. 1990); Matter of Mota, 788 P.2d 538, 542 (Wash. 1990); Snedigar v. Hoddersen, 786 P.2d 781, 787–88 (Wash. 1990); State v. Clark, 875 P.2d 613, 615 n.2 (Wash. 1994); State v. Mierz, 901 P.2d 286, 292 n.10 (Wash. 1995).

This approach goes far beyond a teaching opinion or educational effort such as Vermont's *Jewett* opinion and imposes a prescriptive approach to briefing cases and presenting arguments, similar to the prescriptive effect the criteria approach seems to have had on state courts themselves.[95] As a result, the Washington Supreme Court, over a number of years, appears to have declined to address many important state constitutional arguments actually raised by the parties.[96]

In several cases which utilized a full-blown *Gunwall* criteria analysis, dissenters have disagreed with the way the criteria were analyzed. In *State v. Gocken*, the court performed an elaborate *Gunwall* analysis in a double jeopardy context.[97] Justice Charles Johnson dissented, arguing that the *Gunwall* analysis was flawed.[98] Justice Barbara A. Madsen concurred in part and dissented in part, stating that *Gunwall* should not be treated as "a talisman." "Most importantly, independent state constitutional analysis is lost somewhere in the ever-shifting shadow of the federal courts which are no less political and perhaps more so than our own state courts."[99]

The majority in *Richmond v. Thompson*[100] noted that, although "Thompson's *Gunwall* analysis is incomplete, amicus ACLU-W has presented a factor-by-factor analysis, and the Court of Appeals analyzed the State Constitution."[101] It performed its own complete *Gunwall* analysis, rejecting a claim based on the

[95] Connecticut has not gone quite this far, but is strict with counsel. *See, e.g.*, State v. Zarick, 630 A.2d 565, 574 n.15 (Conn. 1993); State v. Johnson, 630 A.2d 69, 71 (Conn. 1993); State v. Tucker, 629 A.2d 1067, 1070 n.5 (Conn. 1993); State v. Williams, 629 A.2d 402, 409 n.6 (Conn. 1993) ("less than extensive analysis"); State v. Reddick, 619 A.2d 453, 457 n.7, 462 n.22 (Conn. 1993); *see also* Savastano v. Nurnberg, 569 N.E.2d 421, 424 n.7 (N.Y. 1990); State v. Jensen, 818 P.2d 551, 552 n.2 (Utah 1991); State v. Pitsch, 369 N.W.2d 711, 721 (Wis. 1985). *But see* State v. Oquendo, 613 A.2d 1300, 1307 n.6 (Conn. 1992) (although defendant's analysis of state constitution is "less than exhaustive, he has clearly invoked his rights thereunder and, accordingly, we shall consider his claim"); State v. Joyce, 639 A.2d 1007, 1012 (Conn. 1994) ("Under appropriate circumstances, review of state constitutional claims may be undertaken despite the failure of a defendant to brief the state constitutional issue in a prior appeal."); Robert F. Williams, *Foreword: The Importance of an Independent State Constitutional Equality Doctrine in School Finance Cases and Beyond*, 24 Conn. L. Rev. 675, 702 n. 146 (1992).

According to a 1986 poll, 56 percent of the state high court judges were unwilling to entertain state law claims that have not been raised below, and only 15 percent favor the idea of the court raising the matter *sua sponte*. Ronald K.L. Collins et al., *supra* note 18; *see* Griffin v. Eller, 922 P.2d 788, 805 (Wash. 1996) (Talmadge, J., dissenting) ("This Court has the inherent authority to reach constitutional issues that determine a case.").

[96] The Washington Court distinguished between the need to brief the *Gunwall* criteria for new issues of state constitutional law but not for cases where the court has already recognized expanded protections. State v. Hendrickson, 917 P.2d 563, 567 n.1 (Wash. 1996).

[97] 896 P.2d 1269, 1270–73 (Wash. 1995). *See also* State v. Surge, 156 P.3d 208 (Wash. 2007).

[98] *Gocken*, 896 P.2d at 1275–81.

[99] *Id.* at 1274–75; *see also* State v. Rose, 909 P.2d 280 (Wash. 1996) (not using *Gunwall* analysis); State v. Johnson, 909 P.2d 293 (Wash. 1996) (using *Gunwall* analysis); State v. Martin, 252 P.3d 872 (Wash. 2011); State v. Bassett, 428 P.3d 343 (Wash. 2018).

[100] 922 P.2d 1343 (Wash. 1996).

[101] *Id.* at 1349.

right to petition the government. Justice James Dolliver, dissenting, contended that the majority had applied the criteria approach too rigidly: "The court need not fulfill every—or any—*Gunwall* factor to justify a broader reading of a parallel state constitutional provision."[102]

In *State v. Thorne*, the Washington court refused to reach a state constitutional due process claim because of an improper *Gunwall* briefing. Justice Barbara A. Madsen dissented:

> Since this court has already recognized greater protection *in the very context presented in this case*, it is unnecessary for the defendant to present a *Gunwall* argument to receive state constitutional protection. To hold to the contrary, as the majority does, is to elevate form over substance and to unjustly deny the defendant the protections he deserves as a Washington State citizen.[103]

## B. New Jersey

In New Jersey, also, there has been dissatisfaction with the course of state constitutional adjudication. In 1989, in another case coincidentally called *State v. Hunt*,[104] Justice Handler complained of the Court's approach to constitutional questions in death penalty adjudications:

> Its passive acceptance of the Supreme Court's lead on this fundamental issue is both baffling and unsettling for several reasons. First, the Court gravely misunderstands the weight that a state should attribute to the federal constitution with respect to the criminal law of capital-murder. . . . Consequently, this Court's frequent attempts to clone the federal constitution to determine and define critical capital-murder issues and rights is more than a doctrinal distraction. It has become a major barrier to the development of a cohesive body of substantive and procedural law to govern the prosecution of these complex and unique causes.

[102] *Id.* at 1355; *see also* Stage v. Manussier, 921 P.2d 473, 489–90 (Wash. 1996) (Madsen, J., dissenting); State v. Rivers, 921 P.2d 495, 507 (Wash. 1996) (Sanders, J., dissenting) (*Gunwall* approach "has been criticized for placing too much emphasis on the United States constitution as a starting point . . . ; however, it is helpful for present purposes").

[103] 921 P.2d 514, 537 (Wash. 1996). *See also* Grant Co. Fire Prot. Dist. v. City of Moses Lake, 83 P.3d 419, 425–28 (Wash. 2004); McNabb v. Dept. Corrections, 180 P.3d 1257, 1261 (Wash. 2008); *In re* Dependency of MSR, 271 P.3d 234 (Wash. 2012). The Washington courts still apply the *Gunwall* criteria. *See* Matter of Williams, 496 P.3d 289 (Wash. 2021).

[104] 558 A.2d 1259 (N.J. 1989).

> Second, in terms of capital-murder jurisprudence, the Supreme Court's approach boarders on the chaotic. For example, we have only recently rejected the federal court's own shifting constitutional analysis of what culpable state of mind is necessary in order for a murder to rise to the level of a capital offense. We most emphatically pronounced that protections under the New Jersey Constitution are different from and greater than those under the federal Constitution. Yet, in *Ramseur*, on the equally important issue of fair and impartial juries, the Court said that "the protections regarding death qualification afforded under the New Jersey Constitution are no different from or greater than those under the federal Constitution." It should be apparent that the Court has become engaged in the random selection of constitutional protections, sometimes federal, sometimes state; its approach to capital-murder jurisprudence is becoming indistinguishable from the federal approach in its lack of consistency.[105]

In none of the death penalty decisions, and there have been many in New Jersey since capital punishment was upheld in 1987,[106] was there any extended discussion of the *Hunt* criteria and their application to the variety of state constitutional issues in death penalty litigation.[107]

Justice Stewart Pollock, in 1998, noted that, in deciding a search and seizure case, even in favor of the rights claimant based on federal constitutional law, the New Jersey Supreme Court failed to address the state constitutional argument that had been raised:

> Here, defendants rely not only on the fourth amendment to the United States Constitution, but also on *article 1, paragraph 7 of the New Jersey Constitution.* Like its federal counterpart, that article of the State Constitution prohibits unreasonable searches and seizures. I believe that the Court should address both parts of defendants' argument. The failure to analyze defendants' state-law argument may require us to review that argument in the future if the United States Supreme Court should agree that the dissent, not the Court, has correctly applied federal law.[108]

[105] *Id.* at 1291–92 (Handler, J., concurring in part and dissenting in part) (citations omitted).
[106] *See* State v. Ramseur, 524 A.2d 188 (N.J. 1987).
[107] *See, e.g.*, State v. Koedatich, 572 A.2d 622, 627–28 (N.J. 1990). For a law review argument based on the *Hunt* criteria, see Edward Devine et al., *Special Project: The Constitutionality of the Death Penalty in New Jersey*, 15 Rutgers L.J. 261, 310–24, 376–93 (1984).
[108] State v. Lund, 573 A.2d 1376, 1385 (N.J. 1990).

## C. Pennsylvania

Pennsylvania also attempted an application of a criteria approach in the 1991 *Edmunds*[109] case. The Pennsylvania courts, though, have not followed any consistent pattern.[110] Justice Nicholas Papadakos dissenting in a later case noted:

> I am dismayed also at the form of analysis of the Pennsylvania Constitution employed by the majority. It has been my impression for the past year that we had set forth a dramatically new way of assessing state constitutional issues, especially Article I, section 8 cases predicated on independent state grounds. I take the central message of *Edmunds* to be that mere assertions of independent state constitutional grounds are not acceptable: no longer can the state constitution be viewed as an all-purpose surrogate for informed analysis, to be taken from the shelf and opened like a can of beans to feed those who periodically hunger for answers in that document. Instead, *Edmunds* mandated a structured analytical form to be used in applicable cases. . . .
>
> I believe I am quite correct in stating that we decided *Edmunds* in order to guard against precisely this kind of opinion. Even assuming arguendo that the majority could make its case on independent state grounds (which I do not believe), there is no evidence they have done so here. I take very little comfort in the fact that although we adopted a significant and path-breaking analysis one year ago, neither the courts below nor the majority opinion herein have shown any recognition of its existence as precedent. And still we wonder why our courts often are criticized for being like little puppies who chase their own tails rather than run forward.[111]

[109] Commonwealth v. Edmunds, 586 A.2d 887 (Pa. 1991); *see supra* note 55 and accompanying text. *Edmunds* was criticized for denigrating U.S. Supreme Court precedents by including "case-law from other states" as a factor but not mentioning U.S. Supreme Court opinions. Barry Latzer, *Four Half-Truths About State Constitutional Law*, 65 TEMP. L. REV. 1123, 1136–37 (1992). This is, of course, a different critique of the criteria approach from the one made here. Pennsylvania's "horizontal federalism" criterion, however, is different from the New Jersey and Washington approach and does focus attention somewhat away from the glare of the Supreme Court decision.

[110] *See, e.g.*, Comm. v. Gary, 91 A.3d 102 (Pa. 2014); United Artists' Theater Circuit, Inc. v. Philadelphia, 635 A.2d 612, 615–20 (Pa. 1993); Blum by Blum v. Merrell Dow Pharm., Inc., 626 A.2d 537, 541–49 (Pa. 1993); Commonwealth v. Hess, 617 A.2d 307, 313–15 (Pa. 1992); Commonwealth v. Lewis, 598 A.2d 975, 978–79 (Pa. 1991). Professor Ken Gormley supported the *Edmunds* criteria approach in *The Pennsylvania Constitution After* Edmunds, 3 WIDENER J. PUB. L. 55 (1993).

[111] Commonwealth v. Kohl, 615 A.2d 308, 320–21 (Pa. 1992) (Papadakos, J., dissenting) (citations omitted); *see also* Commonwealth v. Rodriguez, 614 A.2d 1378, 1385 (Pa. 1992) (Papadakos, J., dissenting) ("*Edmunds*, however, mandates much more, as I am growing weary of reminding this Court.").

The *Edmunds* approach was applied as a rigid briefing requirement by both the Pennsylvania Supreme Court and the lower courts.[112] Then, in 1995, after a four-year experiment, the Pennsylvania Supreme Court stated:

> In *Edmunds*, this Court set forth certain factors that we found helpful in our analysis herein. We reiterate, the factors set forth are helpful. The failure of a litigant to present his state constitutional arguments in the form set forth in *Edmunds* does not constitute a fatal defect, although we continue to strongly encourage use of that format.[113]

Commenting on this revised approach, Pennsylvania Superior Court Judge Phyllis W. Beck observed, "[A]s access to the court is of primary importance to the individual, it is particularly appropriate that a litigant seeking to enlarge the rights of the individual, via state constitutional law, be free from a technical procedure that may not always serve to advance the inquiry at hand."[114] The Pennsylvania court continues to utilize the *Edmunds* analysis,[115] indicating that it does not apply to all state constitutional cases, but only to those where there are identical or similar state and federal constitutional rights provisions.[116]

## D. Illinois

In *People v. Tisler*,[117] in 1984, after evaluating the state constitutional argument in a search and seizure context,[118] the Illinois Supreme Court stated:

[112] *See, e.g.*, Commonwealth v. Morley, 681 A.2d 1254, 1257–58 (Pa. 1996); Commonwealth v. Breeland, 664 A.2d 1355, 1359 n.3 (Pa. Super. Ct. 1995); Commonwealth v. Herrick, 660 A.2d 51, 57 (Pa. Super. Ct. 1995).

[113] Commonwealth v. Swinehart, 664 A.2d 957, 961 n.6 (Pa. 1995); *see also* Commonwealth v. White, 669 A.2d 896, 899 (Pa. 1995) (referring to dicta in *Edmunds* and noting that it "expresses the idea that it may be helpful to address the concerns listed therein, not that these concerns must be addressed in order for a claim asserted under the Pennsylvania Constitution to be cognizable."). Justice Frank Montemuro concurred but argued that the court should require, and employ, the *Edmunds* analysis, and impose a stronger presumption in favor of following the U.S. Supreme Court. *Id.* at 903–05.

[114] Phyllis W. Beck, *Foreword: Stepping over the Procedural Threshold in the Presentation of State Constitutional Claims*, 68 Temp. L. Rev. 1035, 1038–39 (1995). Judge Beck had enforced the rigid *Edmunds* briefing requirements in *Commonwealth v. Brown*, 654 A.2d 1096, 1099 (Pa. Super. Ct. 1995).

[115] *See, e.g.*, Commonwealth v. Matos, 672 A.2d 769, 772–76 (Pa. 1996); Commonwealth v. Sam, 952 A.2d 565, 585 (Pa. 2008). In *Commonwealth v. Russo*, 934 A.2d 1199, 1205, 1214 (Pa. 2007), all three opinions concerned the *Edmunds* criteria.

[116] Jubelirer v. Rendell, 953 A.2d 514, 522–23 (Pa. 2008).

[117] 469 N.E.2d 147 (Ill. 1984).

[118] *Id.* at 155–57.

> After having accepted the pronouncements of the Supreme Court in deciding fourth amendment cases as the appropriate construction of the search and seizure provisions of the Illinois Constitution for so many years, we should not suddenly change course and go our separate way simply to accommodate the desire of the defendant to circumvent what he perceives as a narrowing of his fourth amendment rights under the Supreme Court's decision. . . . Any variance between the Supreme Court's construction of the provisions of the fourth amendment in the Federal Constitution and similar provisions in the Illinois Constitution must be based on more substantial grounds. We must find in the language of our constitution, or in the debates and the committee reports of the constitutional convention, something which will indicate that the provisions of our constitution are intended to be construed differently than are similar provisions in the Federal Constitution, after which they are patterned.[119]

Justice William Clark concurred specially, noting that although he agreed with the outcome of the majority opinion, he disagreed with the methodology:

> I believe the majority's stance on this issue is dangerous because it limits our power to interpret our own State Constitution in the future. Under the majority's analysis, this court would be precluded from protecting the civil liberties of Illinois citizens should the United States Supreme Court decide to consistently favor police efficiency over the rights of the accused. Although the majority's reasoning may seem harmless today, it would preclude this court from protecting the individual liberties of Illinois citizens should such protection become essential in the future.[120]

Thus, *Tisler* serves both as Illinois' most important teaching opinion and the basis for its criteria approach. This debate about methodology is still going on.

The Illinois court, in 1992, unanimously rejected a state constitutional claim without applying the criteria approach.[121] Later that same year, the court, while denying the necessity of moving "lockstep" with the U.S. Supreme Court, unanimously rejected a state constitutional claim after a detailed criteria analysis.[122] In 1994, a majority of the court embraced broader protection under the Illinois Constitution's face-to-face confrontation clause, language not found in the federal Constitution.[123] The dissenters argued that it was not an adequate criterion

119 *Id.* at 157 (citations omitted); *see also id.* at 161–63 (Ward, J., concurring).

120 *Id.* at 163–64 (Clark, J., concurring specially).

121 People v. Perry, 590 N.E.2d 454, 456 (Ill. 1992).

122 People v. DiGuida, 604 N.E.2d 336, 342–47 (Ill. 1992); *see also* People v. Levin, 623 N.E.2d 317, 327–28 (Ill. 1993).

123 People v. Fitzpatrick, 633 N.E.2d 685 (Ill. 1994).

on which to base a different outcome from that reached by the U.S. Supreme Court.[124]

Late in 1994, the disagreement over methodology began to heat up. In *People v. McCauley*,[125] the court once again rejected the lockstep approach and held that the state constitution did not permit waiver of self-incrimination rights where an attorney was present and seeking to represent the defendant. In dissent, Justice Ben Miller argued that no valid criteria for divergence had been met.[126] In 1995, in *People v. Mitchell*,[127] the court, while once again acknowledging its power to disagree, rejected a state constitutional argument, relying on the *Tisler* criteria approach.[128] Justice James Heiple dissented:

> Before turning to the merits of the "plain touch" doctrine, I note my disagreement with the majority's conclusion that the Illinois Supreme Court, in interpreting the search and seizure clause of the Illinois Constitution, is bound to follow the decisions of the United States Supreme Court which interpret the search and seizure clause of the Federal Constitution. There is no reason for deference in this area of constitutional interpretation. It would be similarly unsupportable to suggest that the United States Supreme Court, in interpreting a provision of the Federal Constitution, is bound by decisions of the Illinois Supreme Court which interpret a similar provision of the Illinois Constitution. Regardless of the language employed in the two documents, they are separate and distinct. The United States Supreme Court has the responsibility to interpret the Federal Constitution; the Illinois Supreme Court has the responsibility to interpret its State constitution. These are nondelegable duties. . . .
>
> Governance involves choices. Every expansion of government power is a diminution of individual liberty. A balance must be struck between lawlessness and personal freedom.[129]

In two 1996 cases, the debate over application of the criteria approach escalated. In *People v. Washington*,[130] the Illinois Supreme Court disagreed with

[124] *Id.* at 690 (Freeman, J., dissenting) ("However, there must, at least, be some substantive basis for our departure. We have not, heretofore, found the difference in phrasing adequate to provide such a basis.").

[125] 645 N.E.2d 923 (Ill. 1994).

[126] *Id.* at 944–45 (Miller, J., concurring in part and dissenting in part).

[127] 650 N.E.2d 1014 (Ill. 1995).

[128] *Id.* at 1017 ("Certain *judicially crafted* limitations, however, define the exercise of that right.") (emphasis added).

[129] *Id.* at 1025 (Heiple, J., dissenting).

[130] 665 N.E.2d 1330 (Ill. 1996). For an instructive discussion of *Washington*, see Michael J. Muskat, Note, *Substantive Justice and State Interests in the Aftermath of* Herrera v. Collins: *Finding an Adequate Process for the Resolution of Bare Innocence Claims Through State Postconviction Remedies*, 75 Tex. L. Rev. 131, 160 (1996).

the U.S. Supreme Court and held that the state constitutional due process clause required a "free-standing" claim of innocence based on new evidence to be heard. Although acknowledging that the tests were identical and that nothing in the Constitutional Convention records of 1970 indicated any intent for a different meaning, the Court rejected the lockstep approach[131] and reached a result different from federal constitutional decisions.[132] Justice Miller dissented:

> The majority fails to explain, as an initial matter, why the due process clause of the Illinois Constitution should be interpreted differently from the due process clause of the United States Constitution. Invoking the flawed decision in *People v. McCauley* the majority simply declares that we are under no obligation to construe provisions of the Illinois Constitution in lockstep with the United States Supreme Court's interpretation of corresponding provisions of the United States Constitution. Before adopting an interpretation that varies from one given by the United States Supreme Court, however, we should seek some legitimate, objective ground for distinguishing the language of the state constitution from that of the United States Constitution. . . .
>
> Although the approach exemplified in *Tisler* has not been without exception, it represents the better analysis, in my view, and one that I would continue to adhere to. In the present case, the majority acknowledges that the language of the federal and state due process guarantees is identical and, further, that there is nothing in the debates of the 1970 state constitutional convention that suggests that the drafters intended the Illinois provision to mean something different from its federal counterpart. The majority nonetheless concludes that the due process clause of the Illinois Constitution requires a different and more expansive meaning than the same language commands under the federal constitution, and that notions of procedural and substantive due process separately sustain the defendant's action here. Neither ground is persuasive.[133]

Later in 1996, in *People v. Krueger*,[134] the court rejected the U.S. Supreme Court's "bare majority"[135] expansion of the good-faith exception to the exclusionary rule.[136] The *Krueger* majority stated: "We acknowledge that this court has long applied the lockstep doctrine to follow Supreme Court decisions in fourth amendment cases. We knowingly depart from that tradition here, for the reasons

[131] *Washington*, 665 N.E.2d at 1335 ("[W]e labor under no self-imposed constraint to follow federal precedent. . . .") (*citing* People v. McCauley, 645 N.E.2d 923 (Ill. 1994)); *see also id.* ("It is no criticism to read *Herrera* as a conflicted decision.").

[132] *See* Herrera v. Collins, 506 U.S. 390 (1993).

[133] *Washington*, 665 N.E.2d at 1341–42 (Miller, J., dissenting) (citations omitted).

[134] 675 N.E.2d 604 (Ill. 1996).

[135] *Id.* at 610.

[136] *See* Illinois v. Krull, 480 U.S. 340 (1987).

set forth below."[137] The court relied on the seventy-year-old Illinois exclusionary rule and rejected the Supreme Court's rationale for the good-faith exception.[138] Again, Justice Miller dissented:

> I do not agree with the majority's conclusion that the Illinois Constitution forbids in this case what the United States Constitution clearly allows. . . .
>
> In the present case, the majority does not point to anything in either the text or history of our state constitution that would warrant this court in reaching a result different from the one reached by the United States Supreme Court in *Krull*. In the absence of a valid ground for distinguishing the language of article I, section 6, of the Illinois Constitution from the fourth amendment, I would adhere to *Krull* and recognize, in our own state constitution, a good-faith exception to the exclusionary rule when searches and seizures are conducted under statutes that are later held invalid.[139]

## E. Connecticut

Connecticut has had an experience similar to, but more recent than, that of Washington. In 1992, in *State v. Geisler*,[140] the Connecticut Supreme Court embarked on criteria analysis. Since then, the court has purported to apply this criteria approach[141] and to require counsel raising state constitutional claims to brief their arguments using *Geisler* criteria.[142]

In 1995, the court linked criteria analysis and required briefing format:

> The *Geisler* factors serve a dual purpose: they encourage the raising of state constitutional issues in a manner to which the opposing party—the state or the defendant—can respond; and they encourage a principled development of our state constitutional jurisprudence. Although in *Geisler* we compartmentalized the factors that should be considered in order to stress that a systematic analysis

[137] *Krueger*, 675 N.E.2d. at 611 (citations omitted).

[138] *Id.* at 612 ("Consequently, to adopt *Krull's* extended good-faith exception would drastically change this state's constitutional law.").

[139] *Id.* at 613.

[140] 610 A.2d 1225, 1232–34 (Conn. 1992).

[141] *See, e.g.*, State v. Miller, 630 A.2d 1315, 1323–24 (Conn. 1993); Benjamin v. Bailey, 662 A.2d 1226, 1231 (Conn. 1995); State v. Morales, 657 A.2d 585, 589 n.10 (Conn. 1995); State v. Linares, 655 A.2d 737, 753 (Conn. 1995); State v. Webb, 680 A.2d 147, 159 (Conn. 1996); Washington v. Meachum, 680 A.2d 262, 275 (Conn. 1996); State v. Trine, 673 A.2d 1098, 1107 n.12 (Conn. 1996); State v. Rizzo, 833 A.2d 363, 393–98 (Conn. 2003); State v. Davis, 929 A.2d 278, 294–303 (Conn. 2007); Contractors' Supply v. Comm'r of EPA, 925 A.2d 1071, 1079 (Conn. 2007); State v. Jose A. B., 270 A.3d 656 (Conn. 2022).

[142] *See supra* note 86.

> is required, we recognize that they may be inextricably interwoven. Finally, not every *Geisler* factor is relevant in all cases.[143]

The Connecticut court has been very rigid on the required briefing format based on criteria.[144]

In *State v. Miller*,[145] in 1993, the Connecticut court, engaging in criteria analysis,[146] reached a result in a search and seizure case that was more protective in the inventory search context than federal constitutional law. Justice Callahan challenged the decision-making process:

> I believe that the majority is reaching to expand the scope of the state constitution when such an expansion has scant support and serves no useful purpose. The majority concedes that neither textually nor historically is there any justification for the application of the state warrant requirement to this set of facts. It, nonetheless, discovers that Connecticut citizens are entitled to greater protection from searches and seizures, when there is probable cause to believe that their motor vehicles are the repositories of weapons or contraband, than that provided by the federal constitution. . . .
>
> . . . . The majority opinion appears to be simply a flexing of state constitutional muscle for its own sake.[147]

In 1996, though, the court once more declined to reach a claim because of the nature of the briefing.[148] Justice Flemming Norcott dissented:

> Although we have articulated several "tools of analysis" that are to be considered "to the extent applicable" in construing the state constitution . . . I have never understood these criteria to be anything other than guidelines for the benefit of counsel, who can use them adequately to alert us to a serious state constitutional claim and provide us with a framework within which to evaluate it. These areas of analysis normally provide informative and even compelling sources

[143] *Morales*, 657 A.2d at 589 n.10 (citations omitted). *See also* Gleason v. Smolinski, 125 A.3d 920, 928 n. 5 (Conn. 2015).

[144] *See* State v. Faust, 678 A.2d 910, 917 n.10 (Conn. 1996); State v. Nixon, 651 A.2d 1264, 1267 n.4 (Conn. 1995); State v. Taheri, 675 A.2d 458, 462 n.5 (Conn. App. Ct. 1996). *But see* State v. Scarpiello, 670 A.2d 856, 862 n.4 (Conn. App. Ct. 1996) ("The defendant has failed to provide us with a separate analysis of his claim under the Connecticut constitution, and we therefore choose not to review this claim under the Connecticut constitution. This failure, however, does not mean that we are not able to afford review of such a claim if we decide to do so.") (citations omitted).

[145] 630 A.2d 1315 (Conn. 1993).

[146] *Id.* at 1323.

[147] *Id.* at 1327, 1328 (Callahan, J., concurring in part and dissenting in part).

[148] State v. Hill, 675 A.2d 866, 875 n.23 (Conn. 1996).

of authority, and the comprehensive, organized exploration of them by the parties is of substantial benefit to the court and is to be encouraged. I do not believe, however, that by identifying these criteria, we established a rigid formula, the components of which must be formally and specifically invoked in order for a claim to be reviewed, despite the functional sufficiency of the analysis presented. To apply them as such would elevate form over substance, and in no case decided since *Geisler* have we indicated that they are to be applied as technical briefing requirements. In fact, this court has never directly and specifically delineated what constitutes a minimally adequate analysis of this type of claim.[149]

The Connecticut court sometimes applies the *Geisler* factors to state constitutional provisions that do not have a federal analog.[150] Scholars have been critical of the Connecticut criteria approach.[151] In Connecticut, as in the other states analyzed here, the criteria approach itself has become the focal point of state constitutional analysis in at least some of the cases.[152] In 2008, the Connecticut Supreme Court performed a full-blown *Geisler* analysis in its decision recognizing same-sex marriage, thus reflecting a debate over the legitimacy of independent state constitutional law itself.[153]

In Washington and Illinois, the criteria approach seems to have taken on a "life of its own" in state constitutional law cases, while in New Jersey and Pennsylvania it does not seem to have resulted in any predictable approach to state constitutional claims.[154] In no instance has it lived up to its billing as a means to ensure consistency in state constitutional adjudication, and possibly it has actually been counterproductive.

[149] *Id.* at 882–83 (Norcott, J., dissenting) (citations omitted).

[150] Honulik v. Town of Greenwich, 980 A.2d 845, 850 n. 9 (Conn. 2009).

[151] *See supra* note 86.

[152] *See, e.g.*, State v. Hamilton, 636 A.2d 760 (Conn. 1994); *Miller*, 630 A.2d at 1315; State v. Lawrence, 920 A.2d 236, 248–53, 268 (Conn. 2007).

[153] Kerrigan v. Commissioner of Public Health, 957 A.2d 407, 421, 462–76 (Conn. 2008).

[154] *See, e.g.*, State v. Hartley, 511 A.2d 80, 97–99 (N.J. 1986); State v. Stever, 527 A.2d 408, 415 (N.J. 1987); State v. DeLuca, 527 A.2d 1355, 1357 (N.J. 1987); State v. Dunne, 590 A.2d 1144, 1148 (N.J. 1991); State v. Sanchez, 609 A.2d 400, 407–09 (N.J. 1992); State v. Smith, 637 A.2d 158, 163 (N.J. 1994); State v. Pierce, 642 A.2d 947, 959–60 (N.J. 1994); Doe v. Poritz, 662 A.2d 367, 414 (N.J. 1995) ("Although plaintiff has presented no argument for justifying expansion of equal protection beyond the federal right in this case, we nevertheless proceed with the state constitutional analysis.") (citations omitted); State v. Muhammad, 678 A.2d 164, 173, 191 (N.J. 1996). For an early analysis, see Jose L. Fernandez, Note, *The New Jersey Supreme Court's Interpretation and Application of the State Constitution*, 15 RUTGERS L.J. 491 (1984).

## VI. CASE STUDY OF CRITERIA IN ACTION: THE NEW JERSEY AND WASHINGTON GARBAGE SEARCH CASES

In *California v. Greenwood*,[155] the U.S. Supreme Court held in a 6–3 decision that the Fourth Amendment does not prohibit police from seizing and searching garbage which has been left out for collection. The Court concluded that garbage was not protected because persons who leave it at the curb had not "manifested a subjective expectation of privacy in their garbage that society accepts as objectively reasonable."[156] Interestingly, as it has done on a number of occasions, the Supreme Court in *Greenwood* reminded us that "[i]ndividual states may surely construe their own constitutions as imposing more stringent constraints on police conduct than does the Federal Constitution."[157]

The New Jersey Supreme Court, in July 1990, rejected the *Greenwood* holding and concluded that warrantless searches of garbage are unconstitutional under Article I, Paragraph 7 of the New Jersey Constitution.[158] Justice Robert Clifford, writing for the majority in *State v. Hempele*, first analyzed the federal *Greenwood* case and then invoked the nautical metaphor quoted earlier in this chapter.[159] Interestingly, his reference to U.S. Supreme Court decisions as providing "valuable sources of wisdom for us" cited Justice Pashman's concurring opinion in *State v. Hunt*, which disagreed with Justice Handler's criteria approach and criticized it as limiting and reflecting a misplaced presumption of correctness for U.S. Supreme Court decisions.[160] Justice Clifford acknowledged the textual similarity between the federal and state search and seizure provisions. He then noted that the Supreme Court may be "hesitant to impose on a national level far-reaching constitutional rules binding on each and every state."[161] He continued:

> The Supreme Court must be especially cautious in fourth-amendment cases. When determining whether a search warrant is necessary in a specific circumstance, the Court must take note of the disparity in warrant-application procedures among the several states, and must consider whether a warrant requirement in that situation might overload the procedure in any one state. In contrast, we are fortunate to have in New Jersey a procedure that allows for

[155] 486 U.S. 35 (1988).

[156] *Id.* at 39.

[157] *Id.* at 43.

[158] State v. Hempele, 576 A.2d 793 (N.J. 1990); *see* Colleen D. Brennan, Comment, *State v. Hempele*, 21 SETON HALL L. REV. 207 (1990).

[159] *See supra* note 13 and accompanying text. *Hempele*, 576 A.2d at 800. This is very much like Justice Pollock's observation in 1982: "Although the state Constitution may encompass a smaller universe than the federal Constitution, our constellation of rights may be more complete." Right to Choose v. Byrne, 450 A.2d 925, 931 (N.J. 1982).

[160] State v. Hunt, 450 A.2d 952, 967 (N.J. 1982).

[161] *Hempele*, 576 A.2d at 800 (*quoting Hunt*, 450 A.2d at 960 (Pashman, J., concurring)).

> the speedy and reliable issuance of search warrants based on probable cause. A warrant requirement is not so great a burden in New Jersey as it might be in other states.[162]

Justice Clifford indicated that, in contrast to the federal test requiring (1) a subjective expectation of privacy, and (2) that the expectation of privacy be one that society is prepared to recognize as reasonable, the New Jersey Constitution required simply that "an expectation of privacy be reasonable."[163] He concluded that it was reasonable for people to prefer that their garbage remain private and that, because the garbage was in containers concealing their contents, people were entitled to such preference.

The question of "reasonableness" in this context is one on which reasonable people may differ. The Justices of the U.S. Supreme Court differed in *Greenwood*. The dissenters in *Hempele* differed from Justice Clifford's majority opinion. The *Hempele* majority differed from the *Greenwood* majority. The important point is that the focus of the whole *Hempele* opinion was on the Supreme Court's opinion in *Greenwood*. The Supreme Court decision did, in fact, cast a shadow over, or glare on, the decision in *Hempele*. In the final analysis, a majority of the New Jersey Supreme Court disagreed with and authoritatively rejected the majority opinion of the U.S. Supreme Court. Justice Clifford concluded:

> Our decision today does not follow the course set by the Supreme Court because "we are persuaded that the equities so strongly favor protection of a person's privacy interest that we should apply our own standard rather than defer to the federal provision." We are aware that our ruling conflicts . . . [with] virtually every other court that has considered the issue. . . . . . As the trial court . . . so eloquently put it, "the trouble with those cases is that they are *flatly and simply wrong* as the matter of the way people think about garbage." Garbage can reveal much that is personal. We do not find it unreasonable for people to want their garbage to remain private and to expect that it will remain private from the meddling of the State.[164]

Justice Daniel O'Hern dissented:

> This case is not about garbage. This case is about the values of federalism. . . . The issue is the basis on which we shall depart from Supreme Court precedent in interpreting counterpart guarantees of our Constitution . . . .

[162] *Id.* at 800–01 (citations omitted). This seems to be an analysis of strategic concerns. *See infra* notes 202–03 and accompanying text.
[163] *Hempele*, 576 A.2d at 801.
[164] *Id.* at 814–15 (emphasis added) (citations omitted).

> For me, it is not enough to say that because we disagree with a majority opinion of the Supreme Court, we should invoke our State Constitution to achieve a contrary result. It sounds plausible, but one of the unanticipated consequences of that supposedly benign doctrine of state-constitutional rights is an inevitable shadowing of the moral authority of the United States Supreme Court. Throughout our history, we have maintained a resolute trust in that Court as the guardian of our liberties.
>
> ....
>
> Respect for law flows from a belief in its objectivity. To the extent possible, we ought not personalize constitutional doctrine. When we do otherwise, we vindicate the worst fears of the critics of judicial activism. The fourth amendment is the fourth amendment. It ought not mean one thing in Trenton and another across the Delaware River in Morrisville, Pennsylvania.
>
> In truth, the constitutional vision that we have shared as a people is not one of state-constitutional guarantees of freedom. Whether God-given or the result of social compact, the content of our freedom under law is drawn from the Bill of Rights. I rather doubt that most American think otherwise. . . . For good or ill, this unique American vision of freedom has been nurtured by the United States Supreme Court. There may come a time when the Supreme Court might abdicate its responsibility and we would have to act, but this is surely not it. Where that Court has drawn the line in this case does not significantly endanger our freedoms. I would abide by its judgment. If there is a New Jersey view on this issue, the legislature can vindicate it in time.[165]

Justice Marie Garibaldi also dissented, based on the focus on the U.S. Supreme Court's *Greenwood* decision. She stated, "An examination of the 'divergence criteria' developed in *State v. Hunt* and reaffirmed in *State v. Williams*, . . . indicates that there are no independent state-constitutional grounds to justify our divergence from federal law in this area."[166]

About four months after the New Jersey *Hempele* decision, the Washington Supreme Court reached the same conclusion, rejecting *Greenwood*. In *State v. Boland*,[167] Justice James Dolliver's majority opinion referred to the *Gunwall* criteria, noting:

> The purpose of these factors is twofold: first, to lend assistance to counsel where briefing might be appropriately directed in cases in which independent state grounds are urged; and second, to help ensure that if the court does use

[165] *Id.* at 815–16.
[166] *Id.* at 817 (citations omitted).
[167] 800 P.2d 1112 (Wash. 1990).

independent state grounds in reaching its conclusion it will consider the six factors to the end that the decision shall be based on well founded legal reasons and not by merely substituting its own notion of justice for that of duly elected legislative bodies or the United States Supreme Court.[168]

The majority found all six *Gunwall* criteria to be fulfilled, as an apparent threshold matter, and then proceeded to "resort to analysis of the issue on independent state grounds."[169] By contrast to New Jersey's approach, in which application of the criteria (when this approach is actually used) is an integral part of resolving the question of whether the state constitution should be interpreted more broadly than its federal counterpart, Washington's approach appears to be a two-stage inquiry. First, are the criteria satisfied? If all of the criteria are satisfied, the court moves on to "independent" interpretation of the state constitution. In *Boland*, Justice Dolliver concluded, "Having found the six *Gunwall* criteria fulfilled in this case, we now resort to an analysis of the issue on independent state grounds."[170] He relied on *Gunwall's* analysis of the first, second, third, and fifth factors (also on search and seizure) and therefore analyzed only the fourth and sixth factors to reach the conclusion that all six were met.

Much of the Washington court's disagreement with the U.S. Supreme Court's *Greenwood* decision, and added justification beyond the New Jersey *Hempele* conclusion, was based on the text of Article I, Section 7, which, in contrast to the Fourth Amendment, provides: "No person shall be disturbed on his private affairs, or his home invaded, without authority of law." This textual analysis, however, seems the same as analyzing the first and second criteria, which had already taken place in *Gunwall* and was accepted as applicable in *Boland*. The court noted:

While there is an identical result in *Hempele* and this case, we note one important doctrinal difference. In the dissent in *Hempele*, Justice Garibaldi attacks the majority opinion on federalism grounds and argues that the test established under federal precedent more appropriately comports with the reasonable expectation of privacy that most New Jersey citizens have in their garbage than the test developed by the majority. This argument has some merit in that the language of the Fourth Amendment and article 1, section 7 of the New Jersey Constitution are identical. The same argument, however, does not apply when comparing Washington's constitution and the Fourth Amendment. Under Const. art. 1, § 7, the focus is whether the "private affairs" of an individual have

[168] *Id.* at 1114 (citation omitted).
[169] *Id.* at 1115.
[170] *Id.*

> been unreasonably violated rather than whether a person's expectation of privacy is reasonable. In rendering our opinion, we acknowledge that the United States Supreme Court has held to the contrary under the Fourth Amendment in *Greenwood*. We also recognize that the opinions of the Supreme Court, while not controlling on state courts construing their own constitutions, are nevertheless important guides on the subjects they squarely address. However, we decline to follow federal precedent for two reasons. First, *Greenwood* is based in part on the fact the court felt society unwilling to accept as objectively reasonable a privacy expectation in garbage left outside the curtilage of the home for collection. As Chief Judge Alexander points out in his dissent below, this court has previously held the location of a search is indeterminative when inquiring into whether the State has unreasonably intruded into an individual's private affairs. Thus, the fact defendant placed his garbage at the curb rather than in his backyard has no bearing on whether an unreasonable intrusion into his private affairs occurred. Second, the reasoning upon which *Greenwood* is based conflicts directly with this court's interpretation of Const. art I, § 7. In explaining why society was unwilling to accept an expectation of privacy in garbage, the Supreme Court analogized to *Smith v. Maryland*, wherein the court held the Fourth Amendment did not prohibit the installation of a pen register at the telephone company for the purpose of recording telephone numbers of a criminal suspect. The main reason for the court's conclusion was that a person voluntarily conveys the numbers to the telephone company, thereby losing all legitimate privacy expectations in the numbers. However, we held to the contrary in *Gunwall*. . . .[171]

It seems from this analysis that Washington constitutional law arguably protects against searches of a person's garbage regardless of what the U.S. Supreme Court held in *Greenwood*. The use of criteria, though, reorients the focus, from Washington's constitutional text and doctrine to a comparison of other states' constitutional text and doctrine and to federal constitutional law. This is a relational approach. It reasonably leads to a question: If a claim is properly made under a state constitution, why would the court bother to discuss what federal constitutional law or the U.S. Supreme Court would conclude about the problem?

In *Boland*, Justice Richard Guy dissented: "I disagree that the factors set forth in *State v. Gunwall* have been met. Therefore, there is no basis upon which the majority can conclude that a broader interpretation of privacy rights, under Article 1, Section 7 of the Washington State Constitution is warranted."[172] The rest of the dissenting opinion consisted of disagreement on the majority's

[171] *Id.* at 1116–17 (citations omitted) (emphasis removed).

[172] *Id.* at 1118 (citation omitted).

findings with respect to the *Gunwall* criteria. Therefore, Justice Guy argued, there was no basis on which the majority could conclude that garbage searches were protected by the Washington Constitution. He maintained that the *Gunwall* criteria were adopted to "ensure that resort to independent state grounds will be based on well founded legal reasons and not by substitution of a court's own notion of justice for that of . . . the United States Supreme Court."[173] Justice Guy therefore ascribed an explicit presumption of correctness to the U.S. Supreme Court decision (*Greenwood*) with the criteria operating to limit contrary results under the state constitution. This approach is exactly what New Jersey Justice Pashman warned of in *State v. Hunt* in 1982, and for which the dissenters in New Jersey's *Hempele* case argued. Majority and dissent here focus their disagreement on the application of the criteria rather than on the content and application of the state constitutional provision at issue. Is a dissenter's accusation that the majority has misapplied the criteria any different from an accusation that the majority has simply resorted to the state constitution in a result-oriented attempt to "evade" U.S. Supreme Court precedent?[174]

The Massachusetts Supreme Judicial Court[175] and the supreme courts of Colorado,[176] Connecticut,[177] North Dakota,[178] Indiana,[179] and Idaho[180] have each upheld garbage searches and followed the U.S. Supreme Court's *Greenwood* decision. The Massachusetts decision was unanimous, with no discussion of the state cases disagreeing with *Greenwood*. The Colorado decision was 4–3, with

[173] *Id.* at 1120 (citations omitted) (emphasis removed). For an analysis of *Boland*, together with a criticism of the *Gunwall* criteria, see James W. Talbot, Comment, *Rethinking Civil Liberties Under the Washington State Constitution*, 66 Wash. L. Rev. 1099 (1991).

[174] *See* Williams, *supra* note 91, at 357–58 (footnotes omitted):

> [S]tate judges may be particularly sensitive, and even defensive, to charges that their decisions are result oriented or that their disagreement with the Supreme Court is based purely on ideological differences. These charges are typically leveled by dissenters or by those who merely disagree with the state court's substantive result. Nevertheless, these are the kinds of pressures that have forced state courts to develop standards or criteria by which to justify an independent state constitutional interpretation which arguably conflicts with a prior Supreme Court interpretation of a similar or identical federal constitutional provision.

[175] Commonwealth v. Pratt, 555 N.E.2d 559, 567–68 (Mass. 1990); *see* Barry Latzer, *Into the'90s*, *supra* note 20, at 27 ("*Hempele* will probably receive much more attention in the literature than *Pratt*. . . ."). The Massachusetts court also held that garbage in a dumpster on commercial property was protected from warrantless searches. Commonwealth v. Krisco Corp., 653 N.E.2d 579 (Mass. 1995).

[176] People v. Hillman, 834 P.2d 1271 (Colo. 1992).

[177] State v. DeFusco, 620 A.2d 746 (Conn. 1993). One commentator reported that there was negative media reaction to the decision but that an attempt to overturn it by a proposed constitutional amendment failed in the legislature. Ann R. Johnson, Note, State v. DeFusco: *Warrantless Garbage Searches Under the Connecticut Constitution*, 14 Quinnipiac L. Rev. 143, 171 n.210, 171–72 (1994).

[178] State v. Rydberg, 519 N.W.2d 306 (N.D. 1994); *see also* State v. Carriere, 545 N.W.2d 773 (N.D. 1996) (reaffirming *Rydberg*).

[179] Moran v. State, 644 N.E.2d 536 (Ind. 1994). *See also* State v. Schwartz, 689 N.W.2d 430 (S.D. 2004).

[180] State v. Donato, 20 P.3d 5, 6–8 (Idaho 2001).

the majority and dissenting opinions analyzing out-of-state cases and law review literature, as well as the *Greenwood* opinions, both majority and dissent. The Connecticut decision was 3–2, and like Colorado, contained a full exploration of both the federal and state cases. The North Dakota case was unanimous and acknowledged the other state cases but followed the federal result. The Indiana case was closely divided and also contained a complete treatment of both the federal and state cases. The Idaho case was unanimous, holding that because none of the "factors" that had supported earlier independent state constitutional interpretation were present, it would follow the U.S. Supreme Court's decision.

In 1996, the Vermont Supreme Court, in a 3–2 decision, followed New Jersey and Washington, rejecting the U.S. Supreme Court's *Greenwood* decision.[181] The majority analyzed both the federal and the state cases. Justice John Dooley's dissent stated that he "strongly agree[d] with the creation of an independent state constitutional jurisprudence that keeps essential decisions about protected liberties as much as possible within Vermont."[182] He quoted from the Vermont Court's famous *State v. Jewett* decision, however,[183] in support of a criteria approach, concluding that the majority opinion was a "restated *Greenwood* dissent."[184]

## VII. CRITIQUE OF THE CRITERIA APPROACH

The truth is that reasonable people—judges, lawyers, political observers, and citizens—can reasonably differ over whether an individual's telephone toll billing records or garbage should be vulnerable to warrantless police searches. They can disagree about most other constitutional questions. There is often—in hard cases—simply no clear or plain constitutional guidance. The debate in the garbage search cases is about people's view of the reasonableness of citizens' expectation of privacy in these matters. But it is not a valid argument to say that a state constitution should not be interpreted, for example, to ban such warrantless searches just because the U.S. Supreme Court has already held that these searches do not violate the federal Constitution, based on its *national* view of "reasonableness."

At its core, the criteria approach reflects the notion that interpretations of the federal Constitution can somehow authoritatively set the meaning for similar

[181] State v. Morris, 680 A.2d 90 (Vt. 1996).

[182] *Id.* at 106 (Dooley, J., dissenting). *See also* State v. Crane, 329 P.3d 689 (N. M. 2014); State v. Lien, 441 P.3d 185 (Or. 2019); State v. Wright, 961 N.W.2d 396 (Iowa 2021).

[183] *See supra* notes 52–54 and accompanying text.

[184] *Morris*, 680 A.2d at 104 (Dooley, J., dissenting); *see also* State v. Read, 680 A.2d 944, 951–53 (Vt. 1996) (applying *Jewett* as a criteria requirement).

provisions of state constitutions. Justice John Paul Stevens has referred to this presumption of correctness as evidence of a "misplaced sense of duty."[185] Justice Hans Linde referred to it as the "non sequitur that the United States Supreme Court's decisions under such a text not only deserve respect but presumptively fix its correct meaning also in state constitutions."[186] State supreme court justices' views of "reasonableness," or other constitutional formulations, applicable only within their own states, are just as valid as those of U.S. Supreme Court Justices. Of course, the decisions of the U.S. Supreme Court deserve a careful, respectful reading. But only when state judges are convinced by their reasoning should they be followed.[187] As Justice Linde observed:

> This court like others has high respect for the opinions of the Supreme Court, particularly when they provide insight into the origins of provisions common to the state and federal bills of rights *rather than only a contemporary "balance" of pragmatic considerations about which reasonable people may differ over time and among the several states.*[188]

The U.S. Supreme Court decisions in *Smith v. Maryland* and *Greenwood v. California*, both rejected by the New Jersey and Washington courts, as well as other state courts, reflect the sort of "contemporary 'balance' of pragmatic considerations about which reasonable people may differ" that Justice Linde was describing. Such decisions are not entitled to a presumption of correctness when a state court interprets its own constitution. Yet the criteria approach, as articulated most clearly in New Jersey and Washington and as applied in practice,

[185] Delaware v. Van Arsdall, 475 U.S. 673, 699 (1986) (Stevens, J., dissenting).

[186] State v. Kennedy, 666 P.2d 1316, 1322 (Or. 1983); *see also* State v. Flick, 495 A.2d 339, 343 (Me. 1985) (*quoting* Justice Linde). Justice Brennan wrote:

> The essential point I am making, of course, is not that the United States Supreme Court is necessarily wrong in its interpretation of the Federal Constitution, or that ultimate constitutional truths invariably come prepackaged in the dissents, including my own, from decisions of the Court. It is simply that the decisions of the Court are not, and should not be, dispositive of questions regarding rights guaranteed by counterpart provisions of state law. . . . Rather, state court judges, and also practitioners, do well to scrutinize constitutional decisions by federal courts, for only if they are found to be logically persuasive and well-reasoned, paying due regard to precedent and the policies underlying specific constitutional guarantees, may they properly claim persuasive weight as guideposts when interpreting counterpart state guarantees.

Brennan, *supra* note 2, at 502.

[187] Frederic S. Le Clercq, *The Process of Selecting Constitutional Standards: Some Incongruities of Tennessee Practice*, 61 Tenn. L. Rev. 573 (1994); Ronald L. Nelson, *Welcome to the "Last Frontier," Professor Gardner: Alaska's Independent Approach to State Constitutional Interpretation*, 12 Alaska L. Rev. 1 (1995); Edmund B. Spaeth Jr., *Toward a New Partnership: The Future Relationship of Federal and State Constitutional Law*, 49 U. Pitt. L. Rev. 729, 741 (1988).

[188] *Kennedy*, 666 P.2d at 1321 (emphasis added). For an exhaustive analysis of balancing in constitutional interpretation, see T. Alexander Aleinikoff, *Constitutional Law in the Age of Balancing*, 96 Yale L.J. 943 (1987).

seems to result in such a presumption of correctness. Although in the garbage search cases, majorities of both the Washington and New Jersey courts did disagree with the Supreme Court's decision, the criteria approach (most pronounced in Washington) shifts the debate away from analyzing the state constitution to a preoccupation with the shadow or glare cast by the U.S. Supreme Court decision. For these reasons, the criteria approach, while appealing to lawyers and judges, ought to be avoided, because the underlying premise on which it is based is invalid. Decisions of the Supreme Court declining to recognize rights should not be accorded special weight in state constitutional interpretation. Indeed, they should not carry any presumptive validity.

The type of criteria, factors, and standards listed by the New Jersey, Washington, Pennsylvania, and other justices, as well as other commentators, do reflect circumstances in which state courts have interpreted their constitutions to provide more extensive rights than their federal counterpart.[189] They properly serve as important guides for scholars, courts, and advocates. Attorney Hugh Spitzer has pointed out the importance of *Gunwall*-type factors for this purpose.[190] But they should not at the same time serve as *limitations* on state court authority to disagree with Supreme Court constitutional analysis, even if none of the factors is present. A state high court has the duty, in considering the supreme law of the state, to adopt a reasoned interpretation of its own constitution despite what the U.S. Supreme Court has said when interpreting a different constitution under different institutional circumstances.[191]

Wisconsin Chief Justice Shirley Abrahamson, in discussing the garbage search cases,[192] addressed the lingering controversial question of disagreement between state judges and the U.S. Supreme Court:

> But should not different opinions about individual rights in search and seizure cases be expected and accepted?. . . . Differences in interpretation of the state and federal constitutions should be viewed, I believe, as examples of the

[189] *See, e.g.*, A.E. Dick Howard, *State Courts and Constitutional Rights in the Day of the Burger Court*, 62 VA. L. REV. 873, 934–44 (1976); Robert F. Williams, *State Constitutional Law Processes*, 24 WM. & MARY L. REV. 169, 185–95 (1983); Kent M. Williams, Note, *Property Rights Protection Under Article I, Section 10 of the Minnesota Constitution: A Rationale for Providing Possessory Crimes Defendants with Automatic Standing to Challenge Unreasonable Searches and Seizures*, 75 MINN. L. REV. 1255, 1273–1300 (1991).

[190] Hugh D. Spitzer, *New Life for the "Criteria Tests" in State Constitutional Jurisprudence:* Gunwall *Is Dead—Long Live Gunwall*, 37 RUTGERS L.J. 1169 (2006).

[191] *See* Commonwealth v. DeJohn, 403 A.2d 1283, 1289 (Pa. 1979) ("As we believe that *Miller* establishes a dangerous precedent, with great potential for abuse, we decline to follow that case when construing the state constitutional protection against unreasonable searches and seizures."). *See also* State v. Alston, 440 A.2d 1311, 1318–19 (N.J. 1981).

[192] Abrahamson, *supra* note 15, at 725–33.

> difficulties of interpreting language, especially the broad phrases of a bill of rights....
>
> We accept division of opinion within the United States Supreme Court on interpretations of constitutional language. . . . Why should state courts not closely examine a federal decision to determine whether it is sufficiently persuasive to warrant adoption into state law?"[193]

These views recognize the legitimacy of a reasoned difference of opinion, not as a "mere" result-oriented disagreement but rather as the product of honestly held alternative ways of looking at a problem of constitutional interpretation and the consequences of resolving it in a certain way. This attitude has to include rejection of the criteria approach. Former Justice Joseph Grodin of California has made a similar point,[194] as have others.[195]

The garbage search cases involve a disagreement about people's reasonable expectation of privacy. Justice Abrahamson reports that she conducted "her own unscientific survey of Wisconsinites' views on garbage." The "general consensus" was that one's garbage is private. "These views raise questions about how a court determines society's reasonable expectation of privacy."[196] Simply to say that protection under a state constitution may be more extensive than under the federal Constitution fails to confront the question of what those protections should and will be. The highest state courts decide what the state constitution means. The dialogue should concern the meaning of the state constitution itself, rather than on comparing it with, or relating it to, the federal Constitution (or even other state

[193] *Id.* at 731.

[194] Joseph R. Grodin, *Commentary: Some Reflections on State Constitutions*, 15 HASTINGS CONST. L.Q. 391, 400 (1988):

> The presence of distinctive language or history obviously presents the most comfortable context for relying upon independent state grounds. In the absence of such factors, however, state courts are still obliged to find meaning in the provisions of the state constitutions. And . . . neither logic nor history requires that they accord state constitutional language the same meaning as the United States Supreme Court has accorded a comparable provision of the federal Constitution.

*See also* Peter Linzer, *Why Bother with State Bills of Rights?* 68 TEX. L. REV. 1573, 1584–85, 1607–08, 1610 (1990).

[195] *See, e.g.*, G. Alan Tarr, *Constitutional Theory and State Constitutional Interpretation*, 22 RUTGERS L.J. 841, 849 (1991):

> [R]ather than blindly following federal precedent, state judges should independently seek their own best interpretation of their state constitutions. This does not mean that they should altogether ignore federal rulings—they may be adopted or rejected, depending on their inherent persuasiveness. But when state judges forthrightly assert their own perspectives, it is argued, the result is a healthier and more vibrant federalism.

*See also id.* at 847 n. 24, 854–55.

[196] Abrahamson, *supra* note 15, at 729 n.26. Justice Abrahamson considered the problem of "legislative facts" concerning the expectation of privacy in *State v. Rewolinski*, 464 N.W.2d 401, 414 n.1 (Wis. 1990) (Abrahamson, J., dissenting).

constitutions).[197] The current, relational, or criteria-based dialogue is focused on the wrong question, unlike Justice Abrahamson's forthright and refreshing recognition of the real locus of discretion in the state high courts.

Professor Neil McCabe characterized the garbage search cases as reflecting differences of opinion among federal and state courts about "legislative or social facts"—whether society views as reasonable a person's expectation of privacy in his garbage.[198] Obviously, state courts interpreting their own state constitutions may make findings on such legislative or social facts that differ from a federal court's findings under the federal Constitution.

In addition to what has already been pointed out with respect to the differences in text and history between the federal and state constitutions, there are a number of other reasons why the presumption of correctness and its resulting criteria approach are mistaken. Professor Lawrence Sager[199] has convincingly demonstrated that the U.S. Supreme Court often underenforces the federal Constitution out of deference to the states.[200] Justice Harlan had warned of this during the debate over incorporation of the Bill of Rights.[201] Thus, federal decisions should hardly be viewed as limiting the interpretation of state constitutional provisions through the presumption of correctness approach.

Professor Sager's "strategic concerns thesis" is another argument against the presumption of correctness.[202] Pointing to the substantial role of "strategic" considerations in judicial enforcement of constitutional norms, Sager identified

[197] *See supra* note 12 and accompanying text.

[198] Neil Colman McCabe, *Legislative Facts as Evidence in State Constitutional Search Analysis*, 65 Temp. L. Rev. 1229, 1245–51 (1992). *See* State v. Mata, 745 N.W.2d 229, 260–61 (Neb. 2008) (rejecting "factual assumptions" underlying Supreme Court's decision upholding electrocution).

[199] Lawrence Gene Sager, *Fair Measure: The Legal Status of Underenforced Constitutional Norms*, 91 Harv. L. Rev. 1212, 1218–20 (1978). Jeffrey Sutton refers to this perspective as a "federalism discount." Jeffrey S. Sutton, 51 Imperfect Solutions: States and the Making of American Constitutional Law 17, 75 (2018).

[200] "While there is no litmus test for distinguishing these norms, there are indicia of underenforcement. These include a disparity between the scope of a federal judicial construct and that of plausible understandings of the constitutional concept from which it derives, the presence in court opinions of frankly institutional explanations for setting particular limits to a federal judicial construct, and other anomalies. . . ." *Id.* at 1218–19. *See* Montoya v. Ulibarri, 163 P.3d 476, 483 (N.M. 2007); State v. Baldon III, 829 N.W.2d 785, 812 (Iowa 2013) (Appel, J., concurring); Godfrey v. State, 894 N.W.2d 844, 855 (Iowa 2017).

[201] Baldwin v. New York, 399 U.S. 117, 136 (1970), *cited in* State v. Wickes, 910 N.W.2d 554, 575 (Iowa 2018) (Appel, J., concurring specialty). *See* J. Harvie Wilkinson III, *Justice John M. Harlan and the Values of Federalism*, 57 Va. L. Rev. 1185 (1971).

[202] Professor Sager asked, "[T]o what extent, if any, should state judges faced with claims under provisions of their state constitutions feel themselves bound to defer to Supreme Court interpretations of equivalent federal constitutional provisions?" Lawrence Gene Sager, *Foreword: State Courts and the Strategic Space Between the Norms and Rules of Constitutional Law*, 63 Tex. L. Rev. 959, 959 (1985); *see also* Linzer, *supra* note 194, at 1580 ("The gut issue, though, is how closely the state courts should follow federal precedents in applying their states' provisions."); David Schuman, *Advocacy of State Constitutional Law Cases: A Report from the Provinces*, 2 Emerging Issues St. Const. L. 275 (1989).

the possibility of state and federal courts employing different "strategies" in constitutional interpretation. State courts, interpreting their own constitutions, may apply similar "norms of political morality" while seeing a real need to employ different strategies. Sager concluded:

> State judges confront institutional environments and histories that vary dramatically from state to state, and that differ, in any one state, from the homogenized, abstracted, national vision from which the Supreme Court is forced to operate. It is natural and appropriate that in fashioning constitutional rules the state judges' instrumental impulses and judgments differ. . . .
>
> In light of the substantial strategic element in the composition of constitutional rules, the sensitivity of strategic concerns to variations in the political and social climate, the differences in the regulatory scope of the federal and state judiciaries, the diversity of state institutions, and the special familiarity of state judges with the actual working of those institutions, variations among state and federal constitutional rules ought to be both expected and welcomed.[203]

In these circumstances, the "jurisdictional redundancy"[204] of a state constitutional "second look"[205] at constitutional questions makes sense.[206] The adoption of different "strategies" in state and federal constitutional interpretation may, as in the search and seizure cases, reflect a difference of opinion about a "contemporary 'balance' of pragmatic considerations."[207]

Justice William J. Brennan Jr., who had earlier served on the New Jersey Supreme Court, experienced the different perspectives of federal and state supreme courts. In 1966, he made the following observation:

> [A] comment recently made to me by one of my former law partners suggested what I think is a wholly appropriate subject. He said he thought some recent opinions of mine indicated that I had changed some views I had expressed when a member of the New Jersey Supreme Court. In reply, I suggested to my

[203] Sager, *supra* note 202, at 975–76; *see also* Robert B. Keiter, *An Essay on Wyoming Constitutional Interpretation*, 21 LAND & WATER L. REV. 527, 535 (1986) (discussing the institutional reasons for the U.S. Supreme Court's narrow view of standing and concluding that "[t]hese institutional differences between the federal and state courts suggest that active judicial review of public law issues at the state level is not as troublesome theoretically as it is at the federal level"); Lawrence G. Sager, *Some Observations About Race, Sex, and Equal Protection*, 59 TULSA L. REV. 928, 936–58 (1985).

[204] Robert M. Cover, *The Uses of Jurisdictional Redundancy: Interest, Ideology, and Innovation*, 22 WM. & MARY L. REV. 639 (1981). The concept of redundancy is common to the understanding of federal systems. *See* Martin Landau, *Federalism, Redundancy and System Reliability*, 3 PUBLIUS: THE J. FEDERALISM 173, 187–96 (Fall 1973).

[205] Williams, *supra* note 91, at 361.

[206] *See generally* Sager, *supra* note 202. *But see* Earl M. Maltz, *The Dark Side of State Court Activism*, 63 TEX. L. REV. 995 (1985).

[207] State v. Kennedy, 666 P.2d 1316, 1321 (Or. 1983).

> old friend that perhaps what to him seems to reflect a changed viewpoint, may with greater accuracy be said to reflect a change of function. For unmistakably, a high state court judge and a United States Supreme Court Justice must often look at the same case with different eyeglasses.[208]

Two years earlier, he had noted the change of "climate" between a state high court and the U.S. Supreme Court:

> These substantive differences between the functions of the two courts are accompanied by a difference in climate; the winds of criticism and controversy that swirl around the Court in Washington are generally of a higher velocity than those blowing in state capitals—and the temperature is hotter.[209]

Of course, in current times the temperature for state Supreme Court justices can get pretty hot![210]

Professor Louis Bilionis noted that "the constitutionally significant facts may be different at the state and federal levels . . . . Indeed, whenever a constitutional methodology admits a need to accommodate institutional considerations, the possibility for different yet equally correct state and federal results exists."[211] By way of example, he cited the reasonable expectation of privacy analysis in search and seizure cases.[212] A state court's view of "constitutionally significant facts" could certainly differ from the U.S. Supreme Court's view, thus yielding a different outcome.

Professor Paul Kahn argued in favor of an independent state constitutional interpretation, not tied to "unique state sources," as part of the shared national enterprise of constitutional interpretation because, in such matters, there can be no absolute truth. Kahn argued:

> [I] abandon the central premise of most previous works, namely, that the interpretation of a state constitution must rely on unique state sources of law. Those sources include the text of the state constitution, the history of its adoption and application, and the unique, historically identifiable qualities of the state

208 William J. Brennan Jr., *State Supreme Court Judge versus United States Supreme Court Justice: A Change in Function and Perspective*, 19 U. Fla. L. Rev. 225, 227 (1966).

209 William J. Brennan Jr., *Some Aspects of Federalism*, 39 N.Y.U. L. Rev. 945, 949 (1964).

210 *See, e.g.*, Neal Devins, *How State Supreme Courts Take Consequences Into Account: Toward a State-Centered Understanding of State Constitutionalism*, 62 Stan. L. Rev. 1629 (2010); Neal Devins & Nicole Mansker, *Public Opinion and State Supreme Courts*, 13 U. Pa. J. Const. L. 455 P. 229 (2010).

211 Louis D. Bilionis, *On the Significance of Constitutional Spirit*, 70 N.C. L. Rev. 1803, 1808–09 (1992); *see also* McCabe, *supra* note 198 ("legislative or social facts").

212 Bilionis, *supra* note 211, at 1808–09.

> community. State constitutional law, it is assumed, can diverge from federal law only if the differences can be traced to one of these sources. . . .
>
> The doctrine of unique state sources dominates the recent literature. . . . That there should be an intersection between state authority and federal sources is ruled out in advance. This intersection, however, is just the position for which I want to argue. It is the position that many state courts find themselves moving toward, not only because of the meager state sources available, but also because state constitutional debate cannot close its eyes to the larger discursive context within which it finds itself.
>
> . . . .
>
> The doctrine of unique state sources is an approach to constitutional interpretation that rests upon two unexamined assumptions. First, it assumes that differences in the narrow constitution—the formal text and its history—of each state reflect differences in each state's larger constitution. Second, it assumes that constitutional adjudication is a matter of presenting what already exists within those state sources. Both assumptions reflect a fear that the only alternative to an interpretation based upon unique state sources is national uniformity. Interpretive diversity within a common enterprise, however, represents a third possibility that dissipates the fear and undermines the assumptions.
>
> . . . .
>
> Of course, different courts can and will reach different conclusions about the meaning of such constitutional values.[213]

The criteria, or presumption of the validity of the federal interpretation approach is, almost by definition, inconsistent with Professor Kahn's views.

These factors make it particularly important for state courts to look first to their own constitutional provisions and judicial doctrines which predate incorporation of federal Bill of Rights provisions. Second, they should look to state constitutional decisions in other jurisdictions for further guidance. U.S. Supreme Court decisions rejecting asserted federal constitutional rights should persuade state courts confronting similar claims under their state constitutions only by their reasoning, discounted for federalism or strategic concerns, or any other type of deference to the states. The decisions should not be followed merely because of the U.S. Supreme Court's institutional position as the highest court in the land for the resolution of federal constitutional claims.[214]

[213] Paul W. Kahn, *Interpretation and Authority in State Constitutionalism*, 106 HARV. L. REV. 1147, 1147, 1152–53, 1160, 1161 (1993) (footnote omitted).

[214] *See* Williams, *supra* note 91, at 396–97.

The relational, criteria approach starts from the federal precedent and considers the question of deviation. Truly independent state constitutional interpretation, by contrast, is based on state court autonomy. Professor Thomas Morawetz explained this distinction:

> On one hand, many judges write as if congruence with the federal rule is the norm, and deviation from the federal norm is an exception that needs to be justified in the light of special reasons. Judges who proceed from this assumption differ among themselves about the kinds of reasons that warrant deviation. On the other hand, many judges imply that autonomy from federal interpretations of federal law is the norm and that congruence between the federal and the state standard is, at best, coincidence.....
>
> Thus, from the standpoint of power and authority, it is appropriate to see state courts as needing to justify deviation from the federal norm, to justify expanding a right. But from the standpoint of interpretive responsibility, state courts are necessarily autonomous, committed by the very nature of the judicial task to offering a compelling account of the rights in question, an account that may or may not dovetail with the federal understanding.[215]

Professor Morawetz referred to the Connecticut criteria analysis[216] as the "smorgasbord" approach.[217]

In 2007, the Utah Supreme Court, in an opinion by Chief Justice Christine Durham, rejected the criteria approach, both as a briefing requirement and as a rigid analytical method.[218] The court declined to require a "formula of some kind for adequate framing and briefing of state constitutional issues"[219] and stated:

> In theory, a claimant could rely on nothing more than plain language to make an argument for a construction of a Utah provision that would be different from the interpretation the federal courts have given similar language. Independent analysis must begin with the constitutional text and rely on whatever assistance legitimate sources may provide in the interpretive process. There is no presumption that federal construction of similar language is correct.[220]

215 Thomas Morawetz, *Deviation and Autonomy: The Jurisprudence of Interpretation in State Constitutional Law*, 26 CONN. L. REV. 635, 638–39, 657 (1994).

216 *See supra* notes 140–53 and accompanying text.

217 Morawetz, *supra* note 215, at 644.

218 State v. Tiedemann, 162 P.3d 1106, 1112–15 (Utah 2007).

219 *Id.* at 1114.

220 *Id.*

## VIII. Continuing LegitimaCy and Methodology Debates

The criteria cases reflect a fundamental debate about the legitimacy of independent state constitutional interpretation in cases where there are also similar or identical federal constitutional guarantees. Despite repeated assurances by the U.S. Supreme Court itself that the practice is unexceptional,[221] the legitimacy debate continues to rage. It is a central question of constitutional theory, albeit one of state rather than federal constitutional theory. These legitimacy questions in state cases "evading"[222] Supreme Court precedent fuel the debate over the need for standards or criteria by which to justify rejection of Supreme Court decisions.[223]

State court justices have continued the debate reflected in the garbage search decisions and in the *Hunt*, *Gunwall*, and *Edmunds* criteria or factor lines of cases. Split high courts in New York,[224] Texas,[225] California,[226] Michigan,[227] and Massachusetts,[228] while deciding important substantive state constitutional questions and serving an important teaching function, have also disputed methodology questions and the situations in which it was legitimate for state courts to diverge from Supreme Court precedent. The Wyoming Supreme Court justices,

[221] *See supra* note 157 and accompanying text. As early as 1945 in *Chase Securities Corp. v. Donaldson*, 325 U.S. 304, 312–13 (1945), the U.S. Supreme Court had advised:

> We are reminded that some state courts have not followed it [a United States Supreme Court decision] in construing provisions of their constitutions similar to the due process clause. Many have, as they are privileged to do, so interpreted their own easily amendable constitutions to give restrictive clauses a more rigid interpretation than we properly could impose upon them from without by construction of the federal instrument which is amendable only with great difficulty and with the cooperation of many States.
> (footnote omitted).

[222] *See* Donald E. Wilkes Jr., *More on the New Federalism in Criminal Procedure*, 63 Ky. L.J. 873, 873 n.2 (1975) (referring to "evasion" cases); Donald E. Wilkes Jr., *The New Federalism in Criminal Procedure: State Court Evasion of the Burger Court*, 62 Ky. L.J. 421 (1974).

[223] This search is not really new. *See* Gabrielli v. Knickerbocker, 82 P.2d 391, 393 (Cal. 1938) ("[C]ogent reasons must exist before a state court in construing a provision of the state constitution will depart from the construction placed by the Supreme Court of the United States on a similar provision in the federal constitution."); *see also* People v. Disbrow, 545 P.2d 272, 283–84 (Cal. 1976) (Richardson, J., dissenting); Zacchini v. Scripps-Howard Broadcasting Co., 376 N.E.2d 582, 583 (Ohio 1978); State v. Florance, 527 P.2d 1202, 1209 (Or. 1974).

[224] People v. Scott, 593 N.E.2d 1328 (N.Y. 1992).

[225] Davenport v. Garcia, 834 S.W.2d 4 (Tex. 1992); *see also Ex parte Tucci*, 859 S.W.2d 1 (Tex. 1993); Star-Telegram, Inc. v. Walker, 834 S.W.2d 54 (Tex. 1992); Texas Dept. Trans. v. Barber, 111 S.W.3d 86, 105–06 (Tex. 2003).

[226] Sands v. Morongo Unified Sch. Dist., 809 P.2d 809 (Cal. 1991). *See generally* Mark R. Drozdowski, Comment, *Building Castles Out of Sands: An Analysis of the Competing Adjudicative Models Used by the California Supreme Court in* Sands v. Morongo Unified School District, 40 UCLA L. Rev. 253 (1992).

[227] People v. Bullock, 485 N.W.2d 866 (Mich. 1992).

[228] Guiney v. Police Comm'r, 582 N.E.2d. 523 (Mass. 1991). *See also* State v. Schwartz, 689 N.W.2d 430, 440–41 (S.D. 2004); Ortiz v. State, 869 A.2d 285, 290–91 n.4 (Del. 2005); State v. Melde, 725 N.W.2d 99, 104 n.5 (Minn. 2006); Fertig v. State, 146 P.3d 492, 496–97 (Wyo. 2006).

for example, engaged in debate through the 1990s on the proper methodology to apply in cases where litigants argued for greater protection under the state constitution. The debate began in 1993 in *Saldana v. State*, which produced four opinions based on methodology.[229] In 1999, the court appeared to settle on the criteria approach,[230] which it now applies.[231]

The New York Court of Appeals had exhibited some tendencies toward the criteria approach as a limiting doctrine.[232] In *People v. P. J. Video, Inc.*,[233] for example, the court distinguished between "interpretive" and "noninterpretive" state constitutional construction, but both approaches sounded like the relational, criteria approach:

> If the language of the State Constitution differs from that of its Federal counterpart, then the court may conclude that there is a basis for a different interpretation of it. . . . Such an analysis considers whether the textual language of the State Constitution specifically recognizes rights not enumerated in the Federal Constitution; whether language in the State Constitution is sufficiently unique to support a broader interpretation of the individual right under State law; whether the history of the adoption of the text reveals an intention to make the State provision coextensive with, or broader than, the parallel Federal provision; and whether the very structure and purpose of the State Constitution serves to expressly affirm certain rights rather than merely restrain the sovereign power of the State. A non-interpretive analysis attempts to discover, for example, any pre-existing State statutory or common law defining the scope of the individual right in question; the history and traditions of the State in its protection of the individual right; any identification of the right in the State Constitution as being one of peculiar State or local concern; and any distinctive attitudes of the State citizenry toward the definition, scope or protection of the individual right.[234]

[229] 846 P.2d 604 (Wyo. 1993).

[230] Vasquez v. State, 990 P.2d 476, 486 (Wyo. 1999).

[231] *See* Mogard v. City of Laramie, 32 P.3d 313 (Wyo. 2001). *See also* Cordova v. State, 33 P.3d 142, 146–47 (Wyo. 2001); Sheesley v. State, 437 P.3d 830, 836-37 (Wyo. 2019).

[232] *See Galie*, *supra* note 46, at 234; *see also* Daniel C. Kramer & Robert Riga, *Acceptance and Rejection of State Constitutional Authority in Civil Liberties Decisions: A Sampling of Findings in the New York Court of Appeals*, St. Const. Commentaries & Notes, Winter 1992, 13.

[233] 501 N.E.2d 556 (N.Y. 1986). Professor Robert M. Pitler provided a thorough and illuminating analysis of New York's experience with the criteria approach. *See* Robert M. Pitler, *Independent State Search and Seizure Constitutionalism: The New York State Court of Appeals' Quest for Principled Decisionmaking*, 62 Brook. L. Rev. 1, 185–322 (1996).

[234] *P.J. Video*, 501 N.E.2d at 560.

Despite these indications of the criteria approach, however, the New York court has not adhered to it in any predictable or uniform way.[235] Methodological problems other than the criteria approach, such as the sequence of state and federal constitutional analysis and whether to engage in both, have also been handled in different ways by the New York court.[236] These issues came to a head in 1992, in a full debate over the legitimacy of independent state constitutional interpretation. In *People v. Scott* and *People v. Keta*,[237] decided together, the New York Court of Appeals disagreed with the U.S. Supreme Court in rejecting, respectively, the "open fields" doctrine and the "administrative search" exception in search and seizure cases. Judge Joseph Bellacosa, with Judge Richard Simons and Chief Judge Sol Wachtler in agreement, wrote a bitter, accusatorial dissent aimed at both the substance and methodology of the majority opinions:[238]

> The doctrine that State courts should interpret their own State Constitutions, where appropriate, to supplement rights guaranteed by the Federal Constitution is not in dispute. Indeed, we have shown our support for that doctrine where appropriate with our votes in a long line of cases.... We do strenuously disagree with the Court, however, that the doctrine is being "cautiously exercised"... and believe that the applications of the doctrine here create a sweeping, new and unsettling interpretation—not mere application of settled principles.[239]

[235] *See, e.g.*, People v. Dunn, 564 N.E.2d 1054 (N.Y. 1990). In *Dunn*, the New York Court of Appeals disagreed with the U.S. Supreme Court and concluded that a "canine sniff" in a hallway was a search under the New York Constitution, but in this case concluded that the search was based on reasonable suspicion. Two judges concurred in the result but stated that they would not hold that there was a search. The majority did not rely on the criteria approach. In several other cases, however, the court has referred to the *P.J. Video* "general rules governing independent State review...." People v. Harris, 570 N.E.2d 1051, 1053 (N.Y. 1991); People v. Reynolds, 523 N.E.2d 291, 293 (N.Y. 1988); *see* Vincent Martin Bonventre, *Court of Appeals—State Constitutional Law Review*, 1991, 14 PACE L. REV. 353, 357–69 (1994) (discussing *Harris*).

[236] Immuno A.G. v. Moor-Jankowski, 567 N.E.2d 1270 (N.Y. 1991). In *Immuno*, Judge Simons, criticizing the majority's methodology of deciding both the federal and state constitutional issues, stated: "As Judge Kaye notes... neither the Court nor its individual Judges have consistently followed any announced standards for departing from Federal law to adopt a different State rule or settled on any preferred methodology for doing so." *Id.* at 1286 n.2 (Simmons, J. concurring) (citations omitted).

[237] 593 N.E.2d 1328 (N.Y. 1992). *See generally* Luke Bierman, *Horizontal Pressures and Vertical Tensions: State Constitutional Discordancy at the New York Court of Appeals*, 12 TOURO L. REV. 633 (1996); Eve Cary & Mary R. Falk, *People v. Scott & People v. Keta: "Democracy Begins in Conversation,"* 58 BROOK. L. REV. 1279 (1993); Pitler, *supra* note 233, at 218.

[238] *Scott*, 593 N.E.2d at 1348–49 (Bellacosa, J., dissenting) ("Simply stated, the common issue is whether this Court has a justifiable basis, within its recently rearticulated method of noninterpretative analysis, to apply New York's mirror equivalent to the Fourth Amendment... differently from the United States Supreme Court in these cases.").

[239] *Id.* at 1356 (Bellacosa, J., dissenting) (emphasis removed). *See also* State v. Kelliher, 873 S.E. 2d 366 (N.C. 2022).

Judge Bellacosa considered the majority view a mere disagreement with the U.S. Supreme Court, after which "New York's adjudicative process is left bereft of any external or internal doctrinal disciplines."[240] The majority, in his view, had simply "superimpose[d] its preferred view of the constitutional universe."[241]

Judge Judith Kaye concurred with the majority opinions to address the methodological issues raised by Judge Bellacosa.[242] Her observations justify careful consideration:

> The dissent in this case is distinctive only in the tone of its expression, most especially its accusation that the Court's legal conclusions and analysis are the product of ideology, simply the imposition of a personally preferred view of the constitutional universe. . . . First, however much we might consider ourselves dispensing justice strictly according to formula, at some point the decisions we make must come down to judgments as to whether . . . constitutional protections we have enjoyed in this State have in fact been diluted by subsequent decisions of a more recent Supreme Court. In that no two cases are identical, it is in the nature of our process that in the end a judgment must be made as to the application of existing precedents to new facts. To some extent that has taken place in the two cases before us. . . . We may disagree in our application of precedents, but our considered judgment hardly justifies attack for lack of principle, or for overthrowing stare decisis.
>
> Second, I disagree with the dissent that, in an evolving field of constitutional rights, a methodology must stand as an *ironclad checklist* to be rigidly applied on pain of being accused of lack of principle or lack of adherence to stare decisis. We must of course be faithful to our precedents, as I believe we are in the cases now before us. But where we conclude that the Supreme Court has changed course and diluted constitutional principles, I cannot agree that we act improperly in discharging our responsibility to support the State Constitution when we examine whether we should follow along as a matter of State law—wherever that may fall on the checklist.
>
> . . . .
>
> Time and again in recent years, the Supreme Court as well as its individual Justices have reminded State courts not merely of their right but also of their responsibility to interpret their own Constitutions, and where in the State courts' view those provisions afford greater safeguards than the Supreme Court would

[240] *Id.* (citations omitted).

[241] *Id.*; *see also id.* at 1348–49 (Bellacosa, J., dissenting). Such attacks on independent state constitutional interpretation are not new. *See* Williams, *supra* note 91, at 357–58; Friedman v. Commissioner of Public Safety, 473 N.W.2d 828, 845–46 (Minn. 1991) (Coyne, J., dissenting).

[242] *See Scott*, 593 N.E.2d at 1346 (Kaye, J., concurring).

> find, to make plain the State decisional ground so as to avoid unnecessary Supreme Court review.
>
> The Supreme Court is not insulted when we do so.[243] . . .
>
> In those instances where we have gone beyond Supreme Court interpretations of Federal constitutional requirements, our objective has been the protection of fundamental rights, consistent with our Constitution, our precedents and own best human judgments in applying them.[244]

This frank, on-the-bench assessment of the human difficulties of judging complex controversies, based on general state and federal constitutional phrases like "unreasonable search and seizure," is refreshing. It mirrors Justice Abrahamson's off-the-bench discussion of the same problem.[245] Of the New York dissenters, in fact, at least two had described independent state constitutional law in glowing terms in off-the-bench writings.[246] In this light, it seems just as likely that the dissent was as "result-oriented" as was the majority. The charge of a result-oriented decision can be made in this context only when one uses the Supreme Court decision as the starting point, or referent, for legal reasoning. As Judge Kaye

[243] *Id.* at 1346–47 (Kaye, J., concurring) (emphasis added). The Supreme Court of Maine quoted Chief Judge Kaye's rejection of the "ironclad checklist" approach. State v. Melvin, 955 A.2d 245, 250 (Me. 2008). Judge Kaye's statement was quoted with approval in *People v. Pavone*, 47 N.E.3d 56, 64 (N.Y. 2015). *See also* State v. Tiedemann, 162 P.3d 1106, 1112–15 (Utah 2007); People v. Davis, 695 N.W.2d 45, 55–56 (Mich. 2005) (Kelly, J., dissenting). *See* Vincent Martin Bonventre, *New York's Chief Judge Kaye: Her Separate Opinions Bode Well for Renewed State Constitutionalism at the Court of Appeals*, 67 Temp. L. Rev. 1163, 1192–96 (1994).

[244] *Scott*, 593 N.E.2d at 1348 (Kaye, J., concurring). For a similar case in New Hampshire, see *State v. Canelo*, 653 A.2d 1097 (N.H. 1995). Justice W. Stephen Thayer's dissent argued that the court's independent approach to state constitutional analysis did not "give us permission to invent new constitutional protections that some may argue are based on the whim of the majority." *Id.* at 1112 (Thayer, J., dissenting). Justice William Johnson concurred specially: "Such heightened rhetoric adds nothing to the jurisprudence of our State. I know of no one on this court—and, I stress, no one—who decides the cases that come before us on a whim." *Id.* at 1106 (Johnson, J., concurring).

In a 1987 dissent, Justice Thayer had made the following point, after criticizing the majority for deciding a case on state constitutional grounds without discussing a contrary U.S. Supreme Court decision:

> Our citizens are entitled, and indeed have the right, to seek redress under our State Constitution. However, when interpreting the State Constitution, this court's analysis should, at the very least, distinguish United States Supreme Court decisions concerning the same issue, especially if an inconsistent holding results. The citizens of this State are entitled to know when their State Constitution is being interpreted in such a way as to give individuals accused of crimes greater rights than these same individuals are given under the Federal Constitution, because our citizens have the constitutional right to correct the imbalance, if they wish, by constitutional revision.
>
> State v. Denney, 536 A.2d 1242, 1250 (N.H. 1987).

[245] Abrahamson, *supra* note 15 and accompanying text; *see also* Beck, *supra* note 114, at 1038.

[246] Joseph W. Bellacosa, *A New York State Constitution: A Touch of Class*, 59 N.Y. St. B.J. 14 (Apr. 1987); Sol Wachtler, *Our Constitutions—Alive and Well*, 61 St. John's L. Rev. 381 (1987); *see also* Pitler, *supra* note 233, at 231 n.909.

pointed out, it was not the effect of result orientation but the exercise of independent judicial judgment that drove the majority.

In the Texas case, striking down an overly broad gag rule, Justice Lloyd Doggett's seventy-footnote treatise on independent state constitutional analysis, generally and with specific reference to Texas, was met with a concurring opinion by Justice Nathan Hecht. His concurrence leveled a broad attack on reliance on the state constitution where there was relevant federal free speech doctrine that would arguably support the same outcome.[247] These opinions taken together provide a very sophisticated treatment of the current issues in judicial federalism. But they focus on legitimacy concerns that should not still be bothering state court justices. The debate would continue in Texas.[248]

In the California case involving prayers at public school graduation, the court held that such prayers were constitutionally impermissible.[249] The five separate opinions, however, disagreed not only as to the merits but as to the methodology to be employed in cases raising both state and federal constitutional claims.[250] Chief Justice Malcolm Lucas concurred but argued that the state constitutional claim should not be reached until the Supreme Court had resolved the federal constitutional issue.[251] He supported the notion of "deference" to Supreme Court decisions and departure from them only for "cogent reasons."[252] Justice Stanley Mosk also concurred but reasoned that state constitutional claims should be reached before federal claims.[253] The dissenting justices analyzed the state constitutional claims.[254]

The Michigan case involved the state constitution's "cruel *or* unusual" punishments clause and imposition of a mandatory life sentence without parole for possession of 650 grams of cocaine.[255] Here, by contrast to the Texas and California cases, the U.S. Supreme Court had already upheld the Michigan life sentence statute.[256] The Michigan court struck down the penalty, though, observing that the Supreme Court decision was only "persuasive authority" for state constitutional interpretation and that "we may in some cases find more persuasive, and choose to rely upon, the reasoning of the dissenting justices of that Court. . . ."[257] Justice Michael Cavanagh's majority opinion held itself to a "compelling reason"[258] standard for disagreement with the Supreme Court but found

[247] Davenport v. Garcia, 834 S.W.2d 4, 24–45 (Tex. 1992) (Hecht, J., concurring).
[248] *See In re* J.W.T., 872 S.W.2d 189 (Tex. 1994).
[249] Sands v. Morongo Unified Sch. Dist., 809 P.2d 809, 810, 820 (Cal. 1991).
[250] *Id.* at 821, 835.
[251] *Id.* at 822, 833 (Lucas, C.J., concurring).
[252] *Id.* at 834 (*quoting* Raven v. Deukmejian, 801 P.2d 1077, 1088 (Cal. 1990)).
[253] *Id.* at 836 (Mosk, J., concurring).
[254] *Id.* at 853–58, 863–64.
[255] People v. Bullock, 485 N.W.2d 866, 867 (Mich. 1992).
[256] Harmelin v. Michigan, 501 U.S. 957 (1991).
[257] *Bullock*, 485 N.W.2d at 870.
[258] *Id.* at 871.

such compelling reasons to be present.[259] This seems like the criteria approach. Justice Dorothy Riley wrote a partial dissent, reasoning that compelling reasons had not been shown sufficiently to justify departure from the Supreme Court decision.[260]

This debate continued in Michigan.[261] In 1996, in *People v. Bender*,[262] the Michigan court held that a confession must be suppressed where an attorney is present and seeking to advise the defendant and the police fail to inform the defendant of this situation, thus rejecting U.S. Supreme Court precedent.[263] The majority declined to apply its "compelling reasons" standard to establish a "conclusive presumption artificially linking state constitutional interpretation to federal law."[264] Justice Patricia Boyle dissented:

> Today, without a single foundation in the language, historical context, or the jurisprudence of this Court, a majority of the Court engrafts its own "enlightened" view of the Constitution of 1963, art. I, § 17, on the citizens of the State of Michigan. With nothing more substantial than a disagreement with the United States Supreme Court as the basis for its conclusion, a majority of the Court ignores our obligation to find a principled basis for the creation of new rights and imposes a benefit on suspects that will eliminate voluntary and knowledgeable confessions from the arsenal of society's weapons against crime...
>
> ... Although we have repeatedly concluded that our constitution should be interpreted differently only if there is a compelling reason for doing so ... the lead opinion is not hindered by traditional principles of constitutional interpretation.[265]

The Massachusetts case dealt with random drug testing of police officers.[266] Like the Michigan case, the federal constitutional issue had been answered against the rights claimants, in federal litigation involving the same litigants.[267] The

[259] *Id.* at 872–77.
[260] *Id.* at 880, 883–89 (Riley, J., concurring in part and dissenting in part).
[261] *See, e.g.*, People v. Mezy, 551 N.W.2d 389, 394 (Mich. 1996); People v. Champion, 549 N.W.2d 849, 852–53 n.3 (Mich. 1996); Kivela v. Department of Treasury, 536 N.W.2d 498, 502–04 (Mich. 1995).
[262] 551 N.W.2d 71 (Mich. 1996).
[263] Moran v. Burbine, 475 U.S. 412 (1986). In *Moran*, the U.S. Supreme Court had noted that "[n]othing we say today disables the States from adopting different requirements for the conduct of its employees and officials as a matter of state law." *Id.* at 428.
[264] *Bender*, 551 N.W.2d at 79 n.17 (*quoting* Sitz v. Department of State Police, 506 N.W.2d 209 (Mich. 1993)).
[265] *Id.* at 84, 86 (Boyle, J., dissenting). *See also* State v. Davis, 79 P.3d 64, 67–68 (Ariz. 2003) ("compelling reason"); People v. Goldston, 682 N.W.2d 479, 485 (Mich. 2004). For cases in other states espousing the criteria approach, *see, e.g.*, McCaughtry v. City of Red Wing, 831 N.W.2d 518, 528 n. 2 (Minn. 2013) (Anderson, J., concurring); Doe v. Wilmington Housing Authority, 88 A.3d 654, 662 (Del. 2014); State v. Fox, 868 N.W.2d 206, 218 (Minn. 2015).
[266] Guiney v. Police Comm'r, 582 N.E.2d 523, 524 (Mass. 1991).
[267] Guiney v. Roache, 873 F.2d 1557 (1st Cir. 1989).

Massachusetts Supreme Judicial Court, despite the federal ruling, struck down the random drug testing under the state constitution in an opinion by Justice Herbert Wilkins.[268] Justice Joseph Nolan's dissenting opinion criticized the majority for finding "some hidden meaning" in the state constitution, without "any standard used to deviate from the position of the Supreme Court."[269] Justice Nolan asserted the lack of "compelling reasons" and the absence of "any coherent rationale for this court to disagree with the Supreme Court."[270] This is a call for the criteria approach.

As these cases in New Jersey, Washington, New York, Texas, California, Michigan, and Massachusetts show, the legitimacy questions associated with independent state constitutional analysis, by contrast to the merits of the outcome of the case under the state constitution, are still argued vigorously. The relational approach abides.

At bottom, the presumption of correctness relegates state constitutional protections to "a mere row of shadows."[271] Justice David H. Souter wrote these words while serving on the New Hampshire Supreme Court. He observed:

> It is the need of every appellate court for the participation of the bar in the process of trying to think sensibly and comprehensively about the questions that the judicial power has been established to answer. Nowhere is the need greater than in the field of State constitutional law, where we are asked so often to confront questions that have already been decided under the National Constitution. If we place too much reliance on federal precedent we will render the State rules a mere row of shadows; if we place too little, we will render State practice incoherent. If we are going to steer between these extremes, we will have to insist on developed advocacy from those who bring the cases before us.[272]

State constitutional provisions need not, and should not, be reduced to a "row of shadows" through too much reliance on federal precedent. Swinging the pendulum in the other direction, however, where too little reliance on federal precedent will "render State practice incoherent," is also unnecessary. It does not make sense to advocate "zero-based" state constitutional interpretation,[273] with no reference at all to U.S. Supreme Court interpretations of the federal Constitution on similar questions. But the overwhelming gravitational pull of

[268] *Guiney*, 582 N.E.2d at 525–26.
[269] *Id.* at 527 (Nolan, J., dissenting).
[270] *Id.* (*citing* Commonwealth v. Cast, 556 N.E.2d 69, 79 (Mass. 1990)).
[271] State v. Bradberry, 522 A.2d 1380, 1389 (N.H. 1986) (Souter, J., concurring specially).
[272] *Id.* (emphasis added).
[273] Maurice Kelman, *Foreword: Rediscovering the State Constitutional Bill of Rights*, 27 Wayne L. Rev. 413, 429 (1981).

those interpretations must be counteracted. With some informed attention to constitutional texts, history, and the lessons of federalism—aided by the insights of practicing and academic lawyers—state courts can and should have coherent, independent doctrines surrounding their state constitutional provisions.[274]

## IX. OTHER PROCEDURAL ISSUES OF THE NEW JUDICIAL FEDERALISM

When state courts are dealing with independent state constitutional rights above or beyond the national minimum standards established by the federal Constitution, as interpreted by the U.S. Supreme Court, they may also be independent on procedural matters such as harmless error, retroactivity, and waiver of rights.

In *Cooper v. California*,[275] the Court held that the California Supreme Court had incorrectly applied a Fourth Amendment precedent and that federal law did not require suppression of the disputed evidence. Justice Black, however, observed:

> Our holding, of course, does not affect the State's power to impose higher standards on searches and seizures than required by the Federal Constitution if it chooses to do so. And when such state standards alone have been violated, the State is free, without review by us, to apply its own state harmless error rule to such errors of state law. There being no federal constitutional error here, there is no need for us to determine whether the lower court properly applied its state harmless error rule.[276]

Questions of retroactivity of state constitutional rulings, as well, can be handled by state courts independently.[277] As stated by the Indiana Supreme Court, "Federal law does not govern retroactivity of a new rule of criminal procedure

[274] Oregon Justice Hans A. Linde said that in order "to make an independent argument under the state clause [it] takes homework—in texts, in history, in alternative approaches to analysis." Hans A. Linde, *First Things First: Rediscovering the States' Bills of Rights*, 9 U. Balt. L. Rev. 379, 392 (1980).

[275] 386 U.S. 58 (1967).

[276] *Id.* at 62. For a discussion of California's constitutional harmless error rule in the field left to it after *Cooper*, see Note, *The California Constitution and the California Supreme Court in Conflict Over the Harmless Error Rule*, 32 Hastings L.J. 687 (1981). *See also* State v. Benoit, 417 A.2d 895, 901 (R.I. 1980); People v. Cahill, 853 P.2d 1037, 1043–60 (Cal. 1993) (California Constitution itself contains a harmless error rule); State v. Harris, 544 N.W.2d 545, 561 (Wis. 1996) (Abrahamson, J., concurring); State v. White, 543 N.W.2d 725 (Neb. 1996); Cassim v. Allstate Insurance Co., 94 P.3d 513, 524–25 (Cal. 2004). Some states constitutionalize the harmless error rule. *See, e.g.*, Oregon Const. art. VII, § 3.

[277] Mary C. Hutton, *Retroactivity in the States: The Impact of* Teague v. Lane *on State Postconviction Remedies*, 44 Ala. L. Rev. 421 (1993).

that derives from the state constitution."[278] In addition, in 2008 the U.S. Supreme Court vindicated the views of a number of state courts and concluded that they could diverge from the retroactivity rules of even *federal* rights decisions.[279]

Waiver issues concerning state constitutional rights may also be analyzed differently from, or independently of, federal constitutional approaches.[280] The West Virginia Supreme Court of Appeals ruled that a union could not waive its members' free speech rights in a union contract.[281] The court relied on the following provision:

> All men are, by nature, equally free and independent, and have certain inherent rights, of which, when they enter into a state of society, they cannot, by any compact, deprive or divest their posterity . . .[282]

## A. Direct Right of Action for Money Damages

A direct right of action for money damages in the absence of authorizing legislation was recognized at the federal level for Fourth Amendment violations.[283] With the rise of the NJF, this question has become very important in state constitutional law,[284] and the states are divided on the issue. The Oregon Supreme Court considered the matter to be one for the legislature and concluded that "Oregon's Bill of Rights provides no textual or historical basis for implying a right to damages for constitutional violations."[285] California, along with other states, has followed this view.[286] Several courts have conditioned their refusal to recognize a cause of action on the availability of statutory or administrative remedies.[287]

[278] Membres v. State, 889 N.E.2d 265, 272 (Ind. 2008). *See generally* Honorable Laura Denvir Stith, *A Contrast of State and Federal Court Authority to Grant Habeas Relief*, 38 VAL. U. L. REV. 421 (2004).

[279] Danforth v. Minnesota, 552 U.S. 264 (2008). *See, e.g.*, Bush v. State, 428 S.W.3d 1, 11–12 (Tenn. 2014); *In re* Haghighi, 309 P.3d 459, 462 (Wash. 2013).

In 2021, however, the Court held that criminal *procedure* decisions would never be retroactive on federal collateral review. Edwards v. Vannoy, 593 U.S. ___ (2021). It remains to be seen whether the *Danforth* rule will pertain in these circumstances.

[280] Lee v. City of Missoula Police Dept., 187 P.3d 609, 612 (Mont. 2008); State v. Stephenson, 878 S.W.2d 530 (Tenn. 1994); Choi v. State, 560 A.2d 1108 (Md. 1989).

[281] Woodruff v. Board of Trustees of Cabell Huntington Hosp., 319 S.E.2d 372 (W. Va. 1984).

[282] W. VA. CONST. art. III, § 1.

[283] Bivens v. Six Unknown Named Agents of Fed. Bur. Of Narcotics, 403 U.S. 388 (1971); Susan Bandes, *Reinventing* Bivens: *The Self-Executing Constitution*, 68 S. CAL. L. REV. 289 (1995).

[284] *See* FRIESEN, *supra* note 26, at ch. 7.

[285] Hunter v. City of Eugene, 787 P.2d 881, 883–84 (Or. 1990).

[286] Katzberg v. Regents of the University of California, 58 P.3d 339 (Cal. 2002); Degrassi v. Cook, 58 P.3d 360 (Cal. 2002); St. Luke Hospital v. Straub, 354 S.W.3d 529 (Ky. 2011); Gordon v. Maesaka-Hirata, 431 P.3d 708 (Haw. 2018) (sovereign immunity); Fields v. Mellinger, 851 S.E.2d 789 (W.Va. 2020).

[287] Provens v. Stark Cty. Bd. of Mental Retardation & Developmental Disabilities, 594 N.E.2d 959 (Ohio 1992). *See* David M. Gareau, *Opening the Courthouse Doors: Allowing a Cause of Action to*

The Supreme Court of North Carolina took the opposite view, concluding that, if constitutional wrongs were to have a remedy, the judiciary must rely on its common-law tradition to implement its "responsibility to protect the state constitutional rights of the citizens. . . ."[288] The New York Court of Appeals took a similar approach.[289] This matter is very important and will arise eventually in any state that does not have legislation, like 42 U.S.C. Section 1983 at the federal level, authorizing a cause of action for damages as a remedy for state constitutional violations.[290] In 2017, Justice Brent Appel of the Iowa Supreme, writing for a divided court, wrote a scholarly opinion holding that there was a private right of action for money damages under the Iowa Constitution. He linked his conclusion to the self-executing nature of the constitution's equality clause.[291] In 2018, the court held, in another thorough opinion, that qualified immunity could apply to such claims.[292] Justice Appel dissented.[293] This question does not normally arise with respect to declaratory and injunctive relief.[294]

## B. State Action

The state action doctrine in federal constitutional law operates as a significant limit on the reach of federal constitutional law.[295] Like so many other doctrines, this one might be viewed differently by courts interpreting and applying state constitutional rights provisions. First, some state constitutional

*Arise Directly from a Violation of the Ohio Constitution*, 43 CLEV. ST. L. REV. 459 (1995). *See also* State, Dept. of Corrections v. Heisey, 271 P.3d 1082, 1096 (Alaska 2012).

[288] Corum v. University of North Carolina, 413 S.E.2d 276, 289–92 (N.C. 1992); John D. Boutwell, *The Cause of Action for Damages Under North Carolina's Constitution*: Corum v. University of North Carolina, 70 N.C. L. REV. 1899 (1992). *See also* Zullo v. State, 205 A.3d 466 (Vt. 2019).

[289] Brown v. State, 674 N.E.2d 1129 (N.Y. 1996). *See* Martin A. Schwartz, *Claims for Damages for Violations of State Constitutional Rights*, 14 TOURO L. REV. 657 (1998); Gail Donoghue & Jonathan I. Edelstein, *Life After* Brown: *The Future of State Constitutional Tort Actions in New York*, 42 N.Y.L. SCH. L. REV. 447 (1998).

[290] *See* Sheldon H. Nahmod, *State Constitutional Torts: Deshaney, Reverse-Federalism and Community*, 26 RUTGERS L.J. 949 (1995); T. Hunter Jefferson, Note, *Constitutional Wrongs and Common Law Principles: The Case for the Recognition of State Constitutional Tort Actions Against State Governments*, 50 VAND. L. REV. 1525 (1997); John M. Baker, *The Minnesota Constitution as a Sword: The Evolving Private Cause of Action*, 20 WM. MITCHELL L. REV. 313 (1994).

[291] Godfrey v. State, 898 N.W.2d 844 (Iowa 2017).

[292] Baldwin v. City of Estherville, 915 N.W.2d 259 (Iowa 2018).

[293] *Id.* at 281 (Appel, J., dissenting).

[294] City of Elsa v. M.A.L., 226 S.W.3d 390, 392 (Tex. 2007).

[295] *See generally* Robert J. Glennon Jr. & John E. Nowak, *A Functional Analysis of the Fourteenth Amendment "State Action" Requirement*, 1976 SUP. CT. REV. 221 (1977); Flagg Bros., Inc. v. Brooks, 436 U.S. 149 (1978); Paul Brest, *State Action and Liberal Theory: A Case Note on* Flagg Brothers v. Brooks, 130 U. PA. L. REV. 1296 (1982).

provisions, by their terms, apply to private action.[296] Further, many state courts apply a less exacting standard than the federal doctrine.[297] The question of whether, and to what extent, state action will be required to trigger state constitutional rights protections remains one of the most important in state constitutional law.[298]

A number of state courts, however, do apply the state action doctrine to avoid, as the Pennsylvania Supreme Court put it, "significant governmental intrusion into private individuals' affairs and relations . . ."[299] The Pennsylvania court rejected a claim of free speech and assembly rights on privately owned property. Similar claims are rejected under the federal Constitution because of the lack of state action.[300] Private property that is open to the public, however, such as shopping malls and private universities, has been required to accommodate expression under free speech and assembly provisions of state constitutions, which are often worded quite differently from the federal First Amendment. In 1982, the New Jersey Supreme Court recognized state constitutional free speech rights on a private university campus. Justice Alan Handler noted:

> A basis for finding exceptional vitality in the New Jersey Constitution with respect to individual rights of speech and assembly is found in part in the *language employed*. Our Constitution *affirmatively* recognizes these freedoms, viz:
>
> > Every person may freely speak, write and publish his sentiments on all subjects, being responsible for the abuse of that right. No law shall be

[296] *See, e.g.*, N.J. CONST. art. I, ¶ 19: "Persons in private employment shall have the right to organize and bargain collectively." *See* also MONT. CONST. art. II, § 4; Gazelka v. St. Peter's Hospital, 420 P.3d 528 (Mont. 2018).

[297] Sharrock v. Dell Buick-Cadillac, Inc., 379 N.E.2d 1169 (N.Y. 1978) (due process); Gay Law Students Ass'n v. Pacific Tel. & Tel. Co., 595 P.2d 592 (Cal. 1979) (equal protection); People v. Zelinski, 594 P.2d 1000 (Cal. 1979) (search and seizure, noting the tremendous rise of private security services); State v. Von Bulow, 475 A.2d 995 (R.I. 1984), *cert. denied*, 469 U.S. 875 (1984) (government extension of private search); Hill v. NCAA, 865 P.2d 633 (Cal. 1994) (privacy); Pacific Radiation Oncology, LLC v. Queen's Medical Center, 375 P.3d 1252, 1257 (Haw. 2016).

[298] On the state action doctrine under state constitutions, see generally FRIESEN, *supra* note 26, at ch. 9; Jennifer Friesen, *Should California's Constitutional Guarantees of Individual Rights Apply Against Private Actors?* 17 HASTINGS CONST. L.Q. 111 (1989); and Scott E. Sundby, *Is Abandoning State Action Asking Too Much of the Constitution?* 17 HASTINGS CONST. L.Q. 139 (1989); Kevin Cole, *Federal and State "State Action": The Undercritical Embrace of a Hypercriticized Doctrine*, 24 GA. L. REV. 327 (1990); John Devlin, *Constructing an Alternative to "State Action" as a Limit on State Constitutional Rights Guarantees: A Survey, Critique and Proposal*, 21 RUTGERS L.J. 819 (1990).

[299] Western Pa. Socialist Workers 1982 Campaign v. Connecticut Gen. Life Ins. Co., 515 A.2d 1331, 1335 (Pa. 1986). *See also* State v. Johnson, 94 A.3d 1173, 1182 (Conn. 2014); State v. Malkuch, 154 P.3d 558, 560 (Mont. 2007); King v. King, 174 P.3d 659, 669–72 (Wash. 2007) (Saunders, J., concurring); Jacobs v. Major, 407 N.W.2d 832, 844 (Wis. 1987).

[300] Lloyd Corp. Ltd. v. Tanner, 407 U.S. 551 (1972).

passed to restrain or abridge the liberty of speech or of the press. [N.J. Const. (1947), Art. I, par. 6.]

The people have the right freely to assemble together, to consult for the common good, to make known their opinions to their representatives, and to petition for redress of grievances. [N.J. Const. (1947), Art. I, par. 18.][301]

Justice Handler also observed that "our State Constitution not only affirmatively guarantees to individuals the rights of speech and assembly, but also expressly prohibits government itself, in a manner analogous to the federal First and Fourteenth Amendments, from unlawfully restraining or abridging 'the liberty of speech.'"[302] The New Jersey court recognized similar rights in regional shopping malls in 1994.[303] The California Supreme Court had recognized state constitutional free speech rights in shopping malls in 1980, a decision upheld by the U.S. Supreme Court against a federal constitutional challenge.[304] These cases, however, reflect a distinct minority view,[305] but litigants will continue to argue for a reduced state action requirement, with a focus on other forms of private property.[306]

The area of search and seizure is another in which there are some more stringent limitations on "private" searches that lead to evidence being presented to law enforcement authorities. For instance, the New Jersey Supreme Court has rejected the "third party intervention doctrine" in searches involving apartments

[301] State v. Schmid, 423 A.2d 615, 626 (N.J. 1982), *app. dis. sub. nom.* Princeton Univ. v. Schmid, 455 U.S. 100 (1982) (emphasis added).

[302] *Id.* at 628.

[303] New Jersey Coalition Against War in the Middle East v. J.M.B. Realty Corp., 650 A.2d 757 (N.J. 1994). In *Green Party of N.J. v. Hartz Mountain Industries, Inc.*, 752 A.2d 315 (N.J. 2000), the New Jersey Supreme Court struck down a mall's required $1 million bond requirement for leafletters.

[304] Robins v. Pruneyard Shopping Center, 592 P.2d 341 (Cal. 1979), *aff'd*, 447 U.S. 74 (1980). This issue has a major impact on union picketing under federal labor law. *See* United Brotherhood of Carpenters and Joiners v. NLRB, 540 F.3d 957 (9th Cir. 2008); Glendale Associates, Ltd. v. NLRB, 347 F.3d 1145 (9th Cir. 2002).

[305] For a critique of the cases finding a state constitutional right to free expression on private property as being insufficiently concerned with the property owners' federal free speech rights (coerced speech), see Julian N. Eule, as completed by Jonathan D. Varat, *Transporting First Amendment Norms to the Private Sector: With Every Wish There Comes a Curse*, 45 UCLA L. Rev. 1537, 1564–80 (1998). *See also* Gregory C. Sisk, *Uprooting the Pruneyard*, 38 Rutgers L.J. 1145 (2007); Jacobs v. Major, 407 N.W.2d 832 (Wis. 1987).

[306] For consideration of state constitutional free speech claims on other forms of private property, see Jennifer A. Klear, *Comparison of the Federal Courts' and the New Jersey Supreme Court's Treatments of Free Speech on Private Property: Where Won't We Have the Freedom to Speak Next?* 33 Rutgers L.J. 589 (2002); Jennifer Niles Coffin, Note, *The United Mall of America: Free Speech, State Constitutions, and the Growing Fortress of Private Property*, 33 U. Mich. J.L. Ref. 615 (2000); Josh Mulligan, Note, *Finding a Forum in the Simulated City: Mega Malls, Gated Towns, and the Promise of Pruneyard*, 13 Cornell J.L. & Pub. Pol'y 533 (2003). In *Golden Gateway Ctr. v. Golden Gateway Tenants Ass'n*, 29 P.3d 797 (Cal. 2001), the California Supreme Court rejected a claim of free speech rights to leaflet in a residential apartment complex.

and motel rooms.[307] New Mexico requires a warrant to "extend" a private search.[308] Even private searches, if conducted by someone "intertwined," or in an agency relationship, with law enforcement, can be subject to suppression.[309] Unlawful private searches, if independent of law enforcement, may be upheld.[310]

## X. SUBSTANTIVE DUE PROCESS AND ECONOMIC REGULATION

It is quite well known that, after the end of the "*Lochner* era,"[311] as a result of the federal "'Constitutional Revolution' of the 1930s,"[312] the federal courts took, and continue to take, a "hands off" approach to federal substantive due process challenges to state economic regulation.[313] Interestingly, however, many state courts have continued to subject state regulation of the economy to fairly searching scrutiny.[314] This form of judicial review can be based on a number of state constitutional provisions. According to Professor A.E. Dick Howard:

> The state courts overturning these laws [state fair trade laws] have used various grounds, including invalid delegation of legislative power, violation of due process of law, limits of the police power, and state constitutional provisions against price fixing or monopolies.[315]

The Florida Supreme Court struck down a statute prohibiting insurance agents from discounting their commissions as exceeding the police power.[316] The Arkansas Supreme Court has struck down, as due process violations, several statutes prohibiting the sale of goods at below cost without evidence of predatory

[307] State v. Shaw, 207 A.3d 229 (N.J. 2019) (motel rooms), and State v. Wright, 114 A.3d 340 (N.J. 2015) (apartments).

[308] State v. Rivera, 241 P.3d 1099 (N.M. 2010); Ladd v. Real Estate Comm., 230 A.3d 1096 (Pa. 2020).

[309] State v. Hunt, 450 A.2d 952 (N.J. 1982); State v. Sines, 379 P.3d 502 (Or. 2016).

[310] State v. Luman, 223 P.3d 1041, 1044 (Or. 2009).

[311] Lochner v. New York, 198 U.S. 45 (1905).

[312] Howard, *supra* note 72, at 880. *See generally* Robert G. McCloskey, *Economic Due Process and the Supreme Court: An Exhumation and Reburial*, 1962 SUP. CT. REV. 34 (1962).

[313] *Id.* at 883.

[314] *Id.* at 879–91. *See also* Monrad G. Paulsen, *The Persistence of Substantive Due Process in the States*, 34 MINN. L. REV. 91 (1950); John A.C. Hetherington, *State Economic Regulation and Substantive Due Process of Law*, 53 NW. U. L. REV. 226 (1958); Peter J. Galie, *State Courts and Economic Rights*, 496 ANNALS AM. ACAD. POL. & SOC. SCI. 76 (1988).

[315] Howard, *supra* note 72, at 883.

[316] Dept. of Ins. v. Date County Consumer Advocate's Office, 492 So.2d 1032 (Fla. 1986).

motive.[317] Equal protection concepts can also have an important impact on judicial review of state economic regulation.[318]

These kinds of constitutional challenges require state judges to subject statutes regulating economic relations to meaningful scrutiny even though it seems to be asking them to return to the discredited *Lochner* era.[319] One commentator noted the dilemma for state judges:

> This judicial revolution has created a real dilemma for the state courts. These courts cannot refuse to enforce state trade regulation which has been enacted for the benefit of particular pressure groups without violating the tenets of a philosophy which bears the endorsement of Holmes, Thayer, Corwin, Hand, and Frankfurter, which has been accepted by the United States Supreme Court, and which is probably regarded as sacred by most of the academic commentators. Yet if the courts enforce such legislation, they will produce results which are pernicious not only for the businessmen whose rights are restricted but also for the public as a whole.[320]

In fact, the state court enforcement of substantive due process in the area of economic regulation seems, in modern times, to be the opposite of *Lochner*, representing the exercise judicial review in order to protect the general public—the *majority*—from special interest, rent-seeking legislation favoring a *minority*. This possibility was pointed out perceptively by the editors of the *Harvard Law Review* in 1982:

> Both courts and commentators have largely ignored the possibility that judicial review might play a radically different role—that of safeguarding the interests of majorities. State constitutional law could be dramatically divorced from its federal counterpart if state courts were to reconceive their purpose in terms of elaborating and employing a theory of majoritarian, rather than antimajoritarian, review. In fact, there is reason to believe that state courts already

[317] Ports Petroleum Co., Inc. v. Tucker, 916 S.W.2d 749 (Ark. 1996); McLane Co. Inc. v. Weiss, 965 S.W.2d 109 (Ark. 1998). *See also* Jackson v. Raffensperger, 843 S.E.2d 576 (Ga. 2020).

[318] Randal S. Jeffrey, *Equal Protection in State Courts, The New Economic Equality Rights*, 17 LAW & INEQUALITY 239, 251–60 (1999); *Jackson*, 843 S.E.2d at 581.

[319] *See generally* Johansen, *supra* note 71.

[320] *Id.* at 314. *See, e.g.*, Racing Assoc. of Central Iowa v. Fitzgerald, 675 N.W.2d 1, 19 n.9 (Iowa 2004) (Cady, J., dissenting):

> The majority's approach and resolution of this appeal echoes the Supreme Court's *Lochner*-era decisions. It must be left to posterity to determine whether the majority opinion will someday be viewed as we now view *Lochner*.

> have undertaken something very much like this change of direction in one area: the review of economic regulation.[321]

This is a very important point for lawyers and judges; it portrays this kind of litigation in a very different light from most constitutional litigation. While it is important not to overstate the reach of these state cases,[322] many of them present a stark departure from federal constitutional doctrine.

## XI. CONCLUSION

The New Judicial Federalism has matured substantially since its inception. An important new literature has been, and continues to be, developed. Each new generation of scholars, judges, and students has the benefit of the lessons learned from the growing pains described in this part of this book. State court personnel are constantly changing so that an approach or methodology announced at one point in time may not be followed by future judges. As we continue to learn about state constitutional law, it is likely that state courts' treatment of it will continue to be "intermittent."[323]

[321] *Developments in the Law—The Interpretation of State Constitutional Rights*, 95 HARV. L. REV. 1324, 1498–99 (1982).

[322] *See, e.g.*, Matter of C.V.S. Pharmacy, 561 A.2d 1160 (N.J. 1989); James C. Kirby Jr., *Expansive Judicial Review of Economic Regulation Under State Constitutions: The Case for Realism*, 48 TENN. L. REV. 241 (1981).

The literature and cases are collected and analyzed in Anthony B. Sanders, *The "New Judicial Federalism" Before Its Time: A Comprehensive Review of Economic Substantive Due Process Under State Constitutional Law Since 1940 and the Reasons for Its Recent Decline*, 55 AM. U. L. REV. 457 (2005).

[323] Justin Long, *Intermittent State Constitutionalism*, 34 PEPP. L. REV. 41 (2006).

# 7

# LOCKSTEPPING STATE CONSTITUTIONAL RIGHTS WITH FEDERAL CONSTITUTIONAL LAW

*Some states appear to be adopting, apparently in perpetuity, all existing or future United States Supreme Court interpretations of a federal constitutional provision as the governing interpretation of the parallel state constitutional provision.*

* * *

*Today's courts are qualifying these precedents; they explain that past adherence to federal decisional law does not signify that the state court is bound to construe the state constitution in accordance with the federal interpretation of the federal constitution for all times and under every circumstance.*

—Honorable Shirley S. Abrahamson, Wisconsin Supreme Court[1]

Since the beginning of the New Judicial Federalism,[2] there has been heated debate over state court interpretation of state constitutional rights provisions that are identical or similar to federal constitutional provisions that have already been interpreted in a certain way by the U.S. Supreme Court.[3] The

[1] Shirley S. Abrahamson, *Criminal Law and State Constitutions: The Emergence of State Constitutional Law*, 63 Tex. L. Rev. 1141, 1166, 1169 (1985).

[2] The matters of state constitutional structure-of-government or distribution-of- powers also raise important questions about the relationship between state and federal constitutional doctrine, but they are different from those in rights cases. *See* Chapter 8.

[3] Federal courts, of course, may be faced with state constitutional questions under their diversity and supplemental jurisdiction. *See* Michael T. Morley, *Litigating Imperfect Solutions: State Constitutional Claims in Federal Court*, 35 Const. Comm. 401 (2020) (reviewing Jeffery S. Sutton, 51 Imperfect Solutions: States and the Making of American Constitutional Law (2018)). *See also* City of Mesquite v. Aladdin's Castle, Inc., 455 U.S. 283, 291, 293–94 (1982); Robert A. Schapiro, *Polyphonic Federalism: State Constitutions in the Federal Courts*, 87 Cal. L. Rev. 1409, 1411–12 (1999); Robert A. Schapiro, Polyphonic Federalism: Toward the Protection of Fundamental Rights 121–50 (2009). For an example of a federal court exercising its discretion not to hear a state constitutional claim asserted under its supplemental jurisdiction (formerly pendent jurisdiction), and dismissing without prejudice under 28 U.S.C. § 1367, see Green v. Zendrian, 916 F. Supp. 493 (D. Md. 1996). *See also* Trump Hotels & Casino Resorts, Inc. v. Mirage Resorts, Inc., 963 F. Supp. 395, 408 (D.N.J. 1997); Snyder v. Murray City Corp., 124 F.3d 1349, 1354–55 (10th Cir.

*The Law of American State Constitutions.* Robert F. Williams and Lawrence Friedman, Oxford University Press.
 DOI: 10.1093/oso/9780190068806.003.0008

"shadow"[4] or "glare"[5] of these U.S. Supreme Court decisions, both as to their substantive outcome and their techniques of constitutional interpretation, seem to raise legitimacy questions about state courts reaching more protective, often more liberal, results when they interpret their own state constitutions.[6] These questions arise from America's system of dual enforcement of constitutional rights norms.

Federal constitutional interpretations often exert a kind of "gravitational pull" on interpretations of identical or similar state constitutional provisions.[7] However, according to Professor Scott Dodson:

> Constitutional law often involves sensitive and important policy matters, on which local preferences tend to be stronger, more unified, and more extreme than national preferences. Further, state constitutions have a different history and erect a different governmental structure than the federal Constitution. Finally, constitutional governance is the most prominent feature of popular sovereignty, a cherished American ideal. These factors suggest that states should exercise independence in state constitutionalism, relying on the preferences of their particular populaces, with sensitivity to the nuances of their state governmental structures.[8]

Much legal literature and many state judicial opinions have addressed questions of state constitutional substance and interpretation, often presenting arguments as to why it is, in fact, legitimate for state courts to "diverge" from the U.S. Supreme Court's interpretation of similar or identical provisions in the federal Constitution. The literature has even differentiated among the federal protections, contending that where the Supreme Court "underenforce[s]" certain federal constitutional norms, such as the Equal Protection Clause,[9] or where "strategic concerns" in enforcing such norms differ between the state and federal systems, state courts are more justified in diverging from the Supreme Court's

1997). Such dismissed claims, of course, would not be subject to claim or issue preclusion arguments. Snyder v. Murray City Corp., 73 P.3d 325, 332–33 (Utah 2003).

[4] Robert F. Williams, *In the Supreme Court's Shadow: Legitimacy of State Rejection of Supreme Court Reasoning and Result*, 35 S.C. L. Rev. 353, 353 (1984).

[5] Robert F. Williams, *In the Glare of the Supreme Court: Continuing Methodology and Legitimacy Problems in Independent State Constitutional Rights Adjudication*, 72 Notre Dame L. Rev. 1015, 1015 (1997).

[6] *Id.* at 1016–17.

[7] Scott Dodson, *The Gravitational Force of Federal Law*, 164 U. Pa. L. Rev. 703, 705 (2016).

[8] *Id.* at 724–25.

[9] Lawrence Gene Sager, *Fair Measure: The Legal Status of Underenforced Constitutional Norms*, 91 Harv. L. Rev. 1212, 1215–19 (1978). *See* King v. State, 818 N.W.2d 1, 86 (Iowa 2012) (Appel, J., dissenting).

interpretation of the federal Constitution.[10] State courts might even agree with the U.S. Supreme Court on the *meaning*—both textually and historically—of identical or similar federal and state constitutional provisions but proceed to *apply* them differently in particular circumstances.[11] These matters are covered in Chapters 5 and 6.

## I. STATE COURT ADOPTION OF FEDERAL CONSTITUTIONAL DOCTRINE: THE FORMS OF LOCKSTEPPING

Much less attention has been devoted, however, to the circumstances where state courts decide to *follow*, rather than *diverge from*, federal constitutional doctrine. This is, in fact, the clear majority of cases[12] and represents an important feature of the dual enforcement of constitutional norms. Professors Michael Solimine and James Walker have argued that the prevalence of lockstepping supports the view that there is "parity" between federal and state courts as effective enforcers of *federal* constitutional norms.[13] G. Alan Tarr has noted that, by contrast to the great question in federal constitutional law about the legitimacy of judicial review itself, the central question in state constitutional law concerns the legitimacy of state constitutional rulings that diverge from, or "go[] 'beyond,'" federal constitutional standards.[14] It is also important to examine the issue of legitimacy as well as other questions about state courts *adopting* federal constitutional standards.[15]

[10] Lawrence Gene Sager, *Foreword: State Courts and the Strategic Space Between the Norms and Rules of Constitutional Law*, 63 TEX. L. REV. 959, 964 (1985).

[11] Professor Williams is indebted to Hans Linde for this important insight.

[12] *See* Michael E. Solimine, *Supreme Court Monitoring of State Courts in the Twenty-First Century*, 35 IND. L. REV. 335, 338–39 (2002); *see also* BARRY LATZER, STATE CONSTITUTIONS AND CRIMINAL JUSTICE 158 (1991); Barry Latzer, *The Hidden Conservatism of the State Court "Revolution,"* 74 JUDICATURE 190, 190 (1991); James A. Gardner, *The Failed Discourse of State Constitutionalism*, 90 MICH. L. REV. 761, 788–93 (1992); Michael Esler, *State Supreme Court Commitment to State Law*, 78 JUDICATURE 25, 29–31 (1994); Michael E. Solimine & James L. Walker, *Federalism, Liberty and State Constitutional Law*, 23 OHIO N.U. L. REV. 1457, 1467 & nn.68–70 (1997); James N.G. Cauthen, *Expanding Rights Under State Constitutions: A Quantitative Appraisal*, 63 ALB. L. REV. 1183, 1194–1201 (2000).

[13] MICHAEL E. SOLIMINE & JAMES L. WALKER, RESPECTING STATE COURTS: THE INEVITABILITY OF JUDICIAL FEDERALISM 93–96 (1999). *See generally* Michael E. Solimine, *The Future of Parity*, 46 WM. & MARY L. REV. 1457 (2005).

[14] G. ALAN TARR, UNDERSTANDING STATE CONSTITUTIONS 174–77 (1998) (citation omitted).

[15] *See* William F. Cook, *The New Jersey Bill of Rights and a "Similarity Factors" Analysis*, 34 RUTGERS L.J. 1125, 1160–66 (2003) (suggesting an approach where state courts must justify their decision to adopt federal constitutional doctrine). *See also* Robert S. Claiborne Jr., *Commonwealth and Constitution*, 48 U. RICHMOND L. REV. 415 (2013); James K. Leven, *A Roadmap to State Judicial Independence Under the Illinois Limited Lockstep Doctrine Predicated on the Intent of the Framers of the 1970 Illinois Constitution and Illinois Tradition*, 62 DEPAUL L. REV. 63 (2012).

What are the implications for state constitutional law when state courts decide to interpret their state constitutional provisions in the same manner—or to reach the same outcome—as the Supreme Court under a similar or identical clause of the federal Constitution? How does this "doctrinal convergence" actually work?[16] Upon closer examination, there is a range of different approaches, each with different implications. As Chief Justice Shirley Abrahamson noted:

> On one side stand the cases intentionally adopting federal decisional law as interpretive of their own constitutions. Some state courts merely say that the texts of the two constitutions are substantially similar and should be similarly construed. Other state courts analyze the state constitution, or the federal doctrine, or both, and explain the reasons for adopting federal decisional law.[17]

She concluded:

> [S]tate cases adopting federal law as state constitutional law will have to be studied carefully to analyze the reasons for and manner of adopting federal law, and to determine whether state courts change their interpretations of the state constitutions as United States Supreme Court and sister state court decisions take new paths.[18]

## A. Judicial Approaches to Adopting Federal Constitutional Doctrine as State Constitutional Law

Many commentators (including us) have denigrated state constitutional law cases adopting federal constitutional interpretations as a form of knee-jerk lockstepping.[19] Justice Hans A. Linde of Oregon described state courts' uncritical adoption of federal constitutional doctrine in interpreting state constitutional provisions as the "non sequitur that the United States Supreme Court's decisions under such a text not only deserve respect but presumptively *fix* its correct

[16] This is Jim Gardner's term. *See* James A. Gardner, *The Positivist Revolution That Wasn't: Constitutional Universalism in the States*, 4 ROGER WILLIAMS U. L. REV. 109 (1998).

[17] Abrahamson, *supra* note 1, at 1181–82.

[18] *Id.* at 1182. Justice Abrahamson continued: "The second group of cases . . . *do* depart from federal precedent. These cases will also have to be studied to analyze the reasons for and manner of the departure." *Id.*

[19] *See, e.g.*, Robert F. Williams, *A "Row of Shadows": Pennsylvania's Misguided Lockstep Approach to Its State Constitutional Equality Doctrine*, 3 WIDENER J. PUB. L. 343, 373–79 (1993) [hereinafter Williams, *Row of Shadows*]; Robert F. Williams, *supra* note 4, at 397–402; Lawrence Friedman, *The Constitutional Value of Dialogue and the New Judicial Federalism*, 28 HASTINGS CONST. L.Q. 93, 143 (2000) (observing that lockstepping approach does not promote dialogue between state and federal courts about meaning of common rights provisions).

meaning also in state constitutions."[20] Justice William J. Brennan Jr. noted that "decisions of the Court are not, and should not be, dispositive of questions regarding rights guaranteed by counterpart provisions of state law."[21] Finally, state court justices have criticized their courts when they "parrot"[22] or "mimic[]"[23] the U.S. Supreme Court approach.

Justices Linde and Brennan are correct: the U.S. Supreme Court cannot "fix"[24] the meaning of a state constitution; neither can its decisions be "dispositive"[25] of state constitutional issues. This does not mean, however, that we should ignore the instances where state courts *choose* to follow federal doctrine. The cases illustrate two extreme points on what is actually a continuum of approaches to adopting federal constitutional doctrine as state constitutional law. These cases, as well as those in many other states, reveal the range of different methods by which state courts may choose to follow Supreme Court interpretations of the federal Constitution. The cases also suggest differing implications of each of these techniques for the bench and bar.

## B. Unreflective Adoptionism

The first approach may be referred to in Professor Barry Latzer's terms: "unreflective adoptionism."[26] He stated that "[i]t is illogical, the argument runs, to retract state constitutional rights simply because the Supreme Court has not found those rights in the U.S. Constitution. This argument is quite persuasive if the premise of unreflective adoptionism is correct."[27] He was referring to state court decisions simply applying federal analysis to a state clause without acknowledging the possibility of a different outcome or considering arguments in favor of such a different, or more protective, outcome. This might be an accurate description of the pre-1993 stance, for example, adopted by the Supreme Court of Ohio. Throughout this period, that court virtually never recognized

[20] State v. Kennedy, 666 P.2d 1316, 1322 (Or. 1983) (emphasis added).

[21] William J. Brennan Jr., *State Constitutions and the Protection of Individual Rights*, 90 Harv. L. Rev. 489, 502 (1977).

[22] Brown v. State, 657 S.W.2d 797, 807 (Tex. Crim. App. 1983) (Clinton, J., concurring) *overruled* by Heitman v. State, 815 S.W.2d 681 (Tex. Crim. App. 1991).

[23] *Id.* at 810 (Teague, J., dissenting).

[24] *Kennedy*, 666 P.2d at 1322.

[25] Brennan, *supra* note 21, at 502.

[26] *See* Barry Latzer, *The New Judicial Federalism and Criminal Justice: Two Problems and a Response*, 22 Rutgers L.J. 863, 864 (1991); *see also* Ronald K.L. Collins & Peter J. Galie, *Models of Post-Incorporation Judicial Review: 1985 Survey of State Constitutional Individual Rights Decisions*, 55 U. Cinn. L. Rev. 317, 323–24 (1986) (discussing the "equivalence model").

[27] Latzer, *supra* note 26, at 864. This can, unfortunately, lead to what Nebraska Supreme Court Justice Thomas M. Shanahan called a "pavlovian conditioned reflex in an uncritical adoption of federal decisions." State v. Havlat, 385 N.W.2d 436, 447 (Neb. 1986) (Shanahan, J., dissenting).

the independent force of the Ohio Constitution, opting instead for lockstepping or "instant agreement" with federal doctrine.[28] Many other state courts have followed this approach as well.

The Maryland Court of Appeals often refers to similar state and federal constitutional provisions as *in pari materia*.[29] Although it is not entirely clear what the court means by its use of this statutory interpretation term, the court seemed to have embraced an "unreflective adoptionism" approach. Nonetheless, on several occasions the Maryland Court of Appeals indicated that the *in pari materia* approach "does *not* mean that the provision will *always* be interpreted or applied in the same manner as its federal counterpart."[30] Thus the court appears to be sending the lower courts and practitioners a form of a "mixed message."[31]

## C. Reflective, Case-by-Case Adoption

The next approach—reflective, case-by-case adoption—describes a state court decision in which the court acknowledges the possibility of different state and federal outcomes; considers the arguments *in the specific case*; and, on balance, decides to apply federal analysis to the state provision.[32] Under this approach, the state court makes an informed decision to conform its analysis, in a particular case, to existing federal constitutional precedents.[33] As Professor Latzer noted:

> [I]f the state courts are not merely presuming that state and federal law are alike, but are coming to this conclusion after independent evaluation of the meaning of the state provision, then the critique collapses. There is nothing improper in concluding that the Supreme Court's construction of similar text is sound. Adoptionism is not per se unjustifiable.[34]

[28] *See* Arnold v. City of Cleveland, 616 N.E.2d 163, 168 n.8 (Ohio 1993); Mary Cornelia Porter & G. Alan Tarr, *The New Judicial Federalism and the Ohio Supreme Court: Anatomy of a Failure*, 45 OHIO ST. L.J. 143 (1984). Professor Williams is indebted to Larry Sager for the "instant agreement" formulation.

[29] *See, e.g.*, WBAL-TV Div., Hearst Corp. v. State, 477 A.2d 776, 781 n.4 (Md. 1984); Lodowski v. State, 513 A.2d 299, 306 (Md. 1986). For a criticism of this approach, see Michael R. Braudes, *When Constitutions Collide: A Study in Federalism in the Criminal Law Context*, 18 U. BALT. L. REV. 55 (1988); Ehrlich v. Perez, 908 A.2d 1220, 1234 (Md. 2006); Hof v. State, 655 A.2d 370, 373 n.3 (Md. 1995). *See also* Richard Boldt & Dan Friedman, *Constitutional Interpretation: A Consideration of the Judicial Function in State and Federal Constitutional Interpretation*, 76 MD. L. REV. 309, 344 n.193 (2017), *But see* Leidig v. State, 256 A.3d 830 (Md. 2021).

[30] Pack Shack, Inc. v. Howard County, 832 A.2d 170, 176 n.3 (Md. 2003) (*quoting* Dua v. Comcast Cable, 805 A.2d 1061, 1071 (Md. 2002)); *see also* Parker v. State, 936 A.2d 862, 878–89 (Md. 2007).

[31] *See infra* notes 113–14 and accompanying text.

[32] *See* Latzer, *supra* note 26, at 864.

[33] *Id.*

[34] *Id.* (footnote omitted). For several examples—among many—of reflective adoptionism, see State v. Stephenson, 878 S.W.2d 530, 544–47 (Tenn. 1994) *abrogated* by State v. Saylor, 117 S.W.3d 239 (Tenn. 2003); State v. McLellan, 817 A.2d 309, 312–13 (N.H. 2003); State v. Scott, 183 P.3d 801,

Professor James A. Gardner has made a strong argument favoring the legitimacy, among state court options, of reflective, case-by-case adoption.[35] Gardner argues that states and their constitutions "are part of an interlocking plan of federalism devised collectively by the people of the nation and maintained by them as part of a comprehensive plan designed to serve the overriding national purpose of protecting the liberty of all Americans."[36] In his view, therefore, state courts can resist what he refers to as abuses of national power reflected in unreasonably narrow rulings on rights by the U.S. Supreme Court by rejecting such rulings in interpreting their state constitutions.[37] The corollary to this assertion, however, is that where state courts are convinced that Supreme Court rulings on federal rights provide adequate protection for the citizens of the states, it is perfectly reasonable for state courts to adopt such federal rulings as part of their state constitutional law. His account of state courts adopting federal constitutional doctrine is as follows:

> The likeliest explanation is undoubtedly the most obvious one: state judges adopt the Supreme Court's approach because they like it and think that it does a perfectly adequate job of protecting the liberty in question. No innovative, pathbreaking, independent analysis of the state constitution is needed because there is no threat to liberty that the state constitution need be invoked to counteract. . . .
>
> . . . [T]here is nothing at all wrong with state judges adopting U.S. Supreme Court terminology and analyses merely because they think the Court's approach does an effective job of protecting the relevant liberties. Quite the contrary. If a state court believes that some individual liberty is being adequately protected under some formulation developed by the U.S. Supreme Court, it has no particular reason to undertake the effort of independently deriving a different, equivalent formulation to protect that same liberty under the state constitution merely for the sake of demonstrating its independence.[38]

829–30 (Kan. 2008). This can take place even after a period of independence or divergence from federal doctrine. *See* State v. Barton, 594 A.2d 917 (Conn. 1991); State v. Werner, 615 A.2d 1010 (R.I. 1992).

[35] James A. Gardner, *State Constitutional Rights as Resistance to National Power: Toward a Functional Theory of State Constitutions*, 91 GEO. L.J. 1003, 1058–61 (2003). *See also* James A. Gardner, *The Theory and Practice of Contestatory Federalism*, 60 WM. & MARY L. REV. 507 (2018).

[36] *Id.* at 1005; *see also* James A. Gardner, *What Is a State Constitution?* 24 RUTGERS L.J. 1025, 1044–54 (1993). Professor Gardner argues that because the federal Constitution limits states in what they may do, state constitutional interpretation must take federal constitutional law into account. *See* James A. Gardner, *Whose Constitution Is It? Why Federalism and Constitutional Positivism Don't Mix*, 46 WM. & MARY L. REV. 1245 (2005); *see also* Lawrence Gene Sager, *Cool Federalism and the Life-Cycle of Moral Progress*, 46 WM. & MARY L. REV. 1385 (2005).

[37] Gardner, *supra* note 35, at 1032–48.

[38] *Id.* at 1059.

Quite obviously, Professor Gardner is talking about *reflective* adoptionism on a case-by-case basis. In other words, "[f]ederalism may require mutual checking, but where there is no abuse of power there is nothing to check. State acquiescence in the *proper* use of national power is no cause for concern."[39]

Professor Gardner seems to conclude, however, that *unreflective* adoptionism would be inappropriate. He reaches this conclusion not because it represents a failure of independent state constitutionalism, but rather because state courts "are failing to discharge the responsibility for monitoring and checking abusive exercises of national power that a well-functioning system of federalism presupposes."[40] Under this view, state courts adopt federal constitutional doctrine "not because they think such rulings presumptively correct, but because, in the *exercise of their independent judgment*, they deem such rulings to provide adequate protection for the liberties at issue."[41] In these circumstances, "a state court might reasonably conclude that there is no need, *at least for the moment*, to explore in any greater depth the possibilities presented by the state constitution to protect liberty any more or less vigorously than it is already protected by the national judicial analysis."[42] Regardless of whether one agrees entirely with Professor Gardner's thesis, it is an important contribution to the study of the dual analysis of constitutional norms, and it contributes to the dialogue on constitutional law between state and federal courts.[43] It also further elaborates the possible reasons for reflective or informed state court adoption of federal constitutional doctrine.

The Ohio Supreme Court decision in *Simmons-Harris v. Goff*,[44] adopting federal establishment of religion doctrine,[45] arguably illustrates the reflective, case-by-case adoptionism approach. This case involved a challenge to the Ohio school voucher statute. The Ohio Supreme Court stated that the federal Establishment Clause and Ohio's religion provisions were "the approximate equivalent."[46] The court noted that it "had little cause to examine" the Ohio clause and had "never enunciated a standard for determining whether a statute violates it."[47] The court then adopted the federal constitutional *Lemon* test,[48] but did not

[39] *Id.* at 1060.
[40] *Id.* (footnote omitted).
[41] *Id.* at 1061 (emphasis added).
[42] *Id.* (emphasis added).
[43] *Cf.* Friedman, *supra* note 19.
[44] 711 N.E.2d 203 (Ohio 1999). *See also* Gilbert v. Flandreau Santee Sioux Tribe, 725 N.W.2d 249, 256–58 (S.D. 2006).
[45] *Simmons-Harris*, 711 N.E.2d at 207–08.
[46] *Id.* at 211.
[47] *Id.*
[48] *Id.* The relevant test for evaluating Establishment Clause challenges is set out in *Lemon v. Kurtzman*, 403 U.S. 602, 612–13 (1971). The U.S. Supreme Court has since abandoned the *Lemon* test. *See* Kennedy v. Bremerton School District, 597 U.S. ___ (2022).

conclude that the federal and state provisions were "coextensive"[49] or commit to "irreversibly tie" itself to the federal constitutional standards.[50] The court concluded by stating: "We reserve the right to adopt a different constitutional standard pursuant to the Ohio Constitution, *whether because the federal constitutional standard changes* or for any other relevant reason."[51] As demonstrated in *Simmons-Harris*, this approach treats U.S. Supreme Court decisions construing similar or identical federal constitutional provisions as only one, albeit very important, source among many. The court looks only at the controversy before it and the existing, relevant legal materials, *including federal doctrine*, and makes a decision for that case.

## D. Prospective Lockstepping

Next, a state court might engage in "prospective lockstepping," where it announces that not only in the instant case, but *in the future*, it will interpret the state and federal clauses the same.[52] Thus, after the U.S. Supreme Court decided *Illinois v. Krall*,[53] the Kansas Supreme Court stated, "We find our case law *tying* the Kansas Constitution Bill of Rights *to* United States Supreme Court precedent *compels* our recognition of the good-faith exception articulated in *Krall*."[54]

This is what the Ohio Supreme Court, as well as a number of other state courts, seemed to do in a number of other cases. In *Eastwood Mall, Inc. v. Slanco*,[55] the Ohio court confronted a question faced by a number of states with regard to their own state constitutions[56] of whether an injunction against picketing and leafleting in a privately owned shopping mall violated Article I, Section 11, of the Ohio Constitution, which provides that "[e]very citizen may freely speak, write, and publish his sentiments on all subjects, being responsible for the abuse of the right; *and* no law shall be passed to restrain or abridge the liberty of speech, or of

[49] *Simmons-Harris*, 711 N.E.2d at 211.

[50] *Id.* at 212. *See also* State v. Stephenson, 878 S.W.2d 530 (Tenn. 1994); Joye v. Hunterton Central Regional High School Bd. of Ed., 826 A.2d 624 (N.J. 2003).

[51] *Id.* (emphasis added).

[52] *See, e.g., In re* Rosenkrantz, 59 P.3d 174, 193 n.6 (Cal. 2002); Digiacinto v. Rectors and Visitors of George Mason University, 704 S.E.2d 365, 368–69 (Va. 2011); Adoption of Riahleigh M., 202 A.3d 1174, 1180, 1184 (Me. 2019); Mosley v. Texas Health and Human Services Comm., 593 S.W.3d 250, 264 (Tex. 2019); Patterson v. State, 314 P.3d 759, 765 (Wyo. 2013); State v. Beauregard, 198 A.3d 1, 11–12 (R.I. 2018); State v. Perry, 548 S.W.3d 292, 298 (Mo. 2018).

[53] 480 U.S. 340 (1987).

[54] State v. Daniel, 242 P.3d 1186, 1193 (Kan. 2010) (emphasis added).

[55] 626 N.E.2d 59 (Ohio 1994).

[56] *See, e.g.*, Jennifer A. Klear, *Comparison of the Federal Courts' and the New Jersey Supreme Court's Treatments of Free Speech on Private Property: Where Won't We Have the Freedom to Speak Next?* 33 Rutgers L.J. 589, 599–601 (2002); *see also* Stanley H. Friedelbaum, *Private Property, Public Property: Shopping Centers and Expressive Freedom in the States*, 62 Alb. L. Rev. 1229, 1243–45 (1999).

the press."[57] The Supreme Court, ruling on an identical claim, had already provided a clear answer to this question under the First Amendment: because there was no state action, there was no constitutional violation.[58]

The Ohio court acknowledged the obvious textual differences between the federal and Ohio provisions and the fact that the U.S. Supreme Court had observed that states might recognize free speech rights in shopping malls.[59] Relying on an Ohio case from 1992,[60] however, it held "that the free speech guarantees accorded by the Ohio Constitution are no broader than the First Amendment, and that the First Amendment is the proper basis for interpretation of Section 11, Article I of the Ohio Constitution."[61] The court also stated:

> Furthermore, while Section 11 has an additional clause not found in the First Amendment, the plain language of this section, when read in its entirety, bans only the passing of a law that would restrain or abridge the liberty of speech. *When the First Amendment does not protect speech that infringes on private property rights*, Section 11 does not protect that speech either.[62]

This is a clear example of a state constitutional decision going well beyond mere case-by-case adoptionism (even if reflective) and adopting a prospective lockstepping approach.

In *State v. Robinette*,[63] the Ohio Supreme Court considered, under state constitutional search and seizure doctrine, whether a police officer must inform a person that he is "free to go" after a valid traffic stop.[64] The court concluded earlier in the same course of litigation that, under *both* federal and state constitutions, such a statement had to be given.[65] The Supreme Court reversed that conclusion

[57] OHIO CONST. art. I, § 11 (emphasis added). For an in-depth analysis of the very similar Pennsylvania provision, see Seth F. Kreimer, *The Pennsylvania Constitution's Protection of Free Expression*, 5 U. PA. J. CONST. L. 12 (2002). *See also* 1 JENNIFER FRIESEN, STATE CONSTITUTIONAL LAW: LITIGATING INDIVIDUAL RIGHTS, CLAIMS AND DEFENSES, ch. 5 (2006).

[58] *Eastwood Mall*, 626 N.E.2d at 60 (*citing* Hudgens v. NLRB, 424 U.S. 507 (1976); Lloyd Corp. v. Tanner, 407 U.S. 551 (1972)).

[59] *Id.* at 60–61 (*citing* Pruneyard Shopping Ctr. v. Robins, 447 U.S. 74 (1980)).

[60] *Id.* at 61 (*citing* State *ex rel.* Rear Door Bookstore v. Tenth Dist. Ct. App., 588 N.E.2d 116, 123 (Ohio 1992); Zacchini v. Scripps-Howard Broad. Co., 376 N.E.2d 582, 583 (Ohio 1978); State v. Kassay, 184 N.E.521, 525 (Ohio 1932)).

[61] *Id.*; *see also* State v. Mendez, 66 P.3d 811, 817 (Kan. 2003) (concluding that the Kansas Constitution and the U.S. Constitution provide identical protection: "If conduct is prohibited by one it is prohibited by the other.").

[62] *Eastwood Mall*, 626 N.E.2d at 61 (emphasis added); *see also* Elliott v. Commonwealth, 593 S.E.2d 263, 269 (Va. 2004) (finding that the free speech provisions in both the federal Constitution and Virginia Constitution are "coextensive"); State v. Farrow, 144 A.2d 1036, 1044 (Vt. 2016).

[63] 685 N.E.2d 762 (Ohio 1997).

[64] *Id.* at 771.

[65] State v. Robinette, 653 N.E.2d 695, 699 (Ohio 1995).

on the federal constitutional ground, remanding the case to the Ohio Supreme Court.[66] The Ohio Supreme Court then went a step beyond its earlier ruling.

Despite a prior decision declaring that the Ohio Constitution was "a document of independent force,"[67] on remand the Ohio Supreme Court reconsidered its earlier conclusion that the state constitution, in addition to the federal Constitution, required a "free to go" statement by law enforcement officials after a valid traffic stop.[68] The court, noting the identical state and federal constitutional texts, and relying on earlier decisions, adopted the U.S. Supreme Court's view of the Fourth Amendment as the authoritative judicial interpretation of the state constitutional search and seizure clause.[69] The court relied specifically on its 1981 decision in *State v. Geraldo*,[70] where it stated:

> It is our opinion that the reach of Section 14, Article I, of the Ohio Constitution with respect to the warrantless monitoring of a consenting informant's telephone conversation is coextensive with that of the Fourth Amendment to the United States Constitution. *As a consequence thereof, appellant's failure to prove a violation of the Fourth Amendment dictates the conclusion that his rights under Section 14, Article I, of the Ohio Constitution have not been violated either.*[71]

The court cited the need for uniformity in this area of criminal procedure, and stated that in the future, absent "persuasive reasons to find otherwise," it would follow the Supreme Court's interpretations of the Fourth Amendment as a matter of Ohio constitutional law.[72] It abandoned its earlier holding in the litigation, that there was a *state* constitutional violation, as a direct reaction to the U.S. Supreme Court's finding that there was no *federal* constitutional violation in the same litigation. The Ohio court thereby moved from at least recognizing state

[66] Ohio v. Robinette, 519 U.S. 33, 40 (1996).

[67] Arnold v. City of Cleveland, 616 N.E.2d 163, 169 (Ohio 1993); State v. Mole, 74 N.E.3d 368 (Ohio 2016).

[68] *Robinette*, 685 N.E.2d at 771.

[69] *Id.* at 767.

[70] 429 N.E.2d 141 (Ohio 1981).

[71] *Id.* at 146 (emphasis added); *see also* State v. Andrews, 565 N.E.2d 1271, 1273 n.1 (Ohio 1991) ("A review of Ohio case law indicates that we have interpreted Section 14, Article I of the Ohio Constitution to protect the same interests and in a manner consistent with the Fourth Amendment to the United States Constitution."); State v. Garcia, 123 S.W.3d 335, 343 (Tenn. 2003) (finding the state and federal search and seizure provisions "identical in intent and purpose") (citation omitted); State v. Morris, 72 P.3d 570, 576 (Kan. 2003) (explaining that the state search and seizure provision "provides protection identical to that provided under the Fourth Amendment to the United States Constitution").

[72] *Robinette*, 685 N.E.2d at 767. The court cited two cases for the proposition that it had applied the "persuasive reasons" approach to several other provisions. *Id.* at 766 (*citing* Eastwood Mall, Inc. v. Slanco, 626 N.E.2d 59, 60 (Ohio 1994); State v. Gustafson, 668 N.E.2d 435, 441 (Ohio 1996)). In fact, although both of these cases interpret the Ohio Constitution coextensively with the U.S. Constitution, neither of them mentions the "persuasive reasons" approach. The "persuasive reasons" approach can be compared to the "criteria approach" discussed in Chapter 6.

constitutional claims in this area to a prospective lockstep or, literally, a *prospective incorporation* approach.[73]

Other state courts have abandoned their state constitutional holdings after the U.S. Supreme Court reversed its interpretations of a similar or identical federal constitutional provision. For example, after the Pennsylvania Supreme Court ruled in a "stop and frisk" case that the conduct had violated both the state and federal constitutional search and seizure provisions,[74] the U.S. Supreme Court vacated the Pennsylvania Supreme Court's judgment on the federal ground[75] and remanded for further consideration in light of an earlier decision.[76] The Pennsylvania Supreme Court then reversed its prior state constitutional interpretation,[77] stating that it had "consistently followed" federal doctrine in this area and saw "no reason at this juncture to embrace a standard other than that adhered to by the United States Supreme Court."[78] Justice Stephen Zappala dissented:

> In our original opinion addressing this matter, we relied upon *both* the Fourth Amendment to the United States Constitution and Article 1, Section 8 of the Pennsylvania Constitution in holding that the police officer here did not possess the requisite cause to stop appellant based upon flight alone. While the United States Supreme Court's decision . . . impacts upon our analysis as it relates to the Fourth Amendment, the Court's decision is not dispositive of our state constitutional analysis. Moreover, regardless of the majority writer's *current* disagreement with his prior disposition of the case pursuant to Article 1, Section 8, principles of *stare decisis* mandate that such disposition, a majority opinion of this Court, remains the law of this case and of the Commonwealth.[79]

A similar state "turnaround" took place in Washington.[80] The California Supreme Court rejected this argument in 2019,[81] as did the Iowa Supreme Court. Iowa Justice Brent Appel stated:

[73] The term "prospective incorporation" is Larry Sager's.

[74] *In re* D.M., 743 A.2d 422, 424 (Pa. 1999).

[75] Pennsylvania v. D.M., 529 U.S. 1126, 1126 (2000).

[76] *Id.* (*citing* Illinois v. Wardlow, 528 U.S. 119 (2000)).

[77] *In re* D.M., 781 A.2d 1161, 1165 (Pa. 2001); *see also* State v. Luck, 312 S.E.2d 791 (Ga. 1984). *Contra* State v. Cook, 135 P.3d 260, 266 (Or. 2006).

[78] *Id.* at 1163; *see also* People v. Dunaway, 88 P.3d 619, 628–31 (Colo. 2004) (applying similar reasoning as *In re* D.M., 781 A.2d 1161 (Pa. 2001)).

[79] *In re* D.M., 781 A.2d at 1165 (Zappala, J., dissenting) (citation omitted).

[80] State v. Catlett, 945 P.2d 700 (Wash. 1997). Other examples, based on careful reflection, include State v. Barton, 594 A.2d 917 (Conn. 1991); State v. Werner, 615 A.2d 1010 (R.I. 1992); State v. Franklin, 308 S.W.3d 799, 809–10 (Tenn. 2010); State v. Burkett, 849 N.W.2d 624 (S.D. 2014); State v. Tuttle, 515 S.W.3d 282 (Tenn. 2017).

[81] People v. Aranda, 437 P.3d 845 (Cal. 2019); Derr v. State, 73 A.3d 254 (Md. 2013).

> In the words of another state supreme court, we do not allow the words of our Iowa Constitution to be "balloons to be blown up or deflated every time, and precisely in accord with the interpretation of the U.S. Supreme Court, following some tortious trail."[82]

Analyzing the same state constitutional "turnaround" phenomenon in Montana in the 1980s, legal scholar Ron Collins referred to this type of changed opinion as the "Montana Disaster."[83] In each of these instances, the state court decided to, in Barry Latzer's words, "retract state constitutional rights simply because the Supreme Court has not found those rights in the U.S. Constitution."[84] As in the Ohio cases of *Eastwood Mall* and *Robinette*, those decisions reflect the prospective lockstepping approach in circumstances of state and federal constitutional textual identity as well as textual distinctiveness.

By contrast, in *State v. Sullivan*, the Arkansas Supreme Court acknowledged what the U.S. Supreme Court had already confirmed—a state supreme court may not interpret the federal Constitution to provide more rights than recognized by the U.S. Supreme Court.[85] In the original adjudication of *Sullivan* in the Arkansas state court system, the Arkansas Supreme Court had required suppression of the fruits of a pretextual arrest, concluding that, even if the U.S. Supreme Court had rejected that result, it could still base its decision on its view of the federal Constitution.[86]

The U.S. Supreme Court reversed.[87] On remand, the Arkansas Supreme Court, by contrast to those courts discussed earlier that abandoned their views of their state constitutions after the Supreme Court reversed on the federal ground,[88] affirmed its earlier decision "on adequate and independent state grounds."[89] The court further noted that it could make this determination, even after stating in earlier opinions that it would follow the U.S. Supreme Court's interpretation of the Fourth Amendment, explaining: "Current interpretation of the United States

[82] State v. Ingraham, 914 N.W.2d 794, 797 (Iowa 2019) (*quoting* Penick v. State, 440 So.2d 547, 552 (Miss. 1983)).

[83] Ronald K.L. Collins, *Reliance on State Constitutions—The Montana Disaster*, 63 Tex. L. Rev. 1095, 1095 (1985). Collins referred to the "Problem of the Vanishing Constitution." *Id.* at 1111.

[84] Latzer, *supra* note 26, at 864. This calls to mind the words of Justice James L. Robertson of the Mississippi Supreme Court: "If it ain't broke, why fix it?" Stringer v. State, 491 So.2d 837, 850 (Miss. 1986) (Robertson, J., concurring) (majority held that state constitution's search and seizure provision permits no "good faith exception" like that recognized in *United States v. Leon*, 468 U.S. 897 (1984)).

[85] State v. Sullivan, 74 S.W.3d 215, 216–17 (Ark. 2002).

[86] State v. Sullivan, 16 S.W.3d 551, 552 (Ark. 2000) ("[T]here is nothing that prevents this court from interpreting the U.S. Constitution more broadly than the United States Supreme Court, which has the effect of providing more rights").

[87] Arkansas v. Sullivan, 532 U.S. 769 (2001).

[88] *See supra* notes 74–82 and accompanying text.

[89] *Sullivan*, 74 S.W.3d at 221.

Constitution in the federal courts no longer mirrors our interpretation of our own constitution."[90]

In 2006, the Illinois Supreme Court engaged in a searching analysis of its "lockstep" approach to search and seizure cases.[91] It concluded, based on indications it perceived in the history of the adoption of the 1970 Illinois Constitution, that the framers did not intend to protect search and seizure rights beyond federal standards,[92] and that it should continue its "limited lockstep" approach,[93] which recognizes the possibility of divergent opinions if certain criteria are met.[94] The Michigan Supreme Court has followed a similar approach, based on a reading of that state's constitutional history.[95]

## E. State Courts Prospectively Adopting a U.S. Supreme Court "Test"

Some state courts have "borrowed" a well-established test, formula, or mode of reasoning developed by the U.S. Supreme Court when interpreting the federal Constitution and announced they will apply this approach in interpreting an identical or similar state constitutional provision in the future. This is slightly weaker than the strong form of prospective lockstepping just discussed, as the state court may apply the federal test but reach a different outcome.[96] The state court's actual decision or outcome in a specific case, in other words, might not

[90] *Id.* at 222 (internal quotations omitted).

[91] *See* People v. Caballes, 851 N.E.2d 26 (Ill. 2006); Thomas B. McAffee, *The Illinois Bill of Rights and Our Independent Legal Tradition: A Critique of the Illinois Lockstep Doctrine*, 12 S. Ill. U. L.J. 1 (1987). *See also* Brigham City v. Stuart, 122 P.3d 506, 510–11 (Utah 2005), *rev'd*, 547 U.S. 398 (2006), and Rainey v. Comm., 197 S.W.3d 89 (Ky. 2006), and for similar discussions.

[92] *Caballes*, 851 N.E.2d at 33, 36, 45, 47; *see also* People v. Rolfingsmeyer, 461 N.E.2d 410, 412–13 (Ill. 1984); Barger v. Peters, 645 N.E.2d 175, 176 (Ill. 1994); State v. Carter, 664 So.2d 367, 381–83 (La. 1995); State v. Johnson, 667 So.2d 510, 513 (La. 1996).

[93] *Caballes*, 851 N.E.2d at 43–46. *See* Leven, *supra* note 15; Timothy P. O'Neill, *Escape from Freedom: Why "Limited Lockstep" Betrays Our System of Federalism*, 48 John Marshall L. Rev. 325 (2014).

[94] *Id.* at 43; *see also In re* Lakisha M., 882 N.E.2d 570, 581 (Ill. 2008). *But see* City of Chicago v. Pooh Bah Enterprises, 865 N.E.2d 133, 168 (Ill. 2006) (evidence that framers intended free speech clause to be broader than First Amendment).

[95] *See, e.g.*, People v. Collins, 475 N.W.2d 684 (Mich. 1991); People v. Goldston, 682 N.W.2d 479, 485–87 (Mich. 2004). The Michigan court reached the same conclusion concerning double jeopardy. People v. Davis, 695 N.W.2d 45, 47–48 (Mich. 2005); People v. Smith, 733 N.W.2d 351, 356 (Mich. 2007). *But see* People v. Ream, 750 N.W.2d 536, 557 (Mich. 2008) (Kelly, J., dissenting) ("I did not agree with the majority that the ratifiers knew how the United States Supreme Court had interpreted the federal Double Jeopardy Clause and that they accepted it."). *See also* State v. Miyasaki, 614 P.2d 915, 922 (Haw. 1980).

[96] *See, e.g.*, *Ex parte* Peterson, 117 S.W.3d 804, 813–20 (Tex. Crim. App. 2003), *overruled by Ex Parte* Lewis, 219 S.W.3d 335 (Tex. Crim. App. 2007); State v. Lyle, 854 N.W.2d 778, 783–84 (Iowa 2014); Hebert v. City of Woonsocket, 213 A.3d 1065, 1085 (R.I. 2019); State v. Lilly, 930 N.W.2d 293, 301 (Iowa 2019).

in all instances conform to federal precedents. Still, this approach operates as an announced doctrine of ongoing, or prospective, deference to federal constitutional doctrine.[97] For example, the Texas Court of Criminal Appeals declared: "Because we have adopted the federal standard for reviewing claims of ineffective assistance of counsel under the corresponding provision of the Texas Constitution, we will analyze both federal and state constitutional claims under *Strickland* [*v. Washington*.]"[98] Similarly, the Connecticut Supreme Court stated: "The determination of whether probable cause exists under the [F]ourth [A]mendment to the federal [C]onstitution, and under article first, § 7, of our state constitution, is made pursuant to a 'totality-of-the-circumstances' test."[99] Although it may apply an earlier *reflective* adoption of the federal test, this technique clearly implies that the court will continue to apply the federal test in the future.[100] It does seem to constitute *state* constitutional law. Often, state courts

[97] The "ongoing deference" formulation is Larry Sager's. This very question is debated by both the majority and dissent in City of Seattle v. Mighty Movers, Inc., 96 P.3d 979 (Wash. 2004).

[98] Thompson v. State, No. 73128, 2003 WL 21466925, at *2 (Tex. Crim. App. June 25, 2003) (citation omitted); *see* James v. State, 271 P.3d 1016, 1018 (Wyo. 2012); Bido v. State, 56 A.3d 104, 111 (R.I. 2012); *see also* Holding v. Municipality of Anchorage, 63 P.3d 248, 251 n.15 (Alaska 2003); State v. Spivey, 579 S.E.2d 251, 254 (N.C. 2003) (adopting the test laid out by the U.S. Supreme Court in *Barker v. Wingo*, 407 U.S. 514 (1972)); State *ex rel.* Myers v. Painter, 576 S.E.2d 277, 280 (W. Va. 2002) (adopting the test in *Strickland v. Washington*); Commonwealth v. Busanet, 817 A.2d 1060, 1066 (Pa. 2002) ("It is well-settled that the test for counsel ineffectiveness is the same" as that applied in *Strickland v. Washington*, under either the Pennsylvania Constitution or the U.S. Constitution); Damron v. State, 663 N.W.2d 650, 654 (N.D. 2003) (adopting the test in *Strickland v. Washington*, 466 U.S. 668 (1984)); State v. Allen, 837 A.2d 324, 326 (N.H. 2003) (adopting the test laid out by the U.S. Supreme Court in *Barker v. Wingo*); State v. Saylor, 117 S.W.3d 239, 246 (Tenn. 2003) (holding that "[t]he standard for a valid invocation of the right to counsel" is the same under the Tennessee Constitution and the U.S. Constitution); State v. Thiel, 665 N.W.2d 305, 313–14 (Wis. 2003) (noting that the court has "consistently" followed the approach in *Strickland v. Washington*); State v. Hicks, 181 P.3d 831, 836 (Wash. 2008) (adopting the *Strickland* test); State v. Owens, 451 P.3d 476, 471 (Kan. 2019); McLemore v. Comm., 590 S.W.3d 229, 241 (Ky. 2019).

[99] State v. Nowell, 817 A.2d 76, 84 (Conn. 2003) (*quoting* Illinois v. Gates, 462 U.S. 213, 238–39 (1983)).

[100] For example, the Supreme Court of Pennsylvania commonly states that the test for ineffective assistance of counsel is the same under the state and the federal Constitution. *See, e.g.*, *Busanet*, 817 A.2d at 1066. The court cited *Commonwealth v. Pierce*, 527 A.2d 973 (Pa. 1987), for this proposition. *Id.* Upon examination, it appears that the earlier decision was fairly reflective. *Pierce*, 527 A.2d at 974–77. For a similar conclusion, *compare* People v. Gherna, 784 N.E.2d 799, 806 (Ill. 2003) (noting that the court has construed the search and seizure provision in the Illinois Constitution "in a manner that is consistent with the [U.S.] Supreme Court's [F]ourth [A]mendment jurisprudence" (*quoting* Fink v. Ryan, 673 N.E.2d 281, 288 (Ill. 1996)), *with* People v. Mitchell, 650 N.E.2d 1014, 1017–19 (Ill. 1995) (concluding that, although the court is "not bound to follow the Supreme Court's interpretation," there is "nothing . . . to support divergence in interpretation of our . . . search and seizure clause from the Federal [F]ourth [A]mendment interpretation"), *and* People v. Tisler, 469 N.E.2d 147, 155–57 (Ill. 1984) (analyzing and adopting the test laid out by the Supreme Court in *Illinois v. Gates*, but noting that the court "may construe [the] terms [of the search and seizure clause] as contained in [the Illinois] constitution differently from the construction the [U.S.] Supreme Court has placed on the same terms in the Federal Constitution").

The Wisconsin Supreme Court adopted the federal double jeopardy approaches as state constitutional law. *See, e.g.*, State v. Davison, 666 N.W.2d 1, 6–7 (Wis. 2003). Peeling back the layers to the 1975 decision adopting this approach reveals virtually no analysis or reflection. *See* State v. Calhoun, 226 N.W.2d 504, 512 (Wis. 1975), *overruled on other grounds*, State v. Copening, 303 N.W.2d 821,

cite older decisions for the proposition that a federal test has been adopted as state constitutional law at an earlier point in time. Courts and counsel must "peel back the layers" of these precedents to see if the initial decision adopting the federal test was reflective or not.

How does this approach differ from one in which state courts adopt their own tests or approaches under the state constitution? Is the state court (as well as lower courts and counsel) obliged to apply the U.S. Supreme Court's future decisions using such well-established, familiar *federal* tests? If the state court misapplies the federal test, will its decision be insulated from Supreme Court review under the doctrine of adequate and independent state grounds? Is there any point for lawyers, scholars, and judges to continue the "homework"[101] involved in developing independent state constitutional arguments under such state constitutional clauses, or are such efforts effectively chilled?

Other state courts, rather than adopting a specific *test* developed by the U.S. Supreme Court, announce that they follow the same approach as the Supreme Court and that its decisions will be applied in interpreting the state constitution.[102] For example, the Wisconsin Supreme Court stated: "Our tradition is to view these provisions as identical in scope and purpose. Consequently, this court accepts decisions of the United States Supreme Court as *controlling* interpretations of the double jeopardy provisions of both constitutions."[103]

## F. Other Forms of Prospective Lockstepping

State courts have adopted a number of other ways to describe their lockstep approach to federal and state constitutional rights without making it entirely clear whether it is a prospective mandate. They have indicated that identical or similar federal and state constitutional provisions have been interpreted "in a manner

827 n.3 (Wis. 1981). In *Calhoun*, the court stated: "With the provisions of both state and federal constitutions as to double jeopardy being identical in scope and purpose, we accept as *completely controlling* the decisions of the United States Supreme Court. . . ." *Id.* (emphasis added). Subsequently, the court has simply followed this approach. *See, e.g.*, Day v. State, 251 N.W.2d 811, 812–13 (Wis. 1977). *See also* Meyers v. State, 124 P.3d 710, 714 (Wyo. 2005) (earlier cases provide no analysis).

[101] "[T]o make an independent argument under the state clause takes homework—in texts, in history, in alternative approaches to analysis." Hans A. Linde, *First Things First: Rediscovering the States' Bills of Rights*, 9 U. Balt. L. Rev. 379, 392 (1980).

[102] This is the Ohio Supreme Court's approach to its state constitutional free speech provision. *See supra* notes 55–62 and accompanying text.

[103] *Davison*, 666 N.W.2d at 6 (internal citation omitted) (emphasis added); *see also* State v. Seefeldt, 661 N.W.2d 822, 827 n.4 (Wis. 2003) (noting that the court is "guided by" federal doctrine); State v. Rexrode, 844 S.E.2d 73, 80 n.8 (W. Va. 2020) (noting that the Court "has traditionally construed article III, § 6 of the West Virginia Constitution in harmony with the Fourth Amendment, because the language is very similar").

that is consistent,"[104] as "substantial equivalents,"[105] "coextensive,"[106] "equivalent,"[107] "synonymous,"[108] "in accord,"[109] "virtually identical,"[110] or having "the same 'scope, import, and purpose,' "[111] among many other formulations. It is unclear to what extent the precise meanings of these characterizations differ from each other and, more important, what messages they send about the utility of making independent state constitutional arguments in future cases.

Some state courts, rather than announcing a firm prospective lockstepping methodology, unintentionally send a form of "mixed message" for future cases to the bar and bench. The Michigan Supreme Court, for example, deciding a state equal protection case, cited a number of earlier cases stating that it had "interpreted this clause to be coextensive with its federal counterpart."[112] It then provided the following caveat in a footnote:

> By this, we do not mean that we are bound in our understanding of the Michigan Constitution by any particular interpretation of the United States Constitution. We mean only that we have been persuaded in the past that interpretations of the Equal Protection Clause of the Fourteenth Amendment have accurately conveyed the meaning of [Michigan's] Const. 1963, art. 1, § 2 as well.[113]

[104] *Gherna*, 784 N.E.2d at 806; *accord* People v. Gonzalez, 789 N.E.2d 260, 264 (Ill. 2003) ("in a manner consistent"), *overruled on other grounds*, People v. Harris, 886 N.E.2d 947, 958–61 (Ill. 2008); State v. Nobles, 584 S.E.2d 765, 768 (N.C. 2003) ("consistent").

[105] State v. Jorgensen, 667 N.W.2d 318, 327 (Wis. 2003); State v. Quintana, 748 N.W.2d 447, 468 (Wis. 2008); *accord* Commonwealth v. Hall, 830 A.2d 537, 545 n.6 (Pa. 2003) ("functional equivalent").

[106] *In re* Interest of Jordan B., 913 N.W.2d 477, 484 (Neb. 2018); Bragg Hill Corp. v. City of Fredericksburg, 831 S.E.2d 483, 493 (Va. 2019). In another case, the Nebraska Supreme Court used the word "lockstep." State v. Baker, 903 N.W.2d 469, 477 (Neb. 2017). *See also* State v. Smith, 816 A.2d 57, 58 (Me. 2002); State v. Martello, 780 N.E.2d 250, 253 (Ohio 2002); Commonwealth v. 5444 Spruce St., 832 A.2d 396, 399 (Pa. 2003); *Ex parte* Ebbers, 871 So.2d. 776, 786 (Ala. 2003); Town of Frye Island v. State, 940 A.2d 1065, 1069 (Me. 2008); Roberto v. Mass. Parole Bd., 133 N.E.3d 792, 798 (Mass. 2019); Clear Channel Outdoor, Inc., v. Director, 247 A.3d 740, 747 (Md. 2021); State v. Allison, 618 S.W.3d 24, 42 (Tenn. 2021).

[107] State v. Wittsell, 66 P.3d 831, 834 (Kan. 2003).

[108] Willis v. Tenn. Dep't of Corr., 113 S.W.3d 706, 711 n.4 (Tenn. 2003); State v. Rheaume, 853 A.2d 1259, 1265 (Vt. 2004).

[109] State v. Ring, 65 P.3d 915, 926 n.4 (Ariz. 2003).

[110] *In re* City of Wichita, 59 P.3d 336, 341 (Kan. 2002); *accord* State v. Davenport, 827 A.2d 1063, 1071 (N.J. 2003) ("substantially identical and coextensive"); State v. Thiel, 665 N.W.2d 305, 314 n.7 (Wis. 2003) ("standard . . . is identical"); State v. Monteiro, 924 A.2d 784, 795 (R.I. 2007) ("identical"); State v. Stanfield, 554 S.W.3d 1, 8–9 (Tenn. 2018) ("identical in intent and purpose); State v. Hamm, 589 S.W.3d 765, 771 (Tenn. 2019) ("identical in intent and purpose); State v. Chavez-Majors, 454 P.3d 600, 604 (Kan. 2019) ("identical").

[111] Master Builders of Iowa, Inc. v. Polk County, 653 N.W.2d 382, 398 (Iowa 2002); *accord* Lutheran Bhd. Research Corp. v. Comm'r of Revenue, 656 N.W.2d 375, 382 (Minn. 2003) ("scope of protection . . . is identical"); *In re* Percer, 75 P.3d 488, 492 (Wash. 2003) ("same scope of protection").

[112] Harvey v. State, 664 N.W.2d 767, 770 (Mich. 2003).

[113] *Id.* at 770 n.3. *See also* People v. Goldston, 682 N.W.2d 479, 485 (Mich. 2004) (noting that the finding of a "compelling reason should not be understood as establishing a conclusive presumption artificially linking state constitutional interpretation to federal law."); People v. Smith, 733 N.W.2d

The footnote may be seen as an admirable recognition of the potential independence of the Michigan equal protection provision, but what are lawyers and lower court judges to do? Is it worth their time to undertake the difficult research in Michigan constitutional text, history, and case law that might be required to make an independent argument, or has the court signaled that such an effort would be a waste? A case from the Indiana Supreme Court provides an interesting example of this dilemma. Responding to a due process challenge to the Indiana Sex and Violent Offender Registry, the court stated that, although it had "previously held that [it would] employ the same methodology . . . as the Supreme Court . . . used to analyze claimed violations of the Due Process Clause," the most recent due process decision from the Supreme Court did not control the present analysis.[114]

Upon careful examination of the wide range of state constitutional cases adopting federal constitutional doctrine, it becomes apparent that there are in fact a large number of points, each one escalating in its level of purported deference to federal constitutional doctrine, on the continuum between the extreme end points represented by the Ohio cases previously discussed.

## II. LOCKSTEPPING EQUALITY DOCTRINE

One of the most common examples of barely reflective, and often prospective, lockstepping occurs with federal equal protection doctrine and state constitutional equality provisions. Most state constitutions do not contain an "equal protection" clause.[115] But they do contain a variety of equality provisions. In some

351, 356 n.7 (Mich. 2007); *In re* Request for Advisory Opinion, 806 N.W.2d 683, 703 n.32 (Mich. 2011); Directv v. Utah State Tax Comm., 364 P.3d 1036, 1050 (Utah 2015).

[114] Doe v. O'Connor, 790 N.E.2d 985, 988 (Ind. 2003). Significantly, the *Doe* court then stated that it would "employ a similar method of analysis and reach a similar result" as the recent Supreme Court case. *Id.* In a similar show of indecision, the Supreme Court of Arizona asserted that "[n]ormally we interpret clauses in the Arizona Constitution in conformity with decisions of the United States Supreme Court and its interpretation of similar clauses in the United States Constitution. However, 'interpretation of the state constitution is, of course, our province.'" State v. Casey, 71 P.3d 351, 354 (Ariz. 2003) (*quoting* Pool v. Superior Court, 677 P.2d 261, 271 (Ariz. 1984)). *See* State v. Castillo-Alvarez, 836 N.W.2d 527, 534–35 (Minn. 2013); Directv v. Utah State Tax Comm., 364 P.3d 1036, 1050 (Utah 2015); State v. Ireland, 121 N.E.3d 285, 294 (Ohio 2018). *See also supra* note 31 and accompanying text.

[115] Jeffrey Shaman reports that fifteen states have equal protection clauses. Jeffrey M. Shaman, Equality and Liberty in the Golden Age of State Constitutional Law 41 (2008). *See generally* Friesen, *supra* note 57, at ch. 3; Randal S. Jeffrey, *Equal Protection in State Courts, The New Economic Equality Rights*, 17 Law & Inequality 239, 25–60 (1999); Martha I. Morgan & Neal Hutchens, *The Tangled Web of Alabama's Equality Doctrine After* Melof: *Historical Reflections on Equal Protection and the Alabama Constitution*, 53 Ala. L. Rev. 135 (2001).

The Ohio Constitution contains an interesting "equal protection and benefit" clause. It provides: "Government is instituted for their equal protection and benefit. . . ." Ohio Const. art. I, § 2. The Vermont Supreme Court relied on a similar "[c]ommon [b]enefits" clause in striking down a

states, broad guarantees of individual rights have been interpreted generally to require equal protection of the laws.[116] Further, most states have provisions prohibiting special and local laws, the grant of special privileges, or discrimination against citizens in the exercise of civil rights or on the basis of sex. Finally, many state provisions guarantee equality in specific or limited instances—from requiring "uniform" or "thorough and efficient" public schools to requiring uniformity in taxation. Virtually all of these provisions differ significantly from the federal Equal Protection Clause. They were drafted differently, adopted at different times, and aimed at different evils. Nonetheless, when confronted with equality issues, many state judges and lawyers resort almost instinctively to federal equal protection analysis.[117] As in other areas of state constitutional law, many state courts have been unwilling—for whatever reason—to depart from federal doctrine; and even courts that reach different results under their state constitutions often do so without acknowledging the differences between state and federal equality guarantees. Some state courts in the past generation, however, have been willing to develop their own analysis, and this situation continues to change as the New Judicial Federalism matures. The broader point, though, is that scholars, courts, and lawyers should be aware of the tendency to equate federal and state equality provisions. They should also be aware that many of the challenges that are brought under the federal provision can be "repackaged"

ban on same-sex marriage. Baker v. State, 744 A.2d 864, 867 (Vt. 1999). *See also* Brown v. State, 182 A.3d 597 (Vt. 2018); Melissa Saunders, *Equal Protection, Class Legislation, and Color Blindness*, 96 MICH. L. REV. 245, 251–68 (1997) (discussing significance of state equality provisions for framers of Equal Protection Clause of Fourteenth Amendment).

[116] New Jersey's "equal protection" doctrine, for example, is based upon a provision stating: "All persons are by nature free and independent, and have certain natural and unalienable rights, among which are those of enjoying and defending life and liberty, of acquiring, possessing, and protecting property, and of pursuing and obtaining safety and happiness." N.J. CONST. art. I, ¶ 1 (1947); *see, e.g.*, Right to Choose v. Byrne, 450 A.2d 925, 933–34 (N.J. 1982). *See also* Conaway v. Deane, 932 A.2d 571, 602 n.33 (Md. 2007). Several states merely refer to multiple provisions as collectively mandating equal protection of the laws. *See, e.g.*, Markendorf v. Friedman, 133 S.W.2d 516, 519 (Ky. 1939); General Pub. Loan Corp. v. Director, Div. of Taxation, 99 A.2d 796, 800–01 (N.J. 1953); Henry v. Bauder, 518 P.2d 362, 364–65 (Kan. 1974); City of Hueytown v. Jiffy Check Co., 342 So.2d 761, 762 (Ala. 1977); Caldor's, Inc. v. Bedding Barn, Inc. 417 A.2d 343, 349 (Conn. 1979); Carson v. Maurer, 424 A.2d 825, 830 (N.H. 1980), *overruled on other grounds*, Cmty. Res. for Justice, Inc. v. City of Manchester, 917 A.2d 707, 717–21 (N.H. 2007); Hageman v. Goshen Co. School Dist. No. 1, 256 P.3d 487, 503 (Wyo. 2011).

[117] As Justice Linde noted:

> People do not claim rights against self-incrimination; they "take the fifth" and expect "*Miranda* warnings." Unlawful searches are equated with fourth amendment violations. Journalists do not invoke freedom of the press; they demand their first amendment rights. All claims of unequal treatment are phrased as denials of equal protection of the laws.

Hans A. Linde, *E Pluribus—Constitutional Theory and State Courts*, 18 GA. L. REV. 165, 174–75 (1984). *See also* SHAMAN, *supra* note 115, at 7.

under more specific, or least significantly different, state constitutional equality provisions.

Specific and limited equality provisions offer especially attractive bases for invalidating state "classifications." By relying on these narrower provisions, courts can avoid the potentially unmanageable implications of invalidating state actions under general equality provisions.[118]

## A. State Constitutional Equality Provisions

A few early state constitutions contained language similar to the classic language of equality in the Declaration of Independence. Section 1 of the Virginia Bill of Rights, written by George Mason and adopted a month before the Declaration of Independence, provided:

> That all men are by nature equally free and independent, and have certain inherent rights, of which, when they enter into a state of society, they cannot by any compact deprive or divest their posterity; namely, the enjoyment of life and liberty, with the means of acquiring and possessing property, and pursuing and obtaining happiness and safety.[119]

A.E. Dick Howard, a leading expert on the Virginia Constitution, noted that "it is to the teachings of natural law, rather than to the dictates of the British constitution, that we owe" this provision.[120] Although only Pennsylvania[121] and Massachusetts[122] initially included broad provisions such as Virginia's,[123] many states now have similarly worded ones.

Several of the early state constitutions contained another type of general equality provision intended to prohibit grants similar to royal privileges. Section 4 of the 1776 Virginia Bill of Rights, for example, provided that "no man, or set of

[118] *See infra* notes 160–64 and accompanying text.

[119] VA. CONST. Bill of Rights § 1 (1776). The question of this provision's application to slavery was apparently considered in the Virginia Convention, with George Mason's draft version being modified to ease many delegates' pro-slavery objections. HELEN HILL MILLER, GEORGE MASON: GENTLEMAN REVOLUTIONARY 147–49 (1975). Interestingly, it was the earlier draft that was widely circulated and copied. *Id.* at 149, 154–55, 338.

[120] A.E. Dick Howard, *"For the Common Benefit": Constitutional History in Virginia as a Casebook for the Modern Constitution-Maker*, 54 VA. L. REV. 816, 823 (1968).

[121] PA. CONST. art. I, § 1 (1776).

[122] MASS. CONST. pt. I, art. I (1780).

[123] Notions of equality, however, permeated the first state constitutions with respect to governmental structure, even if not with respect to individual rights. *See generally* Chapter 2.

men, is entitled to exclusive or separate emoluments or privileges from the community, but in consideration of public services."[124]

In the nineteenth century, many states amended their constitutions to curb the granting of "special" or "exclusive" privileges, after a series of abuses by the relatively unfettered state legislatures responding to powerful economic interests.[125] These provisions were modeled after provisions adopted earlier in other states, such as Section 4 of the Virginia Bill of Rights.[126] For example, Article I, Section 20, of the 1859 Oregon Constitution, which was patterned after Indiana's 1851 constitution,[127] provides: "No law shall be passed granting to any citizen or class of citizens privileges or immunities which, upon the same terms, shall not equally belong to all citizens."[128] These provisions commonly are found in state bills of rights—not in the legislative articles. They reflect the Jacksonian opposition to favoritism and special treatment for the powerful.[129]

Although these provisions may seem to overlap somewhat with federal equal protection doctrine, closer scrutiny reveals significant differences. As Justice Linde of the Oregon Supreme Court noted, Oregon's Article I, Section 20, and the federal Equal Protection Clause "were placed in different constitutions at different times by different men to enact different historic concerns into constitutional policy."[130] Justice Betty Roberts of the same court noted further:

[124] VA. CONST. Bill of Rights § 4 (1776). For a similar provision, see MASS. CONST. pt. 1, art. VI (1780).

[125] *See* J. HURST, THE GROWTH OF AMERICAN LAW: THE LAW MAKERS 24–42 (1950); William F. Swindler, *Minimum Standards of Constitutional Justice: Federal Floor and State Ceiling*, 49 MO. L. REV. 1, 2 (1984). *See also* A.J. Thomas Jr. & Amy Van Wynen Thomas, *The Texas Constitution of 1876*, 35 TEX. L. REV. 907 (1959).

[126] *See supra* note 119 and accompanying text. The concern of the newer provisions was with legislative, rather than royal, favoritism. *See* Hans A. Linde, *Without "Due Process:" Unconstitutional Law in Oregon*, 49 OR. L. REV. 125, 141 (1970).

[127] *Id.*

[128] OR. CONST. art. I, § 20 (1859). *See generally* David Schuman, *The Right to "Equal Privileges and Immunities": A State's Version of "Equal Protection,"* 13 VT. L. REV. 221 (1988); Jonathan Thompson, *The Washington Constitution's Prohibition on Special Privileges and Immunities: Real Bite for "Equal Protection" Review of Regulatory Legislation?* 69 TEMP. L. REV. 1247 (1996).

[129] Historian Rush Welter observed:

> Hence the whole thrust of Jacksonian thought was in the first instance negative, an effort to eliminate institutions and practices that an earlier generation had more or less taken for granted.
>
> The "aristocracy" that Jacksonians complained of consisted of selective access to power, prosperity, or influence. At bottom it was a political rather than a social or economic concept: in Jacksonian eyes, an "aristocrat" was someone who was empowered by law to affect the economic and social welfare of his contemporaries, or who enjoyed legal privileges that he could turn to his own account in an otherwise competitive economy.

RUSH WELTER, THE MIND OF AMERICA: 1820–1860, 77–78 (1975) (footnote omitted).

[130] Linde, *supra* note 126, at 141; *see also* Linde, *supra* note 117, at 182–83 ("Such provisions long antedated the Civil War, and their target, prohibition of special privileges, was quite different from that of the 14th amendment's equal protection clause."). For a listing of similar state provisions, see *id.* at 182 n.43.

> Article I, section 20, of the Oregon Constitution has been said to be the "antithesis" of the equal protection clause of the fourteenth amendment. . . . While the fourteenth amendment forbids curtailment of rights belonging to a particular group or individual, article I, section 20, prevents the enlargements of rights. . . . There is an historical basis for this distinction. The Reconstruction Congress, which adopted the fourteenth amendment in 1868, was concerned with discrimination against disfavored groups or individuals, specifically, former slaves. . . . When article I, section 20, was adopted as a part of the Oregon Constitution nine years earlier, in 1859, the concern of its drafters was with favoritism and the granting of special privileges for a select few.[131]

A provision like Oregon's, then, does not seek equal *protection* of the laws at all. Instead, it prohibits legislative discrimination *in favor of* a minority.

These provisions may differ in other ways from the federal Equal Protection Clause. Justice Linde suggests that Oregon's provision can cover individuals in addition to classes of people,[132] and that it may not apply to corporations or nonresidents.[133] Moreover, the specific reference to the "passage of laws" may preclude its application to executive action.

Many courts interpreting provisions such as Oregon's, however, fail to recognize that they differ in text, origin, and focus from the federal equal protection provision. These courts, and apparently the lawyers practicing before them, seem content to rely on federal equal protection analysis in a common form of lockstepping.

Closely related to the provisions prohibiting grants of special or exclusive privileges are prohibitions on "special" and "local" laws.[134] These provisions, found in the legislative articles of state constitutions rather than in the declarations of rights (Chapter 9) contain either general or detailed limitations on the objects of legislation[135]—special laws, which are those that apply to specified or a limited number of persons; and local laws, which are those that apply to specified or a limited number of localities.[136] In addition, notice requirements are usually included for those subjects that may be dealt with by

[131] Hewitt v. State Accident Ins. Fund Corp., 653 P.2d 970, 975 (Or. 1982) (citations omitted); *see also* Behrns v. Buake, 229 N.W.2d 86, 88 (S.D. 1975) ("more stringent constitutional standard" than Fourteenth Amendment); Comment, 19 Willamette L.J. 757 (1983) (discussing *Hewitt*).

[132] *See* State v. Clark, 630 P.2d 810, 814–15 (Or. 1981); State v. Freeland, 667 P.2d 509, 512 (Or. 1983).

[133] Linde, *supra* note 126, at 142 nn.53 & 54.

[134] *See* James Q. Dealey, Growth of American State Constitutions 224–26 (1915); Hurst, *supra* note 125, at 241–42; Thomas & Thomas, *supra* note 125, at 915.

[135] *See, e.g.*, Fla. Const. art. III, § 11(a)(1).

[136] *See generally* City of Louisville v. Klusmeyer, 324 S.W.2d 831, 833–34 (Ky. 1959) (noting that both territorially and substantively "special" statutes are permissible in certain cases).

local laws, giving residents of localities to be affected at least constructive notice of the legislature's intended action.

Though intended as limitations on the legislative branch to curb legislative abuses, these proscriptions on special and local laws reflect a concern for equal treatment under the law and are often interpreted as rights guarantees. In 1972, the Illinois Supreme Court held that the state's no-fault automobile insurance act violated Article IV, Section 13, of the Illinois Constitution, which provides that "[t]he General Assembly shall pass no special or local law when a general law is or can be made applicable."[137] The statute required only owners of "private passenger automobiles"[138] to purchase no fault insurance but imposed substantial limitations on tort recoveries of persons injured by any type of motor vehicle. In distinguishing Illinois' "equal protection" clause,[139] which had been added in 1970, Justice Schaefer observed:

> While these two provisions of the 1970 constitution cover much of the same terrain, they are not duplicates, as the commentary to section 13 of article IV points out: "In many cases, the protection provided by Section 13 is also provided by the equal protection clause of Article I, Section 2."[140]

He concluded that Article IV, Section 13, imposed a clear constitutional duty on the courts to determine whether a general law "is or can be made applicable" and that "in this case that question must receive an affirmative answer."[141] The constitutionally infirm portions of the statute were therefore invalidated. The Virginia Supreme Court also noted the distinction between equal protection and special laws limitations in striking down the Sunday Closing Law, stating that, although economic regulation received the lowest level of scrutiny under federal equal protection analysis, the special laws provisions were aimed directly at economic favoritism.[142]

The notice provisions for local laws can also provide a basis for invalidating state laws. The U.S. Supreme Court held in *James v. Valtierra*[143] that California's constitutionally required local referendum on low-cost housing did not violate

[137] Ill. Const. art. IV, § 13. The Illinois "special laws" provision declares further that "[w]hether a general law is or can be made applicable shall be a matter for judicial determination." Ill. Const. art. IV, § 13. The Alabama, Alaska, Kansas, Michigan, Minnesota, and Nevada constitutions contain similar provisions. *See* Shaman, *supra* note 115, at 30.

[138] Ill. Rev. Stat. ch. 73, § 1065.150 (1971) (repealed 1974).

[139] Ill. Const. art. I, § 2 provides: "No person shall . . . be denied the equal protection of the laws."

[140] Grace v. Howlett, 283 N.E.2d 474, 479 (Ill. 1974).

[141] *Id.*

[142] Benderson Development Co., Inc. v. Sciortino, 372 S.E.2d 751, 756 (Va. 1988). *See also* People v. Canister, 110 P.3d 380, 382 (Colo. 2005) (special laws ban "more than a redundant equal protection clause").

[143] 402 U.S. 137 (1971).

the federal equal protection clause. Several years later, however, the Florida Supreme Court found a similar statutory referendum requirement, applicable only in one county, unconstitutional for failure to provide the proper notice before its enactment as a "local law."[144]

In the 1960s, a number of state constitutions were amended to include provisions prohibiting discrimination in the exercise of civil rights. Pennsylvania, for example, added a provision in 1967 that directs "[n]either the Commonwealth nor any political subdivisions thereof shall deny to any person the enjoyment of any civil right, nor discriminate against any person in the exercise of any civil right."[145] Similar provisions in other states typically limit this kind of proscription to discrimination on the basis of race, color, or national origin.[146]

These antidiscrimination provisions are products of the civil rights movement in the 1950s and 1960s, nearly a century after adoption of the Fourteenth Amendment. The express proscription of *discrimination* against persons in the exercise of their civil rights, in addition to prohibiting the *denial* of rights, could provide a strong textual basis for extending such protection beyond federal equal protection doctrine. In *Harris v. McRae*,[147] the U.S. Supreme Court held that restrictions on Medicaid funding for abortions did not violate the federal Equal Protection Clause.[148] The Court concluded that a mere failure to fund the exercise of the federal constitutional right to choose abortion did not unconstitutionally burden or limit the exercise of that right.[149] A state provision such as Pennsylvania's, however, comes much closer to reaching such policies as state restrictions of funding for abortions than does the federal Equal Protection Clause.

Prohibiting this type of discrimination has become increasingly important as state governments have expanded from regulation into the provision of services. When state governments merely regulated conduct, prohibiting them from *denying* persons' civil rights was an effective limit—they did not have the leverage of attaching "unconstitutional conditions" to the provision of services;

[144] Housing Auth. v. City of St. Petersburg, 287 So.2d 307 (Fla. 1973); *see also* State *ex rel.* City of Pompano Beach v. Lewis, 368 So.2d 1298, 1301 (Fla. 1979) (holding local law unconstitutional for failure to provide notice).

[145] PA CONST. art. I, § 26. For discussion of similar provisions in other state constitutions, see Albert L. Sturm, *The Development of American State Constitutions*, 12 PUBLIUS: THE J. FEDERALISM 57, 87–88 (Winter 1982); Albert L. Sturm & Kaye M. Wright, *Civil Liberties in Revised State Constitutions*, *in* CIVIL LIBERTIES: POLICY AND POLICY MAKING 179, 182–83 (S. Wasby ed., 1976).

[146] *See, e.g.*, N.J. CONST. art. I, ¶ 5.

[147] 448 U.S. 297 (1980).

[148] This was a Fifth Amendment equal protection case dealing with a *federal* statute. The companion case, *Williams v. Zbaraz*, 448 U.S. 358 (1980), applied identical analysis to a *state* statute under the equal protection clause of the Fourteenth Amendment.

[149] *Harris*, 448 U.S. at 315–17.

therefore, it was not as easy to favor one right over another. When the state acts as a service provider, however, as it does in programs such as Medicaid, it has the opportunity, in Professor Laurence Tribe's words, "to achieve with carrots what [it] is forbidden to achieve with sticks."[150] Thus, these provisions prohibiting *discrimination* against persons in the exercise of their civil rights may be interpreted to keep states from picking and choosing among citizens' rights that they seek to advance or repress.

Several states adopted constitutional provisions banning various forms of gender discrimination at the end of the nineteenth century.[151] Generally speaking, however, the "state ERA [equal rights amendment]" is a phenomenon of the 1970s—the most recent manifestation of equality concerns in state constitutions.[152]

## B. Interpretation of State Constitutional Equality Provisions

Adoption of equality provisions through popular referenda reflects an important social and political movement in our society.[153] As the Maryland Court of Appeals noted:

> [W]e believe that the "broad, sweeping, mandatory language" of the amendment is cogent evidence that the people of Maryland are fully committed to equal rights for men and women. The adoption of the E.R.A. in this state was intended to, and did, drastically alter traditional views of the validity of sex-based classifications.[154]

Despite their powerful mandate, most jurisprudence under these new provisions is dominated by federal equal protection analysis. For example, in 1973, the Supreme Court of Virginia held that a statute exempting from jury duty women responsible for children or other persons needing continuous care did not violate the state ERA.[155] The court stated that the new state constitutional provision was

150 Laurence Tribe, American Constitutional Law § 15-10, at 933 n.77 (1978).

151 These provisions usually concerned only women's suffrage. *See, e.g.*, Utah Const. art. IV, § 1 (1894); Wyo. Const. art. 1, § 3 (1889).

152 For an excellent review of state ERA litigation, see Linda J. Wharton, *State Equal Rights Amendments Revisited: Evaluating Their Effectiveness in Advancing Protection Against Sex Discrimination*, 36 Rutgers L.J. 1201 (2005). *See also* Shaman, *supra* note 115, at 53–61.

153 *See* Linde, *supra* note 126, at 131 (noting that although a constitutional "rule" is applied by judicial decision, "[it] was first a political decision that others deemed worthy of constitutional magnitude").

154 Rand v. Rand, 374 A.2d 900, 905 (Md. 1977) (*quoting* Darrin v. Gould, 540 P.2d 882, 889 (Wash. 1975)).

155 Archer v. Mayes, 194 S.E.2d 707 (Va. 1973). The plaintiffs raised both federal equal protection and state ERA arguments.

"no broader than the equal protection clause of the Fourteenth Amendment"[156] and applied only rational basis scrutiny.[157] Indeed, most state courts addressing gender discrimination claims seem preoccupied with federal equal protection constructs, largely undermining the state provisions.

The Washington Supreme Court, however, adopted what appears to be a truly independent jurisprudence under its ERA. In *Southwest Washington Chapter, National Electrical Contractors Association v. Pierce County*,[158] the court addressed a challenge, under state and federal equal protection provisions as well as the state ERA, to a county affirmative action plan for public works contracting. While holding that the state's ERA does not bar affirmative efforts to create equality in fact, the court noted: "The ERA absolutely prohibits discrimination on the basis of sex and is not subject to even the narrow exceptions permitted under traditional 'strict scrutiny.' . . . The ERA mandates equality in the strongest of terms and absolutely prohibits the sacrifice of equality for *any* state interest, no matter how compelling. . . ."[159] Thus, the Washington court was apparently willing to go beyond the protection provided by the federal equal protection provision and to develop independent doctrine under its ERA.

Although many states have interpreted generally applicable bill of rights provisions to guarantee equality under the law, other provisions, not usually found in bills or rights, expressly require equality in specific and limited instances. When applicable, these provisions offer state courts sound textual bases for invalidating state actions. At the same time, they warrant extending equality guarantees beyond those of federal equal protection doctrine; these provisions allow courts to avoid some of the problems with basing decisions on generally applicable equality provisions.

In *Robinson v. Cahill*,[160] the New Jersey Supreme Court held unconstitutional the state's school financing scheme under a provision in the New Jersey Constitution requiring a "thorough and efficient" education.[161] The provision was added in 1875 partly to reflect public concern over equality in education.[162]

156 *Id.* at 711.

157 *Id.* at 710. The court relied on federal constitutional precedents; at the time, discrimination on the basis of sex was subject to rational basis scrutiny under federal law.

158 667 P.2d 1092 (Wash. 1983).

159 *Id.* at 1102 (emphasis in original). The court concluded: "As long as the law favoring one sex is intended solely to ameliorate the effects of past discrimination, it simply does not implicate the ERA." *Id.* at 1102.One commentator criticized *Pierce County*, asserting that its holding signaled a retreat from *Hanson v. Hutt*, 517 P.2d 599, 603 (Wash. 1973), in which the Washington Supreme Court held sex to be a suspect class under WASH. CONST. art. I, § 12 (1889), the Jacksonian ban on special privileges and immunities. Comment, *Washington's Equal Rights Amendment: It Says What It Means and It Means What It Says*, 8 U. PUGET SOUND L. REV. 461, 471 (1985).

160 303 A.2d 273, 294 (N.J. 1973), *cert. denied*, 414 U.S. 976 (1973). *See* Paul L. Tractenberg, *The Evolution and Implementation of Educational Rights Under the New Jersey Constitution of 1947*, 29 RUTGERS L.J. 827, 896–902 (1998).

161 N.J. CONST. art. VIII, § 4, ¶ 1.

162 *See Cahill*, 303 A.2d at 287–92.

After criticizing the U.S. Supreme Court's approach to federal equal protection cases,[163] the New Jersey court explained why it chose not to base its decision on state "equal protection" doctrine:

> We hesitate to turn this case upon the State equal protection clause. The reason is that the equal protection clause may be unmanageable if it is called upon to supply categorical answers in the vast area of human needs, choosing those which must be met and a single basis upon which the State must act.
>
> .... [W]e stress how difficult it would be to find an objective basis to say the equal protection clause selects education and demands inflexible statewide uniformity in expenditure. Surely no need is more basic than food and lodging.... Essential also are police and fire protection, as to which the sums spent per resident vary with local decision. Nor are water and sundry public health services available throughout the State on a uniform dollar basis.[164]

Thus, the New Jersey court used the state's thorough and efficient education provision as a more "specific and limited" textual basis for its decision on equality and adequacy in education finance.

State prohibitions on special rights and privileges, special and local laws, discrimination against persons in the exercise of civil rights, and discrimination on the basis of sex may similarly be viewed as specific and limited equality provisions. In addition, most states have uniformity in taxation provisions that provide specific grounds for enforcing equality.[165] It is important to note, though, that while these provisions may be limited in focus, they can be far reaching in effect.

Although most states do not have general "equal protection" clauses, many have interpreted various provisions—such as those just outlined—to guarantee equal protection of the laws generally. Of these courts, a significant number follow federal equal protection doctrine without independent analysis

[163] The New Jersey court said:

> In passing we note briefly the reason why we are not prepared to accept that concept for State constitutional purposes. We have no difficulty with the thought that a discrimination which may have an invidious base is "suspect" and will be examined closely. And if a discrimination of that kind is found, the inquiry may well end, for it is not likely that a State interest could sustain such a discrimination. But we have not found helpful the concept of a "fundamental" right.

303 A.2d at 282.

[164] 303 A.2d at 283, 284. In fact, New Jersey has no "equal protection" clause in its constitution. The general state constitutional doctrines of equality arise from N.J. Const. art. I, ¶ 1. *See supra* note 110.

[165] *See generally* Michael M. Bernard, Constitutions, Taxation and Land Policy (1979) (abstracting tax provisions from the federal and all state constitutions); Wade J. Newhouse, Constitutional Equality and Uniformity in State Taxation (2d ed. 1984) (analysis of state tax uniformity and equality provisions, organized into nine prototypical clauses). *See infra* notes 201–03 and accompanying text.

in addressing state equal protection claims.[166] Those that have "rediscovered" state equality provisions, however, decide for themselves whether governmental actions violate the equality policies embodied in their constitutions.

Courts that have employed an independent analysis of state equal protection claims have done so under one of two methodologies. Under the first, the state court adopts the federal frame of analysis but applies those constructs independently.[167] Under the second, courts reject the federal constructs and apply their own analytical frameworks.

Courts that apply the federal constructs independently use the suspect class/fundamental right/level of scrutiny approach but often reach results that conflict with those reached by the federal courts. The California Supreme Court required busing to achieve racial balance in public schools even though it found no intentional discrimination[168]—a necessary element for court ordered busing under federal equal protection doctrine.[169] It has also held gender to be a suspect classification[170] as well as sexual orientation in the same-sex marriage context,[171] and has taken a different view of the doctrine of unconstitutional conditions in its abortion financing decision.[172] Finally, California has held that its equality provisions can be triggered without meeting the federal standard for state action.[173]

166 *See, e.g.*, Opinion of the Justices, 337 A.2d 354, 356 (N.H. 1975); State *ex rel.* Olsen v. Maxwell, 259 N.W.2d 621, 627 (N.D. 1977); AFSCME Councils v. Sundquist, 338 N.W.2d 560, 569 n.11 (Minn. 1983); State v. PPL Montana, LLC, 172 P.3d 1241, 1246 (Mont. 2007); State v. Johnson, 813 N.W.2d 1 (Minn. 2012); Glossip v. Missouri Dept. of Trans. and Highway Patrol, 411 S.W.3d 796, 809 (Mo. 2013); Propst v. State, 788 S.E.2d 484, 490–91 (Ga. 2016); McClay v. Airport Management Services, LLC, 596 S.W.3d 686, 695–96 (Tenn. 2020); MSAD 6 Bd. of Dir. v. Town of Frye Island, 229 A.3d 514, 524 (Maine 2020). A good example of this type of analysis is *White v. Hughes*, 519 S.W.2d 70 (Ark. 1975), in which the court said: "[W]e take the view that if the rule of . . . the highest authority on the equal protection clause 'is to be changed . . . we shall await the views of the United States Supreme Court. . . .'" *Id.* at 71 (*quoting* Justice v. Gatchell, 325 A.2d 97, 102 (Del. 1974)).

167 *See, e.g.*, Hospital Servs., Inc. v. Brooks, 229 N.W.2d 69, 71–75 (N.D. 1975); Bierkamp v. Rogers, 293 N.W.2d 577, 585 (Iowa 1980); Community Resources for Justice, Inc. v. City of Manchester, 917 A.2d 707, 717–21 (N.H. 2007).

168 Crawford v. Bd. of Educ., 551 P.2d 28 (Cal. 1976); *see* Comment, *Proposition 1 and Federal Protection of State Constitutional Rights*, 75 Nw. U. L. Rev. 685, 707–09 (1980).

This was one of the few noncriminal state constitutional rulings to be overruled by constitutional amendment. California's Proposition 1 amended the state constitution's equal protection clause to make it coextensive with interpretations of the federal Constitution in busing matters. Cal. Const. art. I, § 7 (1879, amended 1979); Comment, *California's Anti-Busing Amendment: A Perspective on the Now Unequal Equal Protection Clause*, 10 Golden Gate U. L. Rev. 611 (1980); Comment, *Proposition 1, supra*.

169 *E.g.*, Keyes v. School Dist. No. 1, 413 U.S. 189, 198 (1973).

170 Sail'er Inn, Inc. v. Kirby, 485 P.2d 529, 538–41 (Cal. 1971); *see also* State *ex rel.* Olson v. Maxwell, 259 N.W.2d 621, 627 (N.D. 1977) (finding classifications based on sex "inherently suspect"); Hanson v. Hutt, 517 P.2d 599, 603 (Wash. 1973) (same).

171 *In re* Marriage cases, 183 P.3d 384, 442–44 (Cal. 2008).

172 *See* Committee to Defend Reproductive Rights v. Myers, 625 P.2d 779, 783 (Cal. 1981).

173 Gay Law Students Ass'n v. Pacific Tel. & Tel. Co., 595 P.2d 592, 598–602 (Cal. 1979); *cf.* Peper v. Princeton Univ., 389 A.2d 465 (N.J. 1978) (allowing employee to maintain equal protection action under state constitution against private university). *See* Chapter 6.

More and more states, as in other areas of the New Judicial Federalism, are rejecting the constructs developed by the U.S. Supreme Court in interpreting the federal Equal Protection Clause.[174] In *Carson v. Maurer*,[175] the New Hampshire Supreme Court held that a state statute placing various restrictions on medical malpractice claims violated the state's equality guarantees.[176] The court sought to determine "whether the challenged classifications are reasonable and have a fair and substantial relation to the object of the legislation."[177] In so doing, the court announced: "In interpreting our State constitution, however, we are not confined to federal constitutional standards and are free to grant individuals more rights than the Federal Constitution requires."[178]

Many state constitutions contain a wide variety of equality clauses, yet it is very common for state courts to interpret the disparate provisions as identical to the Equal Protection Clause of the Fourteenth Amendment.[179] Still, other states that initially equated their equality clauses with federal doctrines have begun to move in the direction of independence. States like Indiana,[180] Vermont,[181] Minnesota,[182] Alaska,[183] Idaho,[184] Wisconsin,[185]

[174] *See, e.g.*, Carson v. Maurer, 424 A.2d 825, 830–32 (N.H. 1980), *overruled on other grounds*, Cmty. Res. for Justice, Inc. v. City of Manchester, 917 A.2d 707, 717–21 (N.H. 2007); Right to Choose v. Byrne, 450 A.2d 925, 936–37 (N.J. 1982).

[175] 424 A.2d 825, 830–32 (N.H. 1980).

[176] The court based its equality analysis on two broad provisions of the state's bill of rights, N.H. Const. pt. 1st, arts. 2d & 12th (1783). *Maurer*, 424 A.2d at 830. Neither of these provisions expressly mandates equality.

[177] *Id.* at 831.

[178] *Id.*

[179] *See, e.g., In re* Commitment of Dennis H., 647 N.W.2d 851, 854–55 n.3 (Wis. 2002); Mass. Fed'n of Teachers v. Bd. of Ed., 767 N.E.2d 549, 562 (Mass. 2002); Newport Int'l University, Inc. v. State, 186 P.3d 382, 386–87 (Wyo. 2008); Kottel v. State, 60 P.3d 403, 413–14 (Mont. 2002); City of Memphis v. Hargett, 414 S.W.3d 88, 110 (Tenn. 2013).

[180] *See, e.g.*, Collins v. Day, 644 N.E.2d 72 (Ind. 1994); League of Women Voters v. Rokita 929 N.E.2d 758 (Ind. 2010). The Ohio Supreme Court continues to debate lockstepping. *See* State v. Mole, 74 N.E.3d 368 (Ohio 2016).

[181] *See, e.g.*, Baker v. State, 744 A.2d 864 (Vt. 1999); Brown v. State, 182 A.3d 599 (Vt. 2018). *See also* Robert F. Williams, *Old Constitutions and New Issues: National Lessons from Vermont's State Constitutional Case on Marriage of Same-Sex Couples*, 43 B.C. L. Rev. 73 (2001).

[182] *See, e.g.*, Ann L. Iijima, *Minnesota Equal Protection in the Third Millennium: "Old Formulations" or "New Articulations"?* 20 Wm. Mitchell L. Rev. 337, 348–81 (1994) (discussing deviations between the Minnesota Supreme Court's interpretation of the state and federal Equal Protection Clauses).

[183] *See, e.g.*, Matanuska-Susitna Borough Sch. Dist. v. State, 931 P.2d 391, 402 (Alaska 1997); Braun v. Borough, 193 P.3d 719, 731 (Alaska 2008). Paul E. McGreal, *Alaska Equal Protection: Constitutional Law or Common Law?* 15 Alaska L. Rev. 209 (1998); Ronald L. Nelson, *Welcome to the "Last Frontier," Professor Gardner: Alaska's Independent Approach to State Constitutional Interpretation*, 12 Alaska L. Rev. 1, 11–17 (1995); Michael B. Wise, *Northern Lights—Equal Protection Analysis in Alaska*, 3 Alaska L. Rev. 1 (1986).

[184] *See, e.g.*, Concerned Taxpayers of Kootenai Co. v. Kootenai Co., 50 P.3d 991, 994 (Idaho 2002). *But see* Rudeen v. Cenarrusa, 38 P.3d 598, 606–07 (Idaho 2001).

[185] *See* Ferdon v. Wisconsin Patients Compensation Fund, 701 N.W.2d 440 (Wis. 2005). *See* Lawrence Friedman, *Reconsidering Rational Basis: Equal Protection Review Under the Wisconsin Constitution*, 38 Rutgers L.J. 1071 (2007). Jeffrey Shaman reports that at least twenty-one states have

Washington,[186] Iowa,[187] Utah,[188] Ohio,[189] and New Mexico[190] have been moving to decouple their state constitutional equality doctrines from the formerly dominant federal equal protection analysis.

We can see an application of the prospective lockstepping "test" approach in the Pennsylvania cases interpreting the various state constitutional equality provisions. Here, as noted, the state court cites a variety of state constitutional provisions and announces that they will be interpreted the same way that the U.S. Supreme Court interprets the Equal Protection Clause. The Pennsylvania Constitution, like a number of state constitutions, includes a number of provisions reflecting equality concerns. None of these clauses has the same origins, text, or date of adoption as the Equal Protection Clause of the Fourteenth Amendment to the U.S. Constitution.[191] The Pennsylvania high court, however, has consistently interpreted Pennsylvania's state constitutional equality provisions in lockstep with the federal Equal Protection Clause. The court stated in *Love v. Borough of Stroudsburg*[192] that "the equal protection provisions of the Pennsylvania Constitution are analyzed by this Court under the *same standards* used by the United States Supreme Court when reviewing equal protection claims under the Fourteenth Amendment to the United States Constitution."[193]

now extended their state constitutional equality analysis beyond federal equal protection doctrine. SHAMAN, *supra* note 115, at 17.

[186] *See, e.g.*, Grant Co. Fire Protection Dist. v. City of Moses Lake, 83 P.3d 419 (Wash. 2004); Ventenbergs v. City of Seattle, 178 P.3d 960 (Wash. 2008); Assoc. of Washington Spirits and Wine Distributors v. Wash. St. Liquor Control Bd., 340 P.3d 849, 857 (Wash. 2015).

[187] Racing Assoc. of Central Iowa v. Fitzgerald, 675 N.W.2d 1 (Iowa 2004); King v. State, 818 N.W.2d 1, 64 (Iowa 2012) (Appel, J., dissenting). AFSCME Iowa Council 61 v. State, 928 N.W.2d 21 (Iowa 2019). *See generally* Edward M. Mansfield & Connor L. Wasson, *Exploring the Original Meaning of Article I, Section 6 of the Iowa Constitution*, 66 DRAKE L. REV. 147 (2018).

[188] State v. Drej, 233 P.3d 476, 486 (Utah 2010); Anderson v. Provo City Corp., 108 P.3d 701, 707 (Utah 2005). *But see* Directv v. Utah State Tax Comm., 364 P.3d 1036, 1050 (Utah 2015) (uniform operation of laws clause "state-law counterpart to federal Equal Protection Clause").

[189] Brown v. State, 182 A.3d 599 (Vt. 2018); Stolz v. J&B Steel Erectors, Inc., 122 N.E.3d 1228, 1239 (Ohio 2018) (Fischer, J., concurring):

> By treating the two clauses as functionally equivalent, this court delegates its final authority to interpret the Ohio clause to the United States Supreme Court, which that court exercises whenever it substantially alters its interpretation of the federal clause. This "upward delegation" of the duty to interpret the Ohio Constitution is improper under our federal system and unconstitutional under the Ohio Constitution.

[190] Rodriguez v. Brand West Dairy, 378 P.3d 13 (N.M. 2016).

[191] *See generally* Williams, *Row of Shadows*, *supra* note 19.

[192] 597 A.2d 1137 (Pa. 1991).

[193] *Id.* at 1139 (emphasis added); *see also* Dansby v. Thomas Jefferson Univ. Hosp., 623 A.2d 816, 820 (Pa. Super. Ct. 1993) (utilizing the same approach); Fort Worth Osteopathic Hospital, Inc. v. Reese, 148 S.W.3d 94, 97–98 (Tex. 2004); *In re* Care and Treatment of Coffman, 225 S.W.3d 439, 445 (Mo. 2007). *See generally* SHAMAN, *supra* note 115, at 7, 15.

This view has often been repeated by the Pennsylvania courts regarding nearly all of the state constitutional provisions that reflect equality concerns.[194] For example, the Pennsylvania Supreme Court, interpreting the state constitution's ban on "special laws," concluded:

> The analysis of both federal and state claims is essentially the same. As this court stated in *Laudenberger v. Port Auth. of Allegheny Co.* . . . "'Appellees' contentions concerning the Equal Protection Clause of the federal Constitution and Art. III, § 32 of the Pennsylvania Constitution may be reviewed simultaneously, for the meaning and purpose of the two are sufficiently similar to warrant like treatment."[195]

The Pennsylvania Supreme Court has noted that its "same standards" approach to state constitutional equality cases is a matter of its own choice.[196] The court stated: "In the equal protection area . . . *we have chosen* to be guided by the standards and analysis employed by the United States Supreme Court. . . ."[197]

On at least one occasion, though, the Pennsylvania Supreme Court stated that "the *content* of" the special laws prohibition "is not significantly different from the Equal Protection Clause," and that "we should be guided by the same principles in interpreting our Constitution" but reached a result different from that under the federal Constitution.[198] In *Kroger Co. v. O'Hara Township*, the court struck down the Sunday Closing Laws (a result never reached by the U.S. Supreme Court), with specific reliance on the explicit prohibition in Article

[194] *See generally* Williams, *Row of Shadows*, *supra* note 19. For examples of approaches that are similar to Pennsylvania's, see East Okla. Bldg. & Constr. Trades Council v. Pitts, 82 P.3d 1008, 1012 (Okla. 2003); Park Corp. v. City of Brook Park, 807 N.E.2d 913, 917 (Ohio 2004); Fort Worth Osteopathic Hosp., Inc. v. Reese, 148 S.W.3d 94, 97–98 (Tex. 2004). The Tennessee Supreme Court acknowledged the "historical and linguistic differences between the equal protection provisions" of the state and federal constitutions, but stated that the two provided "*essentially* the same protection." Gallaher v. Elam, 104 S.W.3d 455, 460 (Tenn. 2003) (emphasis added). Montana has changed its view, State v. Ariegwe, 167 P.3d 815, 827 (Mont. 2007), as has Iowa, Racing Assoc. of Central Iowa v. Fitzgerald, 675 N.W.2d 1, 4–6 (Iowa 2004).

[195] Harristown Dev. Corp. v. Commonwealth Dep't of Gen. Servs., 614 A.2d 1128, 1132 (Pa. 1992) (citations omitted) (*quoting* Laudenberger v. Port Auth., 436 A.2d 147, 155 n.13 (Pa. 1981)); *see also* DeFazio v. Civil Serv. Comm'n, 756 A.2d 1103, 1105–06 (Pa. 2000); Big Sky Excavating, Inc. v. Ill. Bell Tel. Co., 840 N.E.2d 1174, 1186 (Ill. 2005); Tindley v. Salt Lake City School Dist., 116 P.3d 295, 302 (Utah 2005) (uniform operation of laws provision). *See generally* Donald Marritz, *Making Equality Matter (Again): The Prohibition Against Special Laws in the Pennsylvania Constitution*, 3 Widener J. Pub. L. 161 (1993).

[196] *See* Fischer v. Dep't of Pub. Welfare, 502 A.2d 114, 121 (Pa. 1985).

[197] Commonwealth v. Parker White Metal Co., 515 A.2d 1358, 1362 (Pa. 1986) (emphasis added); *see infra* note 230 and accompanying text.

[198] Kroger Co. v. O'Hara Township, 392 A.2d 266, 274 (Pa. 1978). *See also* Folta v. Ferro Engineering, 43 N.E.3d 108, 119 (Ill. 2015).

III, Section 32, on special laws regulating "trade."[199] The court found that the numerous amendments over time, creating exceptions, resulted in the Sunday Closing Laws becoming "special."[200] A decision like *Kroger*, in the midst of all the earlier and later proclamations that the Pennsylvania court would apply the "same principles" as federal equal protection doctrine, exposes the court to the charge that its aberrational decision is unprincipled or result-oriented. A well-reasoned, case-specific decision based on reflective adoptionism, however, would not be vulnerable to this charge.

In addition to those equality clauses, Article VIII, Section 1, of the Pennsylvania Constitution provides: "All taxes shall be uniform, upon the same class of subjects, within the territorial limits of the authority levying the tax, and shall be levied and collected under general laws."[201] In the words of the Pennsylvania Supreme Court: "It is well established, however, that in matters of taxation both constitutional standards are relevant, and that allegations of violations of the equal protection clause, and of the Uniformity Clause, are to be analyzed in the same manner."[202] There are examples, however, where the court announces that the state and federal provisions are interpreted in the same manner but proceeds to strike down a tax statute that might well withstand a federal challenge, leading, once again, to the appearance of result-orientation.[203]

[199] *Id.* at 274 ("We therefore find that it is our judicial duty to carefully examine any law regulating trade."). The court did recognize the additional specific language in the Pennsylvania Constitution, noting it was "not free to treat that language as though it was [*sic*] not there." *Id.*

[200] *Id.* at 273. *See also* Benderson Development Co. v. Sciortino, 372 S.E.2d 751 (Va. 1988).

[201] PA. CONST. art. VIII, § 1. *See supra* note 165 and accompanying text.

[202] Leonard v. Thornburgh, 489 A.2d 1349, 1351 (Pa. 1985); *see also In re* Central Illinois Public Services Co., 78 P.3d 419, 428 (Kan. 2003); Minn. Automatic Merch. Council v. Salomone, 682 N.W.2d 557, 561 (Minn. 2004). *Contra* Char Life Interest v. Maricopa Co., 93 P.3d 486, 491 (Ariz. 2004); Pinghua Zhao v. Montoya, 329 P.3d 676, 685 (N.M. 2014); Odunlade v. City of Minneapolis, 823 N.W.2d 638, 647 (Minn. 2012); Murray Energy Corp. v. Steager, 827 S.E.2d 417, 431 (W. Va. 2019).

In decoupling its uniformity in taxation provision from federal equal protection doctrine, the Supreme Court of Iowa observed:

> Another writer has observed that equal protection challenges to state taxation laws and business regulations are "dismissed out of hand" by federal courts, in part due to federal restraint with respect to state matters. Lawrence Gene Sager, *Fair Measure: The Legal Status of Underenforced Constitutional Norms*, 91 HARV. L. REV. 1212, 1216 (1978). This author writes:
>
> Institutional rather than analytical reasons appear to have prompted the broad exclusion of state tax and regulatory measures from the reach of the equal protection construct fashioned by the federal judiciary. This is what creates the disparity between this construct and a true conception of equal protection, and thus substantiates the claim that equal protection is an underenforced constitutional norm.

*Id.* at 1218; *see also* Brennan, 90 HARV. L. REV. at 503 ("With federal scrutiny diminished, state courts must respond by increasing their own.").

Racing Assoc. Central Iowa v. Fitzgerald, 675 N.W.2d 1, 13 (Iowa 2004).

[203] *See, e.g.*, City of Harrisburg v. Sch. Dist., 710 A.2d 49, 52–53 (Pa. 1998) (striking down an attempt by a school district to tax publicly leased properties that were exempt from city taxes).

## III. CRITIQUE OF PROSPECTIVE LOCKSTEPPING

Of course, there are many other reasons given by state courts for adopting federal constitutional doctrine,[204] often including a special concern for "uniformity" in the area of criminal procedure.[205] Throughout the spectrum of state judicial approaches to lockstepping, however, several problems have become apparent. First, even if the prospective lockstepping approach could be seen as "reflective," it purports to decide *too much* and to go beyond the court's authority to adjudicate cases. It could be argued that such an approach cannot even be referred to as a "holding" because it goes beyond the facts of the case and purports to prejudge future cases. In addition, it is not clear if it even qualifies as dictum. Such statements, therefore, should neither bind lawyers in their arguments nor the court itself in future cases. It is beyond the state judicial power to *incorporate* the federal Constitution and its future interpretations into the state constitution. When a court engages in prospective lockstepping, it not only looks *back* at the case before it and the existing, relevant legal materials, including federal doctrine, but it also purports to foresee, and to attempt to control, the *future*. In other words, it is not within the state judicial authority to receive, wholesale, the law of a different sovereign as a part of its domestic law to be applied in the future.[206]

[204] Lawrence Schlam, *State Constitutional Amending, Independent Interpretation, and Political Culture: A Case Study in Constitutional Stagnation*, 43 DePaul L. Rev. 269, 306 (1994).

[205] In 1974, the Oregon Supreme Court stated:

> There are good reasons why state courts should follow the decisions of the Supreme Court of the United States on questions affecting the Constitution of the United States and the rights of citizens under the provisions of that Constitution, as well as under identical or almost identical provisions of state constitutions, as in this case. . . . The law of search and seizure is badly in need of simplification for law enforcement personnel, lawyers and judges, provided, of course, that this may be done in such a manner as not to violate the constitutional rights of the individual. . . . The rule stated in *United States v. Robinson* . . . is a simplification. Not adopting the rule of *Robinson* would add further confusion in that there would then be an "Oregon rule" and a "federal rule." Federal and state law officers frequently work together and in many instances do not know whether their efforts will result in a federal or a state prosecution or both. In these instances two different rules would cause confusion. For these reasons, we overrule our previous decision in *State v. O'Neal* . . . and other previous decisions to the same effect to the extent that they are contrary to the rule which we now adopt.

State v. Florance, 527 P.2d 1202, 1209 (Or. 1974). *See also* State v. Arias, 752 N.W.2d 748, 755 (Wis. 2008).

In *People v. Gonzalez*, 465 N.E.2d 823, 825 (N.Y. 1984), Judge Simons of the New York Court of Appeals stated: "We deem it desirable to keep the law of this State consistent with the Supreme Court's rulings on inventory searches. . . ." Judge Wachtler, dissenting in *Gonzalez*, contended that the U.S. Supreme Court decisions were distinguishable, and noted, "[i]t is often difficult enough to follow the Supreme Court's decisions in the Fourth Amendment area without also trying to anticipate them." *Id.* at 826 (Wachtler, J., dissenting).

[206] This was the conclusion of the Alaska Supreme Court, in a divided opinion. Doe v. State, 189 P.3d 999, 1005 (Alaska 2008). *See also* State v. Jucumin, 778 S.W.2d 430, 435–36 (Tenn. 1989); State v. Jacobson, 545 N.W.2d 152, 153–54 (N.D. 1996) (Vande Walle, C.J. concurring specially); City of West Fargo v. Ekstrom, 938 N.W.2d 915, 921 (N.D. 2020) (Tufte, J., concurring specially); Keysor v. Kentucky, 486 S.W.3d 273, 280 (Ky. 2016).

This problem has received mixed treatment in academic literature. Professor Earl Maltz has argued in favor of lockstepping, or "the theory that state constitutional provisions should be interpreted to provide exactly the same protections as their federal constitutional counterparts."[207] His argument is based on deference to the state legislative and executive branches and on a criticism of judicial activism.[208] He seems clearly, however, to be referring to case-by-case, or reflective, adoptionism rather than either the unreflective or prospective lockstepping approaches.

In contrast, Justice Robert Utter of the Supreme Court of Washington criticized the use of the prospective lockstep approach to interpreting that state's equality provisions, labeling such an approach a virtual "rewrite" of the state constitution without a constitutional convention or the people's consent.[209] Ron Collins argued that prospective lockstepping results in the "Problem of the Vanishing Constitution,"[210] where the state constitution is rendered a nullity and the "Problem of Amending Without Amendments,"[211] where the *court*, in effect, *amends* the state constitution by purporting to link it, prospectively, to federal constitutional analysis. This is not a valid exercise of judicial review. The power to amend the state constitution, even to link its interpretation to federal constitutional doctrine, is reserved to the state's citizens.[212]

Second, prospective lockstepping seems to operate as a form of a "precommitment device" or "prophylactic rule," described by Professor Adrian Vermeule, albeit in the context of free speech doctrine.[213] He explained:

> It is a precommitment device insofar as judges . . . at time 1 worry that at time 2 their own cognition or decision-making processes will be affected by some overpowering influence. . . . So the judges restrict their choices at time 2 by announcing, at time 1, a rule that will prevent their future selves from surrendering to the passions of the moment. It is a prophylactic device insofar as judges . . . at time 1 worry, not about their own future cognition, but about the cognition of other judges deciding future cases, either judges of subordinate courts or future members of the very court that devised the rule at time

[207] Earl M. Maltz, *Lockstep Analysis and the Concept of Federalism*, 496 Annals Am. Acad. Pol. & Soc. Sci. 98, 99 (1988) [hereinafter Maltz, *Lockstep*]; *see also* Earl M. Maltz, *The Dark Side of State Court Activism*, 63 Tex. L. Rev. 995, 1006–23 (1985) [hereinafter Maltz, *Dark Side*].

[208] Maltz, *Lockstep*, *supra* note 207, at 101–02, 106.

[209] State v. Smith, 814 P.2d 652, 661 (Wash. 1991) (en banc) (Utter, J., concurring).

[210] Collins, *supra* note 83, at 1111.

[211] *Id.* at 1116 ("When a state court withdraws from a constitutional provision its independent legal authority over state action, the court assumes a power that has been constitutionally delegated to others. That power is the right of the people to 'alter' their constitution.") (footnote omitted).

[212] Chapter 5 (discussing "lockstep" and "forced linkage" constitutional amendments).

[213] Adrian Vermeule, *The Judicial Power in the State (and Federal) Courts*, 2000 Sup. Ct. Rev. 357, 366 (2001).

> 1. Here the judges formulate legal doctrine in order to restrict other judges' future choices.[214]

The "overpowering influence" or "passions of the moment" would, in the state constitutional law context, be future disagreement with established or probable federal constitutional doctrine. In this sense, prospective lockstepping operates as a form of an irrebuttable presumption that future cases raising state constitutional claims must be decided the same way the U.S. Supreme Court has decided or would decide the same issue under the federal Constitution.

Third, as Professor Maltz has contended:

> The substance of lockstep analysis is entirely consistent with the basic concept of state autonomy. Of course, one can still attack the standard verbal formulations of the lockstep approach, which seem to suggest that U.S. Supreme Court decisions somehow create state constitutional law. For lockstep courts, however, these *flaws in articulation* have little impact on the practical results reached.[215]

Prospective lockstepping, however, goes far beyond mere "flaws in articulation." Rather, it has the effect of snuffing out the independent research, analysis, and reasoning that must be undertaken by lawyers, judges, scholars, professors, and students in order to make the state constitution an independent document. Verbal formulations can, in fact, have important consequences for the development of state constitutional law.

Fourth, as Professor Gardner has stated:

> By engaging in extensive lockstep analysis, many courts have also created an atmosphere in which it is unnecessary to distinguish between the state and federal constitutions because they are generally held to have the same meaning. This reduces state constitutional law to a *redundancy* and greatly discourages its use and development.[216]

[214] *Id.* (*citing* George Ainslie, Picoeconomics: The Strategic Interaction of Successive Motivational States Within the Person 123–79 (1992); Jon Elster, Ulysses and the Sirens: Studies in Rationality and Irrationality 37–47 (1979); David A. Strauss, *The Ubiquity of Prophylactic Rules*, 55 U. Chi. L. Rev. 190 (1988)).

[215] Maltz, *Lockstep*, *supra* note 207, at 102 (emphasis added).

[216] Gardner, *supra* note 12, at 804 (emphasis added); *see also id.* at 788–93 (discussing lockstep analysis). Professor John Devlin criticized the lockstep approach, even with respect to state constitutional rights provisions that were copied from the U.S. Constitution. *See* John M. Devlin, *State Constitutional Autonomy Rights in an Age of Federal Retrenchment: Some Thoughts on the Interpretation of State Rights Derived from Federal Sources*, 3 Emerging Issues St. Const. L. 195, 234–37 (1990).

This is a negative form of redundancy. In contrast, shared responsibility for constitutional decision-making under different constitutions or dual enforcement of constitutional norms is an element of American "jurisdictional redundancy," a term based on the use of redundant systems to protect against technological malfunction and to ensure reliability.[217] Professor Robert Cover asserted that redundancy in federal and state jurisdiction provides a variety of *positive* influences,[218] which differs from the *negative* sense in which Professor Gardner used the term in the preceding quote. Cover noted that "the jurisdictional structure frequently permits recourse to the courts of another system after one system has adjudicated and reached a result."[219]

Cover terms redundancy in constitutional interpretation as either "confirmatory" or "nonconfirmatory."[220] As Professor Tarr explained: "When two sets of interpreters reach the same outcome in a constitutional case, this increases confidence that the result is rooted in law rather than in will."[221] He noted that where there is disagreement, it is either because there is no "right answer" or that one of the interpreters has interpreted the provision "wrongly by mistake or by design."[222] This form of redundancy, particularly with respect to norm articulation, is a positive aspect of federalism. The prospective lockstep approach frustrates this positive aspect. At least reflective, case-by-case adoptionism retains the potential of the beneficial qualities of jurisdictional redundancy in future cases. Of course, while redundant systems need not be used all of the time, they must remain available for use when necessary.

Fifth, the prospective lockstep approach relegates the state constitutional protections to "a mere row of shadows."[223] As Justice David Souter observed, while still a state judge:

> If we place too much reliance on federal precedent we will render the State rules *a mere row of shadows*; if we place too little, we will render State practice *incoherent*. If we are going to steer between these extremes, we will have to insist on developed advocacy from those who bring the cases before us.[224]

[217] *See* Robert M. Cover, *The Uses of Jurisdictional Redundancy: Interest, Ideology, and Innovation*, 22 Wm. & Mary L. Rev. 639, 639–40 (1981). The concept of redundancy is common to the understanding of federal systems. *See* Martin Landau, *Federalism, Redundancy and System Reliability*, 3 Publius: The J. Federalism 173, 187–96 (Fall 1973) (discussing the definition and effects of federalism).

[218] *See* Cover, *supra* note 217, at 642. *But see* Maltz, *Dark Side*, *supra* note 207.

[219] Cover, *supra* note 217, at 648; *see also id.* at 673 ("If there were a unitary source of norm articulation over a given domain, the costs of error or lack of wisdom in any norm articulation would be suffered throughout the domain.").

[220] *Id.* at 674–75.

[221] Tarr, *supra* note 14, at 175–76.

[222] *Id.* at 176.

[223] State v. Bradberry, 522 A.2d 1380, 1389 (N.H. 1986) (Souter, J., concurring).

[224] *Id.* (emphasis added).

A state's constitutional provisions need not, and should not, be reduced to a "row of shadows" through too *much* reliance on federal precedent. Swinging the pendulum in the other direction, however, *little* reliance on federal precedent may "render State practice incoherent." Reflective, case-by-case adoptionism, but not prospective lockstepping, could be seen to meet the requirements set forth by Justice Souter.

Sixth, state court decisions, such as the Ohio cases of *Robinette* or *Eastwood Mall*, purporting to lockstep prospectively with federal constitutional doctrine, will have the effect of chilling scholarship on the associated state constitutional provision and inhibiting independent state constitutional arguments and analysis by lawyers and lower courts. Such decisions seem like binding "holdings,"[225] resolving the question in the future, even possibly despite unanticipated changes in federal constitutional doctrine. Such decisions will render lawyers, scholars, and lower court judges "literally speechless" when it comes to independent state constitutional analysis.[226] This approach may also result, in a circular way, in excusing lawyers for not making independent state constitutional arguments. For example, the Pennsylvania Supreme Court, in describing counsel's arguments in an ineffective assistance of counsel case stated:

> [I]t is not clear whether these offhanded references to prior counsel's alleged ineffectiveness are intended to sound under the Federal or the Pennsylvania Constitution, or both. Since the constitutional test for counsel effectiveness is the same under both charters—*i.e.*, it is the *Strickland* test—we will assume that appellant intends his averments to pose coextensive questions sounding under both charters.[227]

[225] In discussing independent state constitutional rights, Justice Robert F. Utter of the Washington Supreme Court cautioned:

> [O]ne should be neither ignorant of nor intimidated by the case law and doctrines that may be cited by parties opposing independent interpretation. In most cases the problems they present can and should be overcome. For example, a number of Washington cases contain dicta, and sometimes actual holdings, to the effect that provisions of our constitution should be interpreted in exactly the same way that the federal courts interpret the federal Constitution, unless a very good reason for variance can be shown. While the Washington Supreme Court's holdings must of course be followed unless overturned by that court, it is clear from a number of more recent cases that such an approach does not reflect the court's current attitude. Thus, older state supreme court pronouncements should be scrutinized to determine whether they constitute actual holdings and, if not, whether they were based on assumptions that are no longer valid.

Robert F. Utter, *Freedom and Diversity in a Federal System: Perspectives on State Constitutions and the Washington Declaration of Rights*, 7 U. PUGET SOUND L. REV. 491, 507 (1984). There are many examples of state courts re-evaluating earlier "precedents" announcing that the court would apply state and federal constitutional provisions in lockstep. *See, e.g.*, Collins v. Day, 644 N.E.2d 72, 75 (Ind. 1994); State v. Johnson, 719 P.2d 1248, 1254–55 (Mont. 1986); Baker v. State, 744 A.2d 864, 870–79 (Vt. 1999); *see also supra* note 90 and accompanying text.

[226] Linde, *supra* note 101, at 391.

[227] Commonwealth v. Jones, 811 A.2d 994, 1002 (Pa. 2002) (citations omitted).

It is difficult to see how decisions applying such a doctrine could ever be based on an adequate and independent state ground.[228] In effect, prospective lockstepping purports to force future courts to make a "federal case" out of state constitutional claims.

## IV. A QUESTION OF JUDICIAL STRATEGY?

On the other hand, cases engaging in reflective, case-by-case adoptionism, such as *Simmons-Harris*, settle only the immediate question before the court. Such decisions invite and preserve the possibilities for future dialogue about related issues under even the same state constitutional provision. This approach provides at least a partial stimulus for continuing scholarship and independent state constitutional arguments. Furthermore, this approach preserves state court flexibility in the face of future changes in federal constitutional doctrine, while treating the U.S. Supreme Court decision as one source among many available sources for resolution of the problem. Decisions utilizing this approach are much more likely to be viewed as based on an adequate and independent state ground.

Both prospective lockstepping and reflective adoptionism involve "following" the U.S. Supreme Court's interpretation of the federal Constitution, but they do it in very different ways. The differing approaches have drastically divergent future consequences for lawyers and courts.[229] State courts should become more self-conscious about these differing consequences that flow from alternative techniques of adopting federal constitutional doctrine in state constitutional interpretation.

Another point emerges clearly from a recognition that the prospective lockstepping approach is a conscious *choice* made by state courts. The choice to commit prospectively to following federal doctrine and outcomes cannot arise directly from the state constitutional clause that the court is interpreting. This might be possible for reflective adoptionism on a case-by-case basis; prospective lockstepping, however, is not based on interpretation but rather is based on

[228] According to the U.S. Supreme Court:

> [W]hen, as in this case, a state court decision fairly appears to rest primarily on federal law, or to be interwoven with the federal law, and when the adequacy and independence of any possible state law ground is not clear from the face of the opinion, we will accept as the most reasonable explanation that the state court decided the case the way it did because it believed that federal law required it to do so.

Michigan v. Long, 463 U.S. 1032, 1040–41 (1983). *See generally* Collins & Galie, *supra* note 26, at 323–24; Fitzgerald v. Racing Assoc. of Central Iowa, 539 U.S. 103, 106 (2003). *See* Chapter 5.

[229] *See* Jennifer Friesen, *State Courts as Sources of Constitutional Law: How to Become Independently Wealthy*, 72 NOTRE DAME L. REV. 1065, 1073 n.23 (1997) (criticizing prospective lockstepping).

choice or *judicial strategy*.[230] Like judicial precommitment devices and prophylactic rules, the strategic choice to commit to prospective lockstepping reflects the result of a judicial calculation about how best to go about enforcing the state constitutional clause under consideration, beyond the case at hand. This set of calculations by courts should also take into account the negative, chilling effects mentioned earlier in connection with prospective lockstepping.

Even case-by-case, reflective adoptionism may reflect the exercise of strategic choices by state judges. Barry Latzer, commenting on the fact that most state constitutional rights cases follow federal doctrine, speculated as follows:

> It is a sign that the state judges are proceeding cautiously, borrowing generously from federal law, selectively rejecting it in a significant minority of decisions. Even law-ambiguity may be viewed as a mark of caution: perhaps the failure to "commit" state law to a position is a way of preserving future interpretive options, so that the court could someday say that the previous case was not construing the state constitution after all.[231]

By contrast, Ann Althouse has argued that the *Michigan v. Long* "plain statement" requirement eliminates "law ambiguity" as a choice for state judges: "State judges who want to expand the rights of an unpopular group, such as the criminally accused, may not want to call attention to their independence and thereby make themselves targets for political retaliation."[232] However, in the absence of a plain statement that they base their decision on the state constitution, the U.S. Supreme Court might exercise jurisdiction.

The differing techniques of state courts in following federal constitutional interpretation can also be evaluated within the current discussion of judicial "minimalism" and "maximalism."[233] Clearly, prospective lockstepping qualifies as a form of activist, bright-line maximalism,[234] while case-by-case adoptionism

[230] *See also* State v. Schaefer, 746 N.W.2d 457, 473–74 (Wis. 2008); State v. Gardner, 889 N.E.2d 995, 1012 (Ohio 2008). Williams is indebted to Robert Schapiro for this insight. *See also* Jeffrey L. Amestoy, *Pragmatic Constitutionalism: Reflections on State Constitutional Theory and Same-Sex Marriage Claims*, 35 Rutgers L.J. 1249 (2005) (describing prudential reasons for caution by state courts in reaching judicial resolution of state constitutional claims that have not been resolved nationally by the U.S. Supreme Court, partially because state citizens can overrule such decisions by constitutional amendment). *See generally* Sager, *supra* note 9.

[231] Barry Latzer, *Into the '90's: More Evidence that the Revolution Has a Conservative Underbelly*, 4 Emerging Issues St. Const. L. 17, 31–32 (1991).

[232] Ann Althouse, *Variations on a Theory of Normative Federalism: A Supreme Court Dialogue*, 42 Duke L.J. 979, 988–89 (1993).

[233] *See generally* Christopher J. Peters, *Assessing the New Judicial Minimalism*, 100 Colum. L. Rev. 1454 (2000); Cass R. Sunstein, *Foreword: Leaving Things Undecided*, 110 Harv. L. Rev. 6 (1996); Ernest A. Young, *Judicial Activism and Conservative Politics*, 73 U. Colo. L. Rev. 1139 (2002).

[234] Sunstein, *supra* note 233, at 15 (defining activist maximalism as "an effort to decide cases in a way that establishes broad rules for the future").

(although subject to the criticism that it does not reflect independent state constitutional analysis) constitutes a form of judicial minimalism.[235]

## V. CONCLUSION

The implications arising from the *quality* of state constitutional decisions adopting federal doctrine in different ways is important.[236] Is this reading too much into the subtle distinctions in the language of state court opinions? Are these differing methodological approaches adopted by state courts intentional? Do the courts that express the prospective lockstepping approach really mean it? *Can* they really mean it? Rather, are they unintentional products of busy, multimember courts that do not have the luxury of academic reflection?[237] With just a bit of recognition of the impact of these choices and consideration of the future impact of the chosen state constitutional methodology, state courts may avoid choking off advocacy and scholarship in independent state constitutional analysis. Such courts will then recognize that even subtle changes in methodology may have a substantial impact on the future of state constitutional law.

Courts that have been involved in the New Judicial Federalism have spent a good deal of time attempting to inform the bench and bar about how to make independent state constitutional arguments. They need to recognize that, even where they adopt federal constitutional law, they should do so in a way that does not chill, or even cast doubt on the value of, independent state constitutional arguments. State courts should carefully consider their messages to the bench, bar, and academy.[238]

235 Young, *supra* note 233, at 1151 (defining minimalism as "leaving as much as possible undecided for consideration in the next case.").

236 The cases analyzed in this chapter are assessed *qualitatively* rather than *quantitatively*. *See* James N.G. Cauthen, *Expanding Rights Under State Constitutions: A Quantitative Appraisal*, 63 Alb. L. Rev. 1183, 1183–84 (2000).

237 *Cf.* Lawrence Friedman, *Path Dependence and the External Constraints on Independent State Constitutionalism*, 115 Penn. St. L. Rev. 783, 819–25 (2011) (discussing practical impediments to robust independent constitutional analysis by state courts).

238 For a discussion of the related question of whether statutory interpretation methodology decisions should be given prospective, or precedential weight, see Sydney Foster, *Should Courts Give Stare Decisis Effect to Statutory Interpretation Methodology?* 96 Geo. L.J. 1863 (2008); Jordan Wilder Connors, Note, *Treating Like Subdecisions Alike: The Scope of Stare Decisis as Applied to Judicial Methodology*, 108 Colum. L. Rev. 681 (2008).

# PART III

# STRUCTURE OF STATE GOVERNMENT

In Part III, the general approach to state constitutional separation/distribution of powers and checks and balances will be considered. There are virtually no enforceable federal requirements regulating how the states structure their governments and distribute powers within them. None of the federal separation of powers doctrines apply to the states. Further, there is substantial variation among the states as to how governmental power is distributed within them. As a consequence, state separation of powers issues should be resolved in the context of that particular state's governmental arrangements. A general introduction is followed by chapters on the three branches, each of which differs in important ways from the federal executive, legislative, and judicial branches.

# 8

# STATE CONSTITUTIONAL DISTRIBUTION OF POWERS

> *At the revolution . . . [t]he executive and the judicial as well as the legislative authority was now the child of the people; but, to the two former, the people behaved like stepmothers. The legislature was still discriminated by excessive partiality; and into its lap, every good and precious gift was profusely thrown.*
>
> —James Wilson[1]

It is well known that the early state constitutions, although often textually recognizing the doctrine of separation of powers, in fact "tended to exalt legislative power at the expense of the executive and the judiciary."[2] James Wilson's remarks quoted at the beginning of this chapter reflect this experience. James Madison observed in the Constitutional Convention that "[e]xperience had proved a tendency in our governments to throw all power into the Legislative vortex."[3] If Madison had been speaking today, he would probably have asserted that the legislative branch expanded its influence like the gravitational pull of a "black hole." These observations, based on actual experience under the state constitutions of the Revolutionary period, led to the almost unanimous conclusion of contemporaries that state legislatures were "omnipotent."[4] Wilson's experience had been under the "radical" Pennsylvania Constitution of 1776.[5] Thomas

[1] 1 The Works of James Wilson 292–93 (Robert Green McCloskey ed., 1967). *See* G. Alan Tarr, *Interpreting the Separation of Powers in State Constitutions*, 59 N.Y.U. Ann. Surv. Am. L. 329, 334 (2003).

[2] William Wiecek, The Guarantee Clause of the U.S. Constitution 21 (1972); *see also* Gerhard Casper, *An Essay in Separation of Powers: Some Early Versions and Practices*, 30 Wm. & Mary L. Rev. 211, 216–19 (1989) (stating that, although states introduced separation of powers clauses into their constitutions, in reality, the legislature continued to overshadow the executive branch); Rogan Kersh et al., *"More a Distinction of Words Than Things": The Evolution of Separated Powers in the American States*, 4 Roger Williams U. L. Rev. 5 (1998).

[3] 2 The Records of the Federal Convention of 1787, 35 (Max Farrand ed., 2d ed. 1937); *see also* The Federalist No. 48, at 322 (J. Madison) (Sherman F. Mitchell ed., 1937) (cautioning against legislative encroachment).

[4] 2 The Records of the Federal Convention of 1787, *supra* note 3, at 35. Madison stated in the Convention: "The Executives of the States are in general little more than Cyphers; the legislatures omnipotent." *Id.*

[5] *See* Chapter 2.

*The Law of American State Constitutions*. Robert F. Williams and Lawrence Friedman, Oxford University Press.
© Oxford University Press 2023. DOI: 10.1093/oso/9780190068806.003.0009

Jefferson's experience, like Madison's, was with the Virginia Constitution of 1776; they were equally critical of legislative dominance.[6]

## I. ORIGIN AND JUDICIAL ENFORCEMENT OF STATE SEPARATION OF POWERS

When the federal Constitution was adopted, it built on the lessons of legislative dominance learned under the state constitutions during the Revolutionary years.[7] Thereafter, though, the state constitutions continued on a process of evolution distinct from federal constitutional theory.[8] This process followed the experimental model of federalism that had begun in the decade prior to the adoption of the federal Constitution. In that decade, the states, in the words of Jackson Turner Main, "became the laboratories for testing theories, trying the institutions in the various forms that presently appeared in constitutions of the United States and other countries."[9]

Also, during this early period, there came a fundamental shift in conception of the executive branch, particularly the governor. As Gordon S. Wood has observed:

> [T]he Americans went far beyond anything the English had attempted with Magna Carta or the Bill of Rights. They aimed to make the gubernatorial magistrate a new kind of creature, a very pale reflection indeed of its regal ancestor. They wanted effectively to eliminate the magistracy's chief responsibility for ruling the society—a remarkable and abrupt departure from the English constitutional tradition. . . . The powers and prerogatives taken from the Governors were given to the legislatures, marking a revolutionary shift in the traditional responsibility of government.[10]

Therefore, at the same time the revolutionary state constitutions were providing legislative dominance, they were reformulating the governor's position from a policy-making to a policy-implementing role. Bringing the other two branches

[6] *See* David N. Mayer, The Constitutional Thought of Thomas Jefferson 53–88 (1994).
[7] *See* Chapter 2.
[8] *See* James A. Henretta, *Foreword: Rethinking the State Constitutional Tradition*, 22 Rutgers L.J. 819, 821–26 (1991). John Dinan analyzed the debates over separation of powers as the state constitutions evolved. John J. Dinan, The American State Constitutional Tradition 97–136 (2006).
[9] Jackson Turner Main, *The American States in the Revolutionary Era*, *in* Sovereign States in an Age of Uncertainty 1, 23 (Ronald Hofman & Peter J. Albert eds., 1981).
[10] Gordon S. Wood, *Foreword: State Constitution-Making in the American Revolution*, 24 Rutgers L.J. 911, 915, 916 (1993).

to some form of parity, or at least bringing them closer to being "co-equal" with the legislature, continues to occupy state constitutional framers even today.

Some state constitutions are still suffering from the key constitutional problem of the founding decade—namely, the emerging relationship of separation of powers rhetoric and concrete checks and balances mechanisms. Checks and balances put teeth into separation of powers rhetoric. The Pennsylvania Constitution of 1776, for example, contained separation of powers rhetoric but lacked checks and balances. Professor M.J.C. Vile makes this point as follows:

> It is often stated that the Constitution of Pennsylvania did not embody the separation of powers, whereas in fact it was the basis of the whole Constitution. It is the failure to distinguish clearly between the separation of powers on the one hand, and checks and balances on the other, which leads to the confusion. The founders of the 1776 Constitution were bitterly opposed to any semblance of the checks and balances of the monarchic or aristocratic constitution.[11]

Looking specifically at many state constitutions, it is clear that they, by contrast to the federal Constitution, often provide an express, *textual* affirmation of the doctrine of separation of powers.[12] This is true for forty of the states.[13] For example, Article II, Section 3, of the Florida Constitution provides:

> The powers of the state government shall be divided into legislative, executive, and judicial branches. No person belonging to one branch shall exercise any powers appertaining to either of the other branches unless expressly provided herein.

These sorts of statements date from the earliest state constitutions in 1776.[14] They express two related concerns: that the *powers* of government should be separated and that the *persons* who exercise these powers should be separate individuals. State courts have split, in the context of legislative delegations of authority, on the question of whether such an express statement mandates a more strict state constitutional separation of powers doctrine than the federal doctrine.[15]

[11] M.J.C. Vile, Constitutionalism and the Separation of Powers 136 (1967).

[12] "The powers of the government shall be distributed into three separate and distinct departments: the legislative, executive and judicial." R.I. Const. art. V. The three branches are also explicitly recognized in the paragraph introducing the Rhode Island Declaration of Rights. *See* R.I. Const. art. I. *See* King v. Morton, 955 So.2d 1012, 1019–20 (Ala. 2006); Sentence Review Panel v. Moseley, 663 S.E.2d 679, 682–83 (Ga. 2008).

[13] G. Alan Tarr, Understanding State Constitutions 14 (1998).

[14] Robert F. Williams, *Evolving State Legislative and Executive Power in the Founding Decade*, 496 Annals Acad. Pol & Soc. Sci. 43 (1988); *supra* note 2.

[15] *Compare* Askew v. Cross Key Waterways, 372 So.2d 913, 924–25 (Fla. 1978) (applying a strict interpretation of the separation of powers doctrine, which would prohibit the delegation of legislative powers), *and* Quelch v. Daugherty, 306 S.E.2d 233, 235 (W. Va. 1983), *with* Brown v. Heymann,

Concepts such as "legislative" and "executive" power are, of course, indeterminate.[16] One way of looking at modern separation of powers questions, such as implied limits on state legislative power, is conceptual or *formalistic*. This view draws on the idea that one can define the concept of "legislative, judicial or executive power." As one scholar has explained, "[t]he formalist approach is committed to strong substantive separations between the branches of government, finding support in the traditional expositions of the theme of 'pure' separated powers, such as the maxim that 'the legislature makes, the executive executes, and the judiciary construes the law.' "[17] Formalism in this regard has been criticized as yielding mechanical outcomes but providing the benefit of bright-line rules.[18]

The alternative to the formalist approach is a *functionalist* analysis:

> In contrast, advocates of the "functionalist" approach urge the Court to ask a different question: whether an action of one branch interferes with one of the core functions of another. . . . The functionalist view follows a different strand of separation-of-powers tradition from that of the formalists: the American variant that stresses not the independence, but the interdependence of the branches.[19]

The functionalist approach seems to permit much more judicial discretion than the formalist approach.[20]

State constitutional separation of powers questions also call for a *state-specific* form of analysis rather than one applying a more generalized, or universalist, American-constitutional separation of powers doctrine.[21] Each of the states has its own, virtually unique, arrangements concerning the distribution of powers among and within the branches. Any careful analysis of a separation of powers

297 A.2d 572, 576–77 (N.J. 1972) (upholding a delegation which authorized the governor to prepare a reorganization plan for the Department of Labor and Industry). Cases are collected in Jim Rossi, *Institutional Design and the Lingering Legacy of Antifederalist Separation of Powers Ideals in the States*, 52 VAND. L. REV. 1167 (1999) (analyzing different treatment of the nondelegation doctrine, an aspect of the horizontal separation of powers, in state constitutional law). *See* Chapter 9.

[16] *See* William B. Gwyn, *The Indeterminacy of the Separation of Powers in the Age of the Framers*, 30 WM. & MARY L. REV. 263 (1989).

[17] Rebecca L. Brown, *Separated Powers and Ordered Liberty*, 139 U. PA. L. REV. 1513, 1523–24 (1991) (*quoting* Wayman v. Southard, 23 U.S. (10 Wheat.) 1, 46 (1825)).

[18] *See id.* at 1524–26.

[19] *Id.* at 1527–28.

[20] *See id.* at 1528.

[21] *See* James A. Gardner, *The Positivist Revolution That Wasn't: Constitutional Universalism in the States*, 4 ROGER WILLIAMS U. L. REV. 109 (1998). For a very important example of state-specific separation of powers analysis, see Jonathan Zasloff, *Taking Politics Seriously: A Theory of California's Separation of Powers*, 51 UCLA L. REV. 1079 (2004). Professor Zasloff addressed the issues in litigation later decided by the California Supreme Court. *See* Marine Forests Society v. California Coastal Commission, 113 P.3d 1062 (Cal. 2005).

problem in state constitutional law, therefore, must take account of the particular state's specific arrangements.[22] Further, a state's approach to separation of powers may have changed over the years.[23]

So, for example, the New Jersey Supreme Court recognized that the 1947 constitution had transformed the governor from a weak figure to one of the strongest state chief executives in the country—and interpreted his powers accordingly.[24] The California Supreme Court recounted the state constitution's creation of a powerful legislature in upholding legislative appointments to an executive commission.[25] The California court gave its approval, as a general matter, for legislative appointments but indicated that, on a case-by-case basis, such appointments could violate the California separation of powers doctrine if they "viewed from a realistic and practical perspective, operate to defeat or materially impair the executive branch's exercise of its constitutional functions."[26] This is obviously a functional, as opposed to formalist, approach. The Rhode Island Supreme Court stated that its legislature was specifically empowered by a state constitutional amendment to regulate gambling and could therefore appoint members of the Lottery Commission.[27] That court had earlier rendered an advisory opinion that its state constitution did not prohibit dual office holding; did not contain an appointment clause for the governor; created a fragmented executive; and therefore, based on its tradition of legislative supremacy, the legislature could appoint members of executive boards.[28]

Here, as in the rights context, state courts need not, nor should they necessarily, follow federal constitutional separation of powers doctrine.[29] Professor

[22] Tarr, *supra* note 1, at 329 (". . . the political systems created by these documents [state constitutions] are distinct *from each other* and the Federal Constitution.") (emphasis added). *See, e.g.*, Marc E. Elkins, *Treatment of the Separation of Powers Doctrine in Kansas*, 29 U. Kan. L. Rev. 243 (1981); John V. Orth, *"Forever Separate and Distinct": Separation of Powers in North Carolina*, 62 N.C. L. Rev. 1 (1983); L. Scott Stafford, *Separation of Powers and Arkansas Administrative Agencies: Distinguishing Judicial Power and Legislative Power*, 7 U. Ark. Little Rock L.J. 279 (1984); Harold H. Bruff, *Separation of Powers Under the Texas Constitution*, 68 Tex. L. Rev. 1337 (1990); Roy Pulvers, *Separation of Powers Under The Oregon Constitution: A User's Guide*, 75 Or. L. Rev. 443 (1996); Jack M. Sabatino, *Assertion and Self-Restraint: The Exercise of Governmental Powers Distributed Under the 1947 New Jersey Constitution*, 29 Rutgers L.J. 799 (1998).

[23] Tarr, *supra* note 1, at 332–33.

[24] Communications Workers of America, AFL-CIO v. Florio, 617 A.2d 223, 231 (N.J. 1992); Nero v. Hyland, 386 A.2d 846, 853 (N.J. 1978). *See generally* Robert A. Schapiro, *Contingency and Universalism in State Separation of Powers Discourse*, 4 Roger Williams U.L. Rev. 79, 90–92 (1998).

[25] Marine Forests Society v. California Coastal Comm., 113 P.3d 1062, 1078–82 (Cal. 2005).

[26] *Id.* at 1087.

[27] Almond v. Rhode Island Lottery Comm., 756 A.2d 186, 193, 196–97 (R.I. 2000).

[28] *In re* Advisory Opinion to the Governor, 732 A.2d 55, 64–65 (R.I. 1999).

[29] Schapiro, *supra* note 24, at 92 (". . . unlike federal individual rights precedent, federal separation of powers doctrine does not apply directly to the states."); *Marine Forests Society*, 113 P.3d at 1075–76. Although the California court noted that the case turned "solely" on its state constitution, it also cited other state cases based on horizontal federalism. *Id.* at 1085–86.

John Devlin has argued that following federal doctrine in this area of separation of powers is no more required than in other areas:

> The thesis of this article is that there are systematic differences between the federal government and the states with respect to their constitutions and their place in the American scheme of government, and that these differences make the development of an independent theory of state constitutional allocation of governmental powers both possible and desirable.[30]

Based on the differences in the federal and state constitutions that we have seen so far, this should not be a surprise. The differences between the branches of state governments and the branches of the federal government, on the one hand, and the differences in the branches of state government among the various states, on the other hand, will be explored in the following chapters in this part of the book.

The federal Constitution does not mandate a specific separation or distribution of powers for the states. After all, as Justice Oliver Wendell Holmes said:

> We shall assume that when, as here, a state Constitution sees fit to unite legislative and judicial powers in a single hand, there is nothing to hinder, so far as the Constitution of the United States is concerned.[31]

Professor Robert Schapiro has explained perceptively a number of the reasons behind independent state constitutional separation of powers doctrines—reasons that go even beyond those supporting independent state constitutional rights analysis.[32] First, unlike federal constitutional rights provisions, federal separation of powers doctrine has never been "incorporated" or applied to the states,[33] and therefore state courts have little experience with actually applying federal separation of powers doctrines.[34] He noted that "interpreting state constitutions in lockstep with federal separation of powers law would not further the cause of uniformity. Because federal doctrine . . . does not apply to the states, only one body of separation of powers law will exist."[35] He continued, as we see

[30] *See* John Devlin, *Toward A State Constitutional Analysis of Allocation of Powers: Legislators and Legislative Appointees Performing Administrative Functions*, 66 TEMP. L. REV. 1205, 1211 (1993). Devlin continues to argue "that the structural differences between states and the federal government are so significant as to preclude reliance on federal law as a guide to the resolution of state separation of powers problems." *Id.* at 1211–12. *See also* Hon. Ellen A. Peters, *Getting Away From the Federal Paradigm: Separation of Powers in State Courts*, 81 MINN. L. REV. 1543, 1554–62 (1997) (discussing the effects of separation of powers in state courts as compared to federal courts).

[31] Prentis v. Atlantic Coast Line Co., 211 U.S. 210, 255 (1908). *See also* Highland Farms Dairy v. Agnew, 300 U.S. 608, 612 (1937); Sweezy v. New Hampshire, 354 U.S. 234, 255 (1957).

[32] Schapiro, *supra* note 24.

[33] *Id.* at 92–93.

[34] *Id.* at 93.

[35] *Id.*

from Justice Holmes's preceding quote, "[F]ederal law provides no constitutional floor."[36] State courts might be able to exercise more judicial restraint by not following the fairly rigid and formalistic federal separation of powers doctrine.[37] Once again, the states that permit legislative appointments to executive boards, in circumstances where federal law would prohibit the practice,[38] illustrate Schapiro's point. He noted the relative *strength* of each of the federal branches, while each of the branches in many of the states, in comparison, is relatively *weak*.[39] Therefore, state separation of powers doctrine might include a concern that the powers of state actors be interpreted to empower them to meet the needs of modern, complex society.[40] These are all very important considerations to be taken into account by state courts.

Further, as Professor Lawrence Friedman pointed out, state constitutional separation of powers doctrine often includes the important element of *local* government authority:

> Such structural differentiation may be seen, for example, in the provision under many state constitutions for peculiarly local governmental entities—municipalities—that possess specific lawmaking powers and share a relationship with state government that differs from the state-federal relationship under the U.S. Constitution. It follows that the state court seeking guidance from federal precedent should attend with care to such influential concerns as the underlying lattice of institutional arrangements within which courts seek to develop constitutional rules or principles—including, of course, allocations of authority between and among governmental entities of varying degrees of democratic accountability.[41]

Still, however, a number of state courts like the Rhode Island Supreme Court have turned to federal separation of powers doctrine in the absence of state precedent:

> Although no authority bearing directly on this issue has been called to our attention, complainant comments in her brief that the relevant provisions of our constitution have the same meaning as the comparable provisions of the Federal Constitution, and she suggests that "federal cases dealing with executive power

[36] *Id.* at 94.

[37] *Id.*

[38] *Marine Forests Society*, 113 P.3d at 1074.

[39] Schapiro, *supra* note 24, at 101–05.

[40] *Id.* at 105–06.

[41] Lawrence Friedman, *Unexamined Reliance on Federal Precedent in State Constitutional Interpretation: The Potential Intra-State Effect*, 33 Rutgers L.J. 1031, 1055–56 (2002). For an analysis of the use of state legislative authority to preempt local government lawmaking even in state constitutional home rule states, see Daniel B. Rodriguez, *Localism and Lawmaking*, 32 Rutgers L.J. 627, 630 (2001); Richard Briffault, *The Challenge of the New Preemption*, 70 Stan. L. Rev. 1995 (2018).

> establish standards by which to measure the power of the Governor to issue executive orders on Fair Employment Practices." That suggestion commends itself to us. . . .[42]

## II. CASE STUDY IN STATE SEPARATION OF POWERS: LEGISLATIVE APPOINTEES TO ADMINISTRATIVE BOARDS

The issue of legislators, and to a lesser extent their designees, serving on executive boards and commissions can also be seen as a matter of dual office holding—a subcategory of separation of powers concerns. Dual office holding, or "incompatibility," was a major concern of the framers of the first state constitutions.[43] Commentators on these matters concluded:

> It is important to note that broad bans on plural office holding of the type found in the North Carolina, Maryland, and New Jersey Constitutions were conceived first and foremost as anti-corruption measures. Surprisingly, the separation-of-powers aspect of incompatibility seems not to have been the major theme.[44]

The state experience with legislative appointments to executive boards presents an interesting picture. The weight of authority, both under federal and states' separation of powers doctrines, is that legislators and legislative appointees may not serve on executive or administrative boards and commissions.[45] One in-depth academic commentary concluded:

[42] Chang v. University of R.I., 375 A.2d 925, 928 (R.I. 1977); Sheldon Whitehouse, *Appointments by the Legislature Under the Rhode Island Separation of Powers Doctrine: The Hazards of the Road Less Traveled*, 1 ROGER WILLIAMS. U.L. REV. 1, 16 n.80 (1996) (referring to other cases where the Rhode Island Supreme Court has looked to the federal Constitution for guidance); Brown v. Heymann, 297 A.2d 572, 577 (N.J. 1972). Lawrence Friedman provides specific examples and analysis of problems arising from state reliance on federal separation-of-powers doctrine in Friedman, *supra* note 41; *see also* Michael C. Dorf, *The Relevance of Federal Norms for State Separation of Powers*, 4 ROGER WILLIAMS U.L. REV. 51 (1998).

[43] *See* Steven G. Calabresi & Joan L. Larsen, *One Person, One Office: Separation of Powers or Separation of Personnel?* 79 CORNELL L. REV. 1045, 1057–61 (1994).

[44] *Id.* at 1060; *see also* VILE, *supra* note 11, at 134 (noting the separation of powers doctrine was originally used to prohibit dual office holding).

[45] *See generally* Devlin, *supra* note 30, at 1242–50 (discussing the different approaches that various states have taken with respect to legislative appointments); Sheryl G. Snyder & Robert M. Ireland, *The Separation of Governmental Powers Under the Constitution of Kentucky: A Legal and Historical Analysis of L.R.C. v. Brown*, 73 KY. L.J. 165, 210–16 (1984–1985) (discussing the Kentucky Supreme Court's decision which held the power of appointment is an executive function). The Rhode Island and Connecticut constitutions do not contain gubernatorial appointment clauses. Legislative appointments to executive agencies and boards were upheld in those two states. *See* Seymour v. Elections Enforcement Commission, 762 A.2d 880 (Conn. 2000); *In re* Advisory Opinion to the Governor, 732 A.2d 55 (R.I. 1999). *See also* State *ex rel.* McCrory, 781 S.E.2d 248 (N.C. 2016) (with appointment clause); State v. Berger, 781 S.E.2d 248 (N.C. 2016).

> It is generally recognized that the power to appoint Executive Officers is inherently executive, and that to hold otherwise is to deprive the Chief Executive of the right to control his own branch of government. The Governor's obligation to faithfully execute the law implies, as a necessary incident, the power to appoint those *who will act under his direction* in discharging this obligation.[46]

In disputes between the legislature and the executive, what stake is there for the judiciary? Professor Paul Verkuil posed this question in the federal context: "The debate typically arises over congressional and executive initiatives in governmental administration, but the judicial branch has a fundamental stake in the outcome. The question for the judiciary is how closely should it umpire the activities of the policymaking branches."[47]

The problems that often arise from legislative appointments to executive boards are examples of attempted encroachment or intrusion by one branch into the affairs of another, rather than the problem that arises when one branch seeks to abdicate or cede authority to another branch. Encroachment is the more disturbing of the two types of problems. The New Jersey Supreme Court concluded that *encroachment* problems require much greater judicial scrutiny than do *abdication* problems.[48]

As important as the "protection" of one branch from another is, such as the executive from the legislature, the underlying goal of judicial enforcement of separation of powers principles is the liberty of the citizens. The judicial role in separation of powers cases, particularly those involving encroachment, "ought to be as vigilant arbiter of process for the purpose of protecting individuals from the dangers of arbitrary government."[49] When legislators pass laws, including appropriations, and then administer those laws and funding with questionable legislative oversight, there is the potential and even the probable reality of arbitrary government.

Appointment by the legislature of its own members or designees to executive boards constitutes a sort of "reverse delegation"—an encroachment that should be subjected to rigorous judicial scrutiny.[50] If, in fact, legislative appointment of its members or appointees to administrative or executive boards constitutes a form of "reverse delegation," what light is shed on the problem by examining

[46] Snyder & Ireland, *supra* note 45, at 210–11 (emphasis added) (citations omitted). Sheldon Whitehouse points out that the federal "bright-line" rule prohibits legislators and their appointees from serving on independent or executive agencies. *See* Whitehouse, *supra* note 42, at 8.

[47] Paul R. Verkuil, *Separation of Powers, The Rule of Law and the Idea of Independence*, 30 Wm. & Mary L. Rev. 301, 302 (1989).

[48] *See* Communication Workers v. Florio, 617 A.2d 223, 232 (N.J. 1992) ("Although both the giving and taking of power can be constitutional if not excessive, the taking of power is more prone to abuse and therefore warrants an especially careful scrutiny.").

[49] Brown, *supra* note 17, at 1565; *see* Schapiro, *supra* note 24; Verkuil, *supra* note 47, at 302.

[50] *Communication Workers*, 617 A.2d at 232.

the nondelegation doctrine itself? First, reverse delegation is a form of legislative encroachment on the executive, where delegation constitutes, rather, a ceding of authority. It might, therefore, be argued persuasively that reverse delegation should receive more rigorous judicial scrutiny than delegation.

## III. THE STATE DELEGATION DOCTRINE

A commentator who surveyed the state courts' approaches to the delegation doctrine concluded that Rhode Island exemplified a "'loose' standards and safeguards" approach.[51] Citing *Bourque v. Dettore*,[52] this commentator placed Rhode Island in his "Category II":

> Category II states allow delegations of lawmaking power to administrative agencies as long as the statute contains a general rule to guide the agency in exercising the delegated power. Guiding rules may take the form of general standards, procedural safeguards, or a combination of the two. . . . This standard embodies the principle that in modern society, Congress and state legislatures address complex problems in industry, economics, and general public health and safety. Because Congress often is unable or unwilling to deal with these problems, it frequently relies on administrative experts to decide upon the details of such legislation. Consequently, many courts have allowed delegations of broad power to administrative agencies with minimal direction from the legislature.[53]

The nondelegation doctrine is based on separation of powers concerns, underlying which are desires to shield citizens from arbitrary government. In a state like Rhode Island, therefore, which arguably has a relatively loose view of the dangers of broad delegations of legislative power to the executive, there may be even more reason for concern when the legislature goes on to administer statutes, including appropriations, through its own members or their appointees. Arbitrary government can certainly result from broad delegations of legislative *authority*[54] and may be even more likely when joined with reverse delegations to legislative *personnel*.

[51] Gary J. Greco, *Standards or Safeguards: A Survey of the Delegation Doctrine in the States*, 8 ADMIN. L.J. AM. U. 567, 588–91 & n.109 (1994) ("Essentially, in Rhode Island, a delegation is valid if the statute provides for either standards or procedures to confine and guide the agency's discretion." (*citing* Bourque v. Dettore, 589 A.2d 815, 818 (R.I. 1991)). *See supra* note 15 and accompanying text.

[52] 589 A.2d 815 (R.I. 1991).

[53] Greco, *supra* note 51, at 588.

[54] "Category II states shift more power to administrative agencies to determine policy." *Id.* State legislative delegations to *federal* statutes create separate problems. *See* Regan v. Denney, 437 P.3d 15 (Idaho 2019); Chapter 9, section II.

Interestingly, therefore, the nondelegation doctrine is an example of an implied limit on plenary legislative power, inherent in the concept of legislative power. This is one of the many areas where state constitutional doctrine may differ significantly from federal constitutional doctrine. A doctrine prohibiting reverse delegation can also be seen as an inherent limitation on the concept of legislative power. To the extent that mandatory minimum sentencing schemes enable a prosecutor to exercise discretion over whether to seek the mandatory minimum sentence, they raise delegation issues.[55]

## IV. "POWER PLAYS"

In recent years we have seen notable examples of state legislatures controlled by one political party enacting laws, in lame-duck sessions, that drastically limit the power of the incoming governors of the opposite party, while the outgoing governor, of the same party as a majority of the legislature, willingly signs such legislation. Professor Miriam Seifter has referred to such legislative actions in North Carolina and Wisconsin as "power plays."[56]

In both states, separation-of-powers challenges were filed, with mixed results.[57] In North Carolina, for instance, the high court concluded that the General Assembly could not,

> consistent with the textual command contained in Article III, Section 5(4) of the North Carolina Constitution, structure an executive branch commission in such a manner that the Governor is unable, within a reasonable period of time, to "take care that the laws be faithfully executed" because he or she is required to appoint half of the commission members from a list of nominees consisting of individuals who are, in all likelihood, not supportive of, if not openly opposed to, his or her policy preferences while having limited supervisory control over the agency and circumscribed removal authority over commission members.[58]

The emergence of "power plays" may be a development that calls for some form of constitutional amendment limiting such legislative action in lame-duck-sessions.

[55] *Compare* Estebar v. Municipal Court, 485 P.2d 1140 (Cal. 1971), *with* State v. Benitez, 395 So.2d 514 (Fla. 1981). *See also* State v. Second Judicial Dist. Ct., 432 P.3d 154 (Nev. 2018); Chapter 10, section VI.

[56] Miriam Seifter, *Judging Power Plays in the American States*, 97 TEX. L. REV. 1217 (2019).

[57] *See id.* at 1232.

[58] *See* Cooper v. Berger, 809 S.E.2d 98, 114 (N.C. 2018).

## V. CONCLUSION

As Justin Long has demonstrated, state government structure and separation of powers arguments can be utilized to protect what we think of as "rights."[59] Nonetheless, questions of state constitutional separation or distribution of powers have generally been less newsworthy than the more high-profile rights decisions. Interestingly, however, in Rhode Island, the issue attracted sufficient public attention, in the context of legislative appointments to administrative agency boards, to generate a contentious political debate that led to significant amendments to the state constitution.[60] Separation of powers issues are likely to become more important as controversial and fundamental matters of governance continue to be decided at the state level.

[59] Justin R. Long, *State Court Protection of Individual Constitutional Rights: State Constitutional Structures Affect Access to Civil Justice*, 71 RUTGERS U.L. REV. 937 (2018).

[60] *See generally* Carl T. Bogus, *The Battle for Separation of Powers in Rhode Island*, 56 ADMIN. L. REV. 77 (2004). *See generally*, as to the effect of the new amendments, *In re* Request for Advisory Opinion from the House of Representatives (Coastal Resources Management Council), 961 A.2d 930 (R.I. 2008).

# 9

# THE STATE LEGISLATIVE BRANCH

> *State legislatures are, historically, the fountainhead of representative government in this country. A number of them have their roots in colonial times, and substantially antedate the creation of our Nation and our Federal Government. In fact, the first formal stirrings of American political independence are to be found, in large part, in the views and actions of several of the colonial legislative bodies.*
>
> —Chief Justice Earl Warren[1]

Legislative power at the state level is, after all, central to how we govern ourselves as state polities.[2] If major areas of governmental concern which have been handled by the federal government since the 1930s continue to be returned to the states, this will create new stresses and demands on state legislatures.[3] For example, do *federal* funds have to be appropriated by the *state* legislature?[4] States must be prepared to elaborate a fundamental theory of state legislative power under their constitutions, known as the "police power."[5]

[1] Reynolds v. Sims, 377 U.S. 533, 564 (1964).

[2] *See, e.g.*, Daniel J. Elazar, *A Response to Professor Gardner's* The Failed Discourse of State Constitutionalism, 24 RUTGERS L.J. 975 (1993) (discussing states as polities).

[3] John Kincaid traces the ebb and flow of responsibility back and forth between the federal government and the states in John Kincaid, *Foreword: The New Federalism Context of the New Judicial Federalism*, 26 RUTGERS L.J. 913 (1995).

[4] George D. Brown, *Federal Funds and National Supremacy: The Role of State Legislatures in Federal Grant Programs*, 28 AM. U. L. REV. 279 (1979); Donald J. Toumey, Note, *Taking Federalism Seriously: Limiting State Acceptance of National Grants*, 90 YALE L.J. 1694 (1981); Brian Smentkowski, *Legal Reasoning and the Separation of Powers: A State-Level Analysis of Disputes Involving Federal Funds Appropriations*, 16 LAW & POL'Y 395 (1994); Roderick M. Hills Jr., *Dissecting the State: The Use of Federal Law to Free State and Local Officials from State Legislatures' Control*, 97 MICH. L. REV. 1201, 1253–56 (1999); *see generally* Cooper v. Berger, 852 S.E.2d 46 (N.C. 2020). Appropriation of money is a central legislative function. A.B.A.T.E. of Illinois v. Quinn, 957 N.E.2d 876, 883 (Ill. 2011). The same is true of taxation, or the raising of revenue. Most state constitutions, like the federal Constitution, require revenue measures to originate in the lower house. *See* City of Seattle v. Dept. of Revenue, 357 P.3d 979, 985–88 (Or. 2015).

[5] *See* Daniel B. Rodriguez, *Public Health Emergencies and State Constitutional Quality*, 72 RUTGERS U. L. REV. 1223 (2020).

*The Law of American State Constitutions.* Robert F. Williams and Lawrence Friedman, Oxford University Press.
 DOI: 10.1093/oso/9780190068806.003.0010

The state legislative branch was the repository of the lion's share of governmental power in the "first wave" of revolutionary state constitutions.[6] The framers of the federal Constitution, therefore, had extensive experience with the theory and practice of legislative power under state constitutions before 1787.[7] As the historian Gordon Wood has observed, the Revolution changed attitudes about legislative power:

> The revolutionaries' central aim was to prevent power, which they identified with the governors, from encroaching on liberty, which was the possession of the people or their representatives in the legislatures. Most sought to create a balance between power and liberty, the rulers and the ruled. Thus, in all the state constitutions, the much-feared governors were radically weakened and the popular assemblies or houses of representatives greatly strengthened.[8]
>
> ***
>
> Throughout English history, government had been identified exclusively with the crown or the executive; Parliament's responsibility had generally been confined to voting taxes, protecting the people's liberties, and passing corrective and exceptional legislation. Now, however, the new American state legislatures, in particular the lower houses of the assemblies, were no longer to be merely adjuncts of or checks on magisterial power. They were to assume familiar magisterial prerogatives, including the making of foreign alliances and the granting of pardons. Legislatures had rarely exercised such powers.[9]

Despite the legal and political changes that have occurred since 1776, resulting in the types of limitations on the state legislative branch that will soon be described, state legislatures remain extraordinarily powerful. They are the focal point of policymaking in state government.

The transition from early state constitutions providing unfettered legislative power to the more recent constitutions restricting legislative power reflects one of the most important themes in state constitutional law. The clearly established pattern during the founding decade of 1776–1787 was a gradual transition from legislative dominance, or "omnipotence," to an increased role for the executive

[6] Robert F. Williams, *The State Constitutions of the Founding Decade: Pennsylvania's Radical 1776 Constitution and Its Influences on American Constitutionalism*, 62 TEMPLE L. REV. 541, 571–72 (1989).

[7] Robert F. Williams, *"Experience Must Be Our Only Guide": The State Constitutional Experience of the Framers of the Federal Constitution*, 15 HASTINGS CONST. L. Q. 403, 416–17 (1988).

[8] Gordon S. Wood, *Foreword: State Constitution-Making in the American Revolution*, 24 RUTGERS L.J. 911, 914 (1993).

[9] *Id.* at 916.

and judicial branches.[10] The new executive and judicial powers operated as a check on recognized legislative power rather than a sharing of legislative power. A commentator observed in 1892 that "one of the most marked features of all recent State constitutions is the distrust shown of the legislature."[11]

The range of highly visible legislative abuses in the late 1700s, such as suspension of debts, seizure of the property of Loyalists, generous authorization of paper money, and legislative interference with the executive and judicial branches, began to raise concerns. Increased gubernatorial executive veto power came to be viewed as not inconsistent with popular sovereignty but, rather, as a necessary mechanism to limit legislative power. In this way, even within revolutionary republican rhetoric, with its absence of reliance on a hierarchical social structure that had justified "balanced government," the case could be made for checks on the misuse of power by government officials.[12] In Gordon Wood's words, "The Americans' inveterate suspicion and jealousy of political power, once concentrated almost exclusively on the Crown and its agents, was transferred to various state legislatures."[13]

In addition, the legislative articles of modern state constitutions reflect two important characteristics: (1) the insertion of specific policies or "constitutional legislation" or "policy-oriented" provisions into state constitutional texts, thereby supplanting legislative prerogatives and sometimes leading to a limitation of legislative alternatives through judicially discovered "negative implications";[14] and (2) the insertion into state constitutions of detailed procedural requirements that the legislature must follow in the enactment of statutory law. Also, a number of state constitutions make provision for popular, direct lawmaking through the initiative, referendum, and recall.[15]

## I. THE NATURE OF STATE LEGISLATIVE POWER

More so than either the executive or judicial branches, the legislative branch is different at the state level from the Congress at the federal level. State legislative

[10] GORDON S. WOOD, THE CREATION OF THE AMERICAN REPUBLIC, 1776–1787, 452 (1969). *See also* JEFFREY S. SUTTON, WHO DECIDES? STATES AS LABORATORIES OF CONSTITUTIONAL EXPERIMENTATION 234 (2021) ("Much of American constitutional history can be described as the loss of state legislative power to the other state and federal branches.").

[11] Amasa M. Eaton, *Recent State Constitutions*, 6 HARV. L. REV. 109 (1892). *See also* JAMES Q. DEALEY, GROWTH OF AMERICAN STATE CONSTITUTIONS 120, 188–93, 277–84 (1915).

[12] Peter S. Onuf, *State Politics and Ideological Transformations: Gordon S. Wood's Republican Revolution*, 44 WM. & MARY Q. 614 (1987).

[13] WOOD, *supra* note 10, at 409.

[14] *See* Chapter 12.

[15] *In re* Title, Ballot Title and Submission Clause, and Summary for 1999–2000 #255, 4 P.3d 485, 492 (Colo. 2000) (liberal construction of constitutional provisions on initiative process).

power is "plenary,"[16] whereas federal legislative power is enumerated. The prevailing view is illustrated by the Supreme Court of Illinois:

> Under traditional constitutional theory, the basic sovereign power of the State resides in the legislature. Therefore, there is no need to grant power to the legislature. All that needs to be done is to pass such limitations as are desired on the legislature's otherwise unlimited power.[17]

This basic distinction is somewhat oversimplified because state constitutions also contain authorizations for the legislature to act.[18] Still, it is this basic distinction that led to political scientist Walter Dodd's observation that the most important questions of judicial interpretation of the federal Constitution have to do with implied *powers*, while at the state level, implied *limitations* are most important.[19] Also, the need for, and the arguments in favor of, bills of rights will differ depending on whether legislative power under a constitution is plenary, as under state constitutions, or enumerated, as under the federal Constitution.[20]

Given this plenary nature of state constitutional legislative power, a crucial question arises:

> The question becomes whether the fundamental charter does or should incorporate controlling principles neither referred to nor included in the document. In other words, despite the purposefully constructed character of a constitution, the argument for inclusion of unenumerated constraints presumes that the people omitted principles that they nonetheless intended to operate on the government.[21]

[16] Frank P. Grad & Robert F. Williams, 2 State Constitutions for the Twenty-First Century: Drafting State Constitutions, Revisions and Amendments 27 (2006); Michael E. Libonati, *The Legislative Branch*, *in* 3 State Constitutions for the Twenty-First Century: The Agenda of State Constitutional Reform 37, 37 (2006). For what appears to be the lone contrary view, see Richard B. Sanders & Barbara Mahoney, *Restoration of Limited State Constitutional Government; A Dissenter's View*, 59 N.Y.U. Ann. Surv. Am. L. 269 (2003); *see also* Wash. St. Farm Bureau Federation v. Gregoire, 174 P.3d 1142, 1154–57 (Wash. 2007) (Sanders, J., concurring); *id.* at 1145 n.4; Iberville Parish School Bd. v. Louisiana State Bd. of Ed., 248 So.3d 299, 305 (La. 2018).

[17] Client Follow-up Co. v. Hynes, 390 N.E.2d 847, 849–50 (Ill. 1979). *See also* Town of Lincoln v. Lincoln Lodge No. 22, 660 A.2d 710, 715 (R.I. 1995); Bd. of Commissioners of North LaFourche Conservation, Levee and Drainage Dist. v. Bd. of Commissioners of Atchafalaya Basin Levee Dist., 666 So.2d 636, 639 (La. 1996); White v. Davis, 68 P.3d 74, 81–82 (Cal. 2003).

[18] Michael J. Besso, *Connecticut Legislative Power in the First Century of State Constitutional Government*, 15 Quinnipiac L. Rev. 1, 7–8 n.25 (1995).

[19] Walter F. Dodd, *Implied Powers and Implied Limitations in Constitutional Law*, 29 Yale L.J. 137, 160 (1919). Besso, *supra* note 18, at 14–15.

[20] Besso, *supra* note 18, at 11. For an interesting argument that *federal* legislative authority should not be restricted to enumerated powers, see Calvin H. Johnson, *States Rights? What States Rights?: Implying Limitations on the Federal Government from the Overall Design*, 57 Buff L. Rev. 225 (2009).

[21] *Id.* at 17.

One conclusion could be, albeit tentative,[22] that natural law doctrines should not operate as external constraints on state legislative power. The 1818 Connecticut Constitutional Convention rejected an "unenumerated rights" saving clause.[23] Other states, however, do have such clauses, inviting judicial recurrence to external (possibly, but not necessarily, "natural" law) constraints in limiting legislative choices.[24]

Challenges to the exercise of legislative power have arisen in a wide variety of contexts, including to retroactive laws, statutes validating past legally invalid acts, the enactment of statutes in anticipation of constitutional amendments, as well as in a number of separation of powers controversies. One commentator has noted several important conclusions concerning state constitutional legislative power:

> To summarize, the constitution's plenary grant permits the general assembly to execute its legislative function in any manner not prohibited by existing or clearly implied text-based limitations. The breadth of this authority can't be emphasized too much, particularly when examining the actual exercise of the power, and, particularly, when legislative choices are challenged.[25]
>
> * * *
>
> Because power is plenary and unenumerated, it must be presumed, in every case, that the general assembly is acting pursuant to the constitutional grant. Limits contained in the constitution can then be considered for their possible constraining effect.[26]

These perspectives lead to the important and powerful presumption of constitutionality for statutes enacted by the state legislature. Judicial deference to the legislative product surfaces, as we will see later in this chapter, even in the interpretation and application of the state constitutions' *procedural* limitations on the legislature.

[22] *Id.* at 22. Former Justice Hans A. Linde of Oregon argued, in many contexts, against judicially imposed limits on state legislatures in the absence of textual limitations. *See, e.g.*, Hans A. Linde, *State Constitutions Are Not Common Law: Comments on Gardner's* Failed Discourse, 24 Rutgers L.J. 927 (1993).

[23] Besso, *supra* note 18, at 18.

[24] *See* Louis Karl Bonham, Note, *Unenumerated Rights Clauses in State Constitutions*, 63 Tex. L. Rev. 1321 (1985); Suzanna Sherry, *Natural Law in the States*, 61 U. Cinn. L. Rev. 171 (1992); *see also* McCracken v. State, 518 P.2d 85 (Alaska 1974); Pro-Choice Mississippi v. Fordice, 716 So.2d 645 (Miss. 1998); Atwood v. Vilsack, 725 N.W.2d 641, 651–52 (Iowa 2006).

[25] Besso, *supra* note 18, at 24.

[26] *Id.* at 49.

A complete picture of legislative power under a current state constitution must include the later waves of reaction to state legislative abuses, reflected in the procedural and substantive limitations on the legislature adopted over the years.[27] Further, the limitations contained in state constitutional declarations of rights must be included in the picture of state legislative power. Also, the impact of "positive" rights, or mandates, contained in the state constitution itself must be analyzed for their potential, particularly in judicial interpretation, to supplant legislative choices.[28]

The state legislature as an institution does much more than just enact statutes. It may propose amendments to the state constitution, a power not generally considered to be part of the "legislative power."[29] It may ratify proposed federal constitutional amendments but only within the federal Constitution's mandates.[30] The state legislature may conduct investigations without passing any legislation; it may appropriate money; and it may adopt resolutions which do not have the force of law.[31] The state legislatures in a number of states have even been required in recent times to share their power to reapportion themselves with Reapportionment Commissions.[32] Both the advent of term limits for legislators and the adoption of the initiative and referendum change the nature of the state legislative institution.

None of this, however, detracts from the validity and importance for today of the central characteristic of state legislative power: it is plenary. So when one sees what seem like preliminary statements such as the following ones made by the Rhode Island Supreme Court, they should not be viewed as mere platitudes:

> Since the adoption of the constitution, this court has consistently held that the powers of both the Crown and Parliament reside in the Legislature, unless that

[27] Robert F. Williams, *State Constitutional Law Processes*, 24 WM. & MARY L. REV. 169, 201 (1983) ("The transition from early state constitutions granting unfettered legislative power to the more recent constitutions restricting legislative power reflects one of the most important themes in state constitutional law.").

[28] *See* Burt Neuborne, *Foreword: State Constitutions and the Evolution of Positive Rights*, 20 RUTGERS L.J. 881 (1989); Jonathan Feldman, *Separation of Powers and Judicial Review of Positive Rights Claims: The Role of State Courts in an Era of Positive Government*, 24 RUTGERS L.J. 1057 (1993).

[29] Opinion of the Justices, 81 So.2d. 881, 890–91 (Ala. 1955).

[30] Hawke v. Smith, 253 U.S. 221 (1920); Leser v. Garnett, 258 U.S. 130 (1922).

[31] Scudder v. Smith, 200 A.601 (Pa. 1938).

[32] Fonfara v. Reapportionment Commission, 610 A.2d 153 (Conn. 1992). *See* Scott M. Lesowitz, *Independent Redistricting Commissions*, 43 HARV. J. LEGIS. 535 (2006); Nicholas Stephanopoulos, *Reforming Redistricting: Why Popular Initiatives to Establish Redistricting Commissions Succeed or Fail*, 23 J.L. & POL. 331 (2007).

On the redistricting provisions of state constitutions, see James A. Gardner, *Foreword: Representation Without Party: Lessons from State Constitutional Attempts to Control Gerrymandering*, 37 RUTGERS L.J. 881 (2006); David Schultz, *Redistricting and the New Judicial Federalism: Reapportionment Litigation Under State Constitutions*, 37 RUTGERS L.J. 1087 (2006); Bruce E. Cain, *Redistricting Commissions: A Better Political Buffer?* 121 YALE L.J. 1808 (2012). *See* section XI of this chapter.

> power has been subsumed by the Constitution of the United States or has been removed from the General Assembly by the Constitution of the State of Rhode Island. . . . The power of the General Assembly is, therefore, plenary and unlimited, save for the textual limitations to that power that are specified in the Federal or State Constitutions. . . . The State Constitution defines the powers granted to the executive and judicial departments of government, leaving all other powers to the legislative branch, unless prohibited to it by the constitution. . . . Because the General Assembly does not look to the State Constitution for grants of power, we have invariably adhered to the view that the General Assembly possesses all the powers inherent to the sovereign other than those that the constitution textually commits to the other branches of state government.[33]

Such statements are central to our understanding of state constitutional law, to our systems of state government, and to our theory and practice of state judicial review.

## II. IMPLIED LIMITS: THE NONTEXTUAL BOUNDARIES OF LEGISLATIVE POWER

In evaluating state legislative power, it is important to focus on what is meant by "legislative" power and "executive" power.[34] These are both terms of art used in state constitutions.

The legislative power is, itself, conceptually limited to the notion of "legislating." Concepts such as "legislative" and "executive" power are, of course, indeterminate.[35] They can be words of limitation as well as words granting power. There are unwritten limitations, or internal constraints, on this plenary power, such as the "public purpose" doctrine.[36] This implied limitation on legislative power was clearly recognized as early as 1853 in *Sharpless v. Mayor of Philadelphia*,[37] where the Supreme Court of Pennsylvania noted:

> Neither has the legislature any constitutional right to create a public debt, or to lay a tax, or to authorize any municipal corporation to do it, in order to raise funds for a mere *private* purpose. No such authority passed to the Assembly by

33 City of Pawtucket v. Sundlun, 662 A.2d 40, 44 (R.I. 1995).
34 *See* R.I. CONST. art. VI, § 2 (legislative); *id.* art. IX, § 1 (executive).
35 *See* William B. Gwyn, *The Indeterminacy of the Separation of Powers in the Age of the Framers*, 30 WM. & MARY L. REV. 263 (1989).
36 Besso, *supra* note 18, at 14 n.56. Some states do include the public purpose doctrine in the text of their constitutions. *See, e.g.*, ILL. CONST. art. VIII, § 1.
37 21 Pa. 147 (Pa. 1853).

> the general grant of legislative power. This would not be legislation. Taxation is a mode of raising revenue for *public* purposes.[38]

In certain situations, limitations on legislative power are implied and arise from the legal concept of legislative power. Where does legislating end and executing or administering begin? Many years ago, Walter Dodd confronted the question of the concept of "legislative power":

> The view is frequently expressed that state legislatures have inherently all power not denied to them by state and national constitutions. This view is based upon the notion that state legislatures inherited the powers of the British parliament and possess such powers in full unless denied. . . .
>
> The result is very nearly the same whether we say (1) that the state constitution confers "legislative powers," and that this means all power not denied by constitutional texts, or (2) that "legislative power" is inherent, and unlimited except as restricted by constitutional texts. The first statement is perhaps the better, for there is little ground in our history since the Revolution for inherent or original powers in any department of government. In fact, when reference is made to inherent power, what has usually been meant is that "legislative power," granted in general terms, must be interpreted as conferring all governmental power, except so far as restricted by constitutional texts, i.e., that all such power inheres in the general grant.[39]

First, the "public purpose" doctrine has current importance, for example, in such areas as legislation authorizing vouchers for private school education[40] and authorizing the government to pursue child support obligations on behalf of nonindigent persons.[41] Another way of thinking about the limitation of legislative power to public purposes is to analyze the legislature's "police power."[42] This limitation is also not expressly contained in state constitutions but is viewed as an inherent limiting concept within the notion of "legislative power."

A second implied limitation on otherwise plenary state legislative power is the rule that a present legislature cannot bind future legislatures. The Nebraska Supreme Court confronted this issue and, after surveying the doctrine in other

[38] *Id.* at 168–69 (partial emphasis in original).

[39] Walter F. Dodd, *The Function of a State Constitution*, 30 Pol. Sci. Q. 201, 201, 205 (1915).

[40] *See* Davis v. Grover, 480 N.W.2d 460, 474–77 (Wis. 1992).

[41] *See In re* Marriage of Lappe, 680 N.E.2d 380, 388–92 (Ill. 1997).

[42] Besso, *supra* note 18, at 13 n.54. In 1969, the Illinois Supreme Court declared a motorcycle crash-helmet law unconstitutional as outside the legislature's police power. *See* People v. Fries, 250 N.E.2d. 149, 151 (Ill. 1969). Dept. of Ins. v. Dade Co. Consumer Advocate's Office, 492 So.2d 1032 (Fla. 1986) (holding statute prohibiting insurance agents from discounting commissions beyond police power).

jurisdictions, concluded: "The proposition that one legislature cannot bind a succeeding legislature is derived from the constitutional power of the Legislature to legislate."[43] This is an implied restriction, or limit, on plenary legislative power arising from the very concept of what it means to legislate.

Separation of powers is another limit,[44] although by contrast to federal constitutional law, it often has *a textual* basis in state constitutions. One separation of powers limit on legislative authority is the rule in many states that the legislature may not appoint its members or designees to executive branch boards or commissions, the "reverse delegation" problem discussed in Chapter 8. States that do permit this practice impose a less strict separation of powers doctrine than the federal constitutional doctrine.

Another limit on state legislative power is the nondelegation doctrine. There is a wide variety of approaches to this matter under state constitutions.[45] States that follow the nondelegation doctrine enforce separation of powers in a stricter fashion than the federal constitutional doctrine. Some state courts link strict enforcement of the nondelegation doctrine to the presence of a specific textual statement in the state constitution. The Florida Supreme Court stated:

> It should be noted that Article II, Section 3, Florida Constitution, contrary to the Constitutions of the United States and the State of Washington, does by its second sentence contain an express limitation upon the exercise by a member of one branch of any powers appertaining to either of the other branches of government.
>
> . . . .

43 State *ex rel.* Stenberg v. Moore, 544 N.W.2d 344, 349 (Neb. 1996).

44 *See* Chapter 8. The separation of powers doctrine operates as a limit on the legislative branch, as it also limits the other branches. As one commentator has noted, "[i]t is axiomatic that the authority of the state legislature is plenary except as limited by the state constitution and federal law. Separation of powers is one of those limitations." Roy Pulvers, *Separation of Powers Under the Oregon Constitution: A User's Guide*, 75 Or. L. Rev. 443, 449 (1996) (*citing* Brusco Towboat Co. v. State Land Bd., 589 P.2d 712, 717 (Or. 1978), and Ryan v. Harris, 2 Or. 175, 176 (Or. 1866), for the proposition that state legislative authority is limited by its constitution and federal laws; Pulvers also cites State *ex rel.* Oregon State Bar v. Lenske, 407 P.2d 250, 254–55 (Or. 1966) for the proposition that separation of powers is a limitation on legislative power).

45 Gary J. Greco, *Standards or Safeguards: A Survey of the Delegation Doctrine in the States*, 8 Admin. L. Rev. Am. U. 815 (1994). *See also* Michael Asimow, Arthur Earl Bonfield, & Ronald M. Levin, State and Federal Administrative Law 413–19 (2d ed. 1998) (describing the state nondelegation doctrine). For a case exploring the relationship between legislative guidelines or standards for administrative agency action, on the one hand, and procedural safeguards for agency decisions, on the other, see Westervelt v. Natural Resources Comm., 263 N.W.2d 564 (Mich. 1978). *See also* Diemer v. Commonwealth, 786 S.W.2d 861, 864–66 (Ky. 1990) (state nondelegation doctrine more restrictive than federal, even where state statute copied federal statute's standards). Cases are collected in Jim Rossi, *Institutional Design and the Lingering Legacy of Antifederalist Separation of Powers Ideals in the States*, 52 Vand. L. Rev. 1167 (1999) (analyzing different treatment of the nondelegation doctrine, an aspect of the horizontal separation of powers, in state constitutional law). *See generally In re* Certified Question from U.S. Dist. Ct., Western Dist. of Michigan, Southern Division, 958 N.W.2d 1 (Mich. 2020).

> Accordingly, until the provisions of Article II, Section 3 of the Florida Constitution are altered by the people we deem the doctrine of nondelegation of legislative power to be viable in this State.[46]

By contrast, the New Jersey Supreme Court, in a delegation case, stated: "[T]here is no indication that our State Constitution was intended, with respect to the delegation of legislative power, to depart from the basic concept of distribution of the powers of government embodied in the Federal Constitution."[47] The New Jersey Constitution had a provision similar to Florida's, barring a person in one branch from performing the duties of another branch.[48] The Rhode Island Supreme Court has linked its nondelegation doctrine more directly to the concept of *legislative* power.[49]

The Florida Supreme Court held that the legislature could not, through a state statute, delegate to an administrative agency the responsibility to define an element of a crime.[50] The Colorado Supreme Court took the opposite view.[51]

A number of state statues rely on the authority of, or in effect delegate authority to, *federal* agencies and statutes. The Michigan Supreme Court upheld, on a 4–3 vote, a statute that barred products liability actions for drugs approved by the Federal Food and Drug Administration, even in the future.[52] The state courts, as in other nondelegation contexts, take a wide range of views on this kind of delegation.[53]

There have been a number of challenges to state statutes delegating governmental power to *private* individuals or organizations. For example, the New York decision in *Fink v. Cole*[54] struck down a licensing statute for jockeys that delegated authority to a private entity—the Jockey Club. This issue can arise in a wide variety of contexts.[55] The Arkansas Supreme Court struck down

[46] Askew v. Cross Key Waterways, 372 So.2d 913, 924, 925 (Fla. 1978). *See also* Dept. of Business Reg. v. National Manufactured Housing Federation, 370 So.2d 1132, 1135 (Fla. 1979).
[47] Brown v. Heymann, 297 A.2d 572, 577 (N.J. 1972).
[48] *See* Robert M. Martin Jr., *Legislative Delegations of Power and Judicial Review—Preventing Judicial Impotence*, 8 Fla. St. U. L. Rev. 43 (1980).
[49] Bourque v. Dettore, 589 A.2d 815, 817 (R.I. 1991). The court noted that the nondelegation doctrine "stems" from the character of the Rhode Island Constitution as the supreme law of the state and its assignment of the *legislative* power to the *legislative* branch.
[50] B.H. v. State, 645 So.2d 987, 990–93 (Fla. 1994).
[51] People v. Holmes, 959 P.2d 406, 412 (Colo. 1998).
[52] Taylor v. Smithkline Beecham, 658 N.W.2d 127 (Mich. 2003). *Accord* Oklahoma City v. Oklahoma 918 P.2d 26, 30 (Okla. 1995). *Contra* State *ex rel.* Kirschner v. Urquhart, 310 P.2d 261, 264–65 (Wash. 1957); Wallace v. Comm. of Tax, 184 N.W.2d 588, 591–93 (Minn. 1971) (same).
[53] *See* Rossi, *supra* note 45, at 1235–38; Jim Rossi, *Dual Constitutions and Constitutional Duels: Separation of Powers and State Implementation of Federally Inspired Regulatory Programs and Standards*, 46 Wm. & Mary L. Rev. 1343, 1368–69 (2005).
[54] 97 N.E.2d 873 (N.Y. 1951). *Fink v. Cole* and other similar cases are discussed and analyzed in Note, *The State Courts and Delegation of Public Authority to Private Groups*, 67 Harv. L. Rev. 1398 (1954). *See also* Note, *Delegation of Power to Private Parties*, 37 Colum. L. Rev. 447 (1937).
[55] *See* Group Health Ins. of N.J. v. Howell, 193 A.2d 103 (N.J. 1963); State Bd. of Chiropractic Exmrs. v. Life Fellowship of Pa., 272 A.2d 478 (Pa. 1971); Gumbhir v. Kansas State Bd. of Pharmacy,

a legislative delegation to a private entity to impose a tax for rice promotion on both producers and buyers of rice, where only the producers could vote.[56] The Vermont Supreme Court upheld a statute delegating police power ("It is an attribute of sovereignty, or rather it is sovereignty itself.") to the University of Vermont on the ground that it was a sufficiently *public* body.[57] In the workers' compensation context, litigation challenged state legislative enactments directing that monetary awards would be determined by reference to the *private* American Medical Association's "most recent" guidelines.[58] Most states' legislative adoption of the *private* National Association of Insurance Commissioners' guidelines for insurance companies has come under question.[59]

Finally, some states have confronted the question whether the state legislature could "delegate" to the citizen voters the power to decide whether a law should take effect or not. The South Carolina Supreme Court struck down a video gambling statute that was to be submitted to the people for a "yes or no" vote.[60] The Illinois Supreme Court reached a similar result on the basis that the lawmaking power was assigned by the state constitution to the *legislature*.[61] The New Hampshire Supreme Court opined that the legislature could not submit two alternative tax statutes to the people for them to choose which would become law.[62]

## III. PROCEDURAL RESTRICTIONS ON STATE LEGISLATURES

Constitutions, both state and federal, impose a number of substantive limits on what may be enacted by their respective legislative branches. A major factor distinguishing state and federal constitutions, however, is their differing attention to the procedure for enacting legislation. Congress is relatively unfettered;

618 P.2d 837 (Kan. 1980); McCarty v. Arkansas St. Plant Board, 622 S.W.3d 162 (Ark. 2021); *see also* Louis L. Jaffe, *Law Making by Private Groups*, 51 HARV. L. REV. 201 (1937); George W. Liebmann, *Delegation to Private Parties in American Constitutional Law*, 50 IND. L.J. 650 (1975). *See also* David M. Lawrence, *Private Exercise of Governmental Power*, 61 IND. L.J. 647 (1986).

[56] Leathers v. Gulf Rice Arkansas, Inc., 994 S.W.2d 481 (Ark. 1999). *See generally* Ira P. Robbins, *The Impact of the Delegation Doctrine on Prison Privatization*, 35 UCLA L. REV. 911 (1988); Robert A. Ewert, Comment, *Delegations to Private Entities: The Application of the Boll Weevil Eight Factor Test*, 2 TEX. TECH J. TEX. ADMIN. L. 275 (2002).

[57] State v. Curley-Egan, 910 A.2d 200, 203 (Vt. 2006).

[58] *Compare* West Philadelphia Achievement Charter Elem. Sch. v. School Dist. of Philadelphia, 132 A.3d 957, 963–68 (Pa. 2016) (striking down the delegation without reaching its private element), *with* Hill v. American Medical Response, 423 P.3d 1119 (Okla. 2018) (upholding delegation).

[59] Daniel Schwarcz, *Is U.S. Insurance Regulation Unconstitutional?* 25 CONN. INS. L.J. 191 (2018).

[60] Joy Time Distributions and Amusement Co. v. State, 528 S.E.2d 647, 650–54 (S.C. 1999).

[61] People *ex rel.* Thomson v. Barnett, 176 N.E.108 (Ill. 1931). *Accord In re* Municipal Suffrage to Women, 36 N.E.488 (Mass. 1894). *Contra* Hudspeth v. Swayze, 89 A.780 (N.J. App. 1914).

[62] Opinion of the Justices, 725 A.2d 1082 (N.H. 1999).

unrelated measures may often be included in one federal bill or resolution, and unrelated "riders" may be attached to virtually any measure, including amendments to substantive law contained in appropriations bills.[63] Although House and Senate rules may restrict these practices to a certain degree,[64] the federal Constitution does not contain such restrictions.

By contrast, the legislative articles of virtually all state constitutions contain a wide range of limitations on state legislative processes. Generally, these *procedural* limitations did not appear in the first state constitutions. Instead, they were adopted throughout the nineteenth century in response to perceived state legislative abuses. Last-minute consideration of important measures; logrolling; mixing substantive provisions in omnibus bills; low visibility; and hasty enactment of important, and sometimes corrupt, legislation; and the attachment of unrelated provisions to bills in the amendment process—to name a few of these abuses—led to the adoption of constitutional provisions restricting the legislative process. These constitutional provisions seek generally to require a more open and deliberative state legislative process, one that addresses the merits of legislative proposals in an orderly and rational manner.

Georgia's famous Yazoo land scandal, where a virtual giveaway of land was authorized in a bill "smuggled" through the legislature, led to the requirement that a bill must contain a title disclosing its subject.[65] Other familiar examples of state constitutional limitations on the legislature include the requirement that a bill contain only matters on a "single subject,"[66] that all bills be referred to committee;[67] that the vote on a bill be reflected in the legislature's journal;[68] that no bill be altered during its passage through either House so as to change its original purpose;[69] and that appropriations bills contain provisions on no other subject.[70] These procedural restrictions must be distinguished from the common *substantive* limits on state legislation, such as those prohibiting statutes limiting

[63] *See, e.g.*, Louis Fisher, *The Authorization-Appropriation Process in Congress: Formal Rules and Informal Practices*, 29 CATH. U. L. REV. 51 (1979). *See, e.g.*, Robertson v. Seattle Audubon Society, 503 U.S. 429 (1992). State constitutions often ban this practice. *See* Flanders v. Morris, 558 P.2d 769, 771 (Wash. 1977).

[64] *See* Stanley Bach, *Germaneness Rules and Bicameral Relations in the U.S. Congress*, 7 LEGIS. STUD. Q. 341 (1982).

[65] Millard H. Ruud, *"No Law Shall Embrace More Than One Subject,"* 42 MINN. L. REV. 389, 391–92 (1958); Martha Dragich, *State Constitutional Restrictions on Legislative Procedure: Rethinking the Analysis of Original Purpose, Single Subject, and Clear Title Challenges*, 38 HARV. J. ON LEGIS. 103 (2001); *see also* JEFFREY S. SUTTON, WHO DECIDES? STATES AS LABORATORIES OF CONSTITUTIONAL EXPERIMENTATION, ch. 7 (2021).

[66] *See generally id.* Apparently, the concern about "omnibus" bills dates back to Roman times. Edward S. Crowin, *The "Higher Law" Background of American Constitutional Law*, 42 HARV. L. REV. 149, 160 n.36 (1928).

[67] *See, e.g.*, PA. CONST. art. III, § 2.

[68] *See, e.g.*, OHIO CONST. art. II, § 9.

[69] *See, e.g.*, PA. CONST. art. III, § 1.

[70] *See, e.g.*, FLA. CONST. art. III, § 12.

wrongful death recoveries[71] or mandating a certain type of civil service system[72] and from the general limits contained in state bills of rights.

The continued inclusion of procedural restrictions in modern state constitutions has been widely criticized. Professor Frank Grad noted in 1968:

> Commonly, state constitutions provide that the legislature shall determine its own rules of procedure, and then deny it the effective exercise of that right by providing for the conduct of legislative business in such detail as to leave very little to rulemaking. While it may be appropriate to settle constitutionally and inflexibly such essential matters of representative government as the kind of majority required to pass a law, or the vote required to override a veto by the governor, the constitutional requirement of three readings of a bill is clearly obsolete, and requirements governing the style to be followed in a bill, or limiting a bill to a single subject, have caused considerable damage through invalidation of noncomplying laws on technical grounds.[73]

Despite such criticism, the limitations on state legislative procedure survived the wave of state constitutional revision that occurred during the middle of the twentieth century.[74] Therefore, because these limits have in effect been readopted in contemporary state constitutions and continue to reflect important policies relating to the nature of the deliberative process in state legislatures, they should be respected and complied with by the legislative, executive, and judicial branches of state government.

This section explores the differences in state constitutional limits on the legislative process, evaluates the differing approaches to judicial enforcement, and assesses the impact of judicially unenforceable provisions on members of the legislative and executive branches of state government. It will be seen that legislators

[71] Frank P. Grad, *The State Constitution: Its Function and Form for Our Time*, 54 VA. L. REV. 928, 955 n.92 (1968).

[72] *Id.* at 961–62.

[73] *Id.* at 963 (footnotes omitted). Ruud, by contrast, concluded that the benefits of the single-subject rule "are obtained at comparatively little cost in negative results" and recommended that the provisions be retained in state constitutions. Ruud, *supra* note 65, at 452. For further criticisms, see the materials cited in Williams, *supra* note 27, at 204 n.157. Another commentator noted: "Students of legislation believe that most legislative procedure requirements could be stricken from constitutions without impairing the legislative process in the slightest." William J. Keefe, *The Functions and Powers of the State Legislatures*, *in* STATE LEGISLATURES IN AMERICAN POLITICS 37, 50 (A. Heard ed., 1966). For similar perspectives, see Charles W. Shull, *The Legislative Article*, *in* MAJOR PROBLEMS IN STATE CONSTITUTIONAL REVISION 200, 209 (W. Graves ed., 1960); Patricia S. Wirt, *The Legislature*, *in* SALIENT ISSUES OF CONSTITUTIONAL REVISION 68, 77–78 (J. Wheeler ed., 1961) (suggesting exclusion from judicial review).

[74] Illinois in 1970 removed the title requirement from its constitution. *See* Gerald Sramek, Note, *State Statutes: The One-Subject Rule Under the 1970 Constitution*, 6 J. MARSHALL J. PRAC. & PROC. 359 (1973). There have been proposals in other states, such as in New Jersey in 1947, to remove some of these provisions, but they have not been adopted.

often do not follow the legislative procedure requirements of the state constitution, particularly where the legislative proposal is controversial and the courts do not enforce the constitutional restriction. It is suggested that increased judicial enforcement could result in greater legislative compliance with mandatory constitutional requirements.

A careful look at Pennsylvania's state constitutional provisions and their judicial enforcement will illustrate the issues in most states. The Pennsylvania Constitution contains, for example, among many others, two typical limitations on legislative procedure:

> Article III, Sec. 1. Passage of laws No law shall be passed except by bill, and no bill shall be so altered or amended, on its passage through either House, as to change its original purpose. . . .
>
> Article III, Sec. 3. Form of bills No bill shall be passed containing more than one subject, which shall be clearly expressed in its title, except a general appropriation bill or a bill codifying or compiling the law or a part thereof.[75]

These restrictions, together with others contained in Article III of the Pennsylvania Constitution, are similar to those inserted in nearly all state constitutions during the nineteenth century.[76] The provision contained in Article III, Section 3, concerning the form of bills, was added in 1864. The provision now contained in Article III, Section 1, was inserted by the Constitutional Convention that framed the 1874 constitution. This later provision is obviously narrower than Article III, Section 3, and is aimed at a different perceived evil.

Article III, Section 3, which requires single subject and title, was the culmination of efforts dating back to the 1830s to eliminate the evils of "logrolling" and "omnibus bills" and to ensure separate consideration by the legislature for distinct proposals.[77] The title requirement is a disclosure device to give notice of the contents of the bill. Thus, a violation of this provision can take place even if a separate bill is drafted, introduced, and passed if the bill contains "more than one subject" not reasonably germane to each other or if the subject is not "clearly

[75] PA. CONST. art. III, §§ 1, 3.

[76] *See generally* Williams, *supra* note 27, at 201–05. Interestingly, in Pennsylvania, the history of state constitutional provisions concerning openness and fairness in state legislative procedure dates back to 1776. *See* Cecelia Kenyon, *Constitutionalism in Revolutionary America*, *in* NOMOS XX: CONSTITUTIONALISM 101, 103 (R. Pennock & J. Chapman eds., 1979). *See also* J. PAUL SELSAM, THE PENNSYLVANIA CONSTITUTION OF 1776: A STUDY IN REVOLUTIONARY DEMOCRACY 184–85, 192 (1936). Historian Jackson Turner Main made the following comment about Pennsylvania's 1776 legislative procedure requirements: "Prevented from doing harm, [the legislature] might then be trusted with power to do good." JACKSON TURNER MAIN, THE SOVEREIGN STATES, 1775–1783, 152 (1973).

[77] Jefferson B. Fordham & Carroll C. Moreland, *Pennsylvania's Statutory Imbroglio: The Need of Statute Law Revision*, 108 U. PA. L. REV. 1093, 1100–03 (1960). *See generally* Ruud, *supra* note 65.

expressed" in the bill's title. These restrictions concern the authorized *content* of acts of the legislature. Any asserted violation could be determined by examining the final legislative enactment, or enrolled bill, on its face.

The more recent Article III, Section 1, however, is more specific. It is aimed at the *procedure* by which the legislature may enact laws. Its primary limitation is that, once a bill has been introduced, it may not be "so altered or amended on its passage through either House as to change its original purpose."[78] By contrast to Article III, Section 3, however, a violation of Section 1 cannot be detected by examining the enrolled bill on its face. Any alteration by amendment will have already taken place and will be "masked" by the process of engrossing the amendments into the final version of the bill for presentation to the governor.

The question of *judicial* enforcement of the relevant state constitutional limitations to invalidate an act presents the central difficulty in this area. Violations of the procedural limitations contained in many state constitutions can be separated into two categories: (1) those which are apparent from the face of an act,[79] and (2) those which must be shown by resort to other evidence. Pennsylvania's constitution creates two important limitations, the single subject and original purpose rules, which illustrate each of these categories, and demonstrate that judicial enforcement of these provisions can differ significantly.

## A. Single Subject

The single-subject rule serves several functions. Just two years after Article III, Section 3, of the Pennsylvania Constitution was adopted in 1864, the Pennsylvania Supreme Court observed, "It cannot be doubted that this restriction upon the legislature was designed to prevent an evil which had long prevailed in this state as it had done elsewhere, which was the practice of blending in the same law subjects not connected with each other and often entirely different."[80] Single-subject limits also seek to protect the integrity of the governor's veto power. The governor may not veto part of a legislative measure, except with the item veto in the case of certain appropriation bills.[81] Just as the single-subject limitation seeks

[78] PA. CONST. art. III, § 1. A leading commentator referred to Article III, Section 1 as a "technicality of scant policy content" and stated: "The ban on amendments changing the purpose is designed to assure full deliberation on the stuff of a measure. The object is good but I prefer my faith in a body of able representatives than in hard-to-apply procedural restrictions." JEFFERSON B. FORDHAM, THE STATE LEGISLATIVE INSTITUTION 56 (1959).

[79] The Washington Supreme Court has colorfully described this category of procedural limitations by stating that "the bill carries its death warrant in its hand." State *ex rel.* Dunbar v. State Bd. of Equalization, 249 P. 996, 1000 (Wash. 1926).

[80] Blood v. Mercelliott, 53 Pa. 391, 394 (Pa. 1866) (*quoting* Parkinson v. State, 14 Md. 185, 193 (Md. 1859)). *See also* Dorsey's Appeal, 72 Pa. 192, 195 (Pa. 1872) ("The purpose of the amendment is to prevent a number of different and unconnected subjects from being gathered into one act. . . .").

[81] PA. CONST. art. IV, § 16. *See generally* Johnson v. Walters, 819 P.2d 694 (Okla. 1991).

to ensure separate and independent legislative consideration of proposals, it is intended to guarantee the same freedom from "logrolling" during executive review of legislative enactments. Thus, in the context of non-appropriation bills, if the governor desires to veto any of the sections in the legislation, she would have been required to veto the entire act. To do so requires her to sacrifice desirable legislation in order to veto what she considers undesirable legislation.[82]

Legislative enactments that violate the single-subject rule, or the "altered-during-enactment" rule, often present a governor with a "Hobson's Choice." This represents a legislative attempt to present the governor with a "veto-proof" bill. As a result of the development of the governors' veto power, "legislatures continuously attempt to thwart the veto by implementing various devices to veto-proof a bill. Among the most common are logrolling and riders . . . They enable the legislature to eliminate the essential executive check against unwise legislation. . . . The safeguard enacted by virtually all the states is the 'single-subject' rule."[83]

If a governor attempted to veto unrelated subject-matter sections of a bill, which had possibly unconstitutionally altered the original purpose of the bill, the effort would likely be futile, as the Oklahoma governor found out in *Johnson v. Walters*.[84] There, the court reiterated the all-or-nothing character on the governor's veto power over non-appropriation bills.[85]

A violation of Article III, Section 3, requirements would be apparent from the face an act because Section 3 deals with final content, not procedure. Two or more diverse subjects were contained within the final enactment. Pennsylvania cases indicate that plural subjects are permitted unless they contain subjects which are "foreign" or not "germane" to each other.[86] The Pennsylvania courts long maintained a posture of deference to the legislature on single-subject challenges, adopting what appears to be almost an irrebuttable presumption of constitutionality.[87] Courts have gone to great lengths to create broadly defined categories in which to classify bills containing subjects with seemingly tenuous relationships.[88] Because of the generality of the Article III, Section 3, germanity

[82] Dragich, *supra* note 65, at 115, 122–23.

[83] Deborah S. Bartell, Note, *The Interplay Between the Gubernatorial Veto and the One-Subject Rule in Oklahoma*, 19 OKLA. CITY U. L. REV. 273, 276–77 (1994).

[84] 819 P.2d 694, 698 (Okla. 1994).

[85] *See also* Harbor v. Deukmejian, 742 P.2d 1290 (Cal. 1987). On this problem, see generally Jeffrey Gray Knowles, *Enforcing the One-Subject Rule: The Case for a Subject Veto*, 38 HAST. L. REV. 563 (1987). In the absence of such a gubernatorial "subject veto," authorizing governors to "unpack" non-appropriation bills to veto unrelated provisions, only courts can block "various devices to veto-proof a bill," Bartell, *supra* note 83.

[86] Kotch v. Middle Coal Field Poor Dist., 197 A.334 (Pa. 1938); *In re* Road in Borough of Phoenixville, 109 Pa. 44 (Pa. 1885).

[87] *See* Singer v. Sheppard, 346 A.2d 897 (Pa. 1975); Bensalem Township School Dist. v. County Comm'rs, 303 A.2d 258 (Pa. Commw. 1973). *But see* Commonwealth v. Humphrey, 136 A.213 (Pa. 1927).

[88] *See, e.g.*, Booth & Flinn, Ltd. v. Miller, 85 A.457 (Pa. 1912) (sufficient if related to general subject or connected to general purpose); *In re* Gilberts' Estate, 76 A.428 (Pa. 1910) (sufficient if

test, judicial inquiry must of necessity proceed on a case-by-case basis.[89] But the single subject rule is judicially enforceable, and the germanity test is clearly established and consistently held out as the principal method of determining single-subject validity.

Single-subject provisions do not prevent logrolling within broad subject categories, such as education, transportation, or criminal law.[90] This is why legislators must search for "vehicles" concerning the same broad subject matter as their proposed amendments. If the amendment is germane, even if it has nothing to do with the original purpose of the bill, it will not violate the single-subject rule. This can result in an important "chilling effect," inhibiting minor, but necessary amendments in the years following enactment of major, controversial statutes. Sponsors often decline to "open up" the statutes to any changes, fearing the prospect of hostile amendments that would be germane even though beyond the original purpose of the bill containing the minor changes. Under these circumstances, it is obvious that such a provision as the prohibition on alteration to change original purpose aims at a problem quite different from that targeted by the single-subject rule.

Several state supreme courts, frustrated with repeated single-subject violations, have issued warnings to their state legislatures. For example, in 2010 the Oklahoma Supreme Court stated: "We are growing weary of admonishing the Legislature for so flagrantly violating the terms of the Oklahoma Constitution. It is a waste of time for the Legislature and the Court, and a waste of taxpayer's money. The Legislature ignored our earlier opinions. . . ."[91]

A question arises when a significant period of time passes before a single-subject challenge to a statute is asserted. The Pennsylvania Supreme Court was presented with such a claim more than twenty years after the legislation was enacted. Citing reliance issues (although plaintiffs themselves were not guilty of laches), the court rejected the claim.[92] The court also noted, in dictum, that severance was not appropriate in the case of a single-subject violation.[93]

subordinate). *See also* AB v. State, 949 N.E.2d 1204, 1221–29 (Ind. 2011) (Dickson, J., concurring and Sullivan, J., concurring in part).

[89] "Flagrant violations of this requirement may, of course, be apparent, but no test of violation is laid down by the provision itself and none has been developed by judicial action." Walter F. Dodd, *The Problem of State Constitutional Construction*, 20 COLUM. L. REV. 635, 640 (1920). Michael D. Gilbert describes this indeterminacy, defends logrolling, and proposes a solution to reduce indeterminacy in *Single Subject Rules and the Legislative Process*, 67 U. PITT. L. REV. 803 (2006). *Compare* Washington v. Dept. of Pub. Welfare, 188 A.3d 1135 (Pa. 2018), *with* Weeks v. Dept. of Human Services, 222 A.3d 722 (Pa. 2019).

[90] Ruud, *supra* note 65, at 448–49; *see, e.g.*, Wass v. Anderson, 252 N.W.2d 131 (Minn. 1977).

[91] Nova Health Systems v. Edmondson, 233 P.3d 380, 382 (Okla. 2010).

[92] Sernovitz v. Dershaw, 127 A.3d 783, 789–94 (Pa. 2015).

[93] *Id.* at 788–89 ("it would be arbitrary to preserve one set of provisions germane to one topic, and invalidate the remainder of the bill" (*citing* Commonwealth v. Neiman, 84 A.3d 603, 615 (Pa. 2013)). *See also* St. Louis Co. v. Prestige Travel, Inc., 344 S.W.3d 708, 714–15 n.6 (Mo. 2011).

## B. Alteration Changing Original Purpose

Legislative abuses, despite the inclusion of the single-subject clause in 1864, led to the specific limitations on legislative procedure inserted into the Pennsylvania Constitution in 1874.[94] As Justice John Dean observed in 1893, in *Perkins v. Philadelphia*:[95]

> That convention, direct from the people, composed of the ablest and most experienced citizens of the commonwealth, framed this Article 3 on legislation. Assuming, what was the settled law, that the general assembly had all legislative power not expressly withheld from it in the organic law, they set about embodying in that law prohibitions which should in the future effectually prevent the evils the people complained of. Article 3 is almost wholly prohibitory. . . .[96]

In 1877, however, the Pennsylvania Supreme Court in *Kilgore v. Magee*[97] held that Article III, Section 1, was not judicially enforceable:

> In regard to the passage of the law and the alleged disregard of the forms of legislation required by the constitution, we think the subject is not within the pale of judicial inquiry. So far as the duty and the consciences of the members of the legislature are involved the law is mandatory. They are bound by their oaths to obey the constitutional mode of proceeding, and any intentional disregard is a breach of duty and a violation of their oaths. But when a law has been passed and approved and certified in due form, it is no part of the duty of the judiciary to go behind the law as duly certified to inquire into the observance of form in its passage.[98]

[94] The call for a constitutional convention carried by almost a 5–1 popular vote in 1872. ROSALIND L. BRANNING, PENNSYLVANIA CONSTITUTIONAL DEVELOPMENT 56 (1960).

> The Pennsylvania constitution of 1874 . . . was drafted in an atmosphere of extreme distrust of the legislative body. . . . It was the product of a convention whose prevailing mood was one of reform . . . and, overshadowing all else, reform of legislation to eliminate the evil practices that had crept into the legislative process. Legislative reform was truly the dominant motif of the convention and that purpose is woven into the very fabric of the constitution.

*Id.* at 37. The major focus of the 1873 Pennsylvania Constitutional Convention was on the legislative branch. ROBERT WOODSIDE, PENNSYLVANIA CONSTITUTIONAL LAW 578 (1985).

[95] 27 A.356 (Pa. 1893).

[96] *Id.* at 360. Justice Dean's statement was made in the context of what is now Article III, Section 7 of the Pennsylvania Constitution, which relates to special and local bills. Article III, Section 7 was added in 1873.

[97] 85 Pa. 401 (Pa. 1877).

[98] *Id.* at 412.

This approach, relying on the enrolled bill rule, treats the question of compliance with Article III, Section 1, as nonjusticiable, or similar to a "political question."[99] *Kilgore* remains among the leading judicial statements on the issue in Pennsylvania.[100]

Other provisions of Pennsylvania's Constitution bear on the validity of the legislative enactments. For example, Article III, Section 12, requires each House to keep a journal of its proceedings. This requirement has been in the Pennsylvania Constitution since 1776. In light of modern methods, legislative journals provide accurate, verifiable records of the legislative process leading to the enactment of statutes—a clear record of whether a bill has been "so altered or amended as to change its original purpose" in violation of Article III, Section 1.

Another important, and now common, provision, was added to the Pennsylvania Constitution in 1874 and now appears as Article III, Section 2, which provides, "No bill shall be considered unless referred to committee, printed for the use of the members and returned therefrom."[101] Reinforcing the committee system in both the House and the Senate was one of the objectives at which Article III, Section 2, seems to have been aimed.[102]

The provisions in Article III were added to the Pennsylvania Constitution, as well as to the constitutions of other states, to stem legislative abuses and should be read together. More important, these specific limitations on the legislature, the perceived abuser of the public trust in the years leading up to the Constitutional Convention of 1873, should probably not be viewed as judicially unenforceable. The Supreme Court of Pennsylvania, along with many other state high courts, has declared that the state's constitution must be interpreted as "understood by

[99] *See* Chapter 10; Nat Stern, *The Political Question Doctrine in State Courts*, 35 S.C. L. Rev. 405 (1984). Another way of describing this doctrine is to contrast mandatory or prohibitory provisions with directory provisions. Walter Dodd explored differing judicial enforcement of legislative procedural requirements using this formulation in Walter F. Dodd, *Judicially Non-Enforcible Provisions of Constitutions*, 80 U. Pa. L. Rev. 54, 61–72 (1931).

[100] The *Kilgore* decision contained little analysis, but was apparently based on the enrolled bill rule, which prevents judicial inquiry from going beyond the official act as passed by the legislature and considers the enrolled bill conclusive evidence of regularity in its passage. The enrolled bill rule was adopted in Pennsylvania in 1853 in *Speer v. Plank Road Co.*, 22 Pa. 376 (Pa. 1853); *see generally* Woodside, *supra* note 94, at 348–57. *Speer* involved a challenge to an enactment because it was not signed by the leaders of the two Houses before being presented to the governor, a requirement not contained in the Pennsylvania Constitution. *Speer*, 22 Pa. at 377. *See also* Mikell v. School Dist. of Philadelphia, 58 A.2d 339, 344 (Pa. 1948) (characterizing the contention that an act was a revenue measure which did not originate in the House as "purely technical," viewing the constitutional requirement as directory rather than mandatory, and relying on the enrolled bill rule); Murray Egan & James P. Gill, *Constitutional Regulation of the Legislative Procedure in Pennsylvania*, 11 U. Pitt. L. Rev. 670 (1950).

[101] Pa. Const. art. III, § 2.

[102] On the importance of the committee system to legislative deliberations, see, e.g., Felix Frankfurter, *Some Reflections on the Reading of Statutes*, 47 Colum. L. Rev. 527, 545 (1947). Woodrow Wilson referred to committees as "little legislatures." Woodrow Wilson, Congressional Government: A Study in American Politics 83 (1956).

the people who adopted it."[103] While the constitution as presented to and ratified by the voters of Pennsylvania was silent on the question of judicial enforcement of the new procedural restrictions on the legislative branch,[104] the voters who adopted the 1874 Pennsylvania Constitution would certainly have scoffed at the idea that these new limitations were to be left to legislative self-regulation, in effect permitting the legislature to "overrule" the constitution by a majority vote. Consequently, continued judicial abstention in this area is unwarranted.[105]

The enrolled bill rule precludes evidence of the legislative history of challenged legislation that would be the only way to demonstrate an "alteration" in violation of Article III, Section 1.[106] The Pennsylvania Supreme Court indicated

[103] Firing v. Kephart, 353 A.2d 833, 835 (Pa. 1976). *See also* Commonwealth v. Harmon, 366 A.2d 895, 897 (Pa. 1976). The New York Court of Appeals stated:

> We may not . . . construe the words of the Constitution in exactly the same manner as we would construe the words of a will or contract drafted by careful lawyers, or even a statute enacted by the Legislature. It is the approval of the People of the State which gives force to a provision of the Constitution . . . and in construing the Constitution we seek the meaning which the words would convey to an intelligent, careful voter.
>
> Kuhn v. Curran, 61 N.E.2d 513, 517–18 (N.Y. 1945).

[104] An interesting debate in the 1872–1873 Pennsylvania Constitutional Convention concerning the question of judicial enforceability of legislative procedure requirements in the state constitution is illuminating but inconclusive. The Legislation Committee recommended the inclusion of the following provision in the legislative article:

> Any bill passed in disregard of the provisions and directions prescribed in this article shall be void and of no effect; and when the validity of any law passed by the Legislature is questioned in any court of record, it shall be competent for such court to inspect the Journals of either House, and if it does not appear thereon that all the forms of legislation, in both Houses, as hereinbefore prescribed, have been observed in the passage of such law, the same shall be adjudged by such court to be void.
>
> 2 Debates of the Convention to Amend the Constitution of Pennsylvania, 1872–1873, at 758. A lengthy debate followed, during which the delegates fully discussed the pros and cons of judicial enforcement, together with alternatives, such as enforcement by the executive branch. *Id.* at 758–97. At the conclusion of the debate, the Convention simply voted not to accept the recommended language. *Id.* at 797. A similar debate took place at the 1870 Illinois Constitutional Convention. People v. Dunigan, 650 N.E.2d 1026, 1034–36 (Ill. 1995).

[105] The Pennsylvania Supreme Court held that the political question doctrine did not bar judicial review of the expulsion of a member of the Pennsylvania House of Representatives. Sweeney v. Tucker, 375 A.2d 698, 704–12 (Pa. 1977). In dictum, the court cited the Article III restrictions on legislative procedure and noted, "Specific limitations on the Legislature's power to determine its internal operating procedures are imposed elsewhere in the Constitution. *See* Pa. Const. art. III, §§ 1–13. *These limitations are judicially enforceable.*" *Id.* at 708–09 (footnote omitted and emphasis added). The court cited as authority two cases where the legislative violation of the constitutionally required procedure was apparent on the face of the act. *Id.* at 709 (*citing* Scudder v. Smith, 200 A.601 (Pa. 1938); Stewart v. Hadley, 193 A.41 (Pa. 1937)).

[106] The enrolled bill rule was examined by the Common Pleas Court of Dauphin County in *Velasquez v. Depuy*, 46 Pa. D. & C.2d 587 (1969). After a scholarly review, the court concluded: "Whatever the future may hold in store for the Enrolled Bill Rule, we believe it is undoubtedly the law in Pennsylvania today." *Id.* at 621. This case, and the entire question, is examined in Note, *Pennsylvania's Enrolled Bill Rule: A Reappraisal in Light of HB 1413 and Velasquez v. Depuy*, 75 Dick. L. Rev. 123 (1970).

in *Consumer Party of Pennsylvania v. Commonwealth*[107] that it would not, in all cases, adhere to its earlier view that Article III, Section 1, is not judicially enforceable. *Consumer Party* involved a bill which was significantly altered by a conference committee. The court characterized its earlier "restraint" as "abstention" and noted that "it would be a serious dereliction on our part to deliberately ignore a clear constitutional violation."[108] It declined to continue its "blanket doctrine of abstention," recognizing the evils at which the legislative procedure provisions of the 1874 constitution were aimed. Although the court concluded that Article III, Section 1, was mandatory, it held that the conference committee procedure, even if it does result in significant alteration to bills, is such an important component of the legislative process that its use did not render the altered bill unconstitutional.[109]

The court's reading of Article III, Section 1, to permit conference committee bills, is correct. In reaching this result, however, the court characterized the purpose of the provision and the evils at which it was aimed in unnecessarily and inaccurately narrow terms. The only purpose it recognized was "to put the members of the General Assembly and others interested on notice so that they may act with circumspection."[110] In support of this single purpose—to avoid deception—the court cited a 1938 case, *Scudder v. Smith*,[111] which does not deal with the alteration problem under Article III, Section 1, but rather with its requirement that "no law shall be passed except by bill." In *Scudder*, the court struck down an attempt to enact a statute by the arguably deceptive use of a *joint resolution*, rather than a bill, in direct violation of the constitutional provision.[112]

Article III, Section 1, of the Pennsylvania Constitution contains two requirements. First, laws must be enacted only by bills. Any violation of this first provision will be apparent from the face of the act—it will carry its "death

[107] 507 A.2d 323 (Pa. 1986), *abrogated by* Pennsylvanians Against Gambling Fund, Inc. v. Comm., 877 A.2d 383 (Pa. 2005).
[108] *Id.* at 332–33.
[109]

> The practice of sending legislation to a conference committee is by its nature designed to reach a consensus. . . . To unduly restrict this process would inhibit the democratic process in its traditional method of reaching accord and would unnecessarily encumber the heart of the legislative process, which is to obtain a consensus.

*Id.* at 334.
[110] *Id.* at 335.
[111] 200 A.601 (Pa. 1938).
[112]

> The purpose of the constitutional requirements relating to the enactment of *laws* was to put the members of the Assembly and *others interested, on notice*, by the title of the measure submitted, so that they might vote on it with circumspection. What was attempted to be done by the sponsors of this challenged measure was something utterly alien to the proper subject matter of a 'joint resolution.' Its deceptive nomenclature is fatal to its validity as a *law*.

*Id.* at 604 (emphasis in original).

warrant in its hand."[113] This was the problem in *Scutter*. Second, bills may not be altered so as to change their original purpose. Violations of this second provision will not be apparent from the face of the enrolled act, which leads to the problem of judicial enforceability—a problem that would not arise with respect to the first provision.

Courts should not invalidate acts of the legislature unless the evils at which the constitutional restrictions were aimed have taken place.[114] In characterizing the purpose of the entirety Article III, Section 1, by reference only to the evils at which the first provision is aimed (deception), the Pennsylvania Supreme Court in *Consumer Party* unduly narrowed the scope of the constitutional restriction. The purpose of the second provision barring substantial alteration was not primarily to avoid deception but rather to preserve a regularized legislative procedure, including the committee system. The court in later years came to recognize this broader purpose.[115]

## IV. JUDICIAL ENFORCEMENT OF LEGISLATIVE PROCEDURE PROVISIONS

Other state courts have developed a surprisingly wide range of approaches to enforcing restrictions on legislative procedure in circumstances where an act does not violate procedural limitations on its face. Even within single jurisdictions, one can detect inconsistent doctrines and a lack of continuity over time. These widely varying judicial doctrines reflect what are essentially political decisions, made in the context of adjudicating actual controversies and concern the extent of judicial enforcement of state constitutional norms.

This range of approaches can be viewed as a continuum. At one end is the "enrolled bill rule," apparently followed, at least until recently, by Pennsylvania. This is marked by judicial passivity and complete deference to the legislative enactment.[116] At the other end is the "extrinsic evidence rule," characterized by judicial activism and recognition of the written constitution as a binding source of law.[117] Between these two extremes are three intermediate approaches to judicial enforcement: the "slightly modified" enrolled bill rule, the "modified" enrolled

[113] State *ex rel.* Dunbar v. State Bd. of Equalization, 249 P. 996, 1000 (Wash. 1926). *See supra* note 79 and accompanying text.

[114] *See, e.g.*, Wass v. Anderson, 252 N.W.2d 131 (Minn. 1977). *See also infra* text accompanying note 183.

[115] *See* Pennsylvanians Against Gambling Expansion Fund, Inc. v. Commonwealth, 877 A.2d 383, 408–09 (Pa. 2005).

[116] 1 Norman J. Singer, Sutherland's Statutes and Statutory Construction § 15:3 (6th ed. 2002).

[117] *Id.* § 15:6.

bill rule, and the "journal entry rule." All of these have been developed by the courts as they have been called on by litigants to interpret and enforce state constitutional restrictions on legislative procedure. The judicial doctrines prohibiting judicial enforcement, even in the face of clear violations, have been criticized. Those judicial approaches permitting judicial invalidation of legislative acts adopted in clear violation of constitutional restrictions are recommended as the proper approaches to enforcing mandatory state constitutional provisions.

## A. The Enrolled Bill Rule

The "enrolled bill rule" is referred to as the "conclusive presumption rule" because when it applies, it prevents *any* evidence other than the final enrolled bill itself to show constitutional violations occurring during the process of enacting legislation.[118] In his 1977 commentary on the revised Texas Constitution, Professor George Braden asserted that the enrolled bill rule was the majority view.[119] The most common argument advanced in favor of the rule is the separation of powers doctrine.[120] Because the legislature is a coordinate branch of government, the argument contends that the courts should not question the validity of a certified (enrolled) act by looking beyond the face of the bill to determine whether it was enacted in compliance with applicable constitutional limitations. Another argument supporting the rule is the need for finality with respect to the validity of statutes and the concern that citizens be able to rely on such finality. These arguments inevitably concede to the legislature the power to determine whether there has been compliance with limitations contained in the state constitution.

Braden advocates for the enrolled bill rule in his discussion of Article III, Section 30, of the Texas Constitution,[121] which is nearly identical to Article III, Section 1, of the Pennsylvania Constitution. He states, "Members of the legislature are fully capable of enforcing the rule, and it is their sole responsibility to do so under the enrolled bill doctrine."[122] Texas continues to follow the enrolled bill

[118] *Id.* § 15:3. This approach was adopted by the U.S. Supreme Court in 1892. *See* Field v. Clark, 143 U.S. 649, 669–80 (1892). *See* Ittai Bar-Siman-Tov, *Legislative Supremacy in the United States?: Rethinking the "Enrolled Bill" Doctrine*, 97 Geo. L.J. 323 (2009) (urging reversal of *Field*). There are, of course, relatively few procedural challenges to federal statutes. For an exploration of the English antecedents of the enrolled bill rule, see William H. Lloyd, *Pylkinton's Case and Its Successors*, 69 U. Pa. L. Rev. 20 (1920).

[119] I George Braden, The Constitution of the State of Texas, an Annotated and Comparative Analysis 121 (1977).

[120] Singer, *supra* note 116, § 15:3, at 820.

[121] Tex. Const. art. III, § 30: "No law shall be passed, except by bill, and no bill shall be so amended in its passage through either House, as to change its original purpose."

[122] I Braden, *supra* note 119, at 162.

rule, which has been in effect in civil cases[123] since *Williams v. Taylor*[124] was decided in 1892. The court in *Williams* refused to invalidate a statute even though the legislative journals showed that the bill had not been reported out of committee within three days of final adjournment, in violation of Article III, Section 32, of the Texas Constitution.

The Supreme Court of Washington reaffirmed the enrolled bill rule in *Citizens Council Against Crime v. Bjork.*[125] In continuing to apply the rule, the court cited earlier Washington precedents[126] and stated:

> An additional reason of public policy which supports the [enrolled bill] doctrine is that it is necessary in order that the people may rely upon the statutes as setting forth the laws which have been enacted by the legislature. If the enrolled bill were not taken as conclusive evidence that it was regularly and constitutionally enacted, Judge John P. Hoyt (who had served as President of the Constitutional Convention) said, it would be practically impossible for the courts even to determine what was the law, and would render it absolutely impossible for the average citizen to ascertain that of which he must at his peril take notice.[127]

The results of the "finality argument" are mixed. While citizens have laws that they can rely on, they have no guarantee that those laws were enacted constitutionally. Furthermore, as the experience of states that follow the "journal entry rule" or "extrinsic evidence rule" show, the unfavorable consequences that Judge Hoyt foresaw have not come to pass.

## B. The "Slightly Modified" Enrolled Bill Rule

If the enrolled bill rule is placed at the far left of the continuum, the current rule in New Mexico can be found just a short step to the right of it. After observing the enrolled bill rule since 1915, the New Mexico Supreme Court carved out a narrow exception in 1974 in *Dillon v. King.*[128] The court struck down the statute

[123] Interestingly, until 1971 the Texas Court of Criminal Appeals had followed the "journal entry rule," discussed *infra* at notes 144–54 and accompanying text. In *Maldonado v. State*, 473 S.W.2d 26 (Tex. Crim. App. 1971), the Court of Criminal Appeals brought itself in line with the Supreme Court of Texas in adopting the enrolled bill rule and held, "We will not look behind the engrossed [enrolled] bill to see if the Governor issued a proclamation including the subject matter of the enacted legislation," as required by Article III, Section 40 of the Texas Constitution. *Id.* at 28.

[124] 19 S.W.156 (Tex. 1892).

[125] 529 P.2d 1072 (Wash. 1975).

[126] *See, e.g.*, Roehl v. Public Util. Dist. No. 1 of Chelan County, 261 P.2d 92 (Wash. 1953).

[127] Citizens Council Against Crime v. Bjork, 529 P.2d at 1076 n.1 (*citing* State *ex rel.* Reed v. Jones, 34 P. 201, 202 (Wash. 1893)).

[128] 529 P.2d 745 (N.M. 1974) (*overruling* Earnest v. Sargent, 150 P. 1018 (N.M. 1915)).

in question in *Dillon* because it was enacted after the sixtieth calendar day of the legislative session, which violated Article IV, Section 5, of the New Mexico Constitution. The court held that courts may examine "the question of whether or not the act or bill purportedly passed by the Legislature within the constitutional time limitation was in truth and in fact passed within that limitation."[129] The court explicitly held that its decision was to be *prospective* only and only applicable to alleged violations of Article IV, Section 5. In those cases, "the conclusive legal presumption that ordinarily attaches to enrolled bills simply would not attach."[130]

Acknowledging the separation of powers clause in the New Mexico Constitution[131] and disclaiming any intention of "even suggesting to the Legislature how it should conduct its affairs," the *Dillon* court concluded that "it is nevertheless our function and duty to say what the law is and what the Constitution means."[132] The court also clearly stated that it did "*not* intend to herald the complete demise of the enrolled bill rule."[133]

The court's arguments as to why it should look beyond the enrolled bill to determine compliance with Article IV, Section 5, are persuasive. As it noted, "[t]here is not the slightest doubt that the legislators are duty bound to comply with this constitutional directive."[134] However, the New Mexico court appears to have left the enrolled bill rule in place for challenges asserting that a bill was "altered or amended on its passage . . . as to change its original purpose."[135] A violation of this or other provisions would arguably be as unconstitutional as if it had been passed after the constitutionally allotted time for the legislative session had ended. The court did not explain why it considered only violations of Article IV, Section 5, to be egregious enough to warrant an exception to the enrolled bill rule. The arguments advanced in support of this exception seem equally applicable to abolishing the enrolled bill rule altogether.

## C. The Modified Enrolled Bill Rule

Another step to the right on the continuum lies the "modified enrolled bill rule," adopted by the South Dakota Supreme Court in 1936.[136] Under this rule, the

[129] *Id.* 751.

[130] *Id.*

[131] N.M. Const. art. III, § 1.

[132] *Dillon*, 529 P.2d at 751.

[133] *Id.* at 752 (emphasis added).

[134] *Id.* at 751.

[135] *See* N.M. Const. art. IV, § 15.

[136] The rule was enunciated in *Barnsdall Refining Corp. v. Welsh*, 269 N.W.853 (1936), and is discussed in Marion R. Smyser, *Constitutional Limitations on the Enactment of Statutes in South Dakota*, 25 S.D. L. Rev. 14, 33–35 (1980). Ohio adopted the modified enrolled bill rule in a thoughtful

enrolled bill is conclusive evidence of proper enactment, except when an alleged violation arises concerning a provision for which the state constitution specifically requires that a journal entry be made. In these narrow circumstances, the court will look to the journals to determine whether a challenged act was passed properly.

The South Dakota Supreme Court considered the rule again in 1974, in *Independent Community Bankers Association of South Dakota, Inc. v. State.*[137] One of the alleged improprieties of the bill at issue in that case was that it was not "read twice, by number and title once when introduced, and once upon final passage," as required by Article III, Section 17, of the South Dakota Constitution. The court held that "the modified enrolled bill rule precludes plaintiffs from introducing evidence of the legislature's alleged failure to comply with the requirements of Article III, Section 17, because a journal entry noting compliance with that section is not *expressly required* by the Constitution."[138] Even though the journals showed that the bill did not receive a first reading, the journals did not lack any of the required entries on the day the bill was considered and passed. Therefore the court held that the enrolled bill became conclusive proof of its proper enactment.[139]

The weakness of the modified enrolled bill rule was exposed by Justice Frank Henderson in his dissenting opinion in *Independent Community Bankers Association*. The rule effectively insulates intentional violations of the constitution from judicial review, even if the violation appears on the face of the journals, unless a violation occurs with respect to one of the limited exceptions where a specific journal entry is required by the constitution.[140] Justice Henderson favored adopting the "journal entry rule."[141] In support of his view, Justice Henderson cited Article III, Section 13, of South Dakota's constitution, which mandates that "each House shall keep a journal of its proceedings." He also cited the rules apparently followed by the neighboring states of Minnesota and Michigan[142] and concluded that "making laws is the State Legislature's business but protecting the State Constitution is this Court's business. Viewing an enrolled bill and blessing it as being legal is to forsake, oftentimes, truth."[143]

opinion in *Hoover v. Board of County Comm'rs*, 482 N.E.2d 575 (Ohio 1985), *declined to extend* by State v. Voinovich, 631 N.E.2d 582 (Ohio 1994).

[137] 346 N.W.2d 737 (S.D. 1984), *disagreed with by dissent* in Matter of Estate of Wolff, 349 N.W.2d 33 (S.D. 1984).

[138] *Id.* at 743 (emphasis added).

[139] *Id.*

[140] *Id.* at 749 (Henderson, J., dissenting).

[141] *Id.* at 748. The journal entry rule is discussed more fully *infra* at notes 144–54 and accompanying text.

[142] *See* McClellan v. Stein, 201 N.W.209 (Mich. 1924); Bull v. King, 286 N.W.311 (Minn. 1939).

[143] *Independent Community Bankers Assoc.*, 346 N.W.2d at 749 (Henderson, J., dissenting).

## D. The Journal Entry Rule

The middle of the continuum is represented by the "journal entry rule."[144] This rule allows a court to consider any evidence appearing in the legislative journals to help determine the validity of a statute which has been challenged on constitutional grounds,[145] with the enrolled bill being considered only prima facie valid.

Florida follows the journal entry rule, and the decisions of its courts are instructive. In a 1983 case, *State v. Kaufman*,[146] a Florida drug trafficking statute was challenged on the grounds that it had not been properly read before passage as required by Article III, Section 7, of the Florida Constitution. The journals indicated that both Houses of the legislature had properly read the bills before their enactment,[147] but the trial court considered extrinsic evidence, including voice recordings of the legislative proceedings and transcripts generated from those recordings, which contradicted the journals.

In continuing to follow the journal entry rule, the Florida Supreme Court held that the legislative journals were the only evidence "superior in dignity" to enrolled bills.[148] The rationale for the court's holding, and the basis of the journal entry rule, is that the legislative journals are considered to be "public records" because the Florida Constitution mandates that they be kept.[149] Under this view, the journals are at least as reliable as the enrolled bill as evidence of what procedure the legislature actually followed or did not in enacting legislation. Indeed, in Florida, if there is a conflict between an act and the journal, the journal controls.[150]

144 The journal entry rule means that where a statute is challenged on constitutional grounds, the court may look to the legislative journal to determine compliance with the constitutional provision. It should be noted that there are different formulations of this rule. In his revision of Sutherland's treatise, *Statutes and Statutory Construction*, Professor Norman Singer defines the journal entry rule as the reverse of the enrolled bill or conclusive presumption rule, stating that "if constitutional compliance with mandatory provisions is not set forth in the journal there is a conclusive presumption that the proper proceedings were not followed and the presumption is against the validity of the act." SINGER, *supra* note 116, § 15:5, at 827. This is a minority position. *See* cases cited *id.* § 15:5.

145 A further point of clarification is necessary to distinguish the journal entry rule from the "affirmative contradiction rule." The latter "requires that validity be given the enrolled bill unless there *affirmatively* appears in the journals of the legislature a statement that there has not been compliance with one or more of the constitutional requirements." *Id.* § 15:4 (emphasis added). "It generally results, as does the conclusive presumption rule, in sustaining every nearly statute." *Id.* The principal weakness of this rule is that "[a]s a practical matter it would be remarkable for the journal to recite affirmatively that the bill was not read or a vote was not taken or that any required procedural step was not carried out." *Id.* at 826. As a result, an important distinction can be drawn between the affirmative contradiction rule and the journal entry rule. For an application of the affirmative contradiction rule, see Jensen v. Matheson, 583 P.2d 77 (Utah 1978).

146 430 So.2d 904 (Fla. 1983).

147 *Id.* at 905.

148 *Id.*

149 *See* FLA. CONST. art. III, § 4(c).

150 *See Kaufman*, 430 So.2d at 905 n.3.

The *Kaufman* court listed some specific exceptions where extrinsic evidence might be used to impeach the journals.[151] For example, extrinsic evidence is admissible where "clear and legally sufficient allegations of fraud are presented,"[152] or when it is alleged that actions were taken by a legislature after it ceased to be a duly constituted legislature.[153] Absent a challenge based on these circumstances, the legislative journals are the only evidence that can be used to overcome the presumption of constitutionality afforded to enrolled bills in states which, like Florida, follow the journal entry rule.[154]

## E. The Extrinsic Evidence Rule

At the far end of the continuum from the enrolled bill rule is the "extrinsic evidence rule." This rule "accords to the enrolled bill a *prima facie* presumption of validity but permits an attack by 'clear, satisfactory and convincing' evidence establishing that the constitutional requirements . . . have not been met."[155] This rule was adopted by the Supreme Court of Kentucky in 1980 in *D & W Auto Supply v. Department of Revenue*,[156] in a challenge based on Section 46 of the Kentucky Constitution. Although the journals indicated and all parties conceded that only forty-eight votes in a one-hundred-member Kentucky House were cast in favor of a bill containing an appropriation, Section 46 sets out certain procedures for enacting legislation, including a provision that "any act or resolution for the appropriation of money or the creation of debt shall, on its final passage, *receive the votes of a majority of* all the members elected to each House."[157]

*D & W Auto Supply* presented the Supreme Court of Kentucky with the opportunity to reexamine and abandon the enrolled bill rule, which had been in effect since 1896.[158] Before abandoning the enrolled bill rule, the court examined the four historical bases of the doctrine and the criticisms of the rule.[159] A major

[151] *Id.* at 906.

[152] *See* Jackson Lumber Co. v. Walton County 116 So.771 (Fla. 1928). A similar exception in cases of fraud is allowed in Utah. *See* Jensen v. Matheson, 583 P.2d 77, 81 (Utah 1978) (Ellett, C.J., concurring with reservations).

[153] *See* State *ex rel.* Landis v. Thompson, 164 So.192 (Fla. 1935). *See also* Dillon v. King, 529 P.2d 745 (N.M. 1974).

[154] Rhode Island also follows the journal entry rule. *See* State Terminal Corp. v. General Scrap Iron, Inc., 264 A.2d 334 (R.I. 1970). *See also* Elizabeth H. Cobb, *Judicial Review of the Legislative Enactment Process: Louisiana's "Journal Entry" Rule*, 41 LA. L. REV. 1187 (1981).

[155] SINGER, *supra* note 116, § 15.06, at 828.

[156] 602 S.W.2d 420 (Ky. 1980). The extrinsic evidence rule is also followed by Illinois. *See* Yarger v. Board of Regents, 456 N.E.2d 39 (Ill. 1983). *See also* Jensen v. Matheson, 583 P.2d 77, 82 (Utah 1978) (Maughan, J., dissenting).

[157] 602 S.W.2d at 422 (emphasis in original).

[158] The rule was announced in Lafferty v. Huffman, 35 S.W.123 (Ky. 1896).

[159] 602 S.W.2d at 422–24.

argument that the court advanced in favor of rejecting the rule and adopting the extrinsic evidence rule was the sworn duty of the courts under Section 26 of the Kentucky Constitution, "to see that violations of the constitution . . . are brought to light and corrected."[160] The court stated, "To countenance an artificial rule of law that silences our voices when confronted with violations of our constitution is not acceptable to this court."[161] The court concluded that the extrinsic evidence rule is "a more reasonable rule" and one that would best allow the court to fulfill its obligation to "support . . . the Constitution of this Commonwealth."[162]

As this brief review illustrates, a wide range of conflicting judicial attitudes exists toward enforcing state constitutional restrictions on legislative procedure.[163] Determining which of the alternatives previously discussed is the most desirable requires recognition of the interests of the state's citizens in finality and the separation of powers within state government, as well as enforcement of the written constitution. It also requires an honest appraisal of the situations in which a statute is generally challenged. Litigants pressing a statute's invalidity on the basis of alleged procedural defects generally are not neutral, good-government watchdogs seeking enforcement of the state constitution as an abstract value. Rather, they are often directly affected by and opposed to the challenged statute's substantive outcome and are seeking a means to avoid its consequences. They appear to be seeking a judicial rescue after losing in the legislature, which may increase judicial ambivalence toward enforcing state constitutional restrictions on legislative procedure.

The question remains, however, whether, in the absence of legislative adherence and executive enforcement (which may be common with respect to controversial statutes), courts *should* enforce apparently mandatory requirements of the written constitution. Basic questions of justiciability and the judicial function in constitutional interpretation and enforcement are involved. Such questions are often discussed in the context of whether evidence of violations is available or reliable.[164] For example, Professor Wigmore discussed the matter in his treatise on evidence.[165] Although Wigmore favored the enrolled bill rule as a matter of

[160] *Id.* at 424. Section 26 of the Kentucky Constitution provides: "To guard against transgression of the high powers which we have delegated, we declare that everything in this Bill of Rights is excepted out of the general powers of government, and shall forever remain inviolate; *and all laws contrary thereto, or contrary to this Constitution, shall be void.*" KY. CONST. § 26 (emphasis added).

[161] 602 S.W.2d at 424.

[162] *Id.* at 424–25 (*citing* § 228 of the Kentucky Constitution).

[163] Justice Hans A. Linde noted: "When a law is promulgated without compliance with the rules of legitimate lawmaking, is it not a law? Remarkably, we have no coherent national doctrine on this fundamental question." *Due Process of Lawmaking*, 55 NEB. L. REV. 197, 242 (1976).

[164] *See, e.g.*, William J. Lloyd, *Judicial Control of Legislative Procedure*, 4 SYRACUSE L. REV. 6, 7–8, 12–13 (1952).

[165] 4 JOHN H. WIGMORE, EVIDENCE IN TRIALS AT COMMON LAW § 1350, at 815–34 (J. Chadbourn ed., 1972).

judicial policy,[166] he conceded that, as an evidentiary matter, if courts admit any evidence at all, they should consider sources beyond the legislative journals.[167] At bottom, however, the question of judicial enforcement is not merely evidentiary.[168] If evidence of a constitutional violation is neither available nor reliable, then of course a court cannot find a constitutional violation.

One additional reason courts do not commonly use procedural mandates to invalidate statutes is that judges "are reluctant to visit the past sins of its legislative fathers on an otherwise inoffensive statute, especially when to do so seems a windfall for an undeserving but resourceful litigant."[169] However, in cases where a procedural violation appears on the face of the enrolled bill,[170] courts are willing to engage in judicial review, albeit with appropriate deference to the legislative product. When, upon review of a facially offensive statute, a court invalidates the statute, it is just as much a windfall to a possibly undeserving but resourceful litigant as it would be had the same court reviewed a statute that violated a nonobvious procedural restraint in the state's constitution. Furthermore, invalidating a statute on *procedural* grounds and thus permitting legislative reconsideration seems less intrusive than invalidating the *substance* of a statute on constitutional grounds.[171] For these reasons, courts that have refused to enforce many of the state constitutional restrictions on legislative procedure might rethink their approach.

Interestingly, in 1866 the California Supreme Court suggested that, if the enrolled bill rule were to be abandoned, the legislature could delineate "the cases in which, and the circumstances and limitations under which an enrolled statute may be impeached."[172] Not surprisingly, no state legislature seems to have followed the California court's invitation.[173] Perhaps more aggressive judicial enforcement would motivate such legislative action.

Even where there is significant *judicial* "underenforcement" of state constitutional limits on the legislative process, the constitutional limits remain the supreme law of the state.[174] Constitutions have meaning beyond what the courts

[166] *Id.* § 1350, at 833–34.
[167] *Id.* § 1350, at 832.
[168] Linde, *supra* note 163, at 243–45.
[169] *Id.* at 245.
[170] This occurs in the case of a violation of the single subject rule. *See supra* notes 80–93 and accompanying text.
[171] Linde, *supra* note 163, at 243.
[172] Sherman v. Story, 30 Cal. 253, 279 (Cal. 1866).
[173] In 1873, New Jersey did provide a statutory mechanism for judicial resolution of procedural challenges to statutes but it does not address issues such as the enrolled bill rule. *See* J.A.C. Grant, *New Jersey's "Popular Action" In Rem to Control Legislative Procedure*, 4 Rutgers L. Rev. 391 (1950).
[174] Lawrence Sager makes this point in the context of federal constitutional law. "Thus, the legal powers or legal obligations of government officials which are subtended in the unenforced margins of underenforced constitutional norms are to be understood to remain in full force." Lawrence Sager, *Fair Measure: The Legal Status of Underenforced Constitutional Norms*, 91 Harv. L. Rev. 1212, 1221 (1978).

announce,[175] and the courts are not the only enforcers of the state constitution. State constitutional restrictions are aimed in the first instance at the lawmakers themselves, who are bound by their oath of office to uphold the constitution. Legislators are bound by the state constitution. Constitutional law scholar Paul Brest has called on legislators to "determine, as best they can, the constitutionality of proposed legislation."[176] Many of the procedural restrictions discussed in this section are not so vague and general as to escape the understanding of legislative participants.[177] But, as we have seen, in controversial matters, legislative attitudes are not always governed by concern for the merits of the procedural point.[178]

The stage between legislative enactment and judicial review, the executive veto process, creates another arena for controlling procedurally unconstitutional legislation. Justice Hans A. Linde of Oregon has recommended that "[a] governor or a President ought to veto, on constitutional grounds, a bill that he knows to have been adopted in violation of a constitutionally required procedure, even though the courts would not question its enactment."[179] The governor's oath of office includes upholding the constitution. Also, the governor is not bound by judicially created doctrines used by the courts to avoid enforcing constitutional restrictions on legislative procedure. Thus, governors should not hesitate in vetoing procedurally invalid acts.

Citizens are not guaranteed any substantive outcome from the legislative process.[180] But as a result of perceived procedural abuses, many state constitutions were amended in the mid- to late-nineteenth century to require, in mandatory terms, that legislators follow certain procedures. Therefore, citizens are constitutionally entitled to a certain process in the enactment of statutes—in Justice Linde's terms, a "due process of lawmaking."[181] When fundamental elements of this constitutionally mandated process are ignored and not remedied by the legislative or executive branches, the courts should step in and examine reliable evidence of violations. This is not to say that the drastic remedy of statutory invalidation is appropriate in every case. Certainly, as in the cases enforcing

175 *See generally* Sotirios A. Barber, On What the Constitution Means (1984).

176 *See generally* Paul Brest, *The Conscientious Legislator's Guide to Constitutional Interpretation*, 27 Stan. L. Rev. 585, 587 (1975).

177 Linde, *supra* note 163, at 207, 222, 242. Justice Linde points out the availability of the constitutional point of order in legislatures. Linde, *supra* note 163, at 244.

178 *See also id.* 244 n.124.

179 *Id.* at 244. *See also* Sager, *supra* note 174, at 1221, 1227. Of course, if a governor opposes the substance of bill, she may veto it without regard to any procedural defects. For examples of gubernatorial attempts to enforce state constitutional requirements through veto power, see *Commonwealth v. Barnett*, 48 A.976 (Pa. 1901) (appropriations); *Brown v. Firestone*, 382 So.2d 654 (Fla. 1980) (unsuccessful veto of unconstitutional proviso language in appropriations bill).

180 "As a charter of government a constitution must prescribe legitimate processes, not legitimate outcomes. . . ." Linde, *supra* note 163, at 254.

181 *See generally* Linde, *supra* note 163 at 255.

the single subject rule,[182] judicial deference to the legislature is often appropriate. Courts should look to whether the evil at which the constitutionally prescribed procedure was aimed has occurred.[183] If it has, the court should not hesitate to invalidate the act in question, possibly in a ruling that applies only prospectively to avoid the reliance problems. On the other hand, acts of the legislature should not be invalidated when only "harmless error" has occurred. Judicial lines must be drawn, and deference to the legislative branch must be preserved.

One possible solution to the question of when a court should invalidate a statute on procedural grounds would rest on a distinction between prohibitions in the state constitution as opposed to affirmative requirements. If the legislature has breached specific prohibitions, the act in question would be held unconstitutional. If the legislature merely failed to adhere to affirmative requirements, less drastic remedies could be imposed, such as a prospective ruling pending the legislature's opportunity properly to "re-enact" the statute.

The courts should not abdicate their inherent function of interpreting and enforcing the written constitution. Increased judicial enforcement, in appropriate cases, of state constitutional restrictions on legislative procedure would likely result in the long run in increased legislative compliance with such provisions, which is the original goal of the constitutional provisions.

## V. LIMITATIONS ON SPECIAL AND LOCAL LAWS

In the Chapter 7 discussion of lockstepping federal and state equality doctrine, the state constitutional bans on special and local laws were briefly noted. These provisions, although often interpreted and applied as *rights* provisions, actually function as *limits* on the legislative branch.[184]

By the middle of the nineteenth century, many state legislatures were almost entirely consumed with the enactment of special and local laws. In Indiana, for example, by the 1849–1850 legislative session, "about 90% of all the laws passed were special in nature."[185] The Indiana Court noted:

[182] *See supra* note 87 and accompanying text.

[183] *See, e.g.*, Wass v. Anderson, 252 N.W.2d 131 (Minn. 1977). *See supra* note 114 and accompanying text.

[184] Gourley v. Nebraska Methodist Health System, Inc., 663 N.W.2d 43, 66 (Neb. 2003); City of Hammond v. Herman & Kittle Properties, Inc., 119 N.E.3d 70 (Ind. 2019).

[185] Alpha Psi Chapter, Pi Kappa Phi Fraternity v. Anditor of Monroe Co., 849 N.E.2d 1131, 1135 (Ind. 2006).

> The debates also illustrate the importance the delegates placed on saving for topics of wider importance the legislative time consumed in passing local legislation.[186]

The Pennsylvania high court, in discussing the ban on special and local legislation, stated:

> It is certainly not forgotten that the well-nigh unanimous demand which brought the convention of 1873 into existence was prompted by the evils springing from local and special legislation. That convention, direct from the people, composed of the ablest and most experienced citizens of the commonwealth, framed this article 3 on legislation. Assuming, what was settled law, that the general assembly had all legislative power not expressly withheld from it in the organic law, they set about embodying in that law prohibitions which should in the future effectually prevent the evils the people complained of.[187]

Many state constitutions contain both a general prohibition on special and local laws and, in addition, lists of specific topics which may not be dealt with by special or local legislation. Commenting on these differing limits, the Colorado Supreme Court stated:

> Modern approaches to the analysis of whether a statute amounts to special legislation differ depending on whether one of the express prohibitions enumerated in the constitutional provision is implicated . . . When the statute addresses an enumerated prohibition, we must first answer a threshold question of "whether the classification adopted by the legislature is a real or potential class, or whether it is logically and factually limited to a class of one and thus illusory . . ." If the class created by the legislation is illusory, it is prohibited special legislation. . . . Once it is determined that the legislation affects a genuine class, we then address whether the classification is reasonable. . . . Where an enumerated prohibition is not implicated, we are unconcerned with the composition of the class "so long as the legislature has not abused its discretion."[188]

[186] *Id. See also* Robert F. Williams, The New Jersey State Constitution: A Reference Guide 9 (rev. ed. 1997) (similar ratio of special to general laws in 1870s New Jersey).

[187] Perkins v. Philadelphia, 27 A.356, 360 (Pa. 1893). *See generally* Donald Marritz, *Making Equality Matter (Again): The Prohibition Against Special Laws in the Pennsylvania Constitution*, 3 Widener J. Pub. L. 161 (1993). *See also* Dan Friedman, *Applying Federal Constitutional Theory to the Interpretation of State Constitutions: The Ban on Special Laws in Maryland*, 71 Md. L. Rev. 411 (2012); Justin R. Long, *State Constitutional Prohibitions on Special Laws*, 60 Clev. St. L. Rev. 719 (2012); Anthony Schutz, *State Constitutional Restrictions on Special Legislation as Structural Restraints*, 40 J. Legis. 39 (2013–2014); Evan C. Zoldan, *Legislative Design and the Controllable Costs of Special Legislation*, 78 Md. L. Rev. 415 (2019).

[188] People v. Canister, 110 P.3d 380, 383 (Colo. 2005). *See also* People v. Brooks, 426 P.3d 355, 359 (Colo. 2018).

The concern with favoritism and lack of due process and impartiality was another key rationale for bans on special laws.[189] Central questions in determining whether an act is "special" are whether the classification is open-ended,[190] and whether there are persons or entities who are excluded from coverage of the act.[191] Classifications based on population of local governments, if open-ended and deemed reasonable by the courts, will often be upheld.[192] As the Missouri Supreme Court has stated, "The unconstitutionality of a special law is presumed . . ."[193]

Although the state constitutional limits on special and local laws, and the cases interpreting them highlight their negative effects, such laws do have a proper role in legislation under certain circumstances.[194]

## VI. THE STATE LEGISLATURE AND LOCAL GOVERNMENT

The original state constitutions contained virtually no mention of local governments and their powers.[195] Over time, a majority view emerged portraying local governments as "creatures of the State legislature," able to exercise only those powers specifically delegated to them.[196] The U.S. Supreme Court's adoption of this view has been seriously challenged,[197] and it led to the state constitutional home rule movement. Jefferson Fordham explained:

> In the state orientation there is a very important choice between use of the state constitution as the direct instrument for allocating governmental powers and reliance upon the legislature as a continuing power-distribution organ in the state. The devolution of authority to local units has traditionally been a function of the state legislature under the strongly prevailing doctrine of legislative supremacy over local government. It is here that the basic choice of political

[189] Jordan v. Horseman's Benevolent and Protective Assoc., 448 A.2d 462, 468 (N.J. 1982); Haman v. Marsh, 467 N.W.2d 836, 845 (Neb. 1991); Strickland v. Stephens Production Co., 411 P.3d 369, 375–76 (Okla. 2018); City of Hammond v. Herman & Kittle Properties, 119 N.E.3d 70 (Ind. 2019).

[190] Harris v. Missouri Gaming Comm'n., 869 S.W.2d 58, 65 (Mo. 1994).

[191] *Jordan*, 448 A.2d at 467.

[192] City of Enid v. Public Employees Relations Board, 133 P.3d 281 (Okla. 2005).

[193] Harris v. Missouri Gaming Comm'n., 869 S.W.2d 58, 65 (Mo. 1994).

[194] Professor Evan Zoldan analyzes the costs and benefits of special legislation, *supra* note 187.

[195] James E. Herget, *The Missing Power of Local Government: The Divergence Between Text and Practice in Our Early State Constitutions*, 62 VA. L. REV. 909 (1976).

[196] Michael E. Liberati, *Intergovernmental Relations in State Constitutional Law: A Historical Overview*, 496 ANNALS OF ACAD. OF POL. & SOC. SCIENCE 107, 110 (1988).

[197] Kathleen S. Morris, *The Case for Local Constitutional Enforcement*, 47 HARV. C.R.–C.L.L. REV. 1 (2012).

method presents great difficulty. What factors militate in favor of modifying legislative supremacy by constitutional amendment?

***

The prospect of adequate legislative recognition of local problems and needs is considered so slight by the proponents of constitutional home rule that they regard constitutional amendment as the only practical recourse. They say, in effect, that life is too short; local government cannot afford to wait on the vague prospect that the legislative institution will undergo the desired improvement. It is a familiar theme. Let's by-pass the legislature and provide for this or that problem by modifying the organic law.[198]

Many of the state constitutional delegations of legislative authority to local government were limited by the reservation of state legislative power to "preempt" local ordinances. In recent years, both progressive and conservative interests discovered this local government lawmaking power, as limited by the legislature's preemption power. As issues such as minimum wages, environmental protection, union matters, rent control, and the like have become increasingly salient at local levels, the legislative preemption power has further emerged. As noted by the National League of Cities:

> State legislatures have gotten more aggressive in their use of preemption in recent years. Explanations for this increase include lobbying efforts by special interests, spatial sorting of political preferences between urban and rural areas, and single party dominance in most state governments. This last point is particularly important. As preemption efforts often concern a politically divisive issue, they rely on single party dominance to pass through state legislatures.[199]

The increased use of state legislatures' power to preempt local lawmaking has the potential to swallow up meaningful home rule.[200] Furthermore, in non-home-rule states, preemption can occur when local ordinances and state statutes conflict.[201]

In another important state constitutional change, a number of states have amended their constitutions to include legally enforceable restrictions on

[198] Jefferson B. Fordham, Foreword: *Local Government in the Larger Scheme of Things*, 8 Vand. L. Rev. 667, 668, 671 (1955).

[199] National League of Cities, City Rights in an Era of Preemption: A State-by-State Analysis 3 (2017).

[200] Richard Briffault, *The Challenge of the New Preemption*, 70 Stan. L. Rev. 1995 (2018); *see also* Paul Diller, *Intrastate Preemption*, 87 B.U. L. Rev. 1113 (2007).

[201] City of Laredo v. Laredo Merchants Association, 550 S.W.3d 586, 588–89 (2018).

"unfunded mandates" imposed by states on local governments.[202] These constitute *legal* restrictions on what used to be *political* controversies and have added new matters to the state courts' constitutional dockets.[203]

## VII. SUPERMAJORITY VOTING REQUIREMENTS

A number of state constitutions have been amended (by majority vote) to require supermajority legislative votes to enact certain measures, usually concerning taxing and spending.[204] California's Proposition 13, for example, was adopted in 1978 and required a two-thirds vote in the legislature for a state tax increase.[205] A similar restriction was imposed in Michigan.[206] These kinds of provisions operate to modify the usual legislative process.[207]

## VIII. RETROACTIVE STATUTES

A number of state constitutions, in addition to and potentially more restrictively than their ex post facto clauses, explicitly prohibit retroactive laws.[208] Article II, Section 28, of the Ohio Constitution provides that "[t]he general assembly shall have no power to pass retroactive laws." The Ohio Supreme Court, however, has held that "[a] retroactive statute is unconstitutional only if it impairs vested substantive rights, but not if it is merely remedial in nature."[209] Under this

[202] Robert F. Williams & Lawrence Friedman, State Constitutional Law: Cases and Materials 892–94 (5th ed. 2015).

[203] *Id. See* Coast Community College Dist. v. Commission on State Mandates, 514 P.3d 854 (Cal. 2022).

[204] Richard Briffault, *Foreword: The Disfavored Constitution: State Fiscal Limits and State Constitutional Law*, 34 Rutgers L.J. 907, 929–30 (2003).

[205] *Id.* In 1998, the Oregon voters approved an amendment mandating that any proposed state-constitutional amendment imposing a supermajority voting requirement be ratified by at least an equivalent supermajority. Or. Const. art. II, § 23. *See generally* Cody Hoesly, Comment, *Reforming Direct Democracy: Lessons from Oregon*, 93 Cal. L. Rev. 1191 (2005).

[206] Susan P. Fino, *A Cure Worse Than the Disease? Taxation and Finance Provisions in State Constitutions*, 34 Rutgers L.J. 959, 993 (2003).

[207] *See, e.g.*, Guinn v. Legislature of Nevada, 71 P.3d 1269 (Nev. 2003), *decision clarified by* 76 P.3d 22 (Nev. 2003), *overruled* by Nevadans for Nevada v. Beers, 142 P.3d 339, 348 (Nev. 2006). *See* Steve R. Johnson, *Supermajority Provisions,* Guinn v. Legislature *and a Flawed Constitutional Structure*, 4 Nev. L. Rev. 491 (2004).

[208] R.L. v. State of Missouri Dept. of Corrections, 245 S.W.3d 236, 237 (Mo. 2008) ("The 1875 constitutional debates note the constitutional bar on retrospective laws is broader than the ex post facto bars in other states."). *See also* St. Charles Co. Sheriff's Dept. v. Raynor, 301 S.W.3d 56, 68–69 (Mo. 2010); Accident Fund Inc. Co. v. Casey, 550 S.W.3d 76, 81 (Mo. 2018).

[209] Hyle v. Porter, 882 N.E.2d 899, 901 (Ohio 2008); Robinson v. Crown Cork & Seal Co., 335 S.W.3d 126 (Tex. 2011); Marshall J. Tinkle, *Forward Into the Past: State Constitutions and Retroactive Laws*, 65 Temp. L. Rev. 1253 (1992).

distinction, it upheld asbestos-litigation statutes that significantly tightened the requirements for pending cases.[210]

## IX. DIRECT LEGISLATION

The initiative, referendum, and recall movement that emerged in the Progressive Era at the turn of last century was another indication of public dissatisfaction with state legislatures. These forms of direct democracy arose in the states as a popular response to lack of trust in state government, particularly legislatures, which continues today.[211] Initiatives enable the public to bypass unresponsive state legislatures to enact laws, and referenda provide a check on the effect of unpopular statutes. These devices are more sophisticated than the earlier procedural restrictions, most of which reflected general disapproval of legislative actions. The initiative allows the people to take direct, affirmative action when the legislature refuses to act. The referendum enables the people to target specific enactments they wish to block rather than depend on the indirect deterrence of procedural restrictions. Recall permits the voters to oust a government official before the term expires.

Although state constitutions already contained specific provisions requiring a referendum on such questions as assumption of debts and changes in the constitutional text, the people of South Dakota began the process of taking back, or reserving for themselves, a measure of legislative power in a constitutional amendment approved in 1898. Now, more than two dozen states provide for the statutory initiative and/or referenda.[212]

Commentators have predicted that "[t]he more direct legislation you have . . . the greater the body of our judge-made law."[213] This view raises interesting and complex questions of political philosophy, especially today when many major public issues are resolved at the ballot box.[214] As well, legal questions arise with regard to initiated statutes: (1) Can they be amended or repealed by the legislature? (generally yes, unless the state constitution provides to the contrary);[215] (2) Can they be vetoed by the governor? (generally no); (3) Do the title

[210] Ackison v. Anchor Packing Co., 897 N.E.2d 1118, 1124 (Ohio 2008).

[211] Stephen M. Griffin, *California Constitutionalism: Trust in Government and Direct Democracy*, 11 U. PENN. J. CON. L. 551 (2009). *See generally* HENRY S. NOYES, THE LAW OF DIRECT DEMOCRACY (2014).

[212] DAVID MAGLEBY, DIRECT LEGISLATION: VOTING ON BALLOT PROPOSITIONS IN THE UNITED STATES 38–40 (1984). *See generally* THOMAS E. CRONIN, DIRECT DEMOCRACY: THE POLITICS OF INITIATIVE, REFERENDUM AND RECALL (1999).

[213] George Lefcoe & Barney Allison, *The Legal Aspects of Proposition 13: The Amador Valley Case*, 53 S. CAL. L. REV. 173, 173 (1979).

[214] *See* Richard Briffault, *Distrust of Democracy*, 63 TEX. L. REV. 1347 (1985) (reviewing DAVID MAGLEBY, DIRECT LEGISLATION: VOTING ON BALLOT PROPOSITIONS IN THE UNITED STATES (1984)).

[215] People v. Kelly, 222 P.3d 186 (Cal. 2010) (reviewing states and cases).

and single-subject limitations apply? (generally yes); (4) How should courts interpret such statutes? (according to the understanding of the ordinary, intelligent voter).[216]

## X. LEGISLATIVE VETO

A number of state supreme courts declared the "legislative veto" unconstitutional, whereby the legislature purported to enact statutes delegating rulemaking power to executive agencies, but "reserving" the power to disapprove ("veto") agency rules by resolutions.[217] Of course, an administrative rule could be cancelled by the enactment of an actual law.

States like Iowa (1984)[218] and New Jersey (1992)[219] amended their constitutions specifically to authorize the legislative veto by resolution without presentation to the governor. The New Jersey experience is instructive. The state supreme court in *Communications Workers of Am., AFL-CIO v. N.J. Civil Serv. Com'n*[220] ruled that a court may reverse the legislature's invalidation of an agency rule or regulation pursuant to the new Legislative Review Clause if (1) the legislature has not complied with the procedural requirements of the clause; (2) the legislature has incorrectly asserted that the challenged rule or regulation is inconsistent with "the intent of the Legislature as expressed in the language of the statute which the rule or regulation is intended to implement"; or (3) the legislature's action violates a protection afforded by any other provision of the New Jersey Constitution, or a provision of the U.S. Constitution.

## XI. LEGISLATIVE REDISTRICTING

Redrawing of maps for both state and congressional districts, every decade, is one of the important powers of state legislatures. State constitutions contain a number of provisions, independent of federal law, limiting this legislative power in a variety of ways.[221] The U.S. Supreme Court has taken a "hands-off" approach

[216] Much litigation arises over the procedural requirements for initiative lawmaking. *See, e.g.*, Hensley v. Atty. Gen., 53 N.E.3d 639 (Mass. 2016) (single subject); *In re* Initiative Petition, 367 P.3d 472 (Okla. 2016) (same).

[217] State *ex rel.* Barker v. Mauchin, 279 S.E.2d 622 (W. Va. 1981); General Assembly v. Byrne, 448 A.2d 438 (N.J. 1982). L. Harold Levinson, *The Decline of The Legislative Veto: Federal/State Comparisons and Interactions*, 17 PUBLIUS: THE J. FEDERALISM 115 (1987).

[218] IOWA CONST. art. III, §40.

[219] N.J. CONST. art. V, § IV, ¶ 6.

[220] 191 A.3d 643 (N.J. 2018).

[221] *See supra* note 32. *See also* Legislative Research Comm. v. Fischer, 366 S.W.3d 905, 911 (Ky. 2012); Twin Falls County v. Idaho Comm'n on Redistricting, 271 P.3d 1202, 1206–07 (Idaho 2012).

to the issue, holding that partisan gerrymandering presents a nonjusticiable political question for federal courts.[222] Thus, the matter is left to the states. Several states have amended their constitutions to prohibit such gerrymandering.[223]

The Pennsylvania Supreme Court issued a landmark decision in 2018 striking down an extreme partisan gerrymander of congressional districts under the Pennsylvania Constitution's "Free and Equal Elections Clause."[224] This clause, dating from 1776, appears in at least a dozen other state constitutions.[225]

There is a federal constitutional cloud, however, over cases like *League of Women Voters* and even some of the state judicial decisions surrounding the 2020 election. Some advocates have argued for the existence of the so-called "Independent State Legislature Doctrine," based on Article I, Section 4, Clause 1, of the U.S. Constitution, which provides that the "Legislature" of each state make rules for congressional elections. On this theory, the power of state courts, and even state governors, may be limited in respect to state statutes concerning federal elections.[226] In other words, as the argument goes, only statutes enacted by the state legislature, and not state court judicial review, can apply to federal elections.

The U.S. Supreme Court declined, in 2021, to hear a Pennsylvania case in which the state supreme court extended the date for counting mail-in votes because of the COVID-19 pandemic, relying on the Free and Equal Elections Clause of the state constitution.[227] Although Justices Thomas, Alito, and Gorsuch dissented, the Supreme Court has since indicated that it intends to examine this issue.[228] Recent scholarship examining the Independent State Legislature

[222] Rucho v. Common Cause, 588 U.S. ___ (2019).

[223] Fla. Const. art. 10, § 20: "No apportionment plan or individual district shall be drawn with the intent to favor or disfavor a political party or an incumbent . . ."; League of Women Voters v. Detzner, 179 So.3d 258 (Fla. 2015). *See also* Cal. Const. art. 21, §§ 1, 2, & 3; Ohio Const. art. XI, §§ 6(A) and 6(B) (2015 amendment requiring districting to be fair and proportionate); League of Women Voters of Ohio v. Ohio Redistricting Commission, ___N.E.3d ___ (Ohio 2022); Adams v. DeWine, ___N.E.3d ___ (Ohio 2022); Harper v. Representative Destin Hall, 868 S.E.3d 499 (N.C. 2022).

[224] League of Women Voters of Pa. v. Comm., 178 A.3d 737 (Pa. 2018). The court relied on Article I, Section 5: "Elections shall be free and equal; and no power, civil or military, shall at anytime interfere to prevent the free exercise of the right of suffrage." *See generally* Primo J. Cruz, Note, *Pols Gone Wild: Why State Constitutional Equality Provisions Are a Proper Solution to Partisan Gerrymandering*, 32 Rutgers L.J. 727 (2011); Charlie Stewart, *State Court Litigation: The New Front in the War Against Partisan Gerrymandering*, 116 Mich. L. Rev. Online 152 (2018); Benard Grofman & Jonathan R. Cervas, *Can State Courts Cure Partisan Gerrymandering: Lessons from League of* Women Voters v. Commonwealth of Pennsylvania (2018), 17 Election L.J. 364 (2018); Samuel S.-H. Wang, Richard F. Ober, & Ben Williams, *Laboratories of Democracy Reform: State Constitutions and Partisan Gerrymandering*, 22 U. Pa. J. Const. L. 203 (2019); Emily Rong Zhang, *Bolstering Faith with Facts; Supporting Independent Redistricting Commissions with Redistricting Algorithms*, 109 Cal. L. Rev. 987 (2021).

[225] *Id.* at 178 A.3d at 813 n.71.

[226] *See also* U.S. Const. art. II, § 1, cl. 2. *See generally* Michael T. Morley, *The Independent State Legislative Doctrine, Federal Elections, and State Constitutions*, 55 Ga. L. Rev. 1 (2020); Michael T. Morley, *The Independent State Legislature Doctrine*, 90 Fordham L. Rev. 501 (2021).

[227] Republican Party of Pennsylvania v. Degraffenreid, 592 U.S. ___ (2021).

[228] *See* Moore v. Harper, 2022 WL 2347621 (granting petition for certiorari).

Doctrine suggests that, in fact, where elections are concerned, "the Founding generation understood that 'legislatures' would operate as normal legislatures, not independent legislatures, with respect to both procedure and substance."[229]

## XII. CONCLUSION

The state legislative branch is a substantially different entity from its federal counterpart, the U.S. Congress. A state legislature operates with plenary, residual power rather than enumerated power, with some important exceptions. State legislatures are subject to fairly rigid, judicially enforceable procedural limits on their lawmaking processes, arising from a history of legislative abuses. Finally, in states where the people have direct lawmaking power, legislative authority is shared between the legislature and the people.

[229] Hayward H. Smith, *Revisiting the History of the Independent State Legislature Doctrine*, 55 St. Mary's L.J. 445, 580 (2022). *See also* Mark S. Krass, *Debunking the Non-Delegation Doctrine for State Regulation of Federal Elections*, 108 Va. L. Rev. 1091, 1112–29 (2022) (local power was a common feature of election administration in the nation's early years); Eliza Sweren-Becker & Michael Waldman, *The Meaning, History, and Importance of the Elections Clause*, 96 Wash. L. Rev. 997 (2021) (original intent of federal Elections Clause was to limit power of state lawmakers).

# 10
# THE STATE JUDICIAL BRANCH

In the last quarter of the twentieth century, American state courts emerged as major policymakers, taking their place alongside federal courts as important judicial actors in governmental lawmaking. This statement is not intended to raise the "parity" debate over whether state courts are equal to federal courts in protecting constitutional rights.[1] Rather, it is intended to point out the transformation that many state courts have gone through in the fairly recent past and continue to go through today. After all, it has not been long that a conservative American president attacking "activist judges" could have been referring to state courts!

The controversial decision on same-sex marriage by the Massachusetts Supreme Judicial Court, *Goodridge v. Department of Public Health*,[2] which we discussed in the introduction to this book, may be the most broadly influential state court decision, in a wide variety of ways, in recent memory.[3] As discussed in our introductory chapter, a line of state constitutional decisions on marriage equality preceded the U.S. Supreme Court's same-sex marriage case, *Obergefell v. Hodges*.[4] *Goodridge*, together with an earlier Vermont decision[5] and later California, Connecticut, and Iowa rulings,[6] illustrate how state courts in many jurisdictions have developed into major policymaking branches of state government.

[1] *See generally* Burt Neuborne, *The Myth of Parity*, 90 Harv. L. Rev. 1105 (1977); Michael E. Solimine, *The Future of Parity*, 46 Wm. & Mary L. Rev. 1457 (2005).

[2] Goodridge v. Dep't of Pub. Health, 798 N.E.2d 941 (Mass. 2003); Opinions of the Justices to the Senate, 802 N.E.2d 565 (Mass. 2004).

[3] *See generally* Lawrence Friedman, *The (Relative) Passivity of Goodridge v. Department of Public Health*, 14 B.U. Pub. Int. L.J. 1 (2004). The *Goodridge* majority opinion by Chief Justice Margaret Marshall (originally from South Africa) made use of constitutional rulings from Canada. *Goodridge*, 798 N.E.2d at 969. Chief Justice Marshall explained her reliance on constitutional materials from other countries in Margaret H. Marshall, "*Wise Parents Do Not Hesitate to Learn from Their Children*": *Interpreting State Constitutions in an Age of Global Jurisprudence*, 79 N.Y.U. L. Rev. 1633 (2004). *See* Chapter 12.

[4] 576 U.S. 644 (2015).

[5] Baker v. State, 744 A.2d 864 (Vt. 1999); *see also* Robert F. Williams, *Old Constitutions and New Issues: National Lessons from Vermont's State Constitutional Case on Marriage of Same-Sex Couples*, 43 B.C. L. Rev. 73 (2001) [hereinafter *Old Constitutions and New Issues*].

[6] *In re* Marriage Cases, 183 P.3d 384 (Cal. 2008); Kerrigan v. Commissioner of Public Health, 957 A.2d 407 (Conn. 2008); Varnum v. Brien, 763 N.W.2d 862 (Iowa 2009).

*The Law of American State Constitutions*. Robert F. Williams and Lawrence Friedman, Oxford University Press.
 DOI: 10.1093/oso/9780190068806.003.0011

American state courts, not long ago, were seen as institutions primarily concerned with private and criminal law adjudication, operating in a rather narrow, precedent-bound manner.[7] This began to change with the plaintiff-oriented, nonconstitutional innovations in substantive tort law that some state courts began to develop in the 1960s.[8]

Studies have shown a broader transition in the work of state supreme courts.[9] One of these studies concluded that, even by the late 1970s, state supreme court justices had come "to view their role less conservatively" and seemed "to be less concerned with the stabilization and protection of property rights, more concerned with the individual and the downtrodden, and more willing to consider rulings that promote social change."[10] Probably the most important development reflecting the emergence of state courts as policymakers has been the "New Judicial Federalism," covered in Part II of this book.

The courts, of course, did not begin as a coequal branch of government under the original state constitutions. The early state constitutions, although often textually recognizing the doctrine of separation of powers, favored the legislative branch.[11] James Madison observed, at the federal Constitutional Convention, that under the state constitutions, "[e]xperience had proved a tendency in our governments to throw all power into the Legislative vortex."[12]

In Pennsylvania, for example, justices of the state supreme court under the 1776 constitution, "though appointed for a seven-year term at a fixed salary, could be removed by the legislature at any time for 'misbehavior.'"[13] Final judgments of the Pennsylvania courts were regularly overturned by the legislature. Under New Jersey's 1776 constitution, the court of last resort was the upper

[7] Of course, state courts did strike down, in *Lochner*-like fashion, many Progressive Era statutes around the turn of the last century. Many progressives who distrust the potential of judicial review base that distrust on fear of a return to those days.

[8] G. Alan Tarr & Mary Cornelia Aldis Porter, State Supreme Courts in State and Nation 34–40 (1988).

[9] *See, e.g.*, Robert A. Kagan et al., *The Business of State Supreme Courts, 1870–1970*, 30 Stan. L. Rev. 121, 152–55 (1977) [hereinafter Kagan et al., *The Business of State Supreme Courts*] (describing a shift in the focus of state supreme courts from commercial to noncommercial cases); Robert A. Kagan et al., *The Evolution of State Supreme Courts*, 76 Mich. L. Rev. 961, 998–1001 (1978) (suggesting that changes in the structure of state courts have allowed them to focus more on social and economic cases); Lawrence M. Friedman et al., *State Supreme Courts: A Century of Style and Citation*, 33 Stan. L. Rev. 773, 817–18 (1981) (documenting a trend of increasingly elaborate state court opinions).

[10] Kagan et al., *The Business of State Supreme Courts*, *supra* note 9, at 155.

[11] Gerhard Casper, *An Essay in Separation of Powers: Some Early Versions and Practices*, 30 Wm. & Mary L. Rev. 211, 216–19 (1989) (stating that, although states introduced separation of powers clauses into their constitutions, in reality the legislature continued to overshadow the other branches).

[12] 2 The Records of the Federal Convention of 1787, 35 (Max Farrand ed., 2d ed. 1937); *see also* The Federalist No. 48, 322 (J. Madison) (Sherman F. Mitchell ed., 1937) (cautioning against encroachment by the legislature); Robert F. Williams, *The State Constitutions of the Founding Decade: Pennsylvania's Radical 1776 Constitution and Its Influences on American Constitutionalism*, 62 Temp. L. Rev. 541, 574–75 (1989).

[13] Williams, *supra* note 12, at 556.

house of the legislature, providing *political* review of *legal* judgments, and judges were selected by the legislature.[14] In sharp contrast, we find the ringing words of Article XXIX of the 1780 Massachusetts Declaration of Rights, which are still relevant today:

> It is essential to the preservation of the rights of every individual, his life, liberty, property, and character, that there be an impartial interpretation of the laws, and administration of justice. It is the right of every citizen to be tried by judges as free, impartial, and independent as the lot of humanity will admit. It is, therefore, not only the best policy, but for the security of the rights of the people, and of every citizen, that the judges of the supreme judicial court should hold their offices as long as they behave themselves well, and that they should have honorable salaries ascertained and established by standing laws.

Bringing the other two branches to some form of parity, or at least bringing them closer to being "co-equal" with the legislature, would continue to occupy state constitutional framers for at least the next century.[15] As the state constitutions were revised over time, not only was the executive branch strengthened to enable it to stand up to the legislature but the judicial branch was similarly strengthened for the same reason. The primary motivation behind the move to an elected judiciary in many states between 1840 and 1860 was to enable judges to protect property and individual rights from the still powerful, party-dominated state legislatures.[16]

One of the important components of judicial independence, recognized early in Massachusetts, is the prohibition on the reduction in judicial compensation during judges' terms of office. In Illinois, after a complicated series of events led to the cancellation of judges' statutory cost-of-living raise, that action was invalidated under Article VI, Section 14 of the Illinois Constitution.[17] On the other hand, in New Jersey, after the state supreme court struck down statutory increases to judges pension and health-care contributions as a diminution to their "salary,"[18] an amendment was quickly adopted permitting such increases.[19]

[14] Robert F. Williams, The New Jersey State Constitution: A Reference Guide 5 (Rev. ed. 1997).

[15] *See* James A. Henretta, *Foreword: Rethinking the State Constitutional Tradition*, 22 Rutgers L.J. 819, 821–26 (1991).

[16] *Id.* at 834–35. *See infra* note 50 and accompanying text.

[17] Jorgensen v. Blagojevich, 811 N.E.2d 652 (Ill. 2004); Stilp v. Commonwealth, 905 A.2d 918, 939–49 (Pa. 2006).

[18] DePascale v. State of New Jersey, 47 A.3d 690 (N.J. 2012). *Contra* Bransten v. State, 90 N.E.3d 818 (N.Y. 2017).

[19] N.J. Const. art. VI, § VI, ¶ 6.

Cases concerning issues like judicial salary reduction call on state supreme courts to rule on *their own* rights and powers. Relying on "jurisdiction by necessity," such courts will often do so.[20]

## I. THE NATURE OF STATE JUDICIAL POWER

State courts are not simply "little" versions of the federal courts. A large majority of state judges face the electorate in either partisan, nonpartisan, or merit-retention elections.[21] The range of powers allocated to the judicial branch under state constitutions differs both quantitatively and qualitatively from the "judicial power" enumerated in Article III of the U.S. Constitution. One of the most important innovations in state court structure in the twentieth century was the advent of intermediate appeals courts, which are often the courts of last resort for many matters, thereby freeing state supreme courts from some of the pressure of caseloads and allowing them to focus more on broad policy rulings.[22] This structural change is a major contributing factor to state supreme courts' emergence as policymakers.

When the 1947 New Jersey Constitutional Convention revised the judicial article, it designed the state supreme court on the model of the U.S. Supreme Court.[23] This would have been unheard of fifty years earlier. The New Jersey Supreme Court, based partly on its structure and partly on gubernatorial *appointment* practices, has become (not with everyone's approval) one of the leading policymaking state supreme courts in the country.[24] It exercises its powers to make policy, like many other state courts, not only through constitutional adjudication but also through statutory interpretation, common-law cases, and

[20] *See Gabler v. Crime Victims Rights Bd.*, 897 N.W.2d 384 (Wis. 2017).

[21] G. Alan Tarr, *Designing an Appointive System: The Key Issues*, 34 FORDHAM URBAN L.J. 291, 291 (2007).

[22] *See generally* Note, *Courting Reversal: The Supervisory Role of State Supreme Courts*, 87 YALE L.J. 1191, 1200–02 (1978) (discussing the role of intermediate appellate courts in state supreme court decision-making); Project, *The Effect of Court Structure on State Supreme Court Opinions: A Re-Examination*, 33 STAN. L. REV. 951, 961 (1981) (concluding that structural changes to state appellate courts influence the style of opinions); *Symposium, Caught in the Middle: The Role of State Intermediate Appellate Courts*, 35 IND. L. REV. 329 (2002).

[23] *See* TARR & PORTER, *supra* note 8, at 186–96 (tracing the development of the New Jersey Supreme Court).

[24] *See* Stewart G. Pollock, *Foreword: Celebrating Fifty Years of Judicial Reform Under the 1947 New Jersey Constitution*, 29 RUTGERS L.J. 675 (1998); John B. Wefing, *The New Jersey Supreme Court 1948–1998: Fifty Years of Independence and Activism*, 29 RUTGERS L.J. 701 (1998); Kevin M. Mulcahy, *Modeling the Garden: How New Jersey Built the Most Progressive State Supreme Court and What California Can Learn*, 40 SANTA CLARA L. REV. 863 (2000); Jake Dear & Edward W. Jessen, *"Followed Rates" and Leading State Cases, 1940–2005*, 41 U.C. DAVIS L. REV. 683 (2007).

rulemaking.[25] In fact, rights decisions in state high courts that are more protective than federal constitutional law are not only based on state constitutions but on common law or statute.[26]

Some scholars in the past generation have begun to question whether constitutional law-reform litigation in the courts has really been very effective. For example, Professor Gerald Rosenberg contended that courts (primarily federal) are rarely able to produce "significant social reform" through litigated cases because there are three structural constraints on the American judiciary:

1. Constitutional rights are of a limited nature.
2. There is a lack of judicial independence.
3. The judiciary lacks the power to implement its decisions.

Despite these constraints, under these conditions he concluded that litigation may result in significant social change:

1. There is already existing legal precedent for the change that is sought through litigation.
2. The executive and a substantial number of legislators support the change.
3. Some of the citizens support the change, or at least not very many citizens oppose the change, and either:
   a) There are positive incentives for compliance with the court's decree.
   b) Failure to comply will result in costs being imposed.
   c) Market implementation can support compliance with the judicial decision.
   d) Officials or those whose support is crucial for implementing the judicial decision are willing to engage in such implementation, and they see judicial decisions as enabling them to leverage additional resources or as something they can "hide behind" as they implement the judicial decision.

Needless to say, Professor Rosenberg finds that there are very few instances where these constraints can be overcome and the required conditions met.[27]

25 TARR & PORTER, *supra* note 8, at 233–36.

26 Judith S. Kaye, *Foreword: The Common Law and State Constitutional Law as Full Partners in the Protection of Individual Rights*, 23 RUTGERS L.J. 727, 750–52 (1992).

27 *See* GERALD N. ROSENBERG, THE HOLLOW HOPE: CAN COURTS BRING ABOUT SOCIAL CHANGE? 35–36 (1991). Rosenberg has published a new edition, reaffirming his conclusions, and including a section on the state court same-sex marriage litigation. For a similar pessimistic assessment, see STUART A. SCHEINGOLD, THE POLITICS OF RIGHTS: LAWYERS, PUBLIC POLICY, AND POLITICAL CHANGE (1989).

Many other commentators, however, do not share a similar skepticism. Of course, these factors may play out differently in state constitutional law.[28]

In analyzing judicial power under modern state constitutions, Professor Adrian Vermeule has distinguished between "freestanding judicial power" and "specific constitutional provisions that protect or regulate the judiciary's authority and jurisdiction."[29] The former category is the general concept of judicial power arising from a state constitution's assignment of this power to the courts in the judicial article.[30] The latter category covers the more specific state constitutional grants of authority to the judiciary, such as the judicial rulemaking power, the power to regulate the practice of law, and the prohibition on legislative reductions of judicial compensation, as well as the individual's right to a jury trial and a remedy for injuries.[31]

Professor Vermeule surveyed a number of state cases purporting to exercise freestanding judicial power (he did not analyze specific judicial power cases) and concluded that these cases reflected the courts' "paranoid style," including a "tendency to rhetorical excess, in particular a certain belligerence and defensiveness."[32] He further concluded that they "sweep beyond any defensible conception of judicial power."[33] This led him to propose that freestanding judicial power claims be considered nonjusticiable.[34]

As we saw in Chapter 8, two of the ways of looking at separation-of-powers controversies are formal or functional. The functionalist approach seems to permit much more judicial discretion than the formalist approach.[35] The functionalist judge attempts to assess whether there is any actual harm arising from an alleged encroachment. Even if there is a minor encroachment, the functionalist judge may tolerate it if there is no resulting harm. The formalist judge evaluates encroachment claims based on a more abstract, conceptual view of what constitutes "judicial power." Obviously, there is not a clear line of demarcation between these approaches.

Vermeule argued that what has been called the functional approach would be insufficiently protective of judicial power because "case-specific balancing,"[36] where the specifics of the legislative policy are weighed against the allegedly conflicting judicial power, would often compromise judicial power in deference to an urgent legislative public policy. As Professor Vermeule put it:

[28] Robert F. Williams, *Juristocracy in the American States?* 65 Md. L. Rev. 68 (2006).
[29] Adrian Vermeule, *The Judicial Power in the State (and Federal) Courts*, 2000 Sup. Ct. Rev. 357, 357 n.1 (2001).
[30] *Id.* at 359.
[31] *Id.* at 357 n.1.
[32] *Id.* at 360, 387.
[33] *Id.* at 360.
[34] *Id.* at 361.
[35] *Id.* at 363–64.
[36] *Id.* at 365.

The short-term benefits of "innovative action" would predictably appear far more appealing to the judges, in the setting of particular cases, than the seemingly abstract and speculative benefits of judicial independence.[37]

These perspectives are well worth considering in circumstances where state courts must rule on possible encroachments by the legislature or executive on their own judicial power.

## II. JUDICIAL REVIEW

The texts of state constitutions, by contrast to the federal Constitution, may provide for state judicial review of legislative and executive action.[38] For example, Article I, Section 2, Paragraph 5 of the Georgia Constitution provides: "Legislative Acts in violation of this Constitution or the Constitution of the United States are void, and the judiciary shall so declare them." The Illinois Constitution prohibits the legislature from enacting "special" laws where general laws can be made applicable, and states that "[w]hether a general law is or can be made applicable shall be a matter for judicial determination."[39]

In fact, judicial review itself was a phenomenon of state law well before *Marbury v. Madison*.[40] As well, and contrary to the federal experience, most judiciary provisions of state constitutions have been adopted, revised and ratified in the past century without serious struggles over the exercise of judicial review. It must be remembered, in addition, that judicial review in state courts often takes place in the context of executive or administrative actions, including those by individual police officers or officials, rather than challenging the constitutionality of statutes passed by the legislature.[41]

[37] *Id.* at 368.

[38] Judicial review, both state and federal, often begins with expressions of deference to the legislative branch. For a thorough analysis, see Robert A. Schapiro, *Judicial Deference and Interpretative Coordinacy in State and Federal Constitutional Law*, 85 CORNELL L. REV. 656 (2000).

[39] ILL. CONST. art. IV, § 13 (emphasis added); *see also* COLO. CONST. art. II, § 15 (stating that property may not be taken for public or private use without just compensation and that "the question whether the contemplated use be really public shall be a judicial question, and determined as such without regard to any legislative assertion that the use is public").

[40] 5 U.S. (1 Cranch) 137 (1803). *See* Edward S. Corwin, *The Progress of Constitutional Theory Between the Declaration of Independence and the Meeting of the Philadelphia Convention*, 30 AM. HIST. REV. 511, 521 (1925); William E. Nelson, *Commentary, Changing Conceptions of Judicial Review: The Evolution of Constitutional Theory in the States, 1790–1860*, 120 U. PA. L. REV. 1166, 1169–70 (1972); William E. Nelson, *The Eighteenth Century Background of John Marshall's Constitutional Jurisprudence*, 76 MICH. L. REV. 893 (1978); SYLVIA SNOWISS, JUDICIAL REVIEW AND THE LAW OF THE CONSTITUTION (1990); William Michael Treanor, *Judicial Review Before* Marbury, 58 STAN. L. REV. 455 (2005).

[41] *Cf.* Seth F. Kreimer, *Exploring the Dark Matter of Judicial Review: A Constitutional Census of the 1990's*, 5 WM. & MARY BILL RTS. J. 427 (1997).

Several states have sought to restrict judicial review. For example, the North Dakota Constitution provides:

> A majority of the supreme court [consisting of 5 justices] shall be necessary to constitute a quorum or to pronounce a decision, provided that the supreme court shall not declare a legislative enactment unconstitutional unless at least four of the members of the court so decide.[42]

This provision limits judicial review by requiring a supermajority of the court to declare a statute unconstitutional. This approach to judicial review was a product of the Progressive Movement.[43]

Several other states have included provisions in their constitutions expressly *removing* certain questions from the realm of judicial review. In Michigan, for instance, the sufficiency of grounds for recall of a public official "shall be a political rather than a judicial question."[44] In New Jersey, the voters amended the constitution to bar legislative or administrative mandates to local government without the funding to perform such mandatory activities, created a Council on Local Mandates to determine if unfunded mandates have been imposed on local governments, and provided that the Council's decisions "shall be political and not judicial determinations."[45] The Texas voters in 1986 amended the title requirement for bills to provide that "the legislature is solely responsible for determining compliance with the rule" and that "a law . . . may not be held void on the basis of an insufficient title."[46]

All of these distinctions support the conclusion that state judicial review, like so many other elements of state constitutional law, is not simply a little version of the more-familiar federal model.[47]

[42] N.D. Const. art. VI, § 4. *See also* Neb. Const. art. V, § 2. In *Bismarck Pub. Sch. Dist. No. 1 v. State*, 511 N.W.2d 247, 250 (N.D. 1994), the North Dakota Supreme Court rejected a state constitutional challenge to its school financing statutes when three out of the five justices viewed them as unconstitutional.

[43] *See* John Dinan, *Framing a "People's Government": State Constitution-making in the Progressive Era*, 30 Rutgers L.J. 933, 949–57 (1999). *See also* John J. Dinan, The American State Constitutional Tradition 125–34 (2006). For an excellent analysis of Ohio's former supermajority provision, see Jonathan L. Entin, *Judicial Supermajorities and the Validity of Statutes: How* Mapp *Became a Fourth Amendment Landmark Instead of a First Amendment Footnote*, 52 Case W. Res. L. Rev. 441 (2001).

[44] Mich. Const. art. II, § 8.

[45] N.J. Const. art. VIII, § II, ¶ 5.

[46] Tex. Const. art. III, § 35(b), (c). *See* Ford Motor Co. v. Sheldon, 22 S.W.3d 444, 452 (Tex. 2000).

[47] For a very thoughtful analysis of state judicial review, see David Schultz, *State Courts and Democratic Theory: Toward a Theory of State Constitutional Judicial Review*, 45 Mitchell Hamline L. Rev. 575 (2019). Schultz pointed out that both the counter majoritarian and majoritarian questions are different for state rather than federal courts. *See also* Walt Cubberty, *New Foundations for Constitutional Adjudication in State Courts*, 24 App. Advoc. 425 (2012).

## III. JUDICIAL SELECTION

State constitutions govern the judicial branch in many respects. They have been the vehicles for streamlining and unifying state court systems. They usually set forth in some detail the jurisdiction of most state courts. Finally, the method of selection and tenure of state judges is controlled by the state constitution.

By contrast to federal judges with lifetime appointments, most state judges are elected in one format or another. In fact, a leading commentator estimated that "more than eighty-seven percent of state judges go before the voters at some point in their careers."[48] Still, appointment is important because of initial appointments, as well as those to fill unexpired terms.[49] The advent of the elected judiciary, as an element of Jacksonian Democracy, was an attempt to strengthen judges to stand up to the powerful state legislatures.[50] Among the most well-known judicial elections was the 1986 California Supreme Court election, in which three sitting justices, including Chief Justice Rose Bird, were voted out of office.[51] The two objectives, judicial independence and judicial accountability, remain in some tension.[52] Further, elections for state high court justices continue to grow more expensive and controversial.[53] Strong backlashes against state supreme court justices, such as those in Iowa after the state supreme court's marriage equality decision, are more common.[54]

As Professor Charles Geyh has stated, "[W]ithout legitimacy, the judiciary is helpless to thwart defiance of its decisions."[55] If a state installs an appointive system and the "public ceases to trust judges or those who appoint judges," then opting for electoral accountability could "preserve or restore legitimacy." On the other hand, if the public comes to view and electoral system as "including the

48 Roy A. Schotland, *Comment*, 71 LAW & CONTEMP. PROBS. 149, 154–55 (1998).

49 Tarr, *supra* note 21, at 291.

50 Caleb Nelson, *A Re-Evaluation of Scholarly Explanations for the Rise of the Elective Judiciary in Antebellum America*, 37 AM. J. LEGAL HIST. 190 (1993).

51 This election is analyzed by Joseph R. Grodin, himself one of the justices, in IN PURSUIT OF JUSTICE: REFLECTIONS OF A STATE SUPREME COURT JUSTICE (1989). For further analysis, see John T. Wold & John H. Culver, *The Defeat of the California Justices: The Campaign, the Electorate, and the Issue of Judicial Accountability*, 70 JUDICATURE 348 (1987); Robert S. Thompson, *Judicial Retention Elections and Judicial Method: A Retrospective on the California Retention Election of 1986*, 61 S. CAL. L. REV. 2007 (1988). *See also* John B. Wefing, *State Supreme Court Justices: Who Are They?* 32 NEW ENG. L. REV. 47 (1997).

52 *See* G. ALAN TARR, WITHOUT FEAR OR FAVOR: JUDICIAL INDEPENDENCE AND JUDICIAL ACCOUNTABILITY IN THE STATES (2012).

53 *See, e.g.*, *Symposium, The Impact of Dark Money on Judicial Elections and Judicial Behavior*, 67 DEPAUL L. REV. 169 (2018); Hugh D. Spitzer & Philip A. Talmadge, *Amending Codes of Conduct to Impose Campaign Contribution and Expenditure Limits on Judicial Campaigns*, 25 VA. J. SOC. & L. 87 (2018); MELINDA GANN HALL, ATTACKING JUDGES: HOW CAMPAIGN ADVERTISING INFLUENCES STATE SUPREME COURT ELECTIONS (2015).

54 *See, e.g.*, David E. Pozen, *What Happened in Iowa?* 111 COLUM. L. REV. SIDEBAR 90 (2011).

55 Charles Gardner Geyh, *Judicial Selection and the Search for Middle Ground*, 67 DEPAUL L. REV. 333 (2018).

perception that justice is for sale in privately financed judicial campaigns," the pressure will arise for an appointed system.[56] Dr. Alan Tarr has described the controversy over state courts:

> Both sides in the contemporary debate over judicial independence and judicial accountability—we shall refer to them as the Bashers and the Defenders—claim to support the rule of law, but they disagree about what threatens it. Defenders see the danger as coming from external pressures on judges by those who seek to influence or intimidate them or induce them to abandon their commitment to the law in favor of what is popular or politically acceptable. But Bashers view the danger as rooted in the absence of checks on judges, which frees them to pursue their political or ideological or professional or class agendas at the expense of fidelity to the law. Impartial decision making, according to Bashers, is best promoted by the prospect of retribution for judicial activism, which keeps in line judges who might otherwise be tempted to read their own preferences into the law.[57]

## IV. RULES OF PRACTICE AND PROCEDURE

Supreme courts in many states have constitutional authority to promulgate rules of practice and procedure for the courts. Although this power now is explicitly granted in many constitutions, earlier commentators regarded it as an inherent judicial power.[58] Exercise of the rulemaking power reaches such crucial areas of lawyers' and judges' work as discovery and class actions.

To the extent that state constitutions assign to the judiciary the power to promulgate rules of practice and procedure, conflicting statutes enacted by the legislature arguably constitute an unconstitutional encroachment on specifically enumerated judicial power. In a 1950 New Jersey case, *Winberry v. Salisbury*,[59] the court struck down a statute on the timing of appeals in direct conflict with a court rule. Concluding that the matter concerned "practice and procedure," the court invalidated the conflicting statute but indicated that it would "not make substantive law wholesale through the exercise of the rulemaking power."[60] Years

[56] *Id.* at 367–68.

[57] G. ALAN TARR, WITHOUT FEAR OR FAVOR: JUDICIAL INDEPENDENCE AND JUDICIAL ACCOUNTABILITY IN THE STATES 2 (2012).

[58] *See* Roscoe Pound, *The Rulemaking Power of the Courts*, 12 A.B.A. J. 599 (1926); John Henry Wigmore, *All Legislative Rules for Judiciary Procedure are Void Constitutionally*, 23 ILL. L. REV. 276 (1928); *see also* Solomon v. State, 364 P.3d 536 (Kan. 2015); Mendoza v. WIS International, Inc., 490 S.W.3d 298 (Ark. 2016); Brown v. Cox, 387 P.3d 1040 (Utah 2017).

[59] 74 A.2d 406 (N.J. 1950), *cert. denied*, 340 U.S. 877 (1950).

[60] *Id.* at 410. *Winberry* led to a spirited debate in the *Harvard Law Review. See* Benjamin Kaplan & Warren J. Greene, *The Legislature's Relation to Judicial Rule-Making: An Appraisal of* Winberry v. Salisbury, 65 HARV. L. REV. 234 (1951); and Roscoe Pound, *Procedure Under Rules of Court in New*

later, in 1973, the court upheld its own rule providing for prejudgment interest.[61] Against an argument that this was substantive, the court noted that the procedure/substance dichotomy was unclear; there was no conflicting statute as there had been in *Winberry*; and because the court could make substantive law in its adjudicatory role, there should be no complaint when it arguably did so through rulemaking.[62]

In the converse situation, where the legislature enacted an arguably procedural rape shield law and there was no conflicting court rule, the Colorado Supreme Court noted that this was a "mixed" question of substance and procedure, took a functionalist view, and upheld the statute.[63] It stated that:

> [I]f government is to serve the people, each branch must seek to cooperate fully with the other two. Confrontations of constitutional authority are seldom in the long-term public interest and therefore are to be avoided where possible. Rather, mutual understanding, respect and self-restraint, the lubricants of good government, are to be sought.[64]

The Florida Supreme Court, for example, has been willing to accept policy judgments embodied in legislation which, although technically unconstitutional as an incursion into the court's rulemaking power, reflect a needed change or addition to "practice and procedure." It does this by adopting the legislative provision as a court rule.[65]

Should prior judicial interpretations of judicial rules be entitled to more or less precedential value than other precedents? Chief Justice Stanley G. Feldman of the Arizona Supreme Court wrote:

> In matters relating to the interpretation and application of court rules and procedures, this court must pay constant attention to developments in court procedures and changing circumstances in order to fulfill our constitutional role. *See* Ariz. Const. art. 6, § 5. In furtherance of this responsibility, we will

*Jersey*, 66 HARV. L. REV. 28 (1952). An attempt to overrule *Winberry* by state constitutional amendment in 1951 failed. Kaplan & Greene, *supra*, at 252–53.

[61] Busik v. Levine, 307 A.2d 571 (N.J. 1973). The Court later amended the rule to permit the trial court to suspend prejudgment interest in "exceptional cases." Kotzian v. Barr, 408 A.2d 131, 132–33 (N.J. 1979).

[62] *Busik*, 307 A.2d at 583. *See also* Murphy v. Liberty Mutual Insurance Co., 274 A.3d 412 (Md. 2022).

[63] People v. McKenna, 585 P.2d 275 (Colo. 1978).

[64] *Id.* at 279.

[65] *See, e.g.*, *In re* Clarification of Florida Rules of Practice and Procedure, 281 So.2d 204 (Fla. 1973); Avila South Condo. Ass'n v. Kappa Corp., 347 So.2d 599, 607–08 (Fla. 1977). *See also* Busik v. Levine, 307 A.2d 571, 583 n.10 (N.J. 1973).

reevaluate prior decisions regarding court procedures, where principles of stare decisis might counsel otherwise in substantive matters involving common law decision-making or statutory or constitutional interpretation.[66]

## V. REGULATION OF THE PRACTICE OF LAW

Another power initially claimed to be inherent in the judiciary relates to the admission to practice and discipline of attorneys.[67] Many state constitutions now expressly confer this power upon high courts and, again, as a grant of judicial authority, this power serves as a limitation on the legislature. Surprisingly to many people, state legislatures in such states may not pass statutes concerning the admission to practice and discipline of lawyers. A series of cases in Pennsylvania held that the state ethics act could not be applied to lawyers.[68] "Sunset" legislation applying to statutes regulating professions may not apply to the practice of law.

The New Jersey Supreme Court, for example, has held that its power in this area is exclusive.[69] Still, the New Jersey court has indicated a willingness to uphold important legislation even if it touches on the question of attorney discipline, as it did in upholding legislative conflict-of-interest restrictions on public officials, including judges.[70] The court noted that it had not spoken by rule in the area and that, although it had "ultimate power" over the matter, it could "tolerate actions of other branches of government" for legitimate public policy reasons where there is minimal encroachment.[71] The court distinguished the *existence* of judicial power from its *exercise*.[72] This was clearly a functionalist decision, concluding that no harm arose from the minimal legislative encroachment.

Through the exercise of their power to regulate the bar, state courts have promulgated the modern student practice rules that form that basis for clinical

[66] Hedlund v. Sheldon, 840 P.2d 1008, 1009 (Ariz. 1992). *See also* State v. Mendoza, 823 P.2d 51 (Ariz. 1992).

[67] *See* Petition of the Florida State Bar Ass'n, 40 S.2d 902, 905–06 (Fla. 1949), and cases cited therein. *See also* Board of Overseers of the Bar v. Lee, 422 A.2d 998, 1002 (Me. 1980).

[68] *See* Wajert v. State Ethics Comm'n, 420 A.2d 439 (Pa. 1980); Ballou v. State Ethics Comm'n, 424 A.2d 983 (Pa. Commw. Ct. 1981); Kremer v. State Ethics Comm'n, 424 A.2d 968 (Pa. Commw. Ct. 1981) (judges); *contra* Knight v. City of Margate, 431 A.2d 833 (NJ. 1981). *See also* Persels and Associates v. Banking Commissioner, 122 A.3d 592 (Conn. 2015); Injured Workers Assoc. of Utah v. State, 374 P.3d 14 (Utah 2016). *See generally* Joseph D. Robertson & John W. Buehler, *The Separation of Powers and the Regulation of the Practice of Law in Oregon*, 13 WILLAMETTE L.J. 273 (1977).

[69] McKeown–Brand v. Trump Castle Hotel & Casino, 626 A.2d 425 (N.J. 1993).

[70] Knight v. Margate, 431 A.2d 833 (N.J. 1981).

[71] *Id.* at 842, 841.

[72] *Id.* at 841.

legal education.[73] The New Jersey Supreme Court utilized the power to place limits on attorneys' fees for tort cases,[74] and most courts continue grappling with lawyer advertising and specialization. The Florida Supreme Court, now followed by all others, used the power to regulate the practice of law to initiate an innovative program that permits lawyers to place funds entrusted to them in interest-bearing accounts and to use the revenues for various legal services and public service projects.[75]

## VI. INHERENT POWERS OF THE COURTS

The Pennsylvania[76] and Michigan[77] high courts used the technique of drafting and sending a letter (later published in their reporters) to the other two branches indicating that a law purporting to apply the state "open meetings" statute to the court's rulemaking processes was viewed by the court as unconstitutional and unenforceable.

State courts, particularly with respect to budgetary matters, have asserted that, in the words of the Pennsylvania Supreme Court:

> [T]he Judiciary *must possess* the inherent power to determine and compel payment of those sums of money which are reasonable and necessary to carry out its mandated responsibilities, and its powers and duties to administer Justice, if it is to be in reality a co-equal, independent Branch of our Government.[78]

Consider, as well, a West Virginia decision ordering a county to designate parking spaces for the exclusive use of judicial personnel.[79] Major litigation in New York over judicial funding was settled.[80]

[73] *See, e.g.*, art. XVIII, Integration Rule of the Florida Bar, as amended, *cited in* Petition of the Attorney General and Others to Amend Article XVIII of the Integration Rule of the Florida Bar, 339 So.2d 646 (Fla. 1976).

[74] *See* Am. Trial Lawyers Ass'n v. New Jersey Supreme Court, 330 A.2d 350 (N.J. 1974).

[75] *See generally In re* Interest on Trust Accounts, 402 So.2d 389 (Fla. 1981). The concept was upheld in *Brown v. Legal Foundation of Washington*, 538 U.S. 216 (2003).

[76] *In re* Pa. C.S. § 1703, 394 A.2d 444 (Pa. 1978).

[77] *In re* the "Sunshine Law," 1976 PA 267, 255 N.W.2d 635 (Mich. 1977).

[78] Commonwealth *ex rel.* Caroll v. Tate, 274 A.2d 193, 197 (1971); Comment, *State Court Assertion of Power to Determine and Demand Its Own Budget*, 120 U. Pa. L. Rev. 1187 (1972). For another example of the Pennsylvania court's thinking, see Beckert v. Warren, 439 A.2d 638 (Pa. 1981). *See generally* Geoffrey C. Hazard Jr., Martin B. McNamara & Irwin F. Sentilles III, *Court Finance and Unitary Budgeting*, 81 Yale L.J. 1286 (1972); Note, *Judicial Financial Autonomy and Inherent Power*, 57 Cornell L. Rev. 975 (1972).

[79] State *ex rel.* Lambert v. Stephens, 490 S.E.2d 891 (W. Va. 1997). *See* Vermeule, *supra* note 29, at 382–86.

[80] Howard B. Glaser, Wachtler v. Cuomo: *The Limits of Inherent Power*, 14 Pace L. Rev. 111 (1994); Walter E. Swearingen, Wachtler v. Cuomo: *Does New York's Judiciary Have an Inherent Right*

It is commonly understood that it is within the legislature's plenary power to set the sentences for classes of crimes. On the other hand, although there are no specific constitutional provisions, actual imposition of a sentence upon a finding of guilt is viewed as a judicial function. The legislatures in various states developed mandatory minimum sentencing and crime classification statutes in the 1960s and 1970s giving discretionary authority to prosecutors. This gave prosecutors extraordinary bargaining power in plea negotiations because they were the only avenue through which a defendant could avoid imposition of the mandatory sentence or the risk of being charged with a higher classification of offense.

In California, a statute provided that certain offenses could be classified by the court as misdemeanors with the consent of the prosecuting attorney. This statute was challenged as an unconstitutional legislatively authorized, executive encroachment on judicial power in *Esteybar v. Municipal Court*.[81] There, the defendant was charged with first-offense marijuana possession, which could be treated as either a felony or a misdemeanor. The prosecutor, citing the statute, refused to consent to the case being handled as a misdemeanor unless the defendant pled guilty, thus raising the constitutional separation-of-powers issue.[82] The California Supreme Court, relying on earlier related precedent,[83] struck down the statute as a separation-of-powers violation because the exercise of a judicial power (even granted by statute) could not require the judge to "bargain with the prosecutor."[84] The court rejected the state's claim that this was an exercise of the executive charging power, concluding that "when a decision to prosecute has been made, the process which leads to acquittal or to sentencing is fundamentally judicial in nature."[85] Clearly, the California court saw the encroachment on judicial power as an actual threat to the liberty of the people to such an extent that even functionalist judges would be concerned.

The Florida Supreme Court, by contrast, upheld a drug statute imposing a mandatory minimum sentence for certain drug offenses, subject to an "escape valve" pursuant to which the prosecutor could request a reduced or suspended sentence if the defendant cooperated with law enforcement.[86] The court, relying

*of Self-Preservation?* 14 Pace L. Rev. 153 (1994); Justin S. Teff, *The Judges v. The State: Obtaining Adequate Judicial Compensation and New York's Current Constitutional Crisis*, 72 Alb. L. Rev. 191 (2009).

[81] 485 P.2d 1140 (Cal. 1971).
[82] *Id.* at 1142. *See also* Sentence Review Panel v. Moseley, 663 S.E.2d 679, 682–83 (Ga. 2008).
[83] People v. Tenorio, 473 P.2d 993 (Cal. 1970).
[84] *Esteybar*, 485 P.2d at 1143. The court relied on Article III, Section 1 (now 3) of the California Constitution, which reads, "The powers of state government are legislative, executive, and judicial. Persons charged with the exercise of one power may not exercise either of the others except as permitted by this Constitution." *Id.* at 1145.
[85] *Id.* at 1145 (*quoting Tenorio*, 473 P.2d at 996).
[86] State v. Benitez, 395 So.2d 514 (Fla. 1981).

on a New York decision upholding a similar statute, concluded that "[s]o long as a statute does not wrest from the courts the *final* discretion to impose sentence, it does not infringe upon the constitutional division of responsibilities."[87]

The New Jersey Supreme Court adopted a middle-of-the-road approach when confronted with a similar drug statute purporting to authorize the prosecutor to invoke a mandatory minimum sentence provision for repeat drug offenders, "notwithstanding that extended terms are ordinarily discretionary with the court."[88] The court noted that the separation-of-powers doctrine was intended to "prevent the concentration of *unchecked* power in the hands of any one branch."[89] Responding to the statute's purported assignment of unreviewable discretion to prosecutors, the court determined the statute "*would be* unconstitutional, [but that the legislature] did not intend to circumvent the judiciary's power to protect defendants from arbitrary application of enhanced sentences."[90] The court interpreted the statute to require guidelines for the exercise of this prosecutorial discretion to be adopted, reasons for prosecutors' decisions to be stated on the record, and judicial review of such decisions.[91] The court has applied this same saving judicial interpretation to other, similar statutes.[92]

This claim of inherent powers raises important questions of political theory, but the issue of whether the branches of state government exercise delegated or inherent powers is largely academic. Because state constitutions provide that all legislative power resides in the legislature, the important task is to define the legislative power, not to quibble over whether that power is inherent or delegated. State constitutions similarly place the judicial power in the judiciary; consequently, rather than debating whether a court's power is inherent, the inquiry should focus on whether the claimed power is properly and necessarily a judicial function.

## VII. ADVISORY OPINIONS AND CERTIFIED QUESTIONS

Eight state constitutions, by contrast to federal constitutional orthodoxy, authorize or require state supreme courts to render advisory opinions (usually on constitutional questions) to various governmental officials.[93] This is a modified

[87] *Id.* at 519, *quoting* People v. Eason, 353 N.E.2d 587, 589 (N.Y. 1976).
[88] State v. Lagares, 601 A.2d 698, 700 (N.J. 1992), *quoting* N.J.S.A. § 2C:43-6f.
[89] *Id.* at 701 (emphasis in original).
[90] *Id.* at 704 (emphasis added).
[91] *Id.*
[92] *See* State v. Vasquez, 609 A.2d 29 (N.J. 1992); State v. Kirk, 678 A.2d 233 (N.J. 1996).
[93] Mel A. Topf, *State Supreme Court Advisory Opinions as Illegitimate Judicial Review*, 2001 L. Rev. M.S.U.-D.C.L. 101, 101 n.1 (2001); *see* Helen Hershkoff, *State Courts and the "Passive Virtues": Rethinking the Judicial Function*, 114 Harv. L. Rev. 1833, 1844–52 (2001) (noting the ability

form of judicial review. Interestingly, when state supreme courts issue advisory opinions, they act more like European constitutional courts than the U.S. Supreme Court, which cannot render such opinions. Ten other states have rejected or abandoned the practice.[94] States differ, of course, as to which officers may request opinions and when they may do so. The courts tend to construe strictly their authority and obligations under these provisions.[95]

Important questions have arisen as to the precedential value of advisory opinions. After all, advisory opinions are not adjudications of actual controversies and are not considered exercises of the traditional "judicial power." According to the Supreme Court of Delaware:

> In other words, advisory opinions do not decide a case, do not adjudicate a dispute and are not judicial rulings in any sense. . . . For those reasons, they are not binding on any court and do not carry precedential effect.[96]

There seems to be evidence that, in the context of advisory opinions, courts do not accord the same presumption of correctness to the actions of the other branches that they do in adjudicating cases. The advisory opinion can be viewed as an important safety valve, or check, standing in the way of unconstitutional actions.

The advisory opinion originated in the Massachusetts Constitution of 1780[97] and led to major debate in the 1820 Constitutional Convention.[98] Despite the protestations by justices that advisory opinions are not binding precedents, Professor Mel Topf has argued convincingly that they are utilized by judges and lawyers (and in this book) as though they were regular judicial precedents.[99] "Advisory opinions," Topf observed, "are taken as binding by virtually everyone, including at times the advising judges. Like that which looks like a duck, walks

of state courts to issue advisory opinions); State *ex rel.* Morrison v. Sebelius, 179 P.3d 366, 385 (Kan. 2008). What authorization is necessary for state courts to render advisory opinions? *See In re* Opinion of the Justices, 64 A.2d 169 (Vt. 1949) (statutory authorization inadequate); *In re* Advisory Opinion, 335 S.E.2d 890 (N.C. 1985) (constitutional authorization necessary). *See* Margaret M. Bledsoe, Comment, *The Advisory Opinion in North Carolina: 1947 to 1991*, 70 N.C. L. Rev. 1853 (1992).

[94] Mel A. Topf, *The Jurisprudence of the Advisory Opinion Process in Rhode Island*, 2 Roger Williams U.L. Rev. 207, 213 (1997). For the texts of the state constitutional provisions on advisory opinions, see *id.* at 254–56.

[95] *See* Topf, *supra* note 94, at 230–32. *But see In re* Advisory Opinion to the Governor, 732 A.2d 55, 59 (R.I. 1999).

[96] Opinion of the Justices, 413 A.2d 1245, 1248 (Del. 1980). The Florida Constitution provides for "interested persons to be heard on the questions presented." Fla. Const. art. IV, § 1(c).

[97] Mel A. Topf, *The Origins and Early History of Supreme Judicial Court Advisory Opinions in Massachusetts*, 7 Mass. Legal Hist. 21 (2001).

[98] *Id.* at 23, 32–40.

[99] *Id.* at 129–37.

like a duck, and quacks like a duck, advisory opinions have looked, behaved and sounded like adjudicated decisions, and they have, not unreasonably, been perceived and employed, as such."[100]

Despite the view widely held by many commentators reviewed by Topf, it is important for lawyers and judges to remember the *theory* about the nonbinding character of advisory opinions and the rationale. At least older and divided advisory opinions might be revisited without the rhetoric of stare decisis and, possibly, without its actual influence (Chapter 12).

A mechanism related to advisory opinions is state courts' acceptance of certified questions from the federal courts.[101] When those courts are in doubt as to the meaning of state law or where state authority exists, they have the discretion to present a certified question to the state supreme court.[102] State courts do not always comply.[103] When the constitutionality of the Ohio Supreme Court's practice of answering certified questions was raised, it responded that "such a power exists by virtue of Ohio's very existence as a state in our federal system."[104] Chief Justice Randall Shepard of Indiana has provided some cautionary views on certified questions concerning state constitutional law,[105] as has Professor Justin Long.[106]

## VIII. THE POSITION AND FUNCTION OF THE STATE JUDICIARY

State courts' institutional position in state government is different from the U.S. Supreme Court's position in the federal system. The relationship between state supreme courts and state legislatures, therefore, is different from the Supreme Court's relationship to Congress. State supreme courts serve a number of important functions within state government and the legal system. Most familiar is

[100] *Id.* at 129–30. *See also* Mel A. Topf, *The Advisory Opinion on Separation of Powers: The Uncertain Contours of Advisory Opinion Jurisprudence in Rhode Island*, 5 ROGER WILLIAMS U. L. REV. 385, 408–13 (2000); Topf, *supra* note 94, at 245–49. Mel Topf brought together his work on advisory opinions in A DOUBTFUL AND PERILOUS EXPERIMENT (2011).

[101] Larry M. Roth, *Certified Questions from the Federal Courts: Review and Re-proposal*, 34 U. MIAMI L. REV. 1 (1979); Paul A. LeBel, *Legal Positivism and Federalism: The Certification Experience*, 19 GA. L. REV. 999 (1985); Rebecca A. Cochran, *Federal Court Certification of Questions of State Law to State Courts: A Theoretical and Empirical Study*, 29 J. LEGIS. 157 (2003).

[102] Lehman Bros. v. Schein, 416 U.S. 386 (1974); Cochran, *supra* note 89, at 166.

[103] Cochran, *supra* note 101, at 176–83.

[104] Scott v. Bank One Trust Co., 577 N.E.2d 1077, 1079 (Ohio 1991); *See also In re* Certified Questions from the U.S. Court of Appeals for the Sixth Circuit, 696 N.W.2d 687 (Mich. 2005) (reviewing the cases and arguments concerning authority to answer certified questions); Seals v. H&S, Inc., 301 S.W.3d 237, 241 (Tenn. 2010).

[105] Honorable Randall T. Shepard, *Is Making State Constitutional Law Through Certified Questions a Good Idea or a Bad Idea?* 38 VAL. U. L. REV. 327 (2004).

[106] Justin R. Long, *Against Certification*, 78 GEO. WASH. L. REV. 114 (2009).

their role in common-law development and statutory and constitutional interpretation, functions performed in the context of adjudicating cases. Most studies of state courts focus on their adjudicatory function in deciding cases.

A major feature of the study of state constitutional law, however, should be on the nonadjudicatory functions (outside the decision of cases) of state supreme courts. As noted earlier, many state supreme courts create law through rulemaking powers.[107] Once thought to be legislative in nature, these powers have devolved upon state judiciaries during the past century.[108] They also exercise various "inherent powers," usually at the expense of the legislative branch.[109] State courts are arguably closer to state affairs and more accountable than federal courts.[110] Standing and other prudential justiciability barriers are usually lower at the state level.[111] The "political question" doctrine is often applied differently from the federal doctrine in the state courts.[112] New scholarship has explored this matter.[113]

[107] Jeffrey A. Parness, *Correspondence, Public Process and State-Court Rulemaking*, 88 YALE L.J. 1319, 1319–20 (1979).

[108] Robert F. Williams, *State Constitutional Law Processes*, 24 WM. & MARY L. REV. 169, 208 (1983).

[109] Michael L. Buenger, *Of Money and Judicial Independence: Can Inherent Powers Protect State Courts in Tough Fiscal Times?* 92 KY. L.J. 979, 1000–02 (2004).

[110] *Developments in the Law: The Interpretation of State Constitutional Rights*, 95 HARV. L. REV. 1324, 1351 (1982).

[111] Hershkoff, *supra* note 93, at 1852–68; James W. Doggett, Note, *"Trickle Down" Constitutional Interpretation: Should Federal Limits on Legislative Conferral of Standing Be Imported into State Constitutional Law?* 108 COLUM. L. REV. 839 (2008). *See* Toxic Waste Impact Group, Inc. v. Leavitt, 890 P.2d 906 (Okla. 1994); State *ex rel.* Morrison v. Sebelius, 179 P.3d 366 (Kan. 2008); ACLU of New Mexico v. City of Albuquerque, 188 P.3d 1222, 1226 (N.M. 2008); Lansing Schools Educ. Assoc. v. Lansing Bd. of Ed., 792 N.W.2d 686 (Mich. 2010); Alaska Community Action on Toxics v. Hartig, 321 P.3d 360 (Alaska 2014); Forest v. Employees Political Action Committee (EMPAC), 853 S.E.2d 698 (N.C. 2021); *see also* William A. Fletcher, *The "Case or Controversy" Requirement in State Court Adjudication of Federal Questions*, 78 CAL. L. REV. 263 (1990); Brian A. Stern, Note, *An Argument Against Imposing the Federal "Case or Controversy" Requirement on State Courts*, 69 N.Y.U. L. REV. 77 (1994); John Dimanno, Note, *Beyond Taxpayers' Suits: Public Interest Standing in the States*, 41 CONN L. REV. 639 (2008). *But see* West v. Schofield, 468 S.W.3d 482, 490–94 (Tenn. 2015) (lockstepping with federal doctrine); Meyers v. JDC/Firethorne, Ltd., 548 S.W.3d 477 (Tex. 2018) (same).

[112] Justice Hans A. Linde of the Oregon Supreme Court wrote: "If a 'political question doctrine' exists in a state court, I have not heard of it." Hans A. Linde, *E Pluribus-Constitutional Theory and State Courts*, 18 GA. L. REV. 165, 189–90 (1984). *See* Nat Stern, *The Political Question Doctrine in State Courts*, 35 S.C. L. REV. 405 (1984); S. Car. Pub. Int. Foundation v. Judicial Merit Selection Comm., 632 S.E.2d 277 (S.C. 2006); Kromko v. Arizona Bd. of Regents, 165 P.3d 168, 170–71 (Ariz. 2007); Lobato v. State, 218 P.3d 358, 369–70 (Colo. 2009); State *ex rel.* Dickey v. Besler, 954 N.W.2d 425, 444–51 (Iowa 2021) (Appel, J., dissenting).

[113] *See* Daniel B. Rodriguez, *The Political Question Doctrine in State Constitutional Law*, 43 RUTGERS L.J. 573 (2013); Nat Stern, *Don't Answer That: Revisiting the Political Question in State Courts*, 21 J. CONST. L. 153 (2018); Council 13, American Federation of State, County and Municipal Employees, AFL-CIO v. Rendell, 986 A.2d 63, 76 (Pa. 2009) ("political question doctrine is a shield not a sword . . . it does not exist to remove a question of law from the Judiciary's consideration merely because the Executive has forwarded its own opinion of the legal issue in a political context."); *see also* Lawrence Friedman, *Liberty and Privacy Interests Through the Political Question Lens*, 19 TEMPLE POL. & CIVIL RTS. L. REV. 189, 221–24 (2009) (discussing alternatives to political question doctrine under state constitutional law).

In addition to the nonadjudicatory functions of state supreme courts, the state courts differ significantly from federal courts even in respect to adjudication. State courts occupy different institutional positions and perform different judicial functions from their federal counterparts. The typical American state constitution also differs from its federal counterpart in many ways. Consequently, state court judicial review of state statutes or executive actions is, or should be, qualitatively different from federal judicial review of the same statutes or actions. First, as noted earlier, beginning soon after independence the balance of power between state legislatures and judiciaries has been gradually shifting, increasing executive and judicial authority at the expense of legislative authority. In addition, the wide range of detailed restrictions on state governments contained in state constitutions is enforceable by state courts, bringing them into more regular involvement in the workings of other branches. For all these reasons, state courts are often deeply involved in the state's ongoing policymaking processes (constitutional and nonconstitutional).[114] Although the extent of this involvement may vary from state to state,[115] such judicial action nevertheless reflects a very different institutional position from that occupied by the federal courts.

Second, the typical state court's judicial function is different from that of the federal court. For example, state courts have traditionally performed much nonconstitutional lawmaking. As Oregon Justice Hans A. Linde observed:

> When a state court alters the law of products liability, abolishes sovereign or charitable tort immunity, redefines the insanity defense, or restricts the range of self-exculpation in contracts of adhesion, its action is rarely attacked as "undemocratic." Nor is this judicial role peculiar to matters of common law subject to legislative reversal. The accepted dominance of courts in state law extends to their "anti-majoritarian" role in review of their coordinate political branches in state and local governments.[116]

[114] HENRY ROBERT GLICK, SUPREME COURTS IN STATE POLITICS 5 (1971): "State supreme courts are not simply duplications of the national court at a lower level of the judicial hierarchy. Instead, they are distinctive institutions which are integral parts of state political and legal systems." *See also* HERBERT JACOB & KENNETH N. VINES, POLITICS IN THE AMERICAN STATES: A COMPARATIVE ANALYSIS 246 (3d ed. 1976) ("I[t] becomes apparent that the state courts make significant policies in many of the same substantive arenas as the other organs of government.").

[115] Glick, *supra* note 114, at 151; HENRY ROBERT GLICK & KENNETH N. VINES, STATE COURT SYSTEMS (1973). *See generally* TARR & PORTER, *supra* note 8.

[116] Hans A. Linde, *Judges, Critics, and the Realist Tradition*, 82 YALE L.J. 227, 248 (1972). *See also* Lawrence Baum & Bradley C. Canon, *State Supreme Courts as Activists: New Doctrines in the Law of Torts*, *in* MARY CORNELIA PORTER & G. ALAN TARR, STATE SUPREME COURTS: POLICYMAKERS IN THE FEDERAL SYSTEM 83 (1982). The "legitimacy" of such common-law decisions is sometimes attacked as invading the province of the legislature. *See generally* Ralph F. Bischoff, *The Dynamics of Tort Law: Court or Legislature?* 4 VT. L. REV. 35 (1979).

State supreme courts also pursue policy initiatives outside their formal judicial role in the adversary process, including direct and indirect contact with legislators. *See* Henry Robert Glick, *Policy-Making and State Supreme Courts: The Judiciary as an Interest Group*, 5 LAW & SOC'Y REV. 271 (1970).

Federal courts, although they have far-reaching powers to enforce federal law, have been denied this general lawmaking power since 1938, when, in *Erie Railroad v. Tompkins*,[117] the U.S. Supreme Court declared that *federal* courts do not have the power to make substantive common-law decisions binding on *states*. Linde has further pointed out that state courts are much more often involved in intragovernmental, and even intrabranch, power and policy disputes to a degree never seen at the federal level.[118]

The modern state judiciary, therefore, differs from state to state, and state judicial branches are quite different from the federal judiciary.[119] Some of the most significant state-federal distinctions arise, as noted by former Oregon Justice Hans Linde, from the state courts:

- Retention of broad common-law powers of lawmaking
- Day-to-day involvement in the administration of the great majority of criminal cases
- Greater involvement with the litigation of a wide range of issues that cannot be heard in federal courts because of the political question doctrine, as well as the standing, ripeness, and mootness doctrines
- Power to regulate the practice of law and practice and procedure in the courts—both important issues with some public visibility
- Frequent requirement that judges are either elected or retained by some form of popular vote—possibly leading them to feel less constrained, as elected "representatives," in expressing policy views
- Close proximity to their legislatures
- Power, in some states, to render advisory opinions[120]

In many very real respects, state courts are in fact more powerful within their spheres than are federal courts.

Many state supreme courts face different caseload pressures and jurisdictional restrictions than the U.S. Supreme Court. Some state courts even have "reach down" provisions[121] that enable them to obtain jurisdiction quickly over state

[117] 304 U.S. 64 (1938).

[118] Hans A. Linde, *The State and the Federal Courts in Governance: Vive la Différence!* 46 Wm. & Mary L. Rev. 1273, 1274–75 (2005). *See also* Michael Signer, *Constitutional Crisis in the Commonwealth: Resolving the Conflict Between Governors and Attorneys General*, 41 U. Rich L. Rev. 43 (2006); William P. Marshall, *Break Up the Presidency? Governors, State Attorneys General, and Lessons from the Divided Executive*, 115 Yale L.J. 2446, 2455–68 (2006).

[119] Hans A. Linde, *Observations of a State Court Judge*, *in* Judges and Legislators: Toward Institutional comity 117 (Robert A. Katzmann ed., 1988). *See generally* Christine M. Durham, *The Judicial Branch in State Government: Parables of Law, Politics and Power*, 76 N.Y.U. L. Rev. 1601 (2001).

[120] Linde, *supra* note 119, at 117–19.

[121] *See, e.g.*, Arthur J. England Jr., Eleanor Mitchell Hunter, & Richard C. Williams Jr., *Constitutional Jurisdiction of the Supreme Court of Florida: 1980 Reform*, 32 U. Fla. L. Rev. 147, 193 (1980).

constitutional conflicts bubbling in the lower courts and requiring early resolution. Therefore, state courts are able to approach state constitutional analysis on a narrower, more incremental basis than the U.S. Supreme Court, which labors under intense pressure for broader, more sweeping pronouncements.

## IX. CONCLUSION

State courts as a branch of government have become much more "coequal" over the centuries. They operate differently from federal courts not just in their exercise of judicial review but in a wide variety of other ways. Most of the state courts' characteristics of election and appointment of judges, structure and jurisdiction, and the exercise of nonadjudicatory powers can be traced directly to state constitutions.

# 11
# THE STATE EXECUTIVE BRANCH

As noted in Chapter 2, the Revolutionary-era state constitutions, in reaction to British rule, "aimed to make the gubernatorial magistrate a new kind of creature, a very pale reflection indeed of its regal ancestor."[1] This reconception of the governor's role, from policy making to policy implementing, stood in contrast to the dominant reliance placed on state legislatures.[2] The evolution of gubernatorial authority over the centuries has reflected a gradual shift to bring the executive's (and judiciary's) powers closer to those assigned to the legislature, including longer terms of office, increased veto power, and stronger budgetary authority.[3]

At the same time the realignment of the powers of the three branches was taking place, *internal*, intrabranch adjustments were being made within the executive branch. Most states now have a *plural*, fragmented, or "unbundled"[4] executive, with a variety of elected state constitutional executive officers, each with their own statewide constituency, making up the executive branch. Constitutional officers such as attorneys general,[5] secretaries of state, agriculture commissioners, education commissioners, and various fiscal officers are often named and given powers in state constitutions. New Jersey is one of the few states with a single, statewide elected executive.[6] In those states with plural executives, both political and legal conflicts may arise between the state constitutional

[1] Gordon S. Wood, *Foreword: State Constitution-Making in the American Revolution*, 24 Rutgers L.J. 911, 915 (1993).

[2] *See* Chapter 9.

[3] Thad Beyle, *The Executive Branch*, *in* 3 State Constitutions for the Twenty-first Century: The Agenda of State Constitutional Reform 67, 67–72 (2006); Arch T. Allen III, *A Study in Separation of Powers: Executive Power in North Carolina*, 77 N.C. L. Rev. 2049 (1999).

[4] Christopher R. Berry & Jacob E. Gersten, *The Unbundled Executive*, 75 U. Chi. L. Rev. 1385 (2008).

[5] William P. Marshall, *Break Up the Presidency? Governors, State Attorneys General, and Lessons from the Divided Executive*, 115 Yale L.J. 2446, 2449–68 (2006). *See also* Norman R. Williams, *Executive Review in the Fragmented Executive: State Constitutionalism and Same-Sex Marriage*, 154 U. Pa. L. Rev. 565, 571–77 (2006); Beyle, *supra* note 3, at 74–79. Some states consider their attorneys general to be judicial officers. *See* Eric R. Daleo, Note, *The Scope and Limits of the New Jersey Governor's Authority to Remove the Attorney General and Others "For Cause,"* 39 Rutgers L.J. 393, 411–14 (2008). *See generally* Neal E. Devins & Saikrishkna B. Prakash, *50 States, 50 Attorneys General, and 50 Approaches to the Duty to Defend*, 124 Yale L.J. 2100 (2015).

[6] Robert F. Williams, The New Jersey State Constitution: A Reference Guide 26 (2d ed. 2012).

*The Law of American State Constitutions.* Robert F. Williams and Lawrence Friedman, Oxford University Press.
 DOI: 10.1093/oso/9780190068806.003.0012

officers.[7] This may often draw the state judiciary into conflicts within the executive in ways that rarely occur at the federal level.[8]

## I. THE NATURE OF STATE EXECUTIVE POWER

The early decision to invest the state governor only with delegated, rather than inherent, power is still one of the most fundamental aspects of executive authority in the states. In other words, the general view that states have plenary authority in our federal system is really a description of *legislative* rather than *executive* power. Generally speaking, the governor must be able to point to either constitutionally granted or statutorily granted power in order to exercise legal authority.[9] This issue is raised most often when governors seek to make policy decisions without clear constitutional or statutory authority through the use of executive orders.[10] Although in these separation-of-powers cases state courts generally enunciate the rule that governors may not issue binding executive orders without specific, or at least implied, constitutional or statutory authority, often the cases are very difficult to distinguish.

For example, the New York Court of Appeals has made what can be seen as somewhat inconsistent rulings on this issue.[11] *Rapp v. Carey*[12] considered a challenge to an executive order requiring executive branch employees to file financial disclosure forms and not to engage in certain business and political activities in the absence of implied, let alone specific, legislative authorization. The court invalidated the executive order, stating:

7 Hans A. Linde, *The State and Federal Courts in Governance: Vive la Différence!* 46 Wm. & Mary L. Rev. 1273, 1276–78 (2005); Vikram David Amar, *Lessons from California's Recent Experience with Its Non-Unitary (Divided) Executive: Of Mayors, Governors, Controllers, and Attorneys General*, 59 Emory L.J. 469 (2009); Miriam Seifter, *Gubernatorial Administration*, 131 Harv. L. Rev. 483, 526–28 (2017).

8 *See* Chapter 10; Wilder v. Atty. Gen., 439 S.E.2d 398 (Va. 1994); Wilkins v. West, 571 S.E.2d 100, 103 (Va. 2002). *See generally* Linde, *supra* note 7, at 1274–75; Michael Signer, *Constitutional Crisis in the Commonwealth: Resolving the Conflict Between Governors and Attorneys General*, 41 U. Rich L. Rev. 43 (2006); Marshall, *supra* note 5, at 2455–68.

9 Charles C. Thach Jr., The Creation of the Presidency 1775–1789, 105–06 (1923, Johns Hopkins Press reprint 1969).

10 *See generally* Note, *Gubernatorial Executive Orders as Devices for Administrative Discretion and Control*, 50 Iowa L. Rev. 78 (1964); E. Lee Bernick & Charles W. Wiggins, *The Governor's Executive Order: An Unknown Power*, 16 St. & Local Gov't Rev. 3 (1984); Margaret R. Ferguson & Cynthia J. Bowling, *Executive Orders and Administrative Control*, 68 Pub. Admin. Rev. (Special Issue) S20 (2008); Gerald Benjamin & Zachary Keck, *Executive Orders and Gubernatorial Authority to Reorganize State Government*, 74 Alb. L. Rev. 1613 (2010–2011).

11 *Compare* Rapp v. Carey, 375 N.E.2d 745 (N.Y. 1978), *with* Bourquin v. Cuomo, 652 N.E.2d 171 (N.Y. 1995). *See also* Chang v. University of Rhode Island, 375 A.2d 925 (R.I. 1977); Florida House of Representatives v. Crist, 990 So.2d 1035 (Fla. 2008).

12 375 N.E.2d 745 (N.Y. 1978). *See also* Buettell v. Walker, 319 N.E.2d 502 (Ill. 1974) (purpose of executive order appears to be to formulate a new legal requirement rather than to execute an existing one); Note, *supra* note 10.

> The crux of the case is the principle that the Governor has only those *powers* delegated to him by the constitution and the statutes . . . . Under our system of distribution of power with checks and balances, the purposes of the executive order, however desirable, may be achieved only through proper means.[13]

Eighteen years later, the court upheld an executive order authorizing the creation of a private, nonprofit corporation to represent the interests of residential utility customers in rate-making proceedings and with access to state agency mailings.[14] Because this duplicated the statutory mission of other agencies, the court distinguished *Rapp*, concluding that "it is only where the Executive acts inconsistently with the Legislature, or usurps its prerogatives, that the doctrine of separation is violated."[15] The court determined that it would not invalidate an executive order's "mere creation of a new procedural, administrative mechanism . . . to better implement a legislative policy . . ."[16]

Based on the proposition that the executive branch may exercise only those powers delegated to it by the constitution or statute, the question of *implied powers* is therefore often crucial. This consideration may be contrasted with the importance of *implied limitations* on the legislative branch. An exhaustive study of the use of executive orders in New Jersey concluded that the courts had avoided any major pronouncements on the parameters of gubernatorial authority.[17]

Much of what executive constitutional officers do is mandated by statute and governors, of course, must "take care that the laws are faithfully executed." State constitutions also directly assign a number of functions to governors and other executive branch officials and agencies. For example, constitutions often assign the power of executive clemency to the governor, thereby insulating exercise of that power from legislative or judicial interference.[18] In upholding the Illinois governor's "blanket clemency" for all inmates who had been sentenced to death, the Illinois Supreme Court stated:

> As a final matter, we note that clemency is the historic remedy employed to prevent a miscarriage of justice where the judicial process has been exhausted. . . . We believe that this is the purpose for which the framers gave the Governor this power in the Illinois Constitution. The grant of this essentially unreviewable power carries with it the responsibility to exercise it in the manner intended.

[13] *Rapp*, 375 N.E.2d at 750–51. *See also* Whiley v. Scott, 79 So.3d 702 (Fla. 2011) (executive order may not suspend provisions of Administrative Procedure Act).

[14] Bourquin v. Cuomo, 652 N.E.2d 171, 172 (N.Y. 1995).

[15] *Id.* at 173, *quoting* Clark v. Cuomo, 486 N.E.2d 794, 797 (N.Y. 1985).

[16] *Id.* at 175.

[17] Michael S. Herman, *Gubernatorial Executive Orders*, 30 RUTGERS L.J. 987 (1999).

[18] *See, e.g.*, People *ex rel.* Madigan v. Snyder, 804 N.E.2d 546 (Ill. 2004).

> Our hope is that Governors will use the clemency power in its intended manner—to prevent miscarriages of justice in individual cases.[19]

Governors have even been involved in forms of foreign relations,[20] described as follows:

> Governors exercised this limited but important foreign policy power in a variety of contexts. In addition to the power to respond to requests by foreign governments and international institutions, governors also negotiate and execute certain kinds of international agreement in pursuit of regional or international cooperation. Governors and other state executive officials administer insurance regulations and state purchasing regulations in pursuit of certain foreign policy goals. In these admittedly limited but hardly unimportant areas, a gubernatorial foreign policy is beginning to emerge.[21]

At least one commentator has argued that state governors should have, at least with respect to their constitutionally assigned powers, the ability to *interpret* the constitutions for themselves.[22] On a related matter, Professor Jim Rossi has proposed that governors be able to exercise powers not specifically delegated to them when dealing with a disaster, enemy attack, or other event in their states that also has consequences in other states.[23]

Chapter 8, section II covered clashes between legislatures and governors over appointing members of administrative agencies. Gubernatorial appointment powers can be challenged in other ways. When a Democratic governor was elected in North Carolina, the Republican Legislature, in its lame-duck session, enacted a law consolidating a number of administrative agencies and limiting the governor's power to appoint or change the personnel in charge of such agencies. The North Carolina Supreme Court ruled that this law contravened the governor's power to "faithfully execute the laws."[24] Professor Miriam Seifter has referred to governmental power shifts, such as in North Carolina and later in Wisconsin,[25] as "power plays," in states with divided government, where one

[19] *Id.* at 560. By contrast, the Virginia Supreme Court struck down the governor's "blanket" restoration of voting rights to convicted felons. Howell v. McAuliffe, 788 S.E.2d 706 (Va. 2016). That same court, however, ruled that a governor could issue a "partial pardon." Blount v. Clarke, 782 S.E.2d 152 (Va. 2016).

[20] Julian G. Ku, *Gubernatorial Foreign Policy*, 115 Yale L.J. 2380 (2006).

[21] *Id.* at 2383.

[22] Williams, *supra* note 5, at 637–47.

[23] Jim Rossi, *State Executive Lawmaking in Crisis*, 56 Duke L.J. 237 (2006).

[24] Cooper v. Berger, 809 S.E.2d 98 (N.C. 2018).

[25] League of Women Voters v. Evers, 929 N.W.2d 209 (Wis. 2019) (upholding special election restrictions on governor's powers).

party seeks to disadvantage the other as it loses power, often in lame-duck legislative sessions.[26]

In a deeply researched and analytical study, Professor Seifter concluded that many modern state governors "possess new and extensive powers to set state agendas."[27] Through their formal powers of budget authority, to reorganize state government, appoint officials, item veto, control over state administrative agencies, as well as informal powers such as helping to shape national policy, supporting or resisting federal actions on "immigration, environmental law, healthcare, and more,"[28] she concludes:

> in the past century, and especially in recent decades, most governors have gained a spate of powers that eclipse not only their Founding-era authority, but also the domestic powers of modern Presidents.[29]

Most governors are even subject to less interest-group and media scrutiny than the president.[30]

## II. GUBERNATORIAL VETO

In the area of gubernatorial veto power, a number of difficult issues arise concerning the procedure for presentment of bills to the governor and legislative override of executive vetoes. Many of these issues have to do with timing.[31] For example, the New York Court of Appeals struck down a "bicameral recall" practice whereby the legislature could reacquire a bill from the governor's desk prior to its signature or veto.[32] There, the Court referred to the veto process as "a model of civic simplicity," which did not include the recall practice, which "has little more than time and expediency to sustain it."[33] The Court noted:

> The recall practice unbalances the constitutional law-making equation, which expressly shifts power solely to the Executive upon passage of a bill by both houses and its transmittal to the Executive. By the ultra vires recall method, the Legislature significantly suspends and interrupts the mandated regimen and

[26] Miriam Seifter, *Judging Power Plays in the American States*, 97 Tex. L. Rev. 1217 (2019).
[27] Seifter, *supra* note 7, at 485–86.
[28] *Id.* at 486.
[29] *Id.* at 487.
[30] *Id.* at 523–25.
[31] *See, e.g.*, Board of Ed. v. City of New York, 362 N.E.2d 948 (N.Y. 1977); Warburton v. Thomas, 616 A.2d 495 (N.H. 1992); Gilbert v. Gladden, 432 A.2d 1351 (N.J. 1981); State *ex. rel.* Ohio General Assembly v. Brunner, 872 N.E.2d 912 (Ohio 2007).
[32] King v. Cuomo, 613 N.E.2d 950 (N.Y. 1993).
[33] *Id.* at 952–53.

> modifies the distribution of authority and the complimenting roles of the two law-making Branches.[34]

In a related context, the New York Court of Appeals also struck down the legislative practice of retaining bills that have been passed by both Houses and not presenting them to the governor.[35] The Court noted:

> The practice of withholding passed bills while simultaneously conducting discussions and negotiations between the executive and legislative branches is just another method of thwarting open, regular governmental process, not unlike the unconstitutional "recall" policy which, similarly, violated Article IV, § 7.[36]

The "all-or-nothing" quality of the gubernatorial veto began to cause significant difficulty in the area of appropriation bills, which often include many or even hundreds of appropriations of government funds for various programs. As a response to this problem, the "item veto" was devised, whereby the governor could "unpack" an appropriation bill to disapprove of their specific items or parts.[37] Exercises of this constitutional power are often challenged by legislators, usually from the opposite political party, or by recipients of vetoed funds, leading the state judiciary to have to resolve these disputes.[38] Gubernatorial exercise of the item veto, originally intended to prevent legislative "logrolling," therefore presents a range of complex issues. What constitutes an "item" in an appropriations bill? May a governor veto language or restrictions without vetoing the appropriation itself? What constitutes an appropriation bill?[39]

The question as to what constitutes an "item" arises most often when a governor purports to veto *language* in a bill without also vetoing the appropriated *money*. Legislatures often include language ("proviso language") in appropriation bills that supplements or contradicts codified, substantive statutes, hoping to make the change "veto-proof."[40] Although the legislature may validly attach

[34] *Id.* at 954.
[35] Campaign for Fiscal Equity, Inc. v. Marino, 661 N.E.2d 1372 (N.Y. 1995).
[36] *Id.* at 1374. The New Jersey Supreme Court held that a challenge to a similar practice was nonjusticiable. Gilbert v. Gladden, 432 A.2d 1351 (N.J. 1981). Thereafter, the New Jersey Constitution was amended to eliminate the practice. *See* N.J. CONST. art. V, § I, ¶ 14(a).
[37] Richard Briffault, *The Item Veto in State Courts*, 66 TEMP. L. REV. 1171 (1993).
[38] *Id. See* Alaska Leg. Council v. Knowles, 21 P.3d 367 (Alaska 2001); Jubelirer v. Rendell, 953 A.2d 514 (Pa. 2008). *See also* St. John's Well Child and Family Center v. Schwartzenegger, 239 P.3d 651 (Cal. 2010) (upholding gubernatorial reduction in already reduced budget appropriations).
[39] Briffault, *supra* note 37. *See also* Louis Fisher & Neal Devins, *How Successfully Can the States' Item Veto Be Transferred to the President?* 75 GEORGETOWN L.J. 159 (1986); House Committee on Rules, *Item Veto: State Experience and Its Application to the Federal Situation*, 99th Congress, 2nd Session (Committee Print 1986).
[40] Henry v. Edwards, 346 So.2d 153, 158 (La. 1977).

a "condition, limitation, and qualification" to money it appropriates, it can be difficult to separate these from substantive "unrelated riders" on appropriation bills.[41] The Iowa Supreme Court stated that "the line must be drawn solely on the basis of whether the vetoed provision effectively qualified the subject, purpose, or amount of the appropriation either quantitatively or qualitatively. . . ."[42] The court articulated the test as whether the "amount or purpose of the appropriated funds would be affected if, for some reason, that provision was ignored."[43] The Louisiana Supreme Court stated that, although the line was "difficult to draw," it fell between "a condition or limitation properly included in a general appropriation bill and what amounts to a provision which is essentially a matter of general legislation more appropriately dealt with in a separate enactment . . ."[44] Other state courts have insisted that governors exercising the item veto must use it only "negatively" and not to create new law.[45] The New Mexico Supreme Court put it this way:

> The power of partial veto is the power to disapprove. This is a negative power, or a power to delete or destroy a part or item, and is not a positive power, or a power to alter, enlarge or increase the effect of the remaining parts or items. It is not the power to enact or create new legislation by selective deletions.[46]

Wisconsin seems to be the only state in which the item veto has been used creatively, with the approval of the Wisconsin Supreme Court, to create new law.[47]

Although states' general or annual appropriation bills (the "budget" bill) are obviously subject to gubernatorial item veto, other bills may also appropriate funds. Therefore, questions may arise as to whether the governor may veto items in such bills.[48] Also, there is an obvious relationship between "unrelated

[41] *See, e.g.*, Welsh v. Branstad, 470 N.W.2d 644 (Iowa 1991).

[42] *Id.* at 649. *See also* Homan v. Branstad, 812 N.W.2d 623 (Iowa 2012),

[43] *Id.* at 650. *See* Brent R. Appel, *Item Veto Litigation in Iowa: Marking the Boundaries Between Legislative and Executive Power*, 41 Drake L. Rev. 1 (1992).

[44] Henry v. Edwards, 346 So.2d 153, 158 (La. 1977).

[45] State *ex rel.* Sego v. Kirkpatrick, 524 P.2d 975 (N.M. 1974). *See also* State *ex rel.* Smith v. Martinez, 265 P.3d 1276 (N.M. 2011).

[46] *Sego*, 524 P.2d at 981.

[47] *See, e.g.*, State *ex rel.* Wisconsin Senate v. Thompson, 424 N.W.2d 385 (Wis. 1988). For interesting discussions of the use of the partial veto in Wisconsin, written by former governors, see Patrick J. Lucey, Essay: *The Partial Veto in the Lucey Administration*, 77 Marq. L. Rev. 427 (1994); Anthony S. Earl, Essay: *Personal Reflections on the Partial Veto*, 77 Marq. L. Rev. 437 (1994).

In 1990, the people of Wisconsin adopted an amendment to the item veto provision. Article V, Section 10(1)(c):

> (c) In approving an appropriation bill in part, the governor may not create a new word by rejecting individual letters in the words of the enrolled bill.

This is a very rare *reduction* in gubernatorial power by constitutional amendment.

[48] *See* State *ex rel.* Sego v. Kirkpatrick, 524 P.2d 975, 980 (N.M. 1974); Junkins v. Branstad, 448 N.W.2d 480, 482–83 (Iowa 1989); Risser v. Klauser, 558 N.W.2d 108 (Wis. 1997); Appel, *supra* note 43, at 11–17.

riders," subject to gubernatorial item veto, and provisions that violate the "single-subject" or "altered during passage" limitations that are found in the legislative articles of state constitutions, as discussed in Chapter 9.[49]

The states of Alabama, Illinois, Massachusetts, Montana, New Jersey, South Dakota, and Virginia have further refined the gubernatorial veto to provide for a "conditional" or "amendatory" veto. Article VI, Section 10(2), of the Montana Constitution provides:

> The governor may return any bill to the legislature with his recommendation for amendment. If the legislature passes the bill in accordance with the governor's recommendation, it shall again return the bill to the governor for his reconsideration. The governor shall not return a bill for amendment a second time.

It is not clear if this provides a power the governor did not already have, albeit through informal signals rather than a formal act. It may, in fact, reduce the incentive for the governor to give his attention to legislation before it passes.[50]

## III. EXECUTIVE PRIVILEGE

The doctrine of executive privilege is most often associated with federal constitutional law. State courts have not been of one mind as to whether governors enjoy such a privilege. On the one hand, in *Babets v. Secretary of Executive Office of Human Services*,[51] the Massachusetts Supreme Judicial Court concluded that, under the Massachusetts Constitution, there is no such privilege. The court thought it relevant that the proponents of the privilege had

> failed to demonstrate that the Executive does not function effectively because of the lack of the asserted privilege. Moreover, the explicit constitutional grant to the Legislature of a "privilege" as to its deliberations, see art. 21 of the Declaration of Rights of the Massachusetts Constitution, further supports our view that a corresponding privilege in the Executive is not constitutionally required. Had the framers of our government's structure intended to recognize

[49] Deborah S. Bartell, Note, *The Interplay Between the Gubernatorial Veto and the One-Subject Rule in Oklahoma*, 19 OKLA. CITY U. L. REV. 273 (1994); Flanders v. Morris, 558 P.2d 769 (Wash. 1977); Alaska Legis. Council v. Knowles, 21 P.3d 367, 378–83 (Alaska 2001).

[50] All of these issues are addressed in Jack R. Van Der Slik, *Reconsidering the Amendatory Veto in Illinois*, 8 N. ILL. U. L. REV. 753 (1988). For consideration of the Illinois amendatory veto, see Continental Ill. Nat'l Bank & Trust Co. v. Zagel, 401 N.E.2d 491 (Ill. 1979).

[51] 526 N.E.2d 1261 (Mass. 1988).

in our Constitution an executive privilege, it is reasonable to expect that they would expressly have created one.[52]

On the other hand, and more recently, the Arkansas Supreme Court in 2019 held that gubernatorial privilege was a necessary element of separation-of-powers analysis, to protect the "integrity of the governor's decision-making process."[53]

## IV. CONSTITUTIONAL AGENCIES AND OFFICERS

Many states have amended their constitutions over the years to create constitutional agencies or commissions, in addition to officers, with extensive regulatory and adjudicatory powers. Such agencies can be considered part of the executive branch, but are really more like a "fourth branch."[54] The creation of such agencies or commissions, with constitutionally designated powers, operates to displace the legislative branch from policymaking in these designated areas. Once again, this will regularly draw the state courts into disputes where they must resolve questions about conflicts between statutes and the regulatory decisions of constitutional agencies.[55] For example, the Florida Supreme Court invalidated a *statute* prohibiting hunting on Sundays on the ground that it conflicted with an *administrative rule* of the constitutionally established Game and Fish Commission. The rule provided for a one-month hunting season, which included Sundays.[56]

A number of states have constitutionalized bodies such as boards of regents and given them constitutional authority over higher education governance.[57] In

[52] *Id.* at 1263.

[53] Protect Fayetteville v. City of Fayetteville, 566 S.W.3d 105, 110 (Ark. 2019) (citing other state cases); *see also* Freedom Foundation v. Gregoire, 310 P.3d 1252, 1255–60 (Wash. 2013).

[54] *In re* Advisory to the Governor (Ethics Commission), 612 A.2d 1, 5 (R.I. 1992); G. Alan Tarr, Understanding State Constitutions 17–18 (1998). For a discussion of Arizona's constitutionally created Corporation Commission, see Deborah Scott Engelsby, *The Corporation Commission: Preserving Its Independence*, 20 Ariz. St. L.J. 241 (1988). In 1992, the Arizona Supreme Court explained the Commission's origins and constitutional independence in *Arizona Corp. Comm. v. State* ex rel. *Woods*, 830 P. 2d 807, 811–13 (Ariz. 1992). *See also* Residential Utility Consumer Office v. Arizona Corporation Comm., 377 P. 3d 305 (Ariz. 2016).

[55] *See In re* Advisory to the Governor (Ethics Commission), 612 A.2d 1, 8–13 (R.I. 1992).

[56] Whitehead v. Rogers, 223 So.2d 330 (Fla. 1969). *See also* Colorado Ethics Watch v. Independent Ethics Comm., 369 P.3d 270, 271 (Colo. 2016); Old Dominion Committee for Fair Utility Rates v. State Corporation Commission, 803 S.E.2d 758 (Va. 2017); Matter of Application of Okla. Gas and Electric Co. v. Corporation Commission, 417 P.3d 1196 (Okla. 2018); Hill v. Missouri Dept. of Conservation, 550 S.W.3d 463 (Mo. 2018).

[57] *See generally* Harold W. Horowitz, *The Autonomy of the University of California Under the State Constitution*, 25 UCLA L. Rev. 23 (1977); Joseph Beckham, *Constitutionally Autonomous Higher*

litigation over the North Dakota State Board of Education's authority to terminate a professor's employment, the North Dakota Supreme Court observed:

> Because the Board exercises constitutional powers, our review of its substantive decisions is akin to the review we employ when the doctrine of separation of powers applies.[58]

Nevertheless, the court determined that "judicial review similar to that provided in appeals from administrative agency decisions is appropriate in this case."[59] Given the fact that the legislative branch retains the authority to set funding levels for higher education, however, autonomy for higher education with constitutionally specified governance is still not complete.[60] Many state constitutions now provide for lieutenant governors, with various levels of responsibility and authority. Thorny issues may arise over their powers when the governor is out of the state or leaves office.[61]

## V. STATE ADMINISTRATIVE AGENCIES

Jon Marshfield has demonstrated how state constitutional ease of amendment has resulted in the continual reform of state administrative agencies.[62] Although state administrative agencies have grown and evolved over the years, and exercise important powers, they remain relatively low-visibility and "on the whole, less

*Education Governance: A Proposed Amendment to the Florida Constitution*, 30 U. FLA. L. REV. 546 (1978) (fourteen states provide some form of constitutionally autonomous higher education governance); Joseph Beckham, *Reasonable Independence for Public Higher Education: Legal Implications of Constitutionally Autonomous Status*, 7 J.L. & EDUC. 177 (1978).

58 Peterson v. North Dakota University System, 678 N.W.2d 163, 168 (N.D. 2004). *See generally* Richard B. Crockett, *Constitutional Autonomy and the North Dakota State Board of Higher Education*, 54 N.D. L. REV. 529 (1978).

59 *Peterson*, 678 N.W.2d at 169; see Board of Regents of Higher Education v. State, 512 P.3d 748 (Mont. 2022).

60 Regents of the University of Michigan v. State, 235 N.W.2d 1, 9, 12 (Mich. 1975).

61 *See, e.g.*, Commission on the Governorship of California v. Curb, 603 P.2d 1357 (Cal. 1979) (powers of lieutenant governor when governor out of state); Bryant v. English, 843 S.W.2d 308 (Ark. 1992) (succession when Bill Clinton elected president). *See also* Michael L. Tictin, *Succession to the Office of Governor and Separation of Powers: The Unfinished Business of the 1947 Constitution*, 29 RUTGERS L.J. 1021 (1998). T. Quinn Yeargain has analyzed the process of reforming gubernatorial succession in *Democratizing Gubernatorial Succession*, 72 RUTGERS U. L. REV. 1145 (2021).

62 Jonathan L. Marshfield, *Popular Regulation? State Constitutional Amendment and the Administrative State*, 8 BELMONT L. REV. 342 (2021). *See also* Cynthia J. Bowling & Deil S. Wright, *Public Administration in the Fifty States: A Half-Century Administrative Revolution*, 30 ST. & LOC. GOV'T REV. 52 (1998).

transparent than their federal counterparts, less closely followed by watchdog groups, and less tracked by the state-level media."[63]

## VI. CONCLUSION

This brief review shows the ways in which the state executive branch, sometimes plural or fragmented and possibly containing constitutional agencies and officers, can be an entity that is substantially different from the powerful, potentially "unitary" federal executive. Further, as we saw in Chapter 8, the relationship of the state executive branch to the legislative and judicial branches may vary from state to state.

[63] Miriam Seifter, *Further from the People? The Puzzle of State Administration*, 93 N.Y.U. L. Rev. 107 (2018).

# PART IV

# UNIQUE INTERPRETATION ISSUES IN STATE CONSTITUTIONAL LAW

Part IV surveys the range of interpretation issues that arise in state constitutional law, with a specific focus on those that arise from the unique nature of state constitutions. There are, of course, similarities to other forms of textual interpretation, particularly statutory interpretation. As in the rest of the book, the contrasts with federal constitutional law will be highlighted.

Judicial opinions are referred to as illustrating various interpretation approaches without providing the full context of the specific cases. An exhaustive collection for each point is not provided, but enough decisions are referenced so the reader can study the specific contexts of the cases and compare them to the context with which they are currently concerned.

There are, of course, thousands of cases interpreting state constitutions, starting at the time they were first adopted. This part reflects cases discussing interpretation techniques from the past three decades and highlights relatively recent cases, as the goal is to present current techniques. Through these more recent cases, the user of this book can elaborate the specific technique, in a particular state, by tracing the judicial decisions on the point back through time. Also, the user should be able to trace the specific technique horizontally across the states by use of electronic research tools, as further discussed in the bibliographical essay.

# 12

# INTERPRETING STATE CONSTITUTIONS

*Scholarly interest has focused, understandably, on the courts as the most authoritative sources of constitutional interpretation. Mention, however, should also be made of nonjudicial interpreters of constitutional language, including executive and administrative officials, legislators, lobbyists, lawyers, and numerous private citizens. These nonjudicial interpreters make decisions, virtually on a daily basis, about the meaning of their constitutions, subject to relatively infrequent scrutiny by the courts. The techniques and sources of constitutional interpretation are therefore of concern to the nonjudicial as well as the judicial interpreters.*

—L. Harold Levinson[1]

Professor Levinson is correct to call attention to nonjudicial interpreters of state constitutions, but the primary focus of this book is on judicial interpretation. State constitutions, as *constitutional* documents, are much in need of judicial interpretation. As Walter Dodd observed, because a "constitution is a briefer and more general document than a statute, the share of the court in molding the constitution by interpretation is proportionately greater."[2] On the other hand, because of the greater detail and ease of amendment of state constitutions, other observers conclude that, in the state constitutional context, "it is probably true that interpretation has been less important than the more formal processes of amendment and revision."[3] As noted in Chapter 1, moreover, state constitutions

[1] L. Harold Levinson, *Interpreting State Constitutions by Resort to the Record*, 6 Fla. St. U. L. Rev. 567, 568 (1978). *See also* Peter E. Heiser Jr., *The Opinion Writing Function of Attorneys General*, 18 Idaho L. Rev. 9 (1982); Thomas R. Morris, *State Attorneys General as Interpreters of State Constitutions*, 17 Publius: The J. Federalism 133 (Winter 1987); Ark. Prof'l Bail Bondsman Lic. Bd. v. Oudin, 69 S.W.3d 855, 862 (Ark. 2002) (Attorney General's opinions not binding on courts).

[2] Walter F. Dodd, *The Problem of State Constitutional Construction*, 20 Colum. L. Rev. 635, 637 (1920). *See* McKenna v. Williams, 874 A.2d 217, 242 (R.I. 2005) (state constitution "must of necessity deal in generalities) (Suttell, J., concurring in part and dissenting in part).

[3] Elmer E. Cornwell, Jay S. Goodman, & Wayne R. Swanson, State Constitutional Conventions: The Politics of the Revision Process in Seven States 8 (1975).

*The Law of American State Constitutions.* Robert F. Williams and Lawrence Friedman, Oxford University Press.
 DOI: 10.1093/oso/9780190068806.003.0013

are different in a number of ways from the more familiar federal Constitution. Consequently, judicial interpretation of state constitutions can be quite different from their federal counterpart.[4]

Should the ease and frequency with which constitutions are amended influence the way courts interpret them? One commentator contends that "[s]tate judges, by contrast [to Supreme Court Justices], though they should not innovate lightly, should recall that state constitutions are less immutable."[5] Another commentator argues, however, that "[s]tate constitutions are easier to amend and may therefore provide less justification for flexible interpretation."[6] The relative ease of amendment to state constitutions also has implications for the doctrine of stare decisis, discussed later in this chapter.

Most of the focus that has been brought to bear on state constitutional interpretation has centered on *rights* cases and whether state courts should interpret their constitutions to be more protective than the federal Constitution. These matters are covered in Chapters 5–7. While state constitutional rights adjudication is extremely important and the sophistication of this area of the law has developed substantially, there is much involved in state constitutional interpretation beyond rights cases. These issues are treated in this chapter because, in the rights area, so much emphasis has been placed on the relationship between state and federal rights provisions and their judicial interpretation.

In many states, there are judicial opinions setting forth a general approach to state constitutional interpretation, together with a number of specific rules.[7] These courts often set forth these "rules of interpretation" at the beginning of new cases facing state constitutional interpretation issues. The Wisconsin Supreme Court, for example, has stated:

[4] G. Alan Tarr, *State Constitutional Design and State Constitutional Interpretation*, 72 Mont. L. Rev. 7, 8–9 (2011) ("These distinctive elements affect how jurists, public officials, and citizens interpret—or should interpret—a state constitution.").

[5] A.E. Dick Howard, *State Courts and Constitutional Rights in the Day of the Burger Court*, 62 Va. L. Rev. 873, 939 (1976).

[6] Levinson, *supra* note 1, at 568. *See also* Commonwealth v. O'Neal, 339 N.E.2d 676, 694 (Mass. 1975); In the Interest of J.W.T., 872 S.W.2d 189, 201–02 (Tex. 1994) (Cornyn, J., dissenting). For the contrary view, see State v. Baker, 405 A.2d 368, 375–81 (N.J. 1979).

Anyone who has worked with state constitutions knows they are not "easy" to amend. But compared to the process of amending the *federal* Constitution, amendment of state constitutions is simpler and more often successful.

[7] *See, e.g.*, West v. Thomson Newspapers, 872 P.2d 999 (Utah 1994); Randolph Co. Bd. of Educ. v. Adams, 467 S.E.2d 150 (W. Va. 1995); Thompson v. Craney, 546 N.W.2d 123, 127 (Wis. 1996); Boehm v. Town of St. John, 675 N.E.2d 318, 321 (Ind. 1996), State v. City of Oak Creek, 605 N.W.2d 526, 532 (Wis. 2000); City Chapel Evangelical Free, Inc. v. City of South Bend *ex rel.* Dep't of Redevelopment, 744 N.E.2d 443, 447 (Ind. 2001); Mogard v. City of Laramie, 32 P.3d 313, 316 (Wyo. 2001); Mich. United Conservation Clubs v. Sec'y of State, 630 N.W.2d 297 (Mich. 2001); Evenson v. State, 228 P.3d 282, 287 (Haw. 2010).

> In interpreting a constitutional provision, the court turns to three sources in determining the provision's meaning: the plain meaning of the words in the context used; the constitutional debates and the practices in existence at the time of the writing of the constitution; and the earliest interpretation of the provision by the legislature as manifested in the first law passed following adoption.[8]

Questions of state constitutional interpretation are treated as matters of law to be determined de novo by state high courts.[9]

## I. THE VOICE OF THE PEOPLE: INTENT OF THE VOTERS

As noted in Chapter 1, state constitutional provisions in all states but Delaware have origins that are quite different from the federal Constitution. According to the Michigan Supreme Court:

> When construing a constitution, the Court's task is to "divine the 'common understanding' of the provision, that meaning 'which reasonable minds, the great mass of the people themselves, would give it.'" Relevant considerations include the constitutional convention debates, the address to the people, the circumstances leading to the adoption of the provision, and the purpose sought to be accomplished.[10]

The New Jersey Supreme Court put it this way: "It is a familiar rule of construction that where phraseology is precise and unambiguous there is no room for judicial interpretation or for resort to extrinsic materials. The language speaks for itself, and where found in our State Constitution the language is the

[8] *Thompson*, 546 N.W.2d at 127; Dairyland Greyhound Park, Inc. v. Doyle, 719 N.W.2d 408, 445–48 (Wis. 2006) (Prosser, J., concurring in part and dissenting in part). *See also* Priest v. Pearce, 840 P.2d 65, 67 (Or. 1992); Stranahan v. Fred Meyer, Inc., 11 P.3d 228 (Or. 2000); Malone v. Shyne, 937 So.2d 343, 349–51 (La. 2006); *In re* opinion of the Justices to The Governor, 964 N.E.2d 941, 945–46 (Mass. 2012); *In re* Bruno, 101 A.3d 635, 660 n.13 (Pa. 2014); Wielechoski v. State, 403 P.3d 1141, 1146–47 (Alaska 2017).

[9] State v. Cook, 530 N.W.2d 728, 731 (Iowa 1995); Vilhauer v. Horsemen's Sports, Inc., 598 N.W.2d 525, 527 (S.D. 1999); Hynes v. Hale, 776 A.2d 722, 726 (N.H. 2001); MDC Restaurants, LLC v. Eighth Judicial Dist. Ct., 419 P.3 148, 155 (Nev. 2018).

[10] People v. Mezy, 551 N.W.2d 389, 393 (Mich. 1996) (citation omitted). *See also* State *ex rel.* Sanstead v. Freed, 251 N.W.2d 898, 905 (N.D. 1977); Opinion of the Justices, 673 A.2d 1291, 1297 (Me. 1996); *Stranahan*, 11 P.3d at 237; Allred v. McLoud, 31 S.W.3d 836, 839 (Ark. 2000); Cleveland Surgery Center v. Bradley Co. Mem. Hosp., 30 S.W.3d 278, 281–82 (Tenn. 2000); National Pride at Work, Inc. v. Governor, 748 N.W.2d 524, 533 (Mich. 2008); MDC Restaurants, LLC v. Eighth Judicial Dist. Ct., 419 P.3d 148, 155 (Nev. 2018); Saban Rent-a-Car, LLC. v. Arizona Dept. Revenue, 434 P.3d 1168, 1174 (Ariz. 2019).

*voice of the people*."[11] This approach, which is related to, but different from, the interpretation techniques applied to state statutes enacted through the initiative process,[12] is unlike anything in federal constitutional interpretation. State courts often use this approach, in the absence of indications of a technical meaning, to support a strong preference for ordinary or plain-meaning interpretation.[13] The Supreme Court of Colorado explained:

> To determine intent, courts first examine the language of the amendment and give words their plain and commonly understood meaning. Courts should not engage in a narrow or technical reading of language contained in an initiated constitutional amendment if to do such would defeat the intent of the people.[14]

Based on this preference for plain and ordinary language, attorney Lynn M. Boughey of North Dakota advocated "text-based analysis" over "intent-based analysis."[15] Many courts, of course, have indicated that, while a search for the plain meaning of a state constitutional provision is the primary task, it is often difficult to establish plain meaning, and some constitutional terms may have a technical meaning.[16]

[11] Vreeland v. Byrne, 370 A.2d 825, 830 (N.J. 1977) (emphasis added). *See also* Johnson v. Wells County Water Resources Bd., 410 N.W.2d 525, 528 (N.D. 1987); Harris v. City of Little Rock, 40 S.W.3d 214, 217 (Ark. 2001); Farmer v. Kinder, 89 S.W.3d 447, 452 (Mo. 2002); Wielechoski v. State, 403 P.3d 1141, 1146–47 (Alaska 2017).

[12] *See* Elizabeth A. McNellie, Note, *The Use of Extrinsic Aids in the Interpretation of Popularly Enacted Legislation*, 89 COLUM. L. REV. 157 (1989); Jane S. Schacter, *The Pursuit of "Popular Intent": Interpretive Dilemmas in Direct Democracy*, 105 YALE L.J. 107 (1995); Wash. State Dep't of Revenue v. Hoppe, 512 P.2d 1094 (Wash. 1973).

[13] Assoc. Press v. Bd. Public Educ., 804 P.2d 376, 379 (Mont. 1991); *In re* Janklow, 530 N.W.2d 367, 370 (S.D. 1995) ("In the absence of ambiguity, the language in the [C]onstitution must be applied as it reads."); State v. Trump Hotels & Casino Resorts, Inc., 734 A.2d 1160, 1176 (N.J. 1999); Frank v. Barker, 20 S.W.3d 293, 296 (Ark. 2000); Harris v. City of Little Rock, 40 S.W.3d 214, 217 (Ark. 2001); Chapman v. Bevilacqua, 42 S.W.3d 378, 383 (Ark. 2001); Utah Sch. Bds. Ass'n v. Utah State Bd. of Educ., 17 P.3d 1125, 1129 (Utah 2001); Pitts v. Larson, 638 N.W.2d 254, 257 (S.D. 2001).

[14] Zaner v. City of Brighton, 917 P.2d 280, 283 (Colo. 1996) (citations omitted). *See also* Tivolino Teller House, Inc. v. Fagan, 926 P.2d 1208, 1211 (Colo. 1996) (citation omitted):

> Our primary task is to "ascertain and give effect to the intent of those who adopted [the amendment]." In the case of constitutional amendments adopted by popular vote, we must consider the intent of the voters in enacting the provision, and to that end, we must give the words of the amendment their natural and popular meaning.

*Id. See also* Lawnwood Medical Center, Inc. v. Seeger, 990 So.2d 503, 512 (Fla. 2008) (relying on dictionaries); People v. Clemons, 968 N.E.2d 1046, 1054 (Ill. 2012); State v. Mills, 312 P.3d 515, 519 (Or. 2014).

[15] *See* Lynn M. Boughey, *An Introduction to North Dakota Constitutional Law: Content and Methods of Interpretation*, 63 N.D. L. REV. 157, 272–74 (1987) (advocating "text based analysis" as superior to "intent based analysis" for providing modicum of certainty regarding future interpretation of North Dakota Constitution); Lynn M. Boughey, *A Judge's Guide to Constitutional Interpretation*, 66 TEMP. L. REV. 1269 (1993) (same); *see also* Jeremy M. Christiansen, *Originalism: The Primary Canon of State Constitutional Interpretation*, 15 GEO. J. L. & PUB. POL'Y 341 (2017).

[16] State v. Bray, 291 P.3d 727, 733 (Or. 2012) ("well-defined legal meaning); McIntyre v. Wick, 558 N.W.2d 347 (S.D. 1996). *See also* Chittenden School Dist. v. Dept. of Educ., 738 A.2d 539, 551–52 (Vt.

Because resort to voters' intent is completely foreign to federal constitutional interpretation, the variety of evidence state courts look to in interpreting state constitutional provisions is also quite unheard of in federal courts. State courts will often examine, based on arguments submitted by counsel, evidence of the voters' intent derived from official ballot pamphlets and other materials presented to voters prior to the referendum. In this respect, the California Supreme Court noted:

> When, as here, the language of an initiative measure does not point to a definitive resolution of a question of interpretation, " 'it is appropriate to consider indicia of the voters' intent other than the language of the provision itself.' . . . Such indicia include the analysis and arguments contained in the official ballot pamphlet."[17]

Another form of official information supplied to voters prior to their consideration of proposed constitutional amendments is the "Address to the People," which is often drafted by a constitutional convention itself and presented to the voters.[18] Even more unusual to those familiar only with federal constitutional interpretation is the rather frequent reference by state courts to newspaper coverage of the constitutional issue to be voted on.[19] Debates on *legislatively proposed*

1999); Mich. Coalition of State Employee Unions v. Mich. Civil Serv. Comm'n, 634 N.W.2d 692, 698 (Mich. 2001) (term of art, with no plain meaning, interpreted according to its technical meaning at time of adoption); Mich. United Conservation Clubs v. Sec'y of State, 630 N.W.2d 297, 309 (Mich. 2001); Pitts v. Larson, 638 N.W.2d 254, 260 (S.D. 2001) (Gilbertson, C.J., dissenting); Heath v. Kiger, 176 P.3d 690, 692 (Ariz. 2008).

For a revealing debate about ordinary versus technical meaning, see County of Wayne v. Hathcock, 684 N.W.2d 765, 779–81, 788–99 (Mich. 2004). *See* also Silver Creek Drain Dist. v. Excursions Division, Inc., 663 N.W.2d 436, 440 (Mich. 2003); Phillips v. Mirac, Inc., 685 N.W.2d 174, 180–82 (Mich. 2004).

[17] Hill v. Nat'l Collegiate Athletic Ass'n, 865 P.2d 633, 642 (Cal. 1994). *See also* S.F. Taxpayers Ass'n v. Bd. of Supervisors, 828 P.2d 147, 152–53 (Cal. 1992) (declining reliance on a legislative analyst's report); People v. Dean, 677 N.E.2d 947, 953 (Ill. 1997); *In re* Young, 976 P.2d 581, 589 (Utah 1999); East Bay Asian Local Dev. Corp. v. State, 13 P.3d 1122, 1139 (Cal. 2000); Apartment Ass'n of L.A. v. City of Los Angeles, 14 P.3d 930, 936 (Cal. 2001); Ventura Group Ventures v. Ventura Port Dist., 16 P.3d 717, 728 (Cal. 2001); Opinion of the Justices, 765 A.2d 706, 708 (N.H. 2001).

[18] Wood v. State Admin. Bd., 238 N.W.16, 17 (Mich. 1931) (citations omitted) ("Neither in the debates in the Constitutional Convention, nor in the Address to the People, was it suggested. . . ."). *See also* People v. DiGuida, 604 N.E.2d 336, 344 (Ill. 1992); Straus v. Governor, 592 N.W.2d 53, 57 n.2 (Mich. 1999); Opinion of the Justices, 765 A.2d 706, 708 (N.H. 2001); Bd. of County Comm'rs v. Vail Assocs., 19 P.3d 1263, 1277 (Colo. 2001); Michigan United Conservation Clubs v. Secretary of State, 630 N.W.2d 297, 304 n.11 (Mich. 2001); Bd. of County Comm. v. Vail Associates, 19 P.3d 1263, 1277 (Colo. 2001); Embry v. O'Bannon, 798 N.E.2d 157, 161 (Ind. 2003); People v. Rodriguez, 112 P.3d 693, 702 (Colo. 2005).

[19] Client Follow-up Co. v. Hynes, 390 N.E.2d 847, 854 (Ill. 1979); Lipscomb v. State, 753 P.2d 939, 944–46 (Or. 1988); State v. Trump Hotels & Casinos Resorts, Inc., 734 A.2d 1160, 1182–86 (N.J. 1999); Horry County Sch. Dist. v. Horry County, 552 S.E.2d 737, 740 (S.C. 2001); Dairyland Greyhound Park, Inc. v. Doyle, 719 N.W.2d 408, 426–27 (Wis. 2006). *But see* Kalodimos v. Vill. of Morton Grove, 470 N.E.2d 266, 272 (Ill. 1984) (newspaper coverage unreliable where only from one

state constitutional amendments produce the more standard materials associated with "legislative history."[20]

State constitutions' origins, given life by the citizens who voted on them, can have further effect. The "popular sovereignty" provisions, like North Carolina's quoted in Chapter 1, although generally expressions of political philosophy with little "direct influence on constitutional disputes and the resolution of particular cases,"[21] have provided important support for resolving interpretation questions in certain cases. For example, when questions arise concerning the power of the electorate to approve changes in the state constitutions, these provisions are often invoked.[22] The Iowa Supreme Court relied on its popular sovereignty provision in holding that write-in votes for candidates who were not on the ballot had to be counted.[23] The Alaska Supreme Court cited its clause in invalidating misleading ballot language in a vote on whether to call a constitutional convention.[24] The Pennsylvania Supreme Court relied on its provision in holding that the electorate may amend the state constitution to displace an inconsistent existing provision.[25] The Maine Supreme Court relied on its provision to strike down binding decisions by nonelected arbitrators.[26]

## II. STATE CONSTITUTIONAL HISTORY

Setting aside the debate over the authenticity of federal Constitutional Convention records, federal judges will rely on the debates at the federal

part of the state). *See also* State *ex rel.* Sanstead v. Freed, 251 N.W.2d 898, 907 (N.D. 1977); *In re* Advisory Opinion to the Governor, 612 A.2d 1, 11 (R.I. 1992); Westerman v. Cary, 885 P.2d 1067, 1073 (Wash. 1995); Robert F. Utter, *State Constitutional Law, the United States Supreme Court, and Democratic Accountability: Is There a Crocodile in the Bathtub?* 64 WASH. L. REV. 19, 37 (1989). *See infra* notes 57–71.

[20] *See generally* Gerald Benjamin & Melissa Cusa, *Amending the New York State Constitution Through the Legislature, in* DECISION 1997: CONSTITUTIONAL CHANGE IN NEW YORK 385–88 (Gerald Benjamin & Henrik N. Dullea eds., 1997). *See, e.g.*, East Baton Rouge Parish School Bd. v. Foster, 851 So.2d 985, 997 (La. 2003); Malone v. Shyne, 937 So.2d 343, 353–54 (La. 2006); City of Rock Hill v. Harris, 205 S.E.2d 53 (S.C. 2011).

[21] JOHN DINAN, THE VIRGINIA STATE CONSTITUTION: A REFERENCE GUIDE 39 (2006). These provisions have been referred to as "Lockean power clauses" that "give citizens considerable power over their state governments . . ." Steven Gow Calabresi et al., *Individual Rights Under State Constitutions in 2018: What Rights Are Deeply Rooted in a Modern-Day Consensus of the States?* 94 NOTRE DAME L. REV. 49, 133–34 (2018).

[22] Opinion of the Justices, 81 So.2d 881, 883–84 (Ala. 1955); Gatewood v. Matthews, 403 S.W.2d 716, 721 (Ky. 1966); Harvey v. Ridgeway, 450 S.W.2d 281, 288 (Ark. 1970); Smith v. Cenarrusa, 475 P.2d 11, 17 (Idaho 1970); Pryor v. Lowe, 523 S.W.2d 199, 202 (Ark. 1975).

[23] Barr v. Cardell, 155 N.W.312, 313–14 (Iowa 1915).

[24] Boucher v. Bamhoff, 495 P.2d 77, 78 (Alaska 1972).

[25] Commonwealth v. Tharp, 754 A.2d 1251, 1253 (Pa. 2000).

[26] Cape Elizabeth School Bd. v. Cape Elizabeth Teachers Assoc., 459 A.2d 166, 171–72 (Me. 1983).

Constitutional Convention in appropriate cases, even though these materials are scant indeed when compared with state constitutional convention records.[27] Some states had contentious debates over whether to keep records of their constitutional conventions, with the arguments focused primarily on expense.[28] Nonetheless, Dr. John Dinan was "able to locate the records of the debates for 114 state conventions," making it "possible to trace the development of the American state constitutional tradition."[29]

Of course, constitutional conventions are not the only source of state constitutional amendment and revision. Proposals by the legislature and initiative proposals, as well as those by constitutional conventions, may all be based on recommendations of constitutional commissions. Further, each of these processes may be governed by different procedural requirements (see Chapter 13), enforceable by the courts, and they each produce differing kinds of constitutional history that may be relevant in interpreting the new provisions. Despite complaints that state constitutional history is scarce,[30] it is much more available than federal constitutional history.

Alan Tarr has demonstrated the special appeal of "original intent" (as well as textualism) and resort to state constitutional history materials in the rediscovery of state constitutional rights protections related to the New Judicial Federalism.[31] He noted: "Because state constitutions possess a distinctive design, history and underlying theory, it is argued, the critique of federal original-intent jurisprudence does not apply—or at least does not apply with equal force—to a state original intent jurisprudence."[32] Thus, there is a strong incentive to uncover state constitutional history materials.[33] State constitutional history even played a central role in proving intentional racial discrimination in the U.S. Supreme Court's 1985 decision holding unconstitutional the provision of the Alabama

[27] *See, e.g.*, Christopher Collier, *The Historians Versus the Lawyers: James Madison, James Hutson, and the Doctrine of Original Intent*, 112 Pa. Mag. Hist. & Biog. 137 (1988) (discussing views of accuracy of federal Constitutional Convention records and their relationship to the doctrine of original intent); James H. Hutson, *The Creation of the Constitution: The Integrity of the Documentary Record*, 65 Tex. L. Rev. 1 (1986) (same); Mary Sarah Bilder, *How Bad Were the Official Records of the Federal Convention?* 80 Geo. Wash. L. Rev. 1620 (2012); Mary Sarah Bilder, Madison's Hand: Revising the Constitutional Convention (2015).

For a consideration of similar problems regarding state constitutional convention records, see Maureen Brady, *Uses of Convention History in State Constitutional Law*, 2022 Wis. L. Rev. 169.

[28] John J. Dinan, The American State Constitutional Tradition 18–28 (2006).

[29] *Id.* at 28.

[30] Peter J. Teachout, *Against the Stream: An Introduction to the Vermont Law Review Symposium on the Revolution in State Constitutional Law*, 13 Vt. L. Rev. 13, 26 (1988) ("lack of adequate and available historical materials."). For a good example of state constitutional history research, see Charles W. Johnson & Scott P. Beetham, *The Origin of Article I, Section 7 of the Washington State Constitution*, 31 Sea. U. L. Rev. 431 (2008).

[31] G. Alan Tarr, *Constitutional Theory and State Constitutional Interpretation*, 22 Rutgers L.J. 841, 848–56 (1991).

[32] *Id.* at 851.

[33] *Id.* at 852.

Constitution barring voting by persons convicted of crimes involving "moral turpitude."[34] Further, as Tarr has pointed out, a careful look at state constitutional history (in addition to textual differences) could be used to justify an interpretation of the state constitution that is more protective, or recognizes greater rights, than those available at the federal level.[35]

If, however, it is the voters who adopt the state constitutional provision at a referendum, rather than the drafters themselves, whose intent is the focal point of state constitutional interpretation, why are constitutional convention or other materials relevant at all? The Illinois Supreme Court has been particularly concerned with this linkage issue, observing:

> We have previously acknowledged that in construing the Constitution the true inquiry concerns the understanding of the meaning of its provision by the voters who adopted it. However, the practice of consulting the debates of the members of the convention which framed the constitution has long been indulged in by courts in determining the meaning of provisions which are thought to be doubtful.[36]

In a later case, the Illinois court explained: "The insight provided by these comments is critical to our task of discerning the intent of the drafters . . . The reason is that it is only with the consent of the convention that such provisions are submitted to the voters in the first place."[37]

Professor Harold Levinson also explored this question of possible linkage.[38] He suggested the following possibilities: that the people conveyed their views to their delegates, who acted as agents of the people;[39] that there was some kind of informal communication from the delegates back to the people prior to the ratification vote; and that the delegates and the people shared a "general understanding of how language was used."[40] In addition, Professor Levinson made an

[34] Hunter v. Underwood, 471 U.S. 222, 229–31 (1985).

[35] Tarr, *supra* note 31, at 848 ("If a divergent interpretation may be justified by reference to the distinctive origins or purpose of a provision, then state jurists must pay particular attention to the intent of the framers and to the historical circumstances out of which the constitutional provisions arose.").

[36] People v. Tisler, 469 N.E.2d 147, 161 (Ill. 1984).

[37] Cincinnati Ins. Co. v. Chapman, 691 N.E.2d 374, 381 (Ill. 1998). *See also* Monaghan v. Sch. Dist. No. 1, 315 P.2d 797, 801 (Or. 1957); Baker v. Miller, 636 N.E.2d 551, 555 (Ill. 1994); John L. Horwich, MEIC v. DEQ: *An Inadequate Effort to Address the Meaning of Montana's Constitutional Environmental Provisions*, 62 MONT. L. REV. 269, 288 (2001).

[38] Levinson, *supra* note 1.

[39] *Id.* at 569. Professor Williams is indebted to his colleague, Alan Tarr, for pointing out the major distinctions here from the federal constitutional process. There, the state legislatures selected the delegates, and closed debates took place in Philadelphia under a revision mandate rather than a constitutional replacement mandate. Therefore, at the federal level, there was no interaction between voters and delegates the way there is at the state level.

[40] *Id.*

important distinction between a situation where the people cast a single vote for an entire revised state constitution or package of revisions, on the one hand; and where they vote individually on a single amendment, on the other. In the former case, he concluded, "The result is that many electors, in ratifying a package proposal, must have placed considerable trust in the intent of the framers."[41] Finally, in a case of ambiguous state constitutional language where the people's intent is also unclear, the intent of the framers is the only available source of intent and "the most persuasive substitute available."[42]

Some courts, as noted earlier, insist on the presence of an ambiguity in the state constitutional text as a prerequisite for examining constitutional convention records.[43] Sometimes, both the majority and dissenting opinions in state courts rely on the same debate in the state constitutional convention for their differing views.[44] On many occasions, state courts have referred to the *adoption* or *rejection* of amendments proposed by the legislature or during a constitutional convention, or to changes in language, to indicate the meaning of the final adopted provision, just as they might when undertaking statutory interpretation.[45] This

[41] *Id.* at 570.

[42] *Id.*

[43] SJL of Montana Assoc. v. City of Billings, 867 P.2d 1084, 1088 (Mont. 1993) (Trieweiler, J., dissenting) (disagreement in majority and dissent over presence of ambiguity). *See also* State v. Conger, 878 P.2d 1089, 1093 (Or. 1994); Harris v. City of Little Rock, 40 S.W.3d 214, 217 (Ark. 2001); Utah School Bds. Assoc. v. Utah St. Bd. of Ed., 17 P.3d 1125, 1129 (Utah 2001); ASAP Storage, Inc. v. City of Sparks, 173 P.3d 734, 739 (Nev. 2008). Of course, as in statutory interpretation, there can be two kinds of ambiguity:

> The language of La. Const. art. III, § 2(A)(2) relative to tax exemptions and exclusions is, *by itself*, clear and unambiguous. However, we must analyze the language, both of the entire amendment and of the critical portion, in the context of the enactment of the amendment in order to determine if there is more than one reasonable interpretation.
>
> Louisiana Municipal Assoc. v. State, 773 So.2d 663, 667 (La. 2000). *See also* Lipscomb v. State, 753 P.2d 939, 946–47 (Or. 1988).

Interestingly, the Oregon Supreme Court seems to require a finding of ambiguity before going behind the text of a state constitutional *amendment*, but not when it is interpreting a provision of the *original constitution*. Stranahan v. Fred Meyer, Inc., 11 P.3d 228, 239 (Or. 2000). The court explained:

> As to the former, the drafters of the constitution crafted those provisions and submitted them to the people for approval without the benefit of an existing constitutional framework. In contrast, provisions or amendments created through either legislative referral or initiative petition are adopted by the people against the backdrop of an existing constitutional framework. It follows that, with respect to the latter provisions, it is the people's understanding and intended meaning of the provision in question—as to which the text and context are the most important clue—that are critical to our analysis.
>
> *Id. See also* Wittemyer v. City of Portland, 402 P.3d 702, 705–06 (Or. 2017).

[44] Sheff v. O'Neill, 678 A.2d 1267 (Conn. 1996); Temperance League of Ky. v. Perry, 74 S.W.2d 730, 735–36 (Ky. 2002); Idaho Press Club v. State Legislature, 132 P.3d 397, 401, 406 (Idaho 2006).

[45] Mayle v. Pennsylvania Dept. Highways, 388 A.2d 709, 717 (Pa. 1978); Jacobs v. Major, 407 N.W.2d 832, 853 (Wis. 1987) (Abrahamson, J., concurring in part, dissenting in part); House Speaker v. Governor, 506 N.W.2d 190, 203–04 (Mich. 1993); State v. Rivers, 921 P.2d 495, 513 (Wash. 1996) (rejected amendment indicates meaning); Gryczan v. State, 942 P.2d 112, 123 (Mont. 1997) (rejected amendment does not indicate meaning); Fischer v. Governor, 749 A.2d 321, 326 (N.H. 2000); Wis. Prof'l Police Ass'n, Inc. v. Lightbourn, 627 N.W.2d 807, 837–38 (Wis. 2001);

reference to the "gestation" of a state constitutional provision can be very important in determining meaning. The most common references to state constitutional debates are those where the records indicate the purpose of the provision, such as when the Supreme Court of Montana concluded that "(i)t is clear from the minutes of the Constitutional Convention that the second sentence of Section 16 was in response to our decision. . . ."[46]

In state constitutional interpretation, as in statutory interpretation, it is important to distinguish between *general* intent and purpose, as reflected in constitutional history,[47] and *specific* intent, concerning the very interpretation issue before the court, reflected in such materials. Courts rarely make this distinction, although they should. For example, the Montana Supreme Court relied on constitutional convention debates concerning the very question before the court: whether an initiated constitutional amendment could be challenged on procedural grounds after it was ratified by the voters.[48] In *Thies v. State Bd. of Elections*, the Illinois Supreme Court noted: "This case involves one of the rare instances where resorting to the debates of the convention reveals that the exact question presented for review in this court was asked and answered by the delegates to the convention."[49]

Cambria v. Soaries, 776 A.2d 754, 761–62 (N.J. 2001); New Hampshire Motor Transport Assoc. v. State, 846 A.2d 553, 557 (N.H. 2004); Bienkowski v. Brooks, 873 A.2d 1122, 1132–33 (Md. 2005); Idaho Press Club, Inc. v. State Legislature, 132 P.3d 397, 401 (Idaho 2006); Fransen v. City of New Orleans, 988 So.2d 225, 240 (La. 2008); Hernandez v. Bd. of Co. Commissioners, 189 P.3d 638, 643 (Mont. 2008); Gregg v. Rauner, 124 N.E.3d 947, 955 (Ill. 2018); State v. Staker, 489 P.3rd 489, 502–03 (Mont. 2021).

[46] Trankel v. State Dep't of Military Affairs, 938 P.2d 614, 621 (Mont. 1997) (citation omitted). *See also* People v. Diguida, 604 N.E.2d 336, 342 (Ill. 1992); Polk v. Edwards, 626 So.2d 1128, 1137–38 (La. 1993) (constitutional convention records indicate adoption of earlier judicial interpretations); State v. Mendoza, 920 P.2d 357, 362–67 (Haw. 1996); Mont. Envtl. Info. Ctr. v. Dep't. of Envtl. Quality, 988 P.2d 1236, 1246–49 (Mont. 1999); Cmt'y Ins. Co. v. Ohio Dep't of Transp., 750 N.E.2d 573, 580–81 (Ohio 2001); Alaska Legislative Council v. Knowles, 21 P.3d 367, 371–72 (Alaska 2001); Montanans for Equal Application of Initiative Laws v. State *ex rel.* Johnson, 154 P.3d 1202, 1207 (Mont. 2007); Everson v. State, 228 P.3d 282, 287–89 (Haw. 2010); Clear Springs Foods, Inc. v. Sparkman, 252 P.3d 71, 87 (Idaho 2011); Summit Water Distribution Co. v. Utah State Tax Comm., 259 P.3d 1055, 1058–59 (Utah 2011); Davis v. State, 804 N.W.2d 618, 644–46 (S.D. 2011); Bernstein v. State, 29 A.3d 267, 281–83 (Md. 2011); Nelson v. Hawaiian Homes Com'n., 277 P.3d 279, 292 (Haw. 2012); Gregg v. Rauner, 124 N.E.3d 947, 955 (Ill. 2018); Espinoza v. Montana Dept. of Revenue, 435 P.3d 603, 609–10 (Mont. 2018).

The Michigan Supreme Court permitted two former convention delegates to appear as amici curiae to explain their intent with respect to the specific issue before the court. Goldstone v. Bloomfield Public Library, 737 N.W.2d 476, 491 (Mich. 2007).

[47] We use "constitutional history" here in its "legislative history" sense.

[48] Montanans for Equal Application of Initiative Laws v. State *ex rel.* Johnson, 154 P.3d 1202, 1207–08 (Mont. 2007). *See also* Alaska Legislative Counsel v. Knowles, 21 P.3d 367, 372 n.26 (Alaska 2001); Bryan v. Yellowstone County Elementary School Dist. No. 2, 60 P.3d 381, 388 (Mont. 2002); Bourges v. Le Blanc, 777 N.E.2d 239, 240 (N.Y. 2002); State v. Sunderland, 168 P.3d 526, 538 (Haw. 2007); *In re* Davis, 681 N.W.2d 452, 458–59 (S.D. 2004).

[49] 529 N.E.2d 565, 568 (Ill. 1988). *See also* Continental Illinois Nat'l Bank & Trust Co. v. Zagel, 401 N.E.2d 491, 495 (Ill. 1979); Child v. Lomax, 188 P.3d 1103, 1109–10 (Nev. 2008). *Contra* Committee

Some state courts have questioned the reliability of state constitutional convention debates, as illustrated by the New Hampshire Supreme Court's observation:

> The statements made by the delegates to the constitutional convention are not always significant in determining the meaning of a particular amendment. To be entitled to consideration, the delegates' statements must interpret the amendment's language in accordance with its plain and common meaning while being reflective of its known purpose or object.[50]

Professor Levinson proposed standards for reliance on the records of state constitutional deliberative proceedings. He suggested that such materials be deemed persuasive only if they reflect the "collective intent" of the body, based on "an examination of the record as a whole and a compilation of all parts of the record dealing with the specific point being examined."[51] He then proposed that the burden be on the party relying on such materials to search the record as a whole and that the court (with the aid of opposing counsel) independently review the record.[52]

The most common, though rarely acknowledged, difficulty with state constitutional convention materials arises from the tension, mentioned earlier, between the pull of plain meaning interpretation because voters adopt state constitutional provisions, and the desire to look behind text and rely on indications of intent or purpose expressed at the constitutional convention. What if these two approaches point in differing directions?

The New York Court of Appeals was faced with construing a state constitutional provision authorizing the legislature to change judicial district boundaries.[53] The question arose whether this provision permitted the

for Educational Rights v. Edgar, 672 N.E.2d 1178, 1185 (Ill. 1996) ("general statement of principle was not made in reference to" the interpretation issue before the court).

50 N.H. Mun. Trust Worker's Comp. Fund v. Flynn, 573 A.2d 439, 441 (N.H. 1990); *see* Straus v. Governor, 592 N.W.2d 53, 57 n.2 (Mich. 1999) (constitutional history relied on by both sides but "too ambiguous and short-lived"). *See also* House Speaker v. Governor, 506 N.W.2d 190, 202 (Mich. 1993). The Pennsylvania Supreme Court has also questioned the relevance of constitutional convention debates to state constitutional interpretation. Bowers v. Pa. Labor Relations Bd., 167 A.2d 480, 487 (Pa. 1961).

51 Levinson, *supra* note 1, at 570. For an example of such a compilation of "all parts of the record dealing with the specific point being examined," see generally Robert F. Williams, The *New Jersey Equal Rights Amendment: A Documentary Sourcebook*, 16 WOMEN'S RTS. L. REP. 69 (1994).

52 Levinson, *supra* note 1, at 571.

53 Kuhn v. Curran, 61 N.E.2d 513 (N.Y. 1945). *See generally* Mary Ann Barnard, *Enabling and Implementing Legislation and State Constitutional Convention Committee Reports*, 6 U. HAW. L. REV. 523 (1984); C. Albert Bowers, Comment, *Divining the Framers' Intentions: The Immunity Standard for Criminal Proceedings Under the Utah Constitution*, 2000 UTAH L. REV. 135.

legislature to increase the number of judicial districts. The court rejected such an interpretation, premised on the possible understanding and discussions of the lawyers on the Judiciary Committee, including the deletion of language expressly prohibiting the legislature from increasing the number of districts, in the 1894 New York Constitutional Convention. The court concluded that it would not rely on such technical discussions, or upon a "doubtful implication" arising from the deletion of limiting language, of which the public would have had no knowledge. Judge Irving Lehman cautioned:

> We may not, however, construe the words of the Constitution in exactly the same manner as we would construe the words of a will or contract drafted by careful lawyers, or even a statute enacted by the Legislature. It is the approval of the People of the State which gives force to a provision of the Constitution drafted by the convention, and in construing the Constitution we seek the meaning which the words would convey to an intelligent, careful voter. A grant of an enlarged power by the People should not rest upon doubtful implication arising from the omission of a previous express limitation, at least unless it appears that the omission and its significance was called to the attention of the People.[54]

Similarly, in the words of the Pennsylvania Supreme Court: "Where, as here, we must decide between two interpretations of a constitutional provision, we must favor a natural reading which avoids contradictions and difficulties in implementation, which completely conforms to the intent of the framers and which reflects the views of the ratifying voter."[55] This approach seems to mean that even clear constitutional history ("original intent") cannot overcome an apparent "plain meaning" that would have been the understanding of the voters.

Thus, the "voice of the people" approach seems to serve two related functions. First, it sets a general tone of nontechnical interpretation for state constitutions. Second, it provides a rule of preference in the face of competing, even strong,

[54] *Kuhn*, 61 N.E.2d at 517–18. Judge Lewis wrote an interesting dissent, *id.* at 519.

[55] Commonwealth *ex rel.* Paulinski v. Isaac, 397 A.2d 760, 766 (Pa.), *cert. denied*, 422 U.S. 918 (1979). *See also* Pa. Prison Soc'y v. Commonwealth, 776 A.2d 971, 976 (Pa. 2001). The Missouri Supreme Court stated:

> While the debates of the convention are interesting, they neither add to nor subtract from the plain meaning of the constitution's words. Missouri's voters did not vote on the words used in the deliberations of the constitutional convention. The voters voted on the words of the constitution. . . .

Independence National Education Assoc. v. Independence School Dist., 223 S.E.3d 131, 137 (Mo. 2007). *See also* Continental Ill. National Bank & Trust Co. v. Zagel, 401 N.E.2d 491, 495 (Ill. 1979); East Baton Rouge Parish School Bd. v. Foster, 851 So.2d 985, 996 (La. 2003) ("It is the intent of the voting population that controls."); Wielechoski v. State, 403 P.3d 1141, 1146–47 (Alaska 2015).

evidence of contrary intent contained in constitutional convention materials or other records.

Since the middle of the nineteenth century, increased reliance has been placed on state constitutional *commissions* to help prepare for constitutional conventions or to advise the legislature (Chapter 13). Because of the indirect route taken by constitutional changes proposed by these commissions, debates and reports of such commissions arguably do not qualify as "constitutional history" in the direct sense that the debates in a constitutional convention, or in the legislature on proposed amendments, would be considered evidence of the "intent of the framers." Technically, and legally, of course, the appointed members of a constitutional commission are not the "framers" of ratified amendments that are based on their recommendations but actually proposed to the electorate by the legislature or a constitutional convention. But this is too narrow a view of constitutional history. The commission members operate under a direct delegation of power from either the legislature or the governor. Their recommendations are the origins of important state constitutional changes. Of course, neither the legislature nor a constitutional convention is bound to accept the commission's recommendations, or even to limit its consideration only to those recommendations forwarded by the commission. Still, courts routinely rely on the materials prepared by state constitutional commissions.[56]

In several states, important newspaper coverage of state constitutional conventions has been compiled and published in book form to facilitate its use by scholars, lawyers, judges, and others. Indeed, political scientist John Bebout's widely used (but out-of-print) *Proceedings of the New Jersey Constitutional Convention of 1844*, which is the only usable reference work on the origins of and debates on the 1844 New Jersey Constitution, is based almost exclusively on newspaper reports. This compilation was the product of a Federal Writers Project effort nearly one hundred years after the 1844 New Jersey Constitutional Convention. It has been regularly referred to by New Jersey courts and scholars.[57]

[56] *See, e.g.*, Snow v. City of Memphis, 527 S.W.2d 55, 61 (Tenn. 1975), *appeal dismissed*, 423 U.S. 1083 (1976); State v. Manley, 441 So.2d 864, 885 (Ala. 1983) (Beatty, J., dissenting); Claudio v. State, 585 A.2d 1278, 1297 (Del. 1991); *In re* Young, 976 P.2d 581, 587–89 (Utah 1999); Leone v. Medical Bd., 995 P.2d 191, 195 (Cal. 2000); Thompson v. Dept. of Corrections, 18 P.3d 1198, 1201 (Cal. 2001); Opinion of the Justices, 765 A.2d 706, 708 (N.H. 2001); D&M Healthcare, Inc. v. Kernan, 800 N.E.2d 898, 909 (Ind. 2003); Doe v. Nelson, 680 N.W.2d 302, 308–09 (S.D. 2004); *In re* Request of Governor Daugaard, 801 N.W.2d 438, 441 (S.D. 2011); Solomon v. State, 364 P.3d 536 (Kan. 2015); City of Asheville v. State, 794 S.E.2d 759, 779 (N.C. 2016). The Florida Supreme Court relied on the records of the 1966 Constitutional Revision Commission, located in a "special file in the Supreme Court Library." Hayek v. Lee County, 231 So.2d 214, 216 n.7 (Fla. 1970). *See also In re* Constitutionality of HJR 1987, 817 So.2d 819, 834 (Fla. 2002) (Lewis, J., concurring); Cummings v. Mickelson, 495 N.W.2d 493, 499–500 (S.D. 1993); Diamonds v. Greenville Co., 480 S.E.2d 718, 720 (S.C. 1997); State *ex rel.* McCrory v. Berger, 781 S.E.2d 248, 254–55 (N.C. 2016).

[57] *See, e.g.*, Vreeland v. Byrne, 370 A.2d 825, 838 (N.J. 1977) (Hughes, C.J., dissenting); Cambria v. Soaries, 776 A.2d 754, 761 (N.J. 2001).

Scholars have known and made use of this important, albeit unofficial, source of information concerning state constitutional conventions and commissions for many years. For example, Professor Merrill D. Peterson's *Democracy, Liberty, and Property: The State Constitutional Conventions of the 1820's*, published in 1966, made extensive use of newspaper reports, particularly for the Massachusetts convention of 1820–1821.[58]

Most of the reclamation of newspaper coverage has been of constitutional conventions in the nineteenth century. Scholars in states such as Oregon,[59] Wisconsin,[60] Connecticut,[61] Maryland,[62] Texas,[63] and Arizona[64] have produced compilations of newspaper coverage of state constitutional conventions. There

[58] MERRILL D. PETERSON, DEMOCRACY, LIBERTY, AND PROPERTY: THE STATE CONSTITUTIONAL CONVENTIONS OF THE 1820's, at xxiii (1966). *See* also GORDON MORRIS BAKKEN, ROCKY MOUNTAIN CONSTITUTION MAKING: 1850–1912 (1987); DINAN, *supra* note 28, at 26–28.

[59] THE OREGON CONSTITUTION AND PROCEEDINGS AND DEBATES OF THE CONSTITUTIONAL CONVENTION OF 1857 (Charles Henry Carey ed., 1926) [hereinafter OREGON CONSTITUTION]. This work is regularly relied upon by Oregon courts and scholars. *See, e.g.*, State v. Conger, 878 P.2d 1089, 1094 (Or. 1994); Billings v. Gates, 916 P.2d 291, 298 (Or. 1996); Vannatta v. Keisling, 931 P.2d 770, 782 (Or. 1997); State v. Hirsch, 114 P.3d 1104, 1112 (Or. 2005); David Schuman, *The Creation of the Oregon Constitution*, 74 OR. L. REV. 611, 622 (1995). The editor of this work, Charles Carey, stated in the introduction:

> The transactions of the constitutional convention, held at the county courthouse in Salem, Oregon, between August 17 and September 18, 1857, are shown in the official Journal of the Proceedings, and also by the report printed in the Weekly Oregonian and in the Oregon Statesman of the period. These sources are quoted below, in succession, under each legislative date. The Journal is the official report, and in case of difference between the authorities must control, but the newspaper accounts give the debates in greater detail and furnish a valuable supplement to the record. The legislative date of the Proceedings is given at the top of each page.
>
> OREGON CONSTITUTION, *supra*, at 59.

[60] MILO M. QUAIFE, THE CONVENTION OF 1846 (1919). The Wisconsin courts have relied on this source. *See, e.g.*, Jacobs v. Major, 407 N.W.2d 832, 853 (Wis. 1987).

[61] Wesley W. Horton, *Annotated Debates of the 1818 Constitutional Convention*, 65 CONN. B.J. SI-1 (special issue 1991). Connecticut courts and scholars had relied on the newspaper reports even prior to Horton's compilation. *See, e.g.*, Cologne v. Westfarms Assocs., 469 A.2d 1201, 1209 n.9 (Conn. 1984); Jacob Katz Cogan, Note, *The Look Within: Property, Capacity, and Suffrage in Nineteenth-Century America*, 107 YALE L.J. 473, 480–81 nn.53–54 (1997).

[62] PHILIP B. PERLMAN, DEBATES OF THE MARYLAND CONSTITUTIONAL CONVENTION OF 1867 (1923). *See* Hornbeck v. Somerset County Bd. of Educ., 458 A.2d 758, 770, 773–74 (Md. 1983); Bernstein v. State, 29 A.3d 267, 283 n.10 (Md. 2011).

[63] DEBATES IN THE TEXAS CONSTITUTIONAL CONVENTION OF 1875 (Seth Shepard McKay ed., 1930).

[64] THE RECORDS OF THE ARIZONA CONSTITUTIONAL CONVENTION OF 1910 (John S. Goff ed., 1991) [hereinafter ARIZONA CONSTITUTIONAL CONVENTION]. *See* John D. Leshy, *The Records of the Arizona Constitutional Convention of 1910*, 23 ARIZ. ST. L.J. 1163 (1991) (book review). Professor Leshy commented about this volume: "It will help assuage the eyesight and patience of those who heretofore have had to spend hours in front of microfiche or microfilm readers and elsewhere tracking down scattered materials on the deliberations that led to Arizona's first and only constitution." *Id.* at 1163. *See* Clouse v. State, 16 P.3d 757, 760–61 (Ariz. 2001).

does not seem to be such a compilation of the debates of a constitutional commission other than in New Jersey.[65]

These state constitutional convention newspaper reports and their use by scholars, lawyers, and judges must be distinguished from the use of newspaper reports in the judicial interpretation of initiated statutes.[66] It should also be distinguished from the use of newspaper reports in the interpretation of specific amendments to state constitutions.[67]

Newspaper reports are, of course, unofficial. Still, they often provide the most authoritative coverage of nineteenth-century (and even early twentieth-century, as in the case of Arizona) constitutional conventions and commissions. Newspapers often had a political bias, sometimes explicit. The editor of the Arizona materials made the following observation:

> Some remarks made by the delegates are still missing, but others were located in contemporary newspapers. Interpolations are always enclosed in brackets. It can be said with certainty that all of the words included in these pages were uttered on the floor of the convention; what cannot be said is what others may have been spoken.[68]

The Arizona materials point out the extent to which newspapers can play an important role in supplementing official sources that are relatively complete. To illustrate, a major speech on the floor of the convention in opposition to the initiative was omitted from the official record, but found in the *Phoenix Arizona Republican*, and included by the editor.[69] This was also true of another major speech on the initiative and referendum.[70]

Even in states where the newspaper reports of state constitutional conventions have not been compiled and indexed, lawyers, judges, and scholars seek them out and rely on them.[71] But access is difficult, even assuming one knows that

65 Peter J. Mazzei & Robert F. Williams, "Traces of Its Labors": The Constitutional Commission, the Legislature, and Their Influence on the New Jersey Constitution, 1873–1875 (2012), https://dspace.njstatelib.org/xmlui/handle/10929/18741.

66 *See* Schacter, *supra* note 12; McNellie, *supra* note 12; Wash. State Dep't of Revenue v. Hoppe, 512 P.2d 1094 (Wash. 1973).

67 *See supra* note 19.

68 Arizona Constitutional Convention, *supra* note 64, at iv.

69 *Id.* at 198.

70 *Id.* at 205.

71 *See, e.g.*, Dye v. State *ex rel.* Hale, 507 So.2d 332, 340–41 (Miss. 1987); Collins v. Day, 644 N.E.2d 72, 77 (Ind. 1994); Virmani v. Presbyterian Health Servs., Corp., 493 S.E.2d 310, 316 (N.C. Ct. App. 1997); *In re* Certified Question, 72 P.3d 151, 157–58 (Wash. 2003); Owens v. Colo. Cong. of Parents, Teachers and Students, 92 P.3d 933, 938–39 (Colo. 2004); Bienkowski v. Brooks, 873 A.2d 1122, 1131 (Md. 2005); Federal Way School Dist. No. 210 v. State, 219 P.3d 941, 946 (Wash. 2010); Blount v. Clarke, 782 S.E.152, 156 (Va. 2016); Wielechoski v. State, 403 P.3d 1141, 1150 (Alaska 2017); *see supra* note 19.

such relevant newspaper coverage exists. Compilation greatly facilitates the use of these materials, as it has demonstrably in the states where it has occurred. Compilation will make this relatively inaccessible component of state constitutional history much more usable.

The use to which constitutional history is put will differ according to the reason one seeks to rely on it. Scholarly inquiry, delving into either official or unofficial state constitutional convention or commission materials for broader understanding, is relatively noncontroversial. Questions of accuracy, completeness, or political bias may arise. Use of such materials, however, for legal advocacy raises all of the issues associated with use of legal history in constitutional (albeit usually federal) argument and interpretation.

As legal historian Stephen Gottlieb has observed, analysis of state "[c]onstitutional history is valuable whether or not one subscribes to a jurisprudence of original intent."[72] He continued:

> For those who reject a jurisprudence of original intent, constitutional history nevertheless helps us to preserve the lessons embodied in the drafting of the provisions at issue and to explore the consequences of the language chosen. State constitutional history has become more important as the United States Supreme Court has become less protective of individual rights.[73]

Reliance on constitutional convention or commission records or newspaper coverage of state constitutional conventions and commissions would be used, as Professor William Fisher says, in the "contextualist method."[74] This method "asserts that, by attending carefully to the discourse out of which a text grows (the vocabularies available to its author, the concepts and assumptions he took for granted, and the issues he considered contested), one can (and should) ascertain the author's intent."[75] Although Professor Fisher concludes that this approach is

[72] Stephen E. Gottlieb, *Symposium on State Constitutional History: In Search of a Usable Past*, 53 ALB. L. REV. 255, 258 (1989). *See also* Pierre Schlag, *Framer's Intent: The Illegitimate Uses of History*, 8 U. PUGET SOUND L. REV. 283 (1985); TOWARD A USABLE PAST: LIBERTY UNDER STATE CONSTITUTIONS (Paul Finkelman & Stephen E. Gottlieb eds., 1991).

[73] Gottlieb, *supra* note 72, at 258. *See also* David Schuman, *Advocacy of State Constitutional Law Cases: A Report from the Provinces*, 2 EMERGING ISSUES IN STATE CONSTITUTIONAL LAW 275, 283 (1989).

[74] William W. Fisher III, *Texts and Contexts: The Application to American Legal History of the Methodologies of Intellectual History*, 49 STAN. L. REV. 1065, 1104 (1997).

[75] *Id. See also* Martin S. Flaherty, *History "Lite" in Modern American Constitutionalism*, 95 COLUM. L. REV. 523, 550, 589 (1995):

> American constitutional theorists are correct to turn to the history of the Founding for a number of reasons. Most generally, situating ideas in the context in which they arose enables us to comprehend and assess those ideas better than we would by viewing them as free-floating principles. This follows because the original historical setting almost invariably suggests reasons to accept or reject a given idea that would not otherwise be apparent.

flawed,[76] a number of lawyers and judges make use of state constitutional history in this way. Professor Cass Sunstein has described the constitutional lawyer's (by contrast to the historian's) task of presenting a "usable past":

> The search for a useable past is a defining feature of the constitutional lawyer's approach to constitutional history. It may or may not be a part of the historian's approach to constitutional history, depending on the particular historian's conception of the historian's role. The historian may not be concerned with a useable past at all, at least not in any simple sense. Perhaps the historian wants to reveal the closest thing to a full picture of the past, or to stress the worst aspects of a culture's legal tradition; certainly there is nothing wrong with these projects. But constitutional history as set out by the constitutional lawyer, as a participant in the constitutional culture, usually tries to put things in a favorable or appealing light without, however, distorting what actually can be found.[77]

We will not attempt to reach a resolution of the debate over the *use* of constitutional history here; that debate is alive in well in the wake of U.S. Supreme Court decisions focusing on history to fix the meaning of many individual

> . . . .
>
> No longer must American constitutional thinkers look beyond America when seeking insight from the past. Colleagues across the courtyard in history departments, by taking the arguments earlier American constitutionalists made seriously, and by considering arguments other than just those made one summer in Philadelphia, have achieved stunning success in reconstructing the constitutional discourse that led to revolution, to independence, and to the document we live under today. The success presents a singular opportunity to modern theorists.

It is this sort of reconstruction that can take place if newspaper coverage of state constitutional conventions and commissions is compiled and made available.

[76] Fisher, *supra* note 74, at 1105, 1107. For a thoughtful critique of state judges' use of state constitutional history, *see* Jack L. Landau, *A Judge's Perspective on the Use and Misuse of History in State Constitutional Interpretation*, 38 VAL U. L. REV. 451 (2004).

For a very informative exchange on Minnesota state constitutional history, *compare* Russell Pannier, *Essay: Abraham's Theory of Constitutional Interpretation*, 29 WM. MITCHELL L. REV. 265 (2002), *with* Douglas A. Hedin, *The Quicksands of Originalism: Interpreting Minnesota's Constitutional Past*, 30 WM. MITCHELL L. REV. 241 (2003).

[77] Cass R. Sunstein, *The Idea of a Useable Past*, 95 COLUM. L. REV. 601, 603 (1995).

> What I am suggesting is that the constitutional lawyer, thinking about the future course of constitutional law, has a special project in mind, and that there is nothing wrong with that project. The historian is trying to reimagine the past, necessarily from a present-day standpoint, but subject to the discipline provided by the sources and by the interpretive conventions in the relevant communities of historians. By contrast, the constitutional lawyer is trying to contribute to the legal culture's repertoire of arguments and political/legal narratives that place a (stylized) past and present into a trajectory leading to a desired future. On this view, the historically minded lawyer need not be thought to be doing a second-rate or debased version of what the professional historians do well, but is working in a quite different tradition with overlapping but distinct criteria.

*Id.* at 605 (footnote omitted).

rights provisions, including, for example, the Second Amendment's right to bear arms.[78] The point is that, with increased availability, it is time to begin the debate about state constitutional history.[79]

## III. CANONS OF STATUTORY INTERPRETATION AND NEGATIVE IMPLICATION

A number of state courts have identified judge-made canons of state constitutional interpretation that are virtually identical to statutory interpretation canons, such as the "document as a whole";[80] "specific over the general";[81] "later in time";[82] *ejusdem generis*;[83] the "absurd result" exception to the plain meaning rule'[84] strict construction of provisions on, for example, tax exemption and ineligibility for public office;[85] and the mandatory/directory distinction.[86]

78 *See* New York State Rifle & Pistol Assoc. v. Bruen, 597 U.S. ___ (2022).

79 State constitutional history materials are cataloged in Cynthia E. Browne, State Constitutional Conventions, from Independence to the Completion of the Present Union, 1776–1959: A Bibliography (1973) (the materials are contained in a microfiche collection accompanying the bibliography); Susan Rice Yarger, State Constitutional Conventions, 1959–1975: A Bibliography (1976); Bonnie Canning, State Constitutional Conventions, Revisions and Amendments, 1959–1976: A Bibliography (1977); Dinan, *supra* note 28.

80 Geringer v. Bebout, 10 P.3d 514, 520–21 (Wyo. 2000).

81 Greene v. Marin Co. Flood Control & Water Conservation Dist., 231 P.3d 350, 358 (Cal. 2010); *see* Colorado Common Cause v. Bledsoe, 810 P.2d 201, 207 (Colo. 1991); Van Slyke v. Bd. of Trustees, 613 So.2d 872, 876 (Miss. 1993); Denish v. Johnson, 910 P.2d 914, 922 (N. Mex. 1996); Clouse v. State Dept. Pub. Safety, 11 P.3d 1012, 1015 (Ariz. 2000); Alderson v. County of Allegheny, 585 S.E.2d 795, 799 (Va. 2003); Malone v. Shyne, 937 So.2d 343, 352 (La. 2006). *See infra* note 115 and accompanying text on repeal by implication.

82 *Greene*, 231 P.3d 350 at 358. Denish v. Johnson, 910 P.2d 914, 922 (N. Mex. 1996); Malone v. Shyne, 937 So.2d 343, 353 (La. 2006). *See infra* note 112 and accompanying text on repeal by implication.

83 Dawkins v. Meyer, 825 S.W.2d 444, 447 (Tex. 1992); *see* McDonald v. Bowen, 468 S.W.2d 765, 769 (Ark. 1971) (*noscitur a sociis*). The Arkansas Supreme Court has applied the canons of *ejusdem generis* and *noscitur a sociis* to state constitutional interpretation. State v. Oldner, 206 S.W.3d 818, 822 (Ark. 2005). *See also* Graham v. Haridopolos, 108 So.3d 597, 605 (Fla. 2013).

84 Provigo v. Alcoholic Beverage Control Appeals Bd., 869 P.2d 1163, 1166 (Cal. 1994).

85 Carr v. Forst, 453 S.E.2d 274, 275 (Va. 1995) (strict construction mandated in constitutional text); Children's Psychiatric Hosp. v. Revenue Cabinet, 989 S.W.2d 583, 586 (Ky. 1999); Kansas Enterprises, Inc. v. Franz, 6 P.3d 857, 864 (Kan. 2000); *In re* Carlisle, 209 S.W.3d 93, 96 (Tex. 2006) (strict construction of provisions on ineligibility for public office).

86 Hamnierschmidt v. Boone Co., 877 S.W.2d 98, 102 (Mo. 1994); *In re* Nowak, 820 N.E.2d 335, 342–43 (Ohio 2004); State *ex rel.* Ohio Civil Service Employees Assoc. v. State Employment Relations Bd., 818 N.E.2d 688, 701–03 (Ohio 2004). It has been argued that state constitutional *limits*, particularly, should be interpreted as mandatory. John Sunquist, *Construction of the Wisconsin Constitution—Frequent Recurrence to Fundamental Principles*, 62 Marq. L. Rev. 531, 547 (1979).

*Compare* Arnett v. Sullivan, 13 S.W.2d 76 (Ky. 1939) (distinguishing statutory and constitutional interpretation, and holding that constitutional provisions are always mandatory), *with* Armstrong v. King, 126 A.263 (Pa. 1924) (all that is said in the state constitution is not of the same mandatory force). *See generally* Frank P. Grad & Robert F. Williams, 2 State Constitutions for the Twenty-First Century: Drafting State Constitutions, Revisions and Amendments 86–89 (2006).

As noted in Chapter 1, a key factor distinguishing state constitutions from the federal Constitution is that the state charters are basically (though not exclusively) documents that limit state legislative power. By way of illustration of the impact of this distinction on the judicial interpretation of state constitutions, when state constitutional provisions mandate legislative action or grant authority to a state legislature which already has plenary power, courts can transform these apparent grants of authority into judicially created limitations on legislative power. As Professor Frank Grad and Professor Williams have cautioned:

> It must be emphasized that very nearly everything that may be included in a state constitution operates as a restriction on the legislature, for both commands and prohibitions directed to other branches of the government or even to the individual citizen will operate to invalidate inconsistent legislation.
>
> . . . .
>
> . . . In constitutional theory state government is a government of plenary powers, except as limited by the state and federal constitutions. . . . In order to give effect to such special authorizations, however, courts have often given them the full effect of negative implication, relying sometimes on the canon of construction *expressio unius est exclusio alterius* (the expression of one is the exclusion of another).[87]

The general emphasis on implied limits of legislative power in state constitutional law, although oversimplified, illustrates an important, unique feature of state constitutional law that contrasts in important ways from federal constitutional interpretation. This distinction arises from the differing function of state constitutions.

A controversial Florida case illustrates the problems arising from negative implication interpretation. *Bush v. Holmes*[88] involved a challenge to a Florida school voucher program that purported to authorize public school students to transfer to private schools paid for with public education funds. The challengers contended that the program violated, among other provisions, Article IX, Section

[87] Grad & Williams, *supra* note 86, at 82–83. For cases rejecting this approach, see Sch. Comm. v. Town of York, 626 A.2d 935 (Me. 1993); Opinion of the Justices, 623 A.2d 1258, 1263 (Me. 1993); State v. Clay, 481 S.W.3d 531, 537–38 (Mo. 2016); Idaho Press Club, Inc. v. State Legislature, 132 P.3d 397, 406–09 (Idaho 2006) (Jones, J., dissenting); Stetter v. R.J. Corman Derailment Services, L.L.C., 927 N.E.2d 1092, 1100 (Ohio 2010). *But see* Cook v. City of Jacksonville, 823 So.2d 86, 91–92 (Fla. 2002) (finding negative implication); Fox v. Grayson, 317 S.W.3d 1, 8–9 (Ky. 2010); Ramsay v. City of North Las Vegas, 392 P.3d 814 (Nev. 2017). In *Cook*, Justice Anstead's dissent rejected negative implication. 823 So.2d.at 96; Gerberding v. Munro, 949 P.2d 1366, 1372–77 (Wash. 1998) (finding, over dissent, negative implication). Several state constitutions contain clauses designed to avoid negative implication interpretation. *See, e.g.*, Alaska Const. art. 12, § 8; Okla. Const. art. V, § 36; Va. Const. art. IV, § 14.

[88] 919 So.2d 392 (Fla. 2006).

1, mandating that the legislature provide a "system of free public schools."[89] In a divided opinion, the court struck down the voucher program, placing primary reliance on the *expressio unius* canon, and concluded that the mandate to the legislature to provide *public* schools constituted a limit on its ability to provide for vouchers for *private* schools.[90] The dissent challenged this use of the canon, so *Bush v. Holmes* provides a good exposition of the use of negative implication in state constitutional interpretation.[91]

The Idaho Supreme Court confronted the negative implication issue, and the majority distinguished its application to grants, rather than limitations, of power:

> "Our State Constitution is a limitation, not a grant of power, and the Legislature has plenary powers in all matters, except those prohibited by the Constitution.". . . Because the Constitution is not a grant of power, there is no reason to believe that a Constitutional provision enumerating powers of a branch of government was intended to be an exclusive list. The branch of government would inherently have powers that were not included in the list. The converse is true, however, with a respect to provisions limiting power. When the framers drafted a provision expressly limiting certain powers, there is no reason to believe that they intended the limitation to be broader than they drafted it. The purpose of such provision is to define the limitations. It is not reasonable to assume that they intended to impose other, unstated limitations. Had they wanted to impose limitations in addition to those stated, they could easily have done so. Therefore, the rule of construction *expressio unius est exclusio alterius* applies to provisions of the Idaho Constitution that expressly limit power, . . . but it does not apply to provisions that merely enumerate powers. . . .[92]

The dissent contended that the *expressio unius* canon should not be used in state constitutional interpretation of grants or limits of power.[93]

[89] FLA. CONST. art. IX, § 1(a): "The education of children is a fundamental value of the people of the State of Florida. It is, therefore, a paramount duty of the state to make adequate provision for the education of all children residing within its borders. Adequate provision shall be made by law for a uniform, efficient, safe, secure, and high quality system of free public schools that allows students to obtain a high quality education. . . ."

[90] *Bush*, 919 So.2d at 406–07.

[91] *See* Victoria Guilfoyle, *Comment*, 38 RUTGERS L.J. 1329 (2007); Nicolas Hamann, *Comment*, 58 FLA. L. REV. 935 (2006); *Recent Cases*, 120 HARV. L. REV. 1097 (2007). *See also* Mesivtah Eitz Chaim of Bobov, Inc. v. Pike Co. Bd. of Assessment Appeals, 44 A.3d 3 (Pa. 2012); Thomas v. Nevada Yellow Cab Corp., 327 P.3d 518, 521 (Nev. 2014); Lyons v. Sec. of Commonwealth, 182 N.E.3d 1078, 1092 (Mass. 2022).

[92] Idaho Press Club, Inc. v. State Legislature, 132 P.3d 397, 399–400 (Idaho 2006). *See* Michael Salimbene, *Comment*, 38 RUTGERS L.J. 1467 (2007).

[93] *Id.* at 406–09 (Jones, J., dissenting). *See also* Bd. of Ed. of Borough of Union Branch v. New Jersey Education Assoc., 247 A.2d 867 (N.J. 1968); FFW Enterprises v. Fairfax Co., 791 S.E.2d 795, 801 (Va. 2011); State v. Clay, 481 S.W.3d 531, 533–37 (Mo. 2016).

Many state courts have stated that the rules of statutory construction apply equally to state constitutional interpretation.[94] One should, however, be skeptical of this blanket assertion. Other courts recognize subtle or major differences between statutory and state constitutional interpretation. The Missouri Supreme Court expressed some caution: "Though applied more broadly because of the permanent nature of constitutional provisions, rules of statutory construction apply to interpretation of the constitution."[95] Still other courts have rejected statutory interpretation approaches in interpreting state constitutions. For example, the Idaho Supreme Court noted:

> We look to the State Constitution, not to determine what the legislature may do, but to determine what it may not do. . . .
>
> . . . .
>
> There flows from this fundamental concept, as a matter of logic in its application, the inescapable conclusion that the rule of *expressio unius est exclusio alterius* has no application to the provisions of our State Constitution.[96]

The Virginia Constitution itself mandates a similar conclusion.[97]

Lawyers and courts, for these reasons, should take care not to apply uncritically statutory interpretation approaches. Justice David Prosser of Wisconsin noted that his court relied on "statutory meaning" rather than "legislative intent"

94 State *ex rel.* Sanstead v. Freed, 251 N.W.2d 898, 908 (N.D. 1977); Baker v. Miller, 636 N.E.2d 551, 554 (Ill. 1994); Fish Market Nominee Corp. v. G.A.A., Inc. 650 A.2d 705, 708 (Md. 1994); La. Dep't of Agric. & Forestry v. Sumrall, 728 So.2d 1254, 1258 (La. 1999); Brooks v. Wright, 971 P.2d 1025, 1028 (Alaska 1999); *In re* Request of Gov. William J. Janklow, 615 N.W.2d 618, 620 (S.D. 2000); Nevada Mining Ass'n. v. Erdoes, 26 P.3d 753, 757 (Nev. 2001); State *ex rel.* Harvey v. Second Judicial Dist. Court, 32 P.3d 1263, 1269 (Nev. 2001); State v. Webb, 591 S.E.2d 505, 510 (N.C. 2004); Cathcart v. Meyer, 88 P.3d 1050, 1065 (Wyo. 2004); Bienkowski v. Brooks, 873 A.2d 1122, 1133–34 (Md. 2005); Bernstein v. State, 29 A.3d 267, 271 (Md. 2011); People v. Clemons, 968 N.E.2d 1046, 1054 (Ill. 2012); Graham v. Haridopolis, 106 So.3d 597, 603 (Fla. 2013); Brown v. Gianforte, 468 P.3d 548, 557 (Mont. 2021); Boughey *A Judge's Guide to Constitutional Interpretation*, *supra* note 15, at 1283–85. *See infra* notes 103–05 for a discussion of "less exalted" provisions of state constitutions that possibly should be interpreted as though they were statutes.

95 Thompson v. Comm. on Legislative Research, 932 S.W.2d 392, 395 n.4 (Mo. 1996); Pestka v. State, 493 S.W.3d 405, 409 (Mo. 2016). *See also* Goldstone v. Bloomfield Public Library, 737 N.W.2d 476, 488 (Mich. 2007); Hall v. Progress Pig, Inc., 610 N.W.2d 420, 424 (Neb. 2000); *In re* Bruno, 101 A.3d 635, 660 (Pa. 2014); Black v. City of Milwaukee, 882 N.W.2d 333, 358 (Wis. 2016); State v. Misch, 256 A.3d 519, 526 (Vt. 2021).

96 Eberle v. Nielson, 306 P.2d 1083, 1086 (Idaho 1957). *See also* Imbrie v. Marsh, 71 A.2d 352, 371 (N.J. 1950) (Oliphant, J., dissenting); Mayle v. Dept. Highways, 388 A.2d 709, 716–17 (Pa. 1978); Reale v. Bd. of Real Estate Appraisers, 880 P.2d 1205, 1213 (Colo. 1994) (Erickson, J., dissenting). Some courts do apply the *expressio unius* canon. Inquiry Concerning Complaints, 68 P.3d 889, 892 (Mont. 2003); Cathcart v. Meyer, 88 P.3d 1050, 1060 (Wyo. 2004); State v. Clay, 481 S.W.3d 531, 532–38 (Mo. 2016).

97 *See* Va. Const. art. IV, § 14; FFW Enterprises v. Fairfax Co., 701 S.E.2d 795, 801 (Va. 2010).

and placed little reliance on extrinsic sources in statutory interpretation.[98] He continued:

> Our methodology in interpreting a constitutional provision envisions more intense review of extrinsic sources than our methodology in statutory interpretation. The court has explained that:
>
> The purpose of construction of a constitutional [provision] is to give effect to the intent of the framers and the people who adopted it; and it is a rule of construction applicable to all constitutions that they are to be construed so as to promote the objects for which they were framed and adopted . . .
>
> The reasons we employ a different methodology for constitutional interpretation are evident. Constitutional provisions do not become law until they are approved by the people. Voters do not have the same access to the "words" of a provision as the legislators who framed those words; and most voters are not familiar with the debates in the legislature. As a result, voters necessarily consider second-hand explanations and discussion at the time of ratification. In addition, the meaning of words may evolve over time, obscuring the original meaning or purpose of a provision. The original meaning of a provision might be lost if courts could not resort to extrinsic sources. Finally, interpreting a constitutional provision is likely to have a more lasting effect than the interpretation of a statute, inasmuch as statutory language can be more easily changed than constitutional language. Thus, it is vital for court decisions to capture accurately the essence of a constitutional provision.[99]

## IV. INTERPRETATION BY FUNCTION AND QUALITY OF THE PROVISION

Problems arising with respect to interpreting state constitutional provisions should be approached first by considering the *function* of the provision at issue and its *form*. Such analysis will also have to take into consideration the origin of the state constitutional provision. Judicial interpretation can be aided by remembering that state constitutions reflect an ongoing process of lawmaking, and each provision is intended to serve some purpose or accomplish some goal.

[98] Dairyland Greyhound Park, Inc. v. Doyle, 719 N.W.2d 408, 447–48 (Wis. 2006) (Prosser, J., concurring in part and dissenting in part). *See also* Verizon New England v. Bd. of Assessors of Boston, 62 N.E.3d 46 (Mass. 2016).

[99] Dairyland Greyhound Park, Inc., 719 N.W.2d at 447. *See also* Rudd v. Ray, 248 N.W.2d 125, 129 (Iowa 1976) (state constitution must "speak across centuries."); Chittenden School Dist. v. Dept. of Educ., 738 A.2d 539, 551–52 (Vt. 1999); Michigan United Conservation Clubs, Inc. v. Secretary of State, 630 N.W.2d 297, 325 n.6 (Mich. 2001) (Weaver, J., dissenting); *In re* Bruno, 101 A.3d 635, 660 (Pa. 2014).

Tracing the "genealogy" of the provision may reveal several changes over time in its language. Such changes may support a certain interpretation. This is rarely the case in federal constitutional law.

State constitutions are often referred to as if they were a unitary source of law, including a single set of characteristics. This leads to the common assertion that state constitutions contain limits on power whereas the federal Constitution contains grants or enumerations of power. This is a misleading, oversimplified view, although when taken as a general proposition, it illustrates an important characteristic of the function of many state constitutional provisions. For example, once an existing limit on power is in place in a state constitution, a later need for an exception to that limit requires the insertion, by amendment, of an explicit *grant* of power, to remedy the initial limitation. This situation is best illustrated with state constitutional provisions concerning uniformity in taxation and limits on state and local government debt. Many state constitutions contain broad, general *limits* followed by an accumulation of specific *grants*, or authorizations to act, in certain circumstances in spite of the broad limit.

Further, provisions may be included in state constitutions to overcome or even "overrule" judicial interpretations of earlier provisions and to displace statutes. These can be either grants of, or limits on, powers. Such provisions may also be added to state constitutions to eliminate doubt, even in the absence of a definitive judicial ruling.[100] Consider an example of state constitutional interpretation based on function and origin provided by the North Dakota Supreme Court, which concluded "that the quick take provision was added to the constitution, not to grant power to the Board, but to remove the limitation imposed by judicial construction on the authority of the Legislature to enact quick take statutes if the Legislature chose to do so."[101]

An approach to state constitutional interpretation that is closely based on an assessment of the provision's function is a careful consideration of the purpose of the provision. In the words of the Texas Supreme Court: "When determining the purpose of a provision, we will consider the evil to be remedied and the good to be accomplished by that provision."[102] Finally, a number of courts look at the background of the clause or the context of the situation in which it was adopted.

[100] Tucker v. Toia, 371 N.E.2d 449, 452 (N.Y. 1977).

[101] Johnson v. Wells County Water Res. Bd., 410 N.W.2d 525, 529 (N.D. 1987).

[102] Brown v. Meyer, 787 S.W.2d 42, 45 (Tex. 1990). *See also* Foster v. Jefferson County Quorum Court, 901 S.W.2d 809, 817 (Ark. 1995) ("mischief intended to be corrected"); Rudd v. Ray, 248 N.W.2d 125, 130 (Iowa 1976) ("evil sought to be remedied"); Colorado Common Cause v. Bledsoe, 810 P.2d 201, 207 (Colo. 1991); Pray v. Judicial Selection Comm., 861 P.2d 723, 728 (Haw. 1993); Howard v. Schildberg Const. Co., 528 N.W.2d 550, 553 (Iowa 1995); Embry v. O'Bannon, 798 N.E.2d 157, 160 (Ind. 2003); Airlines Parking, Inc. v. Wayne Co., 550 N.W.2d 490, 498–99 (Mich. 1996) (Cavanagh, J., dissenting).

As stated by the Supreme Court of Rhode Island: "And finally, in our examination of the constitution, we must look to the history of the times and examine the state of affairs as they existed when the constitution was framed and adopted."[103]

As noted in Chapter 1, state constitutions have been criticized for being too long and containing too much trivial detail. Nonetheless, Professor James Pope has pointed out that state constitutions do contain "vital" provisions that are truly *constitutional*, by contrast to the more statutory type provisions that have constitutional status merely because they were inserted in the state constitution. He derived this distinction from the 1977 New Jersey case, *Vreeland v. Byrne*,[104] which observed:

> In considering the meaning of this Article, an important principle of constitutional interpretation should not be overlooked. Not all constitutional provisions are of equal majesty. Justice Holmes once referred to the "great ordinances of the Constitution." Within this category would be included the due process clause, the equal protection clause, the free speech clause, all or most of the other sections of the Bill of Rights, as well as certain other provisions. The task of interpreting most if not all of these "great ordinances" is an evolving and ongoing process. The history of the Federal Constitution clearly teaches that what may, for instance, be due process in one decade or in one generation will fail to meet this test in the next. And this is as it should be. The "great ordinances" are flexible pronouncements constantly evolving responsively to the felt needs of the times.
>
> But there are other articles in the Constitution of a different and less exalted quality. Such provisions generally set forth rather simply those details of governmental administration as are deemed worthy of a place in the organic document....
>
> Such constitutional provisions as these, and others like them, important as they doubtless may be, are entirely set apart from the "great ordinances" mentioned above, and as a matter of constitutional interpretation should receive entirely different treatment. Where in the one case the underlying spirit, intent and purpose of the Article must be sought and applied as it may have relevance to the problems of the day, in the other a literal adherence to the words

[103] City of Pawtucket v. Sundlun, 662 A.2d 40, 45 (R.I. 1995). "The context of a constitutional provision includes other provisions in the constitution that were adopted at the same time." Coultas v. City of Sutherlin, 871 P.2d 465, 468 (Or. 1994). *See also Johnson*, 410 N.W.2d at 528 ("the background context of what is displaced"); Chittenden School Dist. v. Dept. of Educ., 738 A.2d 539, 552 (Vt. 1999); Apartment Ass'n of L.A. v. City of Los Angeles, 14 P.3d 930, 934 (Cal. 2001); Embry v. O'Bannon, 798 N.E.2d 157, 162–64 (Ind. 2003); Washington Water Jet Workers Assoc. v. Yarborough, 90 P.3d 42, 46–47 (Wash. 2004).

[104] 370 A.2d 825 (N.J. 1977).

> of the clause is the only way that the expressed will of the people can be assured fulfillment.[105]

Professor Pope proposed a similar distinction, with "vital" state constitutional provisions receiving the Holmesian "great ordinance" approach.[106]

## V. OTHER INTERPRETATION TECHNIQUES

State courts sometimes subject state constitutional provisions to quite close textual analysis and apply interpretative canons more often seen in statutory interpretation,[107] such as approaching state constitutional text with a view that all of the words should be given meaning.[108] Further, constitutional provisions relating to the same subject matter are often construed together and harmonized if conflicts appear.[109] The Supreme Court of Kentucky, in this regard, stated:

> Sections 14, 54 and 241 have been interpreted to work in tandem and to establish a limitation upon the power of the General Assembly to limit common law

[105] *Id.* at 831–32 (*cited in* James Gray Pope, *An Approach to State Constitutional Interpretation*, 24 RUTGERS L.J. 985, 985 (1993)). For a good example of the "great ordinance" approach, see State v. Hirsch, 114 P.3d 1104, 1109 (Or. 2005); Kerrigan v. Commissioner of Public Health, 957 A.2d 407, 416 (Conn. 2008).

[106] Pope, *supra* note 105, at 1001–04. Professor Gardner, although conceding that Professor Pope's analysis had "undeniable appeal," disagreed, concluding that "[w]hat makes something a constitution is not its content or its pedigree, but the current attitude of the people toward it." James A. Gardner, Reply: *What Is a State Constitution?* 24 Rutgers L.J. 1025, 1031, 1032 (1993). In addition, Alan Tarr criticized Pope's approach because it disregards the fact that provisions are actually contained in the state constitution, which certainly makes them "constitutional" regardless of the difficult judgment about their relative importance. Tarr advocates instead that the specific/open-textured approach to constitutional interpretation be followed. G. ALAN TARR, UNDERSTANDING STATE CONSTITUTIONS 190–91 (1998).

[107] Finks v. Sec'y of State, 647 A.2d 402 (Me. 1994); Westerman v. Cary, 892 P.2d 1067, 1073 (Wash. 1995); Armatta v. Kitzhaber, 959 P.2d 49 (Or. 1998). *See also* Spradlin v. Jim Walter Homes, Inc., 34 S.W.3d 578, 580 (Tex. 2000) (doctrine of last antecedent); Clouse v. State, 16 P.3d 757, 760 (Ariz. 2001) (specific provision governs over general provision); *In re* Lietz Const. Co., 47 P.3d 1275, 1284–85 (Kan. 2002).

[108] "One of the fundamental rules of constitutional construction is that no word shall be assumed to be mere surplusage. It is an essential corollary that every word must be given a meaning if possible." Hendricks v. State, 196 N.E.2d 66, 70 (Ind. 1964). *See also Spradlin*, 34 S.W.3d at 580; Comm. v. Mavredakis, 725 N.E.2d 169, 178 (Mass. 2000); Stringer v. Cendant Mortgage Corp., 23 S.W.3d 353, 355 (Tex. 2000); Stringer v. Cendant Mortgage Corp., 23 S.W.3d 353, 355 (Tex. 2000); City of Guymon v. Butler, 92 P.3d 80, 84 (Okla. 2004); Snetsinger v. Montana University System, 104 P.3d 445, 460 (Mont. 2004) (Nelson, J., concurring specially); Forsyth County v. Ga. Transmission Corp., 632 S.E.2d 101, 104 (2006). *But see* Kottel v. State, 60 P.3d 403, 413–14 (Mont. 2002); Fields v. Elected Officials' Retirement Plan, 320 P.3d 1160, 1164 (Ariz. 2014).

[109] Colorado Common Cause v. Bledsoe, 810 P.2d 201, 207 (Colo. 1991); Copeland v. State, 490 S.E.2d 68, 71 (Ga. 1997); Toledo Edison Co. v. City of Bryan, 737 N.E.2d 529, 532 (Ohio 2000); Doody v. Ameriquest Mortgage Co., 49 S.W.3d 342, 344 (Tex. 2001); Town of Frisco v. Baum, 90 P.3d 845, 847 (Colo. 2004).

> rights to recover for personal injury or death. The fact that these provisions might not have been "conceived as some sort of package" does not prevent them from being construed together to arrive at a separate principle.[110]

This view has, however, been subjected to an important caveat by Alan Tarr, who noted:

> For state judges, the penetration of the state constitution by successive political movements makes the task of producing coherence even more difficult than it has been for federal judges.
>
> . . . .
>
> Insofar as a state constitution does not reflect a single perspective, an interpreter cannot always look to the whole to illuminate the meaning of its various parts.[111]

State courts often refer to the evolution of the state constitutional text over time, concluding that meaning or change of meaning may be derived from this layering of state constitutional text.[112] On the other hand, courts have sometimes found that changes in language do not necessarily indicate a change in meaning.[113] This approach may reveal a number of changes over time in the language of the provision. Analyzing the changes leading up to the current text may support a specific interpretation. Such changes in the underlying text are not often present in federal constitutional law, because the federal Constitution has been so rarely amended. Readoption of a state constitutional provision without change is often

[110] Williams v. Wilson, 972 S.W.2d 260, 267 (Ky. 1998) (citation omitted).

[111] TARR, *supra* note 106, at 194.

[112] Dept. of Trans. v. Dietrich, 555 So.2d 1355, 1358–59 (La. 1990); Luppino v. Gray, 647 A.2d 429, 432–33 (Md. 1994); Husebye v. Jaeger, 534 N.W.2d 811, 814–15 (N.D. 1995) ("We assume that the people's decision to change the language of the constitutional provision was intended to also change the meaning."); *see also* Hunt v. Hubbert, 588 So.2d 848 (Ala. 1991); *In re* Advisory Opinion to the Governor, 626 So.2d 684, 687–88 (Fla. 1993); Calvey v. Daxon, 997 P.2d 164, 169–70 (Okla. 2000); Spradlin, 34 S.W.3d at 579–80; Gerawan Farming, Inc. v. Lyons, 12 P.3d 720, 733 (Cal. 2000); Louisiana Municipal Assoc. v. State, 773 So.2d 663, 666–67 (La. 2000); Redman v. State, 768 A.2d 656, 660–61 (Md. 2001); Thompson v. Dep't of Corr., 18 P.3d 1198, 1201 (Cal. 2001); Turner v. City of Evansville, 740 N.E.2d 860, 863 (Ind. 2001) (Boehm, J., concurring); City Chapel Evangelical Free, Inc. v. City of South Bend, 744 N.E.2d 443, 445–47 (Ind. 2001); Wis. Prof'l Police Ass'n., Inc. v. Lightbourn, 627 N.W.2d 807, 832–33 (Wis. 2001); State *ex rel.* Harvey v. Second Judicial Dist. Court, 32 P.3d 1263, 1267–69 (Nev. 2001); City of Chattanooga v. Davis, 54 S.W.3d 248, 257–58 (Tenn. 2001); Opinion of the Justices, 949 A.2d 670, 673–74 (N.H. 2008); State *ex rel.* McCrory v. Berger, 781 S.E.2d 248, 253–55 (N.C. 2016).

[113] Page v. Carlson, 488 N.W.2d 274, 279 (Minn. 1992); State v. Kastanis, 848 P.2d 673, 675 (Utah 1993); Connally v. State, 458 S.E.2d 336, 336–37 (Ga. 1995); Agnew v. State Bd. Equalization, 981 P.2d 52, 61–63 (Cal. 1999); Stranahan v. Fred Meyer, Inc., 11 P.3d 228, 241 (Or. 2001); People v. Rodriguez, 112 P.3d 693, 701–02 (Colo. 2005); People v. Sharpe, 839 N.E.2d 492, 500 (Ill. 2005); Chames v. DeMayo, 972 So.2d 850, 855–56 (Fla. 2007); City of Golden Valley v. Wiebesick, 879 N.W.2d 152, 160 (Minn. 2017).

seen as adopting the existing judicial interpretations of that provision.[114] The adoption of a later amendment to a state constitution that is inconsistent with earlier provisions, if the contrary presumption can be overcome, constitutes a repeal by implication.[115]

A difficult and controversial case in Nevada arose when an older clause mandating a public education came into conflict with a 1996 amendment, adopted through the initiative process, requiring a two-thirds vote to raise revenues. When the legislature failed to fund education adequately, the court ordered the legislature to proceed by majority vote, declaring that substantive provisions governed over conflicting procedural provisions, and later overruling this approach in 2006.[116] After the first case, the legislature had funded education, by two-thirds, and a petition for rehearing was dismissed.[117]

State constitutional interpretation may rely on the fact that the framers of a provision under review copied it from the federal Constitution[118] or from the constitutions of other states.[119] There was much greater availability of state constitutions at state constitutional conventions than has been recognized generally.[120] Interpreting state constitutional provisions copied from other

[114] TARR, *supra* note 106, at 203–04. *See also* Levinson, *supra* note 1, at 574; State *ex rel.* McLeod v. Edwards, 236 S.E.2d 406, 408 (S.C. 1977); Elliot v. State, 824 S.E.2d 265 (Ga. 2019); Williams v. Wilson, 972 S.W.2d 260, 273 (Ky. 1998) (Cooper, J., dissenting); Suzanne L. Abram, Note, *Problems of Contemporaneous Construction in State Constitutional Interpretation*, 38 BRANDEIS L.J. 613, 624, 636–38 (2000).

[115] Floridians Against Casino Takeover v. Let's Help, 363 So.2d 337, 341–42 (Fla. 1978); Jaksha v. State, 486 N.W.2d 858, 863 (Neb. 1992); Hendrick v. Walters, 865 P.2d 1232, 1235, 1240–43 (Okla. 1993); Moore v. McCuen, 876 S.W.2d 237, 238 (Ark. 1994); Duggan v. Beerman, 515 N.W.2d 788, 792 (Neb. 1994); State v. Gentry, 888 P.2d 1105, 1138 (Wash. 1995); Copeland v. State, 490 S.E.2d 68, 71 (Ga. 1997); McKenna v. Williams, 874 A.2d 217, 232–33, 241–42 (R.I. 2005); Okla. City Urban Renewal Auth. v. Medical Technology and Research Auth., 4 P.3d 677, 693 (Okla. 2000) (Summers, J., dissenting); Anderson v. Solvay Minerals, Inc., 3 P.3d 236, 239 (Wyo. 2000); City of Guyman v. Butler, 92 P.3d 80, 84 (Okla. 2004); City of Fayetteville v. Washington Co., 255 S.W.3d 844, 856 (Ark. 2007) (no repeal by implication); Ramsay v. City of North Las Vegas, 392 P.3d 614 (Nev. 2017). *See supra* notes 81–82 and accompanying text on the last-in-time and specific-over-general rules.

[116] Guinn v. Legislature of the State of Nevada, 71 P.3d 1269 (Nev. 2003), *overruled by* Nevadans for Nevada v. Beers, 142 P.3d 339, 348 (Nev. 2006).

[117] Guinn v. Legislature of Nevada, 76 P.3d 22 (Nev. 2003). *See* William D. Popkin, *Interpreting Conflicting Provisions of the Nevada State Constitution*, 5 NEV. L.J. 308 (2004); Steve R. Johnson, *Supermajority Provisions,* Guinn v. Legislature *and a Flawed Constitutional Structure*, 4 NEV. L.J. 491 (2004).

[118] State v. Miyasaki, 614 P.2d 915, 922 (Haw. 1980); State v. Duk Won Lee, 925 P.2d 1091, 1094 n.4 (Haw. 1996).

[119] Westerman v. Cary, 892 P.2d 1067, 1074 (Wash. 1994); State v. Cookman, 920 P.2d 1086, 1091 (Or. 1996); State v. Wicklund, 589 N.W.2d 793, 799 (Minn. 1999); Daye v. State, 769 A.2d 630, 637 n.4 (Vt. 2000); Gerawan Farming, Inc. v. Lyons, 12 P.3d 720, 733 (Cal. 2000); State v. Mikolinski, 775 A.2d 274, 278–79 (Conn. 2001); Harvey v. District Ct, 32 P.3d 1263, 1269 (Nev. 2001); Clouse v. State, 16 P.3d 757, 761 (Ariz. 2001); State v. Hirsch, 114 P.3d 1104, 1118 (Or. 2005); Zahavi v. State, 343 P.3d 595, 602 n.5 (Nev. 2015); *see* Abram, *supra* note 114, at 636–41. It is not always easy to tell from which state a provision was copied. *Id.* at 638–39.

[120] *See* Marsha L. Baum & Christian G. Fritz, *American Constitution-Making: The Neglected State Constitutional Sources*, 27 HASTINGS CONST. L.Q. 199 (2000).

states can be a very important approach where many states assign added, if not binding, authority to the judicial interpretations of the borrowed ("parent") provision.[121] A closely related technique is comparing the judicial interpretation of similar constitutional provisions in other states.[122]

State courts have interpreted new state constitutional provisions by referring to the intent of earlier, failed state constitutional changes. The Court of Appeals of Maryland noted that background materials for a provision in a proposed constitution that was rejected by the voters could be used "only in the case of an amendment to the present Constitution adopting some of the language of the proposed Constitution, as has been done in certain instances."[123] Courts have also derived the meaning of current state constitutional provisions from proposed amendments to clauses that were defeated by the electorate.[124]

[121] *See* G. Alan Tarr, *Understanding State Constitutions*, 65 Temple L. Rev. 1169, 1190–91 (1992); Christian G. Fritz, *The American Constitutional Tradition Revisited: Preliminary Observations on State Constitution-Making in the Nineteenth-Century West*, 25 Rutgers L.J., 977, 983–84 (1994); Howard v. Schildberg Const. Co., Inc., 528 N.W.2d 550, 553 (Iowa 1995); *In re* Ryan, 853 P.2d 424, 432 (Wash. 1993); State v. Marshall, 859 S.W.2d 289, 292 (Tenn. 1993); Turken v. Gordan, 224 P.3d 158, 161–62 (Ariz. 2010); State v. Davis, 256 P.3d 1075, 1079 (2011). *But see* Abram, *supra* note 114, at 639 ("implausible" to ascribe knowledge of judicial interpretations of courts in state from which provision was copied). Riley v. Brown and Root, Inc., 836 P.2d 1298, 1303–1304 (Okla. 1992); (Kauger, J., concurring in part and dissenting in part); Kotterman v. Killian, 972 P.2d 606, 638 (Ariz. 1999) (Feldman, J., dissenting); State v. Brooks, 604 N.W.2d 345, 350 (Minn. 2000); Dickey v. City of Flagstaff, 66 P.3d 44, 47–48 (Ariz. 2003) (decisions construing "parent" clause "very persuasive"); People v. Rodriguez, 112 P.3d 693, 699–700 (Colo. 2005); State v. Hirsch, 114 P.3d 1104, 1116 (Or. 2005); Dairyland Greyhound Park, Inc. v. Doyle, 719 N.W.2d 408, 450 (Wis. 2006) (Prosser, J., concurring in part and dissenting in part); Arizona Together v. Brewer, 149 P.3d 742, 749 (Ariz. 2007). *See* the discussion in Chapter 3.

[122] *See* Clouse *ex rel.* Clouse v. State, 16 P.3d 757, 761 (Ariz. 2001); Cambria v. Soaries, 776 A.2d 754, 762 (N.J. 2001); Gunaji v. Macias, 31 P.3d 1008, 1015–16 (N.M. 2001); Sirrell v. State, 780 A.2d 494, 500–01 (N.H. 2001); City of Chattanooga v. Davis, 54 S.W.3d 248, 257 (Tenn. 2001) (Tennessee constitutional provision unique in the country). *See infra* notes 169–71 and accompanying text.

[123] *In re* Special Investigation No. 244, 459 A.2d 1111, 1114–15 (Md. 1983). *See* Dan Friedman, *Magnificant Failure Revisited: Modern Maryland Constitutional Law from 1967 to 1998*, 58 Md. L. Rev. 528 (1999). *See also* Rasmussen v. South Florida Blood Serv., Inc., 500 So.2d 533, 536 (Fla. 1987); *In re* Legislative Redistricting, 629 A.2d 646, 658 (Md. 1993); State *ex rel.* Harvey v. Second Judicial Dist. Ct., 32 P.3d 1263, 1267–69 (Nev. 2001); Wagner v. Milwaukee Co. Election Comm., 666 N.W.2d 816, 825–30, 853 (Wis. 2003).

[124] "Even less by way of inference is required to ferret out public understanding of section 9(e) of article IV, since the voters themselves have addressed the question we now consider.... This amendment was rejected by the voters in the 1974 referendum." Cont'l Ill. Nat'l Bank & Trust Co. v. Zagel, 401 N.E.2d 491, 496 (Ill. 1979); Clouse *ex rel.* Clouse v. State, 16 P.3d 757, 769–70 (Ariz. 2001). *Contra* State *ex rel.* Lake County v. Zupancic, 581 N.E.2d 1086 (Ohio 1991); Independence National Education Assoc. v. Independence School Dist., 223 S.W.3d 131, 137 n.4 (Mo. 2007); Leonard v. City of Spokane, 897 P.2d 358, 360 (Wash. 1995). *See* St. Charles Co. Sheriff's Dep't. v. Raynor, 301 S.W.3d 56, 68–69 (Mo. 2012) (amendment rejected in convention); Commonwealth v. Simmons, 394 S.W.3d 903, 906–07 (Ky. 2013); Gregg v. Rauner, 124 N.E.3d 947, 955 (Ill. 2018).

## VI. BURDEN OF STATE CONSTITUTIONAL CHALLENGE

Most state courts accord statutes and actions of officials a presumption of constitutionality.[125] Professor Jennifer Friesen has argued that this presumption is misplaced and unnecessary.[126] Some state courts have indicated, moreover, that the presumption of constitutionality is inapplicable to certain kinds of laws. For example, the Hawaii Supreme Court has held that laws which, on their face, classify on the basis of suspect categories are not entitled to the presumption of constitutionality.[127] The Missouri Supreme Court has stated that "[t]he unconstitutionality of a special law is presumed."[128]

Many state courts articulate the standard for a state constitutional challenge as beyond a reasonable doubt.[129] Two experienced Connecticut state constitutional litigators argued this as an improperly heavy burden—a barrier to state constitutional litigation:

> Creating more than a presumption of constitutionality for legislative or executive action places the reaches of those branches almost above the constitution and tends to render the constitution itself subsidiary.
>
> The adoption of this rigorous standard of persuasion obviously equates a statute with a defendant accused of a crime. This equation is faulty. Protection of an assumedly innocent defendant is of more concern than the protection of a statute of questionable constitutionality. The standard also is unsuitable because in constitutional cases the issue is one of law, not of fact.[130]

[125] Cal. Hous. Fin. Agency v. Patitucci, 583 P.2d 729, 731 (Cal. 1978) ("strong" presumption); Caple v. Tuttle's Design-Build, Inc., 753 So.2d 49, 51 (Fla. 2000); Luebbers v. Money Store, Inc., 40 S.W.3d 745, 748 (Ark. 2001); Bailey v. Republic Engineered Steels, Inc., 741 N.E.2d 121, 122 (Ohio 2001). Professor Robert Schapiro examined judicial deference in an exhaustive study in Robert A. Schapiro, *Judicial Deference and Interpretative Coordinacy in State and Federal Constitutional Law*, 85 CORNELL L. REV. 656 (2000).

[126] Jennifer Friesen, *State Courts as Sources of Constitutional Law: How to Become Independently Wealthy*, 72 NOTRE DAME L. REV. 1065, 1090–91 (1997) (presumption of constitutionality misplaced and unnecessary). *Accord* Brown v. Multnomah County Dist. Court, 570 P.2d 52, 56 n.6 (Or. 1977).

[127] Washington v. Fireman's Fund Ins. Cos., 708 P.2d 129, 134 (Haw. 1985), *cert. denied*, 476 U.S. 1169 (1986) (presumption inapplicable to laws which, on their face, classify on the basis of suspect categories). *See also* Baehr v. Lewin, 852 P.2d 44, 64 n.28 (Haw. 1993).

[128] Tillis v. City of Branson, 945 S.W.2d 447, 448–49 (Mo. 1997); *see also* Harris v. Missouri Gaming Comm., 869 S.W.2d 58, 65 (Mo. 1994).

[129] Robinson v. J.C. Stewart, 655 So.2d 866, 867 (Miss. 1995); Hlava v. Nelson, 528 N.W.2d 306, 308 (Neb. 1995); Wis. Retired Teachers Ass'n v. Employee Trust Funds Bd., 558 N.W.2d 83, 90 (Wis. 1997); Finstad v. W.R. Grace & Co., 8 P.3d 778, 781 (Mont. 2000); Carvey v. W. Va. St. Bd. of Ed., 527 S.E.2d 831, 838 (W. Va. 1999); Gluba *ex rel.* Gluba v. Bitzan & Ohren, 735 N.W.2d 713, 719 (Minn. 2007); School Districts' Alliance for Adequate Funding of Special Ed., 244 P.3d 1, 4 (Wash. 2010); Clark v. Bryant, 253 So.3d 297, 301 (Miss. 2018).

[130] Robert Satter & Shelley Geballe, *Litigation Under the Connecticut Constitution—Developing a Sound Jurisprudence*, 15 CONN. L. REV. 57, 67–72 (1982). *See* WESTLEY W. HORTON, THE CONNECTICUT STATE CONSTITUTION: A REFERENCE GUIDE 30–31 (1993); Hugh Spitzer, *Reasoning v. Rhetoric: The Strange Case of "Unconstitutional Beyond a Reasonable Doubt,"* 74 RUTGERS U. L. REV.

Justice Michael Zimmerman of the Supreme Court of Utah also discussed the inapplicability of the "beyond a reasonable doubt" standard, albeit in the context of a city ordinance:

> The City Council argues that we should uphold its practice unless the Separationists show that the practice is unconstitutional "beyond a reasonable doubt." We agree with the Council that the burden of showing the unconstitutionality of the practice is on the Separationists. However, we do not agree that the showing must be made "beyond a reasonable doubt" as that phrase has been interpreted in the criminal law context. . . . We therefore restate the burden to be met by one who challenges an enactment on constitutional grounds: The act is presumed valid, and we resolve any reasonable doubts in favor of constitutionality.[131]

Failing to distinguish the arguments for deference to the elected, representative legislature and the deference that should be afforded executive officials who are not always elected, including administrators, police, and prison officials, may be a mistake. At least a few courts have made a distinction. An Oregon Supreme Court justice stated:

> The approach taken by the court in this case also recognizes the proper position of the courts in reviewing the actions of the police, which are part of the executive branch of government. The courts are part of the judicial branch. As such, the courts have no general authority to review the reasonableness of the executive action. Under the Oregon Constitution, the courts are empowered to scrutinize the "reasonableness" of a particular class of executive conduct, namely searches and seizures, to determine whether such conduct complies with Article I, section 9, of the Oregon Constitution.[132]

1429, 1459–61 (2022); *see also* Jeffrey S. Sutton, Who Decides? States as Laboratories of Constitutional Experimentation 58–62 (2021).

[131] Soc'y of Separationists, Inc. v. Whitehead, 870 P.2d 916, 920 (Utah, 1993) (footnotes & citations omitted). *See also* Davis v. Grover, 480 N.W.2d 460, 485 n.13 (Wis. 1992); Rohlfs v. Klemenhagen, 227 P.3d 42, 67 (Mont. 2009) (Nelson, J., dissenting); Alexander v. Bozeman Motors, Inc. 234 P.3d 880, 890 (Mont. 2010) (Leaphart, J., concurring). For a detailed investigation of the origins of state constitutional standards, see Christopher R. Green, *Clarity and Reasonable Doubt in Early State-Constitutional Judicial Review*, 57 S. Tex. L. Rev. 169 (2015). *See also* Spitzer, *supra* note 130.

[132] State v. Nagel, 880 P.2d 451, 459 (Or. 1994) (Unis, J., concurring). *See also* City of Cleveland v. Trzebuckowski, 709 N.E.2d 1148, 1153 n.2 (Ohio 1999). *See generally* Seth F. Kreimer, *Exploring the Dark Matter of Judicial Review: A Constitutional Census of the 1990's*, 5 Wm. & Mary Bill Rts. J. 427 (1997).

## VII. ARE STATE CONSTITUTIONAL PROVISIONS SELF-EXECUTING?

Another relatively common interpretation question in state constitutional law that is rarely raised in federal constitutional law is whether a particular clause is "self-executing." "A self-executing provision of a constitution is a provision requiring no supplementary legislation to make it effective and leaving nothing to be done by the legislature to put it (into) operation."[133] Sometimes this question can be answered by reference to state constitutional history[134] or the text of the provision itself.[135] A number of state constitutional provisions have been found to be non-self-executing and therefore reliant on either legislative or local government implementation.[136] In these circumstances, the courts will defer to the legislature's implementing statutes.[137]

Interestingly, the judicial view of whether a state constitutional provision is self-executing has changed as the view of the function of state constitutions

133 Most Worshipful Grand Lodge v. Bd. of County Comm'rs, 912 P.2d 708, 712 (Kan. 1996) (citation omitted); *see* People v. Carroll, 148 N.E.2d 875, 877 (N.Y. 1958); City of Missoula v. Mountain Water Co., 419 P.3d 685, 690 (Mont. 2018); State *ex rel.* Lamm v. Neb. Bd. of Pardons, 620 N.W.2d 763, 769 (Neb. 2001); Davidson v. Sandstrom, 83 P.3d 648, 658 (Colo. 2004); Smiler v. Napolitano, 911 A.2d 1035, 1039 (R.I. 2006); Florida Hospital Waterman, Inc. v. Buster, 984 So.2d 478, 485 (Fla. 2008); County of Hawaii v. ALH Loop Homeowners, 235 P.3d 1103, 1122–29 (Haw. 2010); Espina v. Jackson, 112 A.3d 442 (Md. 2015); City of Missoula v. Mountain Water Co., 419 P.3d 685, 690–91 (Mont. 2018).

134 "The record of the debate at the Convention is clear that this was the delegates' intent in amending the provision. The second sentence is mandatory, prohibitive, and self-executing and it prohibits depriving an employee of his full legal redress, recoverable under general tort law, against third parties." Connery v. Liberty Northwest Ins. Corp., 960 P.2d 288, 290 (Mont. 1998). *See also* Cooper v. Nutley Sun Printing Co., 175 A.2d 639 (N.J. 1961); State *ex rel.* Stephan v. Finney, 867 P.2d 1034, 1047–50 (Kan. 1994); Cmty. Ins. Co. v. Dep't of Transp., 750 N.E.2d 573, 581 (Ohio 2001); Community Ins. Co. v. Ohio Dept. Trans., 750 N.E.2d 573, 580–82 (Ohio 2001) (Douglas, J., dissenting).

135 *See* ILL. CONST. art. I, § 17. The official Constitutional Commentary to Article I, Section 18 states the delegates at the constitutional convention included the express self-executing clause in Section 17 to avoid the result reached by the New York Court of Appeals in Dorsey v. Stuyvesant Town Corp., 87 N.E.2d 541 (N.Y. 1949) (holding a New York constitutional provision non-self-executing in the absence of express intent to make it self-executing). *See also* St. John Medical Plans, Inc. v. Gutman, 721 So.2d 717, 719 (Fla. 1998) (constitutional provision included "[T]he manner of recovery and additional damages may be provided by law"); Developmental Pathways v. Ritter, 178 P.3d 524, 531 (Colo. 2008) (absence of express provision not dispositive).

136 Further authority is found in Article 7, Section 6 of the Idaho Constitution, which permits a municipal corporation to assess and collect taxes for all purposes of the corporation. However, that taxing authority is not self-executing and is limited to that taxing power given to the municipality by the legislature.

Idaho Bldg. Contractors Ass'n. v. City of Coeur D'Alene, 890 P.2d 326, 328 (Idaho 1995). *See also* Johnson v. Wells County Water Res. Bd., 410 N.W.2d 525, 528 (N.D. 1997); State *ex rel.* Lamm v. Nebraska Bd. Pardons, 620 N.W.2d 763, 769 (Neb. 2001); State v. Jackson, 811 N.E.2d 68, 73 (Ohio 2004) A.F. Lusi Construction, Inc. v. Rhode Island Convention Center Authority, 934 A.2d 791, 798 (R.I. 2007) (state constitutional provisions "aspirational in nature"); Jose L. Fernandez, *State Constitutions, Environmental Rights Provisions, and the Doctrine of Self-Execution: A Political Question?* 17 HARV. ENVTL. L. REV. 333 (1993).

137 People v. Giordano, 170 P.3d 623, 630 (Cal. 2007) ("great deference").

has evolved. At the beginning of the last century, the California Supreme Court stated:

> As to the question whether the provision is self-executing, it is well to note, at the outset, that the presumption is not precisely as it would have been had such a matter been presented for consideration fifty years ago. When the federal constitution and first state constitutions were formed, the idea of a constitution was, that it merely outlined a government. . . . The law-making power was vested wholly in the legislature. Save as to the assurances of individual rights against the government, the direct operation of the constitution was upon the government only. And such assurances were themselves in part but limitations upon governmental powers.
>
> Latterly, however, all this has been changed. Through distrust of the legislatures and the natural love of power, the people have inserted in their constitutions many provisions of a statutory character. . . .
>
> Under former conditions it was natural that the court should presume that a constitutional provision was addressed to some officer or department of the government, or that it limited the power of the legislature, or empowered, and perhaps directed, certain legislation, to carry into effect a constitutional policy.
>
> Now the presumption is the reverse. Recently adopted state constitutions contain extensive codes of laws, intended to operate directly upon the people as statutes do. To say that these are not self-executing may be to refuse to execute the sovereign will of the people.[138]

A constitutional provision may be partially self-executing and partially non-self-executing.[139] The Supreme Court of Virginia has held that a self-executing state constitutional provision constitutes a waiver of its nonconstitutional sovereign immunity doctrine.[140] Just because a provision of a state constitution is deemed to be self-executing, however, does not mean that the legislature may not pass implementing statutes. Such statutes, of course, may not narrow or contradict the self-executing clause.[141]

[138] Winchester v. Howard, 69 P. 77, 78–79 (Cal. 1902). *See generally* Orrin K. McMurray, *Some Tendencies in Constitution Making*, 2 Cal. L. Rev. 203, 209–11 (1914); Richard A. Goldberg & Robert F. Williams, *Farmworkers' Organizational and Collective Bargaining Rights in New Jersey: Implementing Self-Executing State Constitutional Rights*, 18 Rutgers L.J. 729 (1987).

[139] Most Worshipful Grand Lodge of Ancient Free and Accepted Masons of Kansas v. Bd. of Co. Commissioners, 912 P.2d 708, 714 (Kan. 1996).

[140] Gray v. Virginia Sec. of Trans., 662 S.E.2d 66 (Va. 2008).

[141] *See* Chesney v. Byram, 101 P.2d 1106, 1108 (Cal. 1940) (*quoting* T. Cooley, A Treatise on Constitutional Limitations 100 (6th ed. 1890)):

> However, it does not follow from the determination that the above-mentioned constitutional provision is self-executing, that the legislature did not have the power to enact legislation providing reasonable regulation for the exercise of the right. . . . "but all such legislation must

## VIII. CONTEMPORANEOUS AND LEGISLATIVE CONSTRUCTION

A number of state courts have applied the doctrine of "contemporaneous construction" in interpreting state constitutional provisions. This approach reflects reliance on, and deference to, the views of the meaning of a state constitutional provision held by other, sometimes nonjudicial, actors in the state government, typically prior to or soon after the adoption of the provision in question.[142] For example, the Supreme Court of Kentucky stated that judicial interpretations rendered soon after the adoption of a state constitutional provision were entitled to special deference:

> [T]he prevailing political climate at the time of adoption of the 1891 Constitution and the language used permits an inference that the Constitutional Convention desired to impose limitations upon legislative authority and cases decided contemporaneously or close in time would appear to be persuasive of Delegates' intent. . . .
>
> This Court has endorsed the principle of contemporaneous construction as providing special insight to the Delegates' intent: "The judges recognizing that tradition in their opinions wrote with a direct, firsthand knowledge of the mind set of the constitutional fathers. . . ." Accordingly, our decisions in Louisville & Nashville R.R. v. Kelly's Adm'x, and Illinois Central R. Co. v. Stewart, are entitled to greater weight in our constitutional analysis.[143]

State courts have also expressed deference to interpretation of the state constitution by the state legislature.[144] Of course, non-self-executing provisions

be subordinate to the constitutional provision, and in furtherance of its purpose, and must not in any particular attempt to narrow or embarrass it."

*See also* Hainline v. Bond, 824 P.2d 959, 963 (Kan. 1992); In the Matter of Statement of Sufficiency For 1997–98 #40, 968 P.2d 112, 116 (Colo. 1998).

142 Abram, *supra* note 114, at 615 n.21 ("'Contemporaneous construction' is a term used to describe the theory that a constitutional provision should be interpreted according to the understanding of the provision at the time of its adoption."). This approach has an obvious link to original intent. *Id.* at 635.

143 Williams v. Wilson, 972 S.W.2d 260, 267 (Ky. 1998) (citations omitted). *But see id.* at 273 (Cooper, J., dissenting) (relying on two decisions prior to constitutional convention readopting provision "verbatim and without debate"). *See also* Lyn-Anna Props., Ltd. v. Harborview Dev. Corp., 678 A.2d 683, 688 (N.J. 1996) (judges writing early decisions were familiar with constitutional convention); McNeil v. Legislative Apportionment Comm., 828 A.2d 840, 854–57 (N.J. 2003); *In re* Davis, 681 N.W.2d 452, 456 n.1 (S.D. 2004); State v. Schwartz, 689 N.W.2d 430, 442–43 (S.D. 2004); Greene v. Marin Co. Flood Control & Water Conservation Dist., 231 P.3d 350, 358 (Cal. 2010).

144 State *ex rel.* Sanstead v. Freed, 251 N.W.2d 898, 905–06 (N.D. 1977); Geringer v. Bebout, 10 P.3d 514, 521–22 (Wyo. 2000); Fox v. Grayson, 317 S.W.3d 1, 16–17 (Ky. 2010). *Contra* State *ex rel.* Oregonian Publ'g Co., 613 P.2d 23, 27 (Or. 1980). The Michigan Supreme Court concluded that a *preexisting statute* included a "technical" taxation term, adopted by a constitutional amendment

contemplate, within limits, exactly that. According to the Supreme Court of North Dakota: "A contemporaneous and long-standing legislative construction of a constitutional provision is entitled to significant weight when we interpret the provision."[145] The Supreme Court of Rhode Island linked legislative interpretation to statutes enacted soon after the adoption of the constitutional amendment:

> In construing a constitutional provision, this court properly consults extrinsic sources, including the proceedings of constitutional conventions and any legislation related to the constitutional provision that was enacted at or near the time of the adoption of the constitutional amendment.[146]

State courts sometimes refer to the doctrine of "practical construction" together with the contemporaneous construction approach. The North Dakota Supreme Court stated:

> And finally, as an elementary rule of construction, we note that which is drawn from contemporaneous and practical constructions, and "where there has been a practical construction which has been acquiesced in for a considerable period, considerations in favor of adhering to this construction sometimes present themselves to the courts with a plausibility and force which is not easy to resist."[147]

using that term, so that the legislature could not, at a later date, expand the meaning of the term of art. WPW Acquisition Co. v. City of Troy, 643 N.W.2d 564, 567 (Mich. 2002).

[145] State *ex rel.* Bd. of Univ. & Sch. Lands v. City of Sherwood, 489 N.W.2d 584, 587 (N.D. 1992). *See* Boughey, *A Judge's Guide*, *supra* note 15, at 1281–83; Boughey, *An Introduction to North Dakota Constitutional Law*, *supra* note 15, at 222–25.

[146] City of Pawtucket v. Sundlun, 662 A.2d 40, 45 (R.I. 1995). *See* Rudd v. Ray, 248 N.W.2d 125, 132 (Iowa 1976); Brown v. Firestone, 382 So.2d 654, 671 (Fla. 1980); Hornbeck v. Somerset County Bd. of Educ., 458 A.2d 755, 774–75 (Md. 1983); State v. Hagerty, 580 N.W.2d 139, 145 (N.D. 1998); State v. Trump Hotels & Casino Resorts, Inc., 734 A.2d 1160, 1175 (N.J. 1999). *See also* Thompson v. Craney, 546 N.W.2d 123, 127 (Wis. 1996):

> In interpreting a constitutional provision, the court turns to three sources in determining the provision's meaning: the plain meaning of the words in the context used; the constitutional debates and the practices in existence at the time of the writing of the constitution; and the earliest interpretation of the provision by the legislature as manifested in the first law passed following adoption.

*Id.*; *see In re* Estate of Dionne, 518 A.2d 178, 183 (N.H. 1986) (Souter, J., dissenting); State v. City of Oak Creek, 605 N.W.2d 526, 534–35 (Wis. 2000); Doe v. Nelson, 680 N.W.2d 302, 306–07 (S.D. 2004); Dairyland Greyhound Park, Inc. v. Doyle, 719 N.W.2d 408, 427–28 (Wis. 2006); State *ex rel.* Webb v. Cianci, 591 A.2d 1193, 1201 (R.I. 1991); Halverson v. Miller, 186 P.3d 893, 897 (Nev. 2008).

[147] State *ex rel.* Linde v. Robinson, 160 N.W.514, 516 (N.D. 1916) (*quoting* T. Cooley, A Treatise on Constitutional Limitations (7th ed. 1903)). *See also* State *ex rel.* Bd. of Univ. and School Lands v. City of Sherwood, 489 N.W.2d 584, 587 (N.D. 1992) ("A contemporaneous and long-standing

Some state courts have deferred to even more specific legislative interpretations of the state constitution, going so far as to uphold noncontemporaneous legislative definitions of terms or other interpretations even contrary to prior judicial interpretations. According to the Florida Supreme Court:

> The situation then, as it presents itself in connection with our constitutional provision, is at least that by the decisions of the courts of Florida and other jurisdiction[s] the word "lottery" may have either of several meanings, and that either is reasonable and possible. In such a situation, where a constitutional provision may well have either of several meanings, it is a fundamental rule of constitutional construction that, if the Legislature has by statute adopted one, its action in this respect is well-nigh, if not completely, controlling.[148]

In another situation, the Florida Supreme Court had adopted a fairly restrictive definition of the state constitutional term "charitable," limiting it to financial assistance to the poor or other measures to help those unable to help themselves, holding, for example, that a Presbyterian home for the aged was not entitled to a tax exemption.[149] Subsequently, the Florida Legislature passed a statute[150] specifically exempting homes for the aged, including homes such as those previously denied exemption in the earlier case.

When the statute was attacked by tax officials, the Florida Supreme Court held in *Jasper v. Mease Manor, Inc.*,[151] that the law constituted a definition by the legislature of "charitable" as used in the constitution and that it was within the legislative prerogative to define it this way. The court stated that there must be only a reasonable relationship between the specific statutory exemption and a purpose the constitution required to be served.[152] Thus, since the legislature had declared that certain property was used for charitable purposes, the court abandoned its prior judicial definitions.[153]

On various occasions, therefore, the Florida Legislature has undertaken to define constitutional terms with regard to tax exemptions. This is not an issue as

legislative construction of a constitutional provision is entitled to significant weight when we interpret the provision."); McNeil v. Legislative Apportionment Comm., 828 A.2d 840, 854–57 (N.J. 2003); Taomae v. Lingle, 118 P.3d 1188, 1196 (Haw. 2005).

148 Greater Loretta Improvement Ass'n v. State *ex rel.* Boone, 234 So.2d 665, 669–70 (Fla. 1970). *See also* State v. Bernier, 717 A.2d 652, 656 (Conn. 1998) ("We have recognized that 'statutes may . . . help to define the contours of constitutional rights. . . .'"); Howell v. McAuliffe, 788 S.E.2d 706, 716–19 (Va. 2016).

149 Presbyterian Homes of the Synod of Fla., Inc. v. City of Bradenton, 190 So.2d 771 (Fla. 1966).

150 1965 Fla. Laws ch. 65–438.

151 208 So.2d 821 (Fla. 1968).

152 *Id.* at 825.

153 *Id.*

long as the courts agree with the legislature's definition. In a situation such as was involved in *Mease Manor*,[154] however, the supreme court and the legislature did not initially agree. The court had for several years subscribed to a fairly restrictive definition of "charitable purposes." Then, after the legislature passed a more liberal statute exempting homes for the aged as being used for charitable purposes, the court withdrew from its position and deferred to the legislature.[155] On the other hand, in *Junkins v. Branstad*,[156] the Iowa Supreme Court dealt with a legislative attempt to define in a statute the term "appropriation bill" as it was used in the constitutional item veto provision. The court stated:

> Whatever purposes the legislative definition of "appropriation bill" may serve, it does not settle the constitutional question. In this case, determination of the scope of the governor's authority granted by Article III, section 16, as amended, will require a decision whether the bill involved here was an "appropriation bill" as that term is used in our constitution. This determination, notwithstanding the legislative definition, is for the courts.[157]

Other state courts have exhibited substantial deference to interpretations of state constitutional provisions by the executive branch, particularly the governor. The Supreme Court of South Carolina noted:

> As the Governor notes in his brief, the historical evidence in this case is overwhelming. Indeed, the Governor's exhaustive analysis of all available historical evidence compels the following conclusions:
>
> Since the ratification of the 1895 Constitution, the uniform belief of South Carolina's governors has been that a bill they have declined to sign after *sine die* adjournment does not have the force and effect of law until it is signed, and a bill vetoed in the interim lacks the force and effect of law without a veto override.[158]

[154] *Id.* at 821.

[155] *See also* State v. Ocean Highway & Port Auth., 217 So.2d 103 (Fla. 1968), where the Florida Supreme Court abandoned its established position that revenue bonds could not be issued to construct industrial plants that were to be leased to private industry, because such was not a public purpose. The court based this decision on 1967 Fla. Laws, ch. 67-1748, which stated that the proposed bond issue was for a public purpose.

[156] Junkins v. Branstad, 421 N.W.2d 130 (Iowa 1988). *See also* State v. Nelson, 502 P.2d 841, 846 (Haw. 1972); State v. Bani, 36 P.3d 1255, 1261 (Haw. 2001); Groch v. General Motors Corp., 883 N.E.2d 377, 408 (Ohio 2008).

[157] *Junkins*, 421 N.W.2d. at 135. *See also In re* Advisory Opinion to the Governor, 593 A.2d 943, 947 (R.I. 1991) ("the self-serving recitation of a public purpose contained in the legislation is not conclusive."); Hickel v. Cowper, 874 P.2d 922, 935–36 (Alaska 1994); Gwinnett Co. School Dist. v. Cox, 710 S.E.2d 773, 779–780 (Ga. 2011); Lewis v. Leon County, 73 So.3d 151, 155 (Fla. 2011).

[158] Williams v. Morris, 464 S.E.2d 97, 101 (S.C. 1995). *See also* State *ex rel.* Twitchell v. Hall, 171 N.W.213, 216 (N.D. 1919); State v. Forbes, 481 S.E.2d 780, 793 (W. Va. 1996).

## IX. THE DOCTRINE OF PRECEDENT IN STATE CONSTITUTIONAL INTERPRETATION

To the extent that stare decisis is followed in state constitutional interpretation, it can reduce the indefiniteness inherent in many constitutional provisions.[159] Interestingly, though, different types of provisions can be more or less susceptible to a reduction in their indefiniteness through an accumulation of judicial interpretation. The "single subject" limitation for the enactment of state statutes has been said to gain little more clarity through judicial interpretation.[160] These distinctions may be worth considering when evaluating precedent related to a particular provision. Distinctions are often made as to the force of the doctrine of precedent in common law, statutory interpretation, and constitutional law.[161] Just as the category of constitutional law must be seen as actually having two parts—federal and state—so the doctrine of precedent in constitutional law may be similarly bifurcated. It is possible that our view of the force of precedent, as with many other doctrines, might be different in state constitutional law as compared to federal constitutional law.

The U.S. Supreme Court has suggested that the doctrine of precedent is weaker in constitutional adjudication than it is in common law or statutory interpretation. The standard authority for this proposition is Justice Brandeis' well-known dissenting opinion in *Burnet v. Coronado Oil & Gas Co.*[162] There, he justified a relaxed doctrine of stare decisis because, in federal constitutional cases, Congress could not correct the Court's errors and because *federal* constitutional amendment was an unlikely solution; consequently, the Court had to correct its own mistakes. Importantly, however, Justice Brandeis went on to say:

> The policy of stare decisis may be more appropriately applied to constitutional questions arising under the fundamental laws of those States whose constitutions may be easily amended. The action following the decision in *Ives v. South Buffalo Ry. Co.* shows how promptly a state constitution may be amended to correct an important decision deemed wrong.[163]

State courts routinely cite Justice Brandeis's view without acknowledging his caveat.[164] Indeed, if ease of amendment were the only criterion with which to assess

159 Dodd, *supra* note 2, at 650.

160 *Id.* at 640. *See* Chapter 9.

161 *See, e.g.*, Earl M. Maltz, *The Nature of Precedent*, 66 N.C. L. Rev. 367 (1988).

162 285 U.S. 393, 409 n.5 (1932) (Brandeis, J., dissenting).

163 *Id.* (citation omitted).

164 State *ex rel.* Moore v. Molpus, 578 So.2d 624, 636 n.16 (Miss. 1991); Cook v. State, 841 P.2d 1345, 1354 (Wyo. 1992) (Golden, J., concurring); State v. Lawrence, 920 A.2d 236, 264 (Conn. 2007) (Katz, J., dissenting). The Connecticut Supreme Court engaged in an extended debate about precedent in 2016 without mentioning the difference between federal and state constitutional change. State

the strength of the doctrine of precedent, Justice Brandeis's argument would not apply to state constitutional law. However, according to one commentator:

> Justice Brandeis's rationale is important for what it does not say as well as for what it says. His argument for a relaxation of stare decisis is not grounded in the nature of a constitution as a unique source of law, a source different in form than statutory or judge-made law. If the essence of a constitution as a source of law were what justified the relaxation of stare decisis, presumably a state's highest court should apply only a relaxed version of stare decisis to its own constitutional precedents, regardless of the state's amendment procedure. Yet Justice Brandeis distinguishes the claims of state constitutional precedents, notwithstanding the functional similarities between state constitutions and the [F]ederal Constitution, or the similarities of the oaths binding state judges and Supreme Court Justices to their respective charters. For Justice Brandeis, apparently, the argument for a relaxation of stare decisis is warranted only by the peculiar difficulty of political response to Supreme Court adjudication of federal constitutional issues.[165]

This generalized critique would support a relaxed view of stare decisis in both state and federal constitutional law based not on ease of amenability but the uniqueness of both the state and federal constitutions as sources of law.

The second commentator, by contrast, argued that Brandeis's distinction supports a more rigid application of stare decisis in state constitutional cases:[166]

> Because most state amendment procedures afford meaningful legislative, as well as popular, participation in the state constitutional lawmaking process, state high courts should proceed with circumspection when deciding whether to overrule a state constitutional precedent.
>
> Article 10, section 4 of the Maine Constitution empowers the Legislature to propose constitutional amendments and put them to a popular vote, where a

v. Peeler, 140 A.3d 811 (Conn. 2016). *See also* Commonwealth v. Alexander, 243 A.2d 177, 195–96 (Pa. 2020). More recently, the justices of the Iowa Supreme Court engaged in a spirited debate about the role of stare decisis in constitutional decision-making in a case in which the majority ultimately concluded that, contrary to prior holdings, the state constitution did not protect a woman's right to choose. *See* Planned Parenthood v. Reynolds, 975 N.W.2d 710, 733–34 (Iowa 2022) (discussing "weak constitutional stare decisis" by Iowa Supreme Court); *id.* at 750–52 (arguing that reliance on stare decisis should be the "default course" in constitutional cases) (Christensen, C.J., dissenting).

[165] James C. Rehnquist, Note, *The Power That Shall Be Vested in a Precedent: Stare Decisis, The Constitution and the Supreme Court*, 66 B.U. L. Rev. 345, 351–52 (1986). *See generally* Martin B. Margulies, Comment, *Cologne v. Westfarms Associates: A Blueprint for an Overruling*, 26 Conn. L. Rev. 691 (1994).

[166] Thad B. Zmistowski, *City of Portland v. DePaolo: Defining the Role of Stare Decisis in State Constitutional Decisionmaking*, 41 Me. L. Rev. 201 (1989).

> simple majority is required for ratification. Thus, as compared with the United States Constitution, which requires the approval of three-fourths of all of the state legislatures in order to ratify a proposed amendment, Maine's constitution is easily amendable. Indeed, the state constitution has been amended repeatedly since 1820. Accordingly, the Brandesian view suggests that stare decisis must play a prominent role in Maine constitutional decisionmaking.[167]

Under this view, stare decisis should be stronger in state constitutional law because state constitutions are relatively easier than the federal Constitution to amend. Brandeis's example, the famous New York *Ives* case, illustrates the point. There are many other examples, as we have seen, where state constitutions have been amended to overturn judicial interpretations of state constitutions.

Regardless of the relative ease of amending state constitutions when compared to the federal Constitution, the fact remains that, in an absolute sense, state constitutions are the highest source of law in any given state, and they are much harder to change than common law or statutory law. Also, as pointed out in Chapter 1, state constitutions are clearly *constitutional* documents despite their differences from the federal Constitution. When assessing the doctrine of precedent in state constitutional law, Justice Brandeis's criterion of ease of amendment compared to the federal scheme should not be the only focal point of analysis. Rather, such an assessment should include an understanding of the unique constitutional stature of state constitutions at the top of each state's legal and political system.[168]

## X. MORE INTERPRETATION TECHNIQUES

Many state courts will examine, in respect to the state constitutional issue before it, the constitutional texts and judicial interpretations of other states. This approach, referred to by the term "horizontal federalism," describes state courts looking for guidance to other state courts interpreting similar or identical state constitutional provisions, rather than looking vertically to U.S Supreme Court

[167] *Id.* at 213 (footnotes omitted). *See also* Mark Sabel, *The Role of Stare Decisis in Construing the Alabama Constitution of 1901*, 53 ALA. L. REV. 273 (2001).

[168] Justice Jack L. Landau of the Oregon Supreme Court explains that court's move to a more flexible doctrine of precedent in *Do Precedents Take Precedence? Stare Decisis and Oregon Constitutionalism*, 77 ALB. L. REV. 1347 (2013/2014). *See also* Jack L. Landau, *Some Thoughts About State Constitutional Interpretation*, 115 PENN ST. L. REV. 837, 867–71 (2011). *See* Robinson Twp., Washington County v. Commonwealth, 83 A.3d 901, 946 (Pa. 2013); Horton v. Oregon Health & Science University, 376 P.3d 998, 1046 (Or. 2016) (Landau, J. concurring). For a discussion of prospective lockstepping as binding precedent, see Chapter XIII.

decisions interpreting similar federal constitutional provisions.[169] This is a very common approach[170] and can also be used effectively to *contrast* a state's constitutional provisions with others.[171]

Some state constitutions contain their own "rules" of interpretation. For example, Article I, Section 26, of the California Constitution provides: "The provisions of this Constitution are mandatory and prohibitory, unless by express words they are declared to be otherwise."[172] The Georgia constitutional provision authorizing the creation of a public mass transit system declares that it "shall be liberally construed to effectuate its purpose . . ."[173] Article XII, Section 9, of the Alaska Constitution states that "the provisions of this constitution shall be construed to be self-executing whenever possible. . . ."[174]

Another, sometimes vexing, state constitutional interpretation problem involves the effective date, and possible retroactive application, of state constitutional amendments.[175] This question was central in a Wisconsin case where a defendant charged with the illegal possession of a firearm three days *after* an amendment was adopted by the voters that would have rendered the possession lawful.[176] The Wisconsin Supreme Court decided, relying on a statute, that the amendment did not become effective until the canvass of the vote was

[169] The term was coined by G. Alan Tarr and M.C. Porter. *See Editor's Introduction* to STATE SUPREME COURTS: POLICYMAKERS IN THE FEDERAL SYSTEM, at xxi–xxii (M.C. Porter & G. Alan Tarr eds., 1982). In the words of former New Jersey Supreme Court Justice Stewart G. Pollock, "[H]orizontal federalism, a federalism in which states look to each other for guidance, may be the hallmark of the rest of the century." Stewart G. Pollock, *Adequate and Independent State Grounds as a Means of Balancing the Relationship Between State and Federal Courts*, 63 TEX. L. REV. 977, 992 (1985). *See supra* note 122 and accompanying text. One study of state constitutional rights cases concluded that over one-third of such decisions referred to cases from other states. James N.G. Cauthen, *Horizontal Federalism in the New Judicial Federalism: A Preliminary Look at Citations*, 66 ALB. L. REV. 783, 784 (2003). *See generally* Eric A. Posner & Cass R. Sunstein, *The Law of Other States*, 59 STAN. L. REV. 131 (2006). For a ranking of the rates at which state supreme courts are cited favorably by sibling courts, *see* Jake Dear & Edward W. Jessen, *"Followed Rates" and Leading State Cases, 1940–2005*, 41 U.C. DAVIS L. REV. 683 (2007).

[170] Simms v. Oedekoven, 839 P.2d 381, 384 (Wyo. 1992); Clouse v. State Dept. Pub. Safety, 11 P.3d 1012, 1016 (Ariz. 2000); Cambria v. Soaries, 776 A.2d 754, 762–63 (N.J. 2000); Washington Water Jet Workers Assoc. v. Yarborough, 90 P.3d 42, 53–57 (Wash. 2004); Cost v. State, 10 A.3d 184, 193 (Md. 2010); *see also* Cardiff v. Bismarck Pub. School Dist., 263 N.W.2d 105, 112 (N.D. 1978) (comparing provisions of constitutions of states admitted under the same Enabling Act).

[171] State v. Riggs, 807 S.W.2d 32, 33 (Ark. 1991); Commonwealth v. Johnson, 631 N.E.2d 1002, 1005 (Mass. 1994); McNamee v. State, 672 N.E.2d 1159, 1165 (Ill. 1996); New Castle Co. Council v. State, 688 A.2d 888, 893 n.6 (Del. 1997); Anderson v. Solvay Minerals, Inc., 3 P.3d 236, 239 (Wyo. 2000); Embry v. O'Bannon, 798 N.E.2d 157, 161–62, 165–66 (Ind. 2003); *In re* Nelson, 86 P.3d 374, 377 (Ariz. 2004); State v. Stevens, 734 N.W.2d 344, 348 (Ind. 2007); People v. Clemons, 968 N.E.2d 1046, 1054–55 (Ill. 2012).

[172] *See also* ARIZ. CONST. art. II, § 32.

[173] GA. CONST. art. XVII, § 1.

[174] *See* Glover v. State, Department of Transportation, 175 P.3d 1240, 1249 (Alaska 2008).

[175] People v. Dean, 677 N.E.2d 947, 952–54 (Ill. 1997) (presumption of prospective application).

[176] State v. Gonzales, 645 N.W.2d 264 (Wis. 2002).

complete and certified.[177] State courts have ruled that a state constitutional amendment does not validate, retroactively, a statute that had been declared unconstitutional.[178] The Nebraska Supreme Court reached this conclusion in partial reliance on the presumption of prospective operation of state constitutional amendments in the absence of clear contrary intent.[179] Some state constitutions contain provisions providing for effective dates of amendments in the absence of a clear expression of intent.[180]

Other state courts have looked back to their colonial (original states) or territorial (nonoriginal states) laws and legal structure in interpreting their state constitutions, particularly their first statehood constitution. As an example, the South Dakota Supreme Court noted: "In considering the power of the new Governor to pardon, the constitutional convention looked to existing Territorial law on the subject of sealing pardons."[181] Such reference to territorial law and even pre-statehood common law is necessarily required by many states' guarantee that the right to jury trial "as it has heretofore existed shall be secured to all and remain inviolate,"[182] or "shall be preserved."[183] The same is true for right to remedy or access to court guarantees (Chapter 5).

In a variety of circumstances, state courts have interpreted a state constitutional clause in light of, or together with, another provision. The Montana Supreme Court, for example, interprets the search and seizure clause in light of the textual privacy guarantee.[184] Montana has also interpreted its cruel and

[177] *Id.* at 267–70. *Contra* Commonwealth v. Tharp, 754 A.2d 1251, 1254 (Pa. 2000) (state constitutional amendment effective upon adoption by electorate).

[178] Millennium Solutions, Inc. v. Davis, 603 N.W.2d 406, 410 (Neb. 1999) (collecting cases and relying on horizontal federalism). *Contra* Carey v. Lincoln Loan Co., 157 P.3d 775, 780–81 (Or. 2007) (doctrine of "implied validation" if vested rights not impaired).

[179] *Id. See also* State *ex rel.* Webb v. Cianci, 591 A.2d 1193, 1202 (R.I. 1991); Bolt v. Arapahoe Co. School Dist. No. Six, 898 P.2d 525, 533 (Colo. 1995); People v. Dean, 677 N.E.2d 947, 952–53 (Ill. 1997); State v. Reeves, 604 N.W.2d 151, 159–60 (Neb. 2000); Strauss v. Horton, 207 P.3d 48 (Cal. 2009); Huber v. Colorado Mining Ass'n., 264 P.3d 884, 890–91 (Colo. 2011); State Fay, 238 A.3d 1191 (N.H. 2020).

[180] Fuchs v. Wilkinson, 630 So.2d 1044, 1045 (Fla. 1994). The legislature may condition the effectiveness of a law upon the approval at a referendum of an amendment to the state constitution that would remove some limitation on the enactment of such a law. *See* Ammerman v. Markham, 222 So.2d 423, 426–27 (Fla. 1969).

[181] Doe v. Nelson, 680 N.W.2d 302, 306 (S.D. 2004). On the Territorial system, see Chapter 3. *See also* Debora A. Person, *Wyoming Pre-Statehood Legal Materials: An Annotated Bibliography—Part II*, 7 Wyo. L. Rev. 333 (2007).

[182] N. Mex. Const. art. II, § 2. *See In re* DES Litigation, 591 N.E.2d 226, 229 (N.Y. 1992); Awada v. Shuffle Master, Inc., 173 P.3d 707, 711 (Nev. 2007).

[183] Or. Const. art. VII, § 3; Lakin v. Senco Products, Inc. 987 P.2d 463, 469 (Or. 1999).

[184] State v. $129,970, 161 P.3d 816, 821 (Mont. 2007) ("The right to privacy in Article II, Section 10 of the Montana Constitution augments the protection against unreasonable searches and seizures."); State v. Conley, 415 P.3d 473, 475 (Mont. 2018); *see also* State v. Gibson, 267 P.3d 645, 659 (Alaska 2012). *But see* State v. Loh, 780 N.W.2d 719, 723 (N.D. 2010) (declining to follow Montana precedent on search and seizure because North Dakota does not have a separate privacy guarantee).

unusual punishment clause in light of its provision guaranteeing human dignity.[185] Some courts provide heightened scrutiny, or equality protection (sometimes referred to as a fundamental right), based on another clause in the state constitution.[186]

## XI. STATE CONSTITUTIONS AS SOURCES OF PUBLIC POLICY

There are a number of circumstances in which state constitutions are not directly applicable to a controversy but can still have an *indirect* effect on the legal arguments. In circumstances where there is no state action (and the state court applies that doctrine), a common-law doctrine that relies on public policy may be informed by state constitutional provisions.[187] As noted by a justice of the Pennsylvania Supreme Court:

> No more clear statement of public policy exists than that of a constitutional amendment. The passage of the Pennsylvania Equal Rights Amendment, Article I, § 28 is the expression of public policy.[188]

Professor Helen Hershkoff has thoughtfully explored this interesting use of state constitutions, which she refers to as "indirect horizontal enforcement" of state constitutional norms, in the context of state constitutional social welfare provisions.[189]

[185] Quigg v. Slaughter, 154 P.3d 1217, 1223 (Mont. 2007); Nicodemus v. State, 392 P.3d 408, 416 (Wyo. 2017). For a similar, ultimately unsuccessful argument in New Jersey, see State v. Ramseur, 524 A.2d 188, 213 n.12 (N.J. 1987).

[186] Pauley v. Kelly, 255 S.E.2d 859, 878 (W. Va. 1979); Sheff v. O'Neill, 678 A.2d 1267, 1281–82 (Conn. 1996); Bd. of Ed. of County of Kanawha v. W. Va. Bd. of Ed., 639 S.E.2d 893, 899 (W. Va. 2006); *In re* S.M.K.-S.H., 290 P.3d 718 (Mont. 2012); State v. Kelliher, 873 S.E.2d 366 (N.C. 2022); Matter of Williams, 496 P.3d 289 (Wash. 2021). *See generally* Robert F. Williams, *Enhanced State Constitutional Rights: Interpreting Two or More Provisions Together*, 2021 Wis. L. Rev. 1001.

[187] Hennessey v. Coastal Eagle Point Oil Co., 609 A.2d 11, 16 (N.J. 1992) (wrongful discharge); Ray v. Wal-Mart Stores, Inc., 359 P.3d 614, 621–23 (Utah 2015); James G. Fannon, *The Public Policy Exception to the Employment at Will Doctrine: Searching for Clear Mandates in the Pennsylvania Constitution*, 27 Rutgers L.J. 927 (1996). Other courts have not been willing to look to their state constitutions in contexts similar to that in New Jersey. *See* Painter v. Graley, 639 N.E.2d 51 (Ohio 1994); Drake v. Cheyenne Newspapers, Inc., 891 P.2d 80 (Wyo. 1995); Stein v. Davidson Hotel Co., 945 S.W.2d 714 (Tenn. 1997).

[188] Clay v. Advanced Computer Applications, Inc., 559 A.2d 917, 924 (Pa. 1990) (Zappala, J., concurring):

[189] Helen Hershkoff, *State Common Law and the Dual Enforcement of Constitutional Norms*, *in* Dual Enforcement of Constitutional Rights: New Frontiers of State Constitutional Law (James Gardner & Jim Rossi eds., 2009); Helen Hershkoff, *"Just Words": Common Law and the Enforcement of State Constitutional and Social Rights*, 62 Stan. L. Rev. 1521 (2010).

The Maryland Court of Appeals relied on a state constitutional provision as a source of public policy to support an exception to the doctrine of comity for foreign judgments,[190] but the Texas Supreme Court declined to rely on a state constitutional clause to provide an element of a tort cause of action.[191]

## XII. INTERNATIONAL LAW AND STATE CONSTITUTIONS

Despite controversy over the use of international law in federal constitutional interpretation,[192] state constitutional interpretation has referred to international law in certain contexts, and is likely to continue to do so. For example, in interpreting the Oregon provision banning "unnecessary rigor" in the treatment of prisoners, Justice Hans Linde referred to international law norms.[193] The West Virginia Supreme Court of Appeals cited the Universal Declaration of Human Rights in its state constitutional school funding decision.[194] There is a growing literature on this important technique of interpretation.[195]

## XIII. CONCLUSION

This chapter has sought to point out the uniqueness, on a number of grounds, of American state constitutions as legal documents and then to link these

[190] Telnikoff v. Matusevitch, 702 A.2d 230, 237 (Md. 1997).

[191] City of Beaumont v. Bouillion, 896 S.W.2d 143, 149–50 (Tex. 1995).

[192] *Compare* Lawrence v. Texas, 539 U.S. 558, 576–77 (2003), *with id.* at 598 (Scalia, J., dissenting). *See* Ernest A. Young, *Foreign Law and the Denominator Problem*, 119 Harv. L. Rev. 148 (2005); Daniel A. Farber, *The Supreme Court, the Law of Nations, and Citations of Foreign Law: The Lessons of History*, 95 Cal. L. Rev. 1335 (2007); *Symposium: International Law and the Constitution: Terms of Engagement*, 77 Fordham L. Rev. 399 (2008).

[193] Sterling v. Cupp, 625 P.2d 123, 131 n.21 (Or. 1981).

[194] Pauley v. Kelly, 255 S.E.2d 859, 864 (W. Va. 1979).

[195] *See* Chapter 4, Section III. Ann I. Park, *Human Rights and Basic Needs: Using International Human Rights Norms to Inform Constitutional Interpretation*, 34 UCLA L. Rev. 1195, 1255–63 (1987); Scott T. Johnson, *The Influence of International Human Rights Law on State Courts and State Constitutions*, 90 Am. Soc'y Int'l L. Proc. 259 (1996); Shirley S. Abrahamson & Michael J. Fischer, *All the World's a Court Room: Judging in the New Millennium*, 26 Hofstra L. Rev. 273 (1997); Penny J. White, *Legal, Political, and Ethical Hurdles to Applying International Human Rights Law in the State Courts of the United States (and Arguments for Scaling Them)*, 71 U. Cinn. L. Rev. 937 (2003); Margaret M. Marshall, "*Wise Parents Do Not Hesitate to Learn from Their Children*," *Interpreting State Constitutions in an Age of Global Jurisprudence*, 79 N.Y.U. L. Rev. 1633 (2004); Martha F. Davis, *The Spirit of Our Times: State Constitutions and Human Rights*, 30 N.Y.U. Rev. L. & Soc. Change 359 (2006); Martha F. Davis, *Upstairs, Downstairs: Subnational Incorporation of International Human Rights Law at the End of an Era*, 77 Fordham L. Rev. 411 (2008); Johanna Kalb, *Human Rights Treaties in State Courts: The International Prospects of State Constitutionalism After Medellín*, 115 Penn. St. L. Rev. 1051 (2011); Jonathan L. Marshfield, *Foreign Precedent in State Constitutional Interpretation*, 53 Duq. L. Rev. 413 (2015).

differences to state constitutional interpretation approaches that differ from federal constitutional interpretation. It is not intended as exhaustive, either as to the range of interpretation issues or as to coverage of every or even a majority of states. It is intended to raise issues and to illustrate interpretation approaches that may be applicable in any state and to highlight the fact that state constitutional law is a category of American constitutional law that must be considered and analyzed on its own terms. No single theory of state constitutional interpretation is proposed.

An interpretation problem in state constitutional law will be unique, first because of the unique nature of state constitutions themselves. Second, it will be unique because of the particular text—whether plain, general, a "great ordinance," or ambiguous, and possibly evolving over time—and because of constitutional history materials—constitutional convention, commission, or legislative reports or debates; official ballot statements or pamphlets; and newspaper materials—that are either more or less specific to the particular interpretation question presented. A final ingredient will be the court's view of various canons or judicial approaches to interpreting state constitutions. Each case will bring a different mix of these factors, all of which must be weighed carefully by advocates and judges.

# PART V

# STATE CONSTITUTIONAL AMENDMENT AND REVISION

Part V surveys the range of methods and processes for change in the texts of state constitutions—both individual amendments and more comprehensive revisions. Each of these processes differs from the others and also produces different kinds of constitutional history materials that remain available for the interpretation process, as analyzed in Chapter 12.

In addition, amending and revising state constitutions often leads to litigation over these processes. This leads to a substantial *judicial* involvement in the processes of state constitutional amendment and revision that generates a number of legal doctrines that must be taken into account; similar doctrines are virtually nonexistent in federal constitutional law. The use of state constitutional amendments as elements of governance has become more common in the states.

# 13
# AMENDING AND REVISING STATE CONSTITUTIONS

*More than two-thirds of the states now operate under constitutions that are more than a century old, that were designed to meet the problems of another era, and that are riddled with piecemeal amendments that have compromised their coherence as plans of government. In addition, the public disdain for government at all levels, together with the increasing reliance on direct democracy for policy making in the states, suggests a need for constitutional reforms designed to increase the responsiveness of state institutions and to promote popular involvement that does not preclude serious deliberation about policy options. Many state constitutions would benefit from substantial changes designed to make state governments more effective, equitable, and responsive, and to equip them to deal with the challenges of the twenty-first century.*

—Alan Tarr[1]

Is a state's constitution obsolete? This is a fundamentally different question from whether it contains specific defects. Only a few states have retained their original, albeit often amended, constitutions.[2] The states' constitutions have been amended an average of about 1.25 times per year.[3]

It is possible, under one view, to see any state's constitution as obsolete at the moment of its adoption. The well-known legal scholar James Willard Hurst noted that, at least with respect to specific policies reflected in state constitutions, they "did not direct, but merely recorded, the currents of social change. Most of this constitutional wisdom was the wisdom of hindsight."[4] In the common

[1] G. Alan Tarr, *Introduction*, *in* 3 State Constitutions for the Twenty-First Century: The Agenda of State Constitutional Reform 1, 3–4 (G. Alan Tarr & Robert F. Williams eds., 2006.)

[2] Robert L. Maddex, State Constitutions of the United States 431 (2d ed. 2006); Donald S. Lutz, *Patterns in the Amending of American State Constitutions*, *in* Constitutional Politics in the States: Contemporary Controversies and Historical Patterns 24, 32–34 (G. Alan Tarr ed., 1996) [hereinafter Constitutional Politics in the States]; *see also* Donald S. Lutz, *Toward a Theory of Constitutional Amendment*, 88 Am. Pol. Sci. Rev. 355, 367 (1994) [hereinafter Lutz, *Toward a Theory*].

[3] Lutz, *in* Constitutional Politics in the States, *supra* note 2, at 34–35.

[4] James Willard Hurst, The Growth of American Law: The Law Makers 246 (1950).

*The Law of American State Constitutions.* Robert F. Williams and Lawrence Friedman, Oxford University Press.
 DOI: 10.1093/oso/9780190068806.003.0014

situation where some of the provisions of a state's constitution were "borrowed" from other state constitutions, there is at least further evidence that much of that constitution was already accepted practice.[5] On the other hand, as proposed state constitutional amendments have more recently been presented to the voters at referenda, the content of the state constitution itself becomes a battleground for hot-button, highly contested issues like same-sex marriage, criminal procedure rights, tort "reform," and a number of other matters.

As Frank Grad and Robert Williams have contended, there is no "ideal" state constitution.[6] They characterized state constitutions as tools or instruments of government, the "suitability and adaptability" of which "can only be gauged in the relationship to its set task."[7] Therefore, the question of whether a state's current constitution is obsolete should be analyzed through an evaluation of how it actually functions within the state. This needs to be a hard-nosed assessment in "the trenches," not a library exercise. They concluded:

> The least we may demand of our state constitutions is that they interpose no obstacle to the necessary exercise of state powers in response to state residents' real needs and active demands for service. . . .
>
> Any review of the adequacy of a state's constitution must begin, therefore, not by comparing the state's present constitution with the more recently adopted charter of another state or with the provisions of some "model" draft, but rather by systematically examining the entire machinery and operation of the state's government.[8]

[5] G. Alan Tarr, *Models and Fashions in State Constitutionalism*, 1998 Wis. L. Rev. 729, 729 (1998). As Willard Hurst noted: "There was a sort of stare decisis about this making of constitutions; it was altogether natural in a country in which men moved about readily, taking with them the learning and institutions of their former homes." Hurst, *supra* note 4, at 224–25.

[6] Frank P. Grad & Robert F. Williams, 2 State Constitutions for the Twenty-First Century: Drafting State Constitutions, Revisions, and Amendments 7, 13 (2006).

[7] *Id.* at 8; *see also* Donald S. Lutz, *The Purposes of American State Constitutions*, 12 Publius: The J. Federalism 27, 31 (Winter 1982) ("A written constitution is a political technology. In a sense it is the very embodiment of the technology for achieving the good life." (footnote omitted)). In his new book, Dr. Adam Brown contends, based on significant statistical evidence, that more specific (and therefore longer) state constitutions have negative effects on states. These include the necessity of more amendments, more statutes invalidated through judicial review, and limitations on "policy performance, resulting in lower incomes per capita, higher unemployment rates, greater economic inequality, and reduced policy innovativeness generally." Adam R. Brown, Dead Hand's Grip: How Long Constitutions Bind States 2 (2022).

[8] Grad & Williams, *supra* note 6, at 12; *see also* Terry Sanford, Storm over the States 189 (1967) (suggesting revision of state constitutions which had been "for so long the drag anchors of state progress." Comparisons may, however, be interesting and useful). *See, e.g.*, Jack Stark, *A Comparison of the Wisconsin and Iowa Constitutions*, 31 Rutgers L.J. 1019, 1019 (2000) (concluding that, because Wisconsin has some provisions not found in Iowa, and "Iowa's courts have been more hesitant to declare statutes unconstitutional. . . . Iowa's constitution has had less effect on Iowa's legal system and, thus, less effect on that state than Wisconsin's constitution has had on Wisconsin").

How would one measure the functional effectiveness, or lack thereof, of a state's constitution? It is obvious that any assessment of a current state constitution must take account of the authoritative judicial interpretations, as well as informal adjustments to the state constitution.[9]

In considering the stability of state constitutions, it is clear that all of them have been *changed* through amendment and judicial interpretation, but some have never been *replaced* or *reformed*. These are very important distinctions in the area of state constitutional development. As G. Alan Tarr has explained:

> Of course, it is possible to introduce significant constitutional reform without calling a convention or adopting a new constitution—amendments proposed by constitutional commissions, by initiative, or by state legislatures may also produce constitutional reform. But in thinking about constitutional reform, it is important to distinguish it from the ordinary constitutional change that is so prevalent in the states. Any alteration of a state constitution, no matter how technical or minor, qualifies as constitutional change. In contrast, constitutional reform involves a more fundamental reconsideration of constitutional foundations. It introduces changes of considerable breadth and impact, changes that substantially affect the operation of state government or the public policy of the state. The replacement of one constitution by another obviously qualifies as constitutional reform. So too may major constitutional amendments or interconnected sets of amendments. However, most constitutional change in the states does not qualify.[10]

These are, of course, not perfect, bright-line distinctions, but they are important all the same.[11] Therefore, the fundamental question in evaluating the functionality of a state's constitution is whether "piecemeal amendments . . . have

[9] Michael Besso, *Constitutional Amendment Procedures and the Informal Political Construction of Constitutions*, 67 J. POL. 69, 69 (2005); *see also* Lawrence Friedman, *Rights in Front of Our Eyes: Positive Rights and the American Constitutional Tradition*, 44 RUTGERS L.J. 609, 614 (2014) (arguing that constitutional law "includes the judicial doctrines that animate and operationalize" constitutional commitments).

[10] G. Alan Tarr, *Introduction*, *in* 1 STATE CONSTITUTIONS FOR THE TWENTY-FIRST CENTURY: THE POLITICS OF STATE CONSTITUTIONAL REFORM 1, 2 (G. Alan Tarr & Robert F. Williams eds., 2006); *see also* Bruce E. Cain, *Constitutional Revision in California: The Triumph of Amendment over Revision*, *in* 1 STATE CONSTITUTIONS FOR THE TWENTY-FIRST CENTURY: THE POLITICS OF STATE CONSTITUTIONAL REFORM, *supra*, at 59, 64:

> In theory, constitutional revision should be more comprehensive and qualitatively more significant than a constitutional amendment. But what if revision occurs increasingly through amendment: What is gained and what is lost? The most important advantage should lie in the ability of a Revision Commission to consider how all the pieces fit together. Where the amendment process is piecemeal and sequential, the revision process affords the opportunity to logically relate proposals to goals, and to make the entire package of proposal[s] coherent.

[11] Tarr, *supra* note 10, at 3.

compromised [its] coherence as [a] plan[] of government,"[12] to such an extent that there is a necessity of "fundamental reconsideration of constitutional foundations."[13] Under this view, even if a number of specific problems or defects were identified in the constitution (and people would differ on each of these), those might continue to be addressed by *amendment*, short of state constitutional *reform* or *revision*.

In evaluating a state constitution in an attempt to determine whether it is obsolete and in need of reform or revision, it should not be compared to the U.S. Constitution.[14] There are a variety of reasons for this lack of fit. State constitutions, even the relatively short ones, are substantially longer than the federal Constitution.[15] But the two kinds of constitutions are also called upon to perform different functions. As noted throughout this book, the federal Constitution is incomplete as a governing document; it depends on the state governments to function within it and serves primarily to delegate a limited set of powers to the national government. Each state constitution structures a subnational government—a government functioning within a government—and serves primarily to limit the plenary authority retained by the state at the time of formation of the Union. Accordingly, the federal and state constitutions perform different legal and political functions, and there is simply a wider variety of subject matter to be regulated by a state constitution than there is under the U.S. Constitution.[16]

Further, even by the middle of the nineteenth century, state constitutions had already begun to evolve from basic charters of government and protections of rights to encompass, in addition, *policy* matters that could have been left to state legislatures. Dr. Tarr has noted that "[s]tate constitutions, in contrast [to the U.S. Constitution], deal directly with matters of public policy, sometimes in considerable detail."[17] These sorts of policy provisions may prohibit legislative action, mandate the enactment of certain policies, or directly enact policies.[18] Tarr concluded that, during the nineteenth century, "state constitutions increasingly became instruments of government rather than merely frameworks for government."[19] Do policy-oriented provisions in state constitutions become obsolete or incoherent more quickly than framework-oriented provisions?

[12] Tarr, *supra* note 1, at 3.
[13] Tarr, *supra* note 10, at 2.
[14] *See* GRAD & WILLIAMS, *supra* note 6, at 14.
[15] Christopher W. Hammons, *State Constitutional Reform: Is it Necessary?* 64 ALB. L. REV. 1327, 1329 (2001).
[16] *Id.* at 1329. *See generally* Donald S. Lutz, *The United States Constitution as an Incomplete Text*, 496 ANNALS AM. ACAD. POL. & SOC. SCI. 23 (1988).
[17] G. ALAN TARR, UNDERSTANDING STATE CONSTITUTIONS 20 (1998). *See* Chapter 1, section V.
[18] TARR, *supra* note 17, at 21.
[19] *Id.* at 132; *see also* Hammons, *supra* note 15, at 1332–33.

Some states rejected, though probably not consciously, the Jeffersonian view that state constitutions should be revised once every generation[20] in favor of the Madisonian preference for a more stable state constitution.[21] This conflict between stability and ease of change has persisted through the entire evolution of state constitutions. Professor Stephen Holmes has captured the modern conflict:

> Some theorists worry that democracy will be paralyzed by constitutional straitjacketing. Others are apprehensive that the constitutional dyke will be breached by a democratic flood. Despite their differences, both sides agree that there exists a deep, almost irreconcilable tension between constitutionalism and democracy. Indeed, they come close to suggesting that "constitutional democracy" is a marriage of opposites, an oxymoron.[22]

If state constitutional revision is too difficult, constitutionalism overwhelms democracy; if it is too easy, democracy overwhelms constitutionalism. It is difficult to achieve exactly the right balance, and this point might change over time. Any assessment of a state constitution's obsolescence must also take account of, and consider adjustments in, the processes of changing or revising the constitution.

What about the content of a state's constitution? As noted in Chapter 1, Dr. Christopher Hammons formulated the distinction between "framework-oriented" and "policy-oriented" provisions in state constitutions.[23] He analyzed all of the state constitutions according to this distinction and concluded that the national average was about 40 percent policy-oriented provisions.[24] Of course,

[20] Jefferson's letter on this subject is quoted in Albert L. Sturm, *The Development of American State Constitutions*, 12 PUBLIUS: THE J. FEDERALISM 57, 66 n.24 (Winter 1982). *See also* JOHN R. VILE, THE CONSTITUTIONAL AMENDING PROCESS IN AMERICAN POLITICAL THOUGHT 59–78 (1992); John Dinan, *"The Earth Belongs Always to the Living Generation": The Development of State Constitutional Amendment and Revision Procedures*, 62 REV. POL. 645, 647–51 (2000); Merrill D. Peterson, *Mr. Jefferson's "Sovereignty of the Living Generation,"* 52 VA. Q. REV. 437 (1976).

[21] LAURA J. SCALIA, AMERICA'S JEFFERSONIAN EXPERIMENT: REMAKING STATE CONSTITUTIONS, 1820–1850, 4–5 (1999); *see also* Stephen Holmes, *Precommitment and the Paradox of Democracy*, *in* CONSTITUTIONALISM AND DEMOCRACY 195–97 (Jon Elster & Rune Slagstad eds., 1993).

[22] Holmes, *supra* note 21, at 197. On the problems encountered with state constitutional "rigidity," see William F. Swindler, *State Constitutional Law for the 20th Century*, 50 NEB. L. REV. 577, 596 (1971).

[23] Hammons, *supra* note 15, at 1338:

> Framework provisions are those provisions that deal exclusively with the principles, institutions, powers, and processes of government. They provide the basic building blocks of government. Policy provisions are defined as those provisions that deal with "statute law" or "public-policy" type issues, do not relate to the establishment of the government, are rather specific, typically do not apply to all citizens, and often provide differential benefits. It is these provisions that most political scientists and legal scholars consider "extra-constitutional."

*Id.* at 1351 (examples of each type of provision); *see also* Christopher W. Hammons, *Was James Madison Wrong? Rethinking the American Preference for Short Framework-Oriented Constitutions*, 93 AM. POL. SCI. REV. 837, 846–47 (1999) (more detailed list of examples).

[24] Hammons, *supra* note 15, at 1333; *see also* Hammons, *supra* note 23, at 840 (39 percent).

what constitutes a policy-oriented provision rather than a framework-oriented provision may be in the eyes of the beholder, and neutral, academic observers may not appreciate the important historic and political reasons why state constitutions contain certain detailed provisions.[25] Interestingly, Dr. Hammons concluded that the longer and more policy-oriented a state constitution is, the longer it endures before replacement.[26]

In his 2018 book, *State Constitutional Politics: Governing by Amendment in the American States*,[27] the political scientist John Dinan collects and expands on much of his deep research into this field. The book's title reflects the tendency of the states to modify their constitutions' rights, government structure, and policy provisions at a significant rate.[28] It will be the standard in this field for some time to come. He concludes:

> Amendments can alter institutions in two main ways: by changing the structure of institutions and means of selecting officials or by shifting authority among institutions and officials. Amendments can alter understandings of rights in either of two ways, whether defining rights in advance of court decisions or overturning understandings of rights expressed in court decisions. Policy amendments also take different forms, whether preventing passage of policies, initiating policies, or authorizing policies in the face of constraints preventing their adoption.[29]

Of course, almost none of this constitutional change takes place at the federal level, where amendment, as noted earlier, is almost impossible.[30]

[25] For each provision in a state constitution, no matter how seemingly trivial, there is a story to be told. It may be a political story rather than an epic, "constitutional" story. As Lawrence Friedman noted, "[t]here was a point to every clause in these inflated constitutions. Each one reflected the wishes of some faction or interest group, which tried to make its policies permanent by freezing them into the charter. Constitutions, like treaties, preserved the terms of compromise between warring groups." LAWRENCE M. FRIEDMAN, A HISTORY OF AMERICAN LAW 119 (2d ed. 1985).

[26] Hammons, *supra* note 15, at 1338–41; Hammons, *supra* note 23, at 845. Although this is not always the case. *See* Lawrence Friedman, *The Endurance of State Constitutions: Preliminary Thoughts and Notes on the New Hampshire Constitution*, 60 WAYNE L. REV. 203 (2014) (discussing endurance of the comparatively short New Hampshire Constitution of 1784).

[27] *See* Jonathan L. Marshfield, *The People and Their Constitutions*, 71 RUTGERS U. L. REV. 1233 (2019) (reviewing JOHN DINAN, STATE CONSTITUTIONAL POLITICS: GOVERNING BY AMENDMENT IN THE AMERICAN STATES (2018)).

[28] DINAN, *supra* note 27, at 3 ("distinctive form of constitutional politics in the States."). For a survey of the expanding processes of state constitutional change, see Robert F. Williams, *Evolving State Constitutional Processes of Adoption, Revision and Amendment*, 69 ARK. L. REV. 553 (2016). *See also* Jonathan L. Marshfield, *America's Misunderstood Constitutional Rights*, 170 U. PENN. L. REV. 853 (2022) (state constitutional rights are intended to be amended and extended to keep up with the times.)

[29] DINAN, *supra* note 27, at 280. *See also* ROBINSON WOODWARD-BURNS, HIDDEN LAWS: HOW STATE CONSTITUTIONS STABILIZE AMERICAN POLITICS (2021) (arguing that, in the United States, national issues and conflicts can be decentralized to the states and their easier-to-amend constitutions, thereby preserving federal constitutional stability); JEFFREY S. SUTTON, WHO DECIDES? STATES AS LABORATORIES OF CONSTITUTIONAL EXPERIMENTATION, ch. 10 (2021).

[30] For some ideas on how mechanisms of *state* constitutional change could be adapted to facilitate *federal* Article V constitutional change, see Robert F. Williams, *Unsettling the Settled: Challenging*

Law professor Jonathan Marshfield has completed a number of pieces of his long-range research into state constitutional change and its effect. He extended the study of "informal change" in state constitutions[31] by examining one element of such change: state supreme courts overruling their earlier interpretations of their state constitutions.[32] He has compared the numbers of formal amendments to state constitutions with the informal "amendments" deriving from decisions overruling precedent, concluding that "although formal amendments vastly outnumber informal amendments by courts in the aggregate, informal amendment regarding individual rights was more prevalent than formal amendment. This generally holds true across states and across time; suggesting that there is something special about the relationship between courts, informal amendment, and rights."[33] As Marshfield observes, "[v]arious states with high formal amendment rates also have some of the highest rates of informal amendment by courts."[34] Marshfield has also noted the effect of possible override by amendment of expansive state civil liberties rulings on state judges' considerations, together with a number of other important considerations of state constitutional amendments.[35]

## I. TWENTIETH-CENTURY STATE CONSTITUTIONAL REVISION

There is a good deal that can be learned from states that have addressed the question of revising their state constitutions. Looking at these experiences indicates that a number of different mechanisms have been utilized; there have been successes and failures; and in the final analysis, each state presents its own unique

*the Great and Not-So-Great Compromises in the Constitution*, 91 TEX. L. REV. 1149, 1154–64 (2013) (reviewing SANFORD LEVINSON, FRAMED: AMERICA'S 51 CONSTITUTIONS AND THE CRISIS OF GOVERNANCE (2012)).

[31] "An informal constitutional change occurs where the enforceable meaning of the constitution changes without altering the constitutional text." Richard Albert, *How Unwritten Constitutional Norms Change Written Constitutions*, 38 DUBLIN U. L.J. 387, 388–39 (2015).

[32] Jonathan L. Marshfield, *Courts and Informal Constitutional Change in the States*, 51 NEW ENG. L. REV. 453 (2017).

[33] *Id.* at 490.

[34] *Id.* at 491. Professor Williams expressed a few thoughts on Marshfield's findings in Robert F. Williams, *New Light on State Constitutional Change*, 51 NEW ENG. L. REV. 547 (2018). *See also* Jonathan L. Marshfield, *The Amendment Effect*, 98 BOSTON U. L. REV. 55 (2018) (noting, among other things, that states with high formal amendment rates also experience high rates of informal change by courts).

[35] *See generally* Jonathan L. Marshfield, *Amendment Creep*, 115 MICH. L. REV. 215 (2016) (considering the effect of state constitutional relative ease of amendment on judicial interpretation), *Improving Amendment*, 69 ARK. L. REV. 477 (2016) (improving the process of amendment approval by requiring county debate and approval); and *Forgotten Limits on the Power to Amend State Constitutions*, 114 NW. U. L. REV. 65 (2019) (submitting argument that significant constitutional change may only be presented to voters by constitutional conventions).

set of state constitutional concerns and challenges. The following brief summary is intended to suggest some key features in state constitutional revision attempts across a number of states.

## A. New Jersey (1947)

New Jersey held a highly successful state constitutional convention in 1947, culminating a number of years of attempts at revision, including a legislatively proposed constitution that was voted down in 1944.[36] This constitutional convention took place in the period of postwar optimism and confidence in government. Very strong gubernatorial leadership was a key element in the approval of the constitutional convention and ratification of the convention's recommended revised constitution by the voters.[37] Furthermore, a crucial limitation was placed on the convention, thereby taking the question of reapportionment of the state senate off the table. This divisive issue, threatening the control that small counties had over the state, had stood in the way of state constitutional revision for over a century.[38] The convention met at Rutgers University, not in the state capital, to avoid the appearance of "politics as usual."

The leading commentator on the New Jersey State Constitutional Convention of 1947 concluded:

> First of all, the convention leaders had limited objectives, basically to update the court system and modernize the executive branch. They did not visualize their job as one of righting all the wrongs in New Jersey's political and social system. Rather, they looked at the old constitution, at what history had shown to be its basic weaknesses, and tried to correct those that seemed alterable in terms of the current political milieu. This provided marketability for the document and helped ensure its substantive integrity. The 1947 New Jersey constitution was relatively free from reformist gimmicks and untested panaceas. Limited goals also gave the constitution a more enduring character.[39]

Out of the 1947 process, New Jersey achieved a revised state constitution that gave it one of the best judicial systems in the United States, a very strong

[36] *See generally* Richard J. Connors, The Process of Constitutional Revision in New Jersey: 1940–1947 (1970).

[37] *Id.* at 192–93; Robert F. Williams, The New Jersey State Constitution: A Reference Guide 15–16 (1997).

[38] Connors, *supra* note 36, at 124–25; Williams, *supra* note 37, at 15–16.

[39] Connors, *supra* note 36, at 194.

governor, and modern rights provisions concerning women's rights, collective bargaining, and racial segregation.[40]

## B. Louisiana (1973)

The State of Louisiana, also after a number of attempts and with the help of strong gubernatorial leadership,[41] convened a constitutional convention in 1973. One leading commentator concluded, with respect to the convention's product, "[l]ittle substantive change resulted, but the document was superior technically. It was simplified, shortened, and made more consistent. It was more of a triumph of the legal technicians than of the reformers."[42] There were, however, some interesting modern innovations in the rights provisions of the Louisiana Constitution, including an equal protection clause as well as a provision stating that "[n]o law shall arbitrarily, capriciously, or unreasonably discriminate against a person because of birth, age, sex, culture, physical condition, or political ideas or affiliations."[43]

## C. Virginia (1968–1970)

Substantial revision of the Virginia Constitution was accomplished through the constitutional commission process.[44] The commission, with strong gubernatorial backing,[45] was authorized by the legislature, and its members were named by the governor in 1968.[46] After detailed study, public hearings, and deliberation, the commission submitted its report to the governor and the legislature

40 For an excellent symposium commemorating the fiftieth anniversary of New Jersey's constitution, see *Tenth Annual Issue on State Constitutional Law*, 29 RUTGERS L.J. 673 (1998). For a very interesting analysis of the ban on racial segregation, the first of its kind in the country, see Bernard K. Freamon, *The Origins of the Anti-Segregation Clause in the New Jersey Constitution*, 35 RUTGERS L.J. 1267 (2004).

41 LEE HARGRAVE, THE LOUISIANA STATE CONSTITUTION: A REFERENCE GUIDE 16 (1991).

42 *Id.* at 17.

43 LA. CONST. art. I, § 3; *see* Lee Hargrave, *The Declaration of Rights of the Louisiana Constitution of 1974*, 35 LA. L. REV. 1, 6 (1975); Louis "Woody" Jenkins, *The Declaration of Rights*, 21 LOY. L. REV. 9, 16–17 (1975). Paradoxically, this provision, which stimulated support by the NAACP for the 1974 constitution, was held by the Louisiana Supreme Court to ban all forms of affirmative action. La. Associated Gen. Contractors, Inc. v. State, 669 So.2d. 1185, 1188 (La. 1996); Robert F. Williams, *Shedding Tiers "Above and Beyond" the Federal Floor: Loving State Constitutional Equality Rights to Death in Louisiana*, 63 LA. L. REV. 917, 918 (2003).

44 A.E. Dick Howard, *Adopting a New Constitution: Lessons from Virginia*, *in* 1 STATE CONSTITUTIONS FOR THE TWENTY-FIRST CENTURY: THE POLITICS OF STATE CONSTITUTIONAL REFORM, *supra* note 10, at 74.

45 *Id.* at 74, 101.

46 *Id.* at 74–75.

at the beginning of 1969.[47] Based on the commission's recommendations, the legislature debated the proposals and presented its proposed revisions to the voters in four separate questions, rather than as a "take-it-or-leave-it package in which they were obliged to approve or disapprove all the constitutional changes in a single question."[48] Notably, after the proposals of the commission were debated, revised, and placed before the voters by the legislature, a privately funded committee was created to inform the people of Virginia about the proposed changes and to encourage their support.[49] The leading commentator on Virginia's successful constitutional revision, Professor A.E. Dick Howard (a participant in the process himself), thoughtfully compared that state's success with problems encountered in constitutional revision in other states during this period.[50]

### D. Montana (1967–1972)

In 1967, the legislature in Montana assigned the legislative council to prepare "a study of the Montana Constitution, to determine if it was adequately serving the current needs of the people."[51] Based on the council's recommendation, the legislature created a Constitution Revision Commission in 1969.[52] The Montana Constitution includes the provision requiring an automatic question to be placed on the ballot every twenty years as to whether there should be a constitutional convention.[53] These preparatory actions were taken in anticipation of that vote in 1970, which was approved by a wide margin. Then, pursuant to legislative authorization and creation of another commission to prepare for the convention, the constitutional convention met in 1972.[54] The Montana convention met at a time when it could draw on several trends in state constitutionalism. First was the movement toward "managerial constitutionalism."[55]

[47] *Id.* at 75; COMMISSION ON CONSTITUTIONAL REVISION, THE CONSTITUTION OF VIRGINIA: REPORT (1969).

[48] Howard, *supra* note 44, at 78, 95.

[49] *Id.* at 78–85.

[50] *Id.* at 86–96. *See generally* A.E. Dick Howard, *"For the Common Benefit": Constitutional History in Virginia as a Casebook for the Modern Constitution-Maker*, 54 VA. L. REV. 816 (1968).

[51] LARRY M. ELISON & FRITZ SNYDER, THE MONTANA STATE CONSTITUTION: A REFERENCE GUIDE 8 (2001).

[52] . *Id.*

[53] MONT. CONST. art. XIV, § 3.

[54] ELISON & SNYDER, *supra* note 51, at 9–10.

[55] G. Alan Tarr, *The Montana Constitution: A National Perspective*, 64 MONT. L. REV. 1, 13 (2003).

> These managerial reformers believed that state government had to be restructured to facilitate vigorous action. Failure to create such proactive state governments, they argued, would result in the erosion of state power, as citizens increasingly looked to the national government to address their concerns. To establish an effective state government, they insisted, required a constitution that was flexible and adaptable, that placed few restrictions on how the state government addressed current and future problems.[56]

There was a second, more recent trend:

> The adherents of this newer view, which I call constitutional populism, distrust activist government. They are skeptical about their state legislature becoming a "little Congress," their governor a "little president," or their supreme court a "little Warren Court." They want not a resurgence of state government but greater control over what they perceive as overly expensive and powerful state governments that are insulated from popular concerns and popular control.[57]

Dr. Tarr concluded that the Montana Constitution "reflects a judicious blending of the recommendations of both these reform movements."[58] He concluded that the 1972 Montana constitutional convention went beyond these two themes and included a number of important innovations, including concern for the cultural heritage of Native Americans; support for the right to privacy; and rights against private entities, along with concern for the environment.[59]

Interestingly, the 1972 Montana Constitution, which was submitted as a revised constitution, with separate votes on three controversial issues (a unicameral legislature, the death penalty, and legalized gambling) was adopted by the voters by an extremely narrow margin.[60] The Montana Supreme Court by a 3–2 vote rejected a legal challenge contending that a majority had not actually ratified constitution.[61] Despite its narrow margin of approval, the Montana voters two decades later overwhelmingly rejected the opportunity to call another constitutional convention.[62]

[56] *Id.*

[57] *Id.* at 14.

[58] *Id.* at 15.

[59] *Id.* at 16–17.

[60] ELISON & SNYDER, *supra* note 51, at 14–15.

[61] State *ex rel.* Cashmore v. Anderson, 500 P.2d 921, 929 (Mont. 1972); ELISON & SNYDER, *supra* note 51, at 14–15.

[62] Tarr, *supra* note 55, at 20–21; ELISON & SNYDER, *supra* note 51, at 16. *See generally The Honorable James R. Browning Symposium: The 1972 Montana Constitution: Thirty Years Later*, 64 MONT. L. REV. vii (2003).

## E. Michigan (1961–1962)

After the adoption in 1960 of an initiative amendment to the state constitution easing the requirements for the calling of a state constitutional convention, and requiring the question of whether a constitutional convention should be called to be placed on the ballot in 1961 and every sixteen years thereafter, Michigan held a constitutional convention in 1961–1962.[63] The governor created a study commission to prepare for the convention.[64] After the legislature refused to provide funding for the operation of the commission, a private foundation stepped forward with financing.[65] Slightly over two-thirds of the delegates to the convention were Republican.[66] The convention, by a wide margin, proposed a modernized constitution that was ratified by the voters and, with amendments, is still in effect today.[67]

## F. Georgia (1983)

In Georgia, based on the recommendations of a Constitutional Revision Commission, the legislature engaged in a two-month extraordinary session in 1964 and adopted a new constitution.[68] The document was, however, never submitted to the people because of a federal court decision declaring that it was the product of a malapportioned legislature.[69] Despite the fact that the U.S. Supreme Court ultimately vacated that decision,[70] the new constitution was never submitted to the voters.[71]

In the 1970s, however, strong gubernatorial leadership led to the recommendation that the legislature prepare a revised constitution, but one without substantive revision. This was accomplished, and the voters overwhelmingly adopted the document in 1976.[72]

The legislature immediately embarked on a process leading to substantive revision of the Georgia Constitution. This process was also based on strong gubernatorial leadership.[73] A multiyear legislative process culminated in 1982, and this legislative product was submitted to the people and adopted overwhelmingly.[74]

[63] Susan P. Fino, The Michigan State Constitution: A Reference Guide 20–21 (1996).
[64] *Id.* at 21.
[65] *Id.*
[66] *Id.*
[67] *Id.* at 23–24.
[68] Melvin B. Hill Jr., The Georgia State Constitution: A Reference Guide 14 (1994).
[69] Toombs v. Fortson, 205 F. Supp. 248, 258–59 (N.D. Ga. 1962), *vacated*, 379 U.S. 621 (1965); Hill, *supra* note 68, at 14.
[70] *Toombs*, 379 U.S. at 622.
[71] Hill, *supra* note 68, at 14.
[72] *Id.* at 15.
[73] *Id.* at 16.
[74] *Id.* at 19.

A commentator on the Georgia process concluded:

> Perhaps because the document was supported by the leadership of all three branches of state government, perhaps because there was an organized public education campaign to explain it, perhaps because there was no organized opposition to the proposal, or perhaps just because the people had grown weary of twenty years' worth of "talk" about constitutional revision, the proposed new constitution was approved overwhelmingly at the 1982 election. . . .[75]

## G. Florida (1967, 1977, 1997)

Beginning in 1966, the state of Florida utilized a constitutional commission to prepare a revised draft of that state's 1885 constitution. The commission's product was presented to the legislature, which held an extraordinary session during the summer of 1967 to consider and modify the commission's recommendations. The legislature's recommended revised constitution was adopted by the people and went into effect in 1968.[76] Florida's 1968 constitution contained a unique mechanism for future state constitutional change: an appointed constitution revision commission automatically created every twenty years (ten years for the first cycle), with the power to place its recommendations directly on the ballot for the voters' approval without sending them to the legislature.[77] This new mechanism was unprecedented and constituted "a leap of faith into the future, a license to later generations with no guarantees as to the substantive outcomes that would flow from the new process."[78] This mechanism was highly disturbing to the state legislature, but the people of Florida rejected an amendment to the state constitution to remove the constitution revision commission process.[79] In fact, the Florida Constitution was amended to authorize the same commission procedure, with direct access to the ballot, for budget and finance matters.[80]

[75] *Id.* There was criticism of the Georgia process on the ground that it did not adequately involve the people in "popular sovereignty." James A. Henretta, *Foreword: Rethinking the State Constitutional Tradition*, 22 Rutgers L.J. 819, 830–31 (1991).

[76] Rebecca Mae Salokar, *Constitutional Revision in Florida: Planning, Politics, Policy, and Publicity*, *in* 1 State Constitutions for the Twenty-First Century: The Politics of State Constitutional Reform, *supra* note 10, at 19, 21–22; Talbot D'Alemberte, The Florida State Constitution: A Reference Guide 11–13 (1991).

[77] Robert F. Williams, *The Florida Constitution Revision Commission in Historic and National Context*, 50 Fla. L. Rev. 215, 220 (1998); D'Alemberte, *supra* note 76, at 13; Salokar, *supra* note 76, at 22.

[78] Robert F. Williams, *Foreword: Is Constitutional Revision Success Worth Its Popular Sovereignty Price?* 52 Fla. L. Rev. 249, 255 (2000).

[79] D'Alemberte, *supra* note 76, at 15. There was another vote to abolish the constitution revision commission scheduled for 2022.

[80] Fla. Const. art. XI, § 6. *See generally* Donna Blanton, *The Taxation and Budget Reform Commission: Florida's Best Hope for the Future*, 18 Fla. St. U. L. Rev. 437 (1991). In 2008 the Florida

Several other states have considered Florida's commission mechanism, but none has adopted it.[81]

Florida's initial experience with this constitution revision mechanism ended in failure. The 1977 commission submitted eight separate propositions to the voters, and all were defeated.[82] A casino gambling amendment was also on the ballot, and the governor exerted great energy opposing it, which left him with little time to support the commission's proposals.[83] Further, there was no organization or funding to support the proposed revisions. Interestingly, however, the commission's proposals set the agenda for state constitutional discussions over the next decade, and a number of its recommendations were later adopted through the amendment process.[84]

The 1997 Constitution Revision Commission was much more successful. A preparatory committee developed background research and even proposed rules for the commission.[85] It learned a number of lessons from the unsuccessful commission of twenty years earlier and made a number of recommendations to the voters that were accepted.[86] The commission successfully utilized opinion polling during its deliberations.[87] The proposals were much more moderate than those of 1978 because the commission required of itself a supermajority vote before recommending a state constitutional change, and an organization was put into place to support the proposed revisions.[88]

As a member of the Florida Bar and a native Floridian, Professor Williams had some involvement in these processes; he suggested:

> [T]he question to be asked by Floridians, as well as those in other states who are watching Florida's experiment in the processes of state constitutionmaking, is whether the very expansive deliberative record of the commission, its arguable independence, and its success in convincing the voters to accept its proposals make up for its seemingly reduced legitimacy on account of its appointed, rather than elected, membership.[89]

Supreme Court ruled that this Commission exceeded its authority in proposing amendments to repeal Florida's "Blaine Amendment" and to overrule a decision striking down a school voucher statute. Ford v. Browning, 992 So.2d 132 (Fla. 2008).

[81] Williams, *supra* note 78, at 256–57.

[82] D'ALEMBERTE, *supra* note 76, at 15; Salokar, *supra* note 67, at 26. For a complete analysis of the 1978 commission's proposals, see *Symposium on the Proposed Revisions to the Florida Constitution*, 6 FLA. ST. U. L. REV. 565 (1978).

[83] Salokar, *supra* note 76, at 47.

[84] Williams, *supra* note 78, at 257 n.30.

[85] Salokar, *supra* note 76, at 34.

[86] *Id.* at 35–37, 44.

[87] *Id.* at 48–49.

[88] *Id.* at 35–37, 47; Williams, *supra* note 78, at 260–61.

[89] Williams, *supra* note 78, at 260. The Florida process was criticized for not adequately involving the voters. *See* Joseph W. Little, *The Need to Revise the Florida Constitutional Revision Commission*,

He concluded:

> It is probably safe to say that Florida conducted the most open and accessible review of a state constitution in the history of our country. This is the source of the Commission's legitimacy with the living generation, even in the absence of prospective authorization by the current generation. . . . Popular participation and deliberation have taken the place of popular stimulus in Florida constitutional revision.[90]

Florida's process has been characterized by substantial preparatory work and gubernatorial leadership.[91] The 1997 process, by contrast to that in 1977, included an important post-commission process of publicizing and supporting its proposals.[92]

## H. New York (1967, 1997)

New York had a constitutional convention in 1967 that was highly partisan and dominated by legislative leaders.[93] The revised constitution presented by that convention to the voters was defeated at the polls.[94] One analyst of these events noted:

> Sitting legislators and others in the government industry were heavily represented at the convention. And, especially offensive to some, during the year that the convention met, the constitutional provision for delegate compensation "required" the legislators who were also delegates, and others on public payrolls, to collect two salaries and the attendant pension benefits.[95]

52 Fla. L. Rev. 475 (2000). *See also* Mary E. Adkins, Making Modern Florida: How the Spirit of Reform Shaped a New Constitution (2016); Mary E. Adkins, *What Florida's Constitution Revision Commission Can Teach and Learn from Those of Other States*, 71 Rutgers U. L. Rev. 1177 (2019); Christopher S. Emmanuel, *Limiting Florida's Constitution Revision Commission*, 47 Fla. St. U. L. Rev. 733 (2020).

[90] Williams, *supra* note 78, at 270.

[91] Salokar, *supra* note 76, at 26–33.

[92] *Id.* at 44–51.

[93] Gerald Benjamin, *The Mandatory Constitutional Convention Question Referendum: The New York Experience in National Context*, *in* 1 State Constitutions for the Twenty-First Century: The Politics of State Constitutional Reform, *supra* note 10, at 155. *See generally* Henrik N. Dullea, Charter Revision in the Empire State: The Politics of New York's 1967 Constitutional Convention (1997).

[94] Benjamin, *supra* note 93, at 155; *see* Lewis B. Kaden, *The People: No! Some Observations on the 1967 New York Constitutional Convention*, 5 Harv. J. Legis. 343 (1968); Robert B. McKay, *Constitutional Revision in New York State: Disaster in 1967*, 19 Syracuse L. Rev. 207 (1967).

[95] Benjamin, *supra* note 93, at 155; *see also* Peter J. Galie, The New York State Constitution: A Reference Guide (1991).

In preparation for the 1997 automatic vote in New York on whether to call a constitutional convention, the governor in 1993 appointed a constitutional revision commission to educate the public prior to the vote and to develop possible constitutional proposals to obviate the necessity of calling a constitutional convention. There was no legislative funding, so the commission had to operate with gubernatorial discretionary funds.[96] The commission ultimately recommended a unique action-producing alternative to a state constitutional convention. The commission's report sought to change the focus from the constitutional convention to specific policy areas that were in need of reform. These were "fiscal integrity, state [and] local relations, education, and public safety":[97]

> The Commission proposed the creation of four Action Panels designed to break the political/policy logjam in all of these issue areas. The panels would create integrated packages of legislation and constitutional amendments by the close of the 1996 legislative session. In creating these panels, the Commission also asked that the governor and legislature "clearly commit themselves to take definitive action on these final proposals by a date certain."[98]

When the legislature failed to act, the commission recommended that the voters approve the call for a constitutional convention. Despite a vigorous campaign, including strong gubernatorial support, the voters rejected the call in 1997.[99] Dr. Gerald Benjamin attributed this rejection to a variety of factors: the 1997 vote did not come at a propitious time, the legislators opposed the calling of a convention that was unlimited and not their idea, there was a lack of a strong campaign supporting the constitutional convention call, and there was an array of interest groups who feared a constitutional convention and potential changes to the status quo.[100]

[96] Benjamin, *supra* note 93, at 153.

[97] *Id.* at 157.

[98] *Id.* (*citing* Temporary State Commission on Constitutional Revision, Effective Government Now for the New Century: A Report to the People, the Governor, and the Legislators of New York (1995)); *see also Documents*, 26 Rutgers L.J. 1355, 1394 (1995) (excerpts from the Commission's report).

[99] Benjamin, *supra* note 93, at 158–63.

[100] *Id.* at 159–66. *See generally* Decision 1997: Constitutional Change in New York (Gerald Benjamin & Henrik N. Dullea eds., 1997). On Hawaii's experience with automatic referenda, see Amy K. Trask, *A History of Revision: The Constitutional Convention Question in Hawai'i, 1950–2008*, 31 U. Haw. L. Rev. 291 (2008).

## I. Alabama (1994–Present)

Alabama is still operating under its 1901 constitution. Efforts at reforming it go back many years but saw renewed emphasis in the past decade or so.[101] Despite strong gubernatorial leadership and a broad, grassroots organization supporting constitutional revision, the voters overwhelmingly rejected a package of tax reforms and an amendment permitting the simplification of Alabama's longest-in-nation state constitution.[102] Still, these activities went a long way toward raising the level of civic debate about the state constitution.[103]

## J. Texas (1971–1975)

After the U.S. Supreme Court reapportionment decisions and early gubernatorial support, the Texas Legislature proposed a constitutional amendment that would authorize the legislature itself to serve as a unicameral constitutional convention in 1974.[104] This amendment also provided for a preparatory constitutional revision commission. After approval of this amendment by the voters, the legislature established the constitutional revision commission which was widely representative of the Texas citizenry.[105] The commission engaged in a broadly inclusive process and recommended a revised state constitution to the Texas Legislature, which convened as a constitutional convention for six months in 1974. Ultimately, the convention adjourned "after failing by three votes to approve the final revision package."[106] Dr. Janice May, a member of the Constitutional Revision Commission, explained this failure:

> Several reasons have been put forward to explain the convention's failure to agree on a new constitution. Among the most plausible are the following: the lame-duck status and relative inexperience of the convention president; the legislative political environment in an election year that exacerbated divisive

[101] H. Bailey Thomson, *Constitutional Reform in Alabama: A Long Time in Coming*, *in* 1 State Constitutions for the Twenty-First Century: The Politics of State Constitutional Reform, *supra* note 10, at 113–24. *See generally Symposium on the Alabama Constitution*, 33 Cumb. L. Rev. 187 (2003).

[102] Thomson, *supra* note 101, at 126–38.

[103] *Id.* at 139; *see also Symposium, Celebrating the Centennial of the Alabama Constitution: An Impetus for Reflection*, 53 Ala. L. Rev. 1 (2001). For the latest developments in Alabama constitutional revision efforts, see https://www.constitutionalreform.org.

[104] Janice C. May, The Texas State Constitution: A Reference Guide 24–25 (1996).

[105] *Id.* at 25.

[106] *Id.* at 26; *see also id.* at 422 (*citing* A New Constitution for Texas: Text, Explanation, Commentary (1973); A New Constitution for Texas: Separate Statements of Commission Members (1973)).

> tendencies; several controversial propositions, including a constitutional right-to-work proposal that generated bitter labor union opposition; the solid Black Caucus bloc vote against the final package; a spirited race for the speakership for the next legislature that was going on during the convention; and the two-thirds vote requirement of the authorizing constitutional amendment, which under normal conditions might not have mattered but possibly did in the highly unusual and politically charged situation at the convention.[107]

Interestingly, at its next session, the Texas Legislature submitted most of the proposed changes it had considered, sitting as a constitutional convention, to the voters as eight separate amendments at a special election in 1975. In a very light turnout and after a poorly funded campaign, voters overwhelmingly rejected the proposals.[108]

## K. California (1993–1996)

In California, a constitutional revision commission met beginning in 1993 during a budget crisis and made its recommendations to the legislature in 1996.[109] Dr. Bruce Cain, a member of the commission, noted, "This Commission undertook a comprehensive look at California governance and ultimately proposed some far-reaching and imaginative ideas. But in the end, these recommendations never got to a vote in the legislature, let alone a place on the ballot."[110] Apparently, because of an improved economy, the complexity of some of the issues, and the vested interests of a number of legislators and other elected officials, the revision commission's proposals were essentially doomed when they were sent to the legislature.[111]

## L. Illinois (1968–1970)

The state of Illinois in the 1960s built on several "decades of effort by civic groups to provide a climate of opinion favorable to constitutional reform."[112] Despite

[107] MAY, *supra* note 104, at 26–27.

[108] *Id.* at 27; *see also id.* at 404; Janice C. May, *Texas Constitutional Revision: Lessons and Laments*, 66 NAT'L CIVIC REV. 64 (1977).

[109] Cain, *supra* note 10, at 59, 67.

[110] *Id.* at 60; *see also* CALIFORNIA CONSTITUTION REVISION COMMISSION, FINAL REPORT AND RECOMMENDATIONS TO THE GOVERNOR AND THE LEGISLATURE (1996).

[111] Cain, *supra* note 10, at 65–70; *see also* CONSTITUTIONAL REFORM IN CALIFORNIA: MAKING STATE GOVERNMENT MORE EFFECTIVE AND RESPONSIVE (Bruce E. Cain & Roger G. Noll eds., 1995).

[112] JANET CORNELIUS, CONSTITUTION MAKING IN ILLINOIS 1818–1970, 138 (1972).

the adoption in 1950 of an amendment to the state constitution that liberalized Illinois' constitutional amendment process, substantial revision had not taken place.[113] The Illinois Legislature created a Constitution Study Commission in 1965 and, after several years of deliberation, it recommended the calling of a constitutional convention. The legislature followed this recommendation, together with the commission's other suggestion that no other amendments be submitted to the voters at the 1968 general election.[114] The voters approved the convention call after a privately funded campaign for adoption, which included substantial gubernatorial support. The private group relied on statewide opinion polls in designing its campaign.[115]

After voters approved the convention call, the legislature established a second commission to advise it and the governor on framing the "enabling act for the election of delegates and organization of the convention."[116] There was also a third commission created by the legislature to make preparations immediately before the convention was convened.[117] The constitutional convention delegates, elected on a nonpartisan basis, worked from December 1969 through September 1970.[118] The site of the convention was moved from the legislative chambers to a different location, primarily to make room for the legislative session, but also to put some distance between the convention and "ordinary politics." This had been done successfully with New Jersey's 1947 constitutional convention and Alaska's 1955–1956 convention.[119] The convention succeeded in proposing a modernized constitution for Illinois which was adopted by the voters in December 1970.[120] The president of the Illinois constitutional convention, Samuel Witwer, reflected on the experience:

> From the outset, the convention delegates were reminded, with an eye to ultimate voter approval, that their task was to write not the best possible constitution but rather the best constitution that could possibly be adopted in this politically complex state. I believe that we came close to that goal. But such a choice implies unmet governmental needs and continued opportunities for further constitutional reforms.[121]

[113] *Id.* at 123–37.
[114] *Id.* at 139–40.
[115] *Id.* at 142.
[116] *Id.* at 144.
[117] *Id.* at 144 n.6.
[118] *Id.* at 149–55.
[119] *Id.* at 153.
[120] *Id.* at 162–63. *See generally The Illinois Constitution of 1970: A Symposium Issue*, 6 J. Marshall J. Prac. & Proc. 213 (1973); Ann M. Lousin, *Why Did Illinois Call a Constitutional Convention in 1968?* 72 Rutgers U. L. Rev. 1021 (2020).
[121] Samuel W. Witwer, *Introduction*, 6 J. Marshall J. Prac. & Proc. 213, 213 (1973).

## M. Maryland (1966–1968)

In Maryland, following the U.S. Supreme Court's one-person, one-vote decisions, a constitution commission was formed on the initiative of the governor to prepare for a 1966 automatic (but not always honored by the legislature) referendum on whether to call a constitutional convention.[122] The convention call was approved by the voters, convention delegates were elected, and the convention met from 1967 to early 1968.[123] The convention's proposed constitutional revision was soundly defeated at the polls in 1968.[124] This has led Maryland's experience to be referred to as the "Magnificent Failure."[125] One commentator has summarized the various views about the reasons for this failure:

> Some commentators have blamed the content of the proposed constitution, suggesting that it was "too liberal" for Maryland. Some have argued that the convention delegates themselves were too intellectual or too liberal to represent the Maryland electorate. Some political scientists point to the fact that the entire constitution was submitted to the voters for a single vote, as a "single package deal," and suggest convincingly that this contributed to the defeat. Still others blame the convention delegates and those responsible for the ratification campaign for their lack of political skill. But all commentators agree that the proponents of the constitution failed to persuade the electorate of the necessity of constitutional revision.[126]

The voters' rejection of convention's proposals in 1968 nonetheless formed the basis for a number of specific state constitutional changes over the following generation.[127]

[122] Dan Friedman, *Magnificent Failure Revisited: Modern Maryland Constitutional Law from 1967 to 1998*, 58 Md. L. Rev. 528, 530–32 (1999).

[123] *Id.* at 532–33. *See generally* Wayne R. Swanson et al., Politics and Constitutional Reform: The Maryland Experience, 1967–1968 (1970).

[124] Friedman, *supra* note 122, at 534; *see also* Dan Friedman, The Maryland State Constitution: A Reference Guide 9–10 (2006); Robert J. Martineau, *Maryland's 1967–68 Constitutional Convention: Some Lessons for Reformers*, 55 Iowa L. Rev. 1196 (1970).

[125] John P. Wheeler Jr. & Melissa Kinsey, Magnificent Failure: The Maryland Constitutional Convention of 1967–1968 (1970).

[126] Friedman, *supra* note 122, at 534–35 (citations omitted).

[127] *Id.* at 529. "This Article assesses the success or failure of the Maryland Constitutional Convention in light of the later adoption—by constitutional amendment, statute, or regulation—of many of the important innovations proposed in the 1967–1968 constitution."

## N. Ohio (1969–1977)

After a successful 1912 constitutional convention, Ohio voters turned to constitutionally mandated convention calls every twenty years.[128] In 1969, the legislature created a constitutional revision commission that took a two-step approach, first proposing an amendment liberalizing the amendment process itself.[129] The commission then proceeded to work until 1977, with sixteen of its twenty amendments adopted by the voters.[130]

## O. Lessons

There are a number of lessons that can be learned from this brief review of state constitution making over the past several generations:

1. State constitutional revision can be a long, multistage, difficult process with no guarantee of success, potentially spanning a number of decades.
2. Sometimes the existing processes of state constitutional change must themselves be reformed, even on a one-time basis, to make way for successful state constitutional revision.
3. The timing of state constitutional revision must be right for both citizens and political actors. State constitutional revision, regardless of its merits, can be overshadowed by other matters, such as other proposed constitutional amendments, legislative reapportionment, changing economic conditions, election campaigns, and so forth. This is particularly true with automatic, periodic referenda.[131] Political circumstances can change while state constitutional revision is being considered.
4. People may hesitate to support a constitutional convention without knowing the details of how the election for delegates will be run and financed, how the convention will be structured, and so forth.[132]
5. The federal one-person, one-vote requirement may not apply to state constitutional conventions, but "vote dilution" for minorities may be an issue under the Voting Rights Act.[133]

[128] Steven H. Steinglass, *Constitutional Revision: Ohio Style*, 77 Ohio St. L.J. 281, 354 (2016).
[129] *Id.* at 339–40.
[130] *Id.* at 340. Ohio had a slightly differently constituted commission from 2011 to 2018, which had only moderate success. *Id.* at 345–54.
[131] *See supra* note 100 and accompanying text.
[132] *See* Richard Briffault, *Electing Delegates to a State Constitutional Convention: Some Legal and Policy Issues*, 36 Rutgers L.J. 1125, 1156–57 (2005).
[133] *Id.* at 1127–39.

6. Strong, active gubernatorial leadership is necessary but not always sufficient for successful state constitutional revision.
7. State constitutional revision takes place within the state's existing political structure, and changes in state constitutions involve important political questions.
8. Detailed preparations must be attended to, concerning:
   a) whether a constitutional convention call should be made or a constitutional commission created;
   b) informing and educating the public prior to the vote if a constitutional convention call is to be made;
   c) what should be included within the constitutional convention call (i.e., an unlimited or a limited convention) or commission mandate;
   d) careful consideration of processes for electing delegates if a constitutional convention call is to be made or appointing members if a commission is to be used, with a preference for a nonpartisan approach;[134]
   e) legislative implementation of a positive decision by the voters on a convention call;
   f) background research and the proposal of draft rules, preferably prepared by a separate committee or commission, and prior to a constitutional convention or commission.
9. The legislature may refuse, through an exercise of "legislative passive aggression,"[135] to provide funding for any of these preparatory activities. Under such circumstances, there may be a need for private or gubernatorial funding.
10. The convention or commission must focus on what is politically achievable rather than the best theoretical state constitutional revision. The convention or commission must therefore engage in self-restraint and structure its deliberations and voting so that proposed revisions are recommended by substantial consensus.
11. Leadership in constitutional conventions and commissions is absolutely crucial to the success of such a body.[136]

[134] *Id.*

[135] Gerald Benjamin, *The Mandatory Constitutional Convention Question Referendum: The New York Experience in National Context*, 65 ALB. L. REV. 1017, 1023 (2002); *see* G. Alan Tarr & Robert F. Williams, *Foreword: Getting from Here to There: Twenty-First Century Mechanisms and Opportunities in State Constitutional Reform*, 36 RUTGERS L.J. 1075, 1100 n.130 (2005).

[136] ELMER E. CORNWELL JR., JAY S. GOODMAN, & WAYNE R. SWANSON, STATE CONSTITUTIONAL CONVENTIONS: THE POLITICS OF THE REVISION PROCESS IN SEVEN STATES 199 (1975) ("The key roles played by the presidents of the various conventions emerged unmistakably. All that we know descriptively about convention behavior underscores the vital importance of the role of the presiding officer.").

12. Consideration should be given to holding the convention or commission sessions away from the state capital to avoid the appearance of "politics as usual."
13. Widespread use of modern information technology such as interactive websites; e-mail; and live, streaming video coverage should be used to educate and involve the public in a transparent, deliberative constitutional revision process. Modern public opinion polling and focus group techniques can be used during deliberations to predict the political acceptance of certain proposed constitutional changes and to inform constitution makers of needed modifications prior to adoption and submission of final proposals to the voters.
14. The convention or commission should give serious consideration to separating controversial proposals for their individual presentation to the voters, rather than a single "take-it-or-leave-it" package. On the other hand, if proposals are interdependent as part of a coherent revision, they should be identified as such to the voters and presented together, if possible, under the state's established processes; or, if required to be presented separately, they should be interlocked so that the adoption of each is dependent on the adoption of the other(s).
15. There should be a well-funded organization (probably not governmental) to advocate for the proposed revisions after the convention or commission has made its recommendations.
16. Even a disappointing, apparent "failure" of substantial state constitutional revision or reform may actually have the positive effect of setting the terms of debate concerning piecemeal constitutional change by amendment over the following generation.

These and many other lessons can be drawn from the state constitutional revision experience in the states in the second half of the twentieth century. Such lessons, however, must be applied in the current state context.

## II. STATE CONSTITUTIONAL REVISION IN THE TWENTY-FIRST CENTURY

> *Constitutional revision is not for the faint of heart. It is not a Sunday drive in the mountains. It is an incredibly difficult, sometimes tedious, sometimes exhilarating, always challenging undertaking requiring the cooperation of the leadership of all three branches of state government, of counties, municipalities, and local school boards, of the business community and the labor community, of public interest groups and*

*private interest groups, of people inside the government and people outside the government—in short, it requires the cooperation of just about everybody.*

—Georgia Governor George D. Busbee (1983)[137]

Since the drafting of many states' original constitutions, both the processes for revision and the content of state constitutions have undergone dramatic change. First, the process of state constitutional reform or revision has been transformed from citizens' exercise of popular sovereignty[138] to a more elite and professional exercise. According to Alan Tarr:

> Perhaps the most striking trend is toward the professionalization of state constitutional change. . . . Typically, it has been political elites and professional reformers who have campaigned for constitutional revision, with the populace reduced to rejecting convention calls and proposed constitutions to register its distrust of a process that it no longer feels it controls.[139]

Further, since many states' original constitutions were framed, the content of many of state constitutions has evolved from short, basic documents of government organization and citizen rights, to longer constitutions that have been expanded to include a number of specific policies that could have been left to the legislature.[140] In fact, there has been a major shift in the idea of what the function of a state constitution should be and what matters are important enough to be contained therein.[141] Professor Christian Fritz noted this shift in the attitudes of constitution makers during the nineteenth century, as the American society and economy became more complex, particularly with the rise of powerful corporations.[142] These constitution makers believed that they needed to include more material in state constitutions, even in areas that could, theoretically, be governed by legislation. Professor Fritz concluded:

> The key to explaining the growing length of nineteenth-century constitutions lies in the delegates' understanding of the purpose of constitutions. There was common agreement that the nature and object of constitutions extended

[137] George D. Busbee, *An Overview of the New Georgia Constitution*, 35 MERCER L. REV. 1, 1–2 (1983).

[138] James A. Henretta, *Foreword: Rethinking the State Constitutional Tradition*, 22 RUTGERS L.J. 819, 826 (1991).

[139] TARR, *supra* note 17 at 170.

[140] *Id.* at 9–12.

[141] *Id.* at 132–33.

[142] *See* Christian G. Fritz, *Rethinking the American Constitutional Tradition: National Dimensions in the Formation of State Constitutions*, 26 RUTGERS L.J. 969 (1995) (reviewing DAVID A. JOHNSON, FOUNDING THE FAR WEST: CALIFORNIA, OREGON, AND NEVADA, 1840–1890 (1992)).

> beyond fundamental principles to what delegates called constitutional legislation. Delegates willingly assumed an institutional role that occasionally supplanted the ordinary legislature.[143]

All of the states have a number of available opportunities for state constitutional revision as opposed to piecemeal amendment. Of course, a process of piecemeal amendment may turn out to be adequate for state constitutional problems that exist. In any event, the Texas approach of a one-time state constitutional amendment authorizing the legislature to convene as a constitutional convention and submit its proposed revised constitution to the people, either as a single package or separate propositions, is one possibility. The Michigan and Illinois changes in their processes of constitutional revision are others. These processes would represent a form of staged constitutional revision, utilizing a vote of the people at two points: first, to approve the amendment modifying the process of revising the constitution (even on a one-time basis); and second, at the point of approval or rejection of the revision proposal(s). A variation on this approach would be to propose an amendment adopting a Florida-style appointed constitution revision commission, even on a one-time basis, with authority to submit its proposal(s) directly to the people. This would also involve two exercises of popular sovereignty or votes by the people of a state.

## A. Constitutional Commissions

Next, the "extratextual" approach of a constitution revision commission that would make recommendations to the legislature could be utilized.[144] State constitutional commissions can be created either by the legislature or the governor and receive funding from either source.[145] Such commissions can be limited in their mandate. Legislatures have sometimes authorized state constitutional commissions as a substitute for a constitutional convention that is feared by the legislature.[146] State constitutional commissions can also be utilized to prepare for and assist a constitutional convention.[147] New Jersey utilized a commission ("Task Force") to advise the legislature on how to call and structure a *limited*

[143] Christian G. Fritz, *The American Constitutional Tradition Revisited: Preliminary Observations on State Constitution-Making in the Nineteenth-Century West*, 25 RUTGERS L.J. 945, 964–65 (1994).

[144] Robert F. Williams, *Are State Constitutional Conventions Things of the Past? The Increasing Role of the Constitutional Commission in State Constitutional Change*, 1 HOFSTRA L. & POL'Y SYMP. 1, 2 (1996); *see also* Peter J. Mazzei & Robert F. Williams, *"Traces of Its Labors": The Constitutional Commission, The Legislature, and Their Influence on the New Jersey State Constitution, 1873–1875*, 33 RUTGERS L.J. 1059, 1062–68 (2002).

[145] Williams, *supra* note 144, at 4–5.

[146] *Id.* at 9.

[147] *Id.* at 11.

constitutional convention on property tax.[148] In a number of states, commissions have failed at certain points in time only to succeed in a later generation, and vice versa. Just because commissions failed in a state at some point in the past does not mean one or more of them would fail now. Finally, commissions can evaluate the need for mere change or more extensive revision and the possible processes for each. In this way, these questions can be fully evaluated rather than prejudged without sufficient consideration.

Legal scholar Albert Sturm observed in 1977:

> Increasing use of the constitutional commission as an auxiliary device for initiating both major and minor changes is one of the most significant developments in the procedure of modernizing state constitutions. Constitutional commissions were developed initially, and have been used primarily, as auxiliary staff arms of state legislative assemblies. Their principal function has been to provide expert advice on constitutional problems and issues and to propose and draft amendments, revisions, and even entire constitutions.[149]

Compared to the constitutional convention, the constitutional commission is of relatively recent vintage, dating to the late nineteenth century. In his 1887 *Treatise on Constitutional Conventions*, Judge John Alexander Jameson described the constitutional commission as "a novel device."[150]

Constitutional commissions are "extratextual," as state constitutions generally do not provide for them. Such commissions also are not usually mentioned in the standard list of mechanisms for state constitutional change: elected constitutional convention proposals, amendments and revisions proposed by legislatures, and initiatives proposing state constitutional amendments.[151]

Constitutional commissions can and often do play ancillary roles crucial to each of these recognized mechanisms. It may be that the constitutional *commission* has now overtaken the constitutional *convention* as the most

[148] Tarr & Williams, *supra* note 135, at 1104–05.

[149] Albert L. Sturm, *The Procedure of State Constitutional Change—With Special Emphasis on the South and Florida*, 5 Fla. St. U. L. Rev. 569, 585 (1977).

[150] John Alexander Jameson, A Treatise on Constitutional Conventions: Their History, Powers, and Modes of Proceeding 570 (4th ed. 1887, 1972 Da Capo reprint). Jameson expressed the opinion that the use of constitutional commissions to facilitate constitutional *revision* as opposed to *amendment* was of doubtful constitutionality. *Id.* at 573.

[151] *See, e.g.*, Michael G. Colantuono, *The Revision of American State Constitutions: Legislative Power, Popular Sovereignty, and Constitutional Change*, 75 Cal. L. Rev. 1473, 1477–78 (1987). Colantuono acknowledges the constitutional commission in a footnote. *Id.* at 1478 n.26. *See also* Michael Colantuono, *Pathfinder: Methods of State Constitutional Revision*, 7 Legal Ref. Surv. Q. 45 (No. 2, 1987).

important source facilitating state constitutional change.[152] Any careful study of the processes of state constitutional change should not ignore the role of constitutional commissions.

Since Jameson wrote, at least four distinct permutations of the constitutional commission have evolved, with very different functions and effects. Commissions have been used (1) in conjunction with constitutional conventions, either to help implement their work after a failure at the polls, or through background study and analysis to lay the groundwork for such conventions; (2) as devices for assisting legislatures in avoiding conventions and thus retaining control of constitutional change; (3) to work together with the legislative branch in studying and recommending state constitutional change; and (4) they have begun in Florida to develop as a method for generating and directly recommending constitutional amendments to the people, bypassing both the legislature and the convention.

State constitutional commissions can be created and funded in a variety of ways and be directed to report to different officials.[153] Creation by statute requires assent of both the legislative and the executive and usually assures legislative funding. Creation by legislative resolution accomplishes the task by involving only a single branch. In both of these instances, the report usually will be submitted to the legislature. Constitutional commissions should be distinguished from joint *legislative* study committees and task forces, which are internal to the legislative branch.[154]

Constitutional commissions can also be created by the governor, either by executive order or by less formal means, and required to report to him. Because this method does not involve the legislature, funding cannot necessarily be assumed. In Mississippi, the governor appointed a constitutional commission whose report was to be submitted to him, without issuing an executive order, apparently to provide for a less formal body.[155] In Oklahoma, private funds were raised to

[152] This may be a premature conclusion. In 1957 John Bebout observed:

> A few years ago many people were saying that the constitutional convention was a thing of the past. There was a fifteen year period between adjournment of the Missouri Constitutional Convention of 1922–23 and the meetings of the New York and New Hampshire conventions in 1938 when no state held such an assembly. The last twenty years, however, have seen a distinct revival of the constitutional convention.

John Bebout, *Recent Constitution Writing*, 35 TEX. L. REV. 1071, 1071 (1957). In any event, constitutional conventions are not now commonly used in the states. *See* Thomas Gais & Gerald Benjamin, *Public Discontent and the Decline of Deliberation: A Dilemma in State Constitutional Reform*, 68 TEMPLE L. REV. 1291 (1995).

[153] ALBERT L. STURM, THIRTY YEARS OF STATE CONSTITUTION-MAKING: 1938–1968 (1970).

[154] Bennet M. Rich, *Revision by Constitutional Commission*, *in* MAJOR PROBLEMS IN STATE CONSTITUTIONAL REVISION 86, 88 (W. Brook Graves ed., 1960); WALTER F. DODD, THE REVISION AND AMENDMENT OF STATE CONSTITUTIONS 263 (1910, 1970 Da Capo reprint). Such direct legislative bodies are a very important source of recommended state constitutional changes.

[155] Leslie H. Southwick & C. Victor Welsh III, *Methods of Constitutional Revision: Which Way Mississippi?* 56 MISS. L.J. 17, 27–28 (1986).

support a governor's constitutional commission when the legislature refused to fund it.[156]

The idea to use a constitutional commission seems to have originated in earnest in New York with the 1872 Constitutional Commission, recommended by the governor and appointed by the legislature.[157] Peter Galie, a leading authority on the history and development of the New York Constitution, describes the 1872 Commission as "... an innovation in the state's constitutional history, which seemed to fill a gap between a cumbersome convention and the ad hoc legislative amending process. This method allowed distinguished and informed individuals to recommend constitutional change to the legislature and then to the people."[158]

The 1872 Constitutional Commission in New York was able to revive and recommend some of the ideas (such as a longer gubernatorial term and the item veto) from the proposed constitution that failed at the polls in 1867. After the legislature approved the Commission's proposals, the people ratified them.[159]

In 1873, New Jersey seemingly emulated the New York commission idea. The legislature there, after refusing to pass legislation calling for a constitutional convention to revise the outmoded 1844 constitution, provided for the establishment of a constitutional commission on terms very similar to New York's 1872 statute.[160] This was surely one of the most successful constitutional commissions in history: the New Jersey Legislature (after extensive and lengthy debate of its own) submitted twenty-eight of the constitutional changes recommended by the commission, all of which voters approved in 1875.[161] The mechanism of an appointed commission to study and recommend to the legislature changes in the state constitution was, as in New York, not authorized in the New Jersey Constitution.

The 1873 Constitutional Commission, unlike earlier and later New Jersey constitutional commissions, was not a "limited" commission.[162] It was authorized, and in fact did, explore, debate, and entertain proposed amendments to

[156] A constitutional commission was used in Oklahoma to develop and recommend initiative petitions seeking state constitutional change. In *In re* Initiative Petition No. 344, 797 P.2d 326 (Okla. 1990), and *In re* Initiative Petition No. 342, 797 P.2d 331 (Okla. 1990), the Oklahoma Supreme Court struck from the ballot initiatives developed by the commission that would have revised articles of the Oklahoma Constitution. The court based its decisions on the single-subject rule. *See* Chapter 14.

[157] Jameson, *supra* note 150, at 570.

[158] Galie, *supra* note 95, at 16.

[159] *Id.* at 15. *See also* Kaden, *supra* note 94, at 364. Michigan reflected a similar pattern: after the defeat of the 1867 Michigan Constitutional Convention's proposals, a constitutional commission was created in 1873. Jameson, *supra* note 150, at 570. Jameson reported that the Michigan Commission, consisting of eighteen members, met for seven weeks, and "recommended a large number of amendments, which upon submission to the people, were all rejected." *Id.* at 571–72.

[160] Williams, *supra* note 37, at 9–11; Mazzei & Williams, *supra* note 144.

[161] Williams, *supra* note 37, at 10. A number of scholars have missed this important commission. *See, e.g.*, Jameson, *supra* note 150, at 570; Thomas Raeburn White, *Amendment and Revision of State Constitutions*, 100 U. Pa. L. Rev. 1132, 1148–49 (1952).

[162] Connors, *supra* note 36, at 9–13.

the entire state constitution. The period of 1873–1875, which includes not only the Commission's deliberations but also the legislature's lengthy consideration of its recommendations and the referendum on the legislature's twenty-eight proposed amendments in 1875, "stands behind only three others in significance for state constitutional development in New Jersey: 1776, 1844, and 1947."[163]

The constitutional commissions came into being in New York and New Jersey based on the justifications of efficiency and expertise, neither of which were regarded, according to Galie's analysis, as attributes of the constitutional convention ("cumbersome") or the legislative amendment process ("ad hoc"). The commission, in these circumstances, served as a research and study group (expertise) and as a technique for agenda-setting in the legislature (efficiency).

But despite the similarities between the New York and New Jersey experiences, there seem to have been additional motivations in the use of the commission method in the second case. In New York, the constitutional commission followed a constitutional convention. In New Jersey, by contrast, the commission was a *substitute* for a convention. Legislation introduced in the same session called for a convention and gained substantial support. The commission method appears to have been used to diffuse popular pressure on the legislature to call a constitutional convention, and as a response to fears about the outcome of a convention. The commission mechanism, therefore, retained control for the legislature over the final recommendations to the voters.[164] As noted, most commentators on constitutional commissions have emphasized only the efficiency and expertise rationales.[165] But in New Jersey, neither was central. Rather, the commission was a means for legislative *control* of the process of state constitutional change, in the face of rising popular and gubernatorial pressure for such change.[166]

A Utah law adopted in 1969 created a *permanent* sixteen-member Constitution Revision Study Commission with heavy representation from the legislature.[167] The Utah commission is authorized by law both to undertake its own initiatives and to consider recommendations from state leaders and "responsible segments of the public." But it may not make proposals directly to the

[163] WILLIAMS, *supra* note 37, at 10.

[164] *Id.* at 9.

[165] *See* JAMESON, *supra* note 150, at 574–75; Note, *State Constitutional Conventions: Limitations on Their Powers*, 55 IOWA L. REV. 244, 259 (1969); Southwick & Welsh, *supra* note 155 at 26–28; Dale A. Kimball, Note, *The Constitutional Convention, Its Nature and Powers—The Amending Procedure*, 1966 UTAH L. REV. 390, 392–94; White, *supra* note 161, at 1147–49; Page Keeton, *Methods of Constitutional Revision in Texas*, 35 TEX. L. REV. 901, 904 (1957). *But see* Rich, *supra* note 154, at 86 (criticizing use of constitutional commissions which report to the legislature).

[166] STURM, *supra* note 153, at 84 ("The mounting popularity of constitutional commissions is attributable mainly to their general acceptability to state legislators who prefer to rely on bodies over whose proposals they have control.").

[167] Chapter 54, Section 63–1, Laws of Utah. This seems to be the adoption of W. Brooke Graves' suggestion of "continuous revision" of state constitutions. *See* W. Brooke Graves, *Current Trends in State Constitutional Revision*, 40 NEB. L. REV. 560, 565–58 (1961).

people for constitutional change. Its duties are ". . . to make a comprehensive examination of the Constitution of the State of Utah, and of the amendments thereto, and thereafter to make recommendations to the governor and the legislature as to specific proposed constitutional amendments designed to carry out the commission's recommendations for changes in the constitution."[168] Three of the commission's revised articles were referred by the legislature to the voters and approved in 1992.[169]

In 1982, the political scientists Albert Sturm and Janice May published data on state constitutional commissions reaching back to 1930.[170] They reported that, during the decade of the 1970s, "constitutional commissions wrote the initial drafts of all revised constitutions proposed to state electorates by legislatures."[171] Although noting that the increased use of commissions "has been one of the significant developments in the procedure of state constitutional revision during the past 30 years. . . . ," they also observed that, in 1980–1981, "fewer state constitutional commissions or committees operated than in any biennium of the 1970s."[172]

In 1990, Janice May reported that during the decade of the 1980s, there were only nine commissions created.[173] But, for the 1992–1993 period, she reported that commissions operated in four states, and one was authorized by statute in another state.[174]

Because of the extratextual nature of constitutional commissions, it is not surprising that their use in the process of state constitutional change has been challenged in the courts. These challenges, however, have generally failed in circumstances where commissions were utilized in conjunction with constitutionally established methods of changing the constitution. Georgia,[175] Kentucky,[176]

[168] Chapter 54, Section 63-3, Laws of Utah. For a discussion of the history of the commission and its impact on the state constitution, see REPORT OF THE UTAH CONSTITUTIONAL REVISION COMMISSION, 1994. *See also* REPORT OF THE UTAH CONSTITUTIONAL REVISION COMMISSION (1996).

[169] Janice C. May, *State Constitutional Revision*, 1990–91, 29 THE BOOK OF THE STATES 2, 5 (1992).

[170] Albert L. Sturm & Janice C. May, *State Constitutions and Constitutional Revision: 1980–81 and the Past 50 Years*, 24 THE BOOK OF THE STATES 115 (1982). W. Brooke Graves provided an exhaustive, albeit now somewhat dated, bibliography on state constitutional revision, including many references on state constitutional commissions, in *Selected Bibliography* in Graves, *supra* note 154, at 283.

[171] Sturm & May, *supra* note 170, at 124.

[172] *Id.*

[173] Janice C. May, *State Constitutions and Constitutional Revision, 1988–89 and in the 1980s*, 28 THE BOOK OF THE STATES 19, 23 (1990). *See also* Gais & Benjamin, *supra* note 152, at 1303.

[174] May, *supra* note 169, at 5.

[175] Wheeler v. Board of Trustees, 37 S.E.2d 322, 327–30 (Ga. 1946).

[176] Gatewood v. Matthews, 403 S.W.2d 716 (Ky. 1966). The decision in *Gatewood* was criticized in *Comment*, 81 HARV. L. REV. 693, 695 (1968) on the grounds that it "has the effect of significantly increasing the legislature's power to initiate and control the process of constitutional revision. In fact, the legislature alone decided to have a new constitution drafted." For a detailed analysis of the processes in Kentucky leading to the *Gatewood* decision, see Paul Oberst & J. Kenderick Wells III, *Constitutional Reform in Kentucky—The 1966 Proposal*, 55 KY. L.J. 50 (1966).

Idaho,[177] and Virginia[178] have upheld the practice. The Alabama high court,[179] however, refused to permit it in a case raising other related problems, disagreeing directly with Georgia and Kentucky. Arkansas struck down an attempt by the legislature to authorize a limited, *appointed* constitutional "convention."[180] This general, albeit not unanimous, judicial endorsement of the commission method, used in conjunction with the established, formal mechanisms of state constitutional change will likely contribute to its increasing use.

Constitutional commissions were likely one of the manifestations of the broader Progressive, and later "managerial," views of government.[181] Reliance on scientific expertise and concerns for efficiency, as opposed to the prior party politics and citizen (voter) involvement, led to a broad adoption of the commission mechanism throughout the federal, state, and local governments. The use of state *constitutional* commissions thus fits nicely into this larger political and societal development. It may be, though, that they have now developed a momentum of their own.

## B. Constitutional Conventions

Many states only require that a one-time majority vote of the legislature is necessary to ask the voters to approve or reject a constitutional convention. This leaves maximum flexibility with the legislature to provide for the election of delegates, the timing of the convention, and other details. Only states whose constitutions do not mention constitutional conventions at all possess greater flexibility.[182] By contrast, some states specify the nature of the question to be put to the voters concerning a constitutional convention, the form of which sometimes precludes the possibility of a limited constitutional convention.[183] Therefore, the question arises as to whether a state's constitution would provide a barrier to a limited constitutional convention if the limits were specified by the legislature and approved by the voters.[184] This way, certain controversial or "hot button" topics

[177] Smith v. Cenarrusa, 475 P.2d 11 (Idaho 1970). *See generally* DONALD CROWLEY & FLORENCE HEFFRON, THE IDAHO STATE CONSTITUTION: A REFERENCE GUIDE 18–20 (1994) (describing the commission, the litigation, and the defeat of the commission's recommendations at the polls.) The commission had recommended that the commission method be written into the Idaho Constitution. *See Cenarrusa*, 475 P.2d at 15.

[178] Staples v. Gilmer, 33 S.E.2d 49, 56 (Va. 1945) (dictum). *See also* White, *supra* note 161, at 1148, n.63.

[179] State v. Manley, 441 So.2d 864, 876–77 (Ala. 1983).

[180] Pryor v. Lowe, 523 S.W.2d 199 (Ark. 1975).

[181] Professor Williams is indebted to John Kinkaid for the suggestions forming the basis of this paragraph.

[182] Tarr & Williams, *supra* note 135, at 1086, 1090.

[183] *Id.* at 1086–87.

[184] *See id.* at 1086–92.

could be "taken off the table," leaving room to achieve necessary state constitutional revision.

Political scientists Gerald Benjamin and Thomas Gais have observed what they call "conventionphobia" in this country.[185] Even states with an automatic vote on whether to call a convention have not had recent success. "In the quarter century between 1960 and 1985 automatic convention calls were approved only in New Hampshire, Rhode Island and Alaska. . . . In each of four states that provided for an automatic convention call during the early 1990s—Alaska, New Hampshire, Ohio and Michigan—majorities have rejected the opportunity."[186] This has also occurred in New York, Rhode Island, Illinois, and Montana. Automatic convention calls were defeated by wide margins in 2008 in Illinois (again), Connecticut, and Hawaii. The rejection of convention calls has been occurring at the same time that dissatisfaction with state government has been increasing. The public seems to view a constitutional convention as political business as usual by the "government industry."[187] Constitutional conventions seem to have lost their *legitimacy* in the public mind. At the time many states' original constitutions were drafted, the politicians and special interests were afraid of the *people* acting through constitutional conventions. Now, by contrast, the people are afraid of *politicians* and *special interests* acting through constitutional conventions.

## C. State Constitutional Change Through the Initiative

In states that permit the state constitution to be amended through the initiative, that avenue is likely to be seen by the public as having more popular legitimacy than a convention. The initiative method provides for *independence*, which Gais and Benjamin have concluded may be necessary to achieve meaningful, publicly acceptable state constitutional revision.[188] But the initiative lacks the possibility of *deliberation*.[189] As they noted:

[185] Gerald Benjamin & Thomas Gais, *Constitutional Conventionphobia*, 1 HOFSTRA L. & POL'Y SYMP. 53, 70 (1996).

[186] *Id.* at 69 (citation omitted). Benjamin and Gais had observed a year earlier:

> [T]he number of active constitutional conventions has also dropped from seven between 1968 and 1969, to just two between 1978 and 1979, to none between 1990 and 1991. Moreover, all of the convention calls that some states are required to put on their ballots have gone down to defeat in recent years: New Hampshire, Alaska, and Montana placed such questions before the voters between 1990 and 1992, but all were defeated, as was Michigan's in 1994.

Gais & Benjamin, *supra* note 152, at 1303.

[187] *Id.* at 1304; Benjamin & Gais, *supra* note 185, at 71.

[188] *See* Gais & Benjamin, *supra* note 152, at 1301.

[189] *Id.* at 1299.

> A more important question is whether the constitutional initiative is a deliberative process, one that involves discussion, learning, and accommodation among all citizens or their representatives regarding common problems. Deliberation is crucial in settling constitutional questions. If we want

> What we need instead are constitutional revision procedures that are deliberative as well as legitimate—procedures that command legitimacy by providing for direct citizen participation and control, but that also generate and assess alternative proposals, take into account the best available information about their likely effects, consider the interactions between the proposed changes and the rest of the constitutional structure, and afford opportunities for discussion and accommodation among significant political interests.[190]

The advent of the initiative method of amending some states' constitutions could be seen as a "revision" of the state's constitution.[191] It has certainly *resulted* in many changes in the states' governing documents, constituting a sort of "continuous revision." No doubt any current revision efforts would focus on modifications to the initiative process, at least in the area of state constitutional change.[192] It is quite unlikely that Congress, assuming it has the power to do so, would step in to limit the states' use of the initiative for state constitutional amendments.[193]

Limits on the substance of initiated amendments to state constitutions, championed by Hans Linde, have been foreclosed.[194] He, and others, had convincingly pointed out that when the U.S. Supreme Court, in a 1912 Oregon case, upheld the initiative process against a federal constitutional challenge under the Guarantee Clause,[195] it was dealing with a *statutory* initiative rather than a state *constitutional* initiative. Of course, the statutory initiative merely supplements

people to view a constitution as legitimate, we must be sure they believe the rules and institutions it prescribes to be reasonable and fair. That is not an easy task, particularly now, when government institutions must often make decisions which many citizens and interest groups oppose. *Id.* at 1301.

[190] *Id.* at 1303.

[191] An analogy could be drawn here to the limitation in some states on using the initiative to *revise*, as opposed to *amend*, the state constitution. This can be analyzed both quantitatively and qualitatively. *See* Adams v. Gunter, 238 So.2d 824 (Fla. 1970); Raven v. Deukmejian, 801 P.2d 1077 (Cal. 1990). *See* Chapter 14.

[192] *See* Marvin Krislov & Daniel M. Katz, *Taking State Constitutions Seriously*, 17 CORNELL J.L. & PUB POL'Y 295, 316 n.59 (2008).

[193] Would it be possible for Congress, rather than the federal or state courts, to provide some enforceable limits on state initiatives, along the lines outlined by Justice Linde? *See* Elizabeth R. Leong, Note, *Ballot Initiatives & Identifiable Minorities: A Textual Call to Congress*, 28 RUTGERS L.J. 677 (1997); Catherine Engberg, Note, *Taking the Initiative: May Congress Reform State Initiative Lawmaking to Guarantee a Republican Form of Government?* 54 STAN. L. REV. 569 (2001).

[194] *See, e.g.*, State v. Wagner, 752 P.2d 1136, 1197 n.8 (Or. 1988) (Linde, J., dissenting); State *ex rel.* Huddelston v. Sawyer, 932 P.2d 1145 (Or. 1997), *cert. denied*, 522 U.S. 994 (1997); Hans A. Linde, *When Is Initiative Lawmaking Not "Republican Government?"* 17 HAST. CONST. L.Q. 159 (1989); *When Initiative Lawmaking Is Not "Republican Government": The Campaign Against Homosexuality*, 72 OR. L. REV. 19 (1993); *Practicing Theory: The Forgotten Law of Initiative Lawmaking*, 45 UCLA L. REV. 1735 (1998); David B. Frohnmayer & Hans A. Linde, *State Court Responsibility for Maintaining "Republican Government": An Amicus Curiae Brief*, 39 WILLAMETTE L. REV. 1487 (2003).

[195] Kadderly v. City of Portland, 74 P. 710 (Or. 1903), *reh'g den.* 75 P. 222 (Or. 1904); Pacific States Telephone & Telegraph Co. v. Oregon, 223 U.S. 118 (1912).

the legislature's power, and initiated statutes would still be subject to limits contained in the state constitution.

The state of Florida has what has been referred to as the most amendable state constitution in the country.[196] In one case, a proposed state constitutional amendment to be placed on the ballot by a citizens' initiative, mandating humane treatment for pregnant pigs, was evaluated by the Florida Supreme Court for its validity (a requirement) prior to the referendum.[197] The court approved the proposed amendment, letting it go to the ballot; but Justice Barbara Pariente concurred, noting:

> [T]he issue of whether pregnant pigs should be singled out for special protection is simply not a subject appropriate for inclusion in our State constitution; rather it is a subject more properly reserved for legislative enactment. I thus find that former Justice McDonald's observations made when this Court reviewed the net fishing amendment continue to ring true today: "The merit of the proposed amendment is to be decided by the voters of Florida and this Court's opinion regarding the wisdom of any proposed amendment is irrelevant to its legal validity. I am concerned, however, that the net fishing amendment is more appropriate for inclusion in Florida's statute books than in the state constitution."[198]

One could reasonably predict that at least some other state judges have similar opinions.

Professor Harry Scheiber has argued effectively that the use of the initiative to amend state constitutions does not advance the purposes of federalism.[199] There have, of course, been a host of other arguments both against and in support of direct state constitutional lawmaking, all of which are beyond the scope of this chapter.

In the absence of *legal* limits, what is the likelihood of *politically imposed* limits, through changes to a state's constitution, that would modify either the *processes* for the state constitutional initiative or the *substance* of state constitutional change that can be accomplished through the initiative rather than through the other avenues of state constitutional change? Any detailed analysis of this question must be undertaken within the specific state context and is, in any event,

[196] *See* D'ALEMBERTE, *supra* note 76, at 146 ("The Constitution of Florida has more processes for amendment and revision than any other state constitution.").

[197] *See* Advisory Opinion to the Attorney General Re: Limiting Cruel and Inhumane Confinement of Pigs During Pregnancy, 815 So.2d 597 (Fla. 2002).

[198] *Id.* at 600 (*quoting* Advisory Opinion to the Attorney General Re: Limited Marine Net Fishing, 620 So.2d 997, 999–1000 (Fla. 1993) (McDonald, J., concurring).

[199] Harry N. Scheiber, *Foreword: The Direct Ballot and State Constitutionalism*, 28 RUTGERS L.J. 787 (1997).

beyond the scope of this chapter. It will be difficult to convince the voters to give up, or even modify, their "democratic" rights. Some recommendations, however, do bear brief mention.

Political scientists Marvin Krislov and Daniel M. Katz examined the literature and empirical research on state constitutional amendments through the initiative and concluded that several moderate reforms, with particular reference to voters' confusion and lack of information, should be considered.[200] They concluded generally that state constitutional initiatives were increasing in number,[201] and noted that in many states the incentive structure encouraged interest groups to propose constitutional amendments rather than statutes because the requirements and methods of disclosure to the voters were very similar.[202] In response, they propose a number of *procedural* changes to differentiate constitutional from statutory initiatives, increase the information concerning not only the substance of the proposal and the time for deliberation but also clearer disclosure to the voters that it is the relatively permanent state constitution they are being asked to amend, with the consequence that the state constitution would be eliminated as any limit on the substance of the proposed amendment.[203]

These are sober and moderate recommendations, with a basis in empirical data. These and other proposed reforms of the constitutional initiative should be carefully considered in the states, regardless of the process that is utilized. After all, despite the fact that the initiative is democratic, these are *constitutions* that we are amending.

## D. Limited Constitutional Conventions

Concerns about unlimited constitutional conventions opening a "Pandora's box" have been raised, sometimes sincerely, to argue against calling constitutional conventions.[204] This has proved particularly effective at the federal level, where there has been no experience with a limited constitutional convention, but it has succeeded in the states as well. In addition, powerful groups in state politics—for example, labor unions, tax limitation advocates, and public employees—have often won inclusion in state constitutions provisions that protect their interests;

[200] Krislov & Katz, *supra* note 192. *See also* Glen Staszewski, *The Bait-and-Switch in Direct Democracy*, 2006 Wis. L. Rev. 17. For an assessment of initiatives (not just constitutional) from 1959 to 1993, concluding that they had a very negative impact on the civil rights of minority groups, see Barbara S. Gamble, *Putting Civil Rights to a Popular Vote*, 41 Am. J. Pol. Sci. 245 (1997).

[201] Krislov & Katz, *supra* note 192, at 307–08.

[202] *Id.* at 319.

[203] *Id.* at 329–42.

[204] *See* Peter J. Galie & Christopher Bopst, *The Constitutional Commission in New York: A Worthy Tradition*, 64 Alb. L. Rev. 1285, 1315 (2001).

they do not wish to see these put at risk of change or removal, however remote the political risk might be. This proved to be the case in New York in 1997;[205] in Rhode Island in 2004; and in Illinois, Connecticut, and Hawaii in 2008, where automatic referenda on unlimited conventions were defeated.

To counter these and other sorts of opposition to constitutional conventions, states developed the limited constitutional convention, which cabins the range of matters to be considered by the convention, but allows delegates to propose amendments or revisions in those areas to the existing constitution. The act authorizing the convention, together with the public question approved by voters at the referendum, limits the delegates to consider only certain subjects and/or prohibits them from considering certain subjects. For example, the Constitutional Convention of 1966 in New Jersey was *authorized* to consider only the question of legislative apportionment, whereas the Constitutional Convention of 1947 in New Jersey was *forbidden* to address the state's system of apportionment.[206] Whatever form the limitation takes, the effect is to take certain politically charged topics "off the table" at the convention and to calm fears about the convention's otherwise unlimited mandate to consider all aspects of a state's constitution.[207]

The states have extensive experience with limited constitutional conventions: about 15 percent of all state constitutional conventions were substantially limited, and the proportion increased after World War II.[208] Some state constitutions—for example, those in Kansas, North Carolina, and Tennessee—expressly provide for calling a constitutional convention with a limited agenda.[209] In Tennessee, the legislature can limit a convention's substantive reach but not how it may act on a specified subject once it is called.[210] Other state constitutions, such as Wisconsin's, provide for the calling of conventions but do not address whether the conventions can be limited.[211] Still other state constitutions, such as New Jersey's, contain no provisions whatsoever concerning constitutional conventions, which leaves maximum flexibility to the legislature and the people in deciding whether to call a limited or unlimited convention.

[205] *Id.* at 1285–87.

[206] Henry D. Levine, Note, *Limited Federal Constitutional Conventions: Implications of the State Experience*, 11 HARV. J. LEG. 127, 134 (1973). As the 1947 example makes clear, the line between constitutional revision and constitutional amendment can be hazy. Delegates at a limited constitutional convention may propose a new document, even though certain issues were taken off the table before the convention met. *See* CONNORS, *supra* note 36, at 139–86.

[207] Benjamin & Gais, *Conventionphobia*, *supra* note 185, at 73 ("The limited convention allays the 'Pandora's Box' fear. . . .").

[208] Levine, *supra* note 206, at 133 n.32.

[209] *See, e.g.*, KAN. CONST. art. XIV, § 1; TENN. CONST. art. XI, § 3.

[210] *See* Snow v. City of Memphis, 527 S.W.2d 55, 63 (Tenn. 1975), *appeal dismissed for want of substantial federal question*, 423 U.S. 1083 (1976); Cummings v. Beeler, 223 S.W.2d 913, 921–23 (Tenn. 1949).

[211] *See* WIS. CONST. art. XII, § 2.

Some state constitutions, however, prohibit limited conventions. The Alaska Constitution refers to the power of a convention as "plenary," and says: "No call for a constitutional convention shall limit these powers of the convention."[212] Still others preclude calling limited conventions through particular mechanisms. The Montana Constitution specifies that a convention called through the use of the initiative must be unlimited.[213] Nine automatic referendum states specify the ballot question in their constitutions, thus precluding the imposition of limits on what a convention called through this procedure might consider.[214]

Questions invariably arise about whether a constitutional convention can actually be limited or whether the possibility exists of a "runaway" convention. There may indeed be a question as to whether a *federal* constitutional convention can be limited so as to consider only certain subjects or to exclude certain subjects from its consideration.[215] But one should recognize that this debate about a limited *federal* constitutional convention is based on different legal materials and thus does not pertain to the discussion of limited *state* constitutional conventions. When it comes to constitutional change, we really do have "dual constitutionalism"—two separate federal and state constitutional structures—in this country.[216]

It seems clear, based on legal authorities and state court cases, that if the proper procedures are followed to impose limitations on a *state* constitutional convention, those limits are legally enforceable. A consensus on this issue emerged during the twentieth century. Prior to that time, respected authors of legal treatises on state constitutional conventions disagreed about whether limitations could be placed upon such conventions.[217] This debate was separate and distinct from the debate on the validity of state constitutional conventions that were approved by the people but that did not conform to the constitutional requirements for conventions.[218] The crux of this debate concerned whether the legislature *itself* could limit a state constitutional convention. When the question

[212] ALASKA CONST. art. XIII, § 4.
[213] MONT. CONST. art. XIV, § 2(1).
[214] Benjamin, *supra* note 93, at 169 n.17.
[215] *See* S. REP. No. 98-594, Constitutional Convention Implementation Act of 1984, 1–3 (1984). *See generally* RUSSELL L. CAPLAN, CONSTITUTIONAL BRINKSMANSHIP: AMENDING THE CONSTITUTION BY NATIONAL CONVENTION (1988); PAUL J. WEBER & BARBARA A. PERRY, UNFOUNDED FEARS: MYTHS AND REALITIES OF A CONSTITUTIONAL CONVENTION (1989); Michael Stokes Paulsen, *A General Theory of Article V: The Constitutional Lessons of the Twenty-seventh Amendment*, 103 YALE L.J. 677 (1993).
[216] Peter J. Galie & Christopher Bopst, *Changing State Constitutions: Dual Constitutionalism and the Amending Process*, 1 HOFSTRA L. & POL'Y SYMP. 27, 31 (1996).
[217] *See* Francis H. Heller, *Limiting a Constitutional Convention: The State Precedents*, 3 CARDOZO L. REV. 563, 565 (1982); Lawrence Schlam, *State Constitutional Amending, Independent Interpretation, and Political Culture: A Case Study in Constitutional Stagnation*, 43 DEPAUL L. REV. 269, 347–48 (1994).
[218] Colantuono, *The Revision of American State Constitutions*, *supra* note 151, 1475, 1481.

was reformulated to ask whether the *voters* could by referendum adopt limitations suggested by the legislature as to what their elected delegates could do at a state constitutional convention, a consensus emerged that this was a valid and legally enforceable limit.[219] A.E. Dick Howard summarized this consensus:

> The prevailing view . . . treats a convention as the agent of the people who have called it. Thus, where the people must vote to approve the calling of a convention . . . the people are seen to have given their implicit approval to limitations on the convention's power contained in the enabling legislation that put the question of calling a convention to the people.[220]

The majority of state judicial rulings tend to confirm this point. Thus, the Virginia Supreme Court in 1945 noted:

> [W]here the legislature, in the performance of its representative function, asks the electors if they desire a convention to amend or revise a certain part of the Constitution but not the whole Constitution, an affirmative vote of the people on such a question would have the binding effect of the people themselves limiting the scope of the convention to the very portion of the Constitution suggested to them by the legislature. The wishes of the people are supreme.[221]

In an important 1947 decision, the Kentucky Supreme Court, relying on the fact that the state constitution did not limit the legislature's authority, upheld a "limit" on a constitutional convention that required it to submit its proposed revisions to the electorate for ratification.[222] The court relied on both the legislature's plenary authority and the directions of the voters to their delegates.[223] The Supreme Court of Tennessee reached a similar result in 1949, concluding that it was "[t]he people themselves who by their vote under the terms of this act limit the scope of the convention."[224]

Some states have constitutional provisions or judicial decisions that seem to prohibit the use of a limited constitutional convention. In Alabama's case, this is based on a 1955 advisory opinion, on a 4–3 vote, that utilized questionable

[219] Schlam, *supra* note 217, at 347–48.

[220] 2 A.E. Dick Howard, Commentaries on the Constitution of Virginia 1182 (1974); *see also* Galie & Bopst, *supra* note 216, at 39.

[221] Staples v. Gilmer, 33 S.E.2d 49, 55 (Va. 1945). This case, together with others, is discussed extensively in Heller, *supra* note 217, at 570–72; *see also In re* Opinion to the Governor, 178 A. 433, 452 (R.I. 1935); R.K. Gooch, *The Recent Limited Constitutional Convention in Virginia*, 31 Va. L. Rev. 708, 713–14 (1945).

[222] Gaines v. O'Connell, 204 S.W.2d 425, 431–32 (Ky. 1947); *see* Heller, *supra* note 217, at 572–74.

[223] *Gaines*, 204 S.W.2d at 431–32.

[224] Cummings v. Beeler, 223 S.W.2d 913, 923 (Tenn. 1949); *see* Heller, *supra* note 217, at 574–75.

reasoning and may well not command a current majority of the court.[225] Other states have similar judicial rulings. In such circumstances, of course, the state constitution could be amended to provide for the option of a limited constitutional convention.[226] Nevertheless, a leading modern commentator concluded:

> The state rule, broadly speaking, is that the citizens of a state may limit a convention's agenda by approving limitations in a popular vote. The argument in support of the rule is that the citizens of a state are sovereign, and the sovereign has the power to amend the basic principles by which it has chosen to be governed. Since by definition the sovereign's amending power cannot be limited, the sovereign may delegate its entire amending power to a suitable agent, such as a convention. It follows that the sovereign may validly delegate only a portion of its amending power.[227]

Finally, in a few states whose constitutions contain no provisions whatsoever concerning constitutional conventions, there are no requirements and no restrictions. This leaves maximum flexibility to the legislature and the people.[228] The few states that have judicial rulings prohibiting limited state constitutional conventions reflect the enforcement of provisions restricting the way conventions take place.

If states can impose limits on constitutional conventions, how might they do so? The legislation authorizing New Jersey's 1947 Constitutional Convention illustrates the array of mechanisms available.[229] First, the limitation was expressed in the title of the act.[230] Second, in the act's legislative findings, the authority for the limitation was expressed.[231] Third, the bill imposed a statutory

[225] *See* Opinion of the Justices, 81 So.2d 678, 679–83 (Ala. 1955). Advisory opinions are arguably not entitled to precedential weight. *See* Hamilton v. Antauga Co., 268 So.2d 30, 41 (Ala. 1972); *see also* Howard P. Walthall Sr., *Methods of Constitutional Revision in Alabama*, 33 Cumb. L. Rev. 195, 212–13 (2003). *See* Chapter 10.

[226] *See, e.g.*, Tenn. Const. art. XI, § 3.

[227] Heller, *supra* note 217, at 575–76. Levine, *supra* note 206, provides citations to many more cases.

[228] *See* Colantuono, *The Revision of American State Constitutions*, *supra* note 151, at 1479 n.34 (1987) (noting that forty-one state constitutions contain such provisions). The absence of any provisions in a state constitution concerning conventions further supports the theory that the legislature's plenary power may be used to propose limits that may be adopted by the voters. Heller, *supra* note 217, at 564, 567; *see also* Walter F. Dodd, *State Constitutional Conventions and State Legislative Power*, 2 Vand. L. Rev. 27, 29–34 (1948) (referring to New Jersey's 1947 Convention as a favorable example); Note, *State Constitutional Conventions: Limitations on Their Powers*, 55 Iowa L. Rev. 244, 264 (1969).

[229] *See* Act of Feb. 17, 1947, ch. 8, 1947 N.J. Laws 24–39.

[230] *Id.* at 24 ("An Act to provide for a State constitutional convention so instructed by the legal voters that it shall have no power to propose any change in the present basis of representation in the Legislature, providing for the nomination and election of delegates, at a special election, and for the submission of the proposals of the convention to the people for adoption or rejection, and making an appropriation therefore.").

[231] *Id.* at 25 ("Whereas, The people in the exercise of their sovereign power may commit their delegates to binding restrictions on the scope and subject matter of such a constituent assembly. . . .").

restriction on the powers of the convention.[232] Fourth, the legislation specified that the public question to be presented to the voters contain within it the limitation[233] and required the secretary of state to review the proposals, for conformity with the limitation before submission to the voters.[234] Finally, the legislation specified that the delegates' oath include their commitment to abide by the limitation.[235]

An important, related question concerns the mechanisms available for enforcing limits imposed on state constitutional conventions if they exceed their authority. Consider, for example, a 1975 ruling of the Rhode Island Supreme Court that, despite the valid limits on a constitutional convention proposed by the legislature and adopted by the voters, it was too late, as a matter of mootness, for judicial enforcement of the plaintiff's (a delegate to the convention) challenge after the voters had ratified the convention's proposals that exceeded the limit.[236] The court held that there was no longer a "live" controversy on which it could rule.[237] Although the cases cited earlier, upholding convention limits adopted by the voters, were brought prior to the convention's recommendations and their ratification by the people, this Rhode Island decision seems limited to its specifics, based on claims of a disgruntled former delegate. Of course, it will never be evident if a convention exceeds its limitations until it has completed its deliberations and made its recommendations to the voters. Challenges have been entertained after a favorable popular vote,[238] but it is important to keep in mind the Rhode Island view that a favorable vote may "cure" a constitutional convention's recommendations beyond the limits. Those who contend that a convention has exceeded its authority probably should not risk waiting until after a vote.

Recently, many competing national progressive and conservative groups, because of the rise of the NJF, have discovered the state constitutional

[232] *Id.*; *see also id.* at 37–39.

[233] *Id.* at 29–39.

[234] *Id.* at 36–37.

[235] *Id.* at 35–36. After the 1947 Constitutional Convention convened, it adopted the following Rule 51, limiting itself:

> Rule 51. No proposal for revision, alteration or reformation of the present Constitution which does not comply with the Convention's instructions as voted by the people shall be introduced in, reported by any Committee to, or agreed upon by, the Convention.
>
> II State of New Jersey Constitutional Convention of 1947: Convention Proceedings 983, 989–90 (1951).

[236] Malinou v. Powers, 333 A.2d 420, 422 (R.I. 1975); *cf.* Woods's Appeal, 75 Pa. 59, 69–75 (1874), *overruled in part by* Stander v. Kelley, 250 A.2d 474 (Pa. 1969).

[237] *Malinou*, 333 A.2d at 422.

[238] *See, e.g.*, Snow v. City of Memphis, 527 S.W.2d 55 (Tenn. 1975), *appeal dismissed for want of substantial federal question*, 423 U.S. 1083 (1976).

amendment process as an avenue for pushing *national* subjects. As analyzed by Dr. John Dinan:

> [T]he early twenty-first century has seen a flurry of state constitutional amendments intended to advance state interests in the federal system, whether by enacting policies blocked at the federal level or aiding in the reversal or modification of congressional statutes or court rulings. As will be shown, such amendments have been formally proposed in recent years and, in many cases, have been enacted on a wide range of issues, including eminent domain, affirmative action, minimum-wage policy, stem cell research, abortion, medicinal marijuana, health care, and union organizing.[239]

Again, by contrast to federal constitutional law, state courts are much more deeply involved in the process of state constitutional amendment and revision.[240]

## III. CONCLUSION

Obviously, when considering formal constitutional change, it is important to try to gauge opposition or status quo instincts ahead of time. A massive study of seven constitutional conventions concluded:

> Just as the delegates and the political activists in each state tended to break down, ultimately, into "reformers" and supporters of the "status quo," so the electorate divides in a similar fashion. . . . In short, constitutional revision potentially polarizes state communities, or the attentive portions of them, along predictable lines.[241]

It is clear, however, that in a number of states as a result of perseverance, the proper leadership, and the right timing, opportunities have arisen for the exercise of high levels of statesmanship. In the right circumstances, state political actors have transcended ordinary, short-term politics and embarked on high-level, far-reaching deliberations in reforming their state's constitution for the

[239] John Dinan, *State Constitutional Amendment Processes and the Safeguards of American Federalism*, 115 Penn St. L. Rev. 1007, 1010 (2011); *see also* Sean Beienburg, *Contesting the U.S. Constitution Through State Amendments: The 2011 and 2012 Elections*, 129 Pol. Sci. Q. 55, 55–56 (2014); Justin R. Long, *Guns, Gays, and Ganja*, 69 Ark L. Rev. 453, 453–54 (2016) ("[T]hree law-reform movements . . . have treated state constitutional changes as a tool for advancing their national policy aims."); Justin Long, *State Constitutions as Interactive Expressions of Fundamental Values*, 74 Alb. L. Rev. 1739 (2010/2011).

[240] Tarr, *supra* note 17, at 26.

[241] Cornwell Jr., Goodman, & Swanson, *supra* note 136, at 205–06.

betterment of themselves and future generations. Sometimes this process takes a period of debate and collegiality before a higher level, "constitutional-revision culture" is achieved by members of a constitutional commission or convention. Sometimes it never happens.

Careful consideration must be given to the important connection—the linkage—between the identified problems in the content of a state constitution and the mechanism, or process, chosen to address the problems. The mechanism should be tailored to the nature of the problems. Once again, of course, people may disagree about the nature of the problems, but if a consensus develops on the areas in need of change, that may dictate the process of state constitutional change that should be utilized.

Frank Grad and Robert Williams have argued that the burden of persuasion should be upon those who seek to include material in state constitutions.[242] It can be argued that a similar presumption should be applied to those who advocate for the calling of a state constitutional convention. This is a time-consuming, expensive, and uncertain process. It can yield great rewards for a state, but it can also fail or result in the inclusion of problematic material within a state constitution. There are, as noted herein, a number of less ambitious or even preliminary alternatives, such as legislatively proposed amendments, constitutional commissions, or limited state constitutional conventions to assess the current state constitution.

The issues that would come before a state constitutional convention now, or in the near future, would be substantially different from those associated with reform proposals in earlier decades or generations. The functions and responsibilities of states have evolved over time.[243] As one of the most in-depth studies of state constitutional conventions concluded:

> Doubtless one could take a cluster of constitutional conventions in any era—the Jacksonian period, the years of reconstruction or post-reconstruction, the turn-of-the-century progressive era—and find patterns of issue uniformity in each. In other words, there are broad areas of agreement in any one period as to what "modern," "effective," "democratic" state government consists of, but little such agreement over time. Conventions in one era meet to undo the careful reforms of an earlier generation.[244]

[242] GRAD & WILLIAMS, *supra* note 6, at 30.
[243] *Id.* at 8–14.
[244] CORNWELL JR., GOODMAN, & SWANSON, *supra* note 136, at 203; *see also* GRAD & WILLIAMS, *supra* note 6, at 24–25.

In other words, a state constitutional convention would not only be concerned with revisions of the existing constitution, but would be confronted with the local, regional, and national issues of importance at that point in time.[245]

All of these concerns point to the conclusion that decision makers in a state should carefully evaluate the question of whether state constitutional revision or reform is really called for, and if so, whether the time and expense of a state constitutional convention is merited. Possibly, even if there is a need for reform or revision, a state constitutional commission would be the logical starting point. Further, an initial step might involve some changes, even one-time-only changes, in the mechanisms of state constitutional change. This was utilized in Texas, albeit unsuccessfully, and with more success in Michigan and Illinois. Finally, a careful evaluation should focus on whether the passage of time and the accretion of specific amendments over the years have rendered the state constitution *functionally* incoherent. Is there really a need for "fundamental reconsideration" of "constitutional foundations?"[246] Are any of the state governmental structures so fundamentally flawed in their operation, or is the interrelationship among them so dysfunctional, as to require fundamental reconsideration of their constitutional foundations in an independent, deliberative process such as the "heavy artillery" of a constitutional convention that can assess proposed changes, in terms of their coherence with the rest of the state constitution?[247] If such fundamental flaws do exist, leading to incoherence, are they located in one or several parts of the constitution, such that they could be addressed by a limited constitutional commission or convention to avoid the "Pandora's box" element of "conventionphobia"?[248] How can the legislature be convinced to take any of these steps? It is these difficult questions which must be addressed to determine if a state's constitution is obsolete and in need of fundamental reform and, if so, whether anything can be done about it.[249]

245 For a consideration of current issues in state constitutional change, see generally 3 STATE CONSTITUTIONS FOR THE TWENTY-FIRST CENTURY: THE AGENDA OF STATE CONSTITUTIONAL REFORM, *supra* note 1.

246 *See* Tarr, *supra* note 1, at 2.

247 *See* Robert J. Martin, *Calling in Heavy Artillery to Assault Politics as Usual: Past and Prospective Deployment of Constitutional Conventions in New Jersey*, 29 RUTGERS L.J. 963, 964–65 (1998).

248 Gais & Benjamin, *supra* note 152, at 1304 ("Citizens may fear that constitutional conventions would open up a 'Pandora's box' or 'can of worms' in which delegates would make enormous constitutional changes with little or no public accountability.").

249 Important recommendations for improving the processes of state constitutional change include Jonathan L. Marshfield, *Improving Amendment*, 69 ARK. L. REV. (2016), and *Forgotten Limits on the Power to Amend State Constitutions*, 114 NW. U. L. REV. 65 (2019); and Thomas Andrew Koenig, *Make Politics Local Again: The Case for Pro-Localization State Constitutional Reform*, 73 RUTGERS U. L. REV. 1059 (2021).

# 14

# JUDICIAL INVOLVEMENT IN STATE CONSTITUTIONAL AMENDMENT AND REVISION

*A final distinctive feature of state constitutional practice regarding constitutional change is the involvement of state courts in overseeing the process of change. The reliance on formal constitutional change in the states has prompted opponents of proposed changes to challenge their legality in the courts. Whereas the United States Supreme Court has dismissed procedural challenges to the federal amendment process as "political questions," state courts have proved quite willing to address a wide range of issues associated with state constitutional change.*

—G. Alan Tarr[1]

The processes of state constitutional amendment and revision, by contrast to their federal counterparts, have come to include a significant degree of state judicial involvement.[2] Chapter 4 discussed federal court involvement when the *substance* of state constitutional provisions is challenged as violating the *federal* Constitution or law. As we saw in Chapter 13, state courts played a significant role in determining the legitimacy of limited constitutional conventions. In the introduction to this book, we discussed the litigation in California over the validity of Proposition 8, purporting to overturn California's same-sex marriage decision, which illustrates this trend.[3] This kind of judicial involvement is the likely result of a significant increase in the interest groups' awareness about, and utilization of, state constitutional change as an "instrument of lawmaking."[4]

A number of "hot button" issues in the past several generations has led not only to important public policy debates surrounding state constitutional change but to controversial judicial rulings concerning compliance with the processes

[1] G. Alan Tarr, Understanding State Constitutions 26 (1998).
[2] *Id.* at 26–27, 169.
[3] Strauss v. Horton, 207 P.3d 48 (Cal. 2009) (upholding Proposition 8).
[4] Robert F. Williams, *State Constitutional Law Processes*, 24 Wm. & Mary L. Rev. 169, 175 (1983).

*The Law of American State Constitutions.* Robert F. Williams and Lawrence Friedman, Oxford University Press.
 DOI: 10.1093/oso/9780190068806.003.0015

for state constitutional change. In the 1970s, California's Proposition 13, a substantial and hard-fought change in taxing provisions proposed through an initiative, led to important litigation concerning a number of process points.[5] In the 1990s, also in California, the state supreme court struck down on procedural grounds an initiative that would have linked virtually all of the state constitution's criminal procedure rights to federal constitutional interpretation.[6] Then, after the wave of state constitutional amendments banning same-sex marriage and, in some cases, civil unions, state courts entertained litigation challenging those amendments on procedural grounds,[7] of which California's litigation over Proposition 8 is merely an example.

## I. PROCEDURAL LIMITS ON STATE CONSTITUTIONAL CHANGE

While there are virtually no *substantive* restrictions on state constitutional amendment and revision (other than federal constitutional constraints),[8] there are significant *procedural* requirements. Each of the differing processes leading to amendment or revision has its own specific requirements. The courts have been deeply involved in enforcing these procedural requirements. While the regular involvement of the state judiciary in the citizens' processes of amending their state constitutions has led to criticism,[9] there are still strong incentives for opponents of a particular state constitutional change to attack it on procedural grounds, either before or after the referendum, in the state courts.[10] There is little to lose and everything to gain.

Generally, the *type* or *method* of state constitutional change that is pursued to accomplish a particular result may be challenged, or the adherence to particular

[5] Amador Valley Joint Union High School District v. State Board of Equalization, 583 P.2d 1281 (Cal. 1978).

[6] Raven v. Deukmejian, 801 P.2d 1077 (Cal. 1990). *See infra* note 17.

[7] *See, e.g.*, Perdue v. O'Kelley, 632 S.E.2d 110 (Ga. 2006) (upholding amendment against a single-subject challenge, applying the test for statutes to constitutional amendment). For other issues arising under these state constitutional bans on same-sex marriage, including *interpretation* questions concerning their meaning, see Alaska Civil Liberties Union v. State, 122 P.3d 781 (Alas. 2005); State v. Carswell, 871 N.E.2d 547 (Ohio 2007); National Pride at Work, Inc. v. Michigan, 748 N.W.2d 524 (Mich. 2008). *See also Recent Case*, 122 HARV. L. REV. 1263 (2009). Interpretation issues are covered in Chapter 12.

[8] FRANK P. GRAD & ROBERT F. WILLIAMS, 2 STATE CONSTITUTIONS FOR THE TWENTY-FIRST CENTURY: DRAFTING STATE CONSTITUTIONS, REVISIONS, AND AMENDMENTS 3 (2006). *See, e.g.*, Omaha National Bank v. Spire, 389 N.W.2d 269 (Neb. 1986).

[9] Harry L. Witte, *Rights, Revolution, and the Paradox of Constitutionalism: The Processes of Constitutional Change in Pennsylvania*, 3 WIDENER J. PUB. L. 383 (1993).

[10] *See generally* Stephen B. Niswanger, Comment: *A Practitioner's Guide to Challenging and Defending Legislatively Proposed Constitutional Amendments in Arkansas*, 17 U. ARK. LITTLE ROCK L. REV. 765 (1995).

*procedural requirements* may be the basis of the attack. In the 1950s, for instance, opponents challenged a legislatively proposed amendment to the Alabama Constitution on the ground that the existing constitution required any change in that particular provision to be proposed by a constitutional convention, rather than by the legislature.[11] The Alabama Supreme Court rejected that argument, over a well-reasoned dissenting opinion, in a 4–3 advisory opinion.[12]

## A. Amendment vs. Revision

Another example of a challenge based on the type of constitutional change is the restriction in some states that the initiative may be used only to propose an *amendment* to, rather than a *revision* of, the state constitution. This was the basis for the challenge to California's Proposition 8. The distinction that must be enforced by the courts is somewhat unclear. Thus, the California Supreme Court struck down Proposition 115, an initiative "amendment" that would have linked (a "forced linkage" amendment") virtually all of the state constitution's criminal procedure protections to the interpretation of similar federal constitutional rights by the U.S. Supreme Court.[13] The court concluded that the provision proposed a *revision* of the California Constitution, rather than an amendment that could be accomplished by the initiative, because it contemplated "such a far-reaching change in our governmental framework as to amount to a qualitative constitutional revision, an undertaking beyond the reach of the initiative process."[14] The court stated that a proposed change through the initiative could be an invalid attempt at revision because of either its quantitative effect (the number of changes) or the qualitative effect: "even a relatively simple enactment may accomplish such far reaching changes in the nature of our basic governmental plan as to amount to a revision. . . ."[15] The California court relied on earlier decisions that applied this two-pronged analysis,[16] concluding:

> Proposition 115 contemplates a similar qualitative change. In essence and practical effect, new article I, section 24 would vest all judicial *interpretive* power, as to fundamental criminal defense rights, in the United States Supreme Court. From a qualitative standpoint, the effect of Proposition 115 is devastating. . . . California courts in criminal cases would no longer have authority

[11] Opinion of the Justices, 81 So.2d 881 (Ala. 1955).
[12] *Id.*
[13] Raven v. Deukmejian, 801 P.2d 1077 (Cal. 1990).
[14] *Id.* at 1080.
[15] *Id.* at 1087 (*quoting Amador*, 583 P.2d at 1281).
[16] *See Amador*, 583 P.2d at 1281; McFadden v. Jordan, 196 P.2d 787 (Cal. 1948).

> to interpret the state Constitution in a manner more protective of defendants' rights than extended by the federal Constitution, as construed by the United States Supreme Court.[17]

California's Proposition 13 earlier had survived a similar challenge based both on quantitative and qualitative proposed changes in the state constitution through the initiative process.[18]

Interestingly, the Alaska Supreme Court adopted, with a modification, the California quantitative/qualitative evaluation of the question of whether an *initiative* proposed an amendment or a revision and applied it to *legislatively proposed* constitutional changes linking prisoners' rights only to those guaranteed by the federal Constitution.[19] The court articulated a sliding scale or "hybrid" approach, which reduced the qualitative assessment if the quantitative impact was greater.[20] The court cited with approval the distinction between revisions and amendments made by John A. Jameson in his *Treatise on Constitutional Conventions*:

> Scholars have also concluded that a distinction exists between the two methods of constitutional change. Judge John A. Jameson, in his *Treatise on Constitutional Conventions*, wrote that the legislative process of amending a constitution should be confined to "changes which are few, simple, independent, and of comparatively small importance," whereas a constitutional convention is required for "a general revision of a Constitution, or even for single propositions involving radical changes as to the policy of which the popular mind has not been informed by prior discussion."[21]

In a Florida case, *Adams v. Gunter*, the state supreme court invalidated an "amendment" to the Florida constitution proposed through the initiative process that would have established a unicameral legislature.[22] The court engaged in a

17 *Raven*, 801 P.2d at 1087. *See* Gerald F. Uelmen, *The California Constitution After Proposition 115*, 3 EMERGING ISSUES IN STATE CONST. L. 33 (1990). *See also* Holmes v. Appling, 392 P.2d 636 (Or. 1964); Citizens Protecting Michigan's Constitution v. Sec. of State, 755 N.W.2d 157 (Mich. 2008).

A detailed analysis of state constitutional amendments after *Raven* concluded that many of the reductions in criminal procedure rights were accomplished through individual amendments. David Aram Kaiser & David A. Carillo, *California Constitutional Law: Reanimating Criminal Procedure Rights After the "Other" Proposition 8*, 56 SANTA CLARA L. REV. 33 (2016).

18 *Amador*, 583 P.2d at 1281. *See* George Lefcoe & Barney Allison, *The Legal Aspects of Proposition 13: The Amador Valley Case*, 53 S. CAL. L. REV. 173 (1979); State v. Manley, 441 So.2d 864 (Ala. 1983).

19 Bess v. Ulmer, 985 P.2d 979 (Alaska 1999).

20 *Id.* at 987–88. *See* Senator Dave Donley, with Douglas Baily et al., Bess v. Ulmer—*The Supreme Court Stumbles and the Subsistence Amendment Falls*, 19 ALASKA L. REV. 295, 301 (2002) ("A partial showing on one test can, evidently, reduce the showing required on the other test.").

21 *Bess*, 985 P.2d at 983. *See generally* Jonathan L. Marshfield, *Forgotten Limits on the Power to Amend State Constitutions*, 114 NW. U. L. REV. 65 (2019).

22 238 So.2d 824 (Fla. 1970).

similar qualitative analysis of the relatively short proposed state constitutional change, concluding that it affected many provisions of the constitution and was therefore an invalid revision that could not be accomplished through the initiative process.[23]

In each of these instances, because the court invalidated the proposed change on procedural rather than substantive grounds, supporters of the changes would have been free to repackage their proposals—in the California case, as individual initiatives; and in the Florida case, as a proposal emanating either from the legislature or from a constitutional convention. Of further interest is the fact that the voters in Florida approved a legislatively proposed amendment to ease the restriction enforced in the *Adams* decision, demonstrating once again that state constitutions can be amended to "overrule" judicial decisions interpreting them.[24]

The state of Illinois imposes important substantive restrictions on its initiative process, limiting such proposed amendments to "structural and procedural subjects contained in" the legislative article of the Illinois Constitution.[25] This limitation has been strictly enforced by the Illinois Supreme Court.[26]

Returning to California and the story of Proposition 8: after the California Supreme Court ruled in favor of same-sex marriage,[27] opponents of same-sex marriage proposed, and voters ratified, Proposition 8 (an initiative) to overturn that decision. That amendment was then challenged as an unauthorized *revision*, rather than an amendment. The California Supreme Court rejected this argument, based on the qualitative effect of the amendment.[28]

## B. Single Subject and Separate Vote Requirements

Two additional procedural requirements present in many state constitutions require proposed amendments to cover only a "single subject" and, in a closely related requirement, specify that if more than one amendment is proposed, the voters must be accorded the opportunity to vote separately on them. These

[23] *Id.* at 831–32. The court relied on *Rivera-Cruz v. Gray*, 104 So.2d 501 (Fla. 1958), and the California *McFadden* decision.

[24] *See* Floridians Against Casino Takeover v. Let's Help Florida, 363 So.2d 337, 339–42 (Fla. 1978).

[25] Ill. Const. art. XIV, § 3.

[26] *See* Chicago Bar Ass'n v. State Board of Elections, 561 N.E.2d 50 (Ill. 1990); Ann Lousin, *The 1970 Illinois Constitution: Has It Made a Difference?* 8 N. Ill. U. L. Rev. 571, 578–82 (1988); Lawrence Schlam, *Legislative Term Limitation Under a "Limited" Popular Initiative Provision?* 14 N. Ill. U. L. Rev. 1, 53–69 (1993).

[27] *In re* Marriage Cases, 183 P.3d 384, 553 (Cal. 2008).

[28] Strauss v. Horton, 207 P.3d 48 (Cal. 2009). For an argument that Proposition 8 did unconstitutionally affect the egalitarian *quality* of the California Constitution, see David B. Cruz, *Equality's Centrality: Proposition 8 and the California Constitution*, 19 Rev. L. & Soc. Justice 45 (2010).

provisions, which are judicially enforceable and generate significant litigation, call on the courts to make similar but subtly different evaluations. The Oregon Supreme Court, in *Armatta v. Kitzhaber*, confronted the argument that the two restrictions, both of which appeared in its constitution, imposed the same limitations.[29] Utilizing many of the interpretation techniques discussed in Chapter 12, the court concluded:

> However, the fact that a proposed amendment containing more than one subject would *violate* both the separate-vote and single-subject requirements does not compel the conclusion that the opposite also is true, *i.e.*, that a proposed amendment that contains only one subject would *not* violate the separate-vote requirement. As we have discussed, the separate-vote requirement imposes a *narrower* restriction than the requirement that a proposed amendment embrace only one subject. It follows, therefore, that a proposed amendment that satisfies the broad standard for embracing a single subject nonetheless may violate the separate-vote requirement.[30]

The California Supreme Court, in 2006, undertook a thorough consideration of the two limitations and their relationship, declining to follow Oregon's *Armatta* decision.[31] The California decision also utilized many of the techniques discussed in Chapter 12. After reviewing provisions of other states as they had been judicially interpreted,[32] the court carefully analyzed California's constitutional history on these points,[33] concluding:

> No jurisdiction of which we are aware that allows amendment of its state constitution either by legislative submission *or* voter initiative discriminates in this manner by setting up a higher obstacle for legislative constitutional submissions than for initiative submissions by the voters, and we cannot imagine that doing so was the intent either of the various drafters over the years or of the voters who enacted, reenacted, and amended California's separate-vote provision. By contrast, if we follow the majority rule of our sister states and construe our separate-vote provision as requiring no more (and no less) than the

[29] Armatta v. Kitzhaber, 959 P.2d 49 (Or. 1998). *See also* Marshall v. State *ex rel.* Cooney, 975 P.2d 325, 331 (Mont. 1999).

[30] *Armatta*, 959 P.2d at 64. *See also* Lehman v. Bradbury, 37 P.3d 989, 994–1001 (Or. 2002); Swett v. Bradbury, 43 P.3d 1094, 1099–1101 (Or. 2002).

[31] Californians for An Open Primary v. McPherson, 134 P.3d 299, 300, 317–29 (Cal. 2006). *See also* Cambria v. Soaries, 776 A.2d 754, 758–63 (N.J. 2001); Arizona Together v. Brewer, 149 P.3d 742, 749 (Ariz. 2007).

[32] *McPherson*, 134 P.3d at 305–09.

[33] *Id.* at 309–17.

> constraint effectuated by the single subject rule, we shall avoid creating such an unprecedented and anomalous scheme.[34]

Several state high courts have held that the processes of state constitutional revision and amendment are mandatory and have to be adhered to strictly.[35] Such an approach may invalidate proposed constitutional changes that were not publicized to the voters in the required manner,[36] or subjected to the proper legislative procedure.[37] Moreover, it has been held that the legislative power to propose constitutional amendments to the voters is not within the basic, plenary *legislative* power, but rather must be specifically authorized, and limited, by the state constitution.[38] Also, the states are split on whether the governor can veto a proposed constitutional amendment.[39]

The California cases have distinguished substantive from procedural challenges to proposed state constitutional changes when considering the propriety of pre-election judicial review. In 1999, the court relied on the specific language of the single-subject rule, "[a]n initiative measure embracing more than one subject *may not be submitted* to *the electors* or have any effect," to conclude that a pre-election challenge was proper.[40] The court noted that the presence of an "invalid measure on the ballot steals attention, time and money from the numerous valid propositions. . . ."[41] The court went on to strike down the initiative as a violation of the single-subject rule.[42]

[34] *Id.* at 326. In *In re* Initiative Petition No. 344, 797 P.2d 326 (Okla. 1990), and *In re* Initiative Petition No. 342, 797 P.2d 331 (Okla. 1990), the Oklahoma Supreme Court struck from the ballot initiatives that would have revised articles of the Oklahoma Constitution. The court based its decisions on the single-subject rule. *See* Robert H. Henry, *The Oklahoma Constitutional Revision Commission: A Call to Arms or the Sounding of Retreat?* 17 OKLA. CITY U. L. REV. 177 (1992); Dennis W. Arrow, *Representative Government and Popular Distrust: The Obstruction/Facilitation Conundrum Regarding State Constitutional Amendment by Initiative Petition*, 17 OKLA. CITY U. L. REV. 3, 66–86 (1992). *See also* State *ex rel.* Loontjer v. Gale, 853 N.W.2d 494 (Neb. 2014); In the Matter of Title, Ballot Title, 374 P.3d 460 (Colo. 2016); Montana Assoc. of Counties v. State, 404 P.3d 733 (Mont. 2017) (victim's rights amendment); Oklahoma Indep. Petrolium Assoc. v. Potts, 414 P.3d 351 (Okla. 2018); Martin v. Humphrey, 558 S.W.3d 370, 377–78 (Ark. 2018); Anderson v. Attorney General, 99 N.E.3d 309 (Mass. 2018); League of Women Voters of Pennsylvania v. Boockvar, 219 A.3d 594 (Pa. 2019).

[35] Watland v. Lingle, 85 P.3d 1079, 1090–91 (Haw. 2004) (collecting cases). *See also* Pennsylvania Prison Society v. Commonwealth, 776 A.2d 971, 976 (Pa. 2001).

[36] *Watland*, 85 P.3d at 1091–92.

[37] Taomae v. Lingle, 118 P.3d 1188, 1195–96 (Haw. 2005). The Louisiana Supreme Court struck down a proposed amendment where the version presented to the voters was not identical to that enacted by the legislature. Shepherd v. Schedler, 209 So.3d 752 (La. 2016).

[38] *See* Opinion of the Justices, 81 So.2d 881, 890 (Ala. 1955); Geringer v. Bebout, 10 P.3d 514, 526 (Wyo. 2000) (Lehman, C.J., dissenting) (collecting cases).

[39] *Geringer*, 10 P.3d at 520–21 (approving governor's veto).

[40] Senate of the State of California v. Jones, 988 P.2d 1089, 1096 (Cal. 1999).

[41] *Id.* (*citing* American Federation of Labor v. Eu, 686 P.2d 609, 615 (Cal. 1984)).

[42] *Id.* at 1098–1106. *See also In re* Advisory Opinion to the Attorney General Re the Medical Liability Claimant's Compensation Amendment, 880 So.2d 675 (Fla. 2004) (upholding, against single-subject and inadequate ballot title and summary challenges, amendment limiting lawyers' contingency fees).

The Florida Supreme Court upheld the presentation of the "forced-linkage" search and seizure amendment, discussed in Chapter 5, against a challenge alleging that inadequate information had been presented to the voters,[43] but struck from the ballot an initiated constitutional amendment, on single-subject, title, and ballot summary grounds, that would have abolished joint and several liability in torts, encouraged summary judgments, and capped noneconomic damages.[44]

Both state and federal courts have become involved in questions surrounding the vote on whether to hold a constitutional convention. The Hawaii Supreme Court ruled that the 1996 automatic vote on whether to hold a constitutional convention failed because, although the positive votes outnumbered the negative, blank and overvoted ballots had to be counted as negative.[45] Interestingly, the supporters of a convention asserted *federal* claims, based on substantive due process and free speech grounds.[46] The Ninth Circuit took the claims seriously and reviewed the possible federal constitutional grounds for such a challenge (including lack of notice that blank ballots would be counted as negative) before upholding the Hawaii Supreme Court's interpretation.[47] Finally, in 1992, the Hawaii Supreme Court ruled that the legislature could not submit to the voters *alternative* constitutional amendments, with the one receiving more votes in a primary being submitted to the voters at the general election.[48]

[43] Grose v. Firestone, 422 So.2d 303 (Fla. 1982). *See* Thomas C. Marks, *The Case of the Bogus Ballot Summary:* Grose v. Firestone, 5 ST. THOMAS L. REV. 147 (1992). The Florida court also struck down a proposed "forced linkage" amendment for cruel and unusual punishment, on similar grounds, in *Armstrong v. Harris*, 773 So.2d 7 (Fla. 2000). Proponents then resubmitted the amendment, seemingly with proper information to the voters. FLA. CONST. art. I, § 17. *See* Thomas C. Marks Jr., *Federalism and the Florida Constitution: The Self-Inflicted Wounds of Thrown-Away Independence from the Control of the U.S. Supreme Court*, 66 ALB. L. REV. 701, 711–18 (2003).

[44] Evans v. Firestone, 457 So.2d 1351 (Fla. 1984). The Florida cases, as well as cases from other jurisdictions, are analyzed carefully by Patrick O. Gudridge in *Florida Constitutional Theory*, 48 U. MIAMI L. REV. 809 (1994). *See also* Kahalekai v. Doi, 590 P.2d 543, 554–57 (Haw. 1979) (upholding a complex submission of thirty-four amendments but invalidating several where the content was not mentioned in the information booklet or required newspaper publications); Roberts v. Priest, 20 S.W.3d 376, 380 (Ark. 2000).

[45] Hawaii State AFL-CIO v. Yoshina, 935 P.2d 89, 98 (Haw. 1997) ("a majority of the ballots cast upon such a question"). *See also* Stoliker v. Waite, 101 N.W.2d 299, 301 (Mich. 1960) (majority of electors at "such election" held to require a majority of those voting at the election and not just on the constitution convention question. The court noted that the relative ease of calling a constitutional convention was one for the framers, not the courts.); State *ex rel.* Cashmore v. Anderson, 500 P.2d 921, 925–30 (Mont. 1972).

[46] Bennett v. Yoshina, 140 F.3d 1218 (9th Cir. 1998).

[47] *Id.* at 1225–28.

[48] Blair v. Cayetano, 836 P.2d 1066 (Haw. 1992). The California Constitution provides for this. CAL. CONST. art II, § 10 (b).

## II. CONCLUSION

A 2006 Florida case ties together a number of the themes in this book. The state constitution mandates that the unique, appointed Taxation and Budget Reform Commission, discussed in Chapter 13, meet automatically every twenty years and that proposed changes concerning "taxation or the state budgetary process" be placed directly on the ballot without legislative involvement.[49] The commission accordingly met, held hearings, and proposed a number of changes to be placed on the November 2008 ballot, two of which would have:

1. Repealed Florida's "Blaine Amendment," barring the use of public funds for religious purposes (Chapter 4)
2. Overturned a decision, based on *expressio unius est exclusio alterius* (Chapter 12), barring the use of school vouchers[50]

The Florida Supreme Court, relying on a plain meaning analysis, held these proposals beyond the Commission's constitutional mandate and ordered them struck from the ballot.[51]

These types of issues can arise in any state and will be subject to the specific wording in the state constitution, as well as to the state court's approach to interpreting such provisions. Perhaps unsurprisingly, these cases can involve the state courts in controversial matters, as illustrated by the California litigation over Proposition 8 overturning the same-sex marriage case and purporting to ban such marriages.[52]

[49] FLA. CONST. art. XI, § 6.

[50] Bush v. Holmes, 919 So.2d 392 (Fla. 2006).

[51] Ford v. Browning, 992 So.2d 132 (Fla. 2008). Justice Lewis concurred on the additional ground that the title of one of the proposals failed to disclose that the school voucher case would be overruled. *Id.* at 141–42.

[52] The California Supreme Court upheld Proposition 8 against a challenge that it was an improper attempt to use the initiative to *revise* the state constitution, but rejected an argument that it was retroactive, wiping out thousands of legally valid same-sex marriages. Strauss v. Horton 207 P.3d 48 (Cal. 2009).

# EPILOGUE

## THE FUTURE OF STATE CONSTITUTIONALISM

In this brief epilogue, we consider where some of the features of state constitutionalism we have discussed in these pages may be headed next. Specifically, we look at the potential direction of state constitutional law in two areas: the New Judicial Federalism (NJF) and the increasing use of state constitutional amendment processes in reaction to legal developments at the federal level.

### I. The NJF's Next Stage

In Chapter 5, we discussed the NJF in the context of the "stages" of its embrace by state court judges and practitioners. Professor Williams first sketched this framework nearly two decades ago, in a law review article introducing the stages of doctrinal evolution by state courts regarding individual rights jurisprudence under their state constitutions.[1] At that time, it was possible to identify three distinct stages of the NJF and to speculate about a nascent fourth. Now, nearly two decades later, the NJF may be on the cusp of a fifth stage of development, one that may well differ in significant ways from the stages that have come before it.

Recall that the first stage of the NJF was a reaction to the Burger Court's retreat from its predecessor's expansion of constitutional criminal procedure protections and embrace of a robust understanding of substantive due process.[2] This was the "Thrill of Discovery."[3] There followed, in the second stage, a backlash to the use of state constitutions by state court judges to chart paths of rights-protection that diverged from federal law.[4] As we recounted in Chapter 5, in response to state court decisions that resulted in more expansive rights interpretation, "[a]cademics, government officials, and judges, . . . spoke out in various forums opposing state decisions 'going beyond' the national minimum standards." Critics raised the specter, in other words, that haunts many cases in

[1] Robert F. Williams, *Introduction: The Third Stage of the New Judicial Federalism*, 59 N.Y.U. Ann. Survey Am. L. 211 (2003).

[2] *See* G. Alan Tarr, Understanding State Constitutions 161–65 (1998).

[3] *See* Chapter 5.

[4] *See id.*

*The Law of American State Constitutions.* Robert F. Williams and Lawrence Friedman, Oxford University Press.
 DOI: 10.1093/oso/9780190068806.003.0016

which a state court's exercise of judicial review of a state constitutional challenge results in a declaration that a particular governmental action is invalid because it infringes an individual right—namely, that a state court's decision not to adhere to the U.S. Supreme Court's authoritative interpretations of federal law somehow means that the justices relied at least in part upon their personal assessments of the rightness or wrongness of the Supreme Court's rulings on the same subject.

By the turn of the twenty-first century, the backlash had died down, and independent state constitutionalism had become an accepted feature of the constitutional landscape in many states in one form or another. Then and now, of course, particular state supreme court decisions regarding state rights protections attracted controversy. At the same time, state courts and the lawyers who appeared before them took the work of state constitutional interpretation seriously, and the new judicial federalism entered its third stage: "the long hard task."[5] Among the reasons the task was, in many instances, daunting, was the fact that state courts have tended to be underresourced as compared to their federal counterpart, lacking the same access to historical sources, for example, or even the law clerks necessary to assist the justices in the task of discerning the meaning of a particular state constitutional provision.[6]

Nonetheless, the NJF continued to thrive, and efforts at constitutional dialogue between state and federal courts marked a tentative fourth stage of the NJF's development,[7] as foreshadowed by scholars like Professor Paul Kahn, who argued for a greater engagement between state and federal courts regarding the interpretation of rights common to both state and federal constitutions. He maintained that American constitutionalism should not be seen as "a single set of truths," but an "ongoing national discourse about 'ideas of liberty, equality, and due process.' "[8] Whether a true dialogue is in fact possible remains a subject of debate. Now, more than a dozen years after the first edition of this book was published, it seems increasingly clear that, at the end of the day, it is the unique attributes of a particular state court or a particular state constitution—or both—that remain particularly salient in questions of state constitutional interpretation, especially in cases in which the text of an individual rights provision appears to cover the same ground as the parallel federal provision.

After all, in the context of the NJF, when state courts address the interpretation of parallel individual rights protections under their state constitutions, they do so from a perspective on concepts like liberty, equality, and due process that may

[5] *See id.*

[6] *See* Lawrence Friedman, *Path Dependence and the External Constraints on Independent State Constitutionalism*, 115 Penn State L. Rev. 783, 818–21 (2011).

[7] *See* Chapter 5.

[8] Paul W. Kahn, *Interpretation and Authority in State Constitutionalism*, 106 Harv. L. Rev. 1147, 1147–48 (1993).

derive from textual, historical, or precedential starting points that differ significantly from the federal perspective. This does not mean that discourse between the state and federal courts on the meaning and application of these provisions is impossible, but that it may not resemble a traditional dialogue so much as a version of the board game Scrabble, as each court seeks to build its constitutional jurisprudence from a universe of shared points, with each move in turn taking a particular court in a direction dictated by the text, history, and precedent with which it is working.

Consider, in this regard, the issue of same-sex marriage, which we discussed at length in the introduction to this book. In 2003, the year in which Professor Williams's essay on the stages of the new judicial federalism first appeared, the Massachusetts Supreme Judicial Court became the first court in the nation to strike down, on state constitutional grounds, a prohibition on same-sex marriage in *Goodridge v. Department of Public Health.*[9] Many state courts followed, with some reaching the same result on the basis of different reasoning under their own state constitutions, and other courts embracing different doctrinal approaches that led them to reject the arguments presented by the advocates of marriage equality in Massachusetts.[10]

This state court litigation ultimately led to litigation in the federal courts under the Fourteenth Amendment and to review by the U.S. Supreme Court, which resolved the issue of same-sex marriage in 2015. That year, in *Obergefell v. Hodges*, the high court concluded that marriage is a fundamental interest that states cannot deny to same-sex couples.[11] The Supreme Court notably did not rely on the reasoning of any of the state court decisions that preceded *Obergefell*—it turned instead to approaches derived exclusively from federal constitutional law. The Supreme Court, in other words, did what it has always done, and what we and many other commentators have argued that state courts should do—namely, start the process of interpreting constitutional texts with the words of the provision in question, its history, and relevant precedent, and build from there. Some conceptual frameworks are common across jurisdictions and outcomes might in the end mirror one another; the ultimate result in *Obergefell* was little different from the conclusion the Massachusetts Supreme Judicial Court reached in *Goodridge*. But each court's path to that

[9] 798 N.E.2d 941 (Mass. 2003). As we discuss in the introduction to this book, the Vermont Supreme Court had earlier ruled that a prohibition on same-sex marriage violated the state constitution, but that court left the question of remedy to the state legislature. *See* Baker v. State, 744 A.2d 864 (Vt. 1999); Introduction.

[10] *See* Introduction. *See also* Lenore F. Carpenter & Ellie Margolis, *One Sequin at a Time: Lessons on State Constitutions and Incremental Change from the Campaign for Marriage Equality*, 75 N.Y.U. Ann. Survey Am. L. 255 (2020).

[11] *See* Obergefell v. Hodges, 576 U.S. 644 (2015).

result may be different, reflecting the unique nature of the constitutional text and traditions under consideration, just as the Supreme Court's analysis in *Obergefell* differed from the Supreme Judicial Court's analysis in *Goodridge*.

It is this variety of constitutional experience that may lead, at this writing, to another stage in the development of the NJF. Just as each generation of lawyers seems to discover for itself America's other constitutions, we may be at or near another generational moment, as demonstrated, for example, by the popularity of Judge Jeffrey Sutton's recent and extensive work on state constitutions and the work of state courts.[12] One reason why the NJF may gain newfound attention among advocates and lawmakers relates to the perceived direction of the current U.S. Supreme Court, whose membership, at this writing, includes a core of justices—Clarence Thomas, Samuel Alito, Neil Gorsuch, and Amy Coney Barrett—who claim to adhere to the particular approach to federal constitutional interpretation known as originalism.[13] This approach privileges efforts to determine what these justices view as the original understanding of the federal constitutional text, at the time it was adopted.[14]

Originalism stands in contrast to a pragmatic approach to constitutional interpretation, which tends to favor an understanding of the text commensurate with the view that the framers of the federal Constitution sought primarily to create a workable and enduring governmental structure for the United States.[15] Originalism also stands in contrast to the conservative jurisprudence of the U.S. Supreme Court following the Warren Court, the very time period in the 1970s in which state courts began to embrace the NJF. That kind of conservative jurisprudence, to which the NJF was in no small part a reaction, emphasizes judicial deference toward the democratically accountable political departments of

[12] *See* JEFFREY S. SUTTON, 51 IMPERFECT SOLUTIONS: STATES AND THE MAKING OF AMERICAN CONSTITUTIONAL LAW (2020); JEFFREY S. SUTTON, WHO DECIDES? STATES AS LABORATORIES OF CONSTITUTIONAL EXPERIMENTATION (2021).

[13] With the confirmation of Justice Amy Coney Barrett as an Associate Justice of the Supreme Court, originalism has moved to center stage once more in constitutional debates in the United States. Justice Barrett self-identifies as an originalist. So does Justice Neil Gorsuch, whom President Donald Trump nominated and the Senate confirmed to succeed Justice Antonin Scalia. Justice Clarence Thomas has long argued for judicial decision-making based on "the original public meaning" of the U.S. Constitution.

Richard H. Fallon Jr., *The Chimerical Concept of Original Public Meaning*, 107 VA. L. REV. 1421, 1423–24 (2021) (footnotes omitted). *See also* Scott Kafker, *State Constitutional Law Declares Its Independence: Double Protecting Rights During a Time of Federal Constitutional Upheaval*, 49 HASTINGS CONST. L.Q. 115, 115 (2022) (noting that the new Supreme Court majority "will certainly reshape federal constitutional law in its own image").

[14] *See, e.g.*, United States v. Lopez, 514 U.S. 549, 585 (1995) (Thomas, J., concurring) (in interpreting the reach of Congress's power under the commerce clause, should look to the meaning of the term "commerce" as understood "[a]t the time the original Constitution was ratified").

[15] *See generally* STEPHEN BREYER, ACTIVE LIBERTY: INTERPRETING OUR DEMOCRATIC CONSTITUTION (2005).

state governments in resolving arguments about the scope or extent of individual rights commitments.[16]

An increasingly originalist orientation toward federal constitutional interpretation from the U.S. Supreme Court portends, potentially, two trends. First, a reliance upon originalism, unlike either a pragmatic approach to constitutional interpretation or the judicial conservatism of the 1970s, may lead to more than just an end to rights-expansion at the federal level; it may lead in some instances to rights-deterioration or even rights-elimination.[17] The obvious example is the Supreme Court's 2022 decision in *Dobbs v. Jackson Women's Health Organization*.[18] In *Dobbs*, the court overturned *Roe v. Wade*[19] and *Planned Parenthood v. Casey*,[20] reasoning that the federal Constitution makes no reference to a woman's right to choose and the Fourteenth Amendment was not understood at the time of its framing or ratification to protect such an interest.[21]

Consider, as well, the Fourth Amendment's protection against unreasonable searches and seizures. In a 2018 case, *Carpenter v. United States*, decided before Justices Kavanaugh and Coney Barrett joined the Supreme Court, a slim majority concluded that, under the Fourth Amendment, certain searches of digital devices may require that law enforcement first secure a warrant based upon probable cause.[22] Several justices objected to this conclusion on originalist grounds, suggesting that some of the basic precedential assumptions about how the Fourth Amendment historically has been implemented, and upon which the *Carpenter* majority relied, ought to be re-examined.[23]

Perhaps needless to say, an originalist reimagining of the Fourth Amendment would work a sea change in how the protections of that provision are understood and applied. Like the reaction to the Court's conservative turn in the 1970s, such a development could move rights advocates in criminal cases—where much of

[16] *See, e.g.*, Lawrence Friedman, *The Limitations of Labeling: Justice Anthony M. Kennedy and the First Amendment*, 20 OHIO NORTHERN U. L. REV. 225, 229–31 (1993) (discussing conservative jurisprudential emphasis on judicial restraint in individual rights cases).

[17] *See* ERWIN CHEMERINSKY, THE CONSERVATIVE ASSAULT ON THE CONSTITUTION 177 (2010) (predicting, even before Trump's appointments to the U.S. Supreme Court, that the Court was primed to curtail substantive due process). *See also* Kafker, *supra* note 13, at 126–27 (discussing consequences of a Supreme Court decision to eliminate federal constitutional protection for a woman's right to choose whether to obtain an abortion).

[18] 597 U.S. ___ (2022).

[19] 410 U.S. 113 (1973).

[20] 505 U.S. 833 (1992).

[21] *See also* New York State Rifle & Pistol Association, Inc. v. Bruen, 597 U.S. ___ (2022) (eschewing means-ends balancing in implementing Second Amendment right to self-defense in favor of emphasis on relevant historical practices).

[22] 585 U.S. ___ (2018).

[23] *See* Orin Kerr, *Judge Kavanaugh on the Fourth Amendment*, SCOTUSBLOG (July 20, 2018, 6:16 PM), https://www.scotusblog.com/2018/07/judge-kavanaugh-on-the-fourth-amendment/ (predicting that Justice Kavanaugh likely would accept originalist approach to Fourth Amendment when presented the opportunity to do so).

the work of the NJF has occurred[24]—to shift their attention to state constitutions and the meaning of their search and seizure provisions, many of which are phrased in terms nearly identical to the Fourth Amendment.

Unlike the pragmatic conservative approach of forty years ago, the modern Supreme Court's focus on originalism may present new interpretive problems for state courts, particularly those courts wed to lockstepping—to the jurisprudential position that the state and federal provisions should have the same meaning.[25] It is one thing for a state court to take a principled and realistic approach to the enforcement of the protection against unreasonable searches and seizures, as many lockstepping state courts, following the Supreme Court, have sought to do; it is quite another for state courts to reckon with federal precedent fixing the meaning of a federal constitutional protection through an originalist analysis. This is because, whatever the intent of the framers of the federal Constitution in respect to the Fourth Amendment and other protections contained in the Bill of Rights, or the popular understanding of the words of those provisions in 1789 (or at the time the Fourteenth Amendment was framed and ratified), neither can authoritatively set the meaning of a *state* constitutional provision adopted at a time often far removed from the experience and motivations of the framing generation.

It is possible that the U.S. Supreme Court's turn toward originalism in federal rights jurisprudence might compel some state court justices to pursue more originalist understandings of the individual rights protections of their own state's constitution—or at least such a turn might create incentives for the lawyers arguing before state courts to present originalist arguments about the meaning of the words of the state constitution at the time a provision was framed or ratified. At a minimum, this would require considered attention by state court advocates and judges alike to the origins and history of the provisions in question.[26] Notwithstanding the practical difficulties associated with this effort, such an approach could lead to new arguments and interpretive difficulties about what had been regarded as settled law. As Massachusetts Supreme Judicial Court Justice Scott Kafker has noted, "if the Supreme Court itself is regularly rejecting and revising its own precedents and issuing fractured decisions of its own, the

[24] *See, e.g.*, Robert A. Kagan et al., *The Business of State Supreme Court, 1870–1970*, 30 Stan. L. Rev. 121 (1977).

[25] *See* Chapter 7 (discussing state courts "lockstepping" state constitutional and federal constitutional rights).

[26] In People v. Stovall, 2022 WL 3007491, ___ N.W.2d ___ (Mich. 2022), for example, the chief justice of the Michigan Supreme Court (in a concurring opinion) engaged in a spirited debate with one of her colleagues (in dissent) over the meaning of the state constitution's prohibition on "cruel *or* unusual" punishment and the extent to which the understanding of that provision at the time of its ratification (in 1963) should prevail.

reasons for" lockstepping "state and federal constitutional interpretation will be further diminished."[27]

The second effect of an originalist approach to federal constitutional rights interpretation by the U.S. Supreme Court is, conversely, an absolutism about constitutional meaning that pushes the federal courts toward rights-maximalism in certain circumstances. Such a trend would have implications for state courts considering similar issues raised under state constitutions. Federal free speech jurisprudence provides an illustration, as the Supreme Court has in recent years dismantled some of the doctrinal limits that had permitted greater governmental regulation of expression in such areas as corporate speech and commercial speech.[28] These decisions have led to an understanding of the First Amendment's protection of expression that in many instances leaves less room for the kind of judicial deference toward democratically accountable political actors that was often favored by justices during the span of the Burger and Rehnquist courts.[29] In other words, to the extent the Bill of Rights has been regarded as the floor of protections deemed enforceable under the Fourteenth Amendment, the Supreme Court may be raising the floor in particular areas, leaving less room for rights expansion under state constitutions.

As another example, consider the approach of the current U.S. Supreme Court toward the First Amendment's commitment to the free exercise of religion. The justices have spilled no small amount of ink over the question whether the rule adopted in a case called *Employment Division v. Smith*, from the early 1990s, should continue to control judicial review of general laws that have some arguably negative effect on the free exercise of religion.[30] The Supreme Court has in recent years welcomed free exercise claims that run counter to the understanding adopted in *Smith*—namely, that neutral and generally applicable laws are valid notwithstanding their incidental impact on free exercise. For instance, in its decision in *Roman Catholic Diocese v. Cuomo*,[31] the court struck down COVID-19 pandemic regulations governing religious gatherings that arguably would have been viewed by the federal courts as reasonable just a few years earlier.[32] State courts, by contrast, tended to treat the pandemic decisions of governmental health officials with greater deference under state constitutions.[33]

[27] Kafker, *supra* note 13, at 134.

[28] *See, e.g.*, Citizens United v. FEC, 558 U.S. 310 (2010) (eliminating as inconsistent with First Amendment the federal limit on corporate funding of independent political broadcasts in elections).

[29] *See* Friedman, *supra* note 16, at 229–31.

[30] *See, e.g.*, Fulton v. City of Philadelphia, 593 U.S. ___ (2021) (Barrett, J., concurring) (discussing the textual and structural arguments against *Employment Division v. Smith*).

[31] Roman Catholic Diocese v. Cuomo, 592 U.S. ___ (2020).

[32] *See* Kafker, *supra* note 13, at 122–24 (discussing Supreme Court tendency to favor free exercise claims under the First Amendment).

[33] *See, e.g.*, C.F. v. New York City Department of Health and Mental Hygiene, 139 N.Y.S.3d 273, 288–89 (N.Y. App. 2020) (ruling COVID-19 restrictions did not violate free exercise rights);

Federal rights-maximalism puts state courts and state constitutions in a different position in relation to the federal courts and the federal Constitution than the one they occupied during the earliest stage of the NJF, when Justice William Brennan and others advocates were urging lawyers to press state courts to continue expanding rights and liberties that had stalled, or were anticipated to stall, at the federal level.[34] Indeed, greater protections for individual interests under the federal Constitution may be seen in many ways as the *opposite* of the situation in the 1970s, when the court's conservatism signaled an end to rights expansion in many areas, including free speech, religious liberty, and constitutional criminal procedure protections.[35]

At bottom, rights-maximalism by the U.S. Supreme Court in regard to free speech and the free exercise of religion may deter advocates from pressing state courts to expand state constitutional protections in those areas, because the federal Constitution's reach is already or soon may occupy the field.[36] At the same time, though, it is not unlikely that state courts will be confronted with cases in which they are asked to determine the meaning of parallel provisions of the state constitution. If, as we suggested in Chapter 7, it is not sufficient for a state court to interpret a state constitutional provision in lockstep with the Supreme Court in cases in which the federal high court has adopted a narrow understanding of the right in question, it should not be sufficient for a state court to interpret that provision in lockstep in a case in which the scope of the federal right has been interpreted by the Supreme Court to exceed its state constitutional analog. Even in these cases, state court advocates and judges should remember that they are interpreting a separate and distinct textual provision with its own meaning, and one deserving of the kind of consideration that corresponds to its status as constitutional law.

Finally, the stakes for state courts—and state constitutional law—may be quite different than they were a few decades ago. The federal extension of free speech and free exercise rights in all directions, for example, may not prove to be an unalloyed good.[37] As noted earlier, in the midst of the COVID-19 pandemic,

Desrosiers v. Governor, 158 N.E.3d 827 (Mass. 2020) (upholding pandemic emergency orders imposing restrictions on gatherings).

[34] *See* Chapter 5.

[35] *See generally* Russell W. Galloway Jr., *The Burger Court (1969–1986)*, 27 SANTA CLARA L. REV. 31 (1987).

[36] Consider, for example, the Supreme Court's maximalist interpretation of the individual right to carry firearms for self-defense purposes, as the court defined that interest in New York State Rifle & Pistol Association, Inc. v. Bruen, 597 U.S. ___ (2022).

[37] *See, e.g.*, Konigsberg v. State Bar of Calif., 366 U.S. 36, 49–50 n.10 (1961) (observing that an absolutist interpretation of the First Amendment "cannot be reconciled with the law relating to libel, slander, misrepresentation, obscenity, perjury, false advertising, solicitation of crime, complicity by encouragement, conspiracy, and the like").

many state courts determined that lawmakers reasonably could treat similarly those situations in which the risk of the disease spreading was equally high, regardless of concerns about the possible impact on religious practices.[38] In other words, if the places the modern Supreme Court's originalism takes federal constitutional law prove to be unpopular, it may be that state judges, generally more attuned to the sensibilities of the communities in which they sit, may be reluctant to expand the scope of particular rights under their constitutions in similar ways. As suggested earlier, this means that it is possible that expanded federal constitutional rights in particular areas may lead to situations in which a state court will interpret its own constitution to provide *less* protection than its federal counterpart.[39] Of course, if that is where a state court's interpretation takes it, such a reading of the state provision, even if it would be unenforceable under the Fourteenth Amendment, should not be seen as any less valid as a matter of state constitutional law.

Ironically, it may be in cases in which the protections afforded by a state constitution are eclipsed by those provided by parallel federal constitutional provisions that the original promise of the NJF will be vindicated, as these decisions will offer a definitive response to the criticism that has plagued the NJF from its start—namely, that independent state constitutional interpretation is simply a tool favored by state high court justices who are philosophically sympathetic to the cause of rights expansion. If the promise of the NJF means anything, it is that specific state constitutional commitments to values like liberty, equality, and privacy deserve the kind of attention from state courts that the U.S. Supreme Court gives the corollary commitments under the federal Constitution—attention that respects each state's governing charter as a source of authority distinct from its federal counterpart. After all, no matter how the U.S. Supreme Court interprets the federal Constitution, every state has its own constitution; though some provisions may resemble those of other state constitutions, no American constitution is in its entirely exactly alike another.[40]

## II. The Future of State Constitutional Amendment

We discussed the processes of state constitutional amendment at length in Chapters 13 and 14. Relative ease of amendment remains an important—and often underappreciated—feature of state constitutional law, for its availability

[38] *See supra* note 33 and accompanying text.

[39] *See, e.g.*, Serna v. Superior Court, 707 P.2d 793 (Cal. 1985) (speedy trial); State v. Smith, 725 P.2d 894 (Or. 1986) (*Miranda* rights); State v. Hopper, 822 P.2d 775 (Wash. 1992) (indictment).

[40] Dr. Alan Tarr speculated about the future of the NJF and the relationship between the state and federal courts in *Does the New Judicial Federalism Have a Future?* 74 RUTGERS U.L. REV. 1405 (2022).

means that constitutional change in many states will occur not through judicial decisions but through the process of amendment.[41] Dr. Alan Tarr has observed that "the ease with which state constitutions can be amended is important in thinking about the future of the new judicial federalism. For the ease of state constitutional amendment and the frequency with which it occurs may actually encourage the development of state constitutional law."[42] In recent years, as Dr. John Dinan has noted, "state constitutional amendments have been a regular means of altering institutions, rights, and policies in a way that might be deemed in key respects preferable to the approach at the federal level."[43] Since the first edition of this book, the popular preference in many states for constitutional change through amendment rather than litigation has arguably accelerated, particularly through rights expansion as a reaction to constitutional developments at the federal level.[44]

In a survey of state constitutional amendment efforts in just the 2020s, Dr. Dinan explored the ways in which these efforts have focused on rights-expansion.[45] The citizens of Pennsylvania, for example, in 2021 ratified an amendment[46] expressly prohibiting discrimination on the basis of ethnicity,

[41] *See* Robert F. Williams, *The State of State Constitutional Law, the New Judicial Federalism and Beyond*, 72 RUTGERS U. L. REV. 949, 968 (2020) (noting "one of the key distinctions between federal and state constitutional law is that the latter is subject to change by amendment").

[42] Tarr, *supra* note 40.

[43] JOHN DINAN, STATE CONSTITUTIONAL POLITICS: GOVERNING BY AMENDMENT IN THE AMERICAN STATES 1 (2018).

[44] *See* Kafker, *supra* note 13, at 121 (discussing state constitutional amendments in reaction to the U.S. Supreme Court's takings jurisprudence under the federal Constitution). Political scientists have noted the recent shift to the states as sites of political activity. *See, e.g.*, JACOB M. GRUMBACH, LABORATORIES AGAINST DEMOCRACY: HOW NATIONAL PARTIES TRANSFORMED STATE POLITICS xxi (2022) (noting that the shift to the state level "benefited those who could marshal information to set policy agendas and influence state-level politicians").

[45] John Dinan, *State Constitutional Amendments and Expansion of Rights*, Address at Utah Valley University Center for Constitutional Studies, Orem, UT, Nov. 3, 2021.

Of course, the state constitutional amendment process also may lend itself to rights-contraction. Following the U.S. Supreme Court's conclusion in *Dobbs v. Jackson v. Jackson Women's Health Organization*, 597 U.S. ___ (2022), that the Fourteenth Amendment does not protect a woman's right to choose, Kansas voters resoundingly defeated a ballot proposal to amend the state constitution to allow for extensive legislative regulation of that right, which the state supreme court had held protected under the state constitution in *Hodes & Nauser v. Schmidt*, 440 P.3d 461 (Kan. 2019). *See* Mitch Smith & Katie Glueck, *Kansas Retains Abortion Rights in Critical Post-*Roe *Referendum*, N.Y. TIMES, Aug. 3, 2022, sec. A, 1. The Kansas experience with a woman's right to choose further illustrates the extent to which, going forward, state reactions to federal constitutional rulings may play out in both state constitutional litigation and state constitutional amendment efforts. For recent examples of state constitutional litigation in reaction to the Supreme Court's decision in *Dobbs*, see *Planned Parenthood South Atlantic v. South Carolina*, ___ S.E. 2d ___, 2023 WL 107972 (S.C. 2023) (holding that state constitutional right to privacy protects a woman's right to choose to have an abortion); *Planned Parenthood Great Northwest v. State*, ___ P.3d ___, 2023 WL 110626 (Idaho 2023) (concluding that state constitution does not implicitly protect right to choose and the right is not rooted in the traditions and conscience of the state).

[46] *See* PA. CONST. art. I, § 29 ("Equality of rights under the law shall not be denied or abridged in the Commonwealth of Pennsylvania because of the race or ethnicity of the individual.").

joining states whose constitutions contain provisions prohibiting discrimination on the bases of such individualized characteristics as sex[47] and disability.[48] Further, states have also adopted amendments to expand the protection of religious liberty in the wake of COVID-19 restrictions put in place at the local level.[49] In 2021, for example, Texas voters ratified an amendment prohibiting limitations on religious services.[50]

What these efforts have in common is that they are, in a real sense, representative of popular reactions to a perceived lack of consideration by the federal courts of a particular interest or right, or a perceived need for a more exacting limit on governmental regulation of a right or interest already recognized in a state's constitution. For instance, a majority of the U.S. Supreme Court appears intent on expanding the protection of religious liberty under the First Amendment, and the individual right to bear arms under the Second Amendment. Nonetheless, the continued development of these interests at the federal level is likely to move forward at the glacial pace of federal constitutional litigation. Consider, for example, that it was fourteen years between the decision in *District of Columbia v. Heller*,[51] announcing an individual right to bear arms for purposes of self-defense, and the decision in *New York State Rifle & Pistol Association v. Bruen*,[52] in which the Court explained the scope of that right and the doctrinal analysis that will control Second Amendment challenges to firearms regulations.

The example of search and seizure protections may be even more telling. As noted earlier, the court in 2018 decided *United States v. Carpenter*, which addressed the federal constitutional protection afforded electronic information; the decision revisited but did not expressly reject a decades-old doctrinal framework governing information disclosed to third parties that had evolved in the predigital age—a framework whose utility today may well have been exhausted.[53] In the face of technological and other societal developments, citizens may be motivated to consider and ratify state constitutional amendments specifically

[47] *See, e.g.*, Or. Const. art. I, § 46(1) ("Equality of rights under the law shall not be denied or abridged by the State of Oregon or by any political subdivision in this state on account of sex.").

[48] *See* Mass. Const. art. amend. 114 ("No otherwise qualified handicapped individual shall, solely by reason of his handicap, be excluded from participation in, be denied the benefits of, or be subject to discrimination under any program or activity within the Commonwealth.").

[49] *See* Dinan, *supra* note 45.

[50] *See* Texas Const. art. I, § 6-a ("This state or a political subdivision of this state may not enact, adopt, or issue a statute, order, proclamation, decision, or rule that prohibits or limits religious services, including religious services conducted in churches, congregations, and places of worship, in this state by a religious organization established to support and serve the propagation of a sincerely held religious belief.").

[51] 554 U.S. 570 (2008).

[52] 597 U.S. ___ (2022) (addressing constitutionality under Second Amendment of New York law regulating the carrying of concealed firearms).

[53] *See* Lawrence Friedman, *Doctrinal Dead Ends and State Constitutional Rights Innovation*, 72 Rutgers U. L. Rev. 1179 (2020).

addressing issues not covered by either the text of the Fourth Amendment or the Supreme Court's halting interpretive efforts. In 2018, for instance, New Hampshire voters adopted an amendment to add an express right to information privacy to the state constitution,[54] while in Michigan, in 2021, voters amended their state constitutional protection against unreasonable searches and seizures to safeguard "electronic data[] and electronic communications."[55] A similar legislative proposal to amend the Montana Constitution was on the ballot in 2022.[56] For a state legislature or a citizenry that concludes that privacy protections under the federal Constitution are unacceptably indeterminate, state constitutional change via the amendment process makes sense: the time span of an effort to amend a state's charter is appreciably shorter than that of a litigation effort in the federal courts (and many state courts)—and with a far more certain result.

As we noted earlier, a potential fourth stage of the NJF was dialogue between the state and federal courts about the scope and dimensions of the individual rights commitments contained in our state and federal constitutions. Given the relative difficulty of amendment, the U.S. Supreme Court is, as Justice Kafker put it, "essentially the only constitutional actor under the federal constitution."[57] The incipient trend in the states toward rights-expansion through state constitutional amendment suggests instead that there may be a burgeoning discourse between states as sovereign entities and the U.S. Supreme Court as the arbiter of the meaning of the federal Constitution—in other words, between the Supreme Court and citizens sufficiently animated by its treatment (or lack of treatment) of a particular constitutional issue that they are willing to devote energy into efforts to amend their state's charter to address what the Court has not. This development at a minimum suggests that, whatever result the Supreme Court eventually reaches on the issues with which these amendments are concerned, for citizens in many states the wait will have been too long.[58]

[54] *See* N.H. Const. pt. I, art. 2-b ("An individual's right to live free from governmental intrusion in private or personal information is natural, essential, and inherent."). *See also* Erin Fitzgerald, *No Place for Strict* Katz *in New Hampshire's Right of Privacy*, 56 New Eng. L. Rev. Forum (2021), at https://www.newenglrev.com/forum-56/no-place-for-strict-katz-in-new-hampshires-right-of-privacy (discussing New Hampshire privacy amendment).

[55] Mich. Const. art. I, § 11 ("The person, houses, papers, possessions, electronic data, and electronic communications of every person shall be secure from unreasonable searches and seizures.").

[56] *See* Mont. S.B. 203 (2021) (proposing amendment to Montana Constitution "to explicitly include electronic data and communications in search and seizure protections").

[57] Kafker, *supra* note 13, at 142.

[58] For a thorough analysis of modern state constitutional amendment trends, see generally Jonathan L. Marshfield, *Amendment Creep*, 115 Mich. L. Rev. 215 (2016) (considering the effect of state constitutional relative ease of amendment on judicial interpretation), *Improving Amendment*, 69 Ark. L. Rev. 477 (2016) (improving the process of amendment approval by requiring county debate and approval); and *Forgotten Limits on the Power to Amend State Constitutions*, 114 Nw. U. L. Rev. 65 (2019) (arguing that significant constitutional change may only be presented to voters by constitutional conventions).

As many observers have commented, the NJF is no longer quite so new. That its novelty has worn off does not undermine its central point—that the authority of state courts to interpret their state constitutions independently of the U.S. Supreme Court is an aspect of the separation of powers the U.S. Constitution establishes. Efforts by many states' citizenries and their representatives to effect state constitutional change via the amendment process in response to developments at the federal level is another, tangible expression of federalism. In the early years of the NJF, individual rights commitments were shaped in the first instance by courts, but judicial involvement in rights development is not and has never been a federal or state constitutional requirement. And, while state constitutional amendment as a response or reaction to constitutional developments at the federal level may qualify only loosely as a dialogue, such engagement does highlight a central feature of state constitutional law that distinguishes it from federal constitutional law—namely, the variety of ways in which state constitutions permit the governed to shape their relationships with their governments, and with each other. That variety—the subject of this book—simply has no functional equivalent in federal constitutional law.

# BIBLIOGRAPHICAL ESSAY

The authors gratefully acknowledge the coverage of online sources prepared by Nancy Talley of the Rutgers Law Library in Camden.

This book, like many other law books, utilizes the footnotes to perform a bibliographical function. Therefore, not all of the references (particularly law review articles) included in the footnotes are repeated in this Bibliographical Essay. Rather, this essay is intended to reflect the major sources of information available on state constitutions.

The best place to start with respect to state constitutions is G. Alan Tarr, *Understanding State Constitutions* (1998). It provides a very readable, broad-brush look at the evolution and the political and legal dimensions of state constitutions. Professor Lawrence Friedman is the editor of a fifty-state series covering each state's constitution, published by Oxford University Press: *The Oxford Commentaries on the State Constitutions of the United States*. These volumes all have the same title: *The* ________ *State Constitution*. Each contains an essay addressing the constitutional history of the state, followed by a section-by-section analysis (including citations to leading cases) of the state constitution, together with a bibliographical essay. Nearly every state is represented in the series at this point, with several volumes in revised editions.

*The Constitutionalism of American States* (George E. Connor & Christopher W. Hammons eds., 2008) is an extremely useful single volume, containing chapters on each of the fifty state constitutions. The chapters vary in focus and length and can be used to supplement the information in the Oxford Press volumes. Other useful single volumes on state constitutions are Robert L. Maddex, *State Constitutions of the United States* (2d ed. 2006); James T. McHugh, *Ex Uno Plura: State Constitutions and Their Political Cultures* (2003); *The Constitutions of the States: A State-By-State Guide and Bibliography to Current Scholarly Research* (Bernard D. Reams Jr. & Stuart D. Yoak eds., 1988); and Tim J. Watts, *State Constitutional Law Development: A Bibliography* (1991).

The texts of the state constitutions are best accessed online, as described as follows. Each state's early constitutional documents, as well as each of their constitutions, are contained in the late William F. Swindler's eleven-volume *Sources and Documents of U.S. Constitutions* (1973–1979). This is now the property of Oxford University Press. The state constitutions are also gathered in the seven-volume *Legislative Drafting Research Fund, Columbia University, Constitutions of the United States: National and State* (various dates), which is now also the property of Oxford University Press.

*The Book of the States*, published by the Council of State Governments every year, includes important data on the state constitutions assembled by John Dinan. A three-volume set covers the important process of each state's achievement of statehood. *The Uniting States: The Story of Statehood for the Fifty United States* (three vols., Benjamin F. Shearer ed., 2004). State constitution making, of course, was an important component of the statehood process in both the original thirteen states, and under different circumstances, the following thirty-seven states.

*Rutgers University Law Review* (formerly *Rutgers Law Journal*) has since 1989 devoted one issue per year to state constitutional law, including scholarly articles and student comments on important state constitutional cases. The *Albany Law Review* has also published valuable symposia on state constitutional law.

On the politics of state constitutions, there is very good coverage in *Constitutional Politics in the States: Contemporary Controversies and Historical Patterns* (G. Alan Tarr ed., 1996); and 1 *State Constitutions for the Twenty-first Century: The Politics of State Constitutional Reform* (G. Alan Tarr & Robert F. Williams eds., 2006).

Still the best treatment of the development of state constitutional theory and practice during the Revolutionary period is Gordon S. Wood, *The Creation of The American Republic, 1776–1787* (1969). Marc W. Kruman challenged some of Wood's ideas in *Between Authority and Liberty: State Constitution Making in Revolutionary America* (1997). For Wood's most recent scholarship on constitutionalism, see *Power and Liberty: Constitutionalism in the American Revolution* (2021). For an excellent analysis of the early decades of state constitution making, see generally Willi Paul Adams, *The First American Constitutions: Republican Ideology and the Making of State Constitutions in the Revolutionary Era* (1980); Elisha Douglass, *Rebels and Democrats: The Struggle For Equal Political Rights and the Majority Rule During the American Revolution* (1955); Jackson Turner Main, *The Sovereign States, 1775–1783*, at 143–95 (1973); and Donald Lutz, *Popular Consent and Popular Control: Whig Political Theory in the Early State Constitutions* 1 (1980).

An outstanding study of the evolution of the state constitutional tradition, with a focus on specific topics, from the time of the Revolution to more recent times, is John J. Dinan, *The American State Constitutional Tradition* (2006). For a deeply analytical look at the evolving, and competing, theories of state constitution-making processes, see Christian G. Fritz, *American Sovereigns: The People and America's Constitutional Tradition Before the Civil War* (2008). Other useful works include Laura Scalia, *America's Jeffersonian Experiment: Remaking State Constitutions, 1820–1850* (1999); Daniel J. Hulsebosch, *Constituting Empire: New York and the Transformation of Constitutionalism in the Atlantic World, 1664–1830* (2005).

Important regional studies of state constitutions and constitution making include Amy Bridges, *Democratic Beginnings: Founding the Western States* (2015); David Alan Johnson, *Founding the Far West: California, Oregon, and Nevada, 1840–1890* (1992); John D. Hicks, *The Constitutions of the Northwest States* (1924); Silvana R. Siddali, *Frontier Democracy: Constitutional Conventions in the Old Northwest* (2016); Don E. Fehrenbacher, *Constitutions and Constitutionalism in the Slaveholding South* (1989); Paul E. Herron, *Framing the Solid South: The State Constitutional Conventions on Succession, Reconstruction, and Redemption, 1860–1902* (2017); Fletcher M. Green, *Constitutional Development in the South Atlantic States, 1776–1860* (1930); Gordon Morris Bakken, *Rocky Mountain Constitution Making, 1850–1912* (1987). Eric Foner provides detailed analysis of the Southern Reconstruction state constitutions in *Reconstruction: America's Unfinished Revolution, 1863–1877* (1988).

By far, the most important and useful resource concerning state constitutional rights adjudication is Jennifer Friesen's two-volume *State Constitutional Law: Litigating Individual Rights, Claims and Defenses* (4th ed. 2006). Professor Friesen provides an updated, fifty-state coverage of a variety of state constitutional rights matters, together with an exhaustive bibliography. On the important topic of positive, or affirmative rights, see Emily Zackin, *Looking for Rights in All the Wrong Places: Why State Constitutions Contain America's Positive Rights* (2013). An additional, very useful resource is Barry Latzer, *State Constitutional Criminal Law* (1995), although this work is no longer being regularly supplemented. See also Susan P. Fino, *The Role of State Supreme Courts in the New Judicial Federalism* (1987); Michael E. Solimine & James L. Walker, *Respecting State Courts: The Inevitability of Judicial Federalism* (1999).

A very thorough and analytical coverage of state constitutional equal protection and liberty issues, including privacy, is provided in Jeffrey M. Shaman, *Equality and Liberty in the Golden Age of State Constitutional Law* (2008). *Dual Enforcement of Constitutional Norms* (James A. Gardner & Jim Rossi eds., 2009) is an edited volume with number of very thoughtful chapters concerning issues arising from our dual federal and state systems of rights protections. Robert A. Schapiro's *Polyphonic Federalism: Toward the Protection of Fundamental Rights* (2009) provides, in Chapter 5, a valuable analysis of state constitutional claims in federal courts.

There are a number of works on individual state constitutions. They will not all be listed here, but one of the best examples is the *Pennsylvania Constitution: A Treatise on Rights and Liberties* (Ken Gormley et al. eds., 2d ed. 2021). This volume contains chapters on each of the important state constitutional rights in Pennsylvania and is updated each year. It provides a very useful model for other states to emulate. Other useful volumes include James L. Underwood, *The Constitution of South Carolina* (2 vols. 1989); and Dennis C. Colson, *Idaho's Constitution: The Tie That Binds* (1991); Mary E. Adkins, *Making Modern Florida: How the Spirit of Reform Shaped a New State Constitution* (2016).

The most useful study of state constitutional conventions is by Elmer E. Cornwell Jr., Jay S. Goodman, & Wayne R. Swanson, *State Constitutional Conventions: The Politics of the Revision Process in Seven States* (1975). Other important studies are John P. Wheeler Jr. & Melissa Kinsey, *Magnificent Failure: The Maryland Constitutional Convention of 1967–1968* (1970); Richard J. Connors, *The Process of Constitutional Revision in New Jersey: 1940–1947* (1970); and Henrik N. Dullea, *Charter Revision in the Empire State: The Politics of New York's 1967 Constitutional Convention* (1997). On the topic of drafting and revising state constitutional provisions, see Frank P. Grad & Robert F. Williams, 2 *State Constitutions for the Twenty-first Century: Drafting State Constitutions, Revisions, and Amendments* (2006). See also G. Alan Tarr & Robert F. Williams, "Foreword: Getting from Here to There: Twenty-first Century Mechanisms and Opportunities in State Constitutional Reform," 36 *Rutgers Law Journal* 1075 (2005).

For a review of issues in state constitutional change, see 3 *State Constitutions for the Twenty-first Century: The Agenda of State Constitutional Reform* (G. Alan Tarr & Robert F. Williams eds., 2006).

James A. Gardner's *Interpreting State Constitutions: A Jurisprudence of Function in a Federal System* (2005) is a very interesting book, proposing a provocative new theory for judicial interpretation of state constitutions in both the rights and government powers areas. Gardner proposes that state courts act as "agents of federalism" in interpreting state constitutions in such a way as to enable the states to resist federal abuses of power. Gardner includes, in addition, a number of important perspectives on state constitutions.

John Dinan's book, *State Constitutional Politics: Governing by Amendment in the American States* (2018), provides an assessment of the types of amendments, and their differing purposes and effects. This is a very important element of state constitutional law.

Most recently, Adam Brown contends, in a book-length study based on significant statistical evidence, that more specific (and therefore longer) state constitutions have negative effects on states. These effects include the necessity of more amendments, more statutes invalidated through judicial review, and limitations on "policy performance, resulting in lower incomes per capita, higher unemployment rates, greater economic inequality, and reduced policy innovativeness generally." Adam R. Brown, *Dead Hand's Grip: How Long Constitutions Bind States* (2022). Other recent books considering state constitutional law include Robinson Woodward-Burns, *Hidden Laws: How State Constitutions Stabilize American Politics* (2021); and Anthony B. Sanders, *Baby Ninth Amendments: How Americans Embraced Unenumerated Rights and Why It Matters* (2023).

There are two law school casebooks, each of which provides a wide range of information on state constitutions. Robert F. Williams & Lawrence Friedman, *State Constitutional Law: Cases and Materials* (5th ed. 2015); Randy J. Holland et al., *State Constitutional Law: The Modern Experience* (2d ed. 2016). One of the authors of the latter casebook, Judge Jeffrey S. Sutton, has also published two books exploring the virtues of state constitutionalism, *51 Imperfect Solutions: States and the Making of American Constitutional Law* (2018) and *Who Decides: States as Laboratories of Constitutional Experimentation* (2021).

Professors Katie Eyer and Robert Williams have published a free online supplement for Constitutional Law professors (and others) who want a short, readily available introduction to state constitutional law: *State Constitutional Law Teaching Materials for 1L Constitutional Law Classes (supplement 2019)*, https://papers.ssrn.com/sol3/papers.cfm?abstractid=3418938.

Westlaw currently provides access to annotated versions of the constitutions of all fifty states, the District of Columbia, and Puerto Rico. To access this content, type "[state name] constitution" in Westlaw's main search field and select the result from the drop-down list that appears.

Lexis Advance also provides access to annotated versions of all state constitutions, as well as the constitution of Puerto Rico. Lexis Advance does not currently provide access to the constitution of the District of Columbia. To access Lexis Advance state constitution content, select "Advanced Search" on Lexis' main webpage. Next, click "select a specific content type." Then select the hyperlink for "Constitutions." Finally, type the state name (e.g., "New Jersey") in the search box. The results will be limited to provisions of the state constitution.

On the internet, there are four sources for state constitutions which can generally be trusted. Findlaw.com is one such source. Findlaw is a commercial website owned by Westlaw. They have a page with direct links to available state constitutions at this web page: http://www.findlaw.com/11stategov/indexconst.html. In addition, Findlaw maintains pages of significant legal resources links for each state. The state's constitution is always listed on that page under the category "Primary Materials."

The Cornell Legal Information Institute is a not-for-profit venture of Cornell Law School, which maintains collections of links to significant state resources, including constitutions. The index to its state resources pages is http://www.law.cornell.edu/states/listing.html.

Justia.com is another commercial website with legal resources pages for all fifty states. Their index of all fifty states links to their state resource pages at http://law.justia.com/ . An important distinction between Findlaw and Justia is that Justia has a policy of downloading and preserving a copy of every resource they offer. Because of this, the copy of the constitution they provide (or anything else) will be from the Justia website, not the state government's website.

Finally, the NBER/Maryland State Constitutions Project includes access to unannotated versions of all fifty state constitutions. For some states, it also includes previous versions of the constitutions. You can access the NBER/Maryland State Constitutions Project by visiting http://www.stateconstitutions.umd.edu/Search/Search.aspx.

Other internet sources for historical state constitutional data are available, but they are highly scattered among state archives, historical societies, and universities. The Yale Avalon project has a smattering of historical state constitutions from various states, but even this is not a programmatic collection of state constitutional documents. The website of the Center for State Constitutional Studies (https://statecon.camden.rutgers.edu/) provides a number of links to resources and developments in state constitutional law, including subnational constitutions in other countries.

Oxford University Press provides an online resource, by subscription, giving access to up-to-date versions of the American state and federal constitutions, which are searchable—"Constitutions of the United States: National and State" is the online version of the former Oceana collection (http://www.oceanalaw.com/).

# INDEX

*For the benefit of digital users, indexed terms that span two pages (e.g., 52–53) may, on occasion, appear on only one of those pages.*